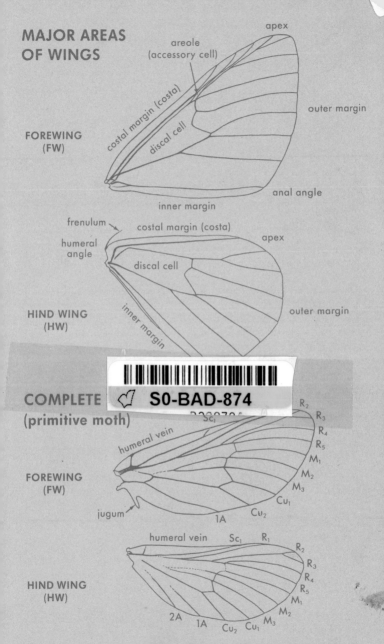

MAJOR AREAS OF WINGS

FOREWING (FW)

apex
areole (accessory cell)
costal margin (costa)
discal cell
outer margin
anal angle
inner margin

HIND WING (HW)

frenulum
humeral angle
costal margin (costa)
apex
discal cell
inner margin
outer margin

COMPLETE (primitive moth)

FOREWING (FW)

humeral vein
jugum
1A
Cu₂
Cu₁
M₃
M₂
M₁
R₅
R₄
R₃
R₂
Sc₁

HIND WING (HW)

humeral vein
Sc₁
R₁
R₂
R₃
R₄
R₅
M₁
M₂
M₃
Cu₁
Cu₂
1A
2A

MAJOR AREAS OF WINGS

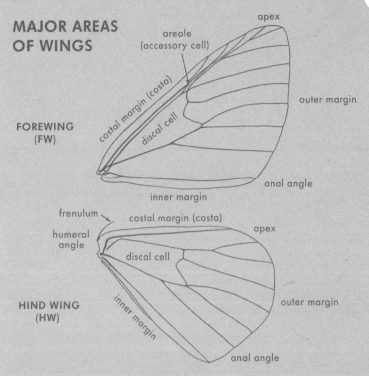

FOREWING (FW)

- areole (accessory cell)
- apex
- costal margin (costa)
- outer margin
- discal cell
- anal angle
- inner margin

HIND WING (HW)

- frenulum
- costal margin (costa)
- humeral angle
- apex
- discal cell
- outer margin
- inner margin
- anal angle

COMPLETE VENATION (primitive moth)

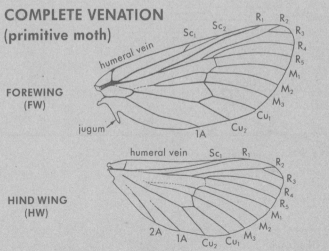

FOREWING (FW)

- humeral vein
- Sc_1
- Sc_2
- R_1
- R_2
- R_3
- R_4
- R_5
- M_1
- M_2
- M_3
- Cu_1
- Cu_2
- jugum
- 1A

HIND WING (HW)

- humeral vein
- Sc_1
- R_1
- R_2
- R_3
- R_4
- R_5
- M_1
- M_2
- M_3
- Cu_1
- Cu_2
- 2A
- 1A

Drawings by Elaine R. (Snyder) Hodges from *Moths of America North of Mexico,* Fasc. 21 (Sphingoidea), courtesy of the artist and the Wedge Entomological Research Foundation

THE PETERSON FIELD GUIDE SERIES
Edited by Roger Tory Peterson

1. Birds—*R.T. Peterson*
2. Western Birds—*R.T. Peterson*
3. Shells of the Atlantic and Gulf Coasts and the West Indies—*Morris*
4. Butterflies—*Klots*
5. Mammals—*Burt and Grossenheider*
6. Pacific Coast Shells (including shells of Hawaii and the Gulf of California)—*Morris*
7. Rocks and Minerals—*Pough*
8. Birds of Britain and Europe—*R.T. Peterson, Mountfort, and Hollom*
9. Animal Tracks—*Murie*
10. Ferns and Their Related Families of Northeastern and Central North America—*Cobb*
11. Trees and Shrubs (Northeastern and Central North America)—*Petrides*
12. Reptiles and Amphibians of Eastern and Central North America—*Conant*
13. Birds of Texas and Adjacent States—*R.T. Peterson*
14. Rocky Mountain Wildflowers—*J.J. Craighead, F.C. Craighead, Jr., and Davis*
15. Stars and Planets—*Menzel and Pasachoff*
16. Western Reptiles and Amphibians—*Stebbins*
17. Wildflowers of Northeastern and North-central North America—*R.T. Peterson and McKenny*
18. Mammals of Britain and Europe—*van den Brink*
19. Insects of America North of Mexico—*Borror and White*
20. Mexican Birds—*R.T. Peterson and Chalif*
21. Birds' Nests (found east of Mississippi River)—*Harrison*
22. Pacific States Wildflowers—*Niehaus and Ripper*
23. Edible Wild Plants of Eastern and Central North America—*L. Peterson*
24. Atlantic Seashore—*Gosner*
25. Western Birds' Nests—*Harrison*
26. Atmosphere—*Schaefer and Day*
27. Coral Reefs of the Caribbean and Florida—*Kaplan*
28. Pacific Coast Fishes—*Eschmeyer, Herald, and Hammann*
29. Beetles—*White*
30. Moths—*Covell*

THE PETERSON FIELD GUIDE SERIES

A Field Guide
to the Moths
of Eastern North America

Charles V. Covell, Jr.

Professor of Biology
University of Louisville
Louisville, Kentucky

Photographic plates by
Tatiana Dominick
and Harold H. Norvell

Drawings by
Elaine R. (Snyder) Hodges
and Charles V. Covell, Jr.

Text photographs by the author

HOUGHTON MIFFLIN COMPANY BOSTON

1984

3839198

Dedication

For Betty, Chuck, Robert, and Elizabeth Katherine.
Also for Edward L. Todd with gratitude,
and in fond memory of Richard B. Dominick.

Library of Congress Cataloging in Publication Data

Covell, Charles V., Jr.
A field guide to the moths of eastern North America.

(The Peterson field guide series)
Bibliography: p.
Includes index.
1. Moths—Atlantic States—Identification.   2. Moths—
United States—Identification.   3. Insects—Identifica-
tion.   4. Insects—Atlantic States—Identification.
5. Insects—United States—Identification.   I. Title.
II. Series.
QL551.A75C68 1984   595.78′1097   83-26523
ISBN 0-395-26056-6
ISBN 0-395-36100-1 (pbk.)

Printed in the United States of America

V 10 9 8 7 6 5 4 3 2 1

Editor's Note

In North America, north of the Mexican border, there are about 765 species of butterflies; this is approximately equal to the number of birds, if we exclude the accidentals. Moths, their nocturnal cousins, outnumber butterflies 14 to 1 with a total of nearly 10,500 known species. Of this galaxy, over 1300 species are treated in this *Field Guide*, which has been prepared with such loving care and scholarship by Charles V. Covell, Jr.

How I wish I had this guide years ago! When I was a teenager, running out of new butterflies to pursue and catch in the hills of western New York state, I turned my attention to the moths. To a net-wielding youth, the big ones — the saturniids, sphinxes, and underwings — held the greatest fascination. The more obscure ones were ignored at first, but not later.

Every evening during the late spring and summer I made the circuit of the old-fashioned arc lights that illuminated the street corners on the north side of town, but there was a problem: Jamestown had a curfew law. Every evening at 8:45 p.m. a siren atop the city hall wailed like a banshee and all boys had to be off the streets. But the moths did not begin to flutter around the lights until 9:15 or 9:30. There was only one way around this dilemma. At the city hall I explained things to Captain Johnson, the Chief of Police, who instructed his secretary to type out a sheet that read: "This permits Roger Peterson to catch moths around street lights until 11 p.m."

I noticed that moths were most numerous around the lights on muggy nights, just before a thunderstorm. On clear, starry nights there were relatively few, sometimes none at all, and I wondered whether they flew toward the shining orb of the moon on such nights rather than to the arc lights.

Today I see very few moths around the lights that line our streets and highways. Could it be that the kind of lights now used do not attract them, or has there been a general decimation because of habitat disruption, pesticides, or other reasons? Butterfly populations are now being monitored by the Xerces Society; it is time for us to pay similar attention to moths as indicators of environmental health.

Regardless of whether you have a specialist's interest in moths or are a generalist, ranging the broad spectrum of nature, take this guide with you on field trips. It will enable you to put names to some of the gentler inhabitants of the night and will give you further insights about our wild world.

Roger Tory Peterson

Preface

Ever since I bought my first edition in 1951 of Klots' *A Field Guide to the Butterflies,* I have recognized the need for a companion guide to the largest and most familiar moths of eastern North America. At a meeting of the Lepidopterists' Society in 1971, its co-founder, Dr. Charles L. Remington of Yale University, suggested that I prepare one. With the green light from Roger Tory Peterson, I was ready to embark upon the adventure of producing this book.

The only other comprehensive illustrated book on North American moths is *The Moth Book,* by W.J. Holland, published in 1903. Although it has now been reprinted by Dover Press, it was out of print for many years and could be found only in libraries and occasionally in used book stores. More recent works provide only limited coverage (see Bibliography, p. 464), and are not generally available to the public through book stores. Much of the information about moths is published in scientific journals, which are not usually read by the beginner.

This book became a viable project when Dr. Richard B. Dominick offered to photograph the plates with the Linhof camera and a special staging apparatus, which he and Harold H. Norvell had developed and refined to make color plates for the *Moths of America North of Mexico* series, which Dr. Dominick initiated in 1967. The superb quality of this photography was evident in the first fascicle of that series, which appeared in 1971 (*Sphingoidea,* by R.W. Hodges). However, both the *Moths of America* project and this Field Guide suffered a great setback when Dr. Dominick died in May 1976. The former series has continued, and I hope that the descriptions of all North American moth species will eventually be updated, and that all species will be shown in color in future volumes. Mrs. Tatiana Dominick had assisted her husband with the photography at their Wedge Plantation in coastal South Carolina. She and Mr. Norvell made and processed the plates you see on these pages (except Pl. 1). Their superb work has brought this book to life, and I am extremely grateful to them for their participation in this project. Most of the South Carolina specimens shown are from the Wedge Plantation collection, and my visits to that beautiful and historic place have provided me with some of my most pleasant memories as a lepidopterist.

A major challenge in creating this guide was that of selecting perfectly spread, well-marked, unfaded, properly identified specimens for the photographs. Some species vary considerably in size, color, and pattern throughout their ranges, but because of space limitations only one specimen could be shown in this guide (except in cases where the male differs markedly from the female). I have tried to select the most typical specimens.

I collected some of the specimens shown, but relied most heavily on material collected and spread by Douglas C. Ferguson, a U.S. Department of Agriculture entomologist working at the U.S. Museum of Natural History in Washington, D.C., where he deposited his collection. Most of the specimens from Nova Scotia, Connecticut, Maryland, and North Carolina are from his collection. In addition, Doug provided a great deal of information and advice, for which I extend my heartfelt thanks.

Other specimens were provided by the U.S. National Museum and represent the work of a variety of collectors. Some of these collectors include specialists who also advised me regarding moth groups in which they have expertise: J.F. Gates Clarke, Don R. Davis, John B. Heppner, Ronald W. Hodges, and Edward L. Todd. Others who provided specimens include H. David Baggett, William R. Black, Jr., André Blanchard, Alan J. Brownell, Carl Cook, the late Carl C. Cornett, Charles V. Covell III, Robert B. Covell, Richard Fellows, John G. Franclemont, Loran D. Gibson, J. Richard Heitzman, Richard A. Henderson, Jack S. Lesshafft, Mogens C. Nielsen, George W. Rawson, Siegfried Scholz, Dale F. Schweitzer, Gerald B. Straley, and William D. Winter, Jr. I wish to thank these colleagues for the use of their fine specimens.

Much of the information needed for the sections on identification, food, range and similar species came from a number of published sources. However, much more came from amateur and professional lepidopterists who took the time to send me data from the collections in their care. Those providing exhaustive information from their parts of the area covered include André Blanchard (Tex.), J. Richard Heitzman (Mo. and Ark.), Bryant Mather (Miss. and other southern states), John S. Nordin (Minn. and S.D.), and William D. Winter, Jr. (Mass.). Many others gave me valuable assistance, including H. David Baggett, Auburn E. Brower, Richard L. Brown, Linda Butler, Ring T. Cardé, Everett D. Cashatt, Terry S. Dickel, Julian P. Donahue, Thomas D. Eichlin, Leslie A. Ferge, Roger G. Heitzman, Roy O. Kendall, the late Charles P. Kimball, Leroy C. Koehn, J. Donald Lafontaine, Ronald H. Leuschner, Gary Marrone, Tim L. McCabe, William C. McGuffin, Eric H. Metzler, Marc Minno, Eugene G. Munroe, Mogens C. Nielsen, Robert W. Poole, Jerry A. Powell, Eric L. Quinter, Frederick H. Rindge, Theodore D. Sargent, the late William E. Sieker, and Barry Wright. I greatly value their contributions, which have helped make this guide more comprehensive and up-to-date.

I am especially indebted to Elaine R. (Snyder) Hodges for her excellent line drawings of anatomical structures of moths, which the Wedge Entomological Foundation so kindly let me adapt from Fasc. 21 of *Moths of America North of Mexico*. The fine color transparencies of caterpillars on Pl. 1 are the work of Alexander B. Klots, John R. MacGregor, and John S. Nordin.

I would also like to thank Rozenna B. Carr, Deborah Harper, and Leah Kohn for clerical assistance, and the following for spiritual and logistical support during the years this book took shape: my parents, Rev. and Mrs. Charles V. Covell; my sister, Alice C. Mahoney; my wife's parents, Capt. (USN, ret.) and Mrs. Robert M. Barnes; Burt L. Monroe, Jr., Chairman of the Biology Department, University of Louisville; my children, Chuck, Robert, and Elizabeth Katherine; and, most of all, my wife Betty, whose patience and encouragement were unstinting.

This book could not have been completed without the competent assistance of the Houghton Mifflin staff. Helen Phillips provided me with my initial "Field Guide training" and inspiration, while others who contributed along the way were Terry Baker, Denny Ehrlich, Lisa Gray Fisher, James P. Thompson, and Harry Foster. Cope Cumpston designed this Field Guide. The last and toughest leg of editing fell to Barbara Stratton, Julia Fellows, and Diane Taraskiewicz, and to them I am deeply grateful.

Finally, my special thanks go to Charles L. Remington for his initial encouragement and matchmaking, and to Roger Tory Peterson for his suggestions and guidance, which resulted in making this a Peterson Field Guide in more than name alone.

                                        Charles V. Covell, Jr.

Contents

Illustrations

Line drawings

Figures 1–76, distributed throughout the book

Color and black-and-white plates

Plates 1–64, grouped after p. 174

Credits

Elaine R. (Snyder) Hodges, endpapers, Figs. 1–6

Alexander B. Klots, Plate 1, Figs. 1, 5, 13, 16, and 17

John R. MacGregor, Plate 1, Figs. 2–4, 6–8, 10, 11, 14, 15, and 18

John S. Nordin, Plate 1, Fig. 9

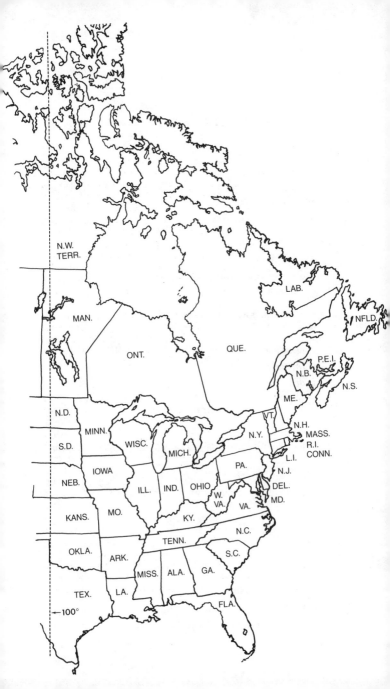

How to Use This Book

This Field Guide is designed mainly to help you identify moths that have been collected and prepared with wings outspread, as shown in the plates at the center of this guide. Techniques for collection and preparation are described in Chapter 3. While you may be able to identify many living moths by their shapes, colors, and patterns, this is usually difficult because moths often rest with their forewings folded over their hind wings. However, after some experience you will become familiar with their characteristic resting poses and will often be able to identify them at least to the family level in the field. Shapes of moths at rest may be quite striking; some examples are shown in silhouette on the rear endpapers.

Since this book is for nonspecialists, highly technical words and microscopic features have been kept to a minimum. However, some of these are necessary to characterize the 59 families and over 1,300 species treated in detail here. Identification keys are not included in this guide, but may be found in many of the works listed in the Bibliography.

Species covered. Of the nearly 94,000 known species of insects in America north of Mexico, the Order Lepidoptera includes over 11,230 species. Only about 760 of these are butterflies; the rest are moths. In addition, many species of moths have yet to be discovered and named, since many are small and unattractive to collectors, and those specialists trained to describe and name insects are few. Because of the great number of moth species and the incomplete nature of our knowledge about them, a Field Guide can include only a fraction and must concentrate on the larger and better-known species. I have tried to select the moths that an eastern North American collector is most likely to encounter and want to identify.

One of the major problems in planning this guide was that of deciding which of the over 10,000 North American moth species to include. I have attempted to introduce you to all the eastern North American families, and to illustrate at least one species from each family. Most people are first attracted to the largest and most strikingly patterned species, so those have been given most thorough treatment. Favorites among beginning collectors include the sphinx or hawk moths (Family Sphingidae), giant silkworm moths (Saturniidae), and the underwings (Noctuidae, genus *Catocala*).

Almost all the species in our area from these families are included in this guide. The large to medium-sized moths commonly found throughout much of our area were given moderately thorough treatment: tiger moths (Arctiidae), the rest of the noctuids, geometer moths (Geometridae), and prominents (Notodontidae). The families generally referred to as microlepidoptera or "micro moths" (families Pterophoridae to Micropterygidae in our order of presentation) are not covered in detail, since beginning collectors are unlikely to collect and study them until they have mastered the identification of the larger moths. Also, the identities of many "micros" remain less well known. As you gain more experience in collecting moths, other books and articles will help you identify many of the species that cannot be included here (see Bibliography, p. 464).

Identification. The best way to identify moths using this guide is to attempt to match a specimen as closely as possible with one in the plates at the center of the book. Then turn to the text for written descriptions and further information on that species. Size, shape, color, and pattern will usually enable you to identify your specimens. Most moths pictured are shown life-size. Those shown in black-and-white are usually drab in color; details about color are described in the text for all species. Each family of moths is described in an introduction to the species of that family, with an emphasis on important diagnostic features such as wing venation. At least one wing venation drawing accompanies each family description; occasionally, other distinctive features of the group are illustrated as well. Distinctions between subfamilies are explained for several of the largest families; however, this level of classification is not used for all the families, particularly among the "micros" (microlepidoptera).

The species treatments and illustrations are the heart of this book. They include the following information:

Common and scientific names. Most of the common names used in this guide follow the 1978 edition of *Common Names of Insects and Related Organisms* by Sutherland; in some cases I have coined common names for species of macro moths that did not have them, such as many of the noctuids. Only previously established common names are given for the micros, most of which are not widely known. Some moths have one common name based on the feeding habits of the caterpillar and another common name derived from characteristics of the adult. Although common names are emphasized in Field Guides, one should try to learn and use the Latin name, since it is the "official" name recognized by scientists worldwide.

In some cases subspecies names are given, indicating that representatives of the species in our area are recognized as being distinct from populations in other parts of the continent or world. Also included in some cases are the Latinized names of certain distinct forms, which have quotation marks around them since these names are not recognized in taxonomic nomenclature. Forms are recognizably different individuals of a species that regularly occur within species populations. Melanic forms are noticeably darker in color than normal—usually blackish—and the wing pattern is often obscured.

After the scientific name, I have listed (in abbreviated form) the name of the author (or joint authors) who first formally described and named each species. Parentheses around the species author's name indicate that subsequent researchers have transferred the species to a genus other than the one in which it was originally described. An index to the abbreviations used for species author names appears on p. 467.

Description. The Identification section includes a brief description of the adult moth. The most distinctive features are highlighted in italics; these features are usually pinpointed with arrows on the plates. Variations in color patterns and any other features that are common and important for identification are also mentioned. The various parts of the body and wings referred to in the descriptive sections are illustrated on the endpapers and in the chapter on Moth Anatomy (Chapter 1).

Abbreviations. A few recurring terms are abbreviated: FW (forewing), HW (hind wing), am. line (antemedial line), pm. line (postmedial line), and st. line (subterminal line).

Measurements. Wingspans are given in centimeters (cm). This is the distance between the tips of the forewings in moths spread as shown in the plates. Measurements given are from specimens in collections, so you may find other specimens with smaller or greater wingspans. A metric rule is included below and on the back cover of this book for your convenience.

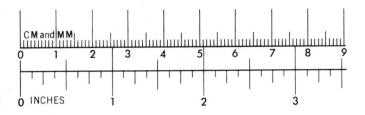

Food. In this section you will find a listing of plants each species is known to eat in its larval form. Unless otherwise indicated, the larva chews the foliage of the plants listed. In most cases, no distinction could be made between plants that larvae feed on in nature and those that people have successfully used to rear them in captivity. Unusual feeding habits, such as stem boring, leaf mining, or leaf folding, are indicated where known. The economic importance of certain species as pests is also briefly noted. Our space limitations do not permit detailed life-cycle information; however, a few examples of common larvae and cocoons are shown on Plates 1 and 2.

References to food plants may be general (such as *oaks* or *poplars*) or very specific (such as *white oak* or *yellow poplar*). If a general name such as "oak" is given in the singular, that vagueness reflects a lack of precision in my sources—in these cases, "oak" may mean "any oak species," or "some unknown species of oak."

Range. This section describes the known geographic limits of the species in the area covered by this book. That area is North America east of the 100th meridian (see map, p. x). Many species covered here may also be found beyond the range described, *i.e.* west of the 100th meridian. This guide is not intended to describe range extensions beyond the midwestern U.S., but it does note when an eastern species is found across Canada or worldwide. Special habitats may also be mentioned (swamp, sand dune, mountain). "Throughout our area" means that one may expect to find the species in appropriate habitat and season anywhere within the scope of this guide. *Holarctic* species are those found in northern Eurasia as well as North America; *neotropical* indicates South America and Central America up to the limits of our own nearctic region, which includes North America down to a line through the Mexican highlands.

The flight season for adult moths is given with the rough center of our area in mind (extending from Virginia west to Kansas). Flight seasons can be expected to be later in northern parts of the range and earlier and possibly longer toward the southern limits of the range. In frost-free areas, moths may fly in all months. The number of generations, or broods, each moth species has per year is given where known. A species may have one brood per year northward, but two or more southward. The exact times when first or second broods begin or end are not usually known, and may shift from year to year due to weather conditions. Much more information needs to be gathered before precise statements can be made about flight seasons and brood numbers in many species.

Abundance. "Abundant" means that the collector can expect to encounter adult moths in great numbers, at least in part of the range. "Common" indicates that you may expect to find the species whenever you are collecting in proper habitat and season, and several specimens can be anticipated. "Uncommon" means that, within proper habitat and season, you may or may not find the species; or that only one or two specimens might be found on a given collecting trip to a specific spot. "Rare" species are seldom encountered, but this designation might also indicate species that live in inaccessible places or that have habits that make them rarer in collections than they truly are in nature.

Similar species. This section is used sparingly since there are so many species of moths similar to the ones shown that listing all of them was not feasible. In this guide, the similar species category often includes fairly common or important species that are not shown but are very close in size, pattern, and other features to species that are illustrated and described in more detail. Brief diagnostic information is given in these cases, along with food and range information. No similar species from outside our area are listed in that section, although there are many moths in western North America that replace certain species in the East.

Finally, please remember that this book is meant as an introduction to eastern North American moths, and includes only a small portion of the species you might encounter. Also, the state of our knowledge of moths is such that no book published at this time can be considered the "last word" on the identity of species, or their life cycles, ranges, and flight periods. I have learned a great deal in preparing this Field Guide for you, and I hope it will lead you to the exciting discoveries awaiting the moth collector and observer.

1

Moth Anatomy

Moths are invertebrate animals that belong to the Phylum Arthropoda, the largest phylum by far in the Animal Kingdom with over a million described species. As arthropods, they possess such characteristic features as a tough exoskeleton, segmented body, and paired, jointed legs.

Within the Phylum Arthropoda, moths belong to the Class Insecta, or Hexapoda. Over 760,000 insect species are known, and many more await discovery. All insects have 3 body regions (head, thorax, and abdomen), 3 pairs of thoracic legs, 2 pairs of wings, 1 pair of antennae, and a tracheal respiratory system (tracheae are flexible, branching tubes that carry air throughout the body). The insects are in turn divided into about 28 orders (this number varies with different classification schemes). One of the most advanced orders is the Lepidoptera (meaning "scale-winged"), which includes the butterflies and moths. Consisting of about 120,000 recognized species worldwide, it is second only in numbers of species to the Coleoptera (beetles).

Most Lepidoptera are easily recognized by the usual presence of *4 membranous wings, fully or partially covered with overlapping scales*; a long, coiled *proboscis* or tongue for sucking liquid food (Fig. 1); and a *caterpillar-type larval form*, usually with *5 pairs of fleshy abdominal prolegs* in addition to the 3 pairs of thoracic legs. They undergo *complete metamorphosis*, consisting of egg, larva, pupa, and adult stages (see Chapter 2).

General insect anatomy is well described in *A Field Guide to the Insects* and other books. A description follows of the adult Lepidoptera, with particular reference to moths.

Head. The moth head is usually covered with scales; Figs. 1 and 2 show it with and without scale covering. The top of the head is the *vertex*, and below it in front is the *frons*. On each side of the frons lie the large compound eyes, which are made up of many individual facets. In some groups of moths the eyes are *hairy* (Fig. 3A); others have long, curving bristles above and below that are referred to as *lashes* (Fig. 3B). A round *ocellus*, or simple eye, may be present at the upper margin of each compound eye (Fig. 2), and some moths have *chaetosemata*—small patches of specialized sensory structures—in that area (Fig. 1).

The antennae are usually conspicuous and are often useful in identification. The first (basal) segment is called the *scape* (Fig. 2).

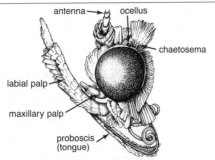

Fig. 1. Head (lateral view), with scale covering.

In some micro moths, the scape is enlarged and densely scaled to form an *eye-cap* (Fig. 4), which can be useful in identifying these moths. The second antennal segment is called the *pedicel* (Figs. 2, 4), and the rest of the segments form the *shaft*. The shaft is often scaled, and its segments are expanded laterally to give the shapes shown on the front endpapers. *Clubbed* (capitate) antennae are found only in butterflies in N. America, and so are one of the best ways to distinguish them from moths. *Simple* (threadlike or filiform) antennae are characteristic of many moth groups, and of the females in groups where males have comblike (*pectinate*) antennae, featherlike (*bipectinate* or *doubly bipectinate*) antennae, or other modified forms of antennae.

Below the antennae are the *labial palps* (Fig. 1), which are often very long and either upturned or project forward. They are usually 3-segmented, and characteristics of the segments and their scale covering may be useful in identification. The smaller *maxillary palps* (Fig. 1) are usually inconspicuous and may be vestigial or absent. Most moths have a long, coiled *proboscis* (Fig. 1), often referred to as the tongue. In some sphinx moths it is extremely

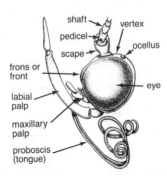

Fig. 2. Head (lateral view), without scale covering.

long (15 or more cm); in others it is quite small or absent. The Micropterigidae (p. 458) and some other primitive moths have chewing mouth parts (mandibles) and no proboscis at all.

Thorax. The thorax consists of 3 segments: the *prothorax*, the *mesothorax*, and the *metathorax* (see rear endpapers). The prothorax is very narrow on top, and usually bears 2 small plates called *patagia* that form the *collar*. The forelegs are attached to the prothorax. The middle legs and forewings are attached to the mesothorax, which is usually the largest part of the thorax; covering the *forewing bases* are the curved *tegulae*, which can move freely and seem to protect the wing-base area. The metathorax, which bears the hind legs and hind wings, is narrower and somewhat bilobed on top. The *tympana*, or "ears," are located toward the lower edges on each side of the metathorax.

The legs consist of several segments (rear endpapers). Their size, number of spines and spurs, and scale covering vary among different families, among species within families, and between males and females within species. The scale covering of the legs is sometimes useful in identification. The *epiphysis*, if present on the inner surface of the foreleg (see rear endpapers), may be used to clean the mouth parts and antennae. Males often have modified hind tibiae and groups of specialized scales (*androconia*) in various locations that help them disperse pheromones (chemicals secreted to make females receptive to mating).

At the tip of each leg is the *pretarsus*, which has 2 claws, usually a central pad (arolium), and a spine (empodium) at the end of the arolium in some species. Two sensory membranes (paronychia) may also be present.

Wings. In a few moth species—mostly in the families Lymantriidae (p. 337), Geometridae (p. 344), and Psychidae (p. 450)—the wings are reduced to small nubs, or are absent. In most moths, the wings are well developed and consist of broad to narrow membranes supported by a network of modified tracheae (air

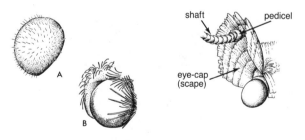

Fig. 3. A (*left*) Eye, hairy. **B** (*right*) Eye, lashed.

Fig. 4. Detail of base of antenna, showing eye-cap.

tubes) called *veins*. The different margins and areas of the fore-wings and hind wings are shown on the front endpapers. The leading edge of each wing is the *costal margin*, which ends at the *apex*. The *outer margin* extends from the apex to the *anal angle*; the *inner margin* extends from the base to the anal angle. Differences in the form of these wing margins and angles are often very useful in identifying families and other categories down to the species level. The *humeral angle* is formed by the curved base of the hind wing in some species.

As in butterflies and other insects, the veins are named and numbered according to the Needham-Comstock System (see front endpapers). The following abbreviations are used: C = Costa, Sc = Subcosta, R = Radius, M = Media, Cu = Cubitus, and A = Anal. The wing venation patterns created by the presence or absence of certain veins and the branches they form are very useful for identification of families and other subgroups of moths, so the characteristic patterns are illustrated for each family in this guide. When veins join together for short or long distances, they may create *cells*, such as the large median *discal cells* and smaller *areoles* (accessory cells), in the wing. If you need to study the wing venation of a specimen, it is best to use a strong hand lens or a microscope.

The forewing and hind wing move together as a unit in flight, so they must be held together in some way. A few primitive families have a *jugum* (see rear endpapers) on the inner margin of the forewing near the base; the jugum catches on the hind wing and holds the two wings together. Most moths, however, have a *frenulum* on the hindwing base that catches in a *retinaculum* on the underside of the forewing to hold the FW and HW together. The frenulum is a single spine in male moths and usually a group of bristles in females. Some moths, like all butterflies, lack both structures, and have a widened *humeral angle* on the hind wing so the forewing will not pop out from below the hind wing (Fig. 18).

The scale covering on the upper and lower surfaces of the wings is the most useful feature in identification. Scales vary in shape, but this usually cannot be seen without magnification of 150X or more. Wing patterns depend on the arrangement and coloration of the scales, and may be so variable within species as to make identification difficult. Some species have raised tufts of specialized scales on wing surfaces, or thumblike clumps of scales projecting from the inner margin of the forewing, as in some owlets (p. 161, Pl. 39) and prominents (p. 330, Pl. 43). The *fringe* is made up of hair-like scales in many of the smallest moths, and may be wider than the wing membrane itself. Specialized folds in the wing membrane and groups of scent-producing scales (androconia) may also be present, usually only in males (see ♂ Notch-winged Geometer, Pl. 46). Some primitive families have tiny spines (*aculeae*) on the wing membrane in addition to scales (not shown).

Wing patterns vary considerably; some moths have a highly complex pattern of lines, spots, and blotches. The forewings are usually more strikingly marked than the hind wings, but there are some exceptions, such as the underwings (*Catocala* species, p. 172). The forewing pattern may continue onto the hind wing, as in many geometer moths (p. 344).

The basic wing pattern found in noctuid moths or owlets (p. 77) and other families is shown on the front endpapers. The major lines that cross the forewing, from the base outward, are the *basal, antemedial (am.), median, postmedial (pm.), subterminal (st.), adterminal,* and *terminal lines* or bands. Lines may be partial, broken, or complete from the costa to the inner margin; they can vary from sharply defined to diffuse, and are sometimes shaded or edged with another color. Sometimes a line is represented only by a vague band (called a *shade line*) or by a series of dots. *Dashes* or daggerlike lines may be present, as in many *Acronicta* species, commonly known as dagger moths (p. 81, Pl. 17). *Basal, apical,* and *anal dashes* are most common, but dashes and streaks may be present in other locations such as the median area. The noctuid moths and some related families typically have at least some suggestion of spots on the forewing: *orbicular* (round), *reniform* (kidney-shaped), *claviform* (club-shaped), and occasionally *subreniform spots* may be present. These spots are often outlined in one color and filled with another, and their shapes may vary from the typical form. Many moths also have a *discal spot* on the hind wing. The coloring of the hindwing fringe is also described whenever it is useful for identification. The patterns on the underside of the wings are occasionally important in confirming identifications, but most moths can be identified using the wing patterns on the upperside of the forewings and hind wings.

Abdomen. Some moths have distinctive color patterns (such as rows of spots) produced by scales on the abdominal segments. In some cases, raised *scale tufts* are present on the dorsal surface of the abdomen. The external organs of reproduction, or *genitalia,* are located on the ventral surface, near the tip of the abdomen. Researchers who are working on the identification and characterization of moth genera and species dissect and stain the genitalia so they can be studied to clarify the taxonomic relationships between closely related species. This technique is not practical for the backyard naturalist, however. If you are having trouble confirming the identification of a moth you have collected, it might be wise to consult with a lepidopterist at a nearby university or natural history museum. Even an expert will find it difficult or impossible to identify a damaged specimen, so be sure to preserve your specimens carefully and to record the place and date of capture (see Chapter 3).

For the serious amateur lepidopterist who has advanced to the point of making genitalic preparations for study, the genitalic features of male and female moths are labeled on the drawings below. The functions of these structures are briefly described on p. 11; for more detailed information, consult Tuxen's *Taxonomist's Glossary of Genitalia in Insects* and Part 1 of Forbes' *Lepidoptera of New York and Neighboring States*.

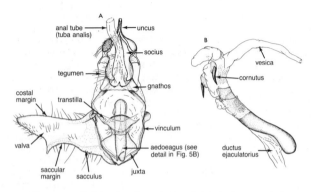

Fig. 5. A (*left*) Genitalia (♂). **B** (*right*) Aedoeagus (♂).

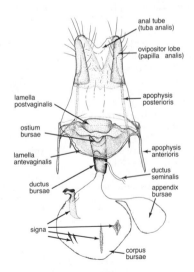

Fig. 6. Genitalia (♀).

2

The Moth Life Cycle

The Lepidoptera undergo complete metamorphosis, consisting of four distinct stages: *egg, larva, pupa,* and *adult.* Metamorphosis means "change in form during postembryonic development." This pronounced change is obvious when you contrast the crawling caterpillar, with chewing mouth parts, with the flying moth, with a sucking proboscis. While all Lepidoptera pass through these stages, there are many differences in details of the life cycle among the thousands of N. American species.

The egg. The egg (ovum) is small, usually less than 1 mm in diameter except in our largest species. Eggs may be somewhat flattened (Fig. 7) or erect (Fig. 8). The shell (chorion) may be smooth or sculptured. Many eggs are ribbed, with the ribs radiating from a tiny hole or group of holes called the micropyle. The micropyle is the opening that admits the sperm that fertilizes the egg nucleus. Microscopic holes (aeropyles) in the shell allow gas exchange between the developing embryo and the atmosphere. Moth eggs vary in color. They are often yellow, green, pink, or mottled when freshly laid, but they usually darken just before hatching.

The female moth usually glues her eggs to a leaf; in some species she inserts the eggs into the stem or branch of a plant, or drops them on the ground. Depending on the species, some females lay their eggs singly; others lay them in masses. The female seems to know instinctively which food plant to lay her eggs on, probably sensing chemical substances characteristic of that plant. Depending on the species and health of the female, the number of eggs laid may vary from just a few to over 18,000.

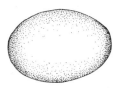

Fig. 7. Egg, flattened.

Fig. 8. Egg, erect.

The embryo usually develops quickly within the egg and may hatch within a week or less. Harsh environmental conditions, such as summer heat or the onset of winter, may curtail the embryo's growth and development for an indefinite period. This period of arrested growth, which can occur at any developmental stage, is called *diapause*. Development resumes when more favorable environmental conditions return.

The caterpillar. In the Lepidoptera, the larval form is commonly known as a caterpillar. When the tiny caterpillar first emerges from the egg, it may eat its eggshell before beginning to feed on its host plant. At first it prefers tender young leaves, but as it grows it may switch to tougher leaves or to a different food plant altogether. Some caterpillars (such as some pinions, p. 112) are known to devour other caterpillars; others feed on soft-bodied insects such as aphids.

Caterpillars have soft, cylindrical bodies; they may be naked, sparsely covered with bristles, or densely hairy. (The word caterpillar comes from the Latin, *catta pilosa,* for "hairy cat.") A few examples of common caterpillars are shown on Pl. 1 at the center of this guide. In a few moth species, such as the Io Moth (p. 49) and the Hag Moth (Monkey Slug, p. 410), the larva (Pl. 1) is covered with stinging hairs. Some sphinx moth larvae, called *hornworms* (Pl. 1), have a spine at the tip of the abdomen, but despite their threatening appearance, these caterpillars do not sting. Strikingly obvious bristles on many other kinds of caterpillars are equally harmless.

The caterpillar has a rounded, hardened *head capsule* (Fig. 9), which is divided by an inverted Y-shaped line or suture into parts that look like two large eyes on each side. These are not true eyes, although caterpillars usually do have about 6 small *ocelli* (simple eyes) in a circular pattern. Antennae and both maxillary and labial palps are small and inconspicuous. The mandibles, the main chewing organs, are well-developed. The thorax bears 3 pairs of legs that are usually short (Fig. 9). The abdomen has several breathing openings (spiracles) on each side and usually 5 pairs of short, fleshy *prolegs* (geometer moths, loopers, and a few others have only 2 pairs of prolegs) equipped with sharp, hooklike *crochets* on their bottom surfaces. The size and arrangement of crochets are often used to identify caterpillars. The only insects with similar larvae are the sawfly group of Hymenoptera (bees, wasps and ants), but their abdominal prolegs lack crochets.

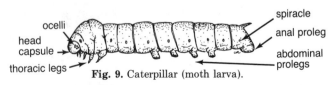

Fig. 9. Caterpillar (moth larva).

Caterpillars usually feed individually, but some species feed in groups for all or part of their larval lives. Some spin communal webs for protection (Fall Webworm, p. 67; Eastern Tent Caterpillar, p. 54). As they feed, they outgrow their exoskeletons. To provide room for further growth, they undergo from 3 to 10 or more (typically 5) molts. Each time they molt, the old exoskeleton cracks along the back and the caterpillar crawls out. The newly formed exoskeleton, which lies beneath the old one, stretches and hardens after the old one is shed. The period between molts is called an *instar,* so a newly hatched caterpillar would be called a *first instar larva.*

The time between hatching from the egg and completion of larval stages varies from species to species. It also depends upon the availability of food, a favorable climate, and other factors. Many moths complete this phase in about a month, but if the species overwinters in the larval stage, that stage lasts much longer. The Isabella Tiger Moth (p. 66) hibernates in its larval stage, known as the Woolly Bear (Pl. 1), and undergoes diapause until spring in a protected place it seeks actively in early fall. Diapause may occur at other times of the year in some species, such as during very hot and dry periods in summer. In the far north, more than one year may be needed for development, since the growing season is so short.

Caterpillar shapes and color patterns may change from one instar to another during the life cycle. The first instar larva of the Cecropia Moth (Pl. 1), for example, is black; the second yellow; the third yellow, orange or green; and the last two are green. In some species certain structures (such as the terminal abdominal "horn" in some hornworms) may disappear in later instars. In other species, the color may vary within an instar. The full-grown caterpillar of the Imperial Moth (p. 45), for example, may be either green or brown.

The pupa. When the caterpillar reaches the proper size and nutritional level, it seeks a protected place where it can pupate. Many species spin a tight or loose cocoon of silk, which they secrete from modified salivary glands and spin from a spinneret located below the mandibles. Bits of frass (larval excrement), plant material, or other debris may be used in the cocoon. If no cocoon is made, a few leaves or bits of debris may be tied together with silk, or the caterpillar may burrow into the soil to form a *cell,* as do the sphinx moths. Cocoons are built by developing larvae and later used for pupation in a few groups (bagworms, p. 450; sack-bearers, p. 57).

All the caterpillars in a certain genus, subfamily, or family of moths usually prepare themselves for pupation in the same way. When the caterpillar is ready to pupate, it molts one last time into the virtually inactive and helpless stage called the *pupa* (Fig. 10). (In butterflies, this stage is called the *chrysalis.*) None of our moth larvae attach themselves to a pad of silk by their terminal abdomi-

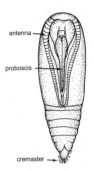

Fig. 10. Pupa.

antenna

proboscis

cremaster →

nal hook (*cremaster*) as do the butterflies (see Klots, *A Field Guide to the Butterflies,* p. 45). However, the cremaster may help the pupa hold its position in its cocoon or cell. In most species, the pupa is *obtect* (has all of its appendages encased against the body), but in some primitive species the pupa is *exarate,* with free-hanging appendages. The proboscis casing hangs free like a jug handle in many sphinx moth pupae, which are otherwise obtect. The exoskeleton is usually shiny brownish to blackish, but may have a mottled pattern in some species.

The pupal period may last a few days to several months. Beneath the exoskeleton, substantial biochemical and anatomical changes occur as larval features are replaced by adult structures such as antennae, proboscis, wings, and sex organs. Part of the time is usually spent in diapause, particularly in species that overwinter as pupae. The adult emerges when fully developed, or when environmental factors such as lengthening days, warmer temperature, and increasing rainfall bring about the end of diapause. In many species, the coordination of the adult moth's emergence from the pupal stage and the hatching of eggs with the leafing of food plants and flowering of nectar sources is remarkably close.

The emerging moth breaks through the pupal exoskeleton and drags itself out. If in a cocoon, it must also penetrate this barrier. Some species secrete a fluid that dissolves the silk to create a hole where the adult can emerge (Silkworm Moth; many giant silkworm moths); some primitive microlepidoptera have a ridge on the head called a *cocoon cutter* for the same purpose. A few, such as the flannel moths, have a trap door in the cocoon that pops open when the moth pushes against it.

Once out of the cocoon or other protective enclosure, the moth crawls onto it or some other support and begins to pump blood into its limp, shriveled wings. Expansion and hardening of the wings may take an hour or more, after which the moth takes flight to seek food, water, or a mate.

Reproduction. Many adult moths mate almost immediately after emerging from the pupal stage; other adults are killed by predators, accidents, or extreme weather conditions before they have a chance to reproduce.

Males are attracted to females of their species by both visual and chemical stimuli. Females usually secrete a chemical substance called a *pheromone* into the air from special glands located toward the tip of the abdomen, which can be exposed at will. This pheromone may be detected by males up to several miles away in large species with special sense organs on their antennae, and they fly upwind toward its source. The pheromone of one species in a genus may be attractive to males of related species, but other mechanisms minimize mistaken identities. In coastal South Carolina, females of the 3 species of *Callosamia* (p. 51) "call" males by releasing pheromone at different times of day: the Sweetbay Silkmoth releases it during the morning and early afternoon, the Promethea Moth from mid-afternoon to dusk, and the Tuliptree Silkmoth from dusk to about midnight. Males usually perform courtship behavior and secrete pheromones themselves to make the female receptive for mating. Pheromones may be secreted from wings, abdomen, and legs, and distributed by means of tufts of special hair-scales on those regions.

If the female is receptive to the male, she permits him to clasp the tip of her abdomen with the flaplike *valves* of his genitalia (Fig. 5, p. 6). The *aedoeagus* (penis) is inserted through her *ostium bursae* and into the *ductus bursae* (Fig. 6). Structural details are usually consistent within each species, but often quite different from one species to another.

Sperm are introduced by the male into the *corpus bursae* of the female. A thin, membranous pouch (*spermatophore*) may be secreted by the male around the sperm mass as it is released, encasing the sperm and perhaps plugging the corpus bursae after mating. Copulation may last up to several hours, after which the two moths part. There is evidence of multiple matings by females in some species.

The spermatophore is later dissolved by enzymes and the sperm travel through the *ductus seminalis* (Fig. 6, p. 6) to another storage sac associated more closely with the ovaries: the *spermatheca*. Here the sperm remain and receive nourishment until they are brought into contact with eggs passing along the common oviduct to the *vagina*. The vagina opens along with the *tuba analis* (anal tube) at the tip of the abdomen between the *ovipositor lobes,* or *papillae anales*. These lobes are typically soft and covered with bristles, but in some species that insert their eggs inside stems and leaves the bristles are hardened and sharp, for piercing plant tissues.

The system described above, with separate openings for copulation and oviposition, is called the *ditrysian type,* and is found in most moths (those that belong to suborder Ditrysia). Females of the primitive suborders Zeugloptera, Dachnonypha, Exoporia, and

Monotrysia (see p. 28) have only a single opening at the tip of the abdomen (*monotrysian* type). Sperm enter and eggs are deposited through a common tube, the *vulva,* which divides inside the ductus bursae and vagina.

The length of adult life under natural conditions is not known for many moth species. Moths may be killed by predators, weather, disease, automobiles, and other forces. Some species live only 2–3 days; others have been reported to live up to 60 days or longer. The Cecropia Moth (p. 52) usually lives 7–14 days, averaging about 10 days for both sexes. Two weeks seems to be a fairly reliable estimate of adult lifespan for medium-sized and large moths, although it is really not safe to generalize on the basis of the little we know about this subject.

Rearing Moths

Many collectors find great satisfaction in obtaining ova (eggs) or larvae and rearing them to the adult stage. Perfect specimens of adult moths can be obtained this way, but more important, new knowledge can be gained about the life history of species reared by collectors. In many cases the larval and pupal stages of moths have not been formally studied and described.

Our knowledge of some species is so limited that not even a single natural food plant (or host plant that is acceptable to larvae reared in captivity) is known. No food plants have been recorded for many of the species treated in this book. If you have never reared moths before, you will probably find it easiest to rear large moths with well-known feeding habits, such as giant silkworm moths (Saturniidae) and sphinx moths (Sphingidae).

Rearing from eggs. You can order eggs from a dealer (see list of biological supply houses on p. 466) or capture females in the wild and confine them in a puffed-out paper bag until they lay eggs. (Check the bag carefully—moth eggs are small and often stick to the bag.) Transfer the eggs to a container where you have placed fresh leaves of a known food plant for the species, so the caterpillars can feed on it when they hatch. If the food plant is unknown, try leaves of many different species. After the larvae begin to feed, you can keep them in a roomy container with a moderately tight lid (if the lid is too loose, the food will dry out). If you prefer to put the sprigs or branches of the food plant in a jar of water to keep them fresh, be sure to cover the jar except where the stem emerges, or the caterpillars may fall in and drown. When rearing moths, I usually put some fresh leaves in a 35 mm film can every day, and snap the cap on over a piece of paper towel that will absorb excess moisture. To obtain eggs from very small moths, I put the female in a baby food jar until she lays her eggs, then transfer the tiny larvae to small tins for their early stages. Some researchers rear individual larvae in screw-capped vials, to make it easier to study the developmental stages. Allow a little air into the rearing container, but not enough to dry out the food plant.

You can feed the larvae fresh leaves or place them on growing plants. If the food plant is a small herbaceous plant, you can often dig it up and grow it in a pot, covering it with a glass or plastic casing such as a lamp chimney. Put a piece of gauze over the top and secure it with a rubber band to keep active larvae from escaping. If your larvae feed on trees or shrubs in the wild, you can use a method called *sleeving* to assure them of a fresh, natural food supply. Slip a tubular piece of netting around a branch containing larvae, and secure the netting at both ends to prevent larvae from escaping and predators and parasites from entering.

Study and measure the caterpillars as they grow; if the life cycle of the species is not known, you may even be able to publish a description of it. To learn techniques for describing developing larvae and pupae, consult McGuffin's *Guide to the Geometridae of Canada.* Keep records of the food plants on which larvae have been collected or successfully reared in captivity. When rearing larvae of unknown species, photograph and keep preserved samples of each stage for later reference.

Rearing from caterpillars. You can collect caterpillars by searching the foliage of plants carefully, or by whacking the branches of a bush or tree with a stick after you have placed a white sheet on the ground underneath. Use the same feeding techniques described above, and try to duplicate natural conditions as closely as is practical. If the species is a leaf miner, you can rear it in the leaves the larvae are mining, but be sure to keep the leaves from drying out by placing them in a nearly airtight container.

Rearing from pupae. Many large and medium-sized moths spin silken cocoons (see Pl. 2) before pupating; others burrow in the ground. If you want to rear moths from a cocoon, try to provide conditions as close as possible to those in nature. Species that overwinter as pupae usually cannot survive indoors. You can keep overwintering larvae or pupae in an overturned glass jar, placed next to your house or some other partly sheltered place.

A word of caution. It is against the law to import or export living insects without a permit from the U.S. Department of Agriculture. The importation of a species not normally part of our North American fauna could result in the introduction of a devastating pest, such as the Gypsy Moth (p. 340). Be sure to comply with all federal, state, and local regulations.

3

Collecting and Preparing Moths

Collecting moths. Since this book emphasizes the identification of pinned, spread moths, it is important to know techniques for proper collection and satisfactory preparation of specimens. Moths occur just about everywhere in the world that plants grow, and vary widely in their habits. While most are *nocturnal* (active at night), a great many are *diurnal* (active only during the day); examples of diurnal moths include some sphinx moths and clear-wing moths. Others, such as many other sphinx moths, are most active at twilight, and are referred to as *crepuscular* species.

Light traps. Collect nocturnal species by using a light to attract them to a sheet or a trap. Different species may be attracted to different wavelengths of light, so some collectors use two or more kinds of bulbs together for better overall effectiveness. The type most commonly used is the black-light fluorescent tube, one that does not emit the most dangerous ultraviolet light that could burn the retinas of your eyes. Other collectors employ mercury vapor bulbs, normal white-light bulbs, or Coleman-type gas lanterns. Use either a regular 110-volt outlet for power, or, in remote areas, a storage battery or small generator. Small 12-volt batteries are available that are not too heavy; you can build a small battery charger into the system to make recharging simple. When using a battery, you will need a converter (inverter) to convert DC current to AC. Suitable equipment may be purchased from supply houses listed on p. 466. You can also collect moths near outdoor lights such as street lamps and building lights, but be sure to alert people nearby to what you are doing so you won't be arrested as a prowler.

If you intend to collect actively from a light, hang a sheet from a rope stretched taut between two supports such as trees, preferably about as high as you can easily reach. Select a clearing, cliff top, or open area near woods where your light can attract moths from a fairly wide area. The sheet should be tightly pegged or weighted down at the bottom corners, with the excess stretched forward to provide a shelf that will catch falling moths (Fig. 11B). Then mount the light on a pole or hang it from a branch or second rope about 2 feet in front of the sheet, so it will cast a glow over most of it.

Lights will attract a variety of insects, including beetles as well as moths. Put the specimens you want for your collection in killing jars (or in live-catch containers if you want eggs), and leave the others alone. You will need a good flashlight or headlamp to see the features of the moths, especially if you use a bluish black-light bulb. Some collectors make their light traps more effective by putting a little amyl acetate or some other chemical that is attractive to moths on the sheet.

A Robinson or garbage-can type light trap (Fig. 11D) is especially useful if you want to perform quantitative sampling. The light sits above a rather large container that may contain small jars charged with a killing agent such as ethyl acetate, with cotton wicks to disperse the fumes. Some collectors use paper bags of cyanide hung inside the container. Four vertical vanes (barely visible in 11D) intercept moths as they fly around the light, and they fall down a funnel into the canister. If no killing agent is used, put layers of egg carton material or a similar irregular cushion on the bottom to provide surfaces where the moths can rest until you can open the trap and select the specimens you want. The advantage of such a trap is that you can collect all night without having to be present, and can perhaps capture species that fly toward dawn. Disadvantages include the possibility of vandalism, and damage to specimens when too many moths and other insects such as beetles mix together in the trap. You may also kill many more moths than you want. If you do not use a killing agent, the insects may hurt themselves while attempting to escape, or crawl over each other and denude each other of scales; but this way you can avoid unnecessary killing of unwanted specimens.

Bait traps. Sugar bait on trees and other supports may attract moths that will not fly to lights. Sugaring is a particularly effective way to collect winter-flying species and underwings (*Catocala* species), and is beautifully described by Holland in his *Moth Book* ("Sugaring for Moths"). Concoct a mixture of beer, brown sugar, and perhaps some rotten fruit or rum and leave it in the sun to ferment for a day or two before your collecting trip. Before dark, paint a swath of the mixture on the trunks of smooth-barked trees, fenceposts, and so on in a wooded area (an old stand of large hardwoods usually is best). Then, after dark, walk the baitline with killing jars and flashlight, bottling the moths you want. Many moths are quick to fly away from bait, so you will have to make your moves quick and sure.

A baitline and two or more well-separated light rigs in a wooded area should assure you of a good night's catch. A poor catch may result if there is too much moonlight or it is too chilly. Hot, humid, moonless summer nights are usually excellent. You can expect your best results in areas where the vegetation is greatly varied, and where there are no competing lights or signs of recent ecological disturbance (floods, pesticide use, land clearing).

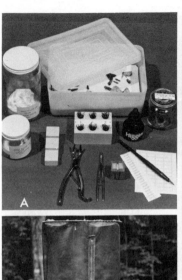

You can also capture moths using a bait trap that is suspended from a tree (Fig. 11C). The trap consists of a cone-shaped funnel that opens into a large cylinder; both can be made by attaching plastic netting or some other kind of mesh to a wire frame that can be hung from a tree. Sew a zipper into the side of the cylinder or make a Velcro-sealed door (flap) that will enable you to remove captured specimens easily. Using wire or cord, suspend the cone inside the cylinder so that the wide end (bottom) of the cone can serve as the entrance to the trap, at the bottom. Hang a wooden platform an inch or two below the entrance and put a dish of sweet bait mixture (described above) at the center of the platform. When moths or butterflies try to leave after being attracted to the bait, they will tend to fly upward through the cone into the cylinder, where they will become trapped. Be sure to empty the trap promptly to avoid damaged specimens and to release any that you do not wish to keep.

Entomologists have developed synthetic sex pheromones for trap bait, which may be bought commercially and put out for selected species in small traps. Pheromones are widely used to collect pest species of clear-wing moths (p. 424). Some collectors cage freshly emerged females of giant silkworm moths such as the Promethea Moth or Cecropia Moth, and collect males that are attracted by the female's pheromones. For satisfactory results, be sure to try this technique at the proper season and time of day or night for the species involved.

Another way to obtain a large sampling of moths is with a Malaise trap (Fig. 11E), which, like the bait trap, takes advantage of the instinct of insects to move upward when they encounter an obstacle. If you stake out a tentlike net in a field or woodland clearing, insects will enter the tent and follow the seams upward until they fall into the container. The container may be designed to keep them alive or may contain a killing agent. As with a light trap, trapping and killing is indiscriminate; many insects other than Lepidoptera will be caught.

Sweeping. To collect day-fliers, you usually have to net them on the wing or as they rest on plants or on the ground. Many diurnal moths stay close to their food plants; try searching carefully for them there. An assortment of microlepidoptera can be collected by sweeping a net through a variety of vegetation, but be careful to empty the net after just a few sweeps or the moths will be ruined. Sometimes rather inactive or well-camouflaged moths can be collected with a jar from the treetrunk or blossom where

Fig. 11. (*opposite*) Collecting equipment: A) relaxing box, B) light trap with sheet, C) bait trap, D) garbage-can light trap, E) Malaise trap, F) Cornell storage drawer with unit pinning trays and Riker mount.

they are resting. You can catch underwings (*Catocala* species) during the day by tapping treetrunks in mature forests with a net handle, then following the moths to nearby trees when they fly.

Many of the crepuscular sphinx moths hover over deep-throated flowers such as trumpet creeper and petunias at twilight to feed. Here a net and quick reflexes will bring good results. In the far north where it never gets completely dark on summer nights, many moths are diurnal but seem to be more active during the night hours. Sweeping with a net is the best collecting technique to use in these areas.

Killing specimens. Many collectors kill butterflies by pinching the thorax, but this technique does not usually work well with moths. Because of their thoracic structure, you may end up just crushing the thorax badly, but not quickly killing them. You can kill very large moths by injecting a killing fluid into the thorax with a hypodermic needle or similar device, but most collectors do not have ready access to hypodermic needles.

Killing jars. Most collectors catch moths in a killing jar. Many fluids do a quick and satisfactory job: diethyl ether, chloroform, or carbon tetrachloride, but these chemicals are dangerous and cannot normally be procured by the layman. The one available fluid that is apparently not too dangerous is ethyl acetate, which may be bought from a large drugstore chain or from a biological supply house.

Soak a pad at the bottom of a jar with fluid, then cover it with a cardboard disc to keep the moths from getting wet. Put cotton, rubber bands, or pieces of blotting paper in the bottom of the jar and pour a layer of plaster of Paris over it. Then add more fluid and let it seep through the plaster into the absorbent bottom. When the plaster surface is dry, the jar is ready for use.

Jars charged with a cyanide compound (potassium, sodium, or calcium cyanide) last longer and kill quickly, but this highly toxic chemical is not usually available to the collector. Put a layer of cyanide in the bottom of a jar and shake it gently to distribute the cyanide evenly, then add a layer of fine sawdust on top. Finally pour in a layer of plaster of Paris to keep the insects separate from the cyanide. If you do have a cyanide jar, tape the bottom to prevent release of the poison if the jar should break. Dispose of an old jar by digging a hole, breaking the jar with a rock or shovel, then covering it. Label all killing jars clearly and keep them in a safe place, away from children, pets, and water supplies.

When a moth is at rest, bring the open killing jar up under it and bring the lid down from the top. The moth will usually jump back and down into the jar.

It is important to keep your specimens in as perfect condition as possible, so ideally you should put one moth in a jar, and when it stops moving, dump it into another large "dump jar" for storage with other specimens until you return to your workroom. Be careful not to jostle the dump jar when it contains many moths. Also, it is best to use separate dump jars for large, medium, and very small moths to prevent damage. Never put hard-bodied insects such as grasshoppers or beetles into the same jar with moths, particularly if the insects are alive; they will ruin your specimens. If you wish to collect other insects with Lepidoptera, use separate killing jars. Leave the insects in the killing jars well after they stop moving, for they can "come to life" again. Leave medium and large moths in a killing jar for at least one half-hour. Do not put moths in alcohol; their colors will fade and they will be worthless as specimens. Caterpillars, however, are normally preserved in special color-retaining fluids like KAAD, obtainable from suppliers (p. 466). A 70% alcohol to 30% water solution will do, but will usually affect colors.

The relaxing box. After specimens are killed, they should be spread as soon as possible after spending a short period of time in a *relaxing box*—a container with high humidity that keeps the muscles relaxed for easy spreading. A plastic refrigerator container (Fig. 11A) makes an ideal relaxing box. Place a layer of absorbent material such as paper towels on the bottom, about $\frac{1}{2}$ in. thick. Saturate it with water, but leave no excess. Add an anti-mold chemical: paradichlorobenzene (moth crystals), carbolic acid (phenol), or thymol. Then put a protective layer of cardboard or file folder paper on top, to keep the moths from getting wet (which would make them useless). Lay the specimens uniformly on this surface, leave them for a few hours, and they will be ready to spread.

If water droplets form on the sides and top of the relaxing box, open it and wipe them off. Be sure not to leave any standing water in the box.

Specimens will remain in good condition in a relaxing box for several days, but will begin to deteriorate if left too long. If you cannot spread them within a few days, you should *field-pin* them (pin them, but let them dry out unspread) or *paper* them (store them in envelopes with their wings folded over their backs). Glassine stamp envelopes or opaque coin envelopes can be bought at hobby or stationery stores, but many collectors fold their own triangular envelopes (Fig. 12), which can be made in any size from almost any kind of paper. Whether you field-pin or paper your specimens, *do not forget to put collection data* (place and date of capture and your name as collector) *on the pin label or envelope.* A rubber stamp or two will save time for dates and places where you collect frequently.

Dried specimens can be placed in a relaxing box and softened for spreading. This takes 1–3 days, depending on the size of the moth and conditions in the relaxing box; the specimen is usually not as flexible as it would be when freshly killed. Satisfactory spreading of medium and large moths is possible even after years of storage in field-pinned or papered condition, but microlepidoptera are very difficult to spread once they have dried. If you must field-pin a micro, try to position the wings *so the hind wings are exposed to view.*

Spreading. Specimens must be dried with wings outspread not only for an attractive display but also to keep the hind wings visible for identification or study. Spreading techniques vary among collectors, and good descriptions are given in both Klots' *Field Guide to the Butterflies* and Borror and White's *Field Guide to the Insects.* My favorite method is described below, along with some variations used by colleagues for high-quality results.

First you will need a spreading board (Fig. 14, p. 23); paper strips for holding down the wings; insect pins, including tiny minuten pins ("minutens") for tiny micros (Fig. 13); and properly relaxed specimens. The boards must have smooth sides and a central notch slightly wider than the body of the moth you wish to spread. If the notch is too narrow, the moth's body will touch the edges of the boards and the wings cannot be pulled easily into place. If the notch is too wide, the moth's wingbases will not be properly supported and may wrinkle or fold. You can buy or make adjustable spreading boards, but serious collectors will usually have many boards with notches of various widths for different-sized moths. The paper strips that hold down the set wings should be wide enough to completely cover the wings of small and medium moths. Fasten extra paper over the wings of large specimens for a perfectly flat result. I use tracing paper (pads cut into lengthwise strips 1 in. wide), but have used waxed paper in a pinch. Translucent papers allow you to see if the wings are evenly spread, but any smooth, strong paper will do if you use a narrow strip and cover the rest of the wings once they are straight.

Insect pins come in a variety of sizes, from #000 (the thinnest) to #7 (the largest). Sizes 1–4 are normally used for medium-small to large moths. For micros, sizes 000–0 may do, but these tend to bend easily when handled. Many collectors use minutens for initial mounting, then double-mount their specimens on tiny blocks of

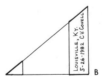

Fig. 12. Triangular envelope for papered moth: **A)** before folding, **B)** folded and labeled, with specimen inside.

polyporous fungus, balsa wood, cork, or other material that is pushed up on a larger insect pin (Fig. 13). Most of the moths in Pls. 63–64 are on minutens. Double-mounts are normally used for moths with wingspans of 1 cm or less, particularly if the thorax is only about 1 mm wide.

Here are the steps (for a right-handed person) in spreading a medium-sized moth. First remove the specimen from the relaxing box. It must be limp enough so that the wings move freely and flutter a bit when you blow on them. Select an insect pin and push it straight down through the high point of the thorax so it makes a right angle to the long axis of the body. The pin must also run straight through the thorax from top to bottom so the specimen is not tilted to the left or right. Push the insect up the pin so that the top of the thorax is from $\frac{1}{3}$ to $\frac{1}{4}$ the distance down from the pinhead (Fig 14A). Grasp the pinhead with the thumb and forefinger of your right hand and push the pin down *perfectly straight* into the soft material at the bottom of the spreading board notch, stopping when the wings can be brought out at right angles to the body and lie flat on the board (Fig. 14B). It is critical that both sets of wings lie flat—*make sure that they do not angle upward or downward* as they lie on the two side pieces of the board.

Place two pieces of tracing paper on the upper surface of the board and fasten the paper at the top with pins (14B). Glass- or plastic-headed florists' pins are ideal for this. Be sure the edges of the paper strips lie $\frac{1}{4}$ to $\frac{1}{8}$ in. from the inner edges of the boards so you can move the wingbases. However, do not put the paper out too far, or too much of the wing surfaces will be exposed. Lay the paper strips over each wing. You may wish to pin them temporarily, to keep the wings down. Place a sturdy insect pin up against

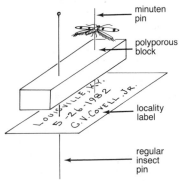

Fig. 13. Micro moth on double mount.

the thorax, just behind the base of the left hind wing (see arrow in 14B), and push the pin into the soft material in the notch, to keep the moth's body from swinging to the left as you pull the left wings into position. Be sure the legs and antennae are out of the way. Now you are ready to position the wings (Fig. 14C, D).

While holding the paper strip in your left thumb and forefinger, insert a sharp, thin insect pin or special mounting pick (I use a shaved-down matchstick with a minuten pushed into one end) behind the costa of the left forewing near the base, and swing the wing toward the head until the inner margin is *at a right angle* to the board notch or body axis (Fig. 14C). Insert the pin through the wing and into the board to hold that wing in position. Then insert another pin or pick through the hind wing, just behind the radial vein near the wingbase, and pull that wing forward until only a *small triangular space* is left between forewing and hind wing (Fig. 14D). Move the pin carefully in an arc to avoid tearing the wings. Pull the paper strip evenly and firmly over the left wings, and secure it with pins above and below the wings, and with another pin where the triangular space separates forewing from hind wing (Fig. 14E).

Repeat this procedure with the right wings. After the paper is secured over all wings, remove the pins or picks used to hold the wings temporarily in place. Use pins against the antennae to gently nudge them into place in front of the head (Fig. 14F). Pins may also be crossed above or below the abdomen to hold it evenly in place.

Some collectors do not put the paper in place until all four wings are temporarily pinned as desired. As a refinement, you can fold the tracing paper back neatly before pinning it over the wings so the edge nearest the body will be rounded and thus will not dig into the scales and leave a line on the wing.

Other collectors use a small wooden block (not shown) with a notch cut to hold the body; the notch is lined with soft material, as in spreading boards. After the moth is pinned into position, blow its wings into position or pull them forward gently as described above. Wrap a thread around each wingbase to hold the wings in place. Then place a bit of paper over each wing and wrap the thread two or more times around each to hold the paper in place over the wings. Specialists often use this method for the tiniest microlepidoptera.

After your first specimen has been spread on the board, you can spread another specimen very close to the first, and so on until the board is filled. Be sure to put collection data on the board (I write it on the tracing paper strips) or make finished pin labels and tuck them under the tracing paper beside each specimen. The spreading date should also be recorded on the paper strips. Then put the

Fig. 14. (*opposite*) Spreading techniques.

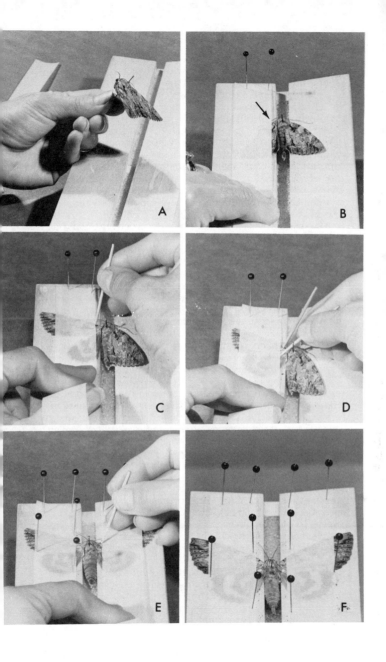

board in a dry, pest-free cabinet or container and leave it for a week or longer. The specimens can then be removed from the board, labeled, identified, and stored.

Labeling. To have any scientific value, specimens must be labeled with the place and date of capture and the collector's name. Print your collecting data with permanent black ink on high-quality cardstock (that contains 50% or more rag or cotton) so the label will not deteriorate over the years. For places you visit often, you can buy printed labels on which you will need to fill in only the date. Keep your labels small so they won't obstruct other specimens or appear unsightly. Each label should be pinned below the insect, roughly $\frac{2}{3}$ of the way down from the pinhead. A 3-step pinning block (Fig. 11A), sold by suppliers, is handy for positioning labels at a uniform height on pins.

The *locality* where you collected the specimen should be given precisely so other collectors can find it. If it is inside a town limit, that town name and state (or province) will suffice. In the country, map coordinates or highway mile markers may be the only points of reference. Road junctions may be used, or distances from well-known, permanent landmarks, such as town limit signs on highways ("Kentucky, Rt. 31-W, 3 miles S. of Ft. Knox"). Abbreviate dates with the month ("Sept.") followed by the day and year, or number the month with a Roman numeral ("V-17-1981" for May 17, 1981). Using Roman numerals will prevent confusion if the European system of giving dates (day before month) is used. Otherwise, "7-8-81" could mean Aug. 7 instead of July 8.

The *determination label* is usually placed below the data label. This label gives the genus and species name, often followed by the species author's name. Beneath that information, specialists usually write their own name and the date of determination: "Det. C.V. Covell Jr. 1981." You can buy determination label blanks printed with your name as the determiner from a supplier.

Storage. Your specimens must be stored away from moisture, light, and pests. Keep pinned specimens in tightly closed insect boxes such as a Schmitt box, or in glass-topped museum storage drawers such as the Cornell, U.S. National Museum, or California Academy of Sciences drawers (Fig. 11F). Unless your specimens are on exhibit, they should not be exposed to light for long periods, as their pigments will fade slowly over months and years. Moisture may relax the specimens and cause pins to rust. This is a particular problem in coastal areas where salty sea air makes pins corrode rapidly.

Some collectors prefer to store their specimens in Riker mounts (Fig. 11F, p. 16), which are shallow cardboard boxes with glass fronts and a cotton cushion inside where the specimen can rest. They can be ordered from supply houses in various sizes and are handy for display, but they tend to squash bodies and flatten wing scales, and specimens cannot be easily handled for study.

You should fumigate your storage drawers and boxes with a chemical to keep out pests. Moth specimens left out in the open may be eaten by mice, voles, cockroaches, and other scavengers. Specimens in loosely closed containers such as cigar boxes may be destroyed by dermestid beetles, booklice, or other small pests. Pests can infest even tightly fitting containers, usually entering when the containers are opened for study. Naphthalene flakes or mothballs are fairly good for preventing infestations, but will not kill pests once they are established. Paradichlorobenzene crystals or "pest strip" chemicals may be used to fumigate infested collections, and will usually kill dermestids and booklice. Be careful not to inhale much of the fumes of any of the chemicals used for fumigation, as they could be harmful.

Identification. After the specimen is spread and the data label affixed, try to identify it to the species level with the help of this and other available literature (see Bibliography, p. 464). A good hand lens or dissecting microscope will help you see small structures, wing venation, and genitalia. If you have access to a major collection, ask permission to search the drawers for a series of moths that match your specimen. Curators of these collections and experienced amateur collectors may help you determine the identity of your specimen. Once you have identified it, you can place your specimen in the appropriate part of your collection.

Arrangement of collections. The families, genera, and species of North American Lepidoptera are arranged according to a checklist (see Classification, p. 28). Series of specimens in big collections are usually stored in unit pinning trays in the drawers (Fig. 11F), and these usually contain a label giving genus and species names of the contents. Thus the groups of specimens of each species can be rearranged easily when additional species are added. If your species are grouped vertically or horizontally in the box or drawer, be sure to leave room to add new specimens without too much rearranging. The most recent classification of moths is reflected in the Hodges *et al. Check List of the Lepidoptera of America North of Mexico*, and each of the 11,233 species has a number assigned to it for easy reference. Although later publications will certainly make changes in the order of species and higher categories, arrangement of collections according to this list will bring them into conformity with most other collections. Your checklist copy may also be marked and used as a catalog to your collection—especially helpful as your collection grows.

Shipping specimens. Specimens sent through the mail must be protected from damage. Firmly layer papered moths in a nest of cotton or similar padding inside a sturdy box, then tape the box thoroughly and wrap it in paper. For further security, place the box inside a larger box, nestled in more padding or plastic foam bits to prevent crushing.

Pinned specimens must be pushed far into a securely anchored pinning bottom in a sturdy wooden or cardboard insect box. Use extra insect pins to hold the body still if it tends to move on the pin. Be sure no loose pins, body parts, or any other loose matter is in the box, for these will destroy the specimens in transit. Some people place a piece of cardboard atop the insect pins and pad the space between that cardboard and the boxtop with cotton or a similar material. The box is then wrapped in paper, taped, and placed in a nest of packing material in a larger carton.

Be sure the address label is securely fastened. It is also a good idea to write on the carton, "Fragile. Dead, dried insect specimens for scientific study; no commercial value." Finally, you may wish to wrap strong string around the package for an extra measure of protection.

Very small lots should be sent first class. Larger ones, sent parcel post, will arrive more quickly if you pay extra for special handling. You might want to use another courier service in some cases. If you are sending specimens to a museum or university, you can probably qualify for Library Rate, the cheapest way to send a package. If you mail specimens out of the country, be prepared to fill out the appropriate customs forms and to comply with possible restrictions (see p. 13).

Communication with other collectors. The best way to contact professional and amateur lepidopterists is through membership in the Lepidopterists' Society. Established in 1947, it has over 1,500 members worldwide. It publishes the *News*, a bimonthly newsletter with notices from members and many items of interest, and the *Journal*, a quarterly scientific magazine. Smaller regional groups include the Society of Kentucky Lepidopterists, the Ohio Lepidopterists, and the Southern Lepidopterists. Their current addresses can be obtained through the Secretary of the Lepidopterists' Society (see p. 466).

4

Classification of Moths

Each organism is known throughout the world by a distinctive combination of Latinized genus and species names, according to a binomial (two-name or two-part) system first utilized in 1758 by the Swedish naturalist, Carolus Linnaeus. Although Linnaeus' system has been refined, the universal scientific name for a species still consists of a Latinized noun (beginning with a capital letter) followed by a Latinized modifier (beginning with a lower case letter). Thus *Sphinx eremitus* is the two-part name, or binomial, which names a distinct biological species, the Hermit Sphinx (p. 34).

A genus may include 1 species or many. For example, this book treats 10 species of the genus *Sphinx,* but only one of *Pachysphinx.* Subspecies, when designated, have the same Latinized genus and species name as the species, plus a third name, resulting in a trinomial combination such as *Dysstroma truncata traversata* (p. 379). The subspecies considered the "type" for the species is given the same species and subspecies name, such as *D. truncata truncata;* all other subspecies are given different third names. Subspecies represent morphologically distinguishable, geographically separate populations within species, such as populations in Europe and North America. While many subspecies have been named in the heavily studied butterflies, they are relatively rare in the North American moths. Few subspecies are mentioned in this book.

Taxonomists working with animals arrange the species within genera to reflect similarities and differences that presumably reflect evolutionary relationships. This is called a *natural* or *phylogenetic classification* (phylogeny is evolutionary history). The genera in turn are grouped into families, the families into orders, the orders into classes, the classes into phyla, and the phyla into kingdoms. Thus the species *Sphinx eremitus* belongs to the genus *Sphinx* in Family Sphingidae, which is part of Order Lepidoptera in Class Insecta, Phylum Arthropoda, and Kingdom Animalia. Intermediate categories between these major levels of classification include suborders, placed just below the order level, and superfamilies. Five suborders are recognized in North American Lepidoptera. Superfamilies, with names ending in *-oidea,* group similar families; 23 appear in the classification scheme below. Since taxonomists are continually publishing results of their research, the numbers of species, genera, and higher categories are constantly changing. The names of genera and species used in this book are as up-to-date as I could make them, but changes will certainly have occurred by the time you read this book. Sometimes two or more species are found to be the same, so the oldest name is used for the species, and later ones become synonyms. On the other hand, what was once thought to be a single species may be split into more than one when new distinguishing features are discovered.

Arrangements of all these categories are occasionally published as checklists, which are useful both for understanding evolutionary relationships and arranging collections (see p. 25). Until recently, North American Lepidoptera were arranged according to the McDunnough *Check List of the Lepidoptera of Canada and the United States of America* (1938–39). However, the arrangement used there has been radically changed in the new *Check List of the Lepidoptera of America North of Mexico,* recently published by Hodges *et al.* That work was being written as I prepared this guide, and I was unable to get information early enough to arrange the plates and text in this guide exactly in accordance with it. The classification of *families* (and of subfamilies in Family Noctuidae) used in this book, therefore, follows McDunnough rather than Hodges *et al.* However, most of the *scientific names* used for families, genera, and species conform to the names in the new checklist, and the genera and species within families are arranged in the Hodges order. (The few differences reflect changes since publication of the Hodges checklist.) To enable you to arrange your collection in the same order as the new checklist, a list of the suborders, superfamilies, and families of North American Lepidoptera is given below, as they appear in Hodges *et al.* Six families of Lepidoptera (marked with an asterisk) are omitted from this book, since they are not known to occur in our area. Moths from the beginning of this list through Family Pterophoridae are considered to be *microlepidoptera,* while all families (including butterflies and skippers) after that point are *macrolepidoptera.* The number of North American species in each family, as included in Hodges *et al.,* is listed after the family name. The butterflies and skippers are also included to show where they appear in this classification scheme, and the numbers of species in those superfamilies is indicated.

ORDER LEPIDOPTERA

Suborder Zeugloptera
 Superfamily Micropterigoidea
  Family Micropterigidae, 2
Suborder Dacnonypha
 Superfamily Eriocranioidea
  Family Eriocraniidae, 12
  Family Acanthopteroctetidae, 3*

*Not known to occur in our area

Suborder Exoporia
    Superfamily Hepialoidea
        Family Hepialidae, 20
Suborder Monotrysia
    Superfamily Nepticuloidea
        Family Nepticulidae, 82
        Family Opostegidae, 7
        Family Tischeriidae, 48
    Superfamily Incurvarioidea
        Family Incurvariidae, 56
        Family Heliozelidae, 31
Suborder Ditrysia
    Superfamily Tineoidea
        Family Tineidae, 174
        Family Psychidae, 26
        Family Ochsenheimeriidae, 1
        Family Lyonetiidae, 122
        Family Gracillariidae, 275
    Superfamily Gelechioidea
        Family Oecophoridae, 225
        Family Elachistidae, 57
        Family Blastobasidae, 121
        Family Coleophoridae, 169
        Family Momphidae, 37
        Family Agonoxenidae, 6
        Family Cosmopterigidae, 180
        Family Scythrididae, 35
        Family Gelechiidae, 630
    Superfamily Copromorphoidea
        Family Copromorphidae, 1*
        Family Alucitidae, 1
        Family Carposinidae, 11
        Family Epermeniidae, 11
        Family Glyphipterigidae, 11
    Superfamily Yponomeutoidea
        Family Plutellidae, 54
        Family Yponomeutidae, 32
        Family Argyresthiidae, 52
        Family Douglasiidae, 5
        Family Acrolepiidae, 3
        Family Heliodinidae, 20
    Superfamily Sesioidea
        Family Sesiidae, 115
        Family Choreutidae, 29
    Superfamily Cossoidea
        Family Cossidae, 45
    Superfamily Tortricoidea
        Family Tortricidae, 1,054
        Family Cochylidae, 110

Superfamily Hesperioidea (skippers), 290
Superfamily Papilionoidea (butterflies), 470
Superfamily Zygaenoidea
 Family Zygaenidae, 22
 Family Megalopygidae, 11
 Family Limacodidae, 52
 Family Epipyropidae, 1
 Family Dalceridae, 1*
Superfamily Pyraloidea
 Family Pyralidae, 1,374
 Family Thyrididae, 12
 Family Hyblaeidae, 1
Superfamily Pterophoroidea
 Family Pterophoridae, 146
Superfamily Drepanoidea
 Family Thyatiridae, 16
 Family Drepanidae, 5
Superfamily Geometroidea
 Family Geometridae, 1,404
 Family Epiplemidae, 8
 Family Sematuridae, 1*
 Family Uraniidae, 1*
Superfamily Mimallonoidea
 Family Mimallonidae, 4
Superfamily Bombycoidea
 Family Apatelodidae, 5
 Family Bombycidae, 1
 Family Lasiocampidae, 35
 Family Saturniidae, 68
Superfamily Sphingoidea
 Family Sphingidae, 124
Superfamily Noctuoidea
 Family Notodontidae, 136
 Family Dioptidae, 2*
 Family Arctiidae, 264
 Family Lymantriidae, 32
 Family Noctuidae, 2,925

*Not known to occur in our area

SPHINX or HAWK MOTHS:
Family Sphingidae

Medium to very large moths. Body very robust; abdomen usually *tapering* to a sharp point. Wings usually narrow; FW sharp-pointed or with an irregular margin (Fig. 15); wingspan

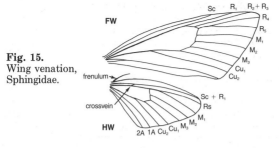

Fig. 15.
Wing venation,
Sphingidae.

2.8–17.5 cm. No ocelli or tympanal organs. Proboscis usually well developed, extremely long in some species (such as *Manduca* species) that feed in flowers with deep calyxes, such as trumpet-creepers. Antennae gradually *thicken* along length, then become *narrower toward tip.* Sc + R₁ of HW *close to and parallel* to Rs along top of discal cell and connected by *oblique crossvein* at about half length of cell. Frenulum present, sometimes short. Members of the subfamily Sphinginae (below) *lack short sensory hairs* on the naked area of the inner surface of the 1st segment of the labial palp, which are present in the subfamily Macroglossinae (p. 38).

Larvae naked except for a few scattered hairs. Most have a prominent *dorsal horn* at tip of abdomen. Larvae feed both day and night on many kinds of woody and herbaceous plants; some are serious pests. Sphinx moths usually pupate in soil, though some form loose cocoons among leaf litter. Adults are among the fastest fliers in the Lepidoptera. Some are active only at night, others at twilight or dawn, and some, such as the clearwings (*Hemaris* species) feed on flowers during the day and resemble bumblebees or hummingbirds. This family is also well represented in the tropics. Since sphinx or hawk moths are both conspicuous and popular with collectors, most species known from our area are included in this guide.

Subfamily Sphinginae

PINK-SPOTTED HAWK MOTH   Pl. 3 (1)
Agrius cingulatus (F.)
Identification: The only sphinx moth in our area with *pink crossbars* on the abdomen. HW gray with black bands and variable pink shading toward base. Wingspan 9.5–12 cm.
Food: Jimsonweed, pawpaw, and sweet-potato.
Range: Throughout our area, but a stray northward. June–Oct. May be locally common, especially Sept.–Oct.

GIANT SPHINX *Cocytius antaeus* (Dru.)   Pl. 7 (8)
Identification: Our largest sphinx moth. FW yellowish gray, often mottled. *HW yellow* at base with *translucent patch* in mid-

dle, black veins, and outer border—black toothlike markings extend from border into translucent area between veins. Wingspan 12.6–17.8 cm; females much larger than males.
Food: Pond apple.
Range: Tropical America; regularly in s. Fla., rare in s. Tex.; strays as far north as Chicago. All months.
Similar species: Duponchel's Sphinx, *C. duponchel* (Poey), not shown, is usually slightly smaller (wingspan 11–15 cm). FW bluish gray; am. and st. lines edged vaguely with whitish. Translucent area of HW ends sharply at black border, *without toothlike markings* between veins. Food: Custard apple. Range: Tropical America; rare in s. Fla. and Tex. All year.

CAROLINA SPHINX *Manduca sexta* (L.)   **Pls. 1 (1), 3 (7)**
Identification: FW gray with black and white markings; usually 6 pairs of yellow spots on abdomen. Lower half of *st. line sinuous.* FW and HW fringes spotted with white. HW has 2 zigzag black median lines that are *indistinct* and *fused together,* with very little white between them. Wingspan 10.5–12 cm.
Food: Larva (**Tobacco Hornworm,** Pl. 1) a pest of potato, tobacco, and tomato plants. Unlike Tomato Hornworm (larva of Five-spotted Hawk Moth, below), the Tobacco Hornworm has 7 *oblique white lines* on each side and a *red-tipped "horn"* at tip of abdomen.
Range: Throughout our area. May–Oct. Common southward.

FIVE-SPOTTED HAWK MOTH   **Pl. 3 (4)**
Manduca quinquemaculata (Haw.)
Identification: Similar to Carolina Sphinx (above), but abdomen has usually 5 (sometimes 6) pairs of yellow spots. Lower half of st. line *nearly straight;* FW and HW fringes gray, *not spotted* with white. Zigzag *median lines* on HW *sharper,* separated by more white. Wingspan 9–13.5 cm.
Food: Larva (**Tomato Hornworm,** not shown) feeds on same plants as Tobacco Hornworm (above), but has 8 L-*shaped lines* on each side and a *black-edged green horn.*
Range: Throughout our area. May–Oct. Less common southward than the Carolina Sphinx, and a less serious pest.

RUSTIC SPHINX *Manduca rustica* (F.)   **Pl. 3 (8)**
Identification: Abdomen has *3 pairs of yellow spots.* FW yellowish to chocolate brown with white at base, in am. and lower median areas, and beyond pm. line. Lines black, *zigzag.* Wingspan 8.7–15 cm.
Food: Bignonia, fringe-tree, jasmine, and various members of the forget-me-not and vervain families.
Range: Me. to Fla., west to Ark. and Tex.; a stray north of Va. July–Oct.; May–Nov. in s. Fla. Common southward.

ASH SPHINX *Manduca jasminearum* (Guér.)   **Pl. 4 (1)**
Identification: FW gray, sometimes shaded with brown; crossed

by indistinct black and white lines. Pm. line most distinct. *Black dash* extends from middle of costa to middle of outer margin; dash often broken around whitish reniform spot. HW black, gray at anal angle. Wingspan 8.4–10.5 cm.
Food: Ash trees.
Range: Conn. and N.Y. to Fla., west to Ark. and Tex. May–Sept. Most common on East Coast.

PAWPAW SPHINX *Dolba hyloeus* (Dru.)   **Pl. 5 (1)**
Identification: FW dark brown with white dusting and black lines, much like a miniature Rustic Sphinx (above, Pl. 3). Some specimens have reddish or yellowish brown blotches in basal and st. areas. Median line zigzag, usually the sharpest line. HW blackish with a *white median line* that becomes *double toward anal angle*. Wingspan 5–6.8 cm.
Food: Blueberries, hollies, pawpaw, and sweetfern.
Range: Me. and s. Ont. to Fla., west to Wisc. and Tex. June–Sept. Common southward.

ELM SPHINX *Ceratomia amyntor* (Geyer)   **Pl. 3 (9)**
Identification: Thorax brown with wide *darker brown stripes* toward edges. All wings light brown with darker brown shading. Whitish pm. line on FW the only complete, distinct line; blackish streaks along veins in outer part of FW. Whitish costal tint and reniform dot. HW brown with dark brown border and incomplete lines. Wingspan 8.8–11.5 cm.
Food: Basswood, birch, cherry, and elm trees.
Range: Common throughout our area. May–Oct.; 2 broods southward.

WAVED SPHINX *Ceratomia undulosa* (Wlk.)   **Pl. 4 (10)**
Identification: FW pale brownish gray with contrasting black streaks and zigzag lines. *Reniform dot large, white with black outline*. HW gray with darker gray shading; lines more diffuse than those on FW. FW of melanic specimens dark gray with obscure lines, or with 2 broad, diffuse blackish bands enclosing pale gray median area. Wingspan 7.8–11 cm.
Food: Ashes, fringe-tree, hawthorn, lilac, oaks, and privet.
Range: Throughout our area. May–Oct.; 2 broods southward. One of our most common sphinxes.

CATALPA SPHINX *Ceratomia catalpae* (Bdv.)   **Pl. 5 (9)**
Identification: FW dull brownish gray with no white scales. Lines blackish brown, indistinct; 4–5 blackish dashes, variably obscure. *Reniform spot black with gray filling*. Vague traces of lines on dark gray HW. Wingspan 6.5–9.5 cm.
Food: Catalpas.
Range: All states in our area plus s. Ont. May–Sept.; 2 broods. Locally common to abundant, except northward.

HAGEN'S SPHINX *Ceratomia hageni* Grt. **Pl. 4 (3)**
Identification: FW gray with a *green to yellowish green tinge.*
Lines zigzag as in Waved Sphinx (Pl. 4), but less distinct; *pale gray patches* along costa above discal spot and at apex. HW gray with blackish shading except at base and outer margin, near anal angle. Wingspan 8–9.2 cm.
Food: Osage-orange.
Range: Ind. to Miss., west to Wisc., Kans., and Tex. April–Sept.; 2 broods. Common where food plant occurs.

CYPRESS SPHINX *Isoparce cupressi* (Bdv.) **Pl. 5 (2)**
Identification: FW gray with 2 broken black dashes, the larger one accented with *orangish brown* above its thickest part. HW uniform dark gray. FW and HW fringes checkered blackish and whitish to yellowish gray. Wingspan 6–6.5 cm.
Food: Baldcypress.
Range: Coastal S.C. to Fla., west to 'Ark. and Tex. March–May and July–Sept.; 2 broods. Common in cypress swamps.

PLEBEIAN SPHINX *Paratraea plebeja* (F.) **Pl. 5 (5)**
Identification: FW gray; blackish pm. line usually most conspicuous line, but often obscure. Series of *black dashes* from base to apex. *Reniform spot white, conspicuous.* HW gray with vague blackish median band and broad outer border. Wingspan 6–7.5 cm.
Food: Trumpet-creeper, Florida yellow-trumpet, lilac, and passionflowers.
Range: Conn. and N.Y. to Fla., west to Minn., Kans., and Tex. April–Oct.; 2 broods southward. Common.

HERMIT SPHINX *Sphinx eremitus* (Hbn.) **Pl. 5 (4)**
Identification: FW grayish brown with black dashes and incomplete zigzag lines. *Reniform spot white* (sometimes double as shown). HW black with *2 distinct, broad white bands;* inner band encloses a *black basal triangle.* Wingspan 6.5–7.5 cm.
Food: Bee-balm, bugleweeds, mints, and sage.
Range: N.S. to N.C., west to Man. and Ark. July–Aug. Uncommon to rare southward; unrecorded in some states within range.

SAGE SPHINX *Sphinx eremitoides* Stkr. **Pl. 5 (6)**
Identification: Similar to Hermit Sphinx (above), but larger. FW pale gray with some yellowish tinges and faint black lines and dashes; reniform spot inconspicuous. *Diffuse black patch* at base of HW. Wingspan 7.6–9 cm.
Food: Sages.
Range: Kans. south to Tex. and westward. April–June and Aug.–Sept.; 2 broods. Locally common.

GREAT ASH SPHINX *Sphinx chersis* (Hbn.) **Pl. 4 (7)**
Identification: FW uniform ash gray; st. line incomplete, with pale gray outer edging. Series of *4 black dashes*—outermost dash

reaches apex. HW black with diffuse pale gray bands. Wingspan 9–13 cm.
Food: Ashes, lilac, privet, *Prunus* species, quaking aspen.
Range: Throughout our area. May–Oct.; 2 broods southward. Rare in Gulf Coast states; uncommon elsewhere.

VASHTI SPHINX *Sphinx vashti* Stkr. **Pl. 4 (5)**
Identification: Similar to the Great Ash Sphinx (above), but smaller; FW lighter gray, with *sharper black st. line. Sharper white bands* on HW. Wingspan 7.5–10 cm.
Food: Snowberry.
Range: Man. to s. Tex. and westward beyond our area; uncommon in our area. May–July.

CANADIAN SPHINX *Sphinx canadensis* Bdv. **Pl. 5 (7)**
Identification: FW very similar to that of Hermit Sphinx (Pl. 5), but *without white reniform spot.* HW more like that of Sage Sphinx (above, Pl. 5), but FW darker and more uniform grayish brown. Wingspan 7–8.5 cm.
Food: Late low blueberry, white ash, and cloudberry (?).
Range: Nfld. to Ky., west to Man. and Ark. May–Sept.; 2 broods southward. Uncommon.

FRANCK'S SPHINX *Sphinx franckii* Neum. **Pl. 4 (4)**
Identification: *Outer margins* of wings *slightly concave* in ♂ (shown) but not in ♀. Costal half of FW *gray,* rest of FW warm *yellowish brown.* Lines obscure except st. line, which is black and broadens to form a diffuse black blotch at anal angle. HW black with brown basal patch and median band. Wingspan 10–12.8 cm.
Food: Elms and white ash.
Range: N.J. to n. Fla., west to Mo. and La. Late June to mid-July; some adults also emerge in Aug.–Sept. southward in some years, as partial 2nd brood. Less rare than once believed, but local and uncommon.

LAUREL SPHINX *Sphinx kalmiae* (J.E. Sm.) **Pl. 4 (6)**
Identification: FW yellowish brown with *black shading along inner margin* and *inside conspicuous whitish st. line.* HW tan with diffuse black basal patch, median line, and outer border. Wingspan 7.5–10.3 cm.
Food: Ashes, fringe-tree, laurels, lilac, poplars, privet.
Range: Nfld. to n. Fla., west to Man., Ark., and La. May–Aug. More common northward than in South.

APPLE SPHINX *Sphinx gordius* Cram. **Pl. 5 (3)**
Identification: *Thorax black with grayish brown edges* near wing bases. FW blackish to gray with white dusting. Lines diffuse, blackish; *white reniform spot* usually distinct. Black and brown HW markings diffuse; HW fringe white with almost no dark checkering (unlike FW). Wingspan 6.8–9.5 cm.
Food: American larch, apple, blueberries, huckleberries, sweetfern and white spruce.

Range: Throughout all of our area except extreme s. Fla. and s. Tex. May–Sept. Common northward; rare in South.

CLEMENS' SPHINX *Sphinx luscitiosa* Clem. **Pl. 4 (2)**
Identification: FW mostly yellowish gray in ♂ (shown); pale gray in ♀, with slight yellow tint. Black shading beyond pm. line widens toward inner margin in both sexes. *HW deep yellow* in ♂ (as shown), *pale yellow* with faint gray median band in ♀; outer border black in both sexes. Wingspan 5.7–7.8 cm.
Food: Apple, ashes, birches, northern bayberry, poplars, wax-myrtle, and willows.
Range: N.S. to N.J., west to Man. and Minn. June–July. Uncommon to rare.

WILD CHERRY SPHINX **Pl. 4 (11)**
Sphinx drupiferarum J.E. Sm.
Identification: FW dark gray to black, with *white edging* along most of costa and beyond st. line. Reniform spot black-edged. St. band of HW narrows toward anal angle. Wingspan 9–11 cm.
Food: Apple, plum, and wild cherry trees, hackberries, and lilac.
Range: Nfld. to Ga., west to Man. and Ark. May–July. Uncommon.

PINE SPHINX *Lapara coniferarum* (J.E. Sm.) **Pl. 5 (10)**
Identification: FW gray, with *2 sharp black dashes* in median area. Lines very diffuse, inconspicuous; st. line blackish, zigzag. FW fringe checkered blackish and white. HW uniform gray, usually paler than FW. Wingspan 5–5.7 cm.
Food: Pines, especially loblolly and longleaf pines in the South.
Range: Se. N.Y. to Fla., west to Minn. and La. Late April–Sept. Locally common in pine forests.

NORTHERN PINE SPHINX **Pl. 5 (8)**
Lapara bombycoides Wlk.
Identification: Similar to the Pine Sphinx (above), but usually smaller. FW *lines much heavier* and more distinct. Wingspan 4.5–6 cm.
Food: Pines (pitch, red, and Scotch) and American larch.
Range: N.S. to Ga., west to Man. and Wisc. June to mid-July. Locally common.

CARTER'S SPHINX *Protambulyx carteri* R. & J. **Pl. 4 (9)**
Identification: *FW yellowish to orangish brown* with vague lines; *no sharp, dark st. line.* HW yellowish to orange, with no brownish shading. Wingspan 9.5–11 cm.
Food: Brazilian pepper.
Range: Cen. to s. Fla.; all months.
Similar species: Streaked Sphinx, *P. strigilis* (L.), not shown, varies greatly in color and markings, but FW has a *distinct st. line.* Food: Brazilian pepper. Range: Tropical; occurs in s. Fla. in all months.

TWIN-SPOTTED SPHINX
Pl. 6 (4)

Smerinthus jamaicensis (Dru.)

Identification: Usually can be distinguished from 4 other sphinxes with blue spots on HW (below; see also Pl. 6) by *black bar usually dividing blue spot* in half; a third small blue spot is present toward base of HW in some specimens. More reliable features are *nearly straight costal margin of HW* and no terminal claw on foretibia. Wingspan 5–7 cm.

Food: Apple, ash, birch, elm, plum, and willow trees.

Range: Throughout our area except in extreme s. Fla. and Tex. April–Oct. Common.

ONE-EYED SPHINX *Smerinthus cerisyi* (Kby.)
Pl. 6 (1)

Identification: Similar to the Twin-spotted Sphinx (above), but usually slightly larger. Foretibia has a *terminal claw.* Crossvein at end of discal cell on FW and other veins toward outer margin are usually *outlined in paler brown.* HW eyespot usually has a *black bull's eye* in middle, as well as a heavy black outer ring. Wingspan 6.2–9 cm.

Food: Pear, plum, poplar, and willow trees.

Range: Nfld. to Ga., west to Man. and Ark. May–July. Uncommon.

BLINDED SPHINX
Pl. 6 (3)

Paonias excaecatus (J.E. Sm.)

Identification: FW deep brown with a *strongly scalloped outer margin.* HW eyespot single. Wingspan 5.5–9.5 cm.

Food: Basswood, birches, elms, oaks, poplars, and *Prunus* species.

Range: Common throughout our area. May–Aug.; 3 broods southward.

SMALL-EYED SPHINX
Pl. 6 (2)

Paonias myops (J.E. Sm.)

Identification: Smaller and darker brown than the Blinded Sphinx (above); *HW yellow.* Outer margin of FW *doubly indented,* not straight as in the Huckleberry Sphinx (below), nor scalloped as in the Blinded Sphinx. Wingspan 4.5–7.5 cm.

Food: Birches, hawthorns, poplars, *Prunus* species, and willows.

Range: Common throughout our area. May–Sept.

HUCKLEBERRY SPHINX
Pl. 6 (6)

Paonias astylus (Dru.)

Identification: Similar to the Small-eyed Sphinx (above) but all wings yellowish orange and pink, often with some brown. Outer margin of FW *nearly straight.* Wingspan 5.5–6.5 cm.

Food: Blueberries, cherries, huckleberries, and willows.

Range: Me. to Fla., west to Mo. and Miss.; distribution westward somewhat spotty. One brood (July) northward; 2 broods (March–June and Sept.) in Fla. Uncommon to rare.

WALNUT SPHINX   **Pl. 6 (5)**
Laothoe juglandis (J.E. Sm.)
Identification: FW and HW the same shade of pale to dark
brown, often with a whitish to pinkish tint. Outer margin of all
wings *scalloped to wavy.* Proboscis very short. Wingspan
4.5–7.5 cm.
Food: Butternut, hickory, *Prunus* species, and walnut trees.
Range: Throughout our area. May–Aug.; 3 broods southward.
Common in most of range.

BIG POPLAR SPHINX or MODEST SPHINX   **Pl. 3 (3)**
Pachysphinx modesta (Harr.)
Identification: Easily recognized by its large size, scalloped outer
margin on FW, and *deep crimson patch* on HW. Bluish gray trian-
gular patch at anal angle of HW bordered with black toward base.
Wingspan 10–12 cm.
Food: Poplars and willows.
Range: Throughout our area. June–July northward; 3 broods in
Gulf states (March–Sept.). May be locally common.

Subfamily Macroglossinae

ALOPE SPHINX *Erinnyis alope* (Dru.)   **Pl. 3 (10)**
Identification: FW and outer border of HW dark brown; basal $\frac{2}{3}$
of *HW bright yellow.* Some lighter streaking on FW, especially
toward anal angle. Wingspan 8.2–10 cm.
Food: Larva has been reared on allamanda (*Allamanda* species),
nettlespurge (*Jatropha* species), and papaya.
Range: Neotropical (Latin America and West Indies); rarely collected in Fla. Occasionally strays northward to N.J. and Kans.
Sept.–Oct. northward; all months in s. Fla.

ELLO SPHINX *Erinnyis ello* (L.)   **Pl. 3 (2)**
Identification: Note the pairs of *black bars* on a gray abdomen
and the *orange HW* bordered with black. FW gray, either marked
only with few black dots toward outer margin, or with heavy
blackish shade lines from base to apex (as shown) and along costa
toward base. Wingspan 7.7–8.5 cm.
Food: Larva has been reared on guava, poinsettia, and on other
spurges; also on saffron plum.
Range: A tropical moth found all year in Fla. and s. Tex. Strays as
far north as N.Y. and Mich. during Aug.–Oct.

OBSCURE SPHINX *Erinnyis obscura* (F.)   **Pl. 6 (18)**
Identification: Similar to Ello Sphinx (above) but smaller, with
no black bars on abdomen. FW shading variable. HW orange with
black border that narrows toward apex. Wingspan 5.6–6.5 cm.
Food: *Cynanchum*, papaya, and white vine.
Range: Tropical; Fla. to Tex., but rare in La. and Miss. Strays

north to Pa., Ky., and Neb. Aug.–Sept. northward; all months in s. Fla. and Tex.

FIG SPHINX *Pachylia ficus* (L.) **Pl. 7 (3)**
Identification: FW brown with *paler brown patch along costa* at apex. HW orangish to brown with black median band and outer border; *white spot* at anal angle (not visible in Pl. 7). Wingspan 12–14 cm.
Food: Various fig species.
Range: Tropical; uncommon in peninsular Fla. and rare in s. Tex.; all months.

FALSE-WINDOWED SPHINX **Pl. 4 (8)**
Madoryx pseudothyreus (Grt.)
Identification: Easily recognized by its brownish gray wings with scalloped margins, and the *large, white V-shaped spot* (surrounded by *2–3 smaller spots*) on the FW. Wingspan 6.6–7 cm.
Food: Unrecorded; possibly an evening-primrose.
Range: Tropical; occurs in cen.-s. Fla. all year.

HALF-BLIND SPHINX *Perigonia lusca* (F.) **Pl. 6 (8)**
Identification: Body and wings brown. FW has darker brown shading in median area, black reniform spot, and bent st. line. HW has *yellowish orange median band* and *anal patch*. Wingspan 5.5–6.5 cm.
Food: Coffee in Peru; reared on *Ilex krugiana* in Fla.
Range: Tropical; locally common in s. Fla. in all months.

TITAN SPHINX *Aellopos titan* (Cram.) **Pl. 5 (11)**
Identification: Note the *pure white band* across the abdomen (characteristic of all our *Aellopos* species). Titan Sphinx is the only moth in this genus with a *black reniform spot* at the end of discal cell and *incomplete, broken median and pm. lines* on dark brown FW. HW blackish brown with creamy white along inner margin and near anal angle. Wingspan 5.5–6.5 cm.
Food: *Randia*, seven-year apple, and other members of the madder family; larva can be reared on pond apple.
Range: The most widely distributed *Aellopos* species in our area: Me. to Fla., west to S.D. and Tex. June–Oct. northward, where it is uncommon to rare. Multibrooded in the Fla. Keys, where it visits such flowers as stoppers and lantana.
Similar species: Three other *Aellopos* species (not shown) occur in our area: (1) Fadus Sphinx, *A. fadus* (Cram.), *lacks black spot* on FW. Food: Unrecorded. Range: Fla. west to Ark. and Tex. Sept.–Dec. (2) Tantalus Sphinx, *A. tantalus* (L.) has *1 row of whitish spots* on FW. Food: Probably madders. Range: N.Y. and s. Que. to Fla., west to Mich. June in north; all months in Fla. (3) Clavipes Sphinx, *A. clavipes* (R. & J.), is very similar to Tantalus Sphinx, but inner surface of tarsal segments 3–5 on foreleg *dark brown* (pale beige in Tantalus Sphinx); segments 3–5 also broad-

ened in ♂ Clavipes Sphinx. Food: Unrecorded. Range: Vicinity of Brownsville, Tex. Aug.

MOURNFUL SPHINX *Enyo lugubris* (L.)   **Pl. 5 (12)**
Identification: Body and wings dark brown; black shading covers upper ⅔ of FW beyond *nearly straight median line*. Reniform spot round, pale tan. Wingspan 5–6 cm.
Food: Grapes.
Range: N.C. to Fla., west to Tex. Strays to s. Mich. Aug.–Oct. northward; all months and common in s. Fla.

HUMMINGBIRD CLEARWING   **Pl. 6 (16)**
Hemaris thysbe (F.)
Identification: This and the other 2 *Hemaris* species (below, Pl. 6) are day-fliers that hover at flowers to drink nectar, and have *large transparent (unscaled) areas* on both FW and HW. In this species the scaled areas are *brown*; inner edge of outer border of FW *uneven*. No reddish brown or black line beneath each wing base. Wingspan 4–5.5 cm.
Food: Hawthorns, honeysuckles, *Prunus* species and snowberry.
Range: Common throughout our area. April–Aug. (1 brood) northward; March–June and Aug.–Oct. (2 broods) in South.

SNOWBERRY CLEARWING   **Pl. 6 (19)**
Hemaris diffinis (Bdv.)
Identification: Easily distinguished from the other 2 *Hemaris* species by *black scaled areas* of wings. Thorax has black lines on ventral surface. Sometimes mistaken for a bumblebee, but does not light on flowers the way a bee does; also, antennae much larger than those of bumblebee. Wingspan 3.5–5 cm.
Food: Dogbane, honeysuckles, and snowberry.
Range: Common throughout our area. April–Aug.; 2 broods.

SLENDER CLEARWING   **Pl. 6 (17)**
Hemaris gracilis (Grt. & Rob.)
Identification: Similar to Hummingbird Clearwing (above) but inner edge of brown border of FW *more even*. Look for *reddish brown line* on ventral surface of thorax, beneath each wing base. Wingspan 4–4.5 cm.
Food: Early low blueberry.
Range: N.S. to Fla., west to Man. and Mich. (Wisc. ?). May–Aug.; possibly 2 broods. Our least common *Hemaris* species.

PANDORUS SPHINX   **Pl. 3 (13)**
Eumorpha pandorus (Hbn.)
Identification: FW *olive green* with darker green *apical patch* and *border along inner margin*, broken near anal angle. Pink streaks along outer ends of veins Cu_1 and Cu_2, and at inner margin. Double black reniform spot. Two blackish patches on HW, and some pink at anal angle. Wingspan 8.7–11.5 cm.
Food: Ampelopsis, grapes, and Virginia creeper.

Range: N.S. to Fla., west to Kans. and Tex. June–Aug. northward; May–Oct. in deep south. Common.

Similar species: (1) Satellite Sphinx, *E. satellitia* (L.), not shown, is pale brownish with a *blackish rectangular patch* midway on inner margin. Food: Reared on grape. Range: Tropical; reported in Brownsville, Tex., mid-June to mid-Nov. (2) Intermediate Sphinx, *E. intermedia* (Clark), not shown, is smaller than our other *Eumorpha* species, and medium to dark olive brown. Dark patches at apex and anal angle of FW *squared off* (not rounded). Food: Probably ampelopsis and grapes. Range: Coastal N.C. to n. Fla., west along Gulf Coast to s. Tex. April–Oct.

ACHEMON SPHINX   Pl. 3 (11)
Eumorpha achemon (Dru.)

Identification: FW pinkish brown with a deep brown apical patch and a squarish patch midway on inner margin. Smaller patch at anal angle. *HW pink with light brown border* and *broken black line* toward anal angle. Wingspan 8.7–9.6 cm.

Food: Ampelopsis and grapes.

Range: Mass. to Fla., west to N.D. and Tex. June–Aug. northward; adults fly earlier southward (2 broods).

VINE SPHINX *Eumorpha vitis* (L.)   Pl. 3 (15)

Identification: FW dark greenish brown with sharp whitish bands and streaks as shown. Note *pink patch at anal angle* of HW. Wingspan 8.5–10.5 cm.

Food: Grapes.

Range: Mass. to Fla., west to Tex. Northern records are strays. April–May and July–Oct.; 2 broods. Common in extreme s. Fla. and s. Tex.

Similar species: Banded Sphinx (below).

BANDED SPHINX *Eumorpha fasciata* (Sulz.)   Pl. 3 (12)

Identification: FW very similar to Vine Sphinx (above), but note pronounced brownish band along costa and darker lower basal area. HW has *pink border along most of outer margin* as well as at anal angle. Wingspan 8.7–9.6 cm.

Food: Primrose-willow and other evening-primroses.

Range: Tropical; sometimes common from Fla. to Ark. and Tex.; strays as far north as N.S. and Mich. Aug.–Nov. northward; May–July and Aug.–Nov. (2 broods) in deep South.

GAUDY SPHINX *Eumorpha labruscae* (L.)   Pl. 3 (6)

Identification: As rare in our area as it is beautiful, the Gaudy Sphinx is easily recognized by its *green body* and FW, and the *red and blue markings* on its HW. Wingspan 11–12 cm.

Food: Ampelopsis, possum grape, Christmasbush eupatorium, and grapes.

Range: Tropical; Fla. to Tex., straying as far north as Me. and Man. Sept–Nov. northward; all months in s. Fla.

GROTE'S SPHINX *Cautethia grotei* Hy. Edw.　　**Pl. 6 (15)**
Identification: FW gray with black lines and shading. *HW deep yellow* with a sharply defined *black outer border* that covers *less* than half of wing. Wingspan 2.8–4 cm.
Food: David's milkberry.
Range: Tropical; common in cen. and s. Fla. all year.
Similar species: Spurious Sphinx, *C. spuria* (Bdv.), not shown, is larger; *yellow* area of HW *blends into black*, which covers *more than half* of HW. Food: Unrecorded. Range: Brownsville, Tex., and vicinity. Oct.; probably all year.

ABBOT'S SPHINX　　**Pl. 6 (9)**
Sphecodina abbottii (Swainson)
Identification: Easily recognized by the dark brown FW with scalloped margins and the *broad yellow* band on HW. Wingspan 5.8–7 cm.
Food: Ampelopsis and grapes.
Range: Me. to Fla., west to Minn., Kans., and Tex. April–July. Comes to flowers, bait, and lights; ♂ flies at dusk, while ♀ seems to fly around midnight. Locally common.

LETTERED SPHINX　　**Pl. 6 (14)**
Deidamia inscripta (Harr.)
Identification: FW narrow, with *deeply scalloped* outer margin; pale brown with darker brown markings. Small *black and white spot* below apex. HW orangish brown with dark brown median line and outer border. Wingspan 4.5–7 cm.
Food: Ampelopsis, grapes, and Virginia creeper.
Range: Mass. and s. Que. to Fla., west to S.D., Mo., and La. March–June. Common.

NESSUS SPHINX　　**Pl. 6 (20)**
Amphion floridensis B.P. Clark
Identification: Easily recognized by the *2 yellow bands* across *dark brown abdomen*. FW and HW chocolate brown. Dark orange median band on HW. Wingspan 3.7–5.5 cm.
Food: Ampelopsis, grapes, and cayenne pepper.
Range: Throughout our area. April–July northward; 2 broods in deep South. At flowers during day and at dusk. Common.
Remarks: Known until recently as *Amphion nessus* (Cram.).

PROUD SPHINX *Proserpinus gaurae* (J.E. Sm.)　　**Pl. 6 (13)**
Identification: FW brown, sometimes with greenish tinge; median area often noticeably darker (as shown). Am. and pm. lines distinct, *curved*. Outer margin of HW bordered with *reddish brown*; rest of HW same color or orange. Underside of HW brown. Pale band across abdomen sometimes present (as shown). Wingspan 4.5–4.8 cm.
Food: Evening-primroses and willow-herbs.
Range: S.C. to n. Fla., west to Mo. and Tex. April–Aug. Local and rare; no records from some states within range.

Similar species: In Juanita Sphinx, *P. juanita* (Stkr.), not shown, outer border of HW is *black*; underside of HW is green to olive green. Food: Evening-primroses and willow-herbs. Range: Mo. and Neb. to Tex. April–Aug. Local and uncommon.

HYDRANGEA SPHINX   **Pl. 6 (7)**
Darapsa versicolor (Harr.)
Identification: FW olive green with *curved,* broken white lines and apical dash. HW orange; some greenish and white near anal angle. Wingspan 5.8–8 cm.
Food: Buttonbush, water-willow, and wild hydrangea.
Range: Me. and s. Que. to Fla., west to Mich., Mo., and e. Tex. June–July. Uncommon to locally common.

HOG SPHINX or   **Pl. 6 (11)**
VIRGINIA CREEPER SPHINX   *Darapsa myron* (Cram.)
Identification: FW pale to dark brown, often with *olive green shading.* Darker brown am. and pm. bands, reniform spot, and *patches at apex* and anal angle. HW orange with small brown to greenish patch at anal angle. Wingspan 5–6.5 cm.
Food: Ampelopsis, viburnums, and Virginia creeper.
Range: S. Que. to Fla., west to N.D. and Tex. April–Sept.; 2 broods. One of our most common sphinxes.

AZALEA SPHINX *Darapsa pholus* (Cram.)   **Pl. 6 (12)**
Identification: Similar to Hog Sphinx (above) but larger; foretibia *spined* (no spine in Hog Sphinx). FW reddish brown with *purplish* (not green) shading. *Pm. line straight* or nearly so, not curved as in Hog Sphinx. Wingspan 5.7–7.5 cm.
Food: Azaleas, blueberries, sour-gum, viburnums, and other plants.
Range: Common throughout our area. April–Aug.; 2 broods.

PLUTO SPHINX *Xylophanes pluto* (F.)   **Pl. 3 (5)**
Identification: *FW olive green* with dull violet shading along lines. *HW black* at base, *yellow* in median area, and *green to brown* at outer margin. Wingspan 5.3–6.5 cm.
Food: *Erythroxylon* species and milkberry.
Range: Tropical; enters s. Fla. and s. Tex.; 1 recorded from La. All months. Sometimes common.

TERSA SPHINX *Xylophanes tersa* (L.)   **Pl. 6 (10)**
Identification: Easily identified by the unusually long, *pointed abdomen,* and the *jagged black markings* on HW, which contrast sharply with the yellowish white median area. FW pale brown with inconspicuous darker brown lines. Wingspan 6–8 cm.
Food: *Manettia* species, smooth buttonplant, and starclusters.
Range: Mass. and s. Ont. to Fla., west to Wisc., Kans., and Tex. A stray northward; June–Oct. Common to abundant in South (Feb.–Nov. in Fla.); comes to lights and flowers.

WHITE-LINED SPHINX *Hyles lineata* (F.) **Pl. 3 (14)**
Identification: FW dark olive brown with an even, *pale tan stripe* extending from base to apex; *white streaks* cover veins. HW black with a pink median band. Wingspan 6.3–9 cm.
Food: Apple trees, four-o'clocks, willow-herbs, and other plants.
Range: Throughout our area; sporadic northward. April–Oct.
Similar species: Galium Sphinx, *H. gallii* (Rottenburg), not shown, has a broader, *more uneven* stripe on FW, and *no white streaks* on veins. The N. American subspecies is *intermedia* (Kby.). Food: Bedstraw and willow-herbs. Range: Holarctic (throughout northern hemisphere); Lab. to Va., west across Can., south to Iowa in our area. May–Aug. Common.

GIANT SILKWORM and ROYAL MOTHS: Family Saturniidae

Medium to very large moths, including the largest moths in our area; wingspan 3–15 cm. Body densely hairy. Head relatively small, held close to thorax. Ocelli absent. Labial palps small; proboscis reduced or absent (adults do not feed). Antennal shaft lacks scales; each antenna usually *quadripectinate* (doubly bipectinate—with 2 pairs of branches per segment) in ♂, bipectinate in ♂ buck moths (*Hemileuca* species). Antennae vary in females (depending on the species)—may be simple, bipectinate, or quadripectinate. Vein *Cu of FW* apparently *3-branched* in all saturniids (Figs. 16, 17); M_2 arising closer to M_1 than to M_3; radial branches reduced to 2, 3, or 4. $Sc + R_1$ of HW *widely separated from Rs*, and not joined to it by crossvein; *frenulum absent.*

Larvae usually very fleshy, with clumps of bristles on raised tubercles; buck moth and io moth caterpillars (*Hemileuca* and *Automeris* species) have sharp, stinging hairs. Caterpillars feed mostly on leaves of trees and shrubs; some may do serious damage. Some giant silkworms (Saturniinae and some Hemileucinae) pupate in a well-built silken cocoon; others (royal moths, Citheroniinae) pupate in a cell in the soil. Adults are active during the day, twilight, or at night, depending on the species.

Note: The commercial Silkworm Moth (*Bombyx mori*), which is not native to North America, belongs to another family (Bombycidae, p. 55).

Of our 3 subfamilies, the royal moths (Citheroniinae) have been considered a separate family until recently. Adults may be identified to subfamily as follows:

Citheroniinae (royal moths), p. 45—Antennae of ♂ *quadripectinate in basal* ½ *to* ⅔ *only*; outer part of each antenna simple. Abdomen *as long as HW* or longer.
Hemileucinae (buck and io moths), p. 48—Antennae of ♂ *bipectinate or quadripectinate all the way to tips*; if quadripec-

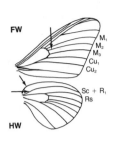

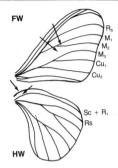

Fig. 16. Wing venation, Saturniidae (Citheroniinae).

Fig. 17. Wing venation, Saturniidae (Saturniinae).

tinate, *outer pair* of branches on a segment *touches inner pair* on succeeding segment; ♀ antennae usually simple. Abdomen no longer than HW, usually shorter.

Saturniinae (giant silkworm moths), p. 49—*Antennae quadripectinate in both sexes; outer pair* of branches on each segment *does not touch inner pair* on succeeding segment in ♂. Abdomen shorter than HW.

Subfamily Citheroniinae

IMPERIAL MOTH *Eacles imperialis* (Dru.)   **Pl. 1 (3), 9 (5)**
Identification: Easily recognized by its large size and *yellow wings*, variably spotted and shaded with *pinkish, orangish*, or *purplish brown*. Males, particularly southward, are more heavily marked than females. Wingspan 8–17.4 cm.
Food: Larva (Pl. 1) feeds on many trees, such as basswood, birches, cedar, elms, maples, oaks, pines, and walnut.
Range: Me. and s. Que. to Fla., west to w. Ont., Kans., and Tex. May–July northward (1 brood); April–Sept. (2 broods) in South.
Remarks: A conifer-feeding subspecies known as the Pine Imperial Moth, *E. imperialis pini* Michener (*smaller*, with *more pink spots* on FW and *strong pm. line on underside* of HW) occurs from Que. to N.Y. and west to w. Ont. and Mich. Another subspecies, the Texas Imperial Moth, *E. imperialis nobilis* Neum., occurs in se. Tex. (⅓ of population is *completely shaded* with *pinkish brown*.) These may be distinct species.

REGAL MOTH or ROYAL WALNUT   **Pls. 1 (18), 9 (2)**
MOTH *Citheronia regalis* (F.)
Identification: FW gray with *yellow spots* and *orange veins*. HW mostly orange with yellow basal patch and median patches at costa and inner margin. Wingspan 9.5–15.5; ♀ larger than ♂.

Food: Larva (**Hickory Horned Devil**, Pl. 1) feeds on ash, cotton, gums, hickories, lilacs, persimmon, sumac, sycamore, and walnut trees. It is often seen in late summer as it leaves foodplant to burrow into the ground to pupate. Although the "horns" give this caterpillar a somewhat threatening appearance, it does not sting. **Range:** Mass. to Fla. west to Kans. and Tex. June–Sept.; 1 brood. Common southward but rare northward. Adults often perch near building and street lights.

PINE-DEVIL MOTH   Pl. 9 (1)
Citheronia sepulcralis Grt. & Rob.

Identification: FW dull brownish violet with a small rose *basal spot* and obscure blackish pm. line and reniform spot. HW rose at base; median line and discal spot blackish. Note faint rose outlines of veins on FW and HW. Wingspan 7–10 cm.

Food: Larva (**Pine-devil**) feeds on pines, including Caribbean, pitch, and white pines.

Range: Me. to Fla., west to Ky. and Miss. June–Aug.; 1 brood. Common southward.

HONEY LOCUST MOTH   Pl. 8 (6, 11, 13)
Sphingicampa bicolor (Harr.)

Identification: FW grayish, yellow to orange, or brown with variable rose shading and dark speckling. Lines obscure; *pm. line reaches costa before apex*. White reniform spot may be double, single, or absent. Wingspan 4.7–6.7 cm.

Food: Honey locust and Kentucky coffee-tree.

Range: N.J. to Ga., west to Ont., Neb., and Tex. April–Sept. Usually 3 broods; 1st brood grayish, 2nd pale yellow to brown; 3rd darker brown with heavier spotting. Common.

BISECTED HONEY LOCUST MOTH   Pl. 8 (3, 4)
Sphingicampa bisecta (Lint.)

Identification: Similar to Honey Locust Moth (above) but *pm. line* straight, more distinct, and *reaches costa at apex*. FW dark yellow to orange with variable dark speckling and rose shading; no white reniform spot. Wingspan 5.3–7.5 cm.

Food: Honey locust and Kentucky coffee-tree.

Range: Mich. to Miss., west to Kans. and Tex. April–Sept.; 2 broods. Less common than Honey Locust Moth.

ROSY MAPLE MOTH   Pl. 8 (15, 16)
Dryocampa rubicunda (F.)

Identification: Body and wings white, cream, or yellow. Bright *pink usually fills all but median area of FW* and forms wide outer border on HW. Wingspan 3.4–5.2 cm.

Food: Larva (**Green-striped Mapleworm**) may be a serious pest on maple and oaks.

Range: N.S. to Fla., west to w. Ont., Neb., and Tex. May–Aug. northward (1 brood); April–Sept. southward (2 broods). Common.

Whitish specimens from Neb. to n. Mo. with little or no pink are subspecies *D. rubicunda alba* Grt.
Similar species: Pink Prominent (p. 336, Pl. 43) has *pink thorax* and *sharply angled am. line.*

SPINY OAKWORM MOTH   Pl. 8 (1, 12)
Anisota stigma (F.)
Identification: FW light to dark rusty brown, *heavily speckled with blackish*; note pink tinge in am. and pm. areas. Reniform spot white. HW same color as FW but with a darker median line. Wingspan 4–7 cm.
Food: Larva (**Spiny Oakworm**) feeds in groups on oaks and hazelnut trees.
Range: Mass. and s. Ont. to Fla., west to Minn., Kans., and Tex. June–July in North; May–Aug. southward. Our only *Anisota* species in which ♂ is common at lights.
Similar species: Large-eyed Oakworm Moth, *A. fuscosa* Fgn. (not shown), has *larger eyes* than other *Anisota* species. FW yellowish brown to deep yellowish orange with heavy *dark speckling*. Food: Oaks, especially post, Spanish, and water oaks. Range: La. and Tex.; May–Oct.

ORANGE-TIPPED OAKWORM MOTH   Pl. 8 (8, 9)
Anisota senatoria (J.E. Sm.)
Identification: FW reddish brown and mostly translucent of ♂; *outer margin of HW concave to straight in* ♂ (not convex as in Spiny Oakworm Moth, above). Female Orange-tipped Oakworm Moth is similar to ♀ Spiny Oakworm Moth but smaller, with less dark speckling and *no* distinct *pm. line on HW.* Wingspan 3–5 cm.
Food: Larva (**Orange-tipped Oakworm**) feeds in groups on oaks, birch (?), and raspberry (?). A pest northward.
Range: Mass. to Ga. (Fla. ?), west to Minn. and e. Tex. June–July northward (1 brood); May–Sept. in South (probably 2 broods). A day-flier, not easily collected.
Similar species: (1) Consular Oakworm Moth, *A. consularis* Dyar, (not shown). Male resembles ♂ Orange-tipped Oakworm Moth, but *outer margin of HW* distinctly *convex*; ♀ darker, *more reddish or pinkish.* Food: Live oak. Range: E. Ga. and Fla. Aug.–Oct. (2) Manitoba Oakworm Moth, *A. manitobensis* McD. (not shown), has *more prominent pink tinge* beyond pm. line, and no dark speckling in both sexes. Food: Bur oak and hazelnut trees. Range: Wisc., and s. Man. June–July. (3) In Finlayson's Oakworm Moth, *A. finlaysoni* Riotte (not shown), ♂ is *sepia brown*; ♀ is dull yellowish brown with almost *no pink* beyond pm. line. Food: White oak and other oaks. Range: Ont., Wisc., and Minn. June–July.

PINK-STRIPED OAKWORM MOTH   Pl. 8 (7, 10)
Anisota virginiensis (Dru.)
Identification: Similar   to   Orange-tipped   Oakworm   Moth

(above), but ♂ FW more pinkish and purplish red, with an almost *transparent median patch*; HW distinctly *convex*. FW and HW of ♀ lacks dark speckling; *heavy pink tinge* beyond pm. line. Wingspan 3.3–4.5 cm.

Food: Larva (**Pink-striped Oakworm**) feeds on oaks, especially red oak.

Range: N.S. to Va., west to Man. and Ark. June–July (1 brood) northward; May–Oct. (2 broods) in South. Common.

Similar species: The following 3 species (not shown) are best distinguished by genitalic features: (1) In ♂ Clear Oakworm Moth, *A. pellucida* (J.E. Sm.) FW is darker reddish brown, outer margin of HW straight. FW *medium reddish brown* in ♀. Food: Oaks, especially Spanish and water oaks. Range: N.C. to Fla., west to La. April–Oct.; 2 broods. (2) Discolored Oakworm Moth, *A. discolor* Fgn., is paler, more dull yellowish brown in both sexes. Food: Oaks, especially mossycup and water oaks. Range: W. La., Okla., and Tex. June–Aug.; 2 broods. (3) In ♂ Peigler's Oakworm Moth, *A. peigleri* Riotte, FW is medium reddish brown with slightly convex outer margin; *HW margin straight*. FW deep orangish yellow with *sprinkling of dark scales* in ♀; purple beyond pm. line. Food: Red, black jack, Spanish, water, and other oaks. Range: N.C. to n. Fla; July–Aug. Common in Piedmont area.

Subfamily Hemileucinae

BUCK MOTH *Hemileuca maia* (Dru.) **Pl. 9 (3)**
Identification: FW and HW black with narrow white median bands. Black-bordered reniform *spot on FW touches black basal patch*. Tip of abdomen red in ♂ (shown), blackish in ♀. Wingspan 5–7.5 cm.

Food: Oaks, especially scrub oak. Larva has stinging hairs.

Range: Me. to Fla., west to Wisc., Kans., and Tex. Oct.–Nov. (Sept. northward; Dec. in Fla.). A rapid day-flier; best sought between noon and 2 P.M. on sunny days in oak forests.

Similar species: Grote's Buck Moth, *H. grotei* Grt. & Rob. (not shown), has a *very narrow white band* on FW, *interrupted* by black border of reniform spot. Food: Live oak. Range: E. Tex. (Bexar, Brown, Edwards, and Kerr counties). Nov.

NEW ENGLAND BUCK MOTH **Pl. 9 (6)**
Hemileuca lucina Hy. Edw.
Identification: Similar to Buck Moth (above) but smaller. Wings paler, more translucent. White band on FW *broader*, completely *surrounding reniform spot*. Wingspan 4.5–6 cm.

Food: Broadleaf spiraea and oaks. Larva has stinging hairs.

Range: Very local in boggy or wet meadows in Me., N.H., and Mass. Sept. (adults of this species always emerge earlier than Buck Moth).

NEVADA BUCK MOTH Pl. 9 (4)
Hemileuca nevadensis Stretch

Identification: Similar in size to the Buck Moth (Pl. 9) but with a wide white median band, as in the New England Buck Moth (above). *Outer border* of white median band on FW *curved*, not straight as in New England Buck Moth. Wingspan 5–7 cm.

Food: Alders and willows. Larva has stinging hairs.

Range: Western U.S. and Canada; now extending east to Man., Wisc., and Tex. Hybrids with the Buck Moth (*H. maia*) have been reported from Ill. and Wisc. Sept.–Dec.

IO MOTH *Automeris io* (F.) Pls. 1 (12), 2 (5), 10 (2,4)
Identification: Easily recognized by the white-centered, black and blue *"bull's-eye" on HW*. In typical specimens, FW is yellow in ♂, red to brownish in ♀. In the Florida Io Moth, *A. io lilith* (Stkr.), not shown, FW is *orange* in ♂, brighter red in ♀. Wingspan 5–8 cm.

Food: Birches, clover, corn, elms, maples, oaks, willows, and many other plants. Larva (Pl. 1) has sharp, stinging spines.

Range: Me. and s. Que. to Fla., west to Man. and Tex. Intermediate forms between typical form and the Florida subspecies (*A. io lilith*) occur from S.C. and Ga. to La. May–Sept.; 1 brood northward, 2–3 in South. Common.

Subfamily Saturniinae

POLYPHEMUS MOTH Pls. 1 (15), 2 (6), 9 (7)
Antheraea polyphemus (Cram.)

Identification: FW reddish to yellowish brown with pink-edged white am. and black pm. lines. *Oval transparent spots* on FW and HW *ringed with yellow, blue, and black*; HW rings broaden much more than those on FW. Wingspan 10–15 cm.

Food: Larva (Pl. 1) feeds on many trees and shrubs, such as ashes, birches, grapes, hickories, maples, oaks, pines, and members of the rose family. Cocoon (Pl. 2) hangs from food plant in winter.

Range: Common throughout our area. May–July (1 brood) northward; April–Sept. (2 broods) in South. Comes to lights.

LUNA MOTH *Actias luna* (L.) Pls. 1 (6), 2 (4), 9 (8)
Identification: One of our most spectacular moths. Wings *pale green*; HW drawn out into *long, sweeping tail*. Transparent spot on each wing. Pink or reddish brown at outer margins in spring brood of southern specimens, yellow in northern and southern summer moths. Wingspan 7.5–10.5 cm.

Food: Larva (Pl. 1) feeds on many trees, including alder, beeches, cherries, hazelnut, hickories, pecan, sweet gum, and willows. Cocoon (Pl. 2) is concealed on ground among leaf litter, so hard to find in winter.

Range: Common throughout our area. May–July (1 brood) northward; March–Sept. (3 broods) southward.

AILANTHUS SILKMOTH *Samia cynthia* (Dru.)   **Pl. 10 (1)**
Identification: Wings olive to brownish with white markings; pink-tinted, white pm. line extends onto HW. *Crescent-shaped, translucent spot* on each wing edged with white and yellow. Note small black spot below apex of FW. Wingspan 10.5–14 cm.
Food: Chinese tree-of-heaven (*Ailanthus altissima*). Larva (**Ailanthus Silkworm**) has also been reared on other plants, including ash, butternut, holly, lilac, privet, *Prunus* species, sassafras, sweet gum, and tulip-trees.
Range: Introduced around 1860 into Philadelphia from China as a possible silk producer. Released deliberately, it has become established primarily in urban areas where tree-of-heaven grows, especially around railroad yards, against factory fences, and in waste areas. Present distribution spotty and not well known—Mass. to Ga., west to Ind. and n. Ky. May or June–Aug.; 2 broods. Adults fly by day and will not come to lights. Look for cocoons attached to main petiole of leaf in early autumn, after leaflets have fallen but before main petioles also fall.

FORBES' SILKMOTH   •   **Pl. 10 (6)**
Rothschildia forbesi Benj.
Identification: The large, *triangular, transparent spots* on each wing identify this as a *Rothschildia* species, but this is the only member of the genus in our area in which the FW spot often *pierces pm. line* (usually more than in specimen shown). Wings reddish brown to dark brown with *olive tinge; pm. line bent* between FW costa and triangular spot. Wingspan 9–12.5 cm.
Food: Larva feeds on ash, lime, prickly ash, and willows in the wild, but can be reared on citrus, privet, wild cherry, and other plants. Cocoon teardrop-shaped, silvery white.
Range: Mexico; sometimes common in extreme se. Tex. Feb.–April; June–July; and Sept.; 3 broods.
Similar species: Two other *Rothschildia* species (not shown) rarely enter se. Tex. from Mexico (food plants and flight seasons similar to those of Forbes' Silkmoth): (1) Jorulla Silkmoth, *R. jorulla* (Westwood) is larger; *pm. line straight* between FW costa and spot; dark specimens have *no olive tinge*. (2) Orizaba Silkmoth, *R. orizaba* (Westwood), is the largest of the 3 species (wingspan up to 15 cm). It has *cinnamon brown* to *pale tan wings* and *straight pm. line* between costa and spot.

CALLETA SILKMOTH   **Pl. 10 (3)**
Eupackardia calleta (Westwood)
Identification: Body and wings blackish brown; collar and rear edge of thorax *red. Triangular white spots* on each wing vary from large and prominent to nearly absent. *Pm. line even, white*, very conspicuous. Wingspan 8–11 cm.
Food: Larva feeds in the wild on catclaw, ceniza, mesquite, and

ocotillo, but can be reared on ash, pepper tree, privet, *Prunus* species, and willows.

Range: Mexico; enters our area in extreme se. Tex. March; Sept.–Nov.; 2 broods.

PROMETHEA MOTH or   **Pls. 1 (7), 2 (2), 10 (9, 12)**
SPICEBUSH SILKMOTH
Callosamia promethea (Dru.)

Identification: *Wings blackish* in ♂, except for faint whitish pm. line, pale tan terminal border, and pink shading around apical spot. *Female bright reddish to dark brown*, usually with well-developed reniform spots. Wingspan 7.5–9.5 cm.

Food: Larva (Pl. 1) feeds on many plants, including apple, ashes, basswood, birches, cherries, lilac, maples, sassafras, spicebush, sweet gum, and tulip-trees. Compact cocoon (Pl. 2) hangs by silken stalk from twig and can be seen easily after leaves have fallen.

Range: Me. and s. Que. to n. Fla., west to Minn. and e. Tex. June–July northward (1 brood); 2 southern broods fly March–May and July–Aug. Females come to lights; males do not. Mating occurs in afternoon to early evening; egg-laying takes place at night. Common in most of range.

TULIP-TREE SILKMOTH   **Pls. 2 (1), 10 (5, 7)**
Callosamia angulifera (Wlk.)

Identification: Usually slightly *larger* than Promethea Moth (above). *Wings dark brown*, not blackish in ♂; whitish pm. line, terminal area, and reniform spots more distinct. Wings *yellowish to orangish brown* in ♀, with *no reddish tint*; FW *reniform spot usually large*. Wingspan 8–11 cm.

Food: Tulip-tree; larva can also be reared on black cherry and sassafras. Cocoon (Pl. 2) not attached to twig by silken stalk, so it falls to the ground with leaves of food plant.

Range: Mass. to n. Fla., west to s. Ont., Mich., Ky. and Miss. One brood (June–Aug.) in North; 2 broods (April–May and July–Aug.) southward. Both sexes are active at night and come to lights.

SWEETBAY SILKMOTH   **Pls. 2 (7), 10 (8, 10)**
Callosamia securifera (Maassen)

Identification: Similar to Promethea Moth and Tulip-tree Silkmoth (above) but wings *more yellowish* brown; triangular *spots tend to be less prominent* or even absent, especially on HW. Underside of HW *not noticeably darker* inside pm. line, as in Promethea Moth, and pm. line *not edged with white* on outer side as in Tulip-tree Silkmoth. Wingspan 7.5–10 cm.

Food: Sweetbay. Cocoon (Pl. 2) is enclosed in leaves of food plant, and remains on tree throughout the winter.

Range: N.C. to cen. Fla., west to Miss. in low coastal swamps and pine flatlands. April–May and July–Sept.; 2 broods. Both sexes fly during day, when mating occurs; females fly also at night. Locally common.

CECROPIA MOTH or   **Pls. 1 (10), 2 (8), 10 (13)**
ROBIN MOTH *Hyalophora cecropia* (L.)
Identification: Easily recognized by its large size and *red body* with *white collar* and *abdominal crossbands*. Wings dark brownish with *red shading* in basal area of FW, in crescent eyespots, and *beyond pm. line* on all wings. Wingspan 11–15 cm.
Food: Larva (Pl. 1) feeds on many trees and shrubs, including apple trees, ashes, beeches, birches, elms, maples, poplars, *Prunus* species, *Ribes* species, white oak, and willows. Loose, brown, spindle-shaped cocoon (Pl. 2) is attached lengthwise on twig, visible in winter.
Range: Throughout our area. May–July; 1 brood. Though adults do fly to lights, they are often found during the day. Increasingly common in urban and suburban areas.

COLUMBIA SILKMOTH   **Pl. 10 (11)**
Hyalophora columbia (S.I. Sm.)
Identification: Very similar to Cecropia Moth (above) but smaller and more drab. *No red shading beyond pm. line* on FW and HW. Wingspan 8–10 cm.
Food: American larch (tamarack).
Range: N.S. to Me. and N.H., west to e. Man. and Minn. June–early July. Found only in boggy northern forests with acid soil and many larch trees.

TENT CATERPILLAR and LAPPET MOTHS: Family Lasiocampidae

Medium-sized moths with hairy bodies that usually exceed HW in length; wingspan 2.5–5.8 cm. Ocelli absent. Proboscis vestigial or absent; adults do not feed. Labial palps vary from small to large and upturned. *Antennae bipectinate to tips* in both sexes. Radius of FW has 4–5 branches; R_5 *stalked with* M_1 (Fig. 18). Vein Cu appears 4-branched; M_2 and M_3 either stalked, or both extend from bottom of discal cell. *Humeral area of HW greatly expanded, supported by 1 or more humeral veins; frenulum absent.* Sc and R_1 either briefly fused with Rs near base, or connected to it by crossvein.

Larvae colorful, longitudinally striped, and densely hairy (Pl. 1). Some species are serious pests in forests and on shade trees. Larvae of some species build communal webs ("tents") in trees, for protection from predators, and leave them to feed on foliage of host tree as well as other deciduous trees and shrubs. These moths pupate in a cocoon. Silk of some species has been used for cloth in some parts of the world, but it is carded and spun (silk of Silkworm Moth, p.

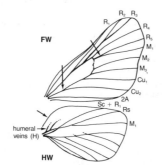

Fig. 18.
Wing venation,
Lasiocampidae.

55, is unraveled). The moths in this family hold their wings like a roof over the body when at rest.

LARGE TOLYPE *Tolype velleda* (Stoll)   **Pl. 8 (17)**
Identification: Body extremely hairy. Head and front and sides of thorax white; middle of thorax black. Abdomen white to gray. Wings pale to dark gray with white veins and lines. *Pm. line broad, almost straight.* Wingspan 3.2–5.8 cm.
Food: Apple, ash, birch, elm, oak, plum, and other trees.
Range: N.S. to cen. Fla., west to Minn., Neb., and Tex. Sept.–Oct. Common.
Similar species: The following 3 species are smaller: (1) Small Tolype (below) has *more wavy pm. line.* (2) Larch Tolype, *T. laricis* (Fitch), not shown, is *blackish gray* in ♂, with lines usually invisible; ♀ looks like a small brownish ♀ of Large Tolype. Food: Larches, firs, pines, and other conifers. Range: N.S. to N.Y., west across Canada, south into northern states. July–Sept. (3) Southern Tolype, *T. minta* Dyar (not shown), is *white* with *gray lines;* broadest line is a shade line beyond pm. line. Food: Probably pines. Range: Coastal S.C. to Fla. April–Dec.; probably 3 broods.

SMALL TOLYPE *Tolype notialis* Franc.   **Pl. 8 (2)**
Identification: Very similar to Large Tolype (above), but usually *much smaller* and more variable in color, ranging from pale to dark smoky gray. Pm. line much *more wavy,* and meets costa at a more perpendicular angle. Wingspan 2.6–3.9 cm.
Food: Conifers. Records confused with those for Large Tolype.
Range: N. Va. to Fla., west to Ky. June–Sept. Common in South.

DOT-LINED WHITE *Artace cribraria* (Ljungh)   **Pl. 11 (6)**
Identification: Easily recognized by its *gleaming white body and wings,* and the *lines of black dots* on its FW. Wingspan 2.5–6.2 cm.
Food: Larvae seem to prefer oaks; will also eat *Prunus* species and roses.
Range: L.I., N.Y. to Fla., west to Ky. and se. Tex. June–Oct. Common in South; uncommon to rare northward.

RILEY'S LAPPET MOTH   Pl. 11 (4)
Heteropacha rileyana Harv.
Identification: Wings dark gray, slightly translucent (almost greasy-looking). Note *whitish gray basal patch;* median area darker gray than area beyond it. Am. line solid; st. line a series of black dots. Fringes of FW and HW checkered. Wingspan 2.7–3.6 cm.
Food: Honey locust.
Range: S. Ont. and w. Pa., to Fla., west to Wisc., Kans., and Tex. March–Nov.; 2 broods. Moderately common.

LAPPET MOTH *Phyllodesma americana* (Harr.)   Pl. 8 (5)
Identification: Easily recognized by the *scalloped outer margins of FW and HW;* note white in "scallops." FW color varies from bluish gray to reddish or yellowish brown; markings white and violet. Reniform spot a black vertical dash when present. Wingspan 2.9–4.9 cm.
Food: Alder, birches, oaks, poplars, members of the rose family, and willows.
Range: N.S. to Ga., west across s. Canada, south to Tex. March–Sept.; 2 broods. Rare to locally common.
Similar species: Southern Lappet Moth, *P. carpinifolia* (Bdv.), not shown, has *white reniform spot on FW.* Food: Unrecorded. Range: Coastal S.C. to Fla., west to Ky. and Tex. March–April; as early as Jan. in Fla.

FOREST TENT CATERPILLAR MOTH   Pl. 11 (3)
Malacosoma disstria Hbn.
Identification: FW dull yellow to yellowish or reddish brown, with *brown am. and pm. lines* in some specimens. Median area may be completely brown (not shown). Wingspan 2.3–3.7 cm.
Food: Many trees and shrubs, especially aspens and maples. Unlike other tent caterpillars, these do not make tentlike webbing, but may be abundant enough to do extensive damage to foliage of forest trees.
Range: Throughout our area. April–Sept. Often common locally; populations move around as adults seek fresh food sources.

EASTERN TENT CATERPILLAR   Pls. 1 (16), 11 (1)
MOTH *Malacosoma americanum* (F.)
Identification: Body and wings warm *fawn brown.* FW with *white am. and pm. lines.* Median area sometimes white. Wingspan 2.2–4.4 cm.
Food: Larva (**Eastern Tent Caterpillar,** Pl. 1) feeds on many trees and shrubs, especially apple and cherry trees, flowering crab-apples, and other members of the rose family. A serious defoliating pest, recognized by the characteristic white webbing ("tents") larvae spin in forks of trees and shrubs in spring. When full-grown, larvae leave host trees and disperse to form loose cocoons in protected places where they pupate. Infestations tend to be cyclic in

severity, worsening for several years until populations "crash" to low levels.

Range: Common throughout our area. Late May–June; 1 brood.

SILKWORM MOTHS:
Family Bombycidae

Heavy-bodied, hairy white moths; wingspan 3.5–5 cm. Labial palps very small; proboscis absent. Vein Cu of both FW and HW appears 3-branched (Fig. 19). Outer margin of FW indented below apex. M_2 arises halfway between M_1 and M_3. Frenulum *small*. *$Sc+R_1$ connected to Rs by oblique crossvein* at about midpoint of top of discal cell.

A family of about 100 species in southern Eurasia. Although these moths are not native to our area, the family is included in this guide because of the Silkworm Moth, which is occasionally reared in North America for teaching, research, and private collections.

Sericulture, or commercial silk culture, was apparently begun in China about 2,697 B.C. The Chinese exported silk, but closely guarded the secret of its production until 555 A.D., when 2 monks smuggled some eggs to Constantinople in the hollow handles of their walking-sticks. The thriving European silk industry was thus begun. Large-scale attempts at sericulture in the U.S. have been largely unsuccessful.

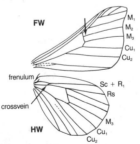

Fig. 19.
Wing venation,
Bombycidae.

SILKWORM MOTH *Bombyx mori* (L.)   **Pl. 13 (14)**
Identification: Easily identified by the *sickle-shaped FW apex* and overall *cream coloring*. Some have partial pale brown lines across wings (not shown). Wingspan 3.5–5 cm.
Food: Mulberry and osage-orange. Early larval instars have been reared successfully on lettuce. In captivity, caterpillars will stay on leaves provided as food, so they do not have to be caged.
Range: This species does not occur in nature; it has been reared in captivity for so long that adults can rarely fly. Eggs can occasion-

ally be purchased from biological supply houses, and larvae can be reared to the adult stage in about 2 months. Conditions for rearing these moths on a large scale apparently do not exist in the U.S.

APATELODID MOTHS:
Family Apatelodidae

A small family of medium-sized moths with small translucent "windows" in FW; probably related to Old World silkmoths (Bombycidae, above). Wingspan 3.2–4.2 cm. Proboscis reduced or absent. Labial palps short, upturned. Antennae bipectinate to tips in both sexes. Vein Cu appears *3-branched,* and M_2 arises *slightly closer to M_1* than to M_3 on all wings (Fig. 20). FW often has R_2 and R_3 stalked, also R_4 and R_5. $Sc + R_1$ and Rs of HW *briefly fused* or very close to each other at about midpoint of top of discal cell, then widely diverging. Frenulum well developed.

Larvae flattened, densely hairy, with abdominal prolegs stretching out laterally. Food plants include many trees and shrubs. These moths usually pupate in a cell in the soil, but some species outside our area spin cocoons. The names Eupterotidae and Zanolidae have been used by some researchers for this family.

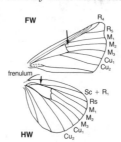

Fig. 20.
Wing venation,
Apatelodidae.

SPOTTED APATELODES   Pl. 8 (19)
Apatelodes torrefacta (J.E. Sm.)
Identification: FW gray with brown lines and shading. Note the *blackish brown patch* near base. Indistinct translucent spot near FW apex. HW reddish brown. Wingspan 3.2–4.2 cm.
Food: Ashes, maples, oaks, *Prunus* species, and other trees.
Range: Me. and s. Ont. to Fla., west to Wisc., Mo., and Tex. May–Aug.; 2 broods southward. Common.

THE ANGEL *Olceclostera angelica* (Grt.)   Pl. 8 (18)
Identification: *Outer margins of FW and HW scalloped.* FW pale gray with brown lines and shading. Note *2 translucent spots* near apex. HW pale brown with darker brown shading. Wingspan 3.2–4.2 cm.
Food: Ash trees and lilac.

Range: Me. and s. Ont. to S.C., west to Wisc. and Mo. May–Sept. Uncommon.

Similar species: Also in our area but not shown are: (1) Indistinct Angel, *O. indistincta* (Hy. Edw.), which is *smaller,* with *less sharply scalloped* outer margins. *Markings less distinct;* HW paler and grayer. Food: Unrecorded. Range: Fla. peninsula. March–June. (2) In The Seraph, *O. seraphica* (Dyar), pm. line of FW is more irregular than in other *Olceclostera* species, and it *curves inward below reniform spot.* No brown on underside of wings as in The Angel. Food: Desert willow. Range: S. and sw. Tex. March; July–Aug.; probably other months.

SACK-BEARERS:
Family Mimallonidae

Medium-sized, hairy moths; wingspan 2–5 cm in our species. Ocelli absent. Proboscis reduced, almost completely absent. Labial palps also reduced. Antennae bipectinate in both sexes. FW hooked below apex; R_2 stalked with R_3, and R_4 with R_5; the 2 *stalks widely separated* (Fig. 21). Cu appears 3-branched on FW and HW. $Sc + R_1$ *fused with Rs* at HW base, then *abruptly and widely separating* from it. Frenulum *very small.*

Larvae thick in middle, tapering toward ends. Later stages build unique, open-ended cases or "sacks" of silk and leaves in which larvae overwinter. Pupation is in late spring.

This family has been known in older books as Lacosomidae. Confined to the western hemisphere; most species are tropical.

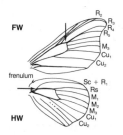

Fig. 21.
Wing venation,
Mimallonidae.

SCALLOPED SACK-BEARER Pl. 11 (2, 5)
Lacosoma chiridota Grt.
Identification: Easily recognized by the *deeply scalloped FW* with a *hooked apex.* FW shaded with dark brown in ♂; FW warm yellowish to reddish brown in ♀. Pm. line and small reniform spot on FW similar in both sexes. Wingspan 2–3.2 cm.
Food: Oaks.
Range: N.H. and s. Ont. to Fla., west to Iowa and Tex. April–Sept. Males rarely come to lights.

MELSHEIMER'S SACK-BEARER   **Pl. 8 (14)**
Cicinnus melsheimeri (Harr.)
Identification: *Apex of FW hooked.* All wings gray to grayish
brown with orangish brown shading and black dusting. Small,
dark grayish reniform spot on FW; pm. line *bends below costa* and
appears to continue onto HW. Wingspan 3.5–5 cm.
Food: Oaks; seems to prefer scrub oak northward.
Range: Mass. and s. Ont. to Fla., west to Wisc. and Tex. May–
July. Most common in sandy, oak-barren habitats.

TIGER, LICHEN, and WASP MOTHS:
Family Arctiidae

Small to medium-sized moths with moderately broad wings; many
are white, yellow, orange, or red with black FW markings. Wingspan 1.2–7 cm. Ocelli present or absent; labial palps short; proboscis usually reduced. Antennae bipectinate or simple with tufts of
hairs (ciliate) in $\male$; simple in $\female$. Tympana on metathorax directed
obliquely toward the rear, with *hood over counter-tympanal cavity*
on base of abdomen lying in front of spiracle. Vein M_2 *arises much
closer to* M_3 than to M_1 on FW and HW. FW has no areoles (Figs.
22 and 23). $Sc + R_1$ either *absent* (as in Ctenuchinae, Fig. 23, p. 59),
or *fused with Rs* for most of basal half of discal cell except at base,
leaving a *small basal areole* (Fig. 22). Sc usually very wide at base
when present.
  Larvae usually very hairy; some in subfamily Arctiinae are
known as woolly bears. Arctiid larvae feed on lichens and many
kinds of herbaceous and woody plants. They pupate in cocoons
made of matted larval hair with little or no silk. Adults may be
day-fliers or nocturnal. A few species are serious forest pests.
  Our 4 subfamilies are characterized as follows:

Pericopinae, p. 59—Medium-sized day-fliers, usually brilliantly
marked. Large, rounded dorsal knob on each side of 1st abdominal
segment.
Lithosiinae (lichen moths), p. 59—Small, pale-colored, slen-
der-bodied; *ocelli absent.* Wing venation resembles that of
Arctiinae (Fig. 22), or is reduced. Most feed on lichens.
Arctiinae (tiger moths), p. 63—Robust, medium-sized; *ocelli
present.* Most have *rows of spots on abdomen.*
Ctenuchinae (wasp moths), p. 75—FW narrow. Color, shape,
and behavior mimic wasps and some beetles. Ocelli present. $Sc + R_1$
of HW absent (Fig. 23).

  These 4 subfamilies were considered separate families until recently. This family is a large one worldwide, particularly in tropical regions.

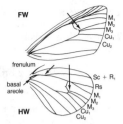

Fig. 22. Wing venation, Arctiidae (Arctiinae).

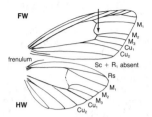

Fig. 23. Wing venation, Arctiidae (Ctenuchinae).

Subfamily Pericopinae

FAITHFUL BEAUTY   Pl. 11 (7)
Composia fidelissima H.-S.
Identification: Easily recognized by the *metallic blue* on its black wings, and the *red border* along FW costa (basal $\frac{1}{3}$). Red border interrupted by 2 black bars. White spots present on FW and HW. Wingspan 4.8–6.4 cm.
Food: Bay bean, leafless cynachum, devil's potato, and oleander.
Range: Fla.; common from Miami through Fla. Keys; rarer north to Indian R. region. All months. A day-flier, best sought at edges of hardwood thickets and woods ("hammocks").

Subfamily Lithosiinae

BICOLORED MOTH *Eilema bicolor* (Grt.)   Pl. 16 (2)
Identification: FW gray with pale *yellow along costa*. Body gray with pale yellow collar, tuft at end of abdomen, and head (some specimens). HW gray. Wingspan 2.4–3.5 cm.
Food: Conifers and lichens growing on conifers. Larvae seem to prefer spruces and firs, but can also be found on cedars, hemlocks, larches, and pines.
Range: Lab. to Mass. and N.Y., west across Canada, south to S.D. Late June–end of Aug. Common.

DARK GRAY LICHEN MOTH   Pl. 16 (7, 9)
Crambidia lithosioides Dyar
Identification: FW gray with pale tan veins in ♂; antennae more broadly bipectinate than in other *Crambidia* species. FW of ♀ very *dark gray with yellow costa*. Collar yellow in ♀; antennae appear sawtoothed. Wingspan 1.2–1.8 cm.
Food: Lichens.
Range: N.C. to Fla., west to Ky. and Miss. June in Ky.; all months and common farther south.

PALE LICHEN MOTH   Pl. 16 (5)
Crambidia pallida Pack.
Identification: Both sexes similar to ♂ Dark Gray Lichen Moth (above), but *antennae simple*. Veins of FW outlined with pale tan,

but no small outline of accessory cell at tip of discal cell, as in ♂ Dark Gray Lichen Moth. Wingspan 1.9–2.5 cm.
Food: Lichens.
Range: N.S. to S.C., west to Man. and Tex. May–Sept.; 2 broods. Common.
Similar species: Uniform Lichen Moth, *C. uniformis* Dyar (not shown), is smaller and *darker gray, almost blackish;* antennae not bipectinate. Food: Lichens. Range: N.J. to Fla., west to Pa. and Ky. June and Sept. Uncommon.

PEARLY-WINGED LICHEN MOTH Pl. 16 (14)
Crambidia casta (Pack.)
Identification: Body and wings *pure white* above and *gray* on underside, but note narrow *white costal border* near base on underside of FW. Western U.S. populations have a more "pearly" cast than those in our area. Wingspan 3–4 cm.
Food: Lichens.
Range: N.S. to N.C., west to Man. and Ky. June–Sept. Uncommon.
Similar species: (1) Pure Lichen Moth, *C. pura* B. & McD. (not shown), is smaller; *underside of FW pure white.* Food: Lichens (?). Range: N.Y. and N.J. to Fla. and Ky. June–July. (2) Yellow-headed Lichen Moth, *C. cephalica* (Grt. & Rob.), not shown, is identical to Pearly-winged Lichen Moth but has *yellow head.* Food: Lichens (?). Range: Tex.; Aug. Specimens from W. Va., N.C., and Ky. may belong to this or an unnamed species.

KENTUCKY LICHEN MOTH Pl. 12 (16)
Cisthene kentuckiensis (Dyar)
Identification: Frons blackish. FW also blackish with a *wide yellowish orange band* in median area; band extends as a thin border along inner margin, *distinctly narrowed* near pm. band. HW pink with black outer border that widens toward apex. Wingspan 1.5–1.9 cm.
Food: Lichens.
Range: N.J. to n. Fla., west to Ky. and Miss. July–Oct. Uncommon.

THIN-BANDED LICHEN MOTH Pl. 12 (13)
Cisthene tenuifascia Harv.
Identification: Identical to Kentucky Lichen Moth (above) except *yellow band* along inner margin of FW *not narrower* where it meets yellow median band. In ♂ (not shown) look for tuft of hairs at anal angle of HW (absent in Kentucky Lichen Moth). Wingspan 1.6–2 cm.
Food: Lichens.
Range: N.J. to Fla., west to Tex. April–Oct. northward; all year in s. Fla. and Tex. Rare northward.

LEAD-COLORED LICHEN MOTH   Pl. 12 (15)
Cisthene plumbea Stretch

Identification: FW pale brownish gray with a yellow to pinkish border along costa and inner margin. Note the *yellow to pinkish patch* (somewhat triangular) at anal angle of FW. HW pink with black outer border, widest at apex. Wingspan 1.7–2.1 cm.
Food: Lichens.
Range: N.Y. to n. Fla., west to Wisc. and Tex. June–Sept.; 2 broods. Common.

STRIATED LICHEN MOTH   Pl. 12 (19)
Cisthene striata Ottolengui

Identification: FW yellowish to pinkish with *gray lines* (striations) along veins; small pink spot on inner margin, near anal angle. HW pale pink with dark gray shading at apex. Wingspan 1.5–2 cm.
Food: Lichens (?); no positive records.
Range: Fla., all months. Locally common in s. Fla.

SUBJECT LICHEN MOTH   Pl. 12 (21)
Cisthene subjecta Wlk.

Identification: FW gray; thin yellow costal border merges into rounded pink patch near apex. Another yellow line extends from base of FW and ends in *rectangular pink patch on inner margin* near anal angle. HW pink with black border, widest near apex. Wingspan 1.3–1.5 cm.
Food: Lichens.
Range: N.J. to Fla., west to Miss. June–Aug.; all year in s. Fla., where it is common. Rare northward.

PACKARD'S LICHEN MOTH   Pl. 12 (18)
Cisthene packardii (Grt.)

Identification: Very similar to Subject Lichen Moth (above) but slightly larger; patch at anal angle more *rounded, yellow and pink* (upper half yellow). Wingspan 1.4–1.9 cm.
Food: Lichens.
Range: N.Y. to Fla., west to Mo. and Tex. May–Sept.; 2 broods in Mo. Common.

BLACK-AND-YELLOW LICHEN MOTH   Pl. 11 (16)
Lycomorpha pholus (Dru.)

Identification: Body and wings bluish black. Tegulae and *bases of FW and HW yellowish orange.* Wingspan 2.5–3.2 cm.
Food: Lichens.
Range: N.S. to N.C., west to S.D. and Tex. July–Sept. A day-flier, often seen on flowers such as goldenrod.
Similar species: Orange-patched Smoky Moth (p. 414, Pl. 57) has *translucent wings;* no yellow on HW. It flies at night.

SCARLET-WINGED LICHEN MOTH Pl. 12 (5)
Hypoprepia miniata (Kby.)

Identification: Body and wings *bright red;* gray shading on abdomen of ♀ (shown). Note *3 broad gray lines* on FW—middle one short. HW has dark gray outer border (absent in some southern specimens). Wingspan 2.8–4 cm.
Food: Tree lichens.
Range: Throughout our area. June–Aug. Common to uncommon.

PAINTED LICHEN MOTH Pl. 12 (2)
Hypoprepia fucosa Hbn.

Identification: Similar to Scarlet-winged Lichen Moth (above) but usually smaller and more common. Look for a *gray dorsal patch on thorax* (present in most specimens). FW has *yellow* along costa and inner margin. HW pale pink with gray outer border (narrower than in Scarlet-winged Lichen Moth). Wingspan 2.5–3.5 cm.
Food: Lichens.
Range: Common throughout our area. May–Sept.

LITTLE WHITE LICHEN MOTH Pl. 16 (12)
Clemensia albata Pack.

Identification: FW white, variably dusted and spotted with brown and black. Lines obscure—am. and median lines usually most distinct. Reniform spot gray with *sharp, black inner half.* HW grayish white with faint, darker gray median line. Wingspan 1.6–2.4 cm.
Food: Lichens.
Range: Common throughout our area. March–Oct.; 2 or more broods.

MOUSE-COLORED LICHEN MOTH Pl. 15 (18)
Pagara simplex Wlk.

Identification: Antennae of ♂ broadly bipectinate, yellow at base; ♀ antennae sawtoothed. Wings broad, translucent grayish brown; bright *yellow at base of FW.* Abdomen yellow with brown middorsal spots. Wingspan 2–2.5 cm.
Food: Larvae have been reared on dandelion and wild lettuce.
Range: Wash., D.C., to Fla., west to s. Mo. and Tex. March–Oct. Apparently uncommon.

CADBURY'S LICHEN MOTH Pl. 31 (13)
Comachara cadburyi Franc.

Identification: FW glossy pale gray with a darker gray basal line; median area dark gray. Pm. line whitish, incomplete; *st. line a series of black dots,* ending in a *large blotch* at inner margin. HW pale gray. Wingspan 2.1–2.3 cm.
Food: Unrecorded.
Range: Mass. to Fla., west to Mo. and Tex. Late April–June.
Similar species: Frigid Owlet (p. 153, Pl. 30), lacks prominent basal line; st. line a more irregular series of black spots, *each spot more squarish.*

Subfamily Arctiinae

BELLA MOTH *Utetheisa bella* (L.)   **Pl. 15 (12)**
Identification: Wing pattern variable but distinctive; the only moth in our area with a *pink and yellow FW* marked with rows of *white-ringed black spots*. HW pink with uneven black border. Wingspan 3–4.4 cm.
Food: Legumes, such as crotalaria, lespedeza, and lupines; also elm trees, fireweed, *Prunus* species, and sweetgale.
Range: N.S. to Fla., west to Minn., Kans., and Tex. July and Sept. broods northward; breeds continuously in deep South. Common southward. A conspicuous day-flier.
Similar species: In Ornate Moth, *U. ornatrix* (L.), not shown, FW is more whitish with sparse black spots, making it look washed-out. Food: Legumes. Range: Tropical; found in s. Fla. and s. Tex. all year.

CLYMENE MOTH *Haploa clymene* (Brown)   **Pl. 15 (15)**
Identification: The boldly patterned FW and *orange-yellow HW* make this the easiest *Haploa* species to identify. FW cream-colored with a partial dark brown border that *extends inward as a "spur"* from inner margin near anal angle. HW has 1–2 dark brown spots near anal angle. Wingspan 4–5.5 cm.
Food: *Eupatorium* species, oaks, peach and willow trees, and other plants.
Range: Me. and Que. to Fla., west to Kans. and Tex. June–Aug. Conspicuous on leaves during the day; active both day and night.

COLONA MOTH *Haploa colona* (Hbn.)   **Pl. 15 (19)**
Identification: HW orange-yellow as in Clymene Moth (above), but usually only 1 small black spot. FW cream-colored with *brown line* extending from *costa before midpoint* to anal angle. Traces of at least 2 other lines extend inward from costa beyond midpoint (pattern varies). Wingspan 4–5.5 cm.
Food: Apple, ash, elms, hackberry, peach, and other plants.
Range: Coastal plain from se. Va. to Fla., west to Tex. April–July. Uncommon.
Similar species: In Reversed Haploa (below), FW pattern may be very similar, but *HW white,* not yellow.

REVERSED HAPLOA   **Pl. 13 (11), 16 (4)**
Haploa reversa (Stretch)
Identification: FW varies: either similar to Colona Moth (above), or *entirely whitish* as in some specimens of Leconte's Haploa (p. 64). Note *whitish HW,* which separates this species from Colona Moth (HW yellow). All-whitish specimens can be identified by association in the field with marked individuals. Wingspan 4–5.5 cm.
Food: Larva may be a pest on peach trees, and feeds on a wide variety of plants, including apple trees.

Range: S. Ont. to se. Va., west to cen. Minn., e. Kans., and Ark. May–July. A common day-flier, but also comes to lights.

THE NEIGHBOR *Haploa contigua* (Wlk.)   **Pl. 16 (1)**
Identification: Wings cream-colored to white. Note *brown line* extending from *costa beyond midpoint* to anal angle of FW, with another line from outer margin meeting it. Costa and inner margins also bordered with brown. Wingspan 3.6–4.9 cm.
Food: Unrecorded; probably a wide variety of plants.
Range: Que. to mts. of Ga., west to S.D., Ark., and Miss. Late May–early Aug.; mostly June–July. Common in Ky.

LECONTE'S HAPLOA   **Pl. 16 (3, 6)**
Haploa lecontei (Guér.)
Identification: FW varies from boldly marked to all cream-colored (not shown). Pattern differs from other *Haploa* species— Note *diagonal dark brown line* (represented by *short spurs* in lighter form shown) extending from outer margin near FW apex to meet dark brown line along inner margin of FW. 1–2 short spurs usually extend inward from costa. All-white individuals indistinguishable from those of Reversed Haploa (above). Wingspan 3.6–5 cm.
Food: Apple, blackberry, peach, spearmint, and other plants.
Range: N.S. to Ga., west to Man. and Ark. May–Aug. Common.

CONFUSED HAPLOA *Haploa confusa* (Lyman)   **Pl. 16 (8)**
Identification: FW similar to Colona Moth (p. 63, Pl. 15) but *smaller,* with *white HW.* Brown markings vary, but usually cover more than half of FW surface. Look for *small whitish spot or dash at anal angle.* HW sometimes has 1 or 2 brown spots near anal angle. Wingspan 3.8–4 cm.
Food: Hound's-tongue.
Range: N. Me. to cen. Pa., west to Man. and S.D. June–Aug.

JOYFUL HOLOMELINA   **Pl. 14 (15)**
Holomelina laeta (Guér.)
Identification: FW ash gray to black. HW red with an *even black outer border.* Wingspan 1.9–2.5 cm.
Food: Larva has been reared on dandelion and plantain.
Range: N.S. to Man., S.D. and Ky. June–Sept. This and other *Holomelina* species may be collected during the day as well as at lights at night.

TAWNY HOLOMELINA   **Pl. 14 (2, 5)**
Holomelina opella (Grt.)
Identification: FW yellowish brown to blackish brown (as shown) in ♂; HW often darker than FW. *Vague discal spots* on all wings; *no orange or red* on underside of FW in ♂. FW dull orangish yellow to blackish brown in ♀; HW *orange* with variable brownish shading and a more conspicuous, *blackish discal spot.* Underside of wings orange to yellowish in ♀. Wingspan 2.2–3.4 cm.

Food: Larva feeds on a variety of low plants and has been reared on dandelion.
Range: S. Que. and Mass. to Fla., west to Minn. and Ark. May–Sept. Common.

BOG HOLOMELINA *Holomelina lamae* (Free.)   **Pl. 14 (4)**
Identification: FW brown with variable orange tinting. Note faint blackish reniform spot and variably sized *orangish yellow spot above inner margin.* HW bright orange with an uneven, blackish border and black discal spot. Wingspan 2–2.3 cm.
Food: Larva has been reared on plantain.
Range: N.S. and Me. west to Wisc. July–Aug. Found only in bogs.

ORANGE HOLOMELINA   **Pl. 14 (8, 13)**
Holomelina aurantiaca (Hbn.)
Identification: Color varies: FW pale yellow to olive brown; HW usually orange. Grayish to black *reniform spot* and *wide st. line* on FW and discal spot and outer border on HW either dark, faint, or absent. *Colors* tend to be *paler* and *markings* more often *absent or faint in* ♂ than in ♀. Wingspan 1.8–2.7 cm.
Food: Corn, dandelion, pigweed, plantain, and other plants.
Range: Common throughout our area. Late May–Sept.

RUDDY HOLOMELINA   **Pl. 14 (11)**
Holomelina rubicundaria (Hbn.)
Identification: Very similar to Orange Holomelina (above) but usually slightly *smaller* and *more reddish orange.* HW markings on ♀ (not shown) more blackish. Wingspan 1.9–2.2 cm.
Food: Unrecorded; probably a wide variety of plants.
Range: Fla. along Gulf Coast to Tex. All year. Common.

RUSTY HOLOMELINA   **Pl. 14 (1, 6)**
Holomelina ferruginosa (Wlk.)
Identification: Very similar to Orange Holomelina (above) but usually *larger.* FW pale orange to dark olive brownish, with or without reniform spot and st. line; *orange spots sometimes present* toward inner margin in dark specimens, as in 14 (6). HW yellowish to orangish, with or without shading. Wingspan 2.5–3 cm.
Food: Larva has been reared on dandelion.
Range: N.S. to Conn., west to S.D. July–Sept.

IMMACULATE HOLOMELINA   **Pl. 14 (3)**
Holomelina immaculata (Reak.)
Identification: FW pale yellow, with or without olive brown shading; *no markings.* HW bright *orange,* unmarked. Least variable of our orangish *Holomelina* species. Wingspan 2.1–2.7 cm.
Food: Unrecorded; probably a wide variety of plants.
Range: Ont. and N.Y. to Ill. and Ky. May–Aug. Locally common.
Remarks: Precise identities, ranges, and other details of this and the 4 preceding *Holomelina* species are confused, and much further study is needed to enable more reliable distinctions.

ISABELLA TIGER MOTH
Pls. 1 (17), 14 (12)
Pyrrharctia isabella (J.E. Sm.)

Identification: Wings orange-yellow to orangish brown. FW pointed; marked with faint brownish am., median, and pm. lines. Note broken black reniform spot and line of st. *spots near apex.* HW usually paler, flushed with pinkish orange in ♀; 2 median and 4 st. patches vary in size. Wingspan 4.5–6.5 cm.

Food: Larva (**Black-ended Bear** or **Woolly Bear,** Pl. 1) eats many plants, including asters, birches, clover, corn, elms, maples, and sunflowers. Colors change as caterpillars molt to successive instars, becoming less black and more reddish as they age. Thus differences in color merely reflect age differences among larvae as they prepare to overwinter and are not a reliable indicator of the severity of the winter to come. Pupation is in spring.

Range: Common throughout our area. April–Aug.; 2 broods.

ECHO MOTH *Seirarctia echo* (J.E. Sm.)
Pl. 13 (9)

Identification: Wings white, with broad, *light brown lines along FW veins.* Legs yellow and black. Wingspan 5–5.7 cm.

Food: Cabbage palm, coontie, crotons, lupine, oaks, and persimmon.

Range: Ga. to s. Fla., west to Miss. Feb.–Dec. in s. Fla., where it is common.

SALT MARSH MOTH
Pl. 13 (13, 16)
Estigmene acrea (Dru.)

Identification: Head and thorax white. *Abdomen orange-yellow with black spots* in both sexes; tip of abdomen white in ♀. FW white, with variable black spots representing bits of usual lines; some specimens have no spots. HW dark orange-yellow in ♂, white in ♀, with 3–4 black blotches in both sexes. Wingspan 4.5–6.8 cm.

Food: Larva (**Salt Marsh Caterpillar**) a pest on many plants, including apple trees, cabbage, clover, corn, cotton, peas, potato, tobacco, and other plants.

Range: Common throughout our area. May–Aug.; 2 broods.

PINK-LEGGED TIGER MOTH
Pl. 13 (3)
Spilosoma latipennis Stretch

Identification: Coxa and femur of foreleg *pink to pinkish orange.* Body and wings pure white, with a trace of black spots on FW of some specimens. Wingspan 3.2–4.7 cm.

Food: Wide variety of plants, including ash trees, dandelions, impatiens, and plantains.

Range: Me. and s. Ont. to Va., west to Neb. and Ark. May–July; 1 brood. Uncommon.

AGREEABLE TIGER MOTH
Pl. 13 (1)
Spilosoma congrua Wlk.

Identification: Pure white and nearly identical to Pink-legged Tiger Moth (above), but coxa and femur of foreleg *yellow,* not

pink. Some specimens have black spots in pm. and st. areas of FW, as shown. Wingspan 2.7–4.7 cm.
Food: Herbaceous plants, including dandelions and pigweed. Larva has also been reported boring into mushroom stems.
Range: Common throughout our area. April–Aug.; longer flight season southward.

DUBIOUS TIGER MOTH   Pl. 13 (7)
Spilosoma dubia (Wlk.)
Identification: Wings white, with *heavy black spotting* representing usual FW lines. Variable black st. patches on HW. Abdomen with some yellow areas and black spots. Wingspan 3.2–3.8 cm.
Food: Wild cherry; larva has been reared on plantain.
Range: N.S. to n. Fla., west across Canada, south to e. Tex. May–July. Rare and local south of N.Y.

VIRGINIAN TIGER MOTH or   Pl. 13 (4)
YELLOW BEAR MOTH *Spilosoma virginica* (F.)
Identification: Coxa and femur of foreleg *white with yellow and black markings.* Wings pure white, usually with several small black spots on FW, and a few spots on HW, especially near anal angle. Note *yellow shading* between middorsal and lateral lines of black spots on abdomen. Wingspan 3.2–5.2 cm.
Food: Larva (**Yellow Bear**) feeds on many plants, such as birches, cabbage, corn, maples, *Prunus* and *Ribes* species, squash, sunflowers, tobacco, walnuts, and willows.
Range: Common throughout our area. April–Oct.; 2 broods.

FALL WEBWORM MOTH   Pl. 13 (2, 5)
Hyphantria cunea (Dru.)
Identification: Very similar to Virginian Tiger Moth (above), but *much smaller.* Wings white; pattern varies from no spots at all (in northern specimens) to heavy grayish brown spots on FW and 1–2 blackish spots on HW (in many southern specimens). Wingspan 2.5–3.9 cm.
Food: Larva (**Fall Webworm**) is a pest that attacks over 100 species of trees, including ash, hickory, maple, oak, and walnut trees, as well as apple trees in neglected orchards. Communal webs built by larvae toward tips of branches can be seen from June to Sept.
Range: Common to abundant throughout our area. April–Aug.; 2 broods southward, 1 in North.

RED-TAILED SPECTER   Pl. 13 (10)
Euerythra phasma Harv.
Identification: Wings and thorax white; most of *abdomen red. Reddish to brownish line* extends from base to outer margin of FW, with branches representing partial am. line and broad pm. line. Veins yellow to reddish near costa. Wingspan 3.1–3.5 cm.
Food: Unrecorded.

Range: Ky. to Fla., west to sw. Mo. and Tex. April–Aug. in Mo.; longer season southward. Uncommon.

THREE-SPOTTED SPECTER   Pl. 13 (12)
Euerythra trimaculata Sm.

Identification: Similar to Red-tailed Specter (above), but usually smaller. FW pattern consists of brownish basal line and bars representing *top and bottom of pm. line.* Reniform spot composed of 1–2 black dots. Wingspan 2.5–3 cm.

Food: Unrecorded.

Range: Fla. to Tex. March–Sept. Uncommon to locally common.

GIANT LEOPARD MOTH   Pl. 16 (13)
Ecpantheria scribonia (Stoll)

Identification: Easily recognized by the white wings with *hollow bluish black spots* on FW. Black shading along inner margin and terminal spots near apex of HW. Wings tend to become translucent toward outer margins with wear. Wingspan 5.7–9.1 cm.

Food: Wide variety, including banana, cabbage, cherry, dandelion, maples, orange, sunflowers, violets, and willows.

Range: Mass. and s. Ont. to Fla., west to Mich., Mo., and Tex. April–Sept. Common southward.

RUBY TIGER MOTH   Pl. 14 (7)
Phragmatobia fuliginosa (L.)

Identification: A holarctic species; the N. American subspecies is *A. fuliginosa rubricosa* (Harr.). Body hairy. Head and thorax dark reddish brown. Abdomen red with rows of black spots. Wings translucent. FW dull reddish brown with *no lines;* only a *black reniform spot.* HW pale pink with black discal spot; uneven black shading along costal and outer margins. Wingspan 2.8–3.4 cm.

Food: Dock, *Eupatorium* species, goldenrod, ironweed, plantain, skunk cabbage, sunflowers, sweetgale, and other plants.

Range: Nfld. to N.J. and Pa., west across Canada, south to N.D. May–Sept.; apparently 2 broods. Locally common.

LINED RUBY TIGER MOTH   Pl. 14 (9)
Phragmatobia lineata Newman & Donahue

Identification: Similar to Ruby Tiger Moth (above), but with faint blackish *am., pm., and st. lines* on FW. Spots and HW borders as in Ruby Tiger Moth. Wingspan 3–3.5 cm.

Food: *Eupatorium* species and probably other low plants.

Range: Me. and Ont. to N.J. and Pa., west across Canada, south to Neb. and Mo. April–Sept.; 2–3 broods.

LARGE RUBY TIGER MOTH   Pl. 14 (10)
Phragmatobia assimilans Wlk.

Identification: Similar to other 2 *Phragmatobia* species (above, Pl. 14) but usually *larger,* with *less translucent wings.* Lines as in Lined Ruby Tiger Moth, but usually less distinct. *No black shad-*

ing along costa of HW (present in other 2 *Phragmatobia* species but hidden by FW). Wingspan 3.5–4.2 cm.
Food: Balsam poplar, *Rubus* species, and white birch; larva has been reared on dandelion and plantain.
Range: N.S. to Conn. and N.Y., west across Canada, south to S.D. Late April–early July; apparently 1 brood. Moderately common.

ST. LAWRENCE TIGER MOTH Pl. 15 (17)
Platarctia parthenos (Harr.)
Identification: FW brown with large *yellowish spots and bars* that represent usual lines. HW yellow with *2 black lines* from base that merge into median spots; black pm. line a series of partially merged spots. Wingspan 5–6.5 cm.
Food: Alder, birches, lettuce, willows, and other plants.
Range: Lab. to mts. of w. N.C., west across Canada, south to Mich. June–Aug. Rare south of N.Y.

GREAT TIGER MOTH *Arctia caja* (L.) Pl. 15 (13)
Identification: Another holarctic species; our subspecies is *A. caja americana* Harr. Similar to St. Lawrence Tiger Moth (above), but *lines* of FW *more complete.* Note *4–5 dark blue spots* outlined with black on HW. Wingspan 5–7 cm.
Food: Alder, apple, cherry, poplars, willows, and other plants.
Range: Lab. to n. N.Y., west across Canada, south to Mich. and Minn. June–Sept. Uncommon to rare.

HARNESSED MOTH Pl. 15 (8, 11)
Apantesis phalerata (Harr.)
Identification: Wing pattern varies, especially on HW. FW mostly black, with *cream-colored costal border and lines* extending from base (as shown in ♂ on Pl. 15); *less cream on* ♀. In specimens from deep South (both sexes), HW usually more yellowish than reddish with little or no black edging. Wingspan 3–4.2 cm.
Food: Clover, corn, dandelion, plantain, and other plants.
Range: Me. and Que. to Fla., west to S.D. and Tex. April–Sept. Common in much of range.

BANDED TIGER MOTH Pl. 15 (5, 7)
Apantesis vittata (F.)
Identification: Nearly identical to Harnessed Moth (above), but no form with entirely yellow HW. Where both species occur, Banded Tiger Moth usually has *more reddish shading* and *broader, more solid black border* on HW. Wingspan 3.2–4.2 cm.
Food: Dandelion and other low plants.
Range: Se. Md. to Fla., west to Ky., Ark., and La. March–Oct. Common, especially southward.

NAIS TIGER MOTH *Apantesis nais* (Dru.) Pl. 15 (9, 10)
Identification: Pattern similar to Harnessed and Banded Tiger moths (above), but *HW yellow* with *broad black outer border*

70 CLASSIFICATION OF MOTHS

(HW red in a few ♀ specimens). Wingspan 3–4 cm.
Food: Clover, grasses, plantain, violets, and other plants.
Range: Me. and Que. to Fla., west to S.D. and Tex. April–Oct.;
most common in June and Aug.
Similar species: (1) Harnessed Moth (p. 69) has *little or no black on HW* when HW is yellow (in specimens from deep South).
(2) Banded Tiger Moth (above) always has *red-washed yellow HW* with *broad black border*. These 3 species are in need of much further taxonomic study, and even experts have difficulty separating them.

LITTLE VIRGIN MOTH   Pl. 14 (18)
Grammia virguncula (Kby.)
Identification: FW black with thick and thin yellowish to cream-colored lines. *Only 1 transverse line* on FW, which extends as a zigzag from costa *near apex;* not 1 or 2 transverse lines nearer base, as in Anna Tiger Moth (below). HW yellow with extensive black shading in both sexes. Look for yellow line on underside of abdomen. Wingspan 3.5–4.6 cm.
Food: Dandelion, knotweed, plantain, and other low plants.
Range: Nfld. to N.C. mts., west to Man. and S.D. June–Aug. Uncommon to rare.

ANNA TIGER MOTH   Pl. 14 (19, 22)
Grammia anna (Grt.)
Identification: Similar to Little Virgin Moth (above), but usually larger. FW pattern includes *2–3 pale lines extending inward from costa*. HW bright yellow with broad black border and black spot near costa, often merged into a curved hook (as shown in ♂). HW entirely black in some females. Little or no yellow on underside of abdomen. Wingspan 4–5.3 cm.
Food: A wide variety of low plants, such as clover and plantain.
Range: Me. to mts. of N.C., west to Neb. and Ark. May–July. Locally common in some areas.

FIGURED TIGER MOTH   Pl. 15 (2, 3)
Grammia figurata (Dru.)
Identification: FW black with variable whitish lines; lines in st. area may form *partial* or *complete triangles* (see Pl. 15). FW usually slightly narrower in ♀ than in ♂. HW usually red with black border and discal spot in ♂, but often without small spots near base. HW may be entirely black in ♀, or marked with a red spot as shown. Wingspan 3–4.3 cm.
Food: Alfalfa, plantain, and other low plants.
Range: N.S. to Ga., west to Minn., Kans., and Tex. April–Sept. 2 broods. Uncommon to locally common.
Similar species: (1) Placentia Tiger Moth (p. 71) is larger; look for *whitish costal border* on FW. (2) Phyllira Tiger Moth (p. 71) is more similar to Placentia Tiger Moth, but *median line curved,* not perpendicular to costa.

PLACENTIA TIGER MOTH
Grammia placentia (J.E. Sm.)

Pl. 15 (4, 6)

Identification: Sexes vary in wing pattern. FW black with distinct white lines in ♂. Costa edged with white; *pm. line straight, perpendicular to costa;* lines toward outer margin form 2 complete triangles. FW black in ♀ except for *small whitish spots* in upper half of wing (as shown). Black border of HW variable in both sexes, but usually thin. Wingspan 3.7–5 cm.
Food: Lupines and other plants; larva can be reared on clover and dandelion.
Range: Southern N.J. to Fla., west to Minn. and Tex. April–Sept.; probably 2 broods. Uncommon.

PHYLLIRA TIGER MOTH
Grammia phyllira (Dru.)

Pl. 15 (1)

Identification: Both sexes similar to ♂ Placentia Tiger Moth (above) but usually smaller. *Pm. line bent, not perpendicular to costa* (pm. line sometimes absent). Am. line may be more complete than in specimen shown. Inner edges of black spots on HW are *same distance from outer margin.* Wingspan 3.5–4 cm.
Food: Corn, lupines, tobacco, and other low plants.
Range: Me. to Fla., west to Wisc. and Tex. May–Sept. Uncommon along Atlantic coast; rarer inland.

OITHONA TIGER MOTH
Grammia oithona (Stkr.)

Pl. 14 (21)

Identification: FW black with fine pale lines along veins, in addition to broader lines and triangles present in other *Apantesis* species (above). *Pm. line straight to slightly curved, not perpendicular to costa.* Midwestern specimens tend to have broader FW lines than those from East Coast. Wingspan 3.5–4.2 cm.
Food: Clover, painted-cup, wild pea, and other low plants.
Range: Me. to Tenn., west to Man. and La. April–early Oct. Common in western part of range.

PARTHENICE TIGER MOTH
Grammia parthenice (Kby.)

Pl. 14 (16, 17)

Identification: Wing pattern similar to that of Oithona Tiger Moth (above), but usually larger. Note the *bend in the whitish st. line* (forming basal side of triangles). Individuals from central part of range (Mass. to n. Fla. and Tex.) tend to be slightly larger, with broader lines on FW, and are considered subspecies *A. parthenice intermedia* (Stretch). Wingspan 3.5–5.5 cm.
Food: Dandelion, ironweed, thistles, and other low plants.
Range: Locally common throughout our area. May–Oct.; 2 broods.

VIRGIN TIGER MOTH *Grammia virgo* (L.)   Pl. 14 (14)
Identification: Easily identified by its large size and the *black spots in median area of HW.* HW and abdomen usually red as in other *Apantesis* species, but are yellow in form "citrinaria"

(Neum. & Dyar), which is uncommon. Wingspan 4.5–7 cm.
Food: *Chenopodium* species, clover, lettuce, plantains, and other low plants.
Range: Nfld. to cen. Fla., west to Man. and Kans. June–Aug., most records in July. Common to uncommon; rare in deep South.

DORIS TIGER MOTH *Grammia doris* (Bdv.)   **Pl. 16 (10)**
Identification: Abdomen and HW pale pinkish; note *large black spots* toward outer margin of HW (♂, not shown, has spots only in terminal area of HW). Pinkish white lines of FW vary. *Black dash* in upper basal area *double*. Note rounded black blotch at top of median area (much thinner in Arge Moth, below). Wingspan 3.5–5 cm.
Food: Dandelion, lettuce, and other low plants.
Range: N.S. to Fla., west to Man. and Tex. May–July. Apparently rare; no records from many states within this area.

ARGE MOTH *Grammia arge* (Dru.)   **Pl. 14 (20)**
Identification: FW predominantly whitish, with small black wedges representing lines, much as in Doris Tiger Moth (above). Upper black *basal dash not double* (as in Doris Tiger Moth), and HW and abdomen have much *less pink*. HW spots usually more numerous but smaller and not as sharp. Wingspan 3.8–5 cm.
Food: Cactus, sunflowers, cotton, grape, and many other plants.
Range: Me. and Que. to Fla., west to Minn., Kans., and Tex. April–Oct.; 2 broods. Common, especially southward.

BANDED TUSSOCK MOTH   **Pl. 12 (6)**
Halysidota tessellaris (J.E. Sm.)
Identification: Body pale orange-yellow with a *bluish green collar and edging on tegula*. Wings paler, translucent yellow. FW has 4 irregular, slightly darker bands with black edges; partial 5th band extends inward from costa over usual position of reniform spot. HW unmarked. Wingspan 4–4.5 cm.
Food: Alder, ashes, birches, elms, hazelnut, hickories, oaks, tuliptree, walnut, willows, and other trees and shrubs.
Range: Common to abundant throughout our area except s. Fla. and s. Tex. May–Oct.; 2 broods.
Similar species: Florida Tussock Moth, *H. cinctipes* Grt. (not shown), is nearly identical, but *lower part of frons brown* (frons entirely yellow in Banded Tussock Moth); bluish green *middorsal stripe on thorax*. Food: Florida trema, hibiscus, and sea grape. Range: Cen. and s. Fla.; all months. Common.

HICKORY TUSSOCK MOTH   **Pl. 12 (7)**
Lophocampa caryae Harr.
Identification: FW yellow with brown shading and *bands of translucent white spots* representing usual lines. HW very pale, translucent yellow; unmarked. Wingspan 3.7–5.5 cm.
Food: Ashes, elms, hickories, maples, oaks, and other trees.
Range: N.S. to N.C. mts., west to Ont., Wisc., and Tex.; absent

from much of midwestern part of range. May–June; locally common.

SPOTTED TUSSOCK MOTH   Pl. 12 (9)
Lophocampa maculata Harr.
Identification: FW deep yellow with 4 brown bands *(usually merged);* partial 5th band extends inward from costa. Partial band *darkest where reniform spot normally occurs.* HW paler yellow, translucent, unmarked. Wingspan 3.5–4.3 cm.
Food: Birches, maples, oaks, poplars, willows, and other trees.
Range: Lab. to N.C. mts., west across Canada, south to Minn. June–July. Locally common.

LONG-STREAKED TUSSOCK MOTH   Pl. 12 (4)
Leucanopsis longa (Grt.)
Identification: Thorax and FW orange-yellow, speckled with brown. Note *dark brown streak* from base to outer margin of FW. HW paler, translucent, unmarked. Wingspan 3.8–4.8 cm.
Food: Only plant recorded is a "wide-bladed marsh grass that grows near freshwater lakes and ponds" (Fla.).
Range: N.C. to s. Fla., west to Miss. All months. Common.

STREAKED CALIDOTA   Pl. 12 (3)
Calidota laqueata (Hy. Edw.)
Identification: Thorax black with 4 tan lines; *abdomen pinkish orange* with rows of black spots. Wings translucent tan. FW streaked with dark brown, with some pinkish orange along inner margin at base. HW edged with brown. Wingspan 4–5 cm.
Food: Velvetseed.
Range: A neotropical moth, found all year in s. Fla. Common.

YELLOW-WINGED PAREUCHAETES   Pl. 12 (14)
Pareuchaetes insulata (Wlk.)
Identification: Body and wings *entirely yellow* except for middorsal and lateral rows of *black spots on abdomen.* HW translucent toward base. Wingspan 2.6–3.8 cm.
Food: *Eupatorium odoratum* and mistflower.
Range: Common from Fla. to Tex.; all months.

UNEXPECTED CYCNIA   Pl. 13 (8)
Cycnia inopinatus (Hy. Edw.)
Identification: Head and abdomen mostly yellow; dorsal and lateral rows of black spots on abdomen. Thorax and wings whitish to gray, with *yellow border along costa of FW*, stopping well before apex. Gray shading may be present along costa on underside of FW, but is not conspicuous. Wingspan 2.8–3.6 cm.
Food: Milkweeds.
Range: N.J. to Fla., west to S.D. and Tex. June–Aug. Uncommon.
Similar species: In Delicate Cycnia (p. 74), *yellow border* along costa of FW is *longer; gray shading* on underside of FW is usually *more conspicuous.*

DELICATE CYCNIA   Pl. 13 (6)
Cycnia tenera Hbn.
Identification: Similar to Unexpected Cycnia (p. 73), but usually larger; *yellow border* on FW costa *more conspicuous, longer* (usually *almost reaching apex*). Gray shading on underside of FW toward costa usually conspicuous. Wingspan 3–4 cm.
Food: Indian hemp and milkweeds.
Range: N.S. to Fla., west to S.D., Ark., and Miss. May–Oct. Locally common; may be found during day on food plants.

OREGON CYCNIA   Pl. 12 (10)
Cycnia oregonensis (Stretch)
Identification: Wings shiny, creamy to yellowish white, but no distinct yellow costal border on FW as in other 2 *Cycnia* species (above). *Wings unmarked*, but *veins of FW stand out* as purer white against off-white ground color in fresh specimens. Abdomen bright yellow with rows of black spots. No gray shading toward costa on underside of FW. Wingspan 3–4 cm.
Food: Indian hemp.
Range: Common from N.S. to S.C., west to Man. and Ark. April–Aug.; 2 broods.

MILKWEED TUSSOCK MOTH   Pl. 12 (17)
Euchaetes egle (Dru.)
Identification: Body and wings mouse gray, with collar, forecoxae, and abdomen yellow; rows of black spots on abdomen. *Wings usually unmarked*, but some individuals have very faint, darker pm. line and reniform spot on FW. Wingspan 3.2–4.3 cm.
Food: Milkweeds; larva easily reared when found in the field.
Range: Me. and s. Canada to Fla., west to Minn. and Tex. May–Sept.; 2 broods. Moths can be found on food plants during day.

SPRAGUE'S PYGARCTIA   Pl. 12 (11)
Pygarctia spraguei (Grt.)
Identification: Thorax and wings mouse gray. Note variable *red shade line along costa and inner margin of FW*. Wings otherwise unmarked. Head, 2 lines on thorax, and abdomen also red; rows of black spots on abdomen. Wingspan 3–3.6 cm.
Food: Painted-leaf spurge.
Range: Ind. to La., west to Wisc., Kans., and Tex. May–June. Local and rare; not recorded in some states within range.

YELLOW-EDGED PYGARCTIA   Pl. 12 (12)
Pygarctia abdominalis Grt.
Identification: Very similar to Sprague's Pygarctia (above), but red markings replaced with *yellow*. Wingspan 3–4 cm.
Food: Unrecorded.
Range: Southern N.J. to s. Fla., in coastal areas. Late March–July; 2 broods southward. Apparently rare.

SNOWY EUPSEUDOSOMA   Pl. 12 (8)
Eupseudosoma involutum (Sepp)
Identification: Head, thorax, and wings *pure, gleaming white.*
Abdomen bright red with white dorsal spots and tip. N. American
subspecies is *E. involutum floridum* Grt. Wingspan 3.5–4 cm.
Food: Guava and Spanish stopper.
Range: Neotropical; southern half of Fla. in all months, but most
common in July.

Subfamily Ctenuchinae

VIRGINIA CTENUCHA   Pl. 12 (1)
Ctenucha virginica (Esper)
Identification: The largest and most broad-winged of our wasp
moths. Body metallic blue; *head and sides of collar orange.* FW
deep grayish brown, metallic blue at base. HW black; fringes on all
wings partly white. Wingspan 4–5 cm.
Food: Grasses, irises, and sedges.
Range: Lab. to Pa., west to Man. and Kans. May–July; apparently 2 broods. Common.

BLACK-WINGED DAHANA   Pl. 11 (13)
Dahana atripennis Grt.
Identification: Abdomen orange, metallic blue at base. FW
brownish black with a *yellow anal dash.* HW black with a metallic
blue tint. Wingspan 3.3–4 cm.
Food: Spanish moss.
Range: Fla.; all year. Adults visit flowers at dusk.

YELLOW-COLLARED SCAPE MOTH   Pl. 11 (12)
Cisseps fulvicollis (Hbn.)
Identification: Body bluish black with an *orange collar* (yellow
in Midwest). FW blackish, slightly translucent in middle. *HW
translucent* except for black veins and margins. Wingspan 2.9–
3.7 cm.
Food: Grasses, lichens, and spike-rushes.
Range: Common to abundant throughout our area. May–Oct. or
first hard frost. Look for adults on fall flowers like goldenrods during daytime. They also come to lights.

EDWARDS' WASP MOTH   Pl. 11 (15)
Lymire edwardsii (Grt.)
Identification: Body and wings light gray; collar and base of
forelegs orange. Rear half of abdomen metallic blue. Note *white
costal edging* on FW, and *translucent HW.* Wingspan 3.6–
4.2 cm.
Food: *Ficus* species and lancewood.
Range: Common to abundant in peninsular Fla. all year.

FLORIDA EUCEREON
Pl. 12 (20)

Eucereon carolina (Hy. Edw.)

Identification: Abdomen brown with unique *yellow markings.* FW dirty white with yellowish brown veins and brownish streaks and spots between veins. HW translucent; whitish with brown shading at outer margin. Wingspan 3.3–3.6 cm.

Food: A vine milkweed (*Cynanchum palustre*) and white vine.

Range: Cen. to s. Fla., Jan.–Aug. Locally common.

Remarks: Note that the common name agrees with the known range of this species, not with the scientific name.

SCARLET-BODIED WASP MOTH
Pl. 11 (9)

Cosmosoma myrodora Dyar

Identification: Easily identified by the *bright red body* and *transparent wings.* Metallic blue middorsal line on abdomen broadens to cover tip. Veins and margins of FW and HW black. Wingspan 3–3.5 cm.

Food: Climbing hempweed.

Range: Fla., west along Gulf coast to La. and probably Tex. All year in s. Fla. Locally common.

DOUBLE-TUFTED WASP MOTH
Pl. 11 (10)

Didasys belae Grt.

Identification: Abdomen red with dorsal line of black dots; note *2 black tufts* at tip of abdomen in ♂ (shown). Wings transparent with black veins and outer margins. Reniform spot *black with red filling*; *red spots* in terminal area of FW. Wingspan 2.2–2.4 cm.

Food: Unrecorded.

Range: Fla., especially in marshy areas. All months except March, Sept., and Dec. Uncommon.

YELLOW-BANDED WASP MOTH
Pl. 11 (11)

Syntomeida ipomoeae (Harr.)

Identification: Note *yellow and metallic blue stripes on abdomen.* Wings bluish black with pale yellow spots. HW transparent near base. Wingspan 3.5–4.2 cm.

Food: Thistles, grapefruit trees, and blossoms of morning-glories.

Range: Fla.; all months except Nov. and Dec. A locally common day-flier.

POLKA-DOT WASP MOTH
Pl. 11 (8)

Syntomeida epilais (Wlk.)

Identification: Wings dark metallic *blue with white spots.* Body metallic blue; abdomen has pair of white spots at base, and *red tip.* N. American subspecies is *S. epilais jucundissima* Dyar. Wingspan 4.2–5.2 cm.

Food: Larva (**Oleander Caterpillar**) is a pest of cultivated oleander, and also feeds on devil's potato.

Range: Neotropical; locally common in all but nw. Fla. in all months. Like most wasp moths, this moth is a day-flier.

LESSER WASP MOTH Pl. 11 (14)
Pseudocharis minima (Grt.)
Identification: Wings and body spotted with white, as in Polka-dot Wasp Moth (above), but this moth is *much smaller.* Abdomen solid blue, *not red-tipped.* Hind legs long; long hair-scales make tibia and tarsus look swollen in ♂ (shown). Wingspan 2.5–2.9 cm.
Food: Christmas berry.
Range: S. Fla. (Broward, Dade, and Monroe counties). All months. Uncommon.

TEXAS WASP MOTH *Horama panthalon* (F.) Pl. 11 (17)
Identification: *Abdomen striped* purplish brown and yellow, white toward base. Wings dull brown with no markings. Hind leg yellow with black base and tuft (hair-scales) in ♂. This moth looks like a paper wasp (*Polistes* species). N. American subspecies is *H. panthalon texana* (Grt). Wingspan 3.2–3.4 cm.
Food: Unrecorded.
Range: S. Tex.; rare in Fla.; all months.

OWLET or NOCTUID MOTHS:
Family Noctuidae

This is the largest family in the Lepidoptera, with about 20,000 species worldwide and about 2,900 species in N. America. Some of these moths are brightly colored, but most are gray to brown with complex patterns of lines and spots (see typical noctuid pattern on front endpapers). The orbicular and reniform spots are usually visible, though sometimes obscure. In most species, the HW pattern is simpler than that of FW, but HW sometimes very striking, especially in the underwing moths (*Catocala* species, p. 172). When at rest, most owlets usually hold their wings rooflike over the body and resemble arrowheads or triangles in lateral view.

These are small to large moths (wingspan 1.2–17 cm); most are medium-sized (2–4.5 cm). Body stout, usually hairy. Ocelli usually present. Labial palps moderately long, upturned; proboscis usually well developed. Antennae simple to bipectinate. Tympanum on side of metathorax below HW base points outward or toward the rear, not downward; counter-tympanal hood located *behind spiracle,* not before it as in tiger moths (Arctiidae, p. 58).

FW usually has 1 areole; Cu appears 4-branched because M_2 arises close to M_3 (Figs. 24, 25). $Sc + R_1$ of HW not greatly swollen at bases as in Arctiidae, but usually *fused with Rs for short distance* beyond small basal areole, then *separating widely.* In some subfamilies, Cu of HW appears 3-branched, with very faint M_2 arising far from M_3 (Fig. 24); in others Cu appears 4-branched, with M_2 well developed and arising close to M_3 (Fig. 25). Frenulum always well developed.

Larvae of most noctuid species feed on foliage of a wide variety

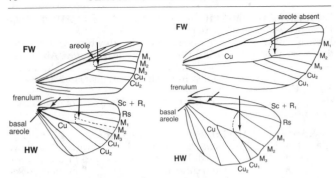

Fig. 24. Wing venation, Noctuidae (vein Cu of HW appears 3-branched).

Fig. 25. Wing venation, Noctuidae (vein Cu of HW appears 4-branched).

of plants, as well as dead leaves, lichens, and fungi. Many are serious pests of forest trees and cultivated plants, and cost us millions of dollars annually in crop losses and pest control expenses. A few species are leaf miners in early larval stages, and some feed in rolled leaves. Some bore into stems, roots, and fruits; others are cutworms that hide in leaf litter during the day and bite off tender plant shoots during the night. A few other species eat scale insects or other caterpillars in addition to feeding on leaves and can thus be considered somewhat beneficial.

These moths pupate in cells in the soil, in cavities in food plants, or in silk cocoons that sometimes include plant parts or other debris. Unlike many tiger moths (Arctiidae) and tussock moths (Lymantriidae, p. 337), owlets do not weave larval hairs into their cocoons. The number of generations per year varies from 1 to 10, but is usually 1 to 4. In the coldest parts of our area, the life cycle may take 2 years or longer to complete. Adults of most species are nocturnal, but many are active during the day.

Researchers have divided this large family of moths into 18 subfamilies on the basis of various external features of the adults (see below), some genitalic features, and some characteristics of the immature stages. In other books, subfamilies Nolinae and Agaristinae have been treated as separate families (Nolidae and Agaristidae); also, the Catocalinae now includes the Erebinae, once considered a distinct subfamily. The arrangement of genera and species within subfamilies in this guide follows the latest classification scheme (the 1983 *Check List of the Lepidoptera of America North of Mexico*), but the arrangement of subfamilies within families is closer to the order in the 1938 McDunnough *Check List*. A brief synopsis of the features of each noctuid subfamily follows, with cross references to pages on which the descriptions of species in each subfamily begin:

Pantheinae, p. 80—Gray above. Eye surface looks *hairy* (Fig. 3A, p. 3) under magnification. Cu of HW appears *4-branched* (Fig. 25).

Acronictinae, p. 81—Usually gray above, with a characteristic *curve in pm. line* of FW; FW often has sharp black dashes ("daggers"). Cu of HW appears 3-branched (Fig. 24). Eye *smooth* (not hairy). Larvae more hairy than those of most other owlets.

Noctuinae, p. 89—FW usually brownish; *orbicular and reniform spots* usually conspicuous. Spines present on middle and (usually) on hind tibiae. Cu of HW appears *3-branched*. Eye *smooth*. Note: This subfamily is known as Agrotinae in many recent publications.

Hadeninae, p. 99—The only other noctuid subfamily besides Pantheinae in which the eye is *hairy*. Cu of HW appears *3-branched*.

Cuculliinae, p. 110—Note the conspicuous *lashes* (rows of bristles) in front of and behind the eye (Fig. 3B, p. 3). Cu of HW appears *3-branched*. Many are active as adults in late fall, winter, or early spring.

Amphipyrinae, p. 121—A large, diverse group. Cu of HW appears *3-branched*. Middle tibia unspined. Larvae vary in appearance and habits, but not hairy as in Acronictinae (above).

Agaristinae, p. 139—The forester moths. More brightly colored and sharply patterned than most other noctuids. Some are diurnal. *Ocelli present* (absent in most other subfamilies). Cu of HW appears *3-branched*.

Heliothinae, p. 140—*All tibiae have spines*. Cu of HW appears *3-branched*. Larvae feed mostly on fruits and flowers. Adults of some species are brightly colored; some species are diurnal.

Acontiinae, p. 145—Most are small and brightly patterned. At rest, some adults resemble *bird droppings* (pp. 148–151). Ocelli present. Cu of HW appears to have *3 or 4 branches*.

Nolinae, p. 151—Small, usually gray. Note the *fanlike tufts of long scales* at middle and end of FW discal cell. Cu of HW appears *3-branched*; M_3 absent.

Sarrothripinae, p. 152—Cu of HW appears to have *3 or 4 branches*. Note size of patch of spines on metascutum (compared to Euteliinae, below)—patch is *more than $\frac{1}{2}$ as long* as width of metascutum.

Euteliinae, p. 153—Cu of HW appears *4-branched*. Patch of spines on metascutum slightly smaller than in Sarrothripinae (*almost $\frac{1}{2}$ as long* as width of metascutum).

Plusiinae, p. 155—Usually brownish with a conspicuous curved *silver or white spot (stigma)* in middle of FW (Pl. 32). Eyes *heavily lashed*. Cu of HW appears *4-branched*. Many species are diurnal.

Catocalinae, p. 159—Our largest subfamily of noctuids, including some of our largest moths. *Middle and hind tibiae* have spines. Eyes *smooth* (not lashed). Cu of HW appears *4-branched*. Some species, such as the underwings (*Catocala* species) have colorful hindwings.

Hypeninae, p. 317—Cu of HW appears *4-branched.* M$_2$ moderately curved and parallel to M$_3$. Eyes *lashed* (Fig. 3B, p. 3). Labial palps *very long* (usually twice as long as head). Mostly blackish with dull patterns. These moths, and those in the 3 subfamilies below, are sometimes called "deltoids" because their wings form a triangle when at rest (in lateral view).

Hypenodinae, p. 320—Our smallest noctuids (wingspan 2 cm or less). No ocelli. Labial palps *very long.* Cu of HW appears *4-branched.* Patterns dark and dull.

Rivulinae, p. 321—Palps *large.* Metascutum *broader and flatter* than in other subfamilies. Cu of HW appears *4-branched.*

Hermeniinae, p. 322—*Ocelli present.* Labial palps *very long;* 2nd segment *bladelike or sickle-shaped,* with long scales. Cu of HW appears *4-branched.*

Subfamily Pantheinae

BLACK ZIGZAG *Panthea acronyctoides* (Wlk.)   Pl. 16 (17)
Identification: *FW white* with *bold black zigzag lines.* Pattern usually visible on white, black (melanic), or more gray-shaded specimens. HW gray. Wingspan 3–3.5 cm.
Food: Firs, hemlocks, larches, pines, and spruces.
Range: Nfld. to e. Ky., west across Canada and south to Mich. May–Aug. Rare southward.

EASTERN PANTHEA *Panthea furcilla* (Pack.)   Pl. 16 (20)
Identification: FW pale and dark gray. Lines black; st. line *turns inward* to meet pm. line as shown. HW dark gray with pale patch at outer margin. Pattern obscure in melanics (FW almost black). Wingspan 3.3–5 cm.
Food: Larches, pines, and spruces.
Range: N.S. to Fla., west to Man. and Ark. May–Aug. Rare in sw. part of range.

YELLOWHORN *Colocasia flavicornis* (Sm.)   Pl. 16 (15)
Identification: Antennae orange. FW gray with variably sharp black lines. Am. and pm. lines usually connected by a black median bar; median area *darker below bar* than above it. Orbicular spot sharper than reniform spot. HW gray. Wingspan 3.3–4 cm.
Food: Larvae have been reared on beech and ironwood.
Range: N.S. to Va. and Ala., west to Mo. and Ark. April–June and Aug; 2 broods. Common to uncommon.

CLOSEBANDED YELLOWHORN   Pl. 16 (11)
Colocasia propinquilinea (Grt.)
Identification: Similar to Yellowhorn (above), but usually slightly larger. Pattern less distinct; *no black bar* between am. and pm. lines. Wingspan 3.5–4.5 cm.

Food: Beech, birches, maples, walnuts, and other trees.
Range: Common from Nfld. to N.C., west to Mo. and Ark. April–July; 2 or more broods southward.

THE LAUGHER *Charadra deridens* (Gn.)   **Pl. 16 (18)**
Identification: FW mottled pale and dark gray. Am. and pm. lines wavy, black; connected across median area by thin black line. Orbicular spot *white-filled, with black dot* at center. HW grayish brown, darker at outer margin. Wingspan 3.8–4.8 cm.
Food: Beech, birches, elms, maples, and oaks.
Range: Throughout our area. March–Oct.; 2 or more broods. Common in most of range; melanic forms fairly common.

ABRUPT BROTHER *Raphia abrupta* Grt.   **Pl. 16 (19)**
Identification: FW bluish gray. Lower halves of am. and pm. lines double; *curve of pm. line flattened* at middle. HW gray; median line continuous; dark patch at anal angle of HW less conspicuous than in The Brother (below). Wingspan 2.8–3.5 cm.
Food: Unrecorded; same as those recorded for The Brother (?).
Range: Me. to Fla., west to Minn. and Tex. March–Sept.; 2 broods southward. Uncommon to locally common.

THE BROTHER *Raphia frater* Grt.   **Pl. 16 (16)**
Identification: Similar to Abrupt Brother (above), but slightly larger. *HW pure white* with *dotted median line* and *dark patch* at anal angle. Wingspan 3.3–3.8 cm.
Food: Alder, birches, cottonwood, poplars, and willows.
Range: Lab. to N.J., west to Man., Minn. and Ill.; old records from Miss. and Tex. probably in error. April–Aug.

Subfamily Acronictinae

Dagger Moths: Genus *Acronicta*

This genus contains 75 species in North America; about 39 of them occur in our area. FW usually gray or grayish brown, with whitish lines that are often double; pm. line *curves outward* below costa. Most species have black dashes or "daggers" on FW (Pl. 17), from which the common name of this group is derived. Melanic individuals are quite common in many of our dagger moth species.

RUDDY DAGGER MOTH   **Pl. 17 (1)**
Acronicta rubricoma Gn.
Identification: FW powdery gray to brownish; pattern usually sharper and *reniform spot* usually *larger and more distinct* than in other dagger moths. Faint black dashes sometimes present in basal area and near anal angle. HW whitish with gray shading; veins blackish. Wingspan 3.8–4.4 cm.
Food: Elms, hackberry, and sumac.

Range: Locally common from N.Y. and s. Ont. to cen. Fla., west to e. Kans. and Tex. April–Oct.; 2 broods.

AMERICAN DAGGER MOTH   Pl. 17 (3)
Acronicta americana (Harr.)
Identification: Our largest dagger moth, easily recognized by its large size and typical dagger moth pattern. FW usually has sharp pm. line; only black dash is in anal area. HW gray with *darker median line*. Wingspan 5–6.5 cm.
Food: Many trees, such as alders, ashes, birches, elms, hickories, maples, oaks, poplars, walnuts, and willows.
Range: Common throughout our area. April–Sept.; 2 or more broods.

FINGERED DAGGER MOTH   Pl. 13 (19)
Acronicta dactylina Grt.
Identification: Distinguished from American Dagger Moth (above) by slightly smaller size and *absence of median line* on HW. HW white in ♂ (shown), gray in ♀. Wingspan 4.5–5 cm.
Food: Alders, birches, poplars, thorn, and willows.
Range: Nfld. to N.C. mts., west to Man. and Ill. May–Aug. Uncommon.

COTTONWOOD DAGGER MOTH   Pl. 13 (17)
Acronicta lepusculina Gn.
Identification: FW whitish; lines faint except for *3 black blotches representing tops of lines* at costa. *Black basal dash* present, but usually no orbicular spot. HW white. Wingspan 4–5 cm.
Food: Aspens, birches, cottonwood, poplars, and willows.
Range: Throughout our area. April–June and Aug.–Sept. 2 broods. Uncommon.

UNMARKED DAGGER MOTH   Pl. 17 (5)
Acronicta innotata Gn.
Identification: Cream white to pale gray. *Bulge* of pm. line *indented* to form 2 small bulges. HW white with diffuse black discal spot, pm. line, and shading. Wingspan 3.5–4 cm.
Food: Alders, birches, hickories, poplars, and willows.
Range: Nfld. to N.C., west to Man. and Ky. May–Aug. Locally common.

BIRCH DAGGER MOTH   Pl. 17 (7)
Acronicta betulae Riley
Identification: Our only dagger moth with a *pale tan FW* and a sharp *right angle* in lower part of pm. line. Much of FW tinged with gray. HW tan. Wingspan 3.5–4 cm.
Food: Birches.
Range: N.H. to Fla., west to Wisc., Miss., and Tex. March–May and Aug.–Sept.; 2 broods. Uncommon to locally common.

RADCLIFFE'S DAGGER MOTH   Pl. 17 (4)
Acronicta radcliffei (Harv.)

Identification: FW smooth, medium to dark gray. Am. and pm. *lines edged with white.* Orbicular spot nearly round, filled with paler gray; reniform spot faint. Basal and anal dashes fine, black. HW yellowish white in ♂ with sparse grayish brown dusting at outer margin; HW entirely grayish brown in ♀. Wingspan 3.5–3.8 cm.

Food: Apple and hawthorn trees, juneberry, and several *Prunus* species.

Range: Nfld. to N.C., west to Man. and Ark. April–June and late July–Aug.; at least 2 broods. Moderately common but local.

TRITON DAGGER MOTH   Pl. 17 (12)
Acronicta tritona (Hbn.)

Identification: FW *purplish gray with brown shading* over reniform spot and beyond pm. line. HW grayish brown, darker in ♀ than in ♂. Wingspan 3.5–4 cm.

Food: Azaleas, blueberries, and rhododendron.

Range: N.S. to Fla., west to Mo. and Tex. April–Sept.; at least 2 broods. Uncommon to rare, especially westward.

GRAY DAGGER MOTH *Acronicta grisea* Wlk.   Pl. 17 (2)
Identification: Similar to Triton Dagger Moth (above), but less purplish and more *powdery gray; dashes slightly heavier. HW white* with brownish shading toward outer margin; more dark shading in ♀ than in ♂. Wingspan 3–3.5 cm.

Food: Alder, apple, birches, elms, poplars, and willows.

Range: Lab. to Conn., west across Canada, south to Minn. May–Aug. May be common northward.

CONNECTED DAGGER MOTH   Pl. 17 (14)
Acronicta connecta Grt.

Identification: FW mottled ash gray; broad, diffuse, black *basal and anal dashes often connected* to form a *continuous band* just above inner margin. HW dirty white, with dark gray veins. Melanics common. Wingspan 3–3.5 cm.

Food: Willows.

Range: N.Y. and Ont. to Fla., west to S.D. and Tex. April–Sept.; 2 broods southward.

FUNERARY DAGGER MOTH   Pl. 17 (6, 9)
Acronicta funeralis Grt. & Rob.

Identification: See Pl. 17—FW powdery pale gray or very dark gray (melanic form). Basal and anal dashes very broad; basal dash long, often joining anal dash; note *tooth on basal dash,* pointing toward costa. HW whitish with dark gray along veins and at outer margin. Wingspan 3.2–4 cm.

Food: Trees such as apples, birches, elms, maples, and willows.

Range: N.S. to Va. and Ky., west across Canada, south to Miss. and Mo. May–Aug.; 2 or more broods. Locally common.

DELIGHTFUL DAGGER MOTH   Pl. 17 (8, 11)
Acronicta vinnula (Grt.)
Identification: A small moth. FW color varies: may be mottled pale gray, dark gray, or green. Note white inside orbicular spot and along pm. line. Pm. line usually *straight below bulge.* HW grayish brown, darker toward outer margin. Wingspan 2.8–3.2 cm.
Food: Elms.
Range: N.S. to Fla., west to Wisc. and Tex. April–Aug.; at least 2 broods. Common in much of range.

SPLENDID DAGGER MOTH   Pl. 17 (10)
Acronicta superans Gn.
Identification: FW pale gray with dark mottling. Diffuse black basal and anal *dashes converge with black shading* in median area; yellowish white patch in lower basal area conspicuous. Wingspan 4–4.6 cm.
Food: Apple, birch, cherry, hazelnut, mountain ash, and plum trees.
Range: Nfld. to mts. of e. Ky., west to Man. and Mich. May–Aug. May be common northward.

PLEASANT DAGGER MOTH   Pl. 17 (13)
Acronicta laetifica Sm.
Identification: FW white, dusted and mottled with pale gray; melanics slate gray. Pm. line with conspicuous white border. Basal dash heavy toward outer end; small anal, subapical, and *orbicular-reniform dashes* also present. Orbicular spot white-filled. Wingspan 3.7–4.3 cm.
Food: Hickories.
Range: N.S. to Fla., west to Man. and Tex. April–Oct.; 2 or more broods. Uncommon to rare.

SPEARED DAGGER MOTH   Pl. 17 (15)
Acronicta hasta Gn.
Identification: Similar to Pleasant Dagger Moth (above), but *FW darker gray* to blackish; *basal dash* ends in *3 prongs.* Wingspan 3.4–4.5 cm.
Food: Wild cherry.
Range: Locally common from Me. and Ont. to Fla., west to Wisc., Kans., Ark., and Miss. April–Sept.; at least 2 broods.

NONDESCRIPT DAGGER MOTH   Pl. 17 (18)
Acronicta spinigera Gn.
Identification: FW pale to medium gray with darker mottling and black basal and anal dashes. *Orbicular spot nearly round,* with an *incomplete outline.* HW medium to dark gray with darker veins. Wingspan 3.7–4.8 cm.
Food: Apple, birch, cherry, elm, linden, and *Rubus* species.
Range: Me. and Que. to Fla., west to Man. and Tex. April–Aug.; 2 or more broods. More common in Midwest than in East.

OCHRE DAGGER MOTH
Pl. 17 (21)

Acronicta morula Grt. & Rob.
Identification: Pale to dark gray above, with an *orange-yellow patch* in center of thorax; orange-yellow below basal dash, beyond pm. line, and covering obscure reniform spot. HW variably dark grayish brown. Wingspan 4–5 cm.
Food: Apple, basswood, and elm trees.
Range: N.S. to Ga., west to Man. and Tex. April–Sept.; 2 or more broods. Common northward.

INTERRUPTED DAGGER MOTH
Pl. 17 (16)

Acronicta interrupta Gn.
Identification: Similar to Ochre and Nondescript Dagger Moths (above), but with *no orange markings*. Basal dash ends in 3 prongs—top prong *turns toward costa* as part of am. line. Anal and subapical dashes present. HW white with gray shading in ♂, all gray in ♀. Wingspan 3.5–4.2 cm.
Food: Apple, birch, elm, hawthorn, and oak trees, and *Prunus* species.
Range: N.S. to Ga. (Fla. ?), west to Man., Neb., and Ark. April–Sept.; 2 or more broods. Common.

LOBELIA DAGGER MOTH
Pl. 18 (3)

Acronicta lobeliae Gn.
Identification: Our second largest dagger moth; size and *heavy black dashes* on gray FW distinctive. Orbicular and reniform spots connected by another black dash. HW grayish brown, darker at outer margin. Wingspan 4.2–6 cm.
Food: Black cherry and oak trees.
Range: Common throughout our area, especially southward. April–Aug.; 2 or more broods.

PRUNUS DAGGER MOTH
Pl. 18 (4)

Acronicta pruni Harr.
Identification: FW mottled gray. Look for a *small tuft* of yellow-tipped bristles on thorax near head (use magnification). Lines and spots blackish, usually inconspicuous; basal and anal *dashes smudgy*. HW grayish brown, darker toward outer margin. Wingspan 3.5–4.3 cm.
Food: Apple, cherry, mountain-ash, plum, and wild cherry.
Range: Me. and Ont. to Fla., west to Neb. and Tex. May–Aug.

FRAGILE DAGGER MOTH
Pl. 17 (20)

Acronicta fragilis (Gn.)
Identification: FW white with heavy gray and black shading. Am. and pm. lines *double, sharply zigzag*. Orbicular spot gray to white with darker center. HW yellowish white with faint gray median line and outer shading. Wingspan 2.9–3.2 cm.
Food: Apple, birch, plum, willow, and white spruce trees.
Range: Nfld. to Fla., west across Canada, south to Ky. and Minn. April–Aug. May be common locally.

EXILED DAGGER MOTH *Acronicta exilis* Grt.   **Pl. 17 (17)**
Identification: FW yellowish gray; look for *yellowish blotch* over reniform spot. Lines and spots inconspicuous. *Basal dash thin* or absent. HW grayish brown. Wingspan 2.6–3.3 cm.
Food: Oaks and other trees.
Range: Me. to Fla., west to Mo. and Tex. May–Sept.; 2 or more broods. Common.

OVATE DAGGER MOTH *Acronicta ovata* Grt.   **Pl. 18 (2)**
Identification: FW mottled gray and yellowish brown. Best identified by the *merged black basal dash and am. line,* forming a conspicuous Y or T toward base. Sharp anal dash also present. HW grayish brown. Wingspan 2.8–3.5 cm.
Food: Beeches, birches, chestnut, and oaks.
Range: Me. and s. Ont. to N.C., west to Man. and Tex. April–July; 2 or more broods. Common.

MEDIUM DAGGER MOTH   **Pl. 18 (1)**
Acronicta modica Wlk.
Identification: Similar to Ovate Dagger Moth (above), but usually larger, more evenly gray. *Basal dash* curves upward into am. line, but *much thinner* than in Ovate Dagger Moth. Anal dash present, sometimes broken toward outer margin. Orbicular and reniform spots paler than FW ground color. HW grayish brown. Wingspan 3.3–4 cm.
Food: Red oak and other oaks.
Range: Mass. and w. Que. to Fla., west to Minn. and Tex. April–Aug.; 2 or more broods. Common.

HESITANT DAGGER MOTH   **Pl. 17 (19)**
Acronicta haesitata (Grt.)
Identification: FW medium gray. Am. and pm. lines usually conspicuously double. Basal dash thick, but usually *not touching small blackish blotch* at middle of am. line. HW grayish brown. Wingspan 3–4.3 cm.
Food: Red and white oaks.
Range: Locally common from Me. and Ont. to S.C., west to Man. and Tex. Late April–Aug.; 2 or more broods.

UNCLEAR DAGGER MOTH   **Pl. 18 (5)**
Acronicta inclara Sm.
Identification: Similar to Ovate Dagger Moth (above) but markings heavier. Basal dash and its extension as part of am. line *usually broader, more diffuse.* Whole basal area often blackish, at least *below basal dash* (as shown). HW grayish brown. Wingspan 2.8–3.6 cm.
Food: Birches, chestnut, and oaks.
Range: Throughout our area. May–Aug.; 2 or more broods. Common in most of range.

RETARDED DAGGER MOTH   Pl. 18 (8)
Acronicta retardata (Wlk.)
Identification: A small, pale gray moth. *Am. line* distinctly *double,* often with a *black spot* midway on its outer side. *Median area usually whitish.* HW whitish with heavy gray shading. Wingspan 2.5–3.2 cm.
Food: Red and sugar maples.
Range: N.S. to Fla., west to Man., Ark., and Miss. April–Aug.; several broods. Uncommon southward.

PUZZLING DAGGER MOTH   Pl. 18 (6)
Acronicta subochrea Grt.
Identification: FW dark powdery gray with blackish mottling that obscures lines. Sharpest marking is *black dash* across lower median area. Orbicular and reniform spots gray with black outlines. HW yellow-bronze. Wingspan 3.8–4.5 cm.
Food: Witch-hazel (?).
Range: N.S. to nw. Fla., west to Wisc. and Ky. April–Aug.; 2 broods. Rare in most of range.

AFFLICTED DAGGER MOTH   Pl. 18 (9)
Acronicta afflicta Grt.
Identification: FW mottled pale gray to coal black (shown). Only sharp marking is *orbicular spot,* which is usually large and whitish, with a darker center. HW white with grayish brown shading at outer margin. Wingspan 3.5–4.5 cm.
Food: Oaks and walnuts.
Range: N.S. to Fla., west to Wisc. and Tex. April–Sept.; 2 or more broods. Locally common in Ky.

YELLOW-HAIRED DAGGER MOTH   Pl. 18 (7)
Acronicta impleta Wlk.
Identification: FW powdery gray. Am. and pm. lines double; note conspicuous *white filling* of pm. line. Orbicular and reniform spots gray, incompletely outlined in black. HW yellowish gray with darker veins. Wingspan 3.8–5 cm.
Food: Birches, elms, maples, oaks, willows, and other trees.
Range: Common throughout our area. April–Aug.; at least 2 broods.

NIGHT-WANDERING DAGGER MOTH   Pl. 18 (12)
Acronicta noctivaga Grt.
Identification: FW white with black shading and markings. Am. and pm. lines double with white filling; orbicular and reniform spots often black with just traces of gray filling. *Black bar* across lower median area usually does *not* touch anal dash. HW dark grayish brown. Wingspan 3.3–3.7 cm.
Food: Poplars.
Range: Throughout our area. May–Aug. Uncommon southward.

LONG-WINGED DAGGER MOTH   Pl. 18 (10)
Acronicta longa Gn.
Identification: FW mottled pale to very dark gray. Am. line incomplete to absent; pm. line a series of very small, widely-spaced crescents, edged with pale gray. Note the *black median border* on inner margin, and the long, thin anal dash. HW white in ♂, gray in ♀ (shown). Wingspan 3.2–4.4 cm.
Food: Birches, blackberry, cherry, oaks, roses, and willows.
Range: Locally common throughout our area. April–Aug.; 2 or more broods.

STREAKED DAGGER MOTH   Pl. 18 (11)
Acronicta lithospila Grt.
Identification: FW dark gray with darker streaks and a *very faint, broken pm. line.* HW white with yellowish brown veins and shading at outer margin. Wingspan 3.4–4.2 cm.
Food: Chestnut, hickory, oak, and walnut trees.
Range: Locally common throughout our area. April–Aug.; 2 or more broods.

SMEARED DAGGER MOTH   Pls. 1 (4), 13 (18)
Acronicta oblinita (J.E. Sm.)
Identification: FW more *narrow* and *pointed* than in our other dagger moths. FW pale to medium gray; obscure broken lines and spot outlines blend with general dark streaking. Note sharp black dotted terminal lines on all wings. HW shiny white. Wingspan 3.6–5.4 cm.
Food: Larva (**Smartweed Caterpillar,** Pl. 1) is a pest of apple and other fruit trees; also reported on clover, corn, cotton, elms, grasses, pines, oaks, smartweed, strawberry plants, and willows.
Range: Common throughout our area. April–Sept.; 2 or more broods.

HENRY'S MARSH MOTH   Pl. 18 (14)
Simyra henrici (Grt.)
Identification: FW narrow and pointed; white with brown filling between veins (looks tan overall). *Three dark brown streaks* extend inward from outer margin, shortest streak near apex. HW pure white without markings. Wingspan 3.5–4 cm.
Food: Cattails, grasses, poplars, sedges, and willows.
Range: Throughout our area in marshes. April–Aug.; 2 or more broods. Sometimes common.

THE GREEN MARVEL   Pl. 26 (16)
Agriopodes fallax (H.-S.)
Identification: *FW pale green* with *lines broken* into *large black spots;* triangular spot near anal angle. HW white with grayish brown markings. Wingspan 3.1–3.6 cm.
Food: Viburnum.
Range: Throughout our area but uncommon. April–Aug.

THE GRAY MARVEL   **Pl. 25 (19)**
Agriopodes teratophora (H.-S.)
Identification: FW dark brownish gray. Lines fine, indistinct. *Reniform spot white, bleeding to costa* and containing some black scaling; small white costal patch near apex. HW grayish brown. Wingspan 1.9–2.5 cm.
Food: Mint and monarda.
Range: Que. to Fla., west to Man. and n. Ark. May–July.

THE HEBREW   **Pl. 26 (20)**
Polygrammate hebraeicum Hbn.
Identification: FW pure white with *black spots and broken lines.* HW whitish with grayish brown shading, darker toward outer margin. Wingspan 2.3–3.9 cm.
Food: Black gum trees.
Range: Common from Me. to Fla., west to Ont., Mo., and Tex. May–Aug.

HARRIS'S THREE-SPOT   **Pl. 18 (13)**
Harrisimemna trisignata (Wlk.)
Identification: FW white with gray shading and irregular or broken black lines. Easily recognized by the *3 large, round, dull red spots*—1 near base, 2 at outer margin. HW white in ♂, gray in ♀. Wingspan 3–3.6 cm.
Food: Woody plants, such as apple trees, lilac, holly, and willows.
Range: Uncommon to common throughout our area. May–Sept.

Subfamily Noctuinae

OLD MAN DART *Agrotis vetusta* Wlk.   **Pl. 19 (4)**
Identification: Thorax and FW pale brownish gray; abdomen and HW white. Only FW markings are *dark gray orbicular and reniform spots* (lower half) and dotted black pm. and terminal lines. Wingspan 3.5–4.2 cm.
Food: Many plants, such as beans, corn, cotton, lettuce, peach trees, tobacco and tomato plants, turnip, and watermelon.
Range: N.S. to Ga., west to Man. and Tex. July–Sept. Uncommon to rare; not reported from some states in range.

SWORDSMAN DART *Agrotis gladiaria* Morr.   **Pl. 19 (2)**
Identification: Wings grayish brown; FW heavily overlaid with black, often less sharply marked than in specimen shown. *Black wedges between veins* in st. area. FW palest in rounded lower basal area and along inner margin. Reniform spot usually obscure; elliptical orbicular and black claviform spots usually sharply defined. Wingspan 2.9–3.8 cm.
Food: Larva (**Clay-backed Cutworm**) eats many wild and cultivated plants, such as beans, berries, corn, and tobacco.

Range: Common throughout our area. Sept.–Oct. Active during day as well as at night.

VENERABLE DART *Agrotis venerabilis* Wlk.　　**Pl. 19 (6)**
Identification: Thorax brown with darker brown collar; tegulae whitish in ♂ (as shown). FW grayish to yellowish brown; lines barely visible. *Blackish shading* along costa usually *extends down over reniform spot,* but rarely reaches apex; 2 smaller black patches in terminal area. *Claviform spot a black dash.* HW grayish brown. Wingspan 3.5–4 cm.
Food: Larva (**Dusky Cutworm**) feeds on alfalfa, chickweed, clover, corn, oats, tobacco, and various other plants.
Range: Throughout our area. Sept.–Oct. Common northward.

VOLUBLE DART *Agrotis volubilis* Harv.　　**Pl. 19 (5)**
Identification: Similar to Venerable Dart (above), but FW smoother grayish to wood brown; lines and spots sharper. Thin *black dash* extends from base *through claviform spot.* HW whitish to dirty grayish brown. Wingspan 3.5–4 cm.
Food: Unrecorded; probably a wide variety of plants.
Range: Nfld. to N.C., west to Man. and Mo. Late May–June; Sept. (2 broods). Uncommon southward.

RASCAL DART *Agrotis malefida* Gn.　　**Pl. 19 (7)**
Identification: FW brownish in ♂, gray to blackish in ♀. Pattern similar to Venerable Dart (above), but this moth is larger and has longer wings. Reniform spot more distinct; *claviform spot short, wide, solid black.* HW gleaming white with some grayish brown at outer margin. Wingspan 4–4.5 cm.
Food: Larva (**Pale-sided Cutworm**) eats many wild and cultivated plants, including clover, corn, peas, and tomato plants.
Range: N.Y. to Fla., west to Mo. and Tex. April–Oct. Locally common southward; a stray in Northeast.

IPSILON DART *Agrotis ipsilon* (Hufn.)　　**Pl. 19 (9)**
Identification: FW yellowish, shaded with dark brown to blackish along costa in ♂, or over most of wing to pm. line in ♀. *Small black wedge* just beyond reniform spot. HW dirty white with grayish brown shading. Wingspan 3.2–5.1 cm.
Food: Larva (**Black Cutworm**) a major pest on many cultivated plants, including clover, corn, lettuce, potatoes, and tobacco.
Range: Worldwide; common to abundant in our area. March–Nov.

SUBTERRANEAN DART　　**Pl. 19 (12)**
Agrotis subterranea (F.)
Identification: FW yellowish to wood brown, with black shading heavier in ♀ than in ♂. Identified by the *black bar between* orbicular and reniform *spots* and the glistening, translucent *white HW* (some gray shading in ♀). Wingspan 3.2–4 cm.
Food: Larva (**Granulated Cutworm**) feeds on wilted and dry

leaves as well as fresh ones of many plants, such as beans, clover, corn, lettuce, peas, potato and tobacco plants, and wheat.
Range: Me. to Fla., west to S.D. and Tex. March–June; Sept.–Nov.; 2 broods. Common southward.

DINGY CUTWORM MOTH   Pl. 19 (8)
Feltia jaculifera (Gn.)
Identification: FW dirty whitish with gray and blackish shading. Note *wide tooth* pointing inward from whitish costal border (at orbicular spot), and *2 sharp wedges* formed as whitish st. coloring extends outward along veins M_3 and Cu_1. HW whitish with grayish brown shading and white fringe. Wingspan 3–4 cm.
Food: Larva (**Dingy Cutworm**) sometimes a serious pest on apple trees, beans, clover, corn, grasses, tobacco, and other plants.
Range: Common throughout our area. Aug.–Nov.; 1 brood.

SUBGOTHIC DART *Feltia subgothica* (Haw.)   Pl. 19 (11)
Identification: Very similar to Dingy Cutworm Moth (above) but slightly larger and darker. Pale st. coloring separated from blackish brown shading beyond by pale st. line; *st. line* irregular but *lacks distinct wedges* on veins M_3 and Cu_1. HW darker than that of Dingy Cutworm Moth. Wingspan 3.2–4.3 cm.
Food: Many plants, including tobacco.
Range: Throughout our area, but less common than Dingy Cutworm Moth, with which it is often confused. Late Aug.–Nov.; 1 brood.

MASTER'S DART *Feltia herilis* (Grt.)   Pl. 19 (10)
Identification: Similar to Dingy Cutworm Moth and Subgothic Dart (above), but *FW dark violet gray to violet brown, including costa.* Pm. line more complete than in other 2 species. St. line as in Subgothic Dart. HW yellowish brown with grayish brown shading. Wingspan 3.4–4.4 cm.
Food: Larva is very similar to the Dingy Cutworm and attacks the same cultivated plants.
Range: Common throughout our area. Late July–Oct.; 1 brood.

KNEE-JOINT DART   Pl. 19 (14)
Feltia geniculata Grt. & Rob.
Identification: *FW gray with purplish brown shading.* Lines usually conspicuous; black shading between orbicular and reniform spots and on basal side of orbicular spot. HW gray with darker gray shading. Wingspan 2.9–3.4 cm.
Food: Unrecorded; probably a wide variety of plants.
Range: Throughout our area but uncommon. Aug.–Oct.

FRINGED DART   Pl. 19 (20)
Eucoptocnemis fimbriaris (Gn.)
Identification: FW smoky or reddish. *Am. and pm. lines* formed of *tiny black and white dots;* reniform spot yellowish, edged with blackish, and surrounded by dark gray scaling. Black terminal line

and patches along costa, at tops of other lines. HW dirty whitish with grayish brown shading and faint median line of dark dots. Wingspan 2.5–3.2 cm.

Food: No confirmed records; probably many low plants.

Range: N.H. to Fla., west to Ind. and Tex. Sept.–Oct.; 1 brood. Uncommon to rare northward and westward.

DIVERGENT DART   Pl. 18 (21)
Euxoa divergens (Wlk.)

Identification: FW dull dark brown. *Costa edged with gray* from base to top of reniform spot; fine grayish line from base to bottom of reniform spot. Orbicular and reniform spots and upper part of am. line grayish. HW pale grayish brown, darker at outer margin. Wingspan 3.1–3.5 cm.

Food: Unrecorded.

Range: Nfld. to Mass. and N.Y., west to Man. and Minn. June–July. Locally common northward.

REAPER DART *Euxoa messoria* (Harr.)   Pl. 18 (16)

Identification: FW brown; lines double, blackish, usually conspicuous. Note *straight lower half of pm. line* and almond-shaped orbicular spot (pointing toward base). Darker brown shading between orbicular and reniform spots in some specimens (not shown). HW whitish with pale brown at margin; fringe white. Wingspan 3.5–4 cm.

Food: Larva (**Dark-sided Cutworm**) a pest of apple trees, cultivated flowers and vegetables, and a wide variety of wild plants.

Range: Nfld. to N.C., west across Canada, south to Mo. Aug.–Sept.; 1 brood. May be common northward.

MIXED DART *Euxoa immixta* (Grt.)   Pl. 19 (3)

Identification: Similar to Reaper Dart (above), but FW duller and less heavily marked. Lines double, *heaviest at costa,* where they are represented by pairs of black spots. Lower half of pm. line *curved;* orbicular spot elliptical. HW grayish brown, darker at outer margin. Wingspan 3.5–4 cm.

Food: Unrecorded.

Range: Mich. to Tenn., west to N.D. and Tex. May–June (our other *Euxoa* species usually fly in late summer). Uncommon.

TESSELLATE DART   Pl. 18 (19)
Euxoa tessellata (Harr.)

Identification: FW variable—usually purplish to grayish brown with conspicuous markings. *Black basal dash* usually present. Note the *small tuft of hair-scales* at FW base (where costa meets thorax); scales yellow in ♂, white in ♀. HW grayish brown, darker at margin. Wingspan 3–3.8 cm.

Food: Larva (**Striped Cutworm**) feeds on many plants and may be a pest of crops such as beans, corn, squash, and tobacco.

Range: Nfld. to Fla., west to Man. and Minn. June–Sept. Local and apparently rare southward.

VIOLET DART *Euxoa violaris* (Grt. & Rob.)   **Pl. 19 (1)**
Identification: FW violet gray with *broad, reddish pm. band.*
Am. and pm. lines even, very conspicuous, dark-edged. Orbicular
spot faint, brown; reniform spot a pale loop filled with grayish
brown. HW pale yellowish, shaded with grayish brown toward
outer margin. Wingspan 3.5–4 cm.
Food: Unrecorded.
Range: Locally common in sandy coastal habitats from Mass. to
N.C. Sept.; 1 brood.

BOSTON DART *Euxoa bostoniensis* (Grt.)   **Pl. 18 (15)**
Identification: FW pale mouse gray. Lines faint, double, incom-
plete, except for a broad, single *median line,* which passes through
faint reniform spot, then angles toward costa. No orbicular spot.
HW white with grayish brown border in ♂; solid grayish brown in
♀. Wingspan 4–4.5 cm.
Food: Larva (**Drab Cutworm**) attacks tobacco and other plants.
Range: Me. and Ont. to N.C., west to Mich. and Mo. Sept.

RUBBED DART *Euxoa detersa* (Wlk.)   **Pl. 18 (20)**
Identification: FW yellowish to dark brown, dark specimens
tinted with gray. Lines double, white-edged. *Orbicular and
reniform spots whitish with dark brown outlines and dots* in their
centers. HW dark brown. Wingspan 3–3.5 cm.
Food: Corn, grasses, cranberry, saltwort, and sea-rocket; sometimes a damaging pest of garden crops and tobacco.
Range: Nfld. to S.C., west to Man. and Neb. Restricted to sandy
habitats such as beaches and river shores. Aug.–Oct.

FILLET DART *Euxoa redimicula* (Morr.)   **Pl. 18 (18)**
Identification: FW bluish gray; median and terminal areas
darker, reddish to blackish. Orbicular and reniform *spots gray,*
with *black area* between both spots and on basal side of orbicular
spot. Black basal dash and claviform spot. HW white with dark
marginal shading. Wingspan 3–3.5 cm.
Food: Blueberries.
Range: Nfld. to se. N.Y., west to Man. and Mo. Mid-Aug.–Sept.
Rare southward.

POLISHED DART *Euxoa perpolita* (Morr.)   **Pl. 18 (17)**
Identification: FW solid blackish; pm. line and orbicular and
reniform *spots sharp, but not much darker* than ground color. St.
line slightly paler; no claviform spot. HW dark grayish brown,
darker at outer margin. Wingspan 3.5–4 cm.
Food: Unrecorded.
Range: Nfld. to N.Y., west to Man. and Mich. Late July–early
Sept. Locally common northward.
Similar species: Fleece-winged Dart, *E. velleripennis* (Grt.), not
shown, has *black claviform spot.* HW white in ♂, dark gray in ♀.
Food: Unrecorded. Range: N.S. to L.I., N.Y., west to Man. and Mo.
Aug.–Sept. Locally common northward.

FLAME-SHOULDERED DART   Pl. 19 (17)
Ochropleura plecta (L.)
Identification: A small dart. FW reddish brown, edged with *cream along costa* from base to reniform spot. Black basal dash and bar extend through gray orbicular and reniform spots. HW white with yellowish brown terminal line and shading at apex. Wingspan 2.5–3.2 cm.
Food: A wide variety of plants, including beets and clover.
Range: Lab. to w. N.C., west across Canada, south to Tex. May–Aug.; 2 broods. Common in northeast; rare in Mo.

SLIPPERY DART *Euagrotis lubricans* (Gn.)   Pl. 20 (2)
Identification: FW gray with *dull reddish shading* that *darkens* beyond indistinct pm. line. Am. and pm. lines black, heaviest at costa. Median band wider, reddish. Reniform spot partly filled with black, usually as 2–3 dots. HW whitish, shaded with grayish brown. Wingspan 3–4 cm.
Food: Unrecorded.
Range: N.C. and s. Ohio to Fla., west to Mo. and Tex. Jan.–May; July–Sept.; presumably 2 broods. Local and uncommon.

SNOWY DART *Euagrotis illapsa* (Wlk.)   Pl. 20 (3)
Identification: Similar to Slippery Dart (above), but *HW almost pure white* (some gray at apex in ♂, shown; more along margin in ♀). Reddish shading on FW paler; lines more sharply defined. Wingspan 2.9–3.5 cm.
Food: Unrecorded.
Range: Common throughout our area. May–Oct.; 2 broods.

GREEN CUTWORM MOTH   Pl. 19 (16)
Anicla infecta (Ochs.)
Identification: FW violet gray with a *dark red border* beyond st. line. Lines indistinct; pm. line usually a series of small dark dots. Reniform spot outlined with whitish and filled with black and reddish spots. HW pearly white with grayish brown at outer margin. Wingspan 3–4 cm.
Food: Larva (**Green Cutworm**) attacks beets, clover, grasses, tobacco, and other low plants.
Range: Me. to Fla., west to Man. and Tex. June–Nov. Common.

VARIEGATED CUTWORM MOTH   Pl. 20 (6)
Peridroma saucia (Hbn.)
Identification: FW brown, sometimes more reddish or grayish brown than specimen shown; costal half sometimes darker than lower half. Lines double, black, indistinct. Orbicular spot may be paler brown or visible only as a thin, elliptical outline. Reniform spot indistinct, usually darker brown. *Dark blotch extends inward from costa* just before apex. HW dirty white, grayish brown at margin. Wingspan 4–5.2 cm.
Food: Larva (**Variegated Cutworm**) is a serious pest and is

known to attack over 100 plants, including alders, cabbage, carrots, clover, corn, fruit trees, maples, tobacco, and wheat.
Range: Worldwide; one of the most widely distributed moths. Common to abundant throughout our area. April–Oct.; 2 broods.

SMALLER PINKISH DART
Pl. 21 (1)
Diarsia jucunda (Wlk.)
Identification: FW yellowish brown with variable reddish brown mottling and blackish markings. *Black blotch* between orbicular and reniform spots *meets reniform spot* in a straight line. Small black claviform spot usually present. HW yellowish brown, darker toward apex. Wingspan 3.2–3.5 cm.
Food: Grasses.
Range: Nfld. to Conn. and N.Y., west to Ont. and Wisc. July–Aug. May be locally common.

FINLAND DART *Actebia fennica* (Tauscher) Pl. 19 (15)
Identification: FW mostly dark gray, brown, or coal black, with yellowish along inner margin, in st. area, and mixed with gray in orbicular and reniform spots. Am. line black, double; claviform spot large, hollow. Note *2 small black wedges* pointing inward from st. line. HW dirty white with grayish brown shading toward margin. Wingspan 3.5–4.5 cm.
Food: Larva (**Black Army Cutworm**) attacks blueberries, elms, clover, onions, peas, and many other trees and low plants.
Range: Lab. to Mass., west across Canada, south to Minn. June–Sept. Uncommon in much of its range.

CLANDESTINE DART
Pl. 19 (13)
Spaelotis clandestina (Harr.)
Identification: Body and FW brown with darker brown collar and head. FW markings generally faint, but note *elliptical orbicular spot* with sharp black outline, open toward costa. Lines strongest as pairs of dots at costa. Black shading between orbicular and reniform spots in some specimens (not shown). HW dirty white with grayish brown shading. Wingspan 4–4.3 cm.
Food: Larva (**W-marked Cutworm**) a pest on apple, beans, blueberries, maples, pines, strawberries, and many other plants.
Range: Nfld. to Va., west to Man., Neb., and Mo. May–Oct.; apparently 2 broods. Common in much of range.

GREATER BLACK-LETTER DART
Pl. 20 (4)
Xestia dolosa Franc.
Identification: FW rose brown in ♂, blackish in ♀ (shown). Black bar from am. line to reniform spot near costa interrupted by *yellowish orbicular spot* that *widens toward costa*. Black blotch angles inward from costa at top of st. line. HW grayish brown, darker in ♀ than in ♂. Wingspan 3.7–4.6 cm.
Food: Larva (**Spotted Cutworm**) feeds on many crops, such as apple, barley, clovers, corn, maples, tobacco, and other plants.

Range: Common from N.S. to N.C. mts., west through s. Ont. to N.D. and Mo. May–early July; Aug.–Oct.; 2 broods.
Similar species: Lesser Black-letter Dart, *X. adela* Franc. (not shown), is usually smaller: FW darker, more marbled in ♂, more vivid black in ♀. HW *paler* in both sexes. Positive identification possible only from examination of genitalia. Food: Same food plants as Greater Black-letter Dart; larva also known as Spotted Cutworm. Range: Canada south to Va., Tenn., and Mo. May–July; Aug.–Sept.; 2 broods. Common northward.
Remarks: These two species were recently described and separated from the European moth, *X. c-nigrum* (L.).

NORMAN'S DART *Xestia normaniana* (Grt.)   **Pl. 19 (19)**
Identification: FW dark gray with reddish mottling. *Orbicular spot narrow, gray*—gray *extends to costa.* Small black dots along am. line, as claviform spot, and on inner edge of reniform spot. Lines double but faint. HW grayish brown. Wingspan 3.5–4.1 cm.
Food: Blueberries, raspberry, wild cherry, and other plants.
Range: Locally common from N.S. to N.C., west to Man., S.D., and Mo. Late July–Oct.

SMITH'S DART *Xestia smithii* (Snell.)   **Pl. 20 (7)**
Identification: FW varies from pinkish to reddish or grayish brown, with slightly darker shading in median area and beyond pm. line. *Small black blotch* on costa near apex is sharpest dark marking. Lines double, grayish, faint. HW grayish brown. Wingspan 3.5–4 cm.
Food: A wide variety of plants, including alders, grapes, and white birch.
Range: Nfld. to Md. and e. Ky., west to Man. and Minn. July–Sept. Locally common northward.

PINK-SPOTTED DART *Xestia bicarnea* (Gn.)   **Pl. 20 (9)**
Identification: FW dark purplish brown with *pinkish orange blotches* near base and at top of pm. line. Lines double, black. Orbicular spot angled, open toward costa, interrupting black bar from am. line to reniform spot. HW grayish brown, darker at outer margin. Wingspan 3.2–4.3 cm.
Food: Many plants, including birches, clovers, and maples.
Range: Nfld. to N.C., west to Man. and Mo. Aug.–Oct. Common in most of range.

COLLARED DART   **Pl. 19 (21)**
Xestia collaris (Grt. & Rob.)
Identification: Thorax and FW dark brown. Note the *blackish head, collar,* and *square shade* between orbicular and reniform spots. Lines sharp, even, yellow; *pm. line curves outward.* HW grayish brown, darker at margin. Wingspan 3–3.6 cm.
Food: No specific records; probably a wide variety of plants.
Range: Nfld. to N.C. mts., west to Man. and Mo. Late Aug.–early Oct. Uncommon to rare.

PALE-BANDED DART *Xestia badinodis* (Grt.) **Pl. 19 (18)**
Identification: Similar to Collared Dart (above), but blackish *shading between* orbicular and reniform *spots paler, less distinct; pm. line more gently curved.* Black dot between am. line and reniform spot, another dot in claviform position. HW dark grayish brown. Wingspan 3–4.2 cm.
Food: Many plants, such as asters, clovers, and tobacco.
Range: Common from Me. and Que. to Ga., west to Ont., Neb., and Tex. Sept.–Oct.

NORTHERN VARIABLE DART **Pl. 20 (10)**
Anomogyna badicollis (Grt.)
Identification: FW gray with slight red or pink shading. Lines sharp to obscure, usually widening into spots at costa. Black shading on basal side of orbicular spot; *reddish brown shading between orbicular and reniform spots,* with *thin black edge* underneath. HW dark grayish brown. Wingspan 3.5–4.5 cm.
Food: Larva a nocturnal feeder on young conifers, such as eastern white cedar, firs, hemlocks, pines, and spruces.
Range: N.S. to N.C., west across s. Canada, south to Mo. July–Oct. May be locally common.
Similar species: (1) Southern Variable Dart, *A. elimata* (Gn.), not shown, is usually slightly larger; FW gray *without red shading.* Food: Conifers. Range: S.C. to Fla. and west along Gulf Coast. Oct.–Dec. Common. (2) Dull Reddish Dart, *A. dilucida* (Morr.), not shown, has dull, uniform reddish FW with no distinct markings except partially filled *dirty white reniform spot.* Food: American larch, black spruce, and other conifers; also a species of blueberry. Range: Locally common from Lab. to Fla., west to Ont. and Ky. Sept.–early Nov.

REDDISH SPECKLED DART **Pl. 20 (5)**
Cerastis tenebrifera (Wlk.)
Identification: FW reddish brown, faintly mottled with gray. Lines gray, inconspicuous, except for partial whitish st. line. Orbicular and reniform *spots whitish with gray centers.* HW grayish brown with faint median line. Wingspan 3–4 cm.
Food: Larva has been reared on dandelion, grape, and lettuce.
Range: Nfld. to e. S.C., west to s. Ont., Neb., and Tex. Uncommon to locally common.

BENT-LINE DART **Pl. 20 (1)**
Choephora fungorum Grt. & Rob.
Identification: All wings pinkish orange. Large brownish shade between faint orbicular and reniform spots. Note *bends* in pm. line, just below costa. Wingspan 3.3–4.7 cm.
Food: Clover, dandelion, tobacco, and other plants.
Range: Locally common from N.Y. and s. Ont. to Fla., west to e. Kans. and Tex. Sept.–Nov.

GREEN ARCHES Pl. 20 (15)
Anaplectoides prasina (D. & S.)
Identification: FW usually mottled olive green and grayish brown, but sometimes pale green, reddish brown or dark gray. *Basal, am., and pm. lines scalloped, double,* black with white filling. Median and st. lines grayish brown. Orbicular and reniform spots brownish with gray centers, partially outlined with black. HW grayish brown with white fringe. Wingspan 4.5–6 cm.
Food: Blueberries, hazelnut, maples, raspberry, and other plants.
Range: Nfld. to N.C. mts., west to cen. Ont. and Iowa. Also occurs in Eurasia. July–Sept. Common northward.

DAPPLED DART *Anaplectoides pressus* (Grt.) Pl. 21 (2)
Identification: FW gray, usually tinted with yellowish to yellow-green. Lines and spots similar to those in Green Arches (above). *St. line thin, curved near apex,* and accented by *3 black wedges.* HW dirty cream with darker veins and faint discal spot and median line. Wingspan 3.5–3.7 cm.
Food: Corn-salad.
Range: Nfld. to N.J., west to Man. and Minn. June–Aug.
Similar species: Brown-lined Dart, *A. brunneomedia* McD. (not shown), is very similar, but FW is gray to green with *heavy black shading between orbicular and reniform spots,* extending downward from costa. Ground color looks whitish in old or worn specimens. Food: Unrecorded. Range: Mts. of Va., N.C., and Ky. July.

BROWN-COLLARED DART Pl. 21 (4)
Protolampra brunneicollis (Grt.)
Identification: Body brown with blackish brown collar. FW narrow; grayish, reddish, or medium brown, with thin, inconspicuous lines and spots. *Blackish blotch near apex* on costa. Some specimens (not shown) have blackish shading on FW except along costa. HW pale brown. Wingspan 3.3–4.3 cm.
Food: Blueberries, clover, tobacco, and other plants.
Range: Common from N.S. to w. N.C., west to Man. and n. Ark. May–Oct.; 2 broods.

SIGMOID DART *Eueretagrotis sigmoides* (Gn.) Pl. 21 (6)
Identification: FW dark brown, with tan costal border, terminal area, filling between double am. and pm. lines, and orbicular and reniform spots. Blackish blotch near apex on costa; *black basal dash almost merges with broad blackish shading* from am. line to reniform spot. HW grayish brown. Wingspan 3.7–4.2 cm.
Food: Unrecorded.
Range: Me. and Que. to w. N.C., west to Man. and Minn. July–Aug. May be common locally.

TWO-SPOT DART Pl. 21 (5)
Eueretagrotis perattenta (Grt.)
Identification: Similar to Sigmoid Dart (above) but smaller; FW paler brown with less mottling. Thin black basal dash usually *well*

separated from shade line between am. line and reniform spot. Small, thin *black wedges* point inward from upper st. line. HW shiny tan. Wingspan 3–3.5 cm.
Food: Blueberries and fire-cherry.
Range: Lab. to N.Y. and Pa., west to Man. and Mich. Late June–Aug. Common northward.
Similar species: Attentive Dart, *E. attenta* (Grt.), not shown, is similar in size and coloring to Two-spot Dart, but *lacks shade line* from am. line to reniform spot. Basal dash is darkest marking. Food: Unrecorded. Range: N.S. to Va., west to Man. and e. Ky. July–Aug. Locally common.

CATOCALINE DART   Pl. 20 (8)
Cryptocala acadiensis (Bethune)
Identification: Our only dart with a *bright yellow HW* which has a *broad blackish border,* similar to HW of some small underwing moths (*Catocala* species, Pl. 33); HW fringe also yellow. FW olive green or various shades of brown, with gray costal border expanding downward to include reniform spot. Wingspan 2.5–3 cm.
Food: Larva has been reared on spreading dogbane.
Range: Lab. to Mass., west to Ont. and Wisc. July–Aug. May be locally common.

GREATER RED DART   Pl. 20 (13)
Abagrotis alternata (Grt.)
Identification: FW reddish, yellowish, or medium brown. Lines double, thin, slightly darker brown; conspicuous *pale band* beyond st. line. Orbicular and reniform spots darker brown. HW dark grayish brown. Wingspan 3.5–4.2 cm.
Food: Larva (**Mottled Gray Cutworm**) climbs in various trees and shrubs, such as apple, ash, cherry, oak, and peach trees.
Range: Common to abundant throughout our area. June–Oct.

Subfamily Hadeninae

THE NUTMEG *Discestra trifolii* (Hufn.)   **Pl. 21 (3)**
Identification: FW yellowish brown to grayish. Lines double, indistinct. Darkest markings are hollow claviform spot, shading in lower half of reniform spot, and *1–3 thin, sharp wedges* pointing inward from st. line. HW dirty whitish with blackish outer margin except for whitish patch at anal angle. Wingspan 3–4 cm.
Food: Larva (**Clover Cutworm**) a pest on clover and many vegetables such as cabbage, lettuce, and peas. Also feeds on elms, poplars, and many other woody and herbaceous plants.
Range: Worldwide in temperate zones; common to uncommon throughout our area. May–Oct.

THE ROSEWING *Sideridis rosea* (Harv.)   **Pl. 20 (19)**
Identification: Head, thorax, and FW light reddish brown; *outer border darker,* beginning outside pm. line. Lines brownish, scal-

loped. Spots brown; lower half of reniform spot blackish. HW yellowish white with grayish median line and marginal shading. Wingspan 3.5–4.5 cm.
Food: Gooseberry, Russian olive, soapberry, and willows.
Range: N.S. to n. N.J., west to Man. and Minn. April–Aug.

THE GERMAN COUSIN   Pl. 20 (22)
Sideridis congermana (Morr.)
Identification: Thorax and FW dull reddish brown. *Orange-yellow middorsal stripe* on thorax. Orange-yellow accents lines and fills terminal area. Orbicular spot small, round, white; reniform spot white, partly filled with black. HW yellowish, blending to brownish at outer margin. Wingspan 3.5–3.8 cm.
Food: Unrecorded.
Range: N.S. and Que. to e. Ky., west to Man. and Mich. May–Sept. Uncommon to rare.

THE MAROONWING *Sideridis maryx* (Gn.)   Pl. 20 (20)
Identification: Easily identified by the uniform *maroon thorax and FW.* Am. and pm. lines a series of *yellowish dots.* Reniform spot filled with gray, but inconspicuous. HW pale grayish brown, darker toward outer margin. Wingspan 3.5–4.2 cm.
Food: Unrecorded.
Range: Nfld. to N.J. and Pa., west to Ont. Late May–July. Uncommon to rare.

STORMY ARCHES *Polia nimbosa* (Gn.)   Pl. 21 (10)
Identification: FW white, mottled with gray and black. Orbicular, reniform, and claviform spots sharp, black; reniform spot *wide, strongly curved.* HW grayish brown, paler outside median line which arises near anal angle. Wingspan 4–6.5 cm.
Food: Alders, huckleberries, *Ribes* species, and vine apple.
Range: Nfld. to N.C. and Ky. mts., west to Man., Wisc., Minn., and N.D. June–early Aug. Locally common.

CLOUDY ARCHES *Polia imbrifera* (Gn.)   Pl. 21 (7)
Identification: Similar to Stormy Arches (above), but more heavily shaded with gray and black; markings more smudged and indistinct. Reniform spot narrower; *black basal dash and white st. line* distinctive. Median line of HW farther from anal angle than in Stormy Arches. Wingspan 4–5.3 cm.
Food: Alders, birches, choke cherry, and willows.
Range: Nfld. to N.C. and Ky. mts., west to sw. Ont. and N.D. June–Aug. Common northward.

PURPLE ARCHES *Polia purpurissata* (Grt.)   Pl. 21 (12)
Identification: FW purplish gray with *brown shading,* especially around *narrow, strongly curved reniform spot.* Lines blackish, double, variably distinct; blackish shading on inside of st. line, *heaviest toward anal angle.* HW grayish brown, darker at outer margin; fringe white. Wingspan 4–5.5 cm.

Food: Alders, blueberries, birches, and other woody plants.
Range: N.S. to N.J. and W. Va., west across s. Canada, south to Mo. and S.D. July–Sept. Common northward.

DISPARAGED ARCHES *Polia detracta* (Wlk.)   **Pl. 21 (14)**
Identification: FW grayish brown; reddish brown blotch beyond claviform spot, which is a *solid, blackish wedge.* Orbicular and reniform spots grayish, indistinct. Lines inconspicuous. Black streaks on veins in terminal area. HW evenly dark grayish brown. Wingspan 3–3.5 cm.
Food: Blueberries, clover, hickories, oaks, and other plants.
Range: N.S. and Que. to N.C., west through s. Canada, south to Ark. and Kans. Late May–early Aug. Common.
Similar species: In Goodell's Arches (below) FW is more solid brown; *claviform spot more slender, hollow.*

GOODELL'S ARCHES *Polia goodelli* (Grt.)   **Pl. 21 (17)**
Identification: Similar to Disparaged Arches (above) but FW warmer brown. Claviform spot longer, narrower, and *usually hollow;* filling of orbicular and reniform spots more whitish. HW dark brown. Wingspan 3–3.5 cm.
Food: Unrecorded.
Range: N.S. and N.B. to n. Fla., west to Man., Mo., and Neb. May–early Sept.
Similar species: In Disparaged Arches (above) FW is distinctly grayish brown; *claviform spot short, solid black.*

FLUID ARCHES *Polia latex* (Gn.)   **Pl. 21 (16)**
Identification: FW very long and narrow. *Orbicular spot large, elongate, white-filled,* separated from brown-filled reniform spot by black shade. HW shiny, light to dark gray. Melanic specimens common. Wingspan 3.9–5.1 cm.
Food: Beech, maples, white elm, and other broadleaved trees.
Range: Common from N.S. to N.C., west to se. Man. and n. Ark. May–Aug.

HITCHED ARCHES *Melanchra adjuncta* (Gn.)   **Pl. 20 (12)**
Identification: FW mottled black and dark greenish; white in basal and st. areas, and along costa. Orbicular spot small, white; *reniform spot large,* white, with *curved black line* in center. HW gray, darker at outer margin. Wingspan 2.9–4 cm.
Food: Asparagus, clover, dandelion, elms, and other plants.
Range: N.S. and Que. to w. N.C., west to Man. and Neb. May–Sept.; 2 broods. Uncommon to common.

ZEBRA CATERPILLAR MOTH   **Pl. 22 (3)**
Melanchra picta (Harr.)
Identification: Head, thorax, and FW deep reddish brown. Upper half of FW dark brown from base to reniform spot; reniform spot indistinct, gray-filled. Broken whitish st. line is only line clearly visible. HW whitish, brown at outer margin. Wingspan 3–4.2 cm.

Food: Many plants, including apple, blueberries, cabbage, carrot, clover, dandelion, peas, *Prunus* species, and willows.

Range: Nfld. and Que. to Va., west through s. Canada, south to Tex. Panhandle. May–Sept.; 2 or more broods. Adult uncommon, but larva (**Zebra Caterpillar**) sometimes a pest.

BLACK ARCHES *Melanchra assimilis* (Morr.)   **Pl. 21 (19)**
Identification: FW blackish brown; spots and lines sharp, coal black, visible under close examination. St. line a series of whitish dots, broadening to form *wavy white mark at anal angle.* HW shiny yellowish white with blackish veins, discal spot, and double border. Wingspan 3–4 cm.
Food: Alder, ash, bracken, goldenrods, St. Johnswort, sweetfern, white birch, and willows.
Range: Nfld. to Va., west across Canada, south to Wisc. and Minn. June–Aug. Uncommon to rare.

SPECKLED CUTWORM MOTH   **Pl. 21 (15)**
Lacanobia subjuncta (Grt. & Rob.)
Identification: FW purplish gray with reddish brown shading, darkest near base and below apex. Black dashes outward from base and across lower median area. St. line obscure, but has *3 sharp black teeth* forming a W-*shaped marking* at its middle. HW brownish. Wingspan 3.4–5 cm.
Food: Larva (**Speckled Cutworm**) a pest on asparagus, blueberries, cabbage, corn, willows, and other plants.
Range: N.S. and Que. to Va., west across Canada, south to Mo. and N.D. May–Sept.; 2 broods. Uncommon southward.

GRAND ARCHES *Lacanobia grandis* (Gn.)   **Pl. 21 (9)**
Identification: FW varies from dull grayish brown, shaded with reddish violet, to pale bluish gray. Markings similar to those in Speckled Cutworm Moth (above), but this moth is larger, and has a *broad white band inside st. line.* HW dark brown with thin blackish terminal line. Wingspan 3.1–4.5 cm.
Food: Alders, cherries, poplars, willows, and other trees.
Range: N.S. to Va., west across Canada, south to Ill. and N.D. May–Aug. Uncommon to moderately common northward.

STRIPED GARDEN CATERPILLAR   **Pl. 20 (17)**
MOTH *Trichordestra legitima* (Grt.)
Identification: Similar to Speckled Cutworm Moth (above) but with more contrast between gray and brown areas on FW; no dashes. *Claviform spot black, sharp, wedge-shaped*, either solid or filled with brown. HW dirty yellowish brown, darker toward outer margin. Wingspan 2.5–3.9 cm.
Food: Larva (**Striped Garden Caterpillar**) a pest on beans, grasses, tobacco, willows, and other plants.
Range: Common throughout our area. June–Sept.

CAPSULE MOTH *Anepia capsularis* (Gn.)   **Pl. 21 (11)**
Identification: FW pale gray shaded with brown. Am. and pm. lines sharp, black, connected by black claviform wedge. Orbicular spot large, round, white with gray center. *Reniform spot touches pm. line.* HW grayish brown with darker median line. Wingspan 2.5–3 cm.
Food: Seed capsules of pinks (Caryophyllaceae).
Range: N.H. to s. Fla., west through s. Ont. to Minn., south to Tex. May–June; April in Fla. Common southward.

THE THINKER *Lacinipolia meditata* (Grt.)   **Pl. 21 (18)**
Identification: FW reddish brown with purplish gray shading, lines, and spots. *Inner margin concave* just before anal angle. FW pattern inconspicuous; sharpest markings usually am. line, orbicular and reniform spots, and st. shading. HW dark grayish brown. Wingspan 2.7–3.3 cm.
Food: Apple trees, clover, dandelion, tobacco, and other plants.
Range: N.S. to S.C., west to Man. and n. Ark. June–Sept.; 2 broods. Usually more common in 2nd brood.

SNAKY ARCHES *Lacinipolia anguina* (Grt.)   **Pl. 21 (13)**
Identification: FW pale ash gray with darker gray median shading. Lines and spots black; *black dash* near anal angle *usually broken* by pale gray line. HW white with brownish shading at outer margin. Wingspan 2.7–3.2 cm.
Food: Unrecorded.
Range: Nfld. to se. Ky., west to Man., Ark. (Ozark Mts.), and Neb. April–June. Rare to locally common.

BRISTLY CUTWORM MOTH   **Pl. 20 (11)**
Lacinipolia renigera (Steph.)
Identification: FW brown with *yellowish green shading* in basal and st. areas. Black basal dash at inner margin and large, solid claviform spot. *Reniform spot* outlined in white, *thicker in lower half.* HW white, brown toward apex. Wingspan 2.1–3 cm.
Food: Larva (**Bristly Cutworm**) eats many wild and cultivated plants, such as apple trees, cabbage, clover, corn, and tobacco.
Range: Common throughout our area except in s. Tex. May–Oct.; 2 or more broods.

BRIDLED ARCHES *Lacinipolia lorea* (Gn.)   **Pl. 20 (21)**
Identification: FW pale yellowish brown with darker median area sharply defined by *slanting* pm. line that *curves inward* just below costa. Orbicular and reniform spots filled with pale yellowish brown. Dark brown costal patch outside top of pm. line. HW dark brown. Wingspan 3–3.5 cm.
Food: Wide variety of plants, including alfalfa, blueberries, clover, dandelion, gray birch, strawberry plants, and sweetfern.
Range: Nfld. to Va., west through s. Canada, south to Mo. and Neb. May–Aug.; 1 brood. Common northward.

OLIVE ARCHES *Lacinipolia olivacea* (Morr.)   **Pl. 20 (14)**
Identification: FW gray, tinged with yellowish green and white; some *pink shading in basal* and *lower st. areas*. Median area dark gray, except reniform spot whitish with greenish filling. HW white with gray shading; darker gray discal spot and median line. Wingspan 2.4–2.5 cm.
Food: Many plants, including dandelion, phlox, and plantain.
Range: Nfld. to N.C., west to Man. and cen. Mo. June–Sept.

IMPLICIT ARCHES   **Pl. 20 (16, 18)**
Lacinipolia implicata McD.
Identification: FW pale green, fading to whitish. Median area blackish, mixed with reddish brown and green, *becoming very narrow toward inner margin*, more so in ♂ than in ♀. HW shiny gray in ♂, gradually becoming darker toward outer margin; entirely *smoky* in ♀. Blackish pm. line and discal spot evident on HW in both sexes. Wingspan 2.5–3.2 cm.
Food: Wide variety; larva will eat dandelion.
Range: Conn. to S.C., west to Ont., Mich., Mo., and Tex. April–Oct.; 2 broods. Usually more numerous in 2nd brood.
Similar species: (1) Explicit Arches, *L. explicata* McD. (not shown), has extensive *blackish shading between basal and am. lines* as well as in *median area*. Less smoky shading on HW; pm. line and discal spot more obscure in both sexes. Food: Unrecorded. Range: Ky. and N.C. to Fla., west to Mo. and Tex. April and Sept.; 2 broods. (2) Laudable Arches, *L. laudabilis* (Gn.), not shown, has no black between basal and am. lines, but *median area wider* at inner margin than in Implicit Arches, and *shaded with reddish brown* with little or no blackish. HW mostly white in ♂, with narrow outer black shading; more black shading in ♀, but less than in other 2 species. Food: An unidentified legume. Range: N.C. to Fla., west to s. Mo. and Tex. May–June and Aug.-Oct.; 2 broods. Locally common.

WHEAT HEAD ARMYWORM MOTH   **Pl. 22 (14)**
Faronta diffusa (Wlk.)
Identification: FW yellowish tan with an *uneven white streak* along vein Cu. Black basal dash, and thin blackish wedge from outer end of white streak to apex. Reniform spot a black dot. HW white with grayish brown shading and veins. Wingspan 2.7–3.6 cm.
Food: Larva (**Wheat Head Armyworm**) a pest of corn, wheat, and other grasses.
Range: Common from Nfld. to Va., west through Canada, south to Tex. April–Oct.; 2–3 broods.

THE PINK-STREAK   **Pl. 24 (1)**
Faronta rubripennis (Grt. & Rob.)
Identification: FW yellowish white, *streaked with dull pink* above and below whitish streak along vein Cu. Outer margin of FW and white HW shaded with dull pink. Wingspan 3.2–3.7 cm.

Food: Unrecorded; probably grasses.
Range: Mass. and Ont. to Fla., west to Minn. and Tex. Aug.–Sept. Rare northward; may be locally common southward.

ARMYWORM MOTH   Pl. 22 (18)
Pseudaletia unipuncta (Haw.)
Identification: FW tan, often tinged with orange and lightly speckled with black; white along veins, especially Cu. Pm. line a series of small, widely spaced black dots; *white dot* where veins Cu_1 and M_3 branch. *Black shade line slants inward* from apex. HW grayish brown with tan fringe. Wingspan 3.5–4.7 cm.
Food: Larva (**Armyworm**) a major pest of many plants, such as alfalfa, corn and other grains, grasses, vegetables, young fruit trees, and ornamentals; also eats many wild plants. Armyworms are named for their feeding habits—they feed in fields by the thousands at night, then migrate in large groups to new areas when their food supply is exhausted.
Range: Virtually worldwide; common to abundant throughout our area. March–Nov.; 2–3 broods.

MANY-LINED WAINSCOT   Pl. 22 (17)
Leucania multilinea Wlk.
Identification: Similar to Wheat Head Armyworm Moth (above, Pl. 22) but with *3 sharp, even gray lines across collar* behind head. FW tan, streaked with fine brown lines; black dot above white streak where Cu_1 and M_3 separate. Pm. line consists of 2–3 black dots. HW white, sometimes with gray shading at outer margin. Wingspan 3.3–5 cm.
Food: Brome, orchard, and quack grasses.
Range: Throughout our area. June–Sept. Uncommon.
Similar species: (1) Scirpus Wainscot (below) *lacks* the 3 *collar stripes.* (2) Phragmites Wainscot, *L. phragmitidicola* Gn. (not shown), has faint collar stripes, but FW darker tan; pm. line consists of *more than 3 black dots*, usually a complete series of dots. Food: Grasses. Range: Throughout our area. April–Oct.; 2 broods. Common in much of range.

SCIRPUS WAINSCOT   Pl. 22 (19)
Leucania scirpicola Gn.
Identification: FW yellowish to dark orangish brown; *white dot* where veins Cu_1 and M_3 diverge. Pm. line curved, a series of widely spaced black dots. HW white, sometimes with grayish brown at outer margin. Wingspan 3.3–4 cm.
Food: Grasses; larva has been reared on orchard grass.
Range: N.S. to Fla., west to Ky. and Tex. April–Oct. Common, but has been confused with other species.
Remarks: Several similar grass-feeding species in our area are easily confused with this and the preceding 3 species. Further study is needed before easy identification and range limits can be properly described.

UNARMED WAINSCOT
Pl. 22 (20)

Leucania inermis (Fbs.)

Identification: *Foretibia moderately hairy* in both sexes. FW yellowish to grayish brown; a trace of pink in fringe. Am. line gray, broken; pm. line evenly curved, consisting of *1–2 rows of dark gray dots*. Reniform spot a gray dot surrounded by pale tan. HW grayish brown with a crescent-shaped discal spot (more conspicuous on underside than upperside). Wingspan 2.8–3.8 cm.

Food: Orchard grass.

Range: N.S. to Va., west to Ont. and Ky. May–Sept.; 2 broods. Locally common.

Similar species: Ursula Wainscot, *L. ursula* (Fbs.), not shown, is nearly identical, but *foretibia of ♂ has heavy tufts*. Very difficult to distinguish ♀. Food: Reared on honeysuckle. Range: Mass. and s. Que. to N.C., west to Ont., Iowa, and Ark. April–Oct.; 2 broods. Locally common.

FALSE WAINSCOT
Pl. 22 (21)

Leucania pseudargyria Gn.

Identification: Similar to Unarmed and Ursula Wainscots (above) but *larger*. FW has stronger pinkish tint. Discal spot faint on upperside of HW, *absent beneath*. Palpi more blackish. Foretibia heavily tufted, as in Ursula Wainscot. Wingspan 4–4.6 cm.

Food: Grasses, including redtop, timothy, and wild rye.

Range: N.S. to N.C., west to Man. and Miss. June–Sept.; most common in July.

RUBY QUAKER *Orthosia rubescens* (Wlk.) Pl. 22 (10)

Identification: Antennae of ♂ bipectinate; otherwise separated from other *Orthosia* species (below) by *heavier reddish to reddish brown shading* of yellowish FW (pattern too variable and indistinct to be useful). HW pale grayish brown, darker toward outer margin; fringe pale. Wingspan 3–4 cm.

Food: Wide variety, including beeches, hemlock, and maples.

Range: N.S. to Va., west to Wisc. and n. Ark. Adults fly during warm periods in winter, but are mostly seen in March–April (scattered records to July). Common to abundant at sugar bait.

GARMAN'S QUAKER
Pl. 22 (16)

Orthosia garmani (Grt.)

Identification: FW reddish brown with sharply defined, pale, sinuous am. and pm. lines and *irregular black st. line*. Terminal line paler brown; spots pale, obscure. HW pale grayish brown with dark discal spot. Wingspan 3.3–4.3 cm.

Food: Choke cherry.

Range: N.H. to Va., west to Minn., Kans., and Tex. Late Feb.–April; a few as late as June. Locally common.

GRAY QUAKER *Orthosia alurina* (Sm.) Pl. 22 (7)

Identification: Antennae of ♂ serrate. FW mouse gray with reddish tinting, especially *between spots* and on *basal side of st. line*.

Lines very inconspicuous, but following same pattern as in Ruby Quaker (above). HW shiny, pale grayish brown with faint discal spot. Wingspan 3.1–4 cm.
Food: Wide variety of plants, including basswood and juneberry.
Range: N.Y. to n. Fla., west to Wisc., Mo., and Tex. Feb.–May, usually April. Locally common to rare.

SPECKLED GREEN FRUITWORM MOTH   Pl. 22 (4)
Orthosia hibisci (Gn.)
Identification: Antennae of ♂ serrate. FW grayish brown with very little reddish tinting. Lines and spots usually distinct, usually accented with vague blackish markings, such as *top of st. line* and *filling in bottom half of reniform spot.* HW grayish brown. Wingspan 3.2–4.2 cm.
Food: Wide variety; larva (**Speckled Green Fruitworm**) attacks apple, crabapple, cherries, plums, and other trees.
Range: Common to abundant throughout our area. Feb–May.
Similar species: (1) In Ruby Quaker (p. 106), FW has more extensive red shading; ♂ has bipectinate antennae. (2) Gray Quaker (above) is very inconspicuously marked. (3) In Subdued Quaker, *O. revicta* (Morr.), not shown, ♂ antennae less serrate than in other *Orthosia* species. FW pale bluish gray to dull reddish brown; st. line sharply defined, with reddish brown to black *outline* beyond it *broken at veins.* Food: Birches, cherries, poplars, and other trees. Range: Nfld. to N.J., west to Man. and Ky. April–May. Common northward.

NORMAN'S QUAKER   Pl. 22 (13)
Crocigrapha normani (Grt.)
Identification: FW brown with darker median area. Am. and pm. lines black with gray edging. Spots inconspicuous; *dark gray* in lower half of *reniform spot.* Gray costal patch near apex. HW whitish, brown at outer margin. Wingspan 3.5–4 cm.
Food: Apple, cherries, oaks, and other trees.
Range: N.S. to S.C., west to Man., Mo., and Miss. March–June. Common northward.

INTRACTABLE QUAKER   Pl. 21 (21)
Himella intractata (Morr.)
Identification: FW grayish to reddish brown; lines yellowish, broken; spots outlined with yellow. *Heavy black spot* on basal line, fainter black spots on am. and pm. lines near inner margin. HW grayish brown, darker toward outer margin. Wingspan 2.5–3.5 cm.
Food: Elms, flowering crabapple, and oaks.
Range: Me. to Fla., west to Mo. and Tex. March–May; a few as late as July. Common.

ALTERNATE WOODLING   Pl. 22 (11)
Egira alternata (Wlk.)
Identification: Abdominal segments tan, with *black band* at base of each segment. FW bluish to greenish gray, darker toward costa.

Lines thin, double, black. Orbicular spot large, filled with pale gray; reniform spot filled with and surrounded by reddish brown. *Squarish black spot* inside pm. line, below reniform spot; 2 black spots inside terminal line. HW grayish brown. Wingspan 2.1–4 cm.
Food: Honeysuckle.
Range: Me. to n. Fla., west to Ky. and Tex. Feb.–June. Common southward, but rare in North.

DISTINCT QUAKER *Achatia distincta* Hbn.   **Pl. 21 (8)**
Identification: Black bar across white to gray frons. FW pale gray with thin black lines and spot outlines. *Bent black bar* connects am. and pm. lines in lower median area. Some brown shading inside reniform spot. HW grayish brown, darker at outer margin. Wingspan 3–3.7 cm.
Food: Flowering crabapple, maples, and red oak.
Range: N.H. and s. Que. to n. Fla., west to Man. and Tex. Late March–early May. Common.

GRAY WOODGRAIN   **Pl. 22 (6)**
Morrisonia mucens (Hbn.)
Identification: Antennae bipectinate in ♂ (serrate in other 2 *Morrisonia* species, below). FW mixed gray and brown, variably dark. Thin basal dash and heavier dash in lower median area. Note *2 blackish triangular patches* at outer margin. HW whitish with heavy grayish brown shading. Wingspan 3–3.5 cm.
Food: Unrecorded.
Range: L.I., N.Y. to Fla., west to Ohio and Tex. March–May. Moderately common southward.

BICOLORED WOODGRAIN   **Pl. 22 (12)**
Morrisonia evicta (Grt.)
Identification: Costal half of FW gray, the rest dark brown to blackish. Orbicular and reniform spots merged; both white, partly filled with reddish brown. *White dash at outer margin,* above anal angle. HW grayish brown. Wingspan 3–3.7 cm.
Food: Larva has been reared on wild cherry.
Range: N.S. to Va., west to Man. and Tex. April–May. Usually uncommon.
Similar species: See Gray Half-spot (p. 130, Pl. 25).

CONFUSED WOODGRAIN   **Pl. 22 (9)**
Morrisonia confusa (Hbn.)
Identification: Thorax pale brown with *dark brown stripes.* FW brown with darker brown veins and shading, creating a woodgrain pattern. Note *2 black dashes* in basal area and black streaks extending inward from outer margin; lines black with white edging, most conspicuous toward inner margin. Orbicular spot elongate, larger than reniform spot. HW grayish brown. Wingspan 3.2–4.5 cm.
Food: Basswood, blueberries, pines, and other woody plants.
Range: Very common throughout our area. April–June.

BRONZED CUTWORM MOTH   Pl. 22 (15)
Nephelodes minians Gn.

Identification: FW color varies: reddish brown (old specimens) to dull ochre, dark reddish, olive green, or dark purple. *Darker ground color* shades outer half of median area beyond median line; reniform spot and edging along costa same color as rest of FW. HW grayish brown with fringe of FW ground color. Wingspan 3.5–5 cm.
Food: Larva **(Bronzed Cutworm)** eats corn and various grasses.
Range: Nfld. to Ga., west to Man. and Tex. Aug.–Oct. Common.

RUDDY QUAKER *Protorthodes oviduca* (Gn.)   Pl. 22 (2)
Identification: FW reddish brown. Am. and pm. lines fine, white, edged with black; *st. line* most conspicuous, *yellowish white, nearly straight.* Spots black with white outlines; orbicular spot touches am. line; reniform spot oval. HW grayish brown with discal spot. Wingspan 2.7–3.2 cm.
Food: Dandelion, grasses, plantains, and other low plants.
Range: Nfld. to Fla., west to Man. and Miss. May–July; Sept. Generally uncommon.

SHEATHED QUAKER *Ulolonche culea* (Gn.)   Pl. 21 (22)
Identification: FW mouse gray to grayish or yellowish brown. Basal, am., and pm. lines sharp, slightly curved, yellowish; angled so that median area *much wider at costa* than at inner margin. Spot outlines yellowish; bottom half of reniform spot filled with gray. HW same color as FW, but paler. Wingspan 3–3.5 cm.
Food: Red oak.
Range: Me. and Que. to n. Fla., west to Mich., Mo., and Tex. April–June. Uncommon to locally common.

SMALL BROWN QUAKER   Pl. 22 (5)
Pseudorthodes vecors (Gn.)

Identification: FW pale to dark reddish brown. Lines grayish, faint, wavy. Am. line zigzagged; dark dots on outer side of pm. line; st. line a series of black dots. Reniform spot *white or orange.* HW grayish brown with faint median line and discal spot. Wingspan 2.2–3.5 cm.
Food: Asters, dandelion, grasses, and other low plants.
Range: Nfld. to N.C., west to Man. and Mo. April–May and July–Oct.; 2 broods. Common.
Similar species: (1) In Cynical Quaker (p. 110, Pl. 22) *reniform spot* is deep brown, not white or orange. Long, curved sex scales on underside of ♂ FW, absent in Small Brown Quaker. (2) In Scurfy Quaker, *Homorthodes furfurata* (Grt.), not shown, FW pattern is almost identical to that of Small Brown Quaker, but ground color differs—*pale brown* (no reddish tint) in North, brown *mottled with orange* in South (subspecies *lindseyi*). Food: Maple and wild cherry. Range: N.S. to N.C., west to Man. and Ark. April–Aug.; apparently 2 broods. Common.

RUSTIC QUAKER *Orthodes crenulata* (Btlr.)   **Pl. 22 (1)**
Identification: FW gray to brown. *Black triangle* in middle of collar. FW lines sharp, yellowish; *pm. line bends toward costa* on vein M$_1$; black dots on veins just beyond it. Orbicular and reniform spots large, often touching. HW dark grayish brown. Wingspan 2.8–3.5 cm.
Food: Wide variety, including dandelion, grasses and willows.
Range: Throughout our area. May–Aug. Locally common.

CYNICAL QUAKER *Orthodes cynica* Gn.   **Pl. 22 (8)**
Identification: Similar to Rustic Quaker (above), but usually with some dull scarlet shading. Lines diffuse, darker than FW ground color. *Pm. line more wavy* than in Rustic Quaker, but with same black dots beyond it; st. line usually accented with dull yellow. Spots large when visible, but rarely touch. HW grayish brown. Wingspan 2.7–3.4 cm.
Food: Larva has been reared on plantain.
Range: N.S. to Fla., west to Man., Ark., and Miss. May–Aug. Common.

SIGNATE QUAKER *Tricholita signata* (Wlk.)   **Pl. 21 (20)**
Identification: FW reddish brown with purplish shading in some specimens, especially southward. Lines thin, dark brown; st. line wavy. Orbicular spot an orange circle; reniform spot filled with ground color, or *white mottled with orange* (as shown). HW grayish brown. Wingspan 2.8–3.8 cm.
Food: Wide variety, including dandelion and plantain.
Range: N.S. to Fla., west to Man., Ark., and Miss. July–Sept. Uncommon.

SPANISH MOTH *Xanthopastis timais* (Cram.)   **Pl. 24 (3)**
Identification: Easily recognized by the *hairy black body* and *pink FW with black markings;* yellow around spots and in terminal area. HW blackish. Wingspan 3.9–4.5 cm.
Food: Figs (*Ficus* species), spider lily, and narcissus. Larva has been reared on iceberg lettuce.
Range: Staten Island, N.Y., and N.J. to Fla., west to Ky., Ark., and Tex. April–July in Miss.; Nov.–May and Sept. in Fla., where it may be common. Rare elsewhere; a stray northward.

Subfamily Cuculliinae

DOT-AND-DASH SWORDGRASS MOTH   **Pl. 24 (9)**
Xylena curvimacula (Morr.)
Identification: Head and collar cream, thorax brown. FW *cream in upper half,* brown in lower half and along costa. Lines indistinct; am. line forms double loops, most conspicuous near coalblack, U-*shaped orbicular spot.* Pm. line consists of tiny black dots. Reniform spot represented by brown crescent beyond orbicu-

lar spot. HW dark grayish brown. Wingspan 4–5 cm.
Food: Alders, dandelion, poplars, willows, and other plants.
Range: Nfld. to s. N.J., west to Man., Ill., and Minn. Sept.–Oct.;
Feb.–May. Adult moth hibernates. Common northward.
Similar species: (1) American Swordgrass Moth, *X. nupera*
(Lint.), not shown, is larger; *black dash* extends from bottom of
reniform spot to st. line; another dash across median area slightly
below end of basal dash. Food: Wild cherry and other plants.
Range: Nfld. to Wash., D.C., west across Canada, south to Minn.
Sept.–Oct.; March–May. (2) Gray Swordgrass Moth, *X. cineritia*
(Grt.), not shown, has *bluish gray FW*. Pale upper half less contrasting than in Dot-and-dash Swordgrass Moth, with salmon tint
toward apex; basal dash absent. Food: Alder, blueberries, willows,
and other plants. Range: Lab. to N.J., west across Canada, south
to Mich. Sept.–Nov.; April–May.

GOAT SALLOW *Homoglaea hircina* (Morr.)   **Pl. 25 (20)**
Identification: Body very hairy. Body and FW dark gray to gray-
ish brown. Am. and pm. lines *double, filled with pale gray;* median
and st. lines darker gray, contrast very slightly with ground color.
Spots inconspicuous. HW paler gray than FW. Wingspan 3–3.5 cm.
Food: Aspen and poplars.
Range: N.S. to n. N.J. and Pa., west to Man. and Wisc. Rarely
Oct.–Nov.; most adults fly in March–April. Fall adults overwinter.

BETHUNE'S PINION   **Pl. 24 (5)**
Lithophane bethunei (Grt. & Rob.)
Identification: FW cream with tan and yellow shading. *Orbicular and reniform spots and st. line yellowish;* other lines represented by tiny black dots on veins. Gray shading between orbicular
and reniform spots and below reniform spot; 2 terminal gray
blotches. HW cream with gray shading except at apex and fringe.
Wingspan 3.2–3.9 cm.
Food: Apple, ash, choke cherry, crabapple, hickory, maple, oak,
witch-hazel, and other trees. Larvae have been observed eating
pupae of Eastern Tent Caterpillar (p. 54).
Range: N.S. to Wash., D.C. and Ky., west to Man. and Mo. Also
Fla.; perhaps a stray. Sept.–Nov.; Feb.–May. Common.

NAMELESS PINION   **Pl. 24 (7)**
Lithophane innominata (Smith)
Identification: FW yellowish tan with dark brown median shade
and st. line. *Very diffuse blackish bar* below reniform spot; *2
blackish blotches* in terminal area; pairs of small black dashes on
veins form am. and pm. lines. HW solid gray; fringe same color as
FW. Wingspan 3.5–3.9 cm.
Food: Alders, apple, firs, oaks, willows, and other trees and shrubs.
Larvae sometimes eat other insects.
Range: N.S. to N.C. mts., west through s. Canada, south to Wisc.
Sept.–Nov.; Feb.–May. Common.

WANTON PINION   Pl. 23 (13), 24 (6)
Lithophane petulca (Grt.)
Identification: FW grayish brown with violet to gray shading along basal half of costa. Two forms—in shaded form (Pl. 24) lower $\frac{2}{3}$ of FW is darker brown with *pale tan along costa;* orbicular and reniform spots also pale tan. Unshaded form (Pl. 23) has reddish brown in median and terminal areas, with a faint dark brown median bar. Am. and median lines zigzagged; pm. line a series of tiny black dots. HW dark grayish brown with pale fringe in both forms. Wingspan 3.5–4.2 cm.
Food: Birches and other trees.
Range: N.S. to N.J. Pine Barrens, west across Canada, south to s. Ohio, Wisc., and Minn. Sept.–Nov.; Feb.–May. Common.
Similar species: See Hemina Pinion (below), especially unshaded form (Pl. 24).

HEMINA PINION *Lithophane hemina* (Grt.)   Pl. 24 (4)
Identification: Similar to Wanton Pinion (above); also has 2 forms—shaded (usually more common) and unshaded. *Median dash* much broader and darker in unshaded form of Hemina Pinion (shown) than in Wanton Pinion. Lower $\frac{2}{3}$ of FW in shaded form usually *darker brown* and costal $\frac{1}{3}$ *more whitish* than in Wanton Pinion. Wingspan 3.4–3.8 cm.
Food: Birches, box elder, oaks, and other trees.
Range: N.S. to s. N.J. and se. Ky., west to Man. and Mo. Sept.–Oct.; Feb.–May. May be common at sugar bait.

BAILEY'S PINION *Lithophane baileyi* Grt.   Pl. 23 (12)
Identification: FW greenish gray with black lines. Black basal dash with white edge on top. *Orbicular spot* ∪*-shaped* (open toward costa), white with black outline. Reniform spot tinged with brown, with some blackish shading between it and orbicular spot that usually does not reach costa. HW dark grayish brown. Wingspan 3.4–3.9 cm.
Food: Apple, birch, cherries, willows, and other trees. Larvae may attack each other when reared in captivity.
Range: N.S. to N.C. mts., west to sw. Ont. and Wisc. Sept.–Oct.; Feb.–April. Uncommon.
Similar species: In Shivering Pinion, *L. querquera* Grt. (not shown), FW greenish gray but *less mottled,* lines barely visible. Black blotch on basal side of reniform spot *extends more completely to costa,* and is *more contrasting.* Two black spots represent st. line. Some specimens have black shading over entire FW except reniform spot and upper st. area. HW dark grayish brown. Food: Many trees; larva has been reared on *Prunus* species, but seems to prefer live prey (including fellow larvae) to foliage. Range: N.H. and se. Ont. to W. Va. and Ky., west to Mo. and Miss. Sept.–Nov.; Feb.–May. Common in northeastern part of range; local south and west of Pa.

ASHEN PINION Pl. 23 (15)
Lithophane antennata (Wlk.)

Identification: FW pale gray; spots and lines black but very thin and inconspicuous. Black basal dash with white edge above; *paler gray area* between basal dash and costa. *Orbicular spot double,* with *pale gray filling; reniform spot* filled with *reddish brown* and a bit of black at lower end. Look for faint black outline of claviform spot. HW grayish brown with slightly darker discal spot and median line. Wingspan 3.5–4.2 cm.

Food: Larva shares its name (**Green Fruitworm**) with larva of Grote's Pinion (below). An occasional orchard pest, attacking young apple, plum, and other fruit trees. Also feeds on ashes, elms, hickories, maples, oaks, wild cherry and willows.

Range: N.B. to S.C., west through Que. and Ont. to Minn., south to Miss. Sept.–May, but less common than other *Lithophane* species in midwinter. Common to abundant except at northeastern limits of range.

GROTE'S PINION *Lithophane grotei* Riley Pl. 23 (16)
Identification: Similar to Ashen Pinion (above) but larger and darker gray; double black lines much more conspicuous, with more black shading. *Orbicular spot whitish; no brown in reniform spot,* but may be lined with white. HW dark grayish brown. Wingspan 4.2–5 cm.

Food: Pin oak, red choke-cherry, and other trees. Larva shares name (**Green Fruitworm**) with larva of Ashen Pinion (above). Cannibalism reported in larvae reared in captivity.

Range: N.S. to N.C., west to Ont., Wisc., Neb. and Mo. Oct.–April; adults often fly during warm periods in winter. Common.

DOWDY PINION Pl. 23 (14)
Lithophane unimoda (Lint.)

Identification: FW a more even deep bluish gray than in Grote's Pinion (above). Lines obscure; st. line most distinct. *White or pale gray orbicular spot* is most conspicuous marking. Reniform spot obscure. HW paler grayish brown than in Grote's Pinion. Wingspan 3.8–4.4 cm.

Food: Mostly black cherry; some other trees.

Range: N.S. to S.C., west through s. Canada, south to Neb. and Mo. Oct.–Dec.; Feb.–May. Common in much of range; comes readily to sugar bait.

MUSTARD SALLOW Pl. 24 (10)
Pyreferra hesperidago (Gn.)

Identification: FW yellow with variable orange shading. Lines darker orange to reddish brown. Am. line and broad median line slightly jagged; *pm. line solid, nearly straight, turns inward* just below costa. HW pale orange with slightly darker orange median band. Wingspan 3.4–3.8 cm.

Food: Witch-hazel and ironwood; sweetgum(?).

Range: N.S. to n. Fla., west to Wisc. and Ark. Sept.–May; rarely June. Abundant in some years; rare in others.

STRAIGHT-TOOTHED SALLOW   Pl. 24 (12)
Eupsilia vinulenta (Grt.)

Identification: FW reddish to brown with purplish lines and shading. *Reniform spot white or orange,* with dots above and below larger middle spot. HW dark grayish brown. *Scales on FW end in 4 straight teeth.* Wingspan 3.3–3.8 cm.

Food: Wide variety, including cherries, maples, and oaks.

Range: N.S. to N.C., west to S.D. and Mo. Sept.–May. Common to abundant; adults fly on warm nights during winter.

Similar species: The following *Eupsilia* species (not shown) are almost identical in color and pattern but have *curled teeth on FW scales* (visible under microscope): (1) Sidus Sallow, *E. sidus* (Gn.), and (2) Franclemont's Sallow, *E. cirripalea* Franc., can be distinguished only by genitalic features. (3) Three-spotted Sallow, *E. tristigmata* (Grt.), has FW mottled with purple, and *dark spot* below orange patch in reniform spot. Food, range, and flight periods of these 3 species same as for Straight-toothed Sallow.

MORRISON'S SALLOW   Pl. 23 (18)
Eupsilia morrisoni (Grt.)

Identification: FW brown, sometimes with reddish tint; lines whitish, even. *Am. line usually heaviest* line, straight to slightly wavy. Narrow reniform spot has dark brown *dot in bottom.* HW grayish brown. Wingspan 3.5–4 cm.

Food: Cherries, elms, maples, oaks, and other woody plants.

Range: N.S. to Wash., D.C. and e. Ky., west to Ont., Minn., and Mo. Sept.–May; adults fly during warm periods in winter. Very common in New England. Will come to sugar bait.

LOST SALLOW *Eupsilia devia* (Grt.)   Pl. 24 (13)

Identification: Thorax and FW mouse gray; *median and st. areas brown.* Lines whitish. Pm. and st. lines thin, inconspicuous; basal and am. lines thicker, as is another whitish line that crosses st. line. *Pm. and st. lines curve slightly outward.* Reniform spot whitish, inconspicuous. HW grayish brown. Wingspan 3–3.5 cm.

Food: Mostly asters and goldenrods; will eat many other plants, such as aspen, oaks, and *Prunus* species.

Range: N.S. to Wash., D.C. and Ky., west through s. Canada, south to Mo. Oct–May. Common to uncommon; may be caught at sugar bait near old fields.

VARIABLE SALLOW   Pl. 23 (22)
Sericaglaea signata (French)

Identification: FW color varies widely: light to dark brown, sometimes reddish brown (note purplish gloss in fresh specimens). Some have *heavy black shading inside irregular st. line* (as shown), with conspicuously paler area outside st. line. Veins and lines usually paler brown, obscure. Sharp *bluish black spot* in lower half of reniform spot. HW brown, grayish brown toward outer margin. Wingspan 3.5-4.3 cm.

Food: Cherry, linden, and oak trees; reared on wild cherry.

Range: Conn. to Fla., west to Mo. and Tex. Oct.-May. May be abundant at sugar bait.

RED-WINGED SALLOW   Pl. 24 (14)
Xystopeplus rufago (Hbn.)

Identification: Note the *straight costal margin* and *sharply pointed apex* on FW. FW dull orange with rose tint. Lines and spots thin, purplish, usually obscure; pm. line darkest—a series of black dots. Reniform spot a figure-8. HW whitish with rose shading. Wingspan 3-3.5 cm.

Food: Oaks; also wild cherry.

Range: Me. to Fla., west to Minn. and Tex. Oct.-May; mostly March-May. Common southward.

UNSATED SALLOW   Pl. 23 (20)
Metaxaglaea inulta (Grt.)

Identification: FW solid warm brown. Am. and pm. lines darker brown, even, curving outward. Orbicular and reniform *spots very large and close together* (sometimes touching). HW darker brown except fringe. Wingspan 4-4.8 cm.

Food: Nannyberry, wayfaring-tree, and other viburnums.

Range: N.S. to N.C., west to Man. and Mo. Late Aug.-Nov. Sometimes common.

FOOTPATH SALLOW   Pl. 24 (22)
Metaxaglaea semitaria Franc.

Identification: FW bright chestnut; median area sometimes slightly paler. Am. and pm. lines purple, scalloped; *pm. line scallops darkest,* at sharp points. Purple shading over am. and pm. lines and in median and st. areas. Spots faint, darker brown; purple in lower end of reniform spot blends into broad median shade line. HW dark grayish brown with chestnut fringe. Wingspan 4-5.4 cm.

Food: Blueberries (young larva will eat unopened buds). Larva can be reared on crabapples, then oaks (catkins preferred).

Range: N.H. to Fla., west to e. Ky. and Miss. Late Sept.-early Dec. Locally common to abundant.

Similar species: Roadside Sallow, *M. viatica* (Grt.), not shown, is nearly identical, but duller brown; ♂ genitalia have long, curved terminal spine on valve (visible by brushing tip of abdomen and observing under magnification); spine of Footpath Sallow is short and broad. Food: Apple, crabapples, mountain ash, and some *Prunus* species. Range: S. Me. to Fla., west to Mo. and Tex. Sept.-Jan. Locally common.

SLOPING SALLOW *Epiglaea decliva* (Grt.)   **Pl. 23 (17)**
Identification: Similar to Footpath Sallow (above) but FW

broader; spots and lines thin, usually more distinct. Pm. line faint but *evenly rounded,* with *black spots* beyond it (not at scallop points of pm. line, as in Footpath Sallow). Dark filling in bottom half of reniform spot more pronounced. HW dark grayish brown. Wingspan 4–5 cm.

Food: Oaks and *Prunus* species.

Range: Me. and s. Ont. to S.C., west to Wisc. and Mo. Oct.–Dec.

Similar species: Pointed Sallow, *E. apiata* (Grt.), not shown, is smaller, with *more pointed apex* on FW; *am. and pm. lines straighter;* st. line more distinct, accented by lighter shading. Food: Cranberry. Range: N.S. to S.C., west across Canada, south to Wisc. Late Aug.–Nov., but mostly Oct. northward, where it may be common and, in Mass. and N.J., a pest.

SILKY SALLOW *Chaetaglaea sericea* (Morr.)　　**Pl. 23 (21)**

Identification: FW brown with sparse black dusting; veins, lines and spots yellowish. Look for a *thin yellow border* along costa and inner margin. Lower half of reniform spot blackish. HW dark grayish brown. Wingspan 3.8–4.5 cm.

Food: Oaks; larvae have been reared on blueberries and cherries.

Range: N.S. to n. Fla., west to Wisc., Mo., and Miss. Sept.–Nov.; to Feb. in S.C. Common.

Similar species: Trembling Sallow, *C. tremula* (Harv.), not shown, is dull pink to various shades of gray or brown. *Am. line toothed,* not evenly rounded as in Silky Sallow. Food: Reared on blueberries, cherries, and oaks. Range: Me. to Fla., west to Ky. and Miss. Mid-Sept. to late Nov.; to Feb. southward.

SCALLOPED SALLOW　　**Pl. 24 (15)**
Eucirroedia pampina (Gn.)

Identification: FW deep yellow, variably shaded with rusty orange. FW and HW *deeply scalloped.* Am. and pm. lines even, lighter yellow, shaded with reddish brown. Orbicular and reniform spots filled with *purplish brown.* HW rose. Wingspan 3.6–4.4 cm.

Food: Black cherry, choke cherry, oaks, poplars, and many other plants. Young larva may feed on tree catkins.

Range: N.S. to Fla., west across s. Canada, south to Mo. and Miss. Late Aug.–Dec.; mostly Sept.–Oct. Locally common.

BICOLORED SALLOW　　**Pl. 24 (17)**
Sunira bicolorago (Gn.)

Identification: FW pale straw yellow to deep orange-yellow, shaded with light brown or gray. Lower half of reniform spot *filled with gray.* Lines usually obscure; pm. line a series of black dots. In some specimens outer half of FW is completely purplish gray. HW paler than FW, shaded with grayish brown. Wingspan 2.8–3.8 cm.

Food: Black cherry, cabbage, crabapple, dock, lawn grasses, maples, scrub oak, tobacco, and other plants.

Range: Common to abundant throughout our area, except in s. Fla. Sept.–Dec.

DOTTED SALLOW   Pl. 24 (20)
Anathix ralla (Grt. & Rob.)
Identification: Similar to Bicolored Sallow (above) but gray filling in lower half of reniform spot *more mottled and diffuse.* Pm. line more conspicuous; row of black dots in st. area. HW pale yellowish with no dark shading. Wingspan 2.6–3.5 cm.
Food: Unrecorded.
Range: Me. and Que. to N.C., west to Ont., Mich., and w. Ky. Aug.–Oct. Common.
Similar species: In Puta Sallow, *A. puta* (Grt. & Rob.), not shown, FW is dull reddish brown, with inconspicuous st. line (dots). Food: Quaking aspen. Range: N.S. to Pa., west across Canada, south to Wisc. and Minn. Aug.–Sept.

PINK-BARRED SALLOW   Pl. 24 (11)
Xanthia togata (Esper)
Identification: Thorax and FW bright yellow; *collar, line fragments,* and *pm. shading purple,* mixed with *reddish brown.* Dotted black st. line. HW white, tinted with pale yellow. Wingspan 3–3.4 cm.
Food: Willows; early stage larva feeds on the catkins.
Range: Nfld. to Conn. and Pa., west across Canada, south to Minn. Aug.–Oct. Locally common.

BROAD SALLOW *Xylotype capax* (Grt.)   Pl. 23 (19)
Identification: FW dark bluish gray, shaded with grayish brown. Lines and spots sharp, black, edged with white. Lower parts of am. and pm. lines w-shaped, connected by a *black median dash.* Brown and black anal dash. HW dark grayish brown. Wingspan 4–4.7 cm.
Food: Blueberries, cherry, crabapple, and red oak trees.
Range: S. Me. to Md. (coast), west to Man. and se. Ky. Aug.–Nov.; mostly Oct.
Similar species: Acadian Sallow, *X. acadia* B. & Benj. (not shown), is smaller, paler, and more whitish gray. Food: Larch. Range: Lab. to Me., west to Man. and Wisc. Aug.–Oct.

COMSTOCK'S SALLOW   Pl. 24 (2)
Feralia comstocki (Grt.)
Identification: FW bright green, sometimes fading to yellowish. Lines scalloped, broken, black, edged with white. Note the *3 squarish black blotches* around reniform spot. HW cream; gray discal spot, partial median line, and broken shade in st. area; some green along black terminal line. Wingspan 3.3–3.6 cm.
Food: Firs, hemlocks, pines, and spruces.
Range: Nfld. to N.C., west across Canada, south to Wisc. and Ky. Late April–early June.
Similar species: (1) Jocose Sallow, *F. jocosa* (Gn.), not shown, has duller green, more evenly colored FW with more conspicuous pm. line and *no black blotches* around reniform spot; median area

gray. HW dark grayish brown except fringe. Food: Eastern white cedar, fir, hemlock, pine, larch, and spruce trees. Range: Nfld. to se. Ky., west across Canada, south to Wisc. April–May. (2) Major Sallow, *F. major* Sm. (not shown), looks like Comstock's Sallow but has *only 1 black blotch,* on basal side of reniform spot. Food: Larch, pine, and spruce trees. Range: N.S. and N.B. to n. Fla., west to Ont., s. Mo., and Tex. March–May.

CHOSEN SALLOW   Pl. 23 (7, 11)
Eutolype electilis (Morr.)
Identification: FW slate gray with obscure black lines (partially edged with white) and white scaling at edge of anal angle. Black *basal dash joins claviform spot* beneath large, round orbicular spot; reniform spot hourglass-shaped. Broad black line extends from base to st. area, sometimes curves up along st. line. Note brown basal and st. shading in form "depilis" (Pl. 23). HW dirty white with dark grayish discal spot, partial median line, and shading toward outer margin. Wingspan 3.1–3.8 cm.
Food: Hickory and walnut trees.
Range: Mass. to Fla., west to Iowa and Tex. March–early May. Locally common.

GRAY SALLOW *Eutolype grandis* Sm.   Pl. 23 (9)
Identification: FW gray, sometimes with violet or brownish tint; lines obscure. *Paler gray in median area* between double am. line and *nearly straight median line;* sometimes almost as pale from base to am. line. HW grayish brown. Wingspan 3.1–4 cm.
Food: Unrecorded.
Range: Mass. to Fla., west to Mo. and Tex. March–April. Uncommon to rare, especially eastward.

ROLAND'S SALLOW *Eutolype rolandi* Grt.   Pl. 23 (10)
Identification: FW uniform dull gray, sometimes a bit brownish. Lines and spots very obscure, darker gray; spots edged with paler gray in some specimens. Markings much like those in Chosen Sallow (above), but *no basal dash or* prominent *white scaling* at anal angle. HW grayish brown. Wingspan 3.1–3.8 cm.
Food: Larva has been reared on oaks.
Range: N.H. and s. Ont. to cen. Fla., west to Iowa and Tex. March–April; Feb. southward. Our most common *Eutolype* species.

FAWN SALLOW *Copipanolis styracis* (Gn.)   Pl. 24 (8)
Identification: FW pale fawn brown, including pale orbicular and reniform spots; rest of median area darker. *Pm. line curves inward* and *parallels costa* before meeting it. Black scaling in median area toward inner margin. HW cream with brownish dusting. Markings very obscure in some specimens, especially southward. Wingspan 3.1–3.6 cm.
Food: Oaks.

Range: Mass. and s. Ont. to Fla., west to Minn., Mo., and Tex. Feb.–April. Common eastward.

FIGURE-EIGHT SALLOW   Pl. 27 (10)
Psaphida resumens Wlk.

Identification: FW mottled pale and dark gray. Orbicular, reniform, and claviform spots large, pale gray; *orbicular and reniform spots usually touch each other,* forming a *figure-8.* Black anal dash crosses broad white st. line. HW grayish brown with darker markings and shading. Wingspan 3.2–3.8 cm.

Food: Maples and oaks.

Range: Mass. and s. Ont. to Fla., west to Minn. and Tex. March–May. Common; sometimes abundant.

GROTE'S SALLOW *Copivaleria grotei* (Morr.)   Pl. 23 (6)
Identification: Thorax and FW *olive green* mixed with black; lines and spots with *variable white edging.* Look for an erect black middorsal tuft on abdomen. FW pattern similar to that of Figure-eight Sallow (above) but *claviform spot less prominent;* spots, st. line, and HW ground color more whitish. Wingspan 3.2–4.2 cm.

Food: Ash.

Range: Common throughout our area. Late March–May.

FINE-LINED SALLOW   Pl. 28 (10)
Catabena lineolata Wlk.

Identification: Frons black; thorax and FW pale gray. Look for 3 thin dark lines across collar. Am. and pm. lines reduced to *small dark dashes* at costa; no other markings except *fine black and white streaks* all over FW. HW white with gray shading and white fringe. Wingspan 2.3–2.6 cm.

Food: Goldenrod and hoary vervain.

Range: S. Me. and sw. Que. to Pa. and Tenn., west to Minn., Kans., and Tex. May–July. Uncommon.

BROWN-LINED SALLOW   Pl. 23 (2)
Homohadena badistriga (Grt.)

Identification: FW brown with variable white scaling and small black streaks in st. area. Am. and pm. *lines very thin, curved. Black basal dash extends to pm. line;* another black dash extends through reniform spot and upper pm. line. HW shiny, whitish; brown toward outer margin. Wingspan 3–3.2 cm.

Food: Honeysuckle.

Range: Throughout our area, but unrecorded between N.J. and Fla. June–July. Apparently quite rare in the Southeast.

BROAD-LINED SALLOW   Pl. 23 (5)
Homohadena infixa (Wlk.)

Identification: Very similar to the Brown-lined Sallow (above) but more grayish; am. and pm. *lines much thicker,* joined by a *thick black median bar.* Median area sometimes solid black below bar. HW grayish brown; fringe whitish. Wingspan 3.1–3.6 cm.

Food: Larva has been reared on black walnut in Mo.
Range: Nfld. to n. Fla., west to Man. and Okla. Late May–June. Locally common.

FRINGE-TREE SALLOW   Pl. 23 (8)
Adita chionanthi (J.E. Sm.)
Identification: FW pale gray with darker gray shading. Am. and pm. lines and spot outlines sharp, black. Orbicular and reniform spots pale gray, darker toward center. Claviform spot *connected to am. line,* forming a *sharp hollow wedge.* Black blotch along costa in median area; thin black anal dash. HW white with narrow grayish brown border. Wingspan 3.3–3.8 cm.
Food: Ash, feverwort, and fringe-tree.
Range: N.S. to Ga., west to S.D. and Kans. Late Aug.–early Oct.

INTERMEDIATE CUCULLIA   Pl. 23 (1)
Cucullia intermedia Speyer
Identification: FW narrow and pointed as in other *Cucullia* species (below). FW dark gray with paler gray streaks that obscure usual FW pattern. Am. and pm. lines partial, terminal line sharp; thin black *basal dash,* thicker *anal dash,* and 2 other *dashes in upper st. area.* HW grayish brown, slightly darker at outer margin. Wingspan 4.2–5.1 cm.
Food: Wild lettuce.
Range: Nfld. to Va., west to Man. and Mich. May–Aug.
Similar species: In Speyer's Cucullia, *C. speyeri* Lint. (not shown) FW streaking is more whitish; *HW white* with grayish brown at outer margin. Food: Colt's-tail and fleabane. Range: S. Me. and Ont. to N.C., west to Man. and S.D. June–Aug.

THE ASTEROID *Cucullia asteroides* Gn.   Pl. 23 (3)
Identification: FW whitish gray with brown and blackish shading along costa that widens toward apex; brown to blackish border of inner margin widens at anal angle. *Pm. line* reduced to *a white crescent* at inner margin. HW white with grayish brown border. Wingspan 4.4–5.6 cm.
Food: Flowers of asters, goldenrods, and other composites.
Range: Nfld. to Fla., west to Man., Ark., and Miss. May–Sept. Common.
Similar species: Omitted Cucullia, *C. omissa* Dod (not shown), has identical FW, but *HW grayish brown,* darker toward outer margin. Food: Asters. Range: Me. and Que. to Pa. and Ky., west to Man. May–Aug.

BROWN-HOODED OWLET or   Pl. 23 (4)
BROWN-BORDERED CUCULLIA
Cucullia convexipennis Grt. & Rob.
Identification: Abdomen brown, with reddish brown middorsal tufts. FW yellowish tan with gray shading and dark streaks (mixed reddish brown, dark brown, and black) along costa and inner margin. *Shaded area widest at FW apex and anal angle.* White frag-

ment of pm. line visible at inner margin. HW dirty white with grayish brown veins and outer margin. Wingspan 4–5 cm.
Food: Flowers of asters, goldenrods, and other low plants.
Range: N.S. to S.C., west to Man. and Mo. Late June–Aug.

Subfamily Amphipyrinae

WOOD-COLORED APAMEA   Pl. 25 (4)
Apamea lignicolora (Gn.)
Identification: FW yellowish with reddish brown shading. Am. and pm. lines obscure; pm. line bends sharply. *St. line forms a* W *at its middle,* dividing black terminal shading into 2 *large patches.* HW grayish brown. Wingspan 4.5–5 cm.
Food: Quack grass and other grasses.
Range: Que. to N.C., west to Man., S.D., and Iowa. Late May–July. Common northward.
Similar species: (1) Airy Apamea, *A. vultuosa* (Grt.), not shown, has light yellow-orange FW, *no st. line or blackish terminal patches.* Food: Grasses. Range: Nfld. to N.J. and Pa., west across Canada, south to N.D. May–early Aug. Uncommon. (2) Common Apamea, *A. vulgaris* (Grt. & Rob.), not shown, has dull brown FW with *orange-yellow in lower and outer parts;* markings as in Wood-colored Apamea. Food: Probably grasses. Range: N.S. to Ky., west to Kans. May–July. Locally common.

YELLOW-HEADED CUTWORM MOTH   Pl. 24 (18)
Apamea amputatrix (Fitch)
Identification: *Median area of FW deep crimson.* Basal and st. areas greenish to whitish gray and warm brown. Note the 2 white dots at lower end of reniform spot. HW yellowish, grayish brown at margin. Melanic specimens deep iridescent chocolate brown. Wingspan 4.4–5 cm.
Food: Larva (**Yellow-headed Cutworm**) attacks cabbage, corn, currants, grasses, lettuce, roses, wheat, and young trees (often fruit trees).
Range: Lab. to N.C. mts., west across s. Canada, south to Mo. June–Aug. Common.

IGNORANT APAMEA   Pl. 25 (1)
Apamea indocilis (Wlk.)
Identification: FW pale brown to gray with darker median area; orbicular and reniform spots pale. Two black basal dashes—upper one Y-shaped, lower one straight; *broad black bar across lower median area.* Two small, rounded black marginal patches. HW grayish brown, darker at margin. Wingspan 3.2–4 cm.
Food: Grasses and sedges.
Range: Nfld. to N.C., west to Man., Minn., and Ky. June–July. Common northward.

BORDERED APAMEA *Apamea finitima* Gn.   **Pl. 25 (2)**
Identification: FW bluish gray to brown; median area darker brown except orbicular and reniform spots. *Black basal dash;* claviform spot a *black loop* extending outward from am. line. HW grayish brown, slightly darker at outer margin. Wingspan 3.5–3.7 cm.
Food: Corn, timothy, wheat, wild rice, and other grasses and sedges.
Range: Lab. to Va., west across Canada, south to Minn. May–July. Moderately common.

DOUBTFUL AGROPERINA   **Pl. 25 (3)**
Agroperina dubitans (Wlk.)
Identification: Thorax chocolate above, with pale middorsal line. FW chocolate; lines and spot outlines black, inconspicuous. St. line heaviest; terminal line a series of white dots. Reniform spot *partially filled with white.* HW grayish brown, darker at margin. Wingspan 4–4.2 cm.
Food: Grasses.
Range: Nfld. to Fla., west across Canada, south to Mo. July–Sept. Common.

YELLOW THREE-SPOT   **Pl. 24 (19)**
Agroperina helva (Grt.)
Identification: FW dull orangish yellow with broken gray lines and *3 gray patches:* at costa above reniform spot, in lower half of reniform spot, and near apex. HW grayish brown with dark dots along orangish yellow outer border. Wingspan 3.5–4.1 cm.
Food: Sod grasses.
Range: Que. to Md. and Ky., west through s. Canada, south to Kans. and Ark. Late July–Sept. Locally common.

GLASSY CUTWORM MOTH   **Pl. 25 (6)**
Crymodes devastator (Brace)
Identification: FW dark gray with variable dark brownish shading. Lines inconspicuous; st. line most prominent. Orbicular and reniform *spots incompletely outlined with white.* HW grayish brown, darker at outer margin; fringe white. Wingspan 3.6–4.1 cm.
Food: Larva (**Glassy Cutworm**) is a pest of sod grasses, grains, and many crops such as alfalfa, beans, cabbage, and tobacco.
Range: Lab. to Va., west through s. Canada, south to Mo. Late June–Sept. Common northward.

DOCK RUSTIC *Luperina passer* (Gn.)   **Pl. 25 (5)**
Identification: FW pale to dark brown, sometimes reddish brown. Spots black; *top of claviform spot thick* and conspicuous; orbicular spot outline thin; reniform spot heavier but broken. Lines inconspicuous, though pm. and terminal lines partially edged with black. HW pale grayish brown. Wingspan 3–4.1 cm.
Food: Dock; larva eats roots.
Range: Nfld. to Va., west across s. Canada, south to Neb. and Miss. May–July; Aug.–Sept.; 2 broods. Common.

BLACK-BANDED BROCADE   Pl. 24 (23)
Oligia modica (Gn.)
Identification: FW pale gray, sometimes bluish gray; warm brown shading in basal and st. areas. Sharp *black wedge* points downward from costa between orbicular and reniform spots, and *nearly touches blackish claviform blotch.* Brown blotch just beyond reniform spot. HW grayish brown. Wingspan 2.5–3.2 cm.
Food: Unrecorded.
Range: Nfld. to Ga., west to Man. and Miss. June–Sept. Common.
Similar species: Broken-lined Brocade, *O. fractilinea* (Grt.), not shown, is brown to blackish. Reniform spot mottled black and white, with *rounded white upper edge.* Black bar connects am. and pm. lines near inner margin. Food: Larva (Lined Stalk Borer) sometimes a pest on corn and timothy. Range: Me. and Que. to Fla., west to Ont., Minn., and Miss. July–Sept. Common.

BRIDGHAM'S BROCADE   Pl. 24 (21)
Oligia bridghami (Grt. & Rob.)
Identification: FW dark reddish with *violet-gray basal and st. areas.* Lines and spots whitish. HW white to gray with grayish brown shading beyond median line. Wingspan 2.8–3.1 cm.
Food: Unrecorded.
Range: N.S. to L.I., N.Y., and Pa., west to Ont., Mich., and Ohio. July–Aug. Uncommon.

WANDERING BROCADE   Pl. 25 (7)
Oligia illocata (Wlk.)
Identification: FW mottled grayish and warm brown. Small basal and broad median black dashes; median dash connects am. and pm. lines near inner margin. Lines variably edged with white. *Reniform spot large, white.* HW grayish brown with faint median line. Wingspan 3.6–4.2 cm.
Food: Alder, birch, and willow trees.
Range: N.S. to se. Ky., west through s. Canada, south to Mo. Aug.–Oct. Common; will come to sugar bait.

OBLONG SEDGE BORER MOTH   Pl. 25 (8)
Archanara oblonga (Grt.)
Identification: FW yellowish with grayish brown shading. Orbicular and reniform spots outlined with ground color. *Pm. line and terminal line* a series *of tiny black dots.* HW colored as FW, but grayish brown shading darker. Wingspan 3.5–5 cm.
Food: Cattails and bulrushes. Young larva a leaf miner, later a stem borer below water line, as in Cattail Borer Moth (p. 128, Pl. 28) and other *Archanara* species (below); considered semiaquatic.
Range: Locally common throughout our area. July–Sept. northward; a second brood Nov.–May in deep South.
Similar species: (1) Cattail Borer Moth (p. 128, Pl. 28) has similar larval habits; FW of moth brown with *tan along costa;* flight season is earlier (May–June northward). (2) Subflava Sedge Borer

Moth, *A. subflava* (Grt.), not shown, *lacks terminal dots.* Food: Bulrushes and rushes. Range: N.S. to N.J., west to Man., Minn., and Ill. July–Sept. (3) Red Sedge Borer Moth, *A. laeta* (Morr.), not shown, is more *reddish,* with *no pm. or terminal lines.* Food: Bur-reed. Range: Me. (?) and s. Que. to N.J., west to Wisc., Ill., and La. June–Sept. Local and rare.

IRIS BORER MOTH Pl. 25 (12)
Macronoctua onusta Grt.

Identification: Thorax blackish. FW dark brown with variable black shading. Lines and spots very thin, black; most conspicuous marking is dash-like *lower end of reniform spot.* HW grayish brown, darker toward margin. Wingspan 4–5.4 cm.

Food: Larva (**Iris Borer**) bores into corms and rhizomes of iris and sometimes gladiolus.

Range: N.S. to S.C., west to Minn., Mo., and Miss. Sept.–Oct.

VEILED EAR MOTH *Amphipoea velata* (Wlk.) Pl. 25 (9)
Identification: FW yellowish to reddish brown with variable darker brown shading, especially in median and st. areas. Lines double, inconspicuous; orbicular and reniform *spot outlines thin,* at least *partially whitish.* HW grayish brown with faint darker brown median line. Wingspan 3–3.5 cm.

Food: Grasses.

Range: Nfld. to S.C., west to Man. and e. Kans. June–Aug. Locally common.

AMERICAN EAR MOTH Pl. 26 (2)
Amphipoea americana (Speyer)

Identification: FW bright rusty orange, shaded with duller orangish brown; veins, lines, and spots darker brown. *Reniform spot filled with white or bright orange* (as shown). HW grayish brown with orange fringe. Wingspan 2.8–3.6 cm.

Food: Grasses and sedges; larva a minor pest on roots of corn.

Range: Nfld. to N.C., west to Man. and Minn. July–Aug. Common.

Similar species: Interoceanic Ear Moth, *A. interoceanica* (Sm.), not shown, is almost identical but usually smaller and more stout-bodied. Pale *filling of reniform spot confined to outer $\frac{2}{3}$ of spot.* Food and range as in American Ear Moth.

BUFFALO MOTH Pl. 26 (15)
Parapamea buffaloensis (Grt.)

Identification: FW dark reddish brown; basal and st. areas *shaded with violet. Am. and pm. lines double, purple;* basal, median, and st. lines single, brownish. Orbicular and reniform spots filled with either ground color (as shown) or white. HW light reddish brown. Wingspan 3–4.2 cm.

Food: Larva bores into roots of lizard's-tail.

Range: N.Y. to Fla., west to Wisc. and e. Tex. Sept. Common.

Genus *Papaipema*

The next 12 moths are *Papaipema* species. FW tends to be brightly marked, often with yellow or orange dominant. Larvae bore in roots, stems, and rhizomes of various herbaceous plants, and can be reared by collecting plants in late summer. Moths emerge in late summer to autumn. Nearly 40 species of this genus occur in our area. Some of the most widespread and easily identified species are described below.

BURDOCK BORER MOTH   Pl. 26 (11)
Papaipema cataphracta (Grt.)

Identification: FW yellow with brown and violet shading (as shown); yellow patch near apex. *Pm. line sharply bent* near costa. Orbicular, reniform, and claviform *spots yellow.* HW yellow with brownish shading and median line. Wingspan 2.9–4.5 cm.

Food: Asters, corn, *Eupatorium* species, burdocks, irises, lilies, sunflowers, tomato, and other plants.

Range: Me. and Que. to Fla., west to Minn. and La. Sept.–Oct. Common in North, but rare southward.

NORTHERN BURDOCK BORER MOTH   Pl. 26 (8)
Papaipema arctivorens Hamp.

Identification: FW light orange with *rusty red shading;* purplish beyond pm. line except for yellow st. line and apical patch. *Orbicular and claviform spots large, white;* reniform spot white, broken into several thin parts. HW yellowish with grayish brown to pinkish shading. Wingspan 2.7–3.9 cm.

Food: Larva bores into rhizomes of thistle, common burdock, teasel, and other plants.

Range: Que. to Va., west to Minn. and Mo. Aug.–Oct. Common.

BRACKEN BORER MOTH   Pl. 26 (4)
Papaipema pterisii Bird

Identification: FW orange with violet-brown shading in am. and st. areas and upper part of median area. Lines sharply defined. *Orbicular and claviform spots fused* to form a *vertical white bar;* reniform spot outlined with small white or yellow fragments. HW straw yellow with slight grayish brown shading. Wingspan 2.8–3.5 cm.

Food: Larva bores into rhizomes of bracken fern.

Range: Nfld. to N.J. and n. W. Va., west to Man. and Iowa. Aug.–Sept. Common northward.

CHAIN FERN BORER MOTH   Pl. 26 (12)
Papaipema stenocelis (Dyar)

Identification: FW orange, with some brown and violet shading. Brown median line slightly bent; pm. line double, rounded. *All 3 spots white, forming narrow vertical bars;* orbicular and claviform spots nearly fused. HW yellow with grayish brown veins and outer shading. Wingspan 3.5–4 cm.

Food: Rhizomes of Virginia chain fern.
Range: Mass. to n. Fla., west along Gulf Coast to La. Aug.–Sept. May be locally common.

OSMUNDA BORER MOTH   Pl. 26 (3)
Papaipema speciosissima (Grt. & Rob.)
Identification: Similar to Chain Fern Borer Moth (above) but larger; FW brighter orange. Median line sharply *bent at right angle;* pm. line more sharply curved than in Chain Fern Borer Moth. Spots white (as shown) or brown. HW orangish with slightly darker shading; median line visible. Wingspan 4.5–5 cm.
Food: Flowering ferns (*Osmunda* species).
Range: Me. to Fla. Keys along coast; through Great Lakes region to Mich. and Ind. inland. Sept.–Oct.
Similar species: Ash Tip Borer Moth, *P. furcata* Sm. (not shown), has *pale yellow FW* with brown lines and shading; median line widest. Spots white; orbicular and claviform *spots large, round, about equal in size,* with another *small spot between them;* reniform spot divided into 6–7 fragments. HW pale yellow with no shading. Wingspan 3.3–4.9 cm. Food: Larva bores into tips of ash tree twigs. Range: N.H. and s. Que. to Ky., west to Minn. and La. Late Aug.–Oct. Locally common.

SENSITIVE FERN BORER MOTH   Pl. 26 (5)
Papaipema inquaesita (Grt. & Rob.)
Identification: Best recognized by the *sharply angled median band.* FW orange, with dull orangish brown shading beyond pm. line except at apex. FW veins outlined with dark purplish brown; spots inconspicuous, orange or whitish. HW yellowish with grayish brown veins and shading. Wingspan 2.9–4 cm.
Food: Sensitive fern.
Range: N.S. to coastal S.C., west to s. Ont., Mo., and La. Sept.–Oct. northward. May be locally common.

PITCHER-PLANT BORER MOTH   Pl. 26 (1)
Papaipema appassionata (Harv.)
Identification: FW straw yellow, nearly *solid dull reddish* beyond pm. line. Orbicular and reniform *spots very large, white.* HW yellow; dull reddish toward outer margin. Wingspan 3–4.1 cm.
Food: Larva bores into stems and roots of pitcher-plants.
Range: N.S. to Fla. along coast; inland through Great Lakes region to Wisc. Found only in peat bogs where pitcher-plants grow. Aug.–Sept.

STALK BORER MOTH   Pl. 26 (7)
Papaipema nebris (Gn.)
Identification: Antennae white; body and wings dark brown. Thin, white pm. line curved slightly below FW costa. White dusting beyond pm. line makes st. area look gray. Look for *5–6 small white spots along costa* near apex. Orbicular, claviform, and

reniform spot groups vary in size and color; may be white (as shown) or blackish and inconspicuous. Wingspan 2.7–4.5 cm.

Food: Larva (**Stalk Borer**) bores into stems of corn and a wide variety of plants (over 129 plant species reported in Iowa alone). Larva a pest of corn and many garden plants.

Range: Throughout our area except Fla.; apparently uncommon in Canada, though common elsewhere. Sept.–Oct.

SUNFLOWER BORER MOTH   Pl. 26 (10)
Papaipema necopina (Grt.)

Identification: Similar to Stalk Borer Moth (above) but FW slightly darker brown and dusted with white scales all over. *No distinct lines or spots,* although white dusting may be slightly heavier in st. area (as shown). HW pale grayish brown, slightly darker at outer margin. Wingspan 3.6–4.5 cm.

Food: Sunflowers (*Helianthus* species).

Range: Conn. and N.Y. to W. Va., west to Minn. and Mo. Sept.–Oct. Common.

RIGID SUNFLOWER BORER MOTH   Pl. 26 (9)
Papaipema rigida (Grt.)

Identification: FW bright yellow with brownish shading beyond pm. line except near apex. *Am. line sharply bent at right angle;* pm. line nearly straight. HW pale yellowish with gray discal spot and outer border. Wingspan 2.5–3.5 cm.

Food: Mostly sunflowers (*Helianthus* species); also burdocks, golden alexander, ox-eye, and sneezeweed.

Range: N.B. to W.Va., west to Man. and Iowa. Sept.–Oct.

IRONWEED BORER MOTH   Pl. 26 (6)
Papaipema cerussata (Grt.)

Identification: Large and stout-bodied. FW violet with dark rust patches in lower median area and near apex. Basal, orbicular, claviform, and reniform spots represented by groups of white spots; note *small white spot on costa* above reniform spot. HW dark grayish brown. Wingspan 4–5.5 cm.

Food: Ironweed.

Range: Mass. to Va., west to Iowa and Miss. Sept.–Nov. Common.

ROSY RUSTIC *Hydraecia micacea* (Esper)   Pl. 24 (16)

Identification: FW pale brown with dark olive brown shading in lower median and terminal areas. *Pm. line* curved at costa, otherwise *straight;* st. line wavy, whitish. HW pale shiny brown with diffuse gray discal spot and median line. Wingspan 3.2–4 cm.

Food: Larva (**Potato Stem Borer**) bores in stems of corn, potato, tomato, and many other plants. A minor pest.

Range: Introduced from Europe; sometimes common from N.S. to Mass., west to Ont. Mid–July to Sept.

Similar species: Hop Vine Borer Moth, *H. immanis* Gn. (not shown), is larger (wingspan 4–5.5 cm); FW more pinkish brown.

Pm. line bent above middle; *st. line double.* All lines edged with dark brown. Food: Larva (Hop Vine Borer) is a pest of cultivated hop plants. Range: Restricted to hop-growing areas from Me. and Que. to Va. and westward. Aug.–Sept.

ELDER SHOOT BORER MOTH　　　　　Pl. 27 (11)
Achatodes zeae (Harr.)
Identification: FW crimson with ash gray shading and bright *orange apical patch.* Look for 3 small white dots along costa near apex. HW grayish brown. Wingspan 2.5–3.5 cm.
Food: Larva (**Elder Shoot Borer**) bores into new growth of elderberries; also alders, corn, dahlias, and wheat.
Range: Common throughout our area. May–Aug.; earlier in South.

WHITE-TAILED DIVER　　　　　Pl. 28 (14)
Bellura gortynoides Wlk.
Identification: FW very long, narrow, orange-yellow. Lines and spots diffuse, brownish. Am. and median lines nearly straight: pm. line jagged, curved below costa. *Brownish blotches* near apex and anal angle. HW yellow with vague darker shading. Anal tuft brown in spring females, white in summer females. Wingspan 3.8–4.2 cm.
Food: Cattails, pickerelweed, and water-lilies. Eggs are laid on leaves above water surface. Larvae are leaf miners in first 3 instars, then become borers in leaf stems. Larvae swim to shore and overwinter in litter, then pupate in late spring; 2nd generation larvae pupate in larval tunnels (reported from Indiana).
Range: N.S. to Fla., west to Mich., Ill., and Ky. May–Sept.; 2 broods. Locally common.

CATTAIL BORER MOTH　　　　　Pl. 28 (18)
Bellura obliqua (Wlk.)
Identification: FW brown with tan to grayish white along costa and in basal area. *Reniform spot long, oblique,* with white edging at base. HW grayish brown with reddish tint. Wingspan 4–5.5 cm.
Food: American lotus, arrowheads, bur-reed, cattails, pickerelweed, and skunk cabbage. First-instar larva mines in leaf; later instars bore into crowns. Larva overwinters; pupates in spring.
Range: N.S. to s. Fla., west to Minn. and Tex. April–Aug.; mostly May. Locally common.

PICKERELWEED BORER MOTH　　　　　Pl. 28 (20)
Bellura densa (Wlk.)
Identification: Similar to Cattail Borer Moth (above), but narrow, oblique *reniform spot partly filled with orange.* Wings reddish brown with pinkish highlights. Lines and median shade darker than ground color. Wingspan 3.5–5 cm.
Food: Cattails, pickerelweed, and water hyacinth.

Range: Wash., D.C. to s. Fla., west to Ind., Mo., and La. June–Aug.; 2 broods southward. Locally common.

AMERICAN ANGLE SHADES Pl. 26 (22)
Euplexia benesimilis McD.
Identification: FW angled; brown, with blackish brown shading in basal and median areas. Lines black, inconspicuous; wide, light brown band beyond pm. line. Reniform spot *white with yellowish filling* in middle, brown at top and bottom. HW grayish brown with darker median line and shading beyond it. Wingspan 2.8–3.6 cm.
Food: A wide variety of plants, including alders, asters, ferns, huckleberries, sunflowers, trilliums, and willows.
Range: Nfld. to N.C., west through s. Canada, south to n. Ark. May–Aug.; 2 broods. Common.

OLIVE ANGLE SHADES Pl. 26 (13)
Phlogophora iris Gn.
Identification: FW strongly angled, with a *deeply scalloped outer margin.* Wings pale yellowish; FW shaded with olive green (fading to greenish yellow with age), brown, and reddish. Lines distinct only in outer half of FW. Note *black edging just outside* reniform spot, broken by pale wing veins. Diffuse brown and reddish bands at outer margin of HW. Wingspan 4–4.5 cm.
Food: Herbaceous plants, such as dandelion, dock, and thistle.
Range: Nfld. to N.J. and Pa., west to Man., Minn., and Ill. May–July. Common northward.

BROWN ANGLE SHADES Pl. 25 (10)
Phlogophora periculosa Gn.
Identification: Outer margin of FW less deeply scalloped than in the Olive Angle Shades (above). FW brown, sometimes slightly shaded with olive green and darker brown. Note the Y-*shaped median patch* (one branch covers reniform spot), which may be blackish brown or only slightly darker than ground color (as shown). HW brown with 3 slightly darker, diffuse lines. Wingspan 4.2–5 cm.
Food: Alders, balsam fir, cranberries, plums, and other plants.
Range: Lab. to S.C., west through Canada, south to Ark. and Miss. Aug.-Oct. Locally common.

EVEN-LINED SALLOW Pl. 25 (11)
Ipimorpha pleonectusa Grt.
Identification: Wings brownish, orangish, or mouse gray, with darker blotches and spots. Am. and pm. *lines straight, even; am. line oblique.* HW paler than FW. Wingspan 3–3.5 cm.
Food: Aspen.
Range: N.S. to e. Ky., west to Man. and e. Mo. July–Aug. Uncommon.

CLOAKED MARVEL   Pl. 25 (14, 17)
Chytonix palliatricula (Gn.)

Identification: FW pale brown with distinct markings, or blackish brown with obscure lines and spots; basal area and lower median area blackish. Typical specimens have a *large white patch* in median area of FW; most others (form "iaspis" Gn.) have only a *short white streak or spot* in lower median area. HW dark grayish brown. Wingspan 2.8–3.3 cm.

Food: Unrecorded; probably grasses.

Range: Common throughout our area. June–Aug.

AMERICAN BIRD'S-WING MOTH   Pl. 25 (16)
Dipterygia rozmani Berio

Identification: Easily recognized by the distinctive *whitish marking near anal angle* of FW, resembling a bird in flight. Whitish area extends along inner margin; rest of FW dark brown with fine black lines. HW grayish brown, paler than FW. Wingspan 3.4–3.9 cm.

Food: Reported on dock and smartweed, but these records may be for the closely related European species, *D. scabriuscula* (L.), now considered a different species.

Range: N.S. to Fla., west to Man., Ark. and Miss. May–Sept.; 2 broods. Uncommon.

COMMON HYPPA *Hyppa xylinoides* (Gn.)   Pl. 25 (15)
Identification: Antennae bipectinate with broad branches in ♂, simple in ♀ (shown). FW gray; am. and pm. lines black, edged with white toward inner margin. Note *black basal and median dashes;* brown shading just above median dash. HW grayish brown. Wingspan 3.3–4.2 cm.

Food: Alders, clover, cranberries, roses, and many other plants.

Range: N.S. to N.C., west to Man. and Minn. May–Sept.; 2 broods. Locally common northward.

GRAY HALF-SPOT *Nedra ramosula* (Gn.)   Pl. 25 (22)
Identification: FW streaked with black, brown, gray and white; usual transverse lines absent. Lower half of reniform spot *outlined in white,* with brown shading around it. HW grayish brown. Wingspan 2.8–4.8 cm.

Food: St. Johnswort.

Range: Common throughout our area. April–Oct.; 2 broods.

Similar species: In Bicolored Woodgrain (p. 108, Pl. 22), *lower half* of FW is *solid brown* except for a *white anal dash;* lower side of reniform spot *elongate* (orbicular and reniform spots merged).

TURBULENT PHOSPHILA   Pl. 25 (13)
Phosphila turbulenta Hbn.

Identification: FW mottled dark brown with *thick black dashes* in st. area, near apex and anal angle. Zigzag pm. line double, filled

with pale brown. Reniform spot pale brown. HW grayish brown with diffuse median line and sharp terminal line. Wingspan 2.3–3.7 cm.
Food: Greenbriar.
Range: S. Me. to Fla., west to Ill. and Tex. May–July and Aug.–Sept.; 2 broods. Common.

SPOTTED PHOSPHILA   Pl. 26 (18)
Phosphila miselioides (Gn.)
Identification: FW olive green to brown with obscure black lines and mottling; ground color yellowish green in faded specimens. *Reniform spot white* (as shown) in lightly marked specimens, *filled with brown* in darker moths. HW grayish brown. Wingspan 3–3.8 cm.
Food: Common greenbriar.
Range: S. Me. to Fla., west to Man. and Tex. April–Aug.; probably 2 broods. Common.

PINK-SHADED FERN MOTH   Pl. 26 (21)
Callopistria mollissima (Gn.)
Identification: FW warm yellowish to reddish brown with broken dark brown lines; *pink shading* inside am. line and beyond pm. line. Note *silvery white outline around most of reniform spot.* St. line yellowish. HW grayish brown. Wingspan 2.1–2.7 cm.
Food: Ferns.
Range: N.S. to cen. Fla., west to Mich., Mo., Ark., and Miss. April–June. Moderately common.
Similar species: Granitose Fern Moth, *C. granitosa* (Gn.), not shown, is duller brown with *no pink shading on FW;* am. and pm. lines double, filled with *silvery white.* Food: Ferns (?). Range: N.J. to Fla. July–Sept.; as early as March in Fla.

SILVER-SPOTTED FERN MOTH   Pl. 26 (14)
Callopistria cordata (Ljungh)
Identification: FW warm brown with *large silver spots* and *silver am. and pm. lines.* HW white to pale grayish brown in northern specimens (shown); dark brown in South. Wingspan 2.5–2.8 cm.
Food: Ferns.
Range: N.S. to cen. Fla., west to Wisc. and Tex. June–early Aug.; as early as March in deep South. Moderately common.

CHOCOLATE MOTH *Acherdoa ferraria* Wlk.   Pl. 29 (2)
Identification: Antennae broadly bipectinate in ♂, simple in ♀. FW chocolate to reddish brown with purplish gray in terminal area. *Lower am. and pm. lines white;* most of *reniform spot edged with white.* HW brownish black. Wingspan 2.1–2.7 cm.
Food: Unrecorded.
Range: N.C. to s. Fla., west to Miss. March–Sept.; all months in s. Fla.

ORBED NARROW-WING   Pl. 28 (11)
Magusa orbifera (Wlk.)

Identification: Note the unusually *long, narrow FW,* which is blackish brown with inconspicuous lines. Some have broad *white border* along inner margin. Rounded *white apical patch* ("orb") not always present, but outline of "orb" visible even in dark form. HW blackish with white fringe. Wingspan 3.2–4.5 cm.

Food: Black ironweed and coyotilla (*Karwinskia humboldtiana*).
Range: Tropical; regularly occurs from Fla. to Tex. in our area, strays north to Me., s. Ont., and Wisc. Aug.–Nov. northward; all year in extreme s. Fla. and Tex. Locally common.

COPPER UNDERWING   Pl. 26 (17)
Amphipyra pyramidoides Gn.

Identification: Easily recognized by the *coppery red HW.* FW pattern varies; pm. line and orbicular spot usually accented with white. Wingspan 3.8–5.2 cm.

Food: Trees and shrubs, including apple, grape, hawthorn, oaks, poplars, raspberry plants, redbud, rhododendrons, and walnuts.
Range: Common throughout our area. July–Nov.

Similar species: The true underwings (*Catocala* species, p. 172) are usually larger, and have either all-black or banded hind wings.

MIRANDA MOTH *Proxenus miranda* (Grt.)   Pl. 27 (19)
Identification: Wings shiny. FW grayish brown with no conspicuous markings except *small reniform spot,* which is *yellowish with black edging.* HW off-white, with grayish brown shading near outer margin. Wingspan 2.3–2.7 cm.

Food: Larvae have been found under matted alfalfa; they have also been reared on dandelion.
Range: N.S. and n. Ont. to S.C., west to N.D. and Tex. May–June and July–Sept.; 2 broods. Common.

THE SLOWPOKE *Anorthodes tarda* (Gn.)   Pl. 27 (5)
Identification: FW variably dark grayish brown; lines darker but usually inconspicuous. *St. line wavy,* with *pale tan to yellowish edging;* spots inconspicuous, blackish. HW paler than FW. Wingspan 2.3–3.5 cm.

Food: Known to eat dead oak leaves.
Range: N.H. to Fla., west to Mo. and Tex. April–Sept.; 2 or more broods. Often abundant.

SPECKLED RUSTIC   Pl. 28 (1)
Platyperigea multifera (Wlk.)

Identification: FW pale gray; lines blackish—series of dots or zigzagged. Note the solid *black orbicular dot,* which *contrasts sharply with the plain ground color* in that part of the median area. Reniform spot black; st. line edged with reddish brown. HW pale gray, with darker border and discal spot. Wingspan 3–3.2 cm.

Food: Unrecorded.

Range: Nfld. to Wash., D.C., west to Man. and Minn. Aug.–Oct.

VERBENA MOTH   Pl. 28 (2)
Crambodes talidiformis Gn.

Identification: FW long and narrow; yellowish tan with dark brown shading and black streaks, including 2 thicker subapical streaks. Lines obscure; *reniform spot small, filled with white.* HW dirty white, shaded with pale grayish brown. Wingspan 2.5–3.3 cm.

Food: Verbena.

Range: Me. and Que. to N.C., west to Minn., Kans. and Tex. May–Oct.; at least 2 broods.

MANY-DOTTED APPLEWORM MOTH   Pl. 28 (3)
Balsa malana (Fitch)

Identification: FW dark gray, paler along costa. Lines very thin, black; am. and pm. lines broader at costa. *Pm. line double* at costa, forming a *broken* Y. HW dirty whitish in ♂; grayish brown in ♀. Wingspan 2.4–3.1 cm.

Food: Larva (**Many-dotted Appleworm**) feeds on leaves of apple, cherry, elm, pear, and plum trees. Not a serious pest.

Range: N.S. to n. Fla., west to Man., Kans., and Miss. April–Sept. Common.

THREE-LINED BALSA   Pl. 28 (4)
Balsa tristrigella (Wlk.)

Identification: Similar to Many-dotted Appleworm Moth (above) but smaller. FW covered with *fine black streaks;* ground color *not* noticeably paler along costa. Most distinct markings are *tops of am. and pm. lines;* pm. line double. HW grayish brown. Wingspan 2–2.4 cm.

Food: Hawthorns.

Range: Me. and s. Que. to N.C., west to Wisc. and Tex. April–June; late July–Aug.; 2 broods. Common.

WHITE-BLOTCHED BALSA   Pl. 28 (6)
Balsa labecula (Grt.)

Identification: Similar to the other 2 *Balsa* species (above), but FW paler gray, with a distinct *greenish white patch* in upper median area. Pm. line double at costa; inner branch *much longer* than in other 2 species. HW pale grayish brown. Wingspan 2.4–3 cm.

Food: Unrecorded.

Range: Me. and Que. to n. Fla., west to Man. and Tex. April–July. Common.

BEET ARMYWORM MOTH   Pl. 28 (15)
Spodoptera exigua (Hbn.)

Identification: FW gray with inconspicuous gray or white markings. Note *round, white orbicular spot* with *gray dot* in center. HW translucent white with gray veins and shading at outer margin. Wingspan 2.5–2.9 cm.

Food: Larva (**Beet Armyworm**) is a pest on many plants, including apple, beans, beets, corn, lettuce, peas, potato, and tomato. **Range:** Me. to Fla., west to Neb. and Tex. Sept.–Oct. northward; adults emerge during any warm period in deep South, where this moth is most common and destructive.

FALL ARMYWORM MOTH   Pl. 28 (9, 12)
Spodoptera frugiperda (J.E. Sm.)
Identification: Sexually dimorphic—in ♀ FW usually plain gray with brown shading and obscure lines and spots; in ♂ FW brown, with an *oblique yellowish line* near the orbicular spot that *does not extend beyond vein Cu.* Male also has a vague whitish mark below reniform spot. *Orbicular spot oblique, elliptical* (not circular) in both sexes. Wingspan 2.5–4 cm.
Food: Larva (**Fall Armyworm**) feeds on a wide variety of plants—often a serious pest on alfalfa, clover, corn, cotton, grains, sorghum, tobacco, and many vegetables. Like other armyworms, this caterpillar is named for its habit of migrating en masse to seek fresh food supplies after denuding crop fields.
Range: Throughout our area; increasingly abundant southward. July–Oct.; 1 brood at northern limits of range, up to 10 broods in deep South.
Similar species: (1) Beet Armyworm Moth (above) is similar to the ♀ Fall Armyworm Moth, but orbicular spot is *circular,* not oblique and elliptical. (2) The Yellow-striped Armyworm Moth (below) resembles the ♂ Fall Armyworm Moth, but oblique yellowish line *extends beyond vein Cu,* nearly to pm. line; white marking below reniform spot forms a *distinct* Y.

YELLOW-STRIPED ARMYWORM MOTH   Pl. 28 (7)
Spodoptera ornithogalli (Gn.)
Identification: FW brown with bluish gray shading inside am. line and near apex and anal angle. *Oblique yellowish shade line* extends from costa across orbicular spot and beyond vein Cu, *almost to pm. line.* White mark below reniform spot *forks* to form a *sideways* Y. Lower median area dark gray or orange-yellow (form "flavimedia" Cram., shown). HW translucent white with blackish veins and terminal line. Wingspan 3.2–4.4 cm.
Food: Larva (**Yellow-striped Armyworm,** also known as **Cotton Cutworm**) feeds on many low plants; often a pest on cotton and other crops, including clover, grasses, potato, and tobacco.
Range: This moth is found throughout our area, but does not overwinter north of L.I. April–Nov.; many broods. Common to abundant southward.

DOLICHOS ARMYWORM MOTH   Pl. 28 (5)
Spodoptera dolichos (F.)
Identification: Similar to Yellow-striped Armyworm Moth (above) but *larger;* easily recognized by the *2 black stripes on the thorax.* FW brown and grayish. White dash extends outward from

top of reniform spot. HW translucent white; only top 2 veins are blackish. Wingspan 3.8–4.6 cm.

Food: Wide variety of plants, including clover, corn, cotton, grasses, hickories, strawberry and tobacco plants, and violets.

Range: Tropical; established in Gulf states, and straying as far north as Me. and Wisc. Aug.–Sept. northward; all months in s. Fla. and Tex. Common southward.

SOUTHERN ARMYWORM MOTH   Pl. 28 (8)
Spodoptera eridania (Cram.)

Identification: FW yellowish brown with very fine black streaks; st. lines a series of black dots. Other markings obscure except *black reniform spot*, which varies from small and fine (as shown) to large and blotchy. Broad black bar (not shown) sometimes extends from reniform spot to outer margin; note thin black basal dash almost at inner margin. HW translucent white with only a trace of a blackish terminal line. Wingspan 2.9–3.4 cm.

Food: Larva (**Southern Armyworm**) seems to prefer careless weed and pokeweed but also attacks a wide variety of crops, including celery, citrus fruit, corn, potato, tobacco, and tomato plants.

Range: Common in Gulf states, straggling north to N.H., Ky., and Mo. Aug.–Oct. northward; all year in Fla.

Nine midgets (*Elaphria* species) occur within our area; the 4 most common ones are described below.

VARIEGATED MIDGET   Pl. 27 (9)
Elaphria versicolor (Grt.)

Identification: FW brown with orange apical patch; median area dark brown except for *thin white edging beyond pm. line* (broader near costa). HW grayish brown. Wingspan 2.2–2.5 cm.

Food: Firs, pines, and spruces.

Range: Throughout our area. April–July. Locally common.

CHALCEDONY MIDGET   Pl. 27 (6)
Elaphria chalcedonia (Hbn.)

Identification: Similar to Variegated Midget (above) but basal and upper median areas *orange-yellow to orangish tan; broad white edging* along entire pm. line. *HW white* with variable grayish brown outer shading. Wingspan 2.4–2.8 cm.

Food: Beardtongue, figwort, monkey-flower, and other members of the snapdragon family.

Range: Me. to Fla., west to Wisc. and Tex. June–Sept. northward; all months in Fla. Common southward.

FESTIVE MIDGET *Elaphria festivoides* (Gn.)   Pl. 27 (7)
Identification: Easily recognized by the distinct *whitish reniform spot*, which interrupts a *broad black dash* in median area of FW. Lower pm. line also whitish. Rest of FW brown—lighter brown with gray mottling near base and along costa, darker

beyond pm. line. HW pale to dark grayish brown. Wingspan 2.1–2.8 cm.

Food: Larva has been reared on Manitoba maple (*Acer negundo*).
Range: Common throughout our area. April–July.

GRATEFUL MIDGET *Elaphria grata* Hbn. **Pl. 27 (24)**
Identification: FW uniform brick red to reddish brown. Lines and spots dull whitish; note the *dark gray dots* in top and bottom of reniform spot and in center of orbicular spot. HW dirty white with variable grayish brown shading. Wingspan 2–2.6 cm.
Food: Clover, oaks, violets; also reported eating dead leaves.
Range: S. Me. and Que. to cen. Fla., west to Wisc. and Tex. April–Oct.; several broods. Common southward.

THE WEDGLING *Galgula partita* Gn. **Pl. 27 (13, 14)**
Identification: Sexes differ in color, but both have a large, *dark spot on costa* and *angled pm. and st. lines*. FW reddish brown to grayish in ♂; shiny dark brownish maroon to blackish in ♀ (markings hardly visible in ♀). HW grayish brown, darker in ♀ than in ♂. Wingspan 2–2.6 cm.
Food: Reported feeding on 2 species of wood-sorrels in Tex.
Range: Common to abundant throughout our area. March–Oct.; several broods.

RED GROUNDLING *Perigea xanthioides* Gn. **Pl. 27 (1)**
Identification: FW mottled brick red and yellow or orange. Note *black dot in bottom of yellow reniform spot* and gray dash extending beneath orbicular and reniform spots. St. line and terminal area gray. HW yellowish, mostly overlaid with grayish brown; orangish at outer margin. Wingspan 2.7–3.2 cm.
Food: Ironweed and sweet joe-pye-weed.
Range: Mass. to Fla., west to S.D. and Tex. May–Sept. Common southward, but uncommon to rare in Northeast.

WHITE-DOTTED GROUNDLING **Pl. 25 (21)**
Platysenta videns (Gn.)
Identification: Wings shiny. FW orange-yellow to reddish brown; *black shade line extends* from base *through white reniform spot.* Pm. line a series of black dots; terminal area and FW fringe black. HW whitish with grayish brown shading at outer margin. Wingspan 2.3–3.5 cm.
Food: Larva has been reported feeding on blossoms of asters, goldenrod, and other composites.
Range: Me. and Que. to Fla., west to Man. and Tex. May–Sept. Common to uncommon.

MOBILE GROUNDLING **Pl. 27 (3)**
Platysenta mobilis (Wlk.)
Identification: FW orangish to reddish brown, with dull brownish lines and mottling. Same FW pattern as in Red Groundling (above, Pl. 27), but duller. Note *prominent white bottom of reni-*

form spot. HW whitish with grayish brown border. Wingspan 2.7–3.4 cm.
Food: Spanish needles.
Range: N.J. to Fla., west to Mo. and Tex. Aug.–Oct.; all months in s. Fla. Common to abundant southward.

DUSKY GROUNDLING   Pl. 27 (2)
Platysenta vecors (Gn.)
Identification: FW mottled dark brown and black. No strong pattern; whitish dots represent am. and terminal lines. Claviform spot solid black; *lower half of reniform spot white.* HW dark grayish brown with whitish fringe. Wingspan 2.9–3.8 cm.
Food: Larva collected in Fla. on lettuce.
Range: Throughout our area. April–Oct. Common southward.

THE COBBLER *Platysenta sutor* (Gn.)   Pl. 27 (4)
Identification: FW brown, shiny, with vague, broken pattern. Pm. line a double series of dark dots followed by a series of white dots; terminal line a series of white dots. *Reniform spot outline whitish,* inconspicuous; look for a small *black median dash* interrupted by lower end of spot. Claviform spot small, black. HW grayish brown; darker toward outer margin. Wingspan 2.9–3.8 cm.
Food: Celery, marigolds, and *Wedelia trilobata* (Fla.).
Range: Lab. to Fla., west to Wisc., Kans., and Tex. May–Nov. Common southward, especially in autumn.

THE CONFEDERATE   Pl. 25 (18)
Condica confederata (Grt.)
Identification: FW pearly to reddish gray with *black basal patch* and *broad claviform spot.* Note pale median area and *2 large pale patches* at outer margin in ♂, most of the rest of FW shaded with dark reddish gray. Dark shading much more extensive in ♀ (not shown), with only am. line, border of inner margin, outlines of orbicular and reniform spots, and 2 patches at outer margin pale. HW grayish brown, darker in ♀ than in ♂. Wingspan 3.2–4 cm.
Food: Spanish needles.
Range: Me. to Fla., west to Wisc. and Tex. Aug.–Oct. northward; all months in Fla. Uncommon northward.

COMMON PINKBAND   Pl. 27 (20)
Ogdoconta cinereola (Gn.)
Identification: FW grayish brown, with a *wide, pale pink band* between pm. and st. lines; some specimens also have some pink in lower basal area. Other markings thin, whitish, inconspicuous. HW grayish brown. Wingspan 2–2.3 cm.
Food: Artichokes, beans, ragweed, and sunflowers.
Range: Common throughout our area. April–Oct.; several broods.

OBTUSE YELLOW *Stiriodes obtusa* (H.-S.)   Pl. 27 (17)
Identification: FW light yellow with *3 large violet-brown costal spots*, and usually 2 small ones. Am., median, and st. lines often

heavier and more complete than in specimen shown. HW paler yellow with 1–3 slightly darker lines. Wingspan 1.8–2.5 cm.
Food: Unrecorded.
Range: N.Y. to Fla., west to Mo. and Tex. June–Aug. Common.

FROTHY MOTH *Stibadium spumosum* Grt.   **Pl. 28 (16)**
Identification: FW brown with white dusting ("froth") and prominent whitish pm. line. Note *abrupt bend in pm. line* below costa. Other lines and spots obscure. HW whitish with grayish brown shading near outer margin. Wingspan 2.8–3.8 cm.
Food: Sunflowers. Larva tunnels in flower head and eats the seeds; sometimes a pest of commercial sunflower crops.
Range: N.J. to Fla., west to Minn., Kans., and Tex. Aug. Common only in Midwest and farther west.
Similar species: In Stalk Borer Moth (p. 126, Pl. 26), FW is same color but *lacks* prominent *pm. line.*

BLACK-BARRED BROWN   **Pl. 28 (13)**
Plagiomimicus pityochromus Grt.
Identification: FW dark gray to brown with sharp, *small black bar* formed from merged orbicular and claviform spots, and dark brown *triangle at apex.* Am. and pm. lines whitish; pm. line abruptly curved below triangle. Reniform spot variably filled with dark gray to brown. HW grayish brown. Wingspan 2.5–3.5 cm.
Food: Giant ragweed.
Range: N.Y. to Fla., west to Minn., Kans., and Tex. Aug.–Sept. Uncommon; rare in Northeast.

GOLDENROD STOWAWAY   **Pl. 27 (8)**
Cirrhophanus triangulifer Grt.
Identification: Body and wings *bright, shiny yellow; FW streaked with orange*; pm. line broadly curved. HW may have slight grayish brown shading. Wingspan 3–4.4 cm.
Food: Spanish needles.
Range: N.Y. to n. Fla., west to Kans. and Tex. Late Aug.–Sept. Adults are often found during the day on yellow flowers such as goldenrods, where they are well concealed.

GOLD MOTH *Basilodes pepita* Gn.   **Pl. 27 (18)**
Identification: *FW pale metallic gold*, with thin brownish lines and spots. Note black dot in reniform spot. Brownish shading in basal area and along outer margin. HW grayish brown. Wingspan 3.5–4.5 cm.
Food: Crown-beard (*Verbesina* species).
Range: N.Y. to Fla., west to Ill., Kans. and Tex. July–early Sept. Moderately common.

FEEBLE GRASS MOTH *Amolita fessa* Grt.   **Pl. 27 (16)**
Identification: FW pointed, tan. Note the *2 brown or grayish brown lines*, one extending from base to apex, the other from inner margin to outer margin. Orbicular and reniform spots represented

by tiny black dots. HW shiny, whitish. Wingspan 2.3–3.2 cm.
Food: Grasses.
Range: N.S. to Fla., west to Wisc. and Tex. April–Sept. Locally common southward.

AMERICAN DUN-BAR   Pl. 27 (21)
Cosmia calami (Harv.)
Identification: FW yellowish. Am. and pm. lines distinct; *am. line nearly straight, oblique; pm. line bent.* FW sometimes heavily mottled with brown, and sometimes has dark brown basal dot and dots in orbicular and reniform spots (as shown). HW pale yellowish cream, slightly darker at outer margin. Wingspan 2.5–3.4 cm.
Food: Oaks (live, red, and white); larva also preys on other caterpillars.
Range: N.S. to n. Fla., west to Man. and Tex. May–Aug. Locally common.

Subfamily Agaristinae

The next 2 moths roll up their wings when at rest, creating a pattern of white and dark that resembles bird droppings. Some of the white and dark moths in subfamily Acontiinae (Pl. 30) also do this.

PEARLY WOOD-NYMPH   Pl. 27 (25)
Eudryas unio (Hbn.)
Identification: Note the *scalloped outer edge of white area* on FW. HW yellow with a broad, even brown border from apex to anal angle. Wingspan 2.6–3.5 cm.
Food: Evening-primrose, grapes, hibiscus, and willow-herbs.
Range: Me. and s. Ont. to Fla., west to Minn. and Tex. June–Aug.; later southward. Common.

BEAUTIFUL WOOD-NYMPH   Pl. 27 (23)
Eudryas grata (F.)
Identification: Larger than Pearly Wood-nymph (above). Edge between white area on FW and brown terminal band *not scalloped.* Brown border of HW does not reach apex. Wingspan 3.5–4.6 cm.
Food: Ampelopsis, buttonbush, grapes, hops, and Virginia creeper.
Range: N.S. to Fla., west through s. Ont. to Minn., south to Tex. May–Aug.; 2 broods in South. Common.

GRAPEVINE EPIMENIS   Pl. 29 (1)
Psychomorpha epimenis (Dru.)
Identification: Body and wings black; note large *white patch on FW* and *red patch on HW.* FW has inconspicuous metallic shading. Wingspan 2.2–2.7 cm.
Food: Grapes.
Range: Mass. to n. Fla., west to Iowa and Tex. Late March–early May. A woodland day-flier, often mistaken for a butterfly.

Similar species: In Florida Psychomorpha, *P. euryrhoda* Hamp. (not shown), *red patch* on HW *extends almost to base.* Food: Unrecorded; probably grapes. Range: Peninsular Fla.; Feb.–April.

EIGHT-SPOTTED FORESTER   Pl. 15 (16)
Alypia octomaculata (F.)

Identification: FW black with *2 pale yellow spots* and inconspicuous metallic blue bands. HW black with *white spots* in basal and median areas. Body black except for pale yellow tegulae and orange on front and middle legs. Wingspan 3–3.7 cm.

Food: Grapes and Virginia creeper; sometimes a pest.

Range: Me. and s. Que. to Fla., west to S.D. and Tex. April–June northward; 2nd Aug. brood in South. A common day-flier.

Similar species: (1) Langton's Forester, *A. langtoni* Couper (not shown), is smaller. FW spots smaller, separated by *more than their width* in ♂ (but not in ♀). Only *1 HW spot* in ♀. Food: Willowherbs. Range: Nfld. to Me., west to Man. and Mich. June–Aug. (2) MacCulloch's Forester, *Androloma maccullochii* (Kby.), not shown, has *3 yellow spots on FW;* all spots interrupted by *black veins.* Food: Fireweed and other willow-herbs. Range: Lab., Que., and westward in Canada. May–Aug.

WITTFELD'S FORESTER   Pl. 15 (14)
Alypia wittfeldii Hy. Edw.

Identification: Similar to Eight-spotted Forester (above), but note *dorsal yellow spots* or bands on some abdominal segments. Inner yellow spot on FW *narrower,* and more like a crossband. Wingspan 2.5–3.5 cm.

Food: Japanese persimmon.

Range: Peninsular Fla. Jan–May. Apparently uncommon.

Subfamily Heliothinae

PINK STAR MOTH *Derrima stellata* Wlk.   **Pl. 27 (15)**

Identification: Easily identified by the dull yellow FW with *pink border along costa and outer margin;* pm. line and orbicular and reniform spots white. HW dull yellowish with dull pink outer border (HW pale brown with a pink outer border in northern specimens). Wingspan 2.4–3 cm.

Food: Unrecorded.

Range: S. Me. to Fla., west to Mo. and Tex. April–May and July–Aug.; 2 broods. Rare northward and uncommon in South.

BORDERED SALLOW *Pyrrhia umbra* (Hufn.)   **Pl. 27 (12)**

Identification: FW rusty orange with dull reddish to grayish brown lines, spot outlines, and veins. *St. area and reniform spot* variably shaded with *purplish red.* HW shiny yellow with purplish red shading. Wingspan 3.2–4 cm.

Food: Alders, cabbage, roses, sumacs, walnuts, and other plants. Larva may eat flowers and fruits as well as foliage.

Range: Nfld. to S.C., west to Man. and Tex. May–Oct. Common.
Similar species: Purple-lined Sallow, *P. exprimens* (Wlk.), not shown, has a dark purple pm. line, and *purplish shading* over all of FW *beyond sharply bent median line.* Border of HW purplish black. Food: *Polygonum* species and sweetfern. Range: Nfld. to N.C., west to Man. and Tex. June–July. Uncommon.

ORANGE SALLOW   Pl. 27 (22)
Rhodoecia aurantiago (Gn.)
Identification: Wings dark orange. *Basal and st. areas* and spots of FW and shading of HW vary from *pale to very dark purple.* Note jagged, blackish pm. and st. lines. Wingspan 2.5–3.3 cm.
Food: Larva bores into seedpods of gerardia and mullein-foxglove.
Range: Me. and s. Ont. to Fla., west to Wisc. and Tex. July–Sept. northward; Aug.-Oct. in Fla. Uncommon northward.

CORN EARWORM MOTH   Pl. 29 (14)
Heliothis zea (Boddie)
Identification: FW yellowish tan with variable reddish brown, olive green, or gray markings and shading (heaviest between pm. and st. lines). Reniform spot usually filled with dark gray. HW whitish with dark gray veins and border, which surrounds *whitish patch at midpoint of outer margin.* Wingspan 3.2–4.5 cm.
Food: Larva (**Corn Earworm,** also known as **Bollworm** and **Tomato Fruitworm**) feeds on a wide variety of plants, and is a major pest of corn, cotton, tomato, and tobacco. This is the caterpillar that feeds on the outer end of the ear beneath the husk. It is known to be cannibalistic.
Range: Throughout our area and most of the world. May–Dec.; several broods. Most common Aug.-Sept. Does not survive winter northward, but quickly repopulates there each season.

SUBFLEXUS STRAW *Heliothis subflexus* Gn.   Pl. 29 (9)
Identification: FW pale green, crossed by 3 lines, each *edged with white* on basal side. *Pm. line continues to apex* by merging with diffuse black apical dash. Reniform spot has almost no dark pigment in outline; outer edge usually nearly straight. HW white, rarely with sparse grayish outer shading. Wingspan 2.7–3.1 cm.
Food: Common nightshade and ground-cherry.
Range: Believed to be identical to that of Tobacco Budworm Moth (below); positively recorded from Ky., S.C., Fla., Mo., Ark., and Miss. May–Oct. Less common than Tobacco Budworm Moth.

TOBACCO BUDWORM MOTH   Pl. 29 (12)
Heliothis virescens (F.)
Identification: FW pale green with 3 nearly parallel lines as in Subflexus Straw (above), but usually *no white edging* on basal side of median line. *Pm. line ends before reaching costa,* and is *not continued to apex* by black dash. Reniform spot outline darker; outer side more curved. HW white, usually with prominent gray outer shading (absent in some males). Wingspan 2.7–3.8 cm.

Food: Larva (**Tobacco Budworm**) a serious pest only on tobacco. First brood larvae eat buds; those of second brood eat flowers and seedpods. Also feeds on ageratum, geraniums, roses, and various members of the nightshade family.
Range: Me. and s. Ont. to Fla., west to Neb. and Tex. May–Oct.; 2 broods. Most common Aug.–Sept.; most damaging in Gulf states.

SPOTTED STRAW   Pl. 29 (4)
Heliothis phloxiphagus Grt. & Rob.
Identification: Wings orangish yellow. FW variably *shaded with dark orange to brown* from median line either to st. line (as shown), or to outer margin. Note *large, dark gray reniform spot.* Dark discal spot and pm. line on HW. Wingspan 2.8–3.4 cm.
Food: Asters, delphiniums, gladiolus, phlox, strawberry, tarweed, and many other plants. Larva eats the flowers.
Range: Me. and s. Ont. to Fla., west to Mo. and Tex. June–Aug. May be locally common.

Flower Moths: Genus *Schinia*

This genus includes some of our most beautiful noctuids. Most are well-camouflaged by their coloring as they rest, feed, and lay eggs on the flowers of their food plants. The larvae eat the flowers, and later the seed capsules. Adults of some species are day-fliers; others will come to lights. Of about 40 species in our area, 14 of the most common and widespread ones are included in this guide.

BINA FLOWER MOTH *Schinia bina* (Gn.)   Pl. 29 (3)
Identification: FW pale *olive* with *rose to purple shading* in all but st. area. HW black with 2 large yellow spots and a small yellow bar along outer margin. Wingspan 1.8–2.5 cm.
Food: Unrecorded.
Range: N.C. to Fla., west to w. Ky. and Miss. July–Aug. Uncommon.

NORTHERN FLOWER MOTH   Pl. 29 (22)
Schinia septentrionalis (Wlk.)
Identification: One of our smallest *Schinia* species. FW dark olive to olive brown with *orange-yellow filling in median and terminal areas.* HW yellow with black border and discal blotch, sometimes mostly black with 2–3 yellow spots. Foretibia has *2 inner claws* and 3 or more outer claws. Wingspan 1.7–2.3 cm.
Food: New England aster (*Aster novae-angliae*).
Range: Me. and Que. to S.C., west to Mo. Sept. Common.

LYNX FLOWER MOTH *Schinia lynx* (Gn.)   Pl. 29 (18)
Identification: Colors and patterns variable. FW marked much like FW of Northern Flower Moth (above), but usually not as dark. *Am. and pm. lines closer together* in median area. HW usually yellow with black border and discal spot. Foretibia has *only 1 claw* (located on inner side). Wingspan 1.8–2.2 cm.

Food: Fleabane.
Range: Me. to Fla., west to Minn. and Tex. May–July. Common.

ARCIGERA FLOWER MOTH   Pl. 29 (20, 21)
Schinia arcigera (Gn.)
Identification: FW dark chocolate brown with grayish brown median and terminal areas. *Am. line broadly rounded; pm. line slightly curved.* HW yellow with blackish border in ♂; entirely blackish in ♀ (see Pl. 29). Wingspan 2.2–2.5 cm.
Food: Asters.
Range: N.S. to Fla., west to Man. and Tex. July–Sept. Common except north of L.I., N.Y. and in s. Fla.

RAGWEED FLOWER MOTH   Pl. 29 (16)
Schinia rivulosa (Gn.)
Identification: FW *powdery ash gray* with conspicuous white lines. Note the deeply *curved pm. line.* Blackish brown shading on basal side of am. line and in st. area. HW grayish brown. Wingspan 2.5–3.1 cm.
Food: Ragweed.
Range: Que. to Fla., west to Neb. and Tex. July–Oct. Common.
Similar species: Thoreau's Flower Moth (below, Pl. 29) is larger; *am. and pm. lines less conspicuous.* Dark shading not as blackish.

BROWN FLOWER MOTH   Pl. 29 (13)
Schinia saturata (Grt.)
Identification: FW reddish to yellowish brown with darker brown shading along curved, *whitish am. and pm. lines.* HW yellowish to dull orange. Wingspan 2.5–2.8 cm.
Food: Unrecorded.
Range: Mass. to Fla., west to S.D. and Tex. Aug.–Sept. Uncommon.

THOREAU'S FLOWER MOTH   Pl. 29 (17)
Schinia thoreaui (Grt. & Rob.)
Identification: Our largest *Schinia* species. FW grayish brown with darker shading in basal and st. areas. *Am. and pm. lines curve toward each other* as in Ragweed Flower Moth (above), but *not as* conspicuously *whitish.* HW grayish brown. Wingspan 2.9–3.7 cm.
Food: Giant ragweed.
Range: N.Y. and s. Ont. to Fla., west to Minn., Kans., and Tex. July–Aug.; as early as April southward. Uncommon.

THREE-LINED FLOWER MOTH   Pl. 29 (7)
Schinia trifascia Hbn.
Identification: FW deep olive green to grayish; median area paler. Note 3 white lines on FW; *am. line sharply bent* toward costa; pm. and st. lines nearly straight. HW greenish white; some grayish brown outer shading in some specimens (as shown). Wingspan 2–3.1 cm.
Food: False boneset and joe-pye-weed.

Range: Cen. N.Y. and s. Ont. to Fla., west to Minn., Neb., and Tex. July–Oct. Sometimes locally common.

PRIMROSE MOTH *Schinia florida* (Gn.)   **Pl. 29 (8)**
Identification: FW *bright pink*, with *yellow* in *lower basal area* and *beyond st. line*. Median area may have much more yellow tinting than shown, with pink reniform spot and st. line more distinct. HW white. Wingspan 2.7–3.6 cm.
Food: Biennial gaura and another species of evening-primrose.
Range: N.S. to n. Fla., west to Minn. and Tex. July–Aug. Uncommon; best collected by looking on flowers of food plants.

CLOUDED CRIMSON   **Pl. 29 (5)**
Schinia gaurae (J.E. Sm.)
Identification: FW yellowish cream with pink to crimson shading in basal and terminal areas. Note the *dark crimson line* slanting downward from costa near apex. HW white with crimson shading at outer margin. Wingspan 2.7–3.2 cm.
Food: Biennial gaura.
Range: Ky. to Fla., west to Neb. and Tex. Aug.–Sept. Uncommon.

GLORIOUS FLOWER MOTH   **Pl. 29 (11)**
Schinia gloriosa (Stkr.)
Identification: FW *pinkish purple* with *dull olive green median area* and large, diffuse purplish reniform spot. Veins form whitish teeth along am. and pm. lines. HW pale grayish brown with darker border. Wingspan 2.9–3.5 cm.
Food: Blazing-star.
Range: N.C. to Fla., west to Ill., Neb., and Tex. July; Sept.–Oct. in Fla. Uncommon.

BLEEDING FLOWER MOTH   **Pl. 29 (15)**
Schinia sanguinea (Gey.)
Identification: Very similar to Glorious Flower Moth (above), but smaller. Median area of FW *darker, less sharply defined*. Basal half of HW *darker*, nearly as dark as border. Wingspan 2.4–2.9 cm.
Food: Unrecorded.
Range: N.C. to Fla., west to Tex.; 1 old record from s. Me. Sept.–Oct. Uncommon.

LEADPLANT FLOWER MOTH   **Pl. 29 (6)**
Schinia lucens (Morr.)
Identification: FW mottled *dark and pale purple* with inconspicuous whitish lines. Note *dark streaking* at outer margin. HW yellow, variably shaded with black. Wingspan 2.5–2.8 cm.
Food: Leadplant (*Amorpha canescens*).
Range: N.C. to Fla., west to Ill., S.D., and Tex. June–July; April–May in Fla. Uncommon to rare.

GOLDENROD FLOWER MOTH   Pl. 29 (10)
Schinia nundina (Dru.)
Identification: FW white with irregular bands of *pale olive green.*
Note *blackish reniform spot.* HW white with olive green discal
spot and outer border. Wingspan 2.4–2.8 cm.
Food: Asters and goldenrods.
Range: Me. and s. Ont. to Fla., west to Minn., Kans., and Tex.
July–Sept. Uncommon.

Subfamily Acontiinae

STRAIGHT-LINED CYDOSIA   Pl. 30 (2)
Cydosia aurivitta Grt. & Rob.
Identification: FW red wth prominent white spots outlined in
black. Reniform spot *divided in half by straight black line.* In
some specimens FW red and bluish black, or bluish black only.
HW of both sexes black. Wingspan 2–2.5 cm.
Food: Unrecorded.
Range: Tropical; enters our area in s. Tex. June.
Similar species: Curve-lined Cydosia, *C. nobilitella* (Cram.), not
shown, has reniform spot *divided by curved line.* HW mostly white
in ♂; entirely black in ♀. Food: Unrecorded. Range: Tropical; occurs all year in Fla. Keys.

THE WHITE-EDGE   Pl. 29 (25)
Oruza albocostaliata (Pack.)
Identification: Note the small body and broad FW, as in some
geometer moths (p. 344). FW pale yellowish to reddish brown with
prominent *white collar* and *band along costa.* Pm. line of FW
continues onto HW. Wingspan 1.8–2.1 cm.
Food: Unrecorded.
Range: Mass. to Fla., west to Mo. and Tex. April–Sept. Common.

AERIAL BROWN *Ozarba aeria* (Grt.)   Pl. 29 (26)
Identification: FW light brown with obscure lines and *dark
brown patches* along costa—*apical patch the largest.* HW grayish
brown. Wingspan 1.6–2 cm.
Food: Clammy cuphea and *Jacobinia* species.
Range: Va. to n. Fla., west to Mo. and Tex. May–Oct.

DOTTED GRAYLET   Pl. 28 (19)
Hyperstrotia pervertens (B. & McD.)
Identification: FW gray with inconspicuous whitish lines.
Reniform spot contains *1–2 black dots.* HW dark grayish brown.
Wingspan 1.7–1.9 cm.
Food: Bur oak and American elm.
Range: N.S. to n. Fla., west to Ky. and Miss. June–Aug. Common.
Similar species: White-lined Graylet, *H. villificans* (B. & McD.),
not shown, has *darker* FW with *more contrasting, white am. and*

pm. lines; lines broadest toward inner margin. Food: American elm. Range: Same range and flight season as for Dotted Graylet. Common.

BLACK-PATCHED GRAYLET Pl. 28 (21)
Hyperstrotia secta (Grt.)

Identification: Almost identical to Dotted Graylet (above), but with a prominent *black patch* in lower median area. Wingspan 1.5–1.9 cm.

Food: Red and white oaks.

Range: Mass. and s. Ont. to N.C. and Ala., west to Mo. and Miss. June–Aug. Common.

Similar species: Yellow-spotted Graylet, *H. flaviguttata* (Grt.), not shown, has a *yellow spot* above a brown median patch. Food: Unrecorded. Range: Mass. to Fla., west to Tex. June–Aug.

BLACK-BORDERED LEMON MOTH Pl. 30 (1)
Thioptera nigrofimbria (Gn.)

Identification: FW lemon yellow. Only markings are blackish brown dots representing claviform, reniform, and sometimes orbicular spots, and *blackish outer border*. HW yellow with light grayish brown outer shading. Wingspan 1.8–2.2 cm.

Food: Crabgrass and morning-glories.

Range: Mass. to Fla., west to Mo. and Tex. June–Sept. Common to abundant, especially southward.

BOG LITHACODIA *Lithacodia bellicula* Hbn. Pl. 30 (3)

Identification: FW gray, with chocolate brown shading in median and terminal areas and an orangish patch in st. area. Spots and pm. line white; pale *orange bar* connects orbicular and reniform spots. HW grayish brown. Wingspan 1.9–2.2 cm.

Food: Unrecorded.

Range: Nfld. to Fla., west to Ill., Kans. and Tex. June–Aug. Local; usually in bogs.

LARGE MOSSY LITHACODIA Pl. 28 (17)
Lithacodia muscosula (Gn.)

Identification: FW whitish, heavily shaded with grayish brown (olive-tinted in fresh specimens) and streaked with black. Lines broken, blackish. Reniform spot partially *outlined in white*. Lower terminal area of FW often white as shown. HW gray. Wingspan 1.9–2.3 cm.

Food: Grasses.

Range: N.S. to n. Fla., west to Mo. and Tex. May–Oct. Common.

Similar species: Small Mossy Lithacodia (p. 147, Pl. 30) is *smaller*. FW more greenish, with rounder, *more conspicuous reniform spot*.

BLACK-DOTTED LITHACODIA Pl. 30 (4)
Lithacodia synochitis (Grt. & Rob.)

Identification: FW white with variable gray shading. Orbicular

spot a *tiny black dot.* Large, *olive green patch* in lower median area; black costal patch at apex. HW white with grayish brown shading and trace of median line. Wingspan 1.7–2.1 cm.
Food: Smartweed.
Range: N.S. to N.C., west to Mich., Kans. and Tex. May–Aug. Common.

RED-SPOTTED LITHACODIA   Pl. 30 (24)
Lithacodia concinnimacula (Gn.)
Identification: FW white and pale green with black orbicular spot and subapical patch. Note *reddish brown reniform and claviform spots.* HW grayish with darker discal spot and median line. Wingspan 2–2.2 cm.
Food: Unrecorded.
Range: N.S. to W. Va., west to Mo. and Miss. May–July. Rare.

SMALL MOSSY LITHACODIA   Pl. 30 (6)
Lithacodia musta (Grt. & Rob.)
Identification: FW dark greenish with blackish shading and lines; green fades to yellowish in old specimens (not shown). *Reniform spot white, with reddish brown and white filling.* Short white line extends upward from inner margin near anal angle. HW gray. Wingspan 1.5–1.9 cm.
Food: Unrecorded.
Range: N.H. to n. Fla., west to Wisc., Mo., and Tex. May–Sept. Common.
Similar species: Large Mossy Lithacodia (p. 146, Pl. 28) is larger. FW whitish with extensive grayish brown shading; reniform spot not as round or conspicuous.

PINK-BARRED LITHACODIA   Pl. 30 (7)
Lithacodia carneola (Gn.)
Identification: FW mostly dark brown from base to pm. line, pale tan beyond it. Prominent *pink to pinkish white bar* extends from costa to just below reniform spot. HW gray. Wingspan 2–2.4 cm.
Food: Dock, goldenrod and smartweed.
Range: Nfld. to Fla., west to Man., n. Ark., and Miss. May–Sept. Common.

BLACK WEDGE-SPOT   Pl. 29 (19)
Homophoberia apicosa (Haw.)
Identification: FW dark grayish brown with cream to pinkish tan reniform spot and st. area. Note coal black, *wedge-like claviform spot* and am. and pm. lines. HW whitish with grayish brown shading and black dot at outer margin. Note cream spot near rear edge of grayish brown thorax. Wingspan 2.1–2.7 cm.
Food: Lady's thumb.
Range: N.S. to Fla., west to Minn., Mo., and Tex. March–Oct. Common.
Similar species: Water-lily Moth, *H. cristata* Morr. (not shown), is *larger* (wingspan 2.7–3.3 cm) and *lacks coal black lines and*

claviform spot. Paler tan reniform spot smaller, triangular; st. area tan, not as contrasting. Antennae bipectinate in ♂; simple in ♀ and in Black Wedge-spot (both sexes). Food: Yellow water-lily. Larva feeds above water on leaves, swims to shore to pupate. Range: Mass. and s. Ont. to Fla., west to Ill. and Ky. June–Aug. Uncommon.

TUFTED BIRD-DROPPING MOTH   Pl. 30 (8)
Cerma cerintha (Tr.)
Identification: Note dark dorsal tufts on abdomen. FW white; lines and shading a mixture of black, gray, reddish brown, and olive green. *Reniform spot white* with olive green filling. HW white with grayish brown border. At rest, this moth resembles a bird dropping. Wingspan 2.8–3.3 cm.
Food: Apple, hawthorn, peach, plum, roses, wild cherry, and other plants in the rose family.
Range: Me. and Que. to Fla., west to Minn., Ark., and Miss. May–Aug. Common.

GREEN LEUCONYCTA   Pl. 26 (19)
Leuconycta diphteroides (Gn.)
Identification: FW *pale green* (whitish in old specimens). Lines *double,* formed by a series of *white dots* (some edged with black). Note black collar and 2 squarish black patches along costa. HW gray with darker gray border. Wingspan 2.7–3.2 cm.
Food: Goldenrod.
Range: N.S. to Fla., west to Man. and n. Ark. April–Oct. Common.

EIGHT-SPOT *Amyna octo* (Gn.)   Pl. 28 (22)
Identification: FW dark brown, chocolate beyond pm. line. Note *white figure-8 outline of reniform spot;* whole lower half often solid white or orangish brown. Lines fine, inconspicuous, yellowish; 6 yellowish spots along costa. HW dark brown, darker toward outer margin. Wingspan 2–2.5 cm.
Food: *Chenopodium* species.
Range: Me. and s. Ont. to Fla., west to Mich., Mo., and Tex. Aug.–Oct. Tropical; migrates northward each year. Moderately common in deep South, but increasingly rare northward.
Similar species: In Hook-tipped Amyna, *A. bullula* (Grt.), not shown, FW outer margin is *hooked;* small *gray patch at apex.* HW has *median line.* Food: Unrecorded. Range: Tropical; strays north to Que. and Ill. Aug.–Oct. Rare northward.

EVERLASTING BUD MOTH   Pl. 29 (23)
Eumicremma minima (Gn.)
Identification: FW cream to tan with fine, slightly darker lines and broad, *olive brown median and st. shade lines.* Median shade continues onto *scale tuft* which projects over HW (shown best on left FW in Pl. 29). Darker apical and anal spots. HW grayish brown, darker at outer margin. Wingspan 1.1–1.5 cm.

Food: Buds of sweet and pearly everlasting; also rabbit tobacco.
Range: N.C. to Fla., west along Gulf Coast to Tex. Strays north to Mass. All months in Fla., where it is common.

STRAIGHT-LINED SEED MOTH   Pl. 29 (24)
Eumestleta recta (Gn.)
Identification: FW pale yellowish with conspicuous, *slightly curved line* from apex to inner margin. Brown shading on basal side of line and toward outer margin. HW shiny yellowish cream. Wingspan 1.5–1.7 cm.
Food: Seeds of bindweed, morning-glory, and sweet potato plants.
Range: S.C. to Fla. Keys, west along Gulf Coast to Tex. All months except July and Aug. in Fla., where it is common.

THE HALF-YELLOW   Pl. 30 (9)
Tarachidia semiflava (Gn.)
Identification: Thorax and basal area of FW *solid yellow*. Rest of FW brown, sometimes with violet tinge. HW shiny light yellowish to grayish brown. Wingspan 1.4–2.4 cm.
Food: Trumpets (*Sarracenia flava*).
Range: N.J. to Fla., west to Man. and Tex. June–Aug. Rare northward; local in rest of range.

OLIVE-SHADED BIRD-DROPPING MOTH   Pl. 30 (19)
Tarachidia candefacta (Hbn.)
Identification: FW white near base and along costa; gray and yellowish *mottling* fills most of *median and st. areas* (creating an *olive green effect*). Note dark grayish bar perpendicular to inner margin. Look for tiny black orbicular dot; reniform spot usually round, outlined with white. HW grayish brown with white fringe. Wingspan 1.8–2.2 cm.
Food: Ragweed.
Range: Throughout our area. April–Sept. Common southward.

SMALL BIRD-DROPPING MOTH   Pl. 30 (17)
Tarachidia erastrioides (Gn.)
Identification: FW white with blackish markings; *no olive green* effect as in Olive-shaded Bird-dropping Moth (above). Large blackish patch *does not reach apex*. Look for a tiny black orbicular dot; reniform spot obscured by mottling. HW whitish with grayish brown shading. Wingspan 1.6–2 cm.
Food: Ragweed.
Range: Me. and s. Que. to n. Fla., west to Minn., Neb., and Tex. May–Sept. Common.

SOUTHERN SPRAGUEIA   Pl. 30 (13)
Spragueia dama (Gn.)
Identification: This and the next 2 *Spragueia* species (below) have bright FW patterns of orange, yellow, and black. *Upper half* of *basal area yellow, lower half black* in this moth; note single blackish *spot at outer margin*. HW grayish brown. Wingspan 1.5–1.6 cm.

Food: Unrecorded.
Range: Ky. and N.C. to Fla., west to Mo. and Tex. May–Sept. Locally common southward.

### BLACK-DOTTED SPRAGUEIA					Pl. 30 (16)
Spragueia onagrus (Gn.)
Identification: Similar to Southern Spragueia (above), but with alternating black and yellow bars *in basal area.* Terminal line *black* except at anal angle. Note *rounded black reniform spot,* unique among our *Spragueia* species. Wingspan 1.5–1.7 cm.
Food: Chinquapin and field corn.
Range: N.C. to Fla., west to Miss. April–Sept. Common.

### COMMON SPRAGUEIA *Spragueia leo* (Gn.)					Pl. 30 (12)
Identification: Basal area and terminal line as in Black-dotted Spragueia (above), but *no round reniform spot.* Note long, black *median dash* which *widens toward apex.* Dash may be solid or interrupted by orange am. and pm. lines (not shown), or by pm. line only (shown). HW dark gray. Wingspan 1.2–1.8 cm.
Food: Bindweed.
Range: Se. Mass. to Fla., west to Kans. and Tex. June–Sept. Common.

### YELLOW SPRAGUEIA					Pl. 30 (10, 14)
Spragueia apicalis (H.-S.)
Identification: Sexes differ in FW color: FW mostly *yellow* with *brown outer margin* and faint tan streak in ♂; FW *dark gray* in ♀. Basal area brown and *apex yellow* in both sexes. HW dark gray. N. American subspecies is *S. apicalis apicella* (Grt.). Wingspan 1.5–1.8 cm.
Food: Broom-snakeroot (*Gutierrezia sarothrae*).
Range: Va. to Fla., west to Ill., Mo., and Tex. Aug.-Sept. northward; Feb.-Nov. in Fla. Common southward.

### EXPOSED BIRD-DROPPING MOTH					Pl. 30 (18)
Acontia aprica (Hbn.)
Identification: Body and wings white. FW of ♂ has *2 blackish costal patches*—outer one merges with general blackish shading beyond pm. line, leaving white patch near apex. FW of ♀ (not shown) blackish except for *2 white costal patches* and some white at base and outer margin. *Black orbicular dot* usually prominent in both sexes. More grayish brown shading at outer margin of HW in ♀ than in ♂. Wingspan 1.5–2.9 cm.
Food: Hollyhocks.
Range: Que. and Ont. to Fla., west to Kans. and Tex. May–Sept. Common southward; can be flushed from plants during the day.

### FOUR-SPOTTED BIRD-DROPPING MOTH					Pl. 30 (15)
Acontia tetragona Wlk.
Identification: FW mostly blackish in both sexes, except for some white at base, and *2 sharp costal patches. Orbicular dot usually*

obscured by blackish median shading, not surrounded by white as in Exposed Bird-dropping Moth (above). *HW yellowish brown.* Wingspan 2.2–2.4 cm.
Food: Unrecorded.
Range: Fla. and Tex. April–Sept.

CURVE-LINED ACONTIA   Pl. 30 (11)
Acontia terminimaculata (Grt.)
Identification: Distinguished by prominent, *curved lower pm. line,* with area beyond a mixture of dark brown, reddish brown, and gray. Sexes differ in color of median area of FW: pale gray *like basal area* in ♂ (not shown), darker gray than basal area in ♀. HW dirty whitish in ♂, grayish brown in ♀. Wingspan 2.5–2.8 cm.
Food: Basswood.
Range: Mass. to Fla., west to Ill. and La. April–Sept. Rare northward; uncommon in South.

DELIGHTFUL BIRD-DROPPING MOTH   Pl. 30 (21)
Acontia delecta Wlk.
Identification: Easily recognized by *yellow HW.* FW white with brown and dark blue basal and st. shading. Shading in upper basal area sometimes extends across median area and merges with shading in lower st. area. Wingspan 2.8–3.2 cm.
Food: Swamp rose-mallow.
Range: Coastal N.Y. to Fla., west to s. Mo. and Tex. May, July, and Sept.; at least 2 broods. May be flushed from flowers in open fields during day. Local and uncommon to rare.

Subfamily Nolinae

These moths usually have *raised scale tufts* on discal cell of FW; see p. 79 for other subfamily characteristics.

CONFUSED MEGANOLA   Pl. 31 (2, 4)
Meganola minuscula (Zell.)
Identification: FW mottled gray and white, with 3 tufts of raised scales in a row toward costa. Lines black, broken; pm. line a series of black dots. Upper *pm. line curves outward* around faint reniform spot. Note 2 black costal patches in form "phylla" Dyar (sometimes listed as a subspecies). HW grayish brown. Wingspan 1.4–2.4 cm.
Food: Oaks and willows.
Range: N.S. to Fla., west to Mo. and Tex. April–Aug.; 2 broods. Common.

BLURRY-PATCHED NOLA   Pl. 31 (9)
Nola cilicoides (Grt.)
Identification: FW white. Note tan am. and st. lines, and *diffuse brown patch* in median area. Look for *metallic black raised scales*

in reniform and upper pm. positions; 2 white scale tufts toward base. HW white with grayish brown discal spot and outer border. Wingspan 1.7–1.8 cm.
Food: Unrecorded.
Range: N.S. to n. Fla., west to Man. and n. Ark. June–Sept.
Similar species: Sharp-blotched Nola, *N. pustulata* (Wlk.), not shown, has a narrow *black costal patch at base* of FW and a larger, more *sharply edged* blackish *median patch* that encloses metallic black orbicular and reniform spots. Food: Unrecorded. Range: Mass. to N.C., west to Mo. and Tex. May–July. Apparently confined to bogs and swamps.

SORGHUM WEBWORM MOTH   Pl. 31 (11)
Nola sorghiella Riley
Identification: FW white, with vague yellowish to brownish *shading along costa and outer margin.* Look for curved pm. and st. lines (close together), dark orbicular spot, and black shading beyond lower st. line. HW gleaming white. Wingspan 1.2–1.8 cm.
Food: Larva (**Sorghum Webworm**) feeds communally in webs spun in seedheads of various grasses; a pest of sorghum.
Range: Tropical; common in southern U.S., becoming less common northward to L.I., N.Y., and Mo. April–Sept.

THREE-SPOTTED NOLA   Pl. 31 (6)
Nola triquetrana (Fitch)
Identification: FW mottled pale and dark gray with *3 black spots along costa.* Each spot partially covers a tuft of raised scales. HW gray with faint discal spot. Wingspan 1.7–1.8 cm.
Food: Witch-hazel.
Range: N.S. to Fla., west to Mo. and Ark. March–May. Common.

Subfamily Sarrothripinae

DOUBLEDAY'S BAILEYA   Pl. 31 (18)
Baileya doubledayi (Gn.)
Identification: All 5 *Baileya* species are gray with a blackish costal patch near the FW apex. Doubleday's Baileya is the most boldly marked, with a *slightly wavy white pm. line* and a black reniform spot shaped like a teardrop. HW whitish to gray. Wingspan 2.4–2.8 cm.
Food: Alders.
Range: N.S. and Que. to n. Fla., west to Wisc. and Miss. May–Aug. Uncommon to rare, especially southward.

EYED BAILEYA *Baileya ophthalmica* (Gn.)   Pl. 31 (23)
Identification: Note the especially *sharp, broken, black apical patch* and the sharp pm. and st. lines in this *Baileya* species. Reniform spot large, with black outline and center. White basal patch conspicuous. HW whitish with darker shading toward outer margin. Wingspan 2.3–3.2 cm.

Food: Beech and ironwood.
Range: N.W. to n. Fla., west to Wisc. and Tex. May–July; common.

SLEEPING BAILEYA   Pl. 31 (22)
Baileya dormitans (Gn.)
Identification: FW uniform dull gray with inconspicuous lines and basal patch (usually gray). Top of st. line *sharply bent*, forming black inner edge of apical patch. *Reniform spot a black dot* (sometimes absent). Wingspan 2.5–3.1 cm.
Food: Ironwood.
Range: Que. and Me. to Fla., west to Wisc., Mo., and Tex. April–Sept. Common.

PALE BAILEYA *Baileya levitans* (Sm.)   Pl. 31 (24)
Identification: FW pale gray, with *grayish white median area. Least distinct apical patch* of any Baileya. Reniform spot with black outline and center, but usually smaller than in Eyed Baileya (above). Lines indistinct. Wingspan 2.5–3.4 cm.
Food: Unrecorded.
Range: Me. and s. Ont. to n. Fla., west to Mich., Mo., Ark., and Miss. Common.

SMALL BAILEYA *Baileya australis* (Grt.)   Pl. 31 (20)
Identification: Smaller than our other *Baileya* species (above). Upper st. line on FW heavy, *nearly straight*. Basal patch white, conspicuous. Reniform spot obscure. Melanic specimens common in Midwest, with less distinct patterns. Wingspan 2.1–2.8 cm.
Food: Unrecorded.
Range: N.Y. and s. Ont. to n. Fla., west to Kans. and Tex. April–Sept.; 3 broods. Common.

FRIGID OWLET *Nycteola frigidana* (Wlk.)   Pl. 30 (25)
Identification: FW long and narrow, shiny gray with bluish to greenish tint in some specimens. Similar to Cadbury's Lichen Moth (p. 62, Pl. 31), but *no contrasting paler basal area* or distinct am. line; *st. line black, irregular, not wider at inner margin* as in Cadbury's Lichen Moth. HW grayish. Wingspan 2.2–2.5 cm.
Food: Poplars and willows.
Range: Nfld. to n. Fla., west across s. Canada, south to n. Ark. and Miss. April–Sept. Common, but rarely collected at lights.

Subfamily Euteliinae

DARK MARATHYSSA   Pl. 28 (23)
Marathyssa inficita (Wlk.)
Identification: Male (shown) has *serrate (sawtoothed) antennae.* FW gray and chocolate brown with *crimson toward apex.* Pm. line meets inner margin at *right angle.* HW grayish brown with darker

veins and shading. Wingspan 2.5–2.8 cm.
Food: Staghorn sumac.
Range: Common throughout our area. May–Sept.

LIGHT MARATHYSSA   Pl. 28 (24)
Marathyssa basalis Wlk.
Identification: Similar to Dark Marathyssa (above), but ♂ *antennae bipectinate,* and *broader.* FW more yellowish brown; general appearance paler. Pm. line meets inner margin at a *more oblique angle.* Wingspan 2.5–3.2 cm.
Food: Poison ivy.
Range: Me. and e. Ont. to Fla., west to Mo. and Tex. April–June. Less common than Dark Marathyssa.

EYED PAECTES *Paectes oculatrix* (Gn.)   Pl. 31 (16)
Identification: The *rounded pattern toward outer margin* of FW created by *curved pm. line* identifies this species. FW gray with black markings and pink-tinted white basal dashes and outer accents. HW dark to light grayish brown. Wingspan 2.3–2.5 cm.
Food: Poison ivy.
Range: Locally common throughout our area. Late May–Aug.; 2 or more broods.

PYGMY PAECTES *Paectes pygmaea* Hbn.   Pl. 30 (20)
Identification: FW blackish brown. *Basal area pale gray, oval.* Median area shaded with bluish gray. Pm. line curves evenly outward from inner margin toward apex, then *angles sharply to costa.* HW blackish with white fringe. Wingspan 1.9–2.3 cm.
Food: Sweetgum.
Range: Mass. to Fla., west to Kans., Ark., and Miss. May–Aug.; at least 2 broods. Common.

LARGE PAECTES *Paectes abrostoloides* (Gn.)   Pl. 30 (23)
Identification: Similar to Pygmy Paectes (above), but *larger.* FW dark brown with bluish gray shading; lower basal area often pale brown (as shown). Note *more scalloped pm. line* and *black blotch near apex.* Fringe of HW checkered. Wingspan 2.7–3.2 cm.
Food: Sweetgum.
Range: Common from Mass. to Fla., west to Mo. and Tex. April–Oct.; at least 2 broods.

BEAUTIFUL EUTELIA   Pl. 30 (5)
Eutelia pulcherrima (Grt.)
Identification: Easily recognized by the *hooked FW* and complex pattern of white, reddish brown, and black. Wingspan 2.3–3.6 cm.
Food: Poison sumac.
Range: Mass. to Fla., west to e. Mo. and Tex. April–July. Local and uncommon.
Similar species: Florida Eutelia, *E. furcata* (Wlk.), not shown, has identical wing shape and size, but *wings darker, more purplish brown.* Food: Unrecorded. Range: Florida; March–May.

Subfamily Plusiinae

GOLDEN LOOPER MOTH   Pl. 32 (1)
Argyrogramma verruca (F.)
Identification: FW mostly deep gold, with brownish lines and shading. *Stigma* (usually silver mark in median area characteristic of looper moths) *small, filled with gold;* tiny 2nd silver spot farther out in some specimens. Wingspan 2.8–3.4 cm.
Food: Arrowhead, curled dock, tobacco, and other low plants.
Range: Tropical; common in South, rarely extending north to Me., s. Ont., and Kans. May–Oct.; 2 or more broods southward.

PINK-WASHED LOOPER MOTH   Pl. 32 (5)
Argyrogramma basigera (Wlk.)
Identification: *FW pinkish brown* with darker brown in lower median and apical areas. Am. and pm. lines sharply defined. Stigma consists of *2 small silver spots:* inner spot usually hollow and attached to am. line, outer spot usually solid. HW grayish brown with pinkish fringe. Wingspan 2.8–3.3 cm.
Food: Unrecorded.
Range: Me. to Fla., west to s. Mo. and Tex. June–Sept. Rare northward.

CABBAGE LOOPER MOTH   Pl. 31 (10)
Trichoplusia ni (Hbn.)
Identification: FW mottled light and dark brown, with black, deeply scalloped pm. line. Stigma consists of *small, U-shaped inner spot,* usually not touching solid outer spot. HW gleaming grayish brown, darker in outer half. Wingspan 3–3.6 cm.
Food: Wide variety. Larva (**Cabbage Looper**) is a pest of asparagus, cabbage, corn, tobacco, watermelon, and other crops.
Range: Variably common throughout our area. Adults may be found in any warm season; 3 or more broods per year.

SHARP-STIGMA LOOPER MOTH   Pl. 31 (17)
Agrapha oxygramma (Gey.)
Identification: FW grayish brown, less mottled and glossier than in Cabbage Looper Moth (above). Note nearly straight, tan, *barlike stigma* with *silver edges* and *pointed bottom end.* HW grayish brown, darker toward outer margin. Wingspan 3.3–4.2 cm.
Food: Asters, goldenrods, horseweed, and tobacco.
Range: Me. and s. Ont. to Fla., west to Mo. and Tex. Aug.–Oct. Tropical; common in South, but a stray northward.

SOYBEAN LOOPER MOTH   Pl. 31 (15)
Pseudoplusia includens (Wlk.)
Identification: FW grayish brown with bronze luster in most of median and st. areas. Stigma divided into 2 parts that usually do not touch; *pale shade line extends from basal part to costa.* Pm. line sharply bent. HW grayish brown. Wingspan 2.8–3.9 cm.
Food: Larva (**Soybean Looper**) feeds on many plants, including

beans, coleus, goldenrods, lettuce, soybeans, and tobacco.
Range: N.S. to Fla., west to Mo. and Tex. April–Nov. Common.

GRAY LOOPER MOTH *Rachiplusia ou* (Gn.)   **Pl. 31 (8)**
Identification: FW glossy ash gray with some brownish shading
and blackish lines. Scalloped st. line thin, distinct only at apex,
curves toward stigma. Stigma consists of thin U-shaped inner part
which may touch solid or hollow outer spot. *HW orangish brown,*
becoming grayish brown toward outer margin. Wingspan 3.1–
4.1 cm.
Food: Clover, corn, cosmos, mint, and several other plants.
Range: N.S. to Fla., west to Minn., Neb., and Tex. May–Oct.
Common in South, rare northward; 2 or more broods.

UNSPOTTED LOOPER MOTH   Pl. 32 (7)
Allagrapha aerea (Hbn.)
Identification: *FW hooked at anal angle,* dull brown with olive
and orangish shading, paler at base and outer margin. Lines dark
brown, wavy, inconspicuous. *No stigma or distinct spots.* HW
grayish brown, yellowish toward costa. Wingspan 2.8–4.2 cm.
Food: Low plants, such as asters, dandelion, and stinging nettle.
Range: Common throughout our area. April–Sept.; 2 broods.
Similar species: In Dark-spotted Looper Moth, *Diachrysia
aereoides* (Grt.), not shown, FW is orangish brown with *pink tint.*
Lines are straighter and parallel; brown outlines of *orbicular and
reniform spots distinct.* Food: Asters, meadowsweet, and wild
mint. Range: N.S. to Pa., west across Canada, south to Mich. and
Wisc. July.

STRAIGHT-LINED LOOPER MOTH   Pl. 32 (4)
Pseudeva purpurigera (Wlk.)
Identification: *FW pink with brown and gold shading.* Note
straight pm. line, angled sharply below costa. No stigma. HW yel-
lowish white with grayish brown shading. Wingspan 2.8–3.1 cm.
Food: Meadow-rue.
Range: Nfld. to Del., west to Man. and Mo. June–July. Uncom-
mon to rare southward.

FORMOSA LOOPER MOTH   Pl. 32 (8)
Chrysanympha formosa (Grt.)
Identification: FW grayish white, sometimes with pinkish tint.
Lower median area metallic brown. Darkest markings are black
top of am. line and *evenly curved st. line.* No distinct stigma. HW
grayish brown, darker at outer margin. Wingspan 3–3.5 cm.
Food: Blueberry and dwarf huckleberry.
Range: Nfld. to N.C., west to Man. and cen. Ky. May–July. Lo-
cally common northward.

PINK-PATCHED LOOPER MOTH   Pl. 32 (9)
Eosphoropteryx thyatyroides (Gn.)
Identification: FW gray with *pink in basal and lower st. areas.*

Dark brown dashes above basal patch, across median area, and near apex, tending to merge. Stigma consists of 2 small, usually separate spots: inner spot hollow, outer spot solid. HW grayish brown with pale median line. Wingspan 3.1–3.8 cm.

Food: Meadow-rue.

Range: N.S. to Va. and Ky., west through s. Canada, south to Mo. and N.D. June–Aug.; probably 2 broods. Uncommon to rare.

BILOBED LOOPER MOTH   Pl. 31 (12)
Autographa biloba (Steph.)

Identification: Easily recognized by the *large, bilobed stigma,* larger than in any other of our looper moths. FW light brown with dark metallic brown shading. Am. and pm. lines and partial reniform spot silver. HW grayish brown. Wingspan 3.4–4 cm.

Food: Low plants, such as alfalfa, cabbage, and tobacco.

Range: Common throughout our area. March–Nov.; several broods.

COMMON LOOPER MOTH   Pl. 31 (14)
Autographa precationis (Gn.)

Identification: FW grayish brown with bronze luster; similar to Soybean Looper Moth (p. 155, Pl. 31), but hollow *inner part of stigma more* V-*shaped,* often *connected to outer part.* Pm. line does not bend on vein M_3 as in Soybean Looper Moth. HW grayish brown. Wingspan 3–3.8 cm.

Food: Many plants, such as beans, cabbage, dandelion, hollyhock, plantain, sunflowers, thistles, and verbena.

Range: Common from N.S. to Ga., west to Minn., Neb., and Kans. April–Oct.; at least 3 broods.

TWO-SPOTTED LOOPER MOTH   Pl. 31 (5)
Autographa bimaculata (Steph.)

Identification: FW yellowish to pinkish brown with chocolate shading and st. line. Stigma consists of *nearly solid inner part shaped like a* G or chemist's retort, usually separate from solid outer part. Metallic brown patch over center of st. line. Bottoms of am. and pm. lines gold and black. HW grayish brown, with darker outer border. Wingspan 3.8–4 cm.

Food: Dandelion.

Range: Nfld. to N.J. and N.Y., west through s. Canada, south to Minn. and S.D. July–Aug. Common.

LARGE LOOPER MOTH   Pl. 31 (3)
Autographa ampla (Wlk.)

Identification: FW gray except for *dark brown apical dash and sharply defined lower median area.* Stigma white, forming upper border of dark median patch. HW grayish brown. Our largest looper moth. Wingspan 3.9–4.2 cm.

Food: Alder, birch, poplars, willows and other woody plants.

Range: Nfld. to N.C. mts., west across Canada, south to Ky. July–Aug. Common.

CELERY LOOPER MOTH   Pl. 31 (7)
Anagrapha falcifera (Kby.)
Identification: FW smooth gray to grayish brown in basal, costal, and terminal areas; median area warm brown, darker toward inner margin. Silvery white *am. line* curves outward and *merges with stigma.* HW yellowish with grayish brown basal and terminal shading. Wingspan 3.2–4 cm.
Food: Larva (**Celery Looper**) feeds on beets, blueberries, clover, corn, lettuce, plantain, viburnum, and other low plants.
Range: Common to abundant throughout our area. March–Nov.; 2–3 broods. Active both day and night.

SALT-AND-PEPPER LOOPER MOTH   Pl. 31 (1)
Syngrapha rectangula (Kby.)
Identification: FW dark gray with sharp silver and pale gray markings. Note *jagged black st. line.* Stigma, if present, may merge with silver costal patch (as shown). HW yellowish with grayish brown in basal and terminal areas. Wingspan 3–3.5 cm.
Food: Firs, hemlocks, pines, spruces, and other conifers.
Range: Nfld. to Pa., west through Canada, south to Minn. July–Aug. Active during the day, as well as at dusk and at night.

PUTNAM'S LOOPER MOTH   Pl. 32 (3)
Plusia putnami Grt.
Identification: FW dark and light orange, crossed by dark orangish brown lines. Stigma consists of 2 *separate, solid silver triangles* (basal one larger). Note silver dash near apex. HW grayish brown. Wingspan 3.2–3.5 cm.
Food: Bur-reed, grasses, and sedges.
Range: Lab. to Va., west to Man. and Minn. June–Oct. Locally common northward in grassy habitats.

CONNECTED LOOPER MOTH   Pl. 32 (6)
Plusia contexta Grt.
Identification: Similar to Putnam's Looper Moth (above), but FW more yellowish. *Stigma parts merged;* silver dash near apex larger. HW yellowish. Wingspan 3–3.5 cm.
Food: Grasses.
Range: Que. to L.I., N.Y., west to Ont., S.D., and Iowa. June–early Oct.; 2 or more broods. Locally common.

WHITE-STREAKED LOOPER MOTH   Pl. 32 (2)
Plusia venusta Wlk.
Identification: *Costal ⅓ of FW pinkish cream;* rest of FW brown, with sharp *white lengthwise streak* and cream along inner and outer margins. HW pinkish cream with grayish brown shading. Wingspan 3–3.5 cm.
Food: Swamp sedges or grasses (?).
Range: Nfld. to Wash., D.C., west to Man. and S.D. June–Aug. Uncommon; found only in wetlands.

Subfamily Catocalinae

This large group includes the underwings (*Catocala* species, p. 172), which are known for their colorful hindwings (see Pls. 32–37).

DECORATED OWLET   Pl. 39 (15)
Pangrapta decoralis Hbn.
Identification: FW and HW mottled yellowish, dark and light brown, and violet. Markings often less distinct than in specimen shown. Note *black-dotted reniform spot* and *curved, double pm. line* on FW and *scalloped margin* on HW. Sharp median line and discal spot on HW. Wingspan 2–2.8 cm.
Food: Blueberries.
Range: Common throughout our area. May–Sept.

LOST OWLET *Ledaea perditalis* (Wlk.)   Pl. 40 (7)
Identification: FW pale grayish brown to tan. *Pm. line blackish, thick in lower half* in ♂ (as shown), or all the way to apex in ♀ (not shown). St. and adterminal lines usually distinct. Variable lines and shading along outer margin on HW. Wingspan 2.3–2.6 cm.
Food: Woolgrass (*Scirpus cyperinus*).
Range: Me. to Fla., west to Mo. and Tex. April–Aug. Common.

THIN-LINED OWLET *Isogona tenuis* (Grt.)   Pl. 40 (9)
Identification: FW mouse gray, darker toward costa and somewhat mottled. Veins, lines, and reniform spot outline yellowish white. Am. line nearly straight; *pm. line Y-shaped,* with branches diverging to apex and costa. HW dark grayish with yellowish white median line. Wingspan 2.8–3 cm.
Food: Hackberry.
Range: Md. and s. Ohio to Fla., west to Mo. and Tex. One record from N.H. May–Aug. May be locally common.

COMMON FUNGUS MOTH   Pl. 39 (17)
Metalectra discalis (Grt.)
Identification: Wings yellowish, heavily shaded with light to dark blackish brown. Markings usually obscure; *blackish patches* represent reniform spot on FW and discal spot on HW. Wingspan 2–2.9 cm.
Food: Larva reported to feed on dry fungus.
Range: Me. and Ont. to Fla., west to Mo. and Tex. May–Sept. Common.

FOUR-SPOTTED FUNGUS MOTH   Pl. 42 (5)
Metalectra quadrisignata (Wlk.)
Identification: FW and HW dull grayish brown; usually not mottled, but highlighted with iridescent purplish to reddish. Darkest markings are double blackish median lines on FW and HW, diffuse *blackish reniform spot* on FW, and *discal spot* on HW. Wingspan 2.5–3.5 cm.

Food: Has been recorded feeding on a species of bracket fungus.
Range: Common throughout our area. June–early Aug.

BLACK FUNGUS MOTH   Pl. 42 (22)
Metalectra tantillus (Grt.)
Identification: Much like Common Fungus Moth (above, Pl. 39), but FW *black* with some *broken whitish lines.* FW reniform spot and HW discal spots deeper black. Wingspan 2–2.2 cm.
Food: Larva reared on bark of dead maple (probably fed on fungus).
Range: L.I., N.Y. to Fla., west to Mo. and Tex. Late May–Aug. Uncommon.

RICHARDS' FUNGUS MOTH   Pl. 39 (24)
Metalectra richardsi Brower
Identification: Similar to Common Fungus Moth (above), but much smaller. HW distinctly *paler than FW,* unlike HW of our other fungus moths (*Metalectra* species). Wingspan 1.5–1.7 cm.
Food: Unrecorded; probably fungus.
Range: Martha's Vineyard, Mass. to S.C. and Fla. (?); west to Ky. Late May–Aug. Locally common.

COMMON ARUGISA   Pls. 39 (23), 40 (5)
Arugisa latiorella (Wlk.)
Identification: FW glossy tan with dark brownish am., pm. and st. lines, variably irregular; black dots in pm. line. Note *brown blotch over center of am. line.* Orbicular and reniform spots are black dots. HW dark gray. Wingspan 1.6–2.1 cm.
Food: Living and dead grasses, such as Ky. bluegrass.
Range: Va. to Fla., west to Mo. and Tex. June–Aug.; all months except Dec. in s. Fla. Common.
Similar species: Watson's Arugisa, *A. watsoni* Richards (not shown) is larger; lines are more complete, *without black dots* over pm. line. Food: Grasses (?). Range: N.C. to Fla.; March–May.

DEAD-WOOD BORER MOTH   Pl. 40 (8)
Scolecocampa liburna (Gey.)
Identification: FW pale tan, reddish in some Fla. specimens. Lines brownish, faint, except for some black accenting of pm. and st. lines and series of black dots representing terminal line. Note black-edged *reniform spot,* single black basal and orbicular dots, and *diffuse double blackish patch* over upper st. line. HW dark gray. Wingspan 3.5–4.3 cm.
Food: Larva bores in decaying logs and stumps of chestnuts, oaks, and hickories. Food may actually be fungus growing there.
Range: Common from N.Y. to Fla., west to Mo. and Tex. April–Oct.

CURVE-LINED OWLET   Pl. 39 (13)
Phyprosopus callitrichoides Grt.
Identification: FW orangish brown to purplish gray; one color

often blends into the other as shown. Note *thin brown pm. line bordered by white* on both sides, curving *from apex to midpoint of inner margin.* Other markings indistinct. HW yellowish with variable dark shading. Wingspan 2.8–3.5 cm.
Food: Greenbriars.
Range: N.H. to Fla., west to Mo. and Tex. May–Aug. Uncommon.

LARGE NECKLACE MOTH Pl. 39 (7)
Hypsoropha monilis (F.)
Identification: FW warm light brown, orange at base and along outer margin. Note *4 whitish spots* inside lower half of pm. line, and fainter whitish spots beyond st. line, near apex. Antennae bipectinate in both sexes. HW pale orangish, darker toward outer margin. Wingspan 3.2–4.2 cm.
Food: Persimmon.
Range: Ky. and N.C. to Fla., west to cen. Mo. and Tex. One old record from Me. April–Aug. Common southward.

SMALL NECKLACE MOTH Pl. 39 (9)
Hypsoropha hormos Hbn.
Identification: Smaller than Large Necklace Moth (above), and *FW dark brown* with variable violet gray tinting. Look for *3–4 white spots* extending in curved line from inner margin. Antennae simple. HW paler brown than FW. Wingspan 2.5–3.4 cm.
Food: Persimmon and sassafras.
Range: N.H. to Fla., west to Kans. and Tex. May–Aug. Common.

MOONSEED MOTH Pl. 39 (11)
Plusiodonta compressipalpis Gn.
Identification: FW grayish brown with brown shading and distinctive *gold loops* in basal and anal areas. Median shading tapers downward, ending in a *large scale tuft* projecting from inner margin. HW yellowish brown. Wingspan 2.5–3.3 cm.
Food: Moonseed vine.
Range: Common from N.Y. and e. Ont. to n. Fla., west to Man. and Tex. May–Sept.

CANADIAN OWLET Pl. 39 (6)
Calyptra canadensis (Bethune)
Identification: Antennae bipectinate in both sexes. FW light brown with darker brown bands. *Pm. line sharp, nearly straight, slanting* from apex to inner margin. Note *2 scale tufts* on inner margin. HW grayish brown. Wingspan 3.3–4 cm.
Food: Tall meadow-rue.
Range: N.S. to N.C. mts., west to Man. and Tex. June–Sept.; 2 broods. Uncommon.

YELLOW SCALLOP MOTH Pl. 39 (14)
Anomis erosa Hbn.
Identification: Note *scalloped outer margin* of yellow FW. Violet gray shading beyond pm. line more or less extensive than shown.

Am. and pm. lines meet near inner margin. Small *orbicular spot white*, ringed with brown. Wingspan 2.7–3.6 cm.

Food: Mallow family, including cotton, hibiscus, and okra.

Range: S. Me. and Que. to Fla., west to Man. and Tex. Aug.–Oct. northward; all months in Fla. Common.

Similar species: Tropical Anomis, *A. flava* (F.), not shown, is almost identical, but $\male$ *antennae bipectinate* (simple in *A. erosa*); 3rd segment of each labial palp = *more than* $\frac{2}{3}$ *length of 2nd segment* (less than $\frac{2}{3}$ second segment in *A. erosa*). N. American subspecies is *A. flava fimbriago* (Steph.). Food: Cotton and okra. Range: Tropical; N.H. to Fla., west to Ill. and Tex. in our area. Aug.–Oct. in North; all months in Fla.

COTTON MOTH *Alabama argillacea* (Hbn.)   **Pl. 39 (10)**
Identification: *FW pointed at apex*, brown, often with pinkish or olive tint. Lines thin, broken, usually inconspicuous. Orbicular spot a white dot; *reniform spot dark gray*, sometimes with some whitish inside. HW grayish brown. Wingspan 3–3.5 cm.

Food: Larva (**Cotton Leafworm**) is a serious pest of cotton.

Range: Cen. and S. America, migrating into s. U.S. each spring. Adults from successive broods continue migration northward, sometimes reaching N.S. to Man., occasionally in swarms in Sept.–Nov. Adults feed on peaches, grapes, and other fruits.

THE HERALD *Scoliopteryx libatrix* (L.)   **Pl. 39 (12)**
Identification: Easily recognized by the *scalloped outer margins* of FW and HW. FW gray with white lines (pm. line double). Note *bright orange patches* and white flecks in basal and median areas. HW dark grayish brown. Wingspan 3.8–4.5 cm.

Food: Poplars and willows.

Range: Holarctic; locally common throughout our area. July–May; adults overwinter, often in caves.

PALMETTO BORER MOTH   **Pl. 39 (8)**
Litoprosopus futilis (Grt. & Rob.)
Identification: FW dark brown with broken, double am. and pm. lines. Metallic *blue and black spot on HW*. Wingspan 4–4.8 cm.
Food: Saw palmetto. Larva bores into flower stalks, and forms cocoon from bits of cloth, fiberglass, and other manmade materials after leaving food plant. It can be a minor household pest.
Range: S.C. to Fla., west to at least Miss. All months.

HIEROGLYPHIC MOTH   **Pl. 39 (5)**
Diphthera festiva (F.)
Identification: FW yellow with distinctive *metallic blue lines*. HW smoky. Wingspan 3.7–4.8 cm.
Food: Pecan and other trees; sweet potato.
Range: Tropical; locally common from S.C. through Fla., west to Tex. along Gulf Coast. Strays recorded as far north as Mich. and Mo. April–Nov. in Gulf states.

VELVETBEAN CATERPILLAR MOTH   Pl. 39 (4)
Anticarsia gemmatalis Hbn.
Identification: Extremely variable. Wings pale to dark grayish brown or olive; often mottled (as shown). Note *blackish pm. line from apex to inner margin*, continuing as median line of HW. Short line also curves from costa to apex of FW. HW often has 2 black spots on faint st. line (not shown). Wingspan 3.3–4 cm.
Food: Larva (**Velvetbean Caterpillar**) is a pest of alfalfa, peanut, soybean, velvetbean, and related plants; also black locust.
Range: Common to abundant throughout our area. Sept.–Nov.

RED-LINED PANOPODA   Pl. 39 (3)
Panopoda rufimargo (Hbn.)
Identification: FW and HW dull orange-yellow, usually shaded with brown or dull reddish. Fine yellow am. and pm. *lines edged with red to grayish brown.* Orbicular spot gray. *Reniform spot narrow, yellowish*; lower half sometimes covered with a round, black blotch. Pm. line continues onto HW. Wingspan 4–4.6 cm.
Food: Beeches and oaks.
Range: Me. and Que. to Fla., west to Minn. and Tex. May–Sept. Common in most of range.

BROWN PANOPODA   Pl. 40 (6)
Panopoda carneicosta Gn.
Identification: FW and HW dark brown, tinted with violet gray. Thin brown am., median, and pm. lines on FW. Note black orbicular dot and L-*shaped reniform spot* (both sometimes reduced or absent). Pm. line continues onto HW. Wingspan 3.8–4.6 cm.
Food: Basswood, hickories, oaks, and willows.
Range: S. Me. to Fla., west to e. Kans. and Tex. May–Aug. Common.

ORANGE PANOPODA   Pl. 39 (2)
Panopoda repanda (Wlk.)
Identification: Wings reddish to orangish, often tinted with orange-yellow to brownish; pink luster when fresh. Am. and pm. lines paler than ground color. Note *tiny black dots* where veins cross pm. line. Black blotch at bottom of diffuse median line in some specimens (as shown). Wingspan 3.7–4.3 cm.
Food: Live oak and Para grass (*Panicum purpurascens*).
Range: N.C. to Fla., west to Ky. and Tex. April–June; Aug.; all months in s. Fla. Common to abundant southward.

COMMON OAK MOTH   Pl. 40 (1)
Phoberia atomaris Hbn.
Identification: FW pale to dark gray or brownish, with *yellowish veins and am. and pm. lines.* Median line, reniform spot, and shading inside irregular st. line darker than ground color. HW grayish brown. Wingspan 3.2–4.7 cm.
Food: Oaks.

Range: Mass. to Fla., west to e. Kans. and Tex. Late March–early May. Common to abundant in oak forests.

Similar species: Greater Red Dart (p. 99, Pl. 20) is warmer brown, with *broken, double am. and pm. lines* and a conspicuous *pale band* beyond st. line. Adults fly later (June–Oct.).

BLACK-DOTTED BROWN   Pl. 39 (1)
Cissusa spadix (Cram.)

Identification: FW grayish to reddish brown, with inconspicuous whitish lines. Note *1-2 sharp black spots* next to st. line below apex. HW pale brown, darker at margin. Wingspan 3–4.1 cm.

Food: Unrecorded.

Range: Me. and Ont. to Fla., west to Wisc., Mo., and Tex. April–July. Common, though rare northward.

INDOMITABLE MELIPOTIS   Pl. 40 (3)
Melipotis indomita (Wlk.)

Identification: FW blackish with *oblique whitish median band* shaded with brown. Whitish reniform spot crossed by blackish streaks along veins. Sinuous pm. line has whitish to gray shading beyond it. HW whitish with blackish shading and outer border; note *black blotch in white fringe*. Wingspan 4–5 cm.

Food: Mesquite.

Range: Southern Me. to Fla., west to Minn., Kans., and Tex. May–Sept. Common.

JANUARY MELIPOTIS   Pl. 40 (13)
Melipotis januaris (Gn.)

Identification: Very similar to Indomitable Melipotis (above, Pl. 40) but usually smaller. *Am. line* and *pale, oblique median band* beyond it *curved*. Markings of ♀ (not shown) contrast less with ground color than those of ♂. Wingspan 3–4 cm.

Food: Unrecorded.

Range: Central to s. Fla.; all months. Locally common.

MERRY MELIPOTIS   Pl. 40 (11)
Melipotis jucunda Hbn.

Identification: FW gray, with black, brown, and white streaks that obscure usual pattern. Look for an *outward bulge in pm. line below costa*. HW whitish with blackish shading, leaving 2 white spots along outer margin. Wingspan 3.3–4.3 cm.

Food: Catclaw and willows.

Range: N.J. to Fla., west to Man. and Tex. March–Sept. southward; June–July in North, where it is uncommon.

GRAPHIC MOTH *Drasteria graphica* Hbn.   Pl. 32 (20)
Identification: FW may be uniform gray (not shown) or light and dark gray with black am. and pm. lines. Note how pm. line merges with outer edge of reniform spot. *HW yellow* (as shown) or orange with *black bands and shading*. Wingspan 3–3.5 cm.

Food: Blueberries.

Range: Me. to Fla., west to Miss.; coastal, in sand dune habitats. May–Aug. Locally common.
Similar species: In Occult Drasteria, *D. occulta* (Hy. Edw.), not shown, *st. line is merely a boundary* (not a distinct line) between blackish st. and gray terminal areas; reniform spot a *distinct blackish patch,* lined with whitish. Food: Blueberries; larva sometimes very injurious. Range: Me. to N.J. and Pa.; May–Aug.

FIGURE-SEVEN MOTH   Pl. 32 (17)
Synedoida grandirena (Haw.)
Identification: FW gray and blackish. Whitish and brown median band and reniform spot merge to form a *"7" on FW.* HW black with 3 white bars. Wingspan 3.5–3.8 cm.
Food: Witch-hazel.
Range: N.S. to Fla., west to Wisc. and Tex. May–Aug. Active both day and night; locally common.

OWL MOTH *Thysania zenobia* (Cram.)   Pl. 7 (1)
Identification: *Outer margins* of gray FW and HW *scalloped.* Many *zigzag lines* distinctive. Black streaks in ♂, absent in ♀ (not shown). Wingspan 10–15 cm.
Food: Legumes (?).
Range: Tropical; regularly present from Fla. to Tex., straying northward rarely to Me., s. Ont., Mich., and Mo. Adults fly mostly in Sept.–Nov. northward; all months in s. Fla. and s. Tex.

BLACK WITCH *Ascalapha odorata* (L.)   Pl. 7 (2, 5)
Identification: Easily recognized by its *large size and pointed FW,* which is blackish to brownish with typical noctuid pattern of lines and spots. Note *large oval patch at outer margin,* containing *2 rounded spots.* Pinkish white bands beyond pm. lines of FW and HW in ♀, absent in ♂. Wingspan 11–15 cm.
Food: Cassia and catclaw.
Range: Tropical; regularly present in s. Fla. and s. Tex. in all months. Individuals migrate northward as far as Nfld. and Minn., usually July–Oct. Found northward more often than Owl Moth (above).

DETRACTED OWLET   Pl. 40 (12)
Lesmone detrahens (Wlk.)
Identification: Wings dark purplish gray to brown; lines darker but often inconspicuous. Pm. line fine, sharply bent just below costa; st. shade line *straight on basal side,* irregular on outer side, with *broad tooth* at about midpoint. Pattern less distinct in ♀ (not shown). Wingspan 2.7–3.1 cm.
Food: Unrecorded.
Range: L.I., N.Y. to Fla., west to e. Kans. and Tex. April–Oct.; common southward.

LUNATE ZALE *Zale lunata* (Dru.)   Pl. 37 (8, 10)
Identification: The *largest* and usually the *most common* of the

20 *Zale* species in our area. FW and HW dark brown with blackish brown shading. Pattern variable, with many vague wavy lines; reniform spot black, lunate. Pm. line of FW thin, black, doubly bulged in upper half (indistinct in some specimens). *Black st. line curves from outer to inner margin* and continues onto HW. Whitish to greenish white terminal patches distinguish form "edusa" (Dru.), Pl. 37 (10). Wingspan 4–5.5 cm.
Food: Many trees and shrubs, such as maples, plums, and willows.
Range: Common throughout our area. March–Nov. or frost.

MAPLE ZALE *Zale galbanata* (Morr.)   **Pl. 37 (17)**
Identification: FW and HW pale gray to grayish brown, often with orange-yellow tint in median area of FW. Lines fine, black; pm. line has *2 bulges* in upper half; *st. line heaviest line,* but usually only from inner margin to lower bulge of pm. line. Some white tint beyond st. line and its continuation onto HW in some specimens (not shown). Wingspan 2.9–4.1 cm.
Food: Maples.
Range: N.H. and e. Ont. to n. Fla., west to Man. and Tex. April–Sept.; 2 broods. Locally common.

GREEN-DUSTED ZALE   **Pl. 37 (15)**
Zale aeruginosa (Gn.)
Identification: FW and HW blackish brown to coal black, variably *dusted with pale green* and sometimes whitish (as shown), mostly beyond am. line, and in st. and terminal areas. Lines fine, black; lower st. line heaviest. Wingspan 3.5–4.2 cm.
Food: Live oak, white oak, and spruce.
Range: N.S. to Fla., west to s. Mo. and Tex. April–Aug.; 2 broods. Locally common.

BLACK ZALE *Zale undularis* (Dru.)   **Pl. 38 (13)**
Identification: Wings blackish brown with inconspicuous, wavy black lines. Similar to Green-dusted Zale (above), but without green or white dusting. *Yellowish blotch* outside upper st. line of FW is only pale mark. Wingspan 3.8–4.6 cm.
Food: Black locust and honey locust.
Range: Me. and e. Ont. to Fla., west to Minn. and Ark. April–Sept. Uncommon in Midwest.

COLORFUL ZALE *Zale minerea* (Gn.)   **Pl. 37 (12)**
Identification: Much like Lunate Zale (above, Pl. 37) but usually slightly smaller and more mottled and brightly marked. Pattern variable; usually some *yellow in median area,* especially in ♂. Many specimens have whitish tinting (as shown), like "edusa" form of Lunate Zale. Note black patches near apex and middle of outer margin of FW. Wingspan 3.7–5 cm.
Food: Beech, birches, maples, poplars, and other trees.
Range: Common throughout our area. April–Aug.

GRAY-BANDED ZALE   **Pl. 38 (12)**
Zale squamularis (Dru.)
Identification: Wings dark brownish gray with broad, *bluish gray band* between am. and median lines. Gray patches in terminal areas of FW and HW. Look for an inconspicuous reddish brown reniform spot. Wingspan 3.5–4 cm.
Food: Pines.
Range: L.I., N.Y. to Fla., west to Ky. and Miss. April–June.
Similar species: (1) Oblique Zale, *Z. obliqua* (Gn.), not shown, has less contrasting pattern; *no bluish gray band*. Food: Pines. Range: N.Y. to Fla., west to Minn. and Tex. May–June. Uncommon. (2) See Brown-spotted Zale and Bethune's Zale (below).

BROWN-SPOTTED ZALE *Zale helata* (Sm.)   **Pl. 38 (15)**
Identification: Very similar to Gray-banded Zale (above, Pl. 38) but *without pale gray basal area*. Am. line *more widely zigzag* (note higher peaks). General warm brown shading most conspicuous in *diffuse spot beyond black reniform spot*. Wingspan 3.5–4.1 cm.
Food: Larch and pines (jack, scrub, and white).
Range: Me. and w. Que. to n. Fla., west to Man. and Tex. May–June. Locally common.

BETHUNE'S ZALE *Zale bethunei* (Sm.)   **Pl. 38 (16)**
Identification: Similar to Brown-spotted and Gray-banded Zales (above, Pl. 38), but shading darker brown and pattern more diffuse. Look for *solid black median band* and *warm brown blotch* beyond reniform spot. Wingspan 3.1–4 cm.
Food: Virginia pine.
Range: Me. to N.C., west to Mich. and Tenn. March–June; late July–Aug.; 2 broods. Locally common.

WASHED-OUT ZALE *Zale metatoides* McD.   **Pl. 38 (18)**
Identification: Wings dull light brown with overall violet tint. Very similar to Brown-spotted Zale (above), but looks washed out; *all lines faint except lower st. line*. Orangish blotch beyond reniform spot prominent. Wingspan 3.2–4 cm.
Food: Scrub pine.
Range: Central N.Y. to N.C., west to Ky. and Miss. May–July.

BOLD-BASED ZALE *Zale lunifera* (Hbn.)   **Pl. 38 (21)**
Identification: Wings gray to brown with variable white dusting (usually more than in specimen shown). Note *dark basal area* and *2 sharp bends* in *am. line*. Reniform spot whitish. Wingspan 3.7–4.5 cm.
Food: Black cherry and white pine.
Range: Common throughout our area. April–May and July–Aug.

DOUBLE-BANDED ZALE   **Pl. 38 (20)**
Zale calycanthata (J.E. Sm.)
Identification: Wings blackish brown. Note *whitish bands*

dusted with blackish outside am. line of FW, and in terminal areas of FW and HW. St. line of FW bulged. Wingspan 4.2–4.5 cm.
Food: Cherry and oaks; report of allspice possibly in error.
Range: Eastern N.J. to Fla., west to Man. and Tex. March–May. Locally common southward.

ONE-LINED ZALE *Zale unilineata* (Grt.)   **Pl. 37 (19)**
Identification: Wings warm brown. Lines inconspicuous except sharp *red and yellow double pm. line* on FW and incomplete black st. line on HW. Look for a tiny black orbicular dot. Note gray tint in terminal areas of FW and HW. Wingspan 4–5 cm.
Food: Black locust.
Range: Me. and Que. to W.Va., west to Man., Iowa, and n. Ark. April–June. Common.

HORRID ZALE *Zale horrida* Hbn.   **Pl. 38 (19)**
Identification: *Undulating st. line* of FW and scalloped st. line of HW divide wings into blackish brown inner area and dirty whitish outer area. Whitish areas dusted with brown. Tops of am. and pm. lines whitish at costa. Wingspan 3.5–4 cm.
Food: Nannyberry.
Range: Throughout our area; most common in beech woods. May–July.

LOCUST UNDERWING   **Pl. 37 (5)**
Euparthenos nubilis (Hbn.)
Identification: Easily recognized by the *4 wavy black bands* on deep yellow HW. FW gray with darker gray and brown lines and shading. Heavy whitish tinting beyond am. line in ♂ (not shown); white confined mostly to patch at top of st. line in ♀. Rare melanics are all blackish; pattern vague. Wingspan 5.6–7 cm.
Food: Locusts, particularly black locust.
Range: Me. and Ont. to n. Fla., west to Neb. and n. Ark. April–Sept.; 2 broods. Common.
Similar species: True underwings (*Catocala* species) with banded HW have only 2–3 black bands.

FALSE UNDERWING   **Pl. 32 (11)**
Allotria elonympha (Hbn.)
Identification: Identified by the deep yellow HW with an *even black border*. FW gray, variably mottled and lined with black. Look for a black orbicular dot (barely visible in melanic specimen shown), which distinguishes this from true underwings (*Catocala* species). FW almost entirely black in some melanic specimens. Wingspan 3.3–4.5 cm.
Food: Black gum, sour-gum, hickories, and walnuts.
Range: S. Me. to Fla., west to s. Mo. and Tex. March–Sept. Common to abundant.
Similar species: Messalina Underwing, *Catocala messalina* (Gn.), p. 311, has similar HW pattern but lines on FW *incomplete*. A southwestern moth (not shown), *rare* in our area.

SMITH'S DARKWING   Pl. 31 (19)
Dysgonia smithii (Gn.)

Identification: FW light brown with blackish shading inside am. and pm. lines; note *2 broad, sharp teeth* on pm. line, and black apical marking. HW dark grayish brown with 2 faint lines. Wingspan 3.8–4 cm.

Food: Unrecorded.

Range: N.J. to Fla., west to Mo. and Tex. April–Sept. Rare northward.

MAPLE LOOPER MOTH   Pl. 31 (21)
Parallelia bistriaris Hbn.

Identification: FW dark brown with 2 distinct yellowish lines: *am. line straight, pm. line slightly wavy.* Note whitish dusting beyond pale, diffuse st. line. HW dark brown with white dusting along outer margin. Wingspan 3.3–4.3 cm.

Food: Larva (**Maple Looper**) feeds on yellow birch, red and white maples, and black walnut.

Range: N.S. to Fla., west to Minn., Kans., and Tex. April–Sept. Common.

TOOTHED SOMBERWING   Pl. 38 (1)
Euclidia cuspidea (Hbn.)

Identification: FW purplish gray and brown; note distinctive *black pm. triangle, basal and apical spots, and am. band.* HW yellowish brown, with 2 blackish lines and basal shading. Wingspan 3–4 cm.

Food: Clover, grasses, lupine, and sweetfern.

Range: Me. and Que. to Fla., west to Man., Kans., and n. Ark. April–Sept.; at least 2 broods. Active day and night; often found in clover fields.

VETCH LOOPER MOTH   Pl. 38 (5)
Caenurgia chloropha (Hbn.)

Identification: FW pale grayish brown in ♂, orangish yellow-brown in ♀. Lines fine, inconspicuous; lower pm. line *bulges inward.* Note diffuse dark patch beyond pm. line—darker in ♀ (shown) than in ♂. HW yellowish with 2 gray bands in both sexes. Wingspan 2.7–3.6 cm.

Food: Vetch.

Range: S. Ont. to Fla., west to Kans. and Tex. April–Oct. Common southward.

CLOVER LOOPER MOTH   Pl. 38 (3)
Caenurgina crassiuscula (Haw.)

Identification: FW mouse gray; ♂ has 2 *diffuse dark bands* which almost meet near inner margin and *touch inner margin.* The ♀ (not shown) is larger, with a similar but even more obscure pattern. Wingspan 3–4 cm.

Food: Larva (**Clover Looper**) feeds on clover, grasses, and lupines.

Range: Abundant throughout our area, especially in clover fields; active day and night. Mar.–Nov.; several broods.

FORAGE LOOPER MOTH   Pl. 38 (2, 6)
Caenurgina erechtea (Cram.)

Identification: Similar to the Clover Looper Moth (above), and equally common. In ♂ of this species, FW has *2 dark bars* that are clearly defined but *do not touch* each other or inner margin. The ♀ is larger than the ♂, with deep brownish wings and only faint traces of lines—no dark bars. Wingspan 3–4.2 cm.

Food: Larva (**Forage Looper**) feeds on alfalfa, clover, grasses, and great ragweed.

Range: Abundant throughout our area. Mar.–Nov.; several broods. Active day and night.

SMALL MOCIS *Mocis latipes* (Gn.)   Pl. 38 (7)

Identification: FW yellowish brown, variably shaded with darker brown; ♀ (not shown) usually more yellowish to reddish than ♂. Am. and pm. lines nearly straight. Look for *large, round subreniform spot* with a blackish outline, just below reniform spot. Some have a black spot (shown) on inner margin (size varies). HW yellowish brown with dark brown shading and 2 faint lines. Wingspan 3.3–4.3 cm.

Food: Grasses, including rice and corn; beans and turnip.

Range: S. Ont. to Fla., west to Mo. and Tex. June–Oct. Common only in South; a stray northward.

TEXAS MOCIS *Mocis texana* (Morr.)   Pl. 38 (4)

Identification: Larger than Small Mocis (above); FW pale grayish to violet brown, with even brown shading along costa and beyond pm. line. Reniform spot distinct, but *no subreniform spot*. Some specimens have a small black spot (not shown) on inner margin. Wingspan 4.2–5 cm.

Food: Larva has been reared on crabgrass.

Range: S. Ont. to Fla., west to Minn. and Tex. April–Sept. Common southward.

Similar species: (1) Yellow Mocis, *M. disseverans* (Wlk.), not shown, is *more yellowish; lines nearly absent.* Food: Sugar cane and other grasses. Range: Coastal S.C. to Fla., west to Tex.; strays northward. All year. (2) Withered Mocis, *M. marcida* (Gn.), not shown, has conspicuous lines: *pm. line bulges inward* just above inner margin. Food: Probably grasses. Range: Same as for Yellow Mocis. (3) See Small Mocis (above).

BLACK BIT MOTH *Celiptera frustulum* Gn.   Pl. 38 (9)

Identification: FW gray; note *rounded black spot* at inner margin, and *other small black "bits"* near base and along am. line. Yellow edging along straight, dark pm. line makes it look double; reniform spot also lined with yellow. HW grayish brown with lines at inner margin. Wingspan 3.4–4.1 cm.

Food: Larva has been reared on black locust.

Range: N.Y. and s. Ont. to Fla., west to Wisc., Kans., and Tex. May–June; Aug.; 2 broods. Moderately common.

COMMON PTICHODIS Pl. 38 (8)
Ptichodis herbarum (Gn.)
Identification: FW light grayish to grayish brown. Am. and pm. lines thin, yellow, shaded with dark brown. Both lines *straight in* ♂; am. line gently *curved in* ♀. *Black dot near base* on inner margin in ♀ (shown). HW grayish brown, darker beyond pale median line. Wingspan 2.8–3.6 cm.
Food: Lespedeza.
Range: N.Y. to Fla., west to Mo. and Tex. May–Oct. Common.
Similar species: (1) Southern Ptichodis (below) has *no median line* on HW. (2) Black-tipped Ptichodis, *P. vinculum* (Gn.), not shown, is more purplish gray from base to pm. line of FW, and has *black apical spot.* Food: Unrecorded. Range: N.Y. to Fla., west to Mo. and La. June–July. Common southward.

SOUTHERN PTICHODIS Pl. 38 (10)
Ptichodis bistrigata Hbn.
Identification: FW violet gray with straight lines and *no black spots;* note brown edging along yellow am. and pm. lines. HW grayish brown with *no median line.* Usually smaller than our other *Ptichodis* species; wingspan 2.7–3.2 cm.
Food: Unrecorded.
Range: Eastern N.J. to Fla., west to Mo. and Tex. April–July.

FOUR-LINED CHOCOLATE Pl. 38 (14)
Argyrostrotis quadrifilaris (Hbn.)
Identification: Easily recognized by the *2 sharp, complete white lines* crossing each dark chocolate FW. Lines blackish instead of white in form "obsoleta" (Grt.), not shown. HW blackish brown with white fringe. Wingspan 2.8–3 cm.
Food: Cotton.
Range: N.H. to Fla., west to Wisc. and Miss. April; July–Aug. Rare northward.

SHORT-LINED CHOCOLATE Pl. 38 (17)
Argyrostrotis anilis (Dru.)
Identification: Similar to Four-lined Chocolate (above), but *am. line more oblique; pm. line incomplete,* slightly curved. Wingspan 2.7–3.7 cm.
Food: Reported on *Sabatia* species.
Range: Mass. to Fla., west to Minn., Kans. and Tex. April–Sept.; at least 2 broods. May be locally common.

DOUBLE-LINED DORYODES Pl. 38 (11)
Doryodes bistrialis (Gey.)
Identification: FW *very narrow, pointed;* yellowish tan with white-edged *brown streak* extending from base to apex. Tiny black orbicular and reniform dots. HW cream. Wingspan 3–3.8 cm.

Food: Salt-meadow grass (*Spartina patens*).

Range: Coastal habitats from P.E.I. to Fla. May–Oct. Locally common.

Similar species: In Dull Doryodes, *D. spadaria* Gn. (not shown), FW is *dull brown*. Food: Unrecorded. Range: S.C. to s. Fla. All year.

MOON-LINED MOTH *Spiloloma lunilinea* Grt.   **Pl. 40 (4)**
Identification: Wings pale gray, with variable light brown shading in lower st. and terminal areas of FW and on most of HW. Lines most conspicuous as 5 *blackish spots* along costa. Note blackish collar. Wingspan 4.4–5.4 cm.

Food: Honey locust.

Range: Mass. to n. Fla., west to Mo. and Tex. April–Aug. Common in most of range.

Underwings: Genus *Catocala*

Easily recognized by the *hind wings,* which are *all black, or brightly colored with black bands.* FW, with typical noctuid pattern, resembles bark of trees. HW apparently startles predators when the well-camouflaged moths are discovered at rest on treetrunks. Of 110 N. American species, this guide includes 76 (most of those known to occur in our area).

THE BETROTHED *Catocala innubens* Gn.   **Pl. 36 (1, 2)**
Identification: FW mottled gray, white, and brown. Subreniform spot usually *white,* with *pale bar* passing through it. Vague blackish bar from base of FW to outer margin (darkest below apex). Most of FW dark brown to st. line in form "scintillans" Grt. (Pl. 36). HW black with orange bands and fringe in both forms. Wingspan 5.5–7.2 cm.

Food: Honey locust.

Range: S. Ont. and N.Y. to Fla., west to S.D. and Tex. June–Sept. Uncommon to common.

THE PENITENT *Catocala piatrix* Grt.   **Pl. 37 (11)**
Identification: FW grayish brown, with an oblique *whitish bar* extending from costa *through subreniform spot.* Note broad tooth on basal side of am. line, near inner margin. HW banded orange and black. Wingspan 6.8–8.4 cm.

Food: Ash, butternut, hickory, pecan, persimmon, and walnut trees.

Range: Me. to Fla., west through s. Ont. to S.D. and Tex. July–early Nov. Uncommon to common.

THE CONSORT *Catocala consors* (J.E. Sm.)   **Pl. 36 (3)**
Identification: FW evenly dull grayish brown; purplish tint in some specimens. Am. and pm. lines sharp, black; outline of subreniform spot distinct. HW yellowish orange with narrow me-

dian black band; *bands scalloped more deeply* than in other underwings. Wingspan 6-7 cm.
Food: Hickories.
Range: Me. to cen. Fla., west to Iowa, Kans., and Tex. June-July; May in Gulf states. Common to uncommon; rare in Northeast.

EPIONE UNDERWING   Pl. 34 (3)
Catocala epione (Dru.)
Identification: FW dark gray and blackish with *chocolate edging* along sharp, black am. and pm. lines and chocolate filling in reniform spot. *Subreniform spot whitish.* HW black with fringe white, black at anal angle. Wingspan 5.5-6.5 cm.
Food: Hickories.
Range: Me. and s. Ont. to Fla., west to Kans. and Tex. June-Sept. Common.

THE LITTLE WIFE   Pl. 36 (4)
Catocala muliercula Gn.
Identification: Easily recognized by the *reddish brown FW;* lines black, except for whitish midsection of pm. line. HW banded black and yellowish orange. Wingspan 5.4-7 cm.
Food: Common waxmyrtle.
Range: Coastal Conn. to Fla., west along Gulf Coast to Tex. May-July. Local; uncommon to common.

WAYWARD NYMPH or SWEETFERN   Pl. 33 (4)
UNDERWING *Catocala antinympha* (Hbn.)
Identification: FW glossy; usually *bluish black* with black lines and some brown shading, especially beyond pm. line. Subreniform spot sometimes whitish (as shown). HW banded yellowish orange and black; most of fringe blackish. A small underwing; wingspan 4.5-5.5 cm.
Food: Sweetfern.
Range: N.S. and Que. to Md., west to s. Ont. and Mich. July-Sept. Common in acid-soil habitats along coast; rare inland.

THE OLD MAID   Pl. 36 (6)
Catocala coelebs Grt.
Identification: FW gray, with light or heavy brown to black shading inside am. and st. lines. Subreniform spot *clearly defined;* usually *open* on outer side and filled with brown. HW yellowish orange and black (bands nearly even). Wingspan 5-6 cm.
Food: Sweetgale.
Range: N.S. and Que. to N.Y. (Adirondacks), west through Ont. to Wisc. Aug. Local and rare.

BAY UNDERWING or BADIA UNDERWING   Pl. 36 (5)
Catocala badia Grt. & Rob.
Identification: Easily recognized by the smooth brown FW with

darker brown, inconspicuous lines. Note *paler brown area beyond nearly straight st. line.* HW orange and black. Wingspan 5–6 cm.
Food: Waxmyrtle.
Range: Me. to N.J. in coastal habitats. July–early Oct. May be locally common where waxmyrtle abounds.

HABILIS UNDERWING Pl. 36 (8)
Catocala habilis Grt.
Identification: FW light gray. Note *whitish scalloped st. line* and white accents along black am. and pm. lines. Black basal dash present in some specimens; *lower pm. line forms a dash* near inner margin. HW banded orange and black. Wingspan 5.5–6.7 cm.
Food: Hickories and walnuts.
Range: Me. and Que. to N.C., west to S.D., Kans., and Ark. July–Oct. Uncommon to common.

SERENE UNDERWING Pl. 33 (1)
Catocala serena Edw.
Identification: Look for *dark brown collar* on brownish gray thorax. FW smooth brownish gray with thin black lines. Zigzag pm. line indents around *open subreniform spot.* HW yellowish orange with black bands. Wingspan 5–6.2 cm.
Food: Unrecorded so far; probably hickories and walnuts.
Range: S. Mass. to N.C., west to Mich., Mo., and Miss. June–Oct. Uncommon to common.

ROBINSON'S UNDERWING Pl. 35 (1, 2)
Catocala robinsoni Grt.
Identification: See 2 forms on Pl. 35: FW usually pale gray as in Habilis Underwing (above, Pl. 36); not much contrast between pattern and ground color. *No dash on lower pm. line;* ♀ (not shown) has a basal dash. In rare form "missouriensis" Schwarz (Pa. to Fla.), FW has a *broad black bar* extending from base to outer margin (below apex), broken only by gray reniform and subreniform spots. HW black with white fringe in both forms. Wingspan 7–8 cm.
Food: Hickories and walnuts (?).
Range: N.H. and s. Ont. to W. Va. and Ala., west to Mo., Ark. and Miss. Aug.–Nov. Uncommon to locally common; rare northward.

JUDITH'S UNDERWING Pl. 34 (6)
Catocala judith Stkr.
Identification: Of our medium-sized underwings with black HW, only this species has *entirely gray fringe on HW* (no white, even at apex). FW gray with inconspicuous lines. Wingspan 4.5–5.5 cm.
Food: Hickories and walnuts.
Range: N.H. and s. Ont. to N.C., west to Wisc. and Mo. June–Aug. Uncommon to locally common (Ky.).

(*Text continues on p. 304*)

Plates

The moths illustrated in this guide are pinned, spread specimens, because it is easiest to study wing patterns and other details needed for identification in specimens that have been spread on a spreading board (see p. 23). You may be able to identify some living or unspread moths, however, by their characteristic resting poses (see examples on rear endpapers) and forewing patterns. The first step is to familiarize yourself with the lines and spots that are present, to varying degrees, in moth wing patterns (see front endpapers). Color alone is rarely sufficient, since many moths have drab colors that help them blend in with their surroundings, and some have two or more color variations within the species. These variations are illustrated on the plates when space permits and are described in the text. Use size and overall wing shape—especially the shape of the outer margins, which may be nearly straight, slightly curved, or scalloped—to get to the right group of moths. As you become more familiar with moth families, you can use the index below as a shortcut. Check the scale (indicated at upper right on each legend page) to make sure that you are comparing moths of roughly the same size; most moths in this guide are shown life-size. Then check the field marks—the distinctive features of each species, which are pinpointed with arrows on the plates, as in other Peterson Field Guides. When you think you have found a close match for your specimen, turn to the text for information on geographic range, flight season, and other details that will help confirm your identification. In addition to providing the common and scientific names and the sex of each specimen shown on the plates, the legends indicate the collection site and the date when the moth was collected, if available. Note that some of the moths shown on the plates have been reared by collectors, so the months when those adult moths emerged in captivity may vary from the normal flight season for the species in nature.

SHORTCUT INDEX TO PLATES

Caterpillars

PLATE 2 x ⅔

Cocoons

1. **TULIP-TREE SILKMOTH,**   p. 51
   Callosamia angulifera

2. **PROMETHEA MOTH or SPICEBUSH**   p. 51
   SILKMOTH, *Callosamia promethea*

3. **EVERGREEN BAGWORM MOTH,**   p. 450
   Thyridopteryx ephemeraeformis

4. **LUNA MOTH,** *Actias luna*   p. 49

5. **IO MOTH,** *Automeris io*   p. 49

6. **POLYPHEMUS MOTH,** *Antheraea polyphemus*   p. 49

7. **SWEETBAY SILKMOTH,** *Callosamia securifera*   p. 51

8. **CECROPIA MOTH or ROBIN MOTH,**   p. 52
   Hyalophora cecropia

All of these cocoons are from the Wedge Plantation, McClellan-ville, S.C., and were collected or reared by the late Richard B. Dominick.

PLATE 3   x ½

Sphinx or Hawk Moths (1)

PLATE 4 x ⅔

Sphinx or Hawk Moths (2)

PLATE 5 x ⅔

Sphinx or Hawk Moths (3)

1. **PAWPAW SPHINX,** *Dolba hyloeus,* ♂, S.C., April   p. 33

2. **CYPRESS SPHINX,** *Isoparce cupressi,* ♂, S.C., March   p. 34

3. **APPLE SPHINX,** *Sphinx gordius,* ♀, Conn., April   p. 35

4. **HERMIT SPHINX,** *Sphinx eremitus,* ♂, N.Y.   p. 34

5. **PLEBEIAN SPHINX,** *Paratraea plebeja,* ♂, Ky., May   p. 34

6. **SAGE SPHINX,** *Sphinx eremitoides,* ♂, Kans., May   p. 34

7. **CANADIAN SPHINX,** *Sphinx canadensis,* ♂, Maine, June   p. 35

8. **NORTHERN PINE SPHINX,** *Lapara bombycoides,* ♂, N.S., June   p. 36

9. **CATALPA SPHINX,** *Ceratomia catalpae,* ♂, Ky., June   p. 33

10. **PINE SPHINX,** *Lapara coniferarum,* ♂, S.C., Aug.   p. 36

11. **TITAN SPHINX,** *Aellopos titan,* ♂, Texas, Nov.   p. 39

12. **MOURNFUL SPHINX,** *Enyo lugubris,* ♀, S.C., Dec.   p. 40

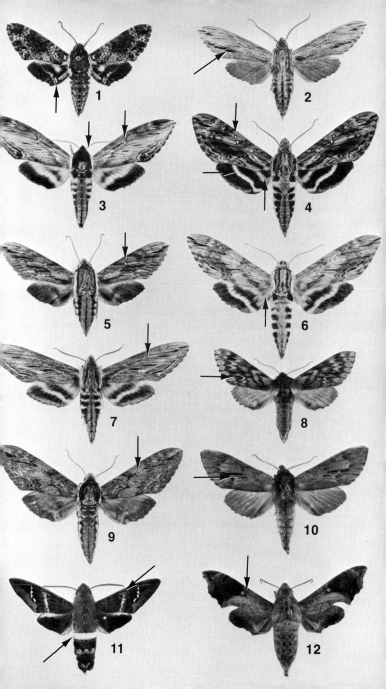

PLATE 6 x ⅔

Sphinx or Hawk Moths (4)

1. **ONE-EYED SPHINX,** *Smerinthus cerisyi,* ♂, N.S., July — p. 37

2. **SMALL-EYED SPHINX,** *Paonias myops,* ♂, N.S., June — p. 37

3. **BLINDED SPHINX,** *Paonias excaecatus,* ♂, Ky., July — p. 37

4. **TWIN-SPOTTED SPHINX,** *Smerinthus jamaicensis,* ♂, Colo. — p. 37

5. **WALNUT SPHINX,** *Laothoe juglandis,* ♂, Ky., Sept., reared — p. 38

6. **HUCKLEBERRY SPHINX,** *Paonias astylus,* ♂, N.Y., July — p. 37

7. **HYDRANGEA SPHINX,** *Darapsa versicolor,* ♂, Ky., July — p. 43

8. **HALF-BLIND SPHINX,** *Perigonia lusca,* ♂, Fla., May — p. 39

9. **ABBOT'S SPHINX,** *Sphecodina abbottii,* ♂, Ky., April — p. 42

10. **TERSA SPHINX,** *Xylophanes tersa,* ♂, Fla., April — p. 43

11. **HOG SPHINX or VIRGINIA CREEPER SPHINX,** *Darapsa myron,* ♂, Ky., May — p. 43

12. **AZALEA SPHINX,** *Darapsa pholus,* ♂, Ky., May — p. 43

13. **PROUD SPHINX,** *Proserpinus gaurae,* ♀, Texas, June — p. 42

14. **LETTERED SPHINX,** *Deidamia inscripta,* ♂, Ky., April — p. 42

15. **GROTE'S SPHINX,** *Cautethia grotei,* ♂, Fla., May — p. 42

16. **HUMMINGBIRD CLEARWING,** *Hemaris thysbe,* ♂, Va., Aug. — p. 40

17. **SLENDER CLEARWING,** *Hemaris gracilis,* ♀, N.Y., May — p. 40

18. **OBSCURE SPHINX,** *Erinnyis obscura,* ♂, Fla., May — p. 38

19. **SNOWBERRY CLEARWING,** *Hemaris diffinis,* ♂, Ky., April — p. 40

20. **NESSUS SPHINX,** *Amphion floridensis,* ♂, N.Y., June — p. 42

PLATE 7 x ½

Large Sphinxes, Noctuids, and Others

1. **OWL MOTH,** *Thysania zenobia,* ♂   p. 165

2. **BLACK WITCH,** *Ascalapha odorata,* ♂, Fla.,   p. 165
   May

3. **FIG SPHINX,** *Pachylia ficus,* ♂, Fla., Nov.   p. 39

4. **PECAN CARPENTERWORM MOTH,**   p. 423
   Cossula magnifica, ♀, Fla., April

5. **BLACK WITCH,** *Ascalapha odorata,* ♀, Fla.,   p. 165
   May

6. **CARPENTERWORM MOTH,**   p. 423
   Prionoxystus robiniae, ♀, N.Y., July

7. **LITTLE CARPENTERWORM MOTH,**   p. 423
   Prionoxystus macmurtrei, ♀, Ky., June

8. **GIANT SPHINX,** *Cocytius antaeus,* ♀, Texas, Oct.   p. 31

9. **CARPENTERWORM MOTH,**   p. 423
   Prionoxystus robiniae, ♂, April, reared

10. **SILVER-SPOTTED GHOST MOTH,**   p. 457
    Sthenopis argenteomaculatus, ♀, N.Y.

PLATE 8   x ⅔

Giant Silkworm Moths (1)
and Relatives

PLATE 9 x ⅔

Giant Silkworm Moths (2)

1. **PINE-DEVIL MOTH,** *Citheronia sepulcralis,* ♂,   p. 46
S.C., Aug.

2. **REGAL MOTH or ROYAL WALNUT MOTH,**   p. 45
Citheronia regalis, ♂, Ky., July

3. **BUCK MOTH,** *Hemileuca maia,* ♂, Wash., D.C.   p. 48

4. **NEVADA BUCK MOTH,** *Hemileuca nevadensis,*   p. 49
♂, Calif., Nov.

5. **IMPERIAL MOTH,** *Eacles imperialis,* ♂, S.C.,   p. 45
July

6. **NEW ENGLAND BUCK MOTH,**   p. 48
Hemileuca lucina, ♂, Me., Sept.

7. **POLYPHEMUS MOTH,** *Antheraea polyphemus,*   p. 49
♂, Ky., March, reared

8. **LUNA MOTH,** *Actias luna,* ♂, S.C., March   p. 49

PLATE 10　　　　　　　　　　　　x ½

Giant Silkworm Moths (3)

1. **AILANTHUS SILKMOTH,** *Samia cynthia, ♂,* p. 50
   reared

2. **IO MOTH,** *Automeris io, ♂,* Ky., July　　　p. 49

3. **CALLETA SILKMOTH,** *Eupackardia calleta, ♂,* p. 50
   Texas, Nov., reared

4. **IO MOTH,** *Automeris io, ♀,* Ky., Sept., reared　p. 49

5. **TULIP-TREE SILKMOTH,** p. 51
   Callosamia angulifera, ♂, S.C., May, reared

6. **FORBES' SILKMOTH,** *Rothschildia forbesi, ♂,* p. 50
   Texas, July

7. **TULIP-TREE SILKMOTH,** p. 51
   Callosamia angulifera, ♀, S.C., May, reared

8. **SWEETBAY SILKMOTH,** *Callosamia securifera,* p. 51
   ♂, S.C., April

9. **PROMETHEA MOTH or SPICEBUSH** p. 51
   SILKMOTH, *Callosamia promethea, ♂,* S.C., July,
   reared

10. **SWEETBAY SILKMOTH,** *Callosamia securifera,* p. 51
    ♀, S.C., May, reared

11. **COLUMBIA SILKMOTH,** *Hyalophora columbia,* p. 52
    ♂, Mich., May

12. **PROMETHEA MOTH or SPICEBUSH** p. 51
    SILKMOTH, *Callosamia promethea, ♀,* S.C., Aug.,
    reared

13. **CECROPIA MOTH or ROBIN MOTH,** p. 52
    Hyalophora cecropia, ♂, Ky., April, reared

PLATE 11   life-size

Tent Caterpillar Moths,
Wasp Moths (1), and Others

PLATE 12   life-size

Wasp Moths (2) and Arctiid Moths

1. **VIRGINIA CTENUCHA,** *Ctenucha virginica,* ♂,   p. 75
   N.S., July

2. **PAINTED LICHEN MOTH,** *Hypoprepia fucosa,*   p. 62
   ♀, S.C., Aug.

3. **STREAKED CALIDOTA,** *Calidota laqueata,* ♀,   p. 73
   Fla., April

4. **LONG-STREAKED TUSSOCK MOTH,**   p. 73
   Leucanopsis longa, ♀, Fla., May

5. **SCARLET-WINGED LICHEN MOTH,**   p. 61
   Hypoprepia miniata, ♀, S.D., July

6. **BANDED TUSSOCK MOTH,**   p. 72
   Halysidota tessellaris, ♀, Ky., May, reared

7. **HICKORY TUSSOCK MOTH,**   p. 72
   Lophocampa caryae, ♂, Va., May

8. **SNOWY EUPSEUDOSOMA,**   p. 75
   Eupseudosoma involutum floridum, ♀, Fla., Nov.

9. **SPOTTED TUSSOCK MOTH,**   p. 73
   Lophocampa maculata, ♀, N.C., June

10. **OREGON CYCNIA,** *Cycnia oregonensis,* ♀, N.S.,   p. 74
    June

11. **SPRAGUE'S PYGARCTIA,** *Pygarctia spraguei,*   p. 74
    ♂, Ind., Feb., reared

12. **YELLOW-EDGED PYGARCTIA,**   p. 74
    Pygarctia abdominalis, ♀, N.C., July, reared

13. **THIN-BANDED LICHEN MOTH,**   p. 60
    Cisthene tenuifascia, ♀, S.C., June

14. **YELLOW-WINGED PAREUCHAETES,**   p. 73
    Pareuchaetes insulata, ♀, Fla., May

15. **LEAD-COLORED LICHEN MOTH,**   p. 60
    Cisthene plumbea, ♀, Ky., June

16. **KENTUCKY LICHEN MOTH,**   p. 60
    Cisthene kentuckiensis, ♀, S.C., Sept.

17. **MILKWEED TUSSOCK MOTH,** *Euchaetes egle,*   p. 74
    ♂, S.C., May

18. **PACKARD'S LICHEN MOTH,**   p. 61
    Cisthene packardii, ♂, S.C., Aug.

19. **STRIATED LICHEN MOTH,** *Cisthene striata,* ♂,   p. 61
    Fla., April

20. **FLORIDA EUCEREON,** *Eucereon carolina,* ♂,   p. 76
    Fla., May

21. **SUBJECT LICHEN MOTH,** *Cisthene subjecta,* ♂,   p. 61
    Fla., March

PLATE 13   life-size

Tiger Moths (1), Dagger Moths (1), and Others

1. **AGREEABLE TIGER MOTH,**   p. 66
   Spilosoma congrua, ♂, N.S., June

2. **FALL WEBWORM MOTH,** *Hyphantria cunea,* ♂,   p. 67
   S.C., March

3. **PINK-LEGGED TIGER MOTH,**   p. 66
   Spilosoma latipennis, ♂, Conn., March, reared

4. **VIRGINIAN TIGER MOTH or YELLOW BEAR**   p. 67
   MOTH, *Spilosoma virginica,* ♂, N.C., June

5. **FALL WEBWORM MOTH,** *Hyphantria cunea,* ♂,   p. 67
   S.C., May

6. **DELICATE CYCNIA,** *Cycnia tenera,* ♂, Ky., May   p. 74

7. **DUBIOUS TIGER MOTH,** *Spilosoma dubia,* ♂,   p. 67
   N.S., June

8. **UNEXPECTED CYCNIA,** *Cycnia inopinatus,* ♂,   p. 73
   S.C., June

9. **ECHO MOTH,** *Seirarctia echo,* ♂, Fla., May   p. 66

10. **RED-TAILED SPECTER,** *Euerythra phasma,* ♂,   p. 67
    Kans., April

11. **REVERSED HAPLOA,** *Haploa reversa,* ♀, Ky.,   p. 63
    July

12. **THREE-SPOTTED SPECTER,**   p. 68
    Euerythra trimaculata, ♂, Tex., March

13. **SALT MARSH MOTH,** *Estigmene acrea,* ♂, Fla.,   p. 66
    April

14. **SILKWORM MOTH,** *Bombyx mori,* ♀, Mo., July,   p. 55
    reared

15. **WHITE FLANNEL MOTH,** *Norape ovina,* ♂,   p. 413
    Ky., July

16. **SALT MARSH MOTH,** *Estigmene acrea,* ♀, May   p. 66

17. **COTTONWOOD DAGGER MOTH,**   p. 82
    Acronicta lepusculina, ♂, N.Y., May

18. **SMEARED DAGGER MOTH,** *Acronicta oblinita,*   p. 88
    ♂, N.S., June

19. **FINGERED DAGGER MOTH,**   p. 82
    Acronicta dactylina, ♂, N.S., June

PLATE 14   life-size

Tiger Moths and Other Arctiids (2)

PLATE 15   life-size

Tiger Moths and Other Arctiids (3); Foresters

1. **PHYLLIRA TIGER MOTH,** *Grammia phyllira,*   p. 71
   ♂, N.C., July, reared

2. **FIGURED TIGER MOTH,** *Grammia figurata,* ♂,   p. 70
   N.J., Aug., reared

3. **FIGURED TIGER MOTH,** *Grammia figurata,* ♀,   p. 70
   N.J., Aug., reared

4. **PLACENTIA TIGER MOTH,**   p. 71
   Grammia placentia, ♂, Fla., July, reared

5. **BANDED TIGER MOTH,** *Apantesis vittata,* ♂,   p. 69
   Fla., March

6. **PLACENTIA TIGER MOTH,**   p. 71
   Grammia placentia, ♀, N.C., Aug., reared

7. **BANDED TIGER MOTH,** *Apantesis vittata,* ♂,   p. 69
   S.C., Sept., reared

8. **HARNESSED MOTH,** *Apantesis phalerata,* ♂,   p. 69
   S.C., Oct., reared

9. **NAIS TIGER MOTH,** *Apantesis nais,* ♂, Conn.,   p. 69
   Aug., reared

10. **NAIS TIGER MOTH,** *Apantesis nais,* ♀, Conn.,   p. 69
    Aug., reared

11. **HARNESSED MOTH,** *Apantesis phalerata,* ♀,   p. 69
    S.C., Oct., reared

12. **BELLA MOTH,** *Utetheisa bella,* ♀, S.C., Nov.   p. 63

13. **GREAT TIGER MOTH,** *Arctia caja americana,*   p. 69
    ♂, Wisc., Aug.

14. **WITTFELD'S FORESTER,** *Alypia wittfeldii,* ♀,   p. 140
    Fla., April

15. **CLYMENE MOTH,** *Haploa clymene,* ♀, Ky., July   p. 63

16. **EIGHT-SPOTTED FORESTER,**   p. 140
    Alypia octomaculata, ♀, Ky., May

17. **ST. LAWRENCE TIGER MOTH,**   p. 69
    Platarctia parthenos, ♀, N.S., July

18. **MOUSE-COLORED LICHEN MOTH,**   p. 62
    Pagara simplex, ♂, S.C., Sept., reared

19. **COLONA MOTH,** *Haploa colona,* ♂, S.C., June   p. 63

PLATE 16   life-size

Arctiids and Noctuids

PLATE 17   life-size

Dagger Moths (2)

PLATE 18   life-size

Dagger Moths (3) and Darts (1)

PLATE 19   life-size

Darts (2)

PLATE 20   life-size

Darts (3) and Other Noctuids

PLATE 21 life-size

Darts (4) and Other Noctuids

1. **SMALLER PINKISH DART,** *Diarsia jucunda,* ♂, Mich., July — p. 95

2. **DAPPLED DART,** *Anaplectoides pressus,* ♂, N.S., July — p. 98

3. **THE NUTMEG,** *Discestra trifolii,* ♀, N.S., Aug. — p. 99

4. **BROWN-COLLARED DART,** *Protolampra brunneicollis,* ♀, Ky., Sept. — p. 98

5. **TWO-SPOT DART,** *Eueretagrotis perattenta,* ♂, Pa., July — p. 98

6. **SIGMOID DART,** *Eueretagrotis sigmoides,* ♂, N.C., July — p. 98

7. **CLOUDY ARCHES,** *Polia imbrifera,* ♀, Ky., July — p. 100

8. **DISTINCT QUAKER,** *Achatia distincta,* ♀, Ky., April — p. 108

9. **GRAND ARCHES,** *Lacanobia grandis,* ♂, N.Y., July — p. 102

10. **STORMY ARCHES,** *Polia nimbosa,* ♂, Ky., July — p. 100

11. **CAPSULE MOTH,** *Anepia capsularis,* ♂, S.C., April — p. 103

12. **PURPLE ARCHES,** *Polia purpurissata,* ♂, Ont., Aug. — p. 100

13. **SNAKY ARCHES,** *Lacinipolia anguina,* ♂, Conn., May — p. 103

14. **DISPARAGED ARCHES,** *Polia detracta,* ♀, Ky., June — p. 101

15. **SPECKLED CUTWORM MOTH,** *Lacanobia subjuncta,* ♂, N.H. — p. 102

16. **FLUID ARCHES,** *Polia latex,* ♀, N.C., July — p. 101

17. **GOODELL'S ARCHES,** *Polia goodelli,* ♂, Pa., June — p. 101

18. **THE THINKER,** *Lacinipolia meditata,* ♀, S.C., Sept. — p. 103

19. **BLACK ARCHES,** *Melanchra assimilis,* ♂, Conn., July — p. 102

20. **SIGNATE QUAKER,** *Tricholita signata,* ♀, N.S., Aug. — p. 110

21. **INTRACTABLE QUAKER,** *Himella intractata,* ♂, Conn., May — p. 107

22. **SHEATHED QUAKER,** *Ulolonche culea,* ♂, Conn., April — p. 109

PLATE 22   life-size

Armyworm Moths (1)
and Other Noctuids

1. **RUSTIC QUAKER,** *Orthodes crenulata,* ♂, N.S.,   p. 110
   June
2. **RUDDY QUAKER,** *Protorthodes oviduca,* ♂,   p. 109
   N.S., June
3. **ZEBRA CATERPILLAR MOTH,**   p. 101
   Melanchra picta, ♂, N.S., June
4. **SPECKLED GREEN FRUITWORM MOTH,**   p. 107
   Orthosia hibisci, ♂, Ky., March
5. **SMALL BROWN QUAKER,**   p. 109
   Pseudorthodes vecors, ♂, N.S., June
6. **GRAY WOODGRAIN,** *Morrisonia mucens,* ♀,   p. 108
   S.C., March
7. **GRAY QUAKER,** *Orthosia alurina,* ♂, Ky., April   p. 106
8. **CYNICAL QUAKER,** *Orthodes cynica,* ♂, N.S.,   p. 110
   May
9. **CONFUSED WOODGRAIN,** *Morrisonia confusa,*   p. 108
   ♀, N.S., May
10. **RUBY QUAKER,** *Orthosia rubescens,* ♂, Ky.,   p. 106
    April
11. **ALTERNATE WOODLING,** *Egira alternata,* ♀,   p. 107
    Fla., March
12. **BICOLORED WOODGRAIN,** *Morrisonia evicta,*   p. 108
    ♀, N.S., May
13. **NORMAN'S QUAKER,** *Crocigrapha normani,* ♂,   p. 107
    N.S., May
14. **WHEAT HEAD ARMYWORM MOTH,**   p. 104
    Faronta diffusa, ♂, N.S., July
15. **BRONZED CUTWORM MOTH,**   p. 109
    Nephelodes minians, ♂, Md., Sept.
16. **GARMAN'S QUAKER,** *Orthosia garmani,* ♂,   p. 106
    Mo., March
17. **MANY-LINED WAINSCOT,** *Leucania multilinea,*   p. 105
    ♀, N.S., July
18. **ARMYWORM MOTH,** *Pseudaletia unipuncta,* ♀,   p. 105
    Conn., Oct.
19. **SCIRPUS WAINSCOT,** *Leucania scirpicola,* ♂,   p. 105
    Fla., March
20. **UNARMED WAINSCOT,** *Leucania inermis,* ♀,   p. 106
    N.S., June
21. **FALSE WAINSCOT,** *Leucania pseudargyria,* ♀,   p. 106
    N.Y.

PLATE 23   life-size

Pinions (1), Sallows, and Other Noctuids

PLATE 24 life-size

Pinions (2) and Other Noctuids

PLATE 25   life-size

Amphipyrine Noctuids

PLATE 26   life-size

Borer Moths and Other
Amphipyrine Noctuids

1. **PITCHER-PLANT BORER MOTH,**   p. 126
   Papaipema appassionata, ♂, S.C., Nov.
2. **AMERICAN EAR MOTH,**   p. 124
   Amphipoea americana, ♂, N.S., Aug.
3. **OSMUNDA BORER MOTH,**   p. 126
   Papaipema speciosissima, ♀, N.J., Sept.
4. **BRACKEN BORER MOTH,** *Papaipema pterisii,*   p. 125
   ♂, N.S., Sept.
5. **SENSITIVE FERN BORER MOTH,**   p. 126
   Papaipema inquaesita, ♂, S.C., July
6. **IRONWEED BORER MOTH,**   p. 127
   Papaipema cerussata, ♀, N.Y.
7. **STALK BORER MOTH,** *Papaipema nebris,* ♀,   p. 126
   Md., Sept.
8. **NORTHERN BURDOCK BORER MOTH,**   p. 125
   Papaipema arctivorens, ♂, Ky., Aug.
9. **RIGID SUNFLOWER BORER MOTH,**   p. 127
   Papaipema rigida, ♀, N.Y., Sept.
10. **SUNFLOWER BORER MOTH,**   p. 127
    Papaipema necopina, ♀, Ill., Sept.
11. **BURDOCK BORER MOTH,**   p. 125
    Papaipema cataphracta, ♂, S.C., Oct.
12. **CHAIN FERN BORER MOTH,**   p. 125
    Papaipema stenocelis, ♀, S.C., Aug.
13. **OLIVE ANGLE SHADES,** *Phlogophora iris,* ♂, p. 129
    Conn., May
14. **SILVER-SPOTTED FERN MOTH,**   p. 131
    Callopistria cordata, ♂, N.S., June
15. **BUFFALO MOTH,** *Parapamea buffaloensis,* ♂, p. 124
    N.J., Sept.
16. **THE GREEN MARVEL,** *Agriopodes fallax,* ♂,   p. 88
    N.S., July
17. **COPPER UNDERWING,**   p. 132
    Amphipyra pyramidoides, ♀, S.C., June
18. **SPOTTED PHOSPHILA,** *Phosphila miselioides,* p. 131
    ♂, N.C., June
19. **GREEN LEUCONYCTA,**   p. 148
    Leuconycta diphteroides, ♀, N.C., June
20. **THE HEBREW,** *Polygrammate hebraeicum,* ♂,   p. 89
    Ky., July
21. **PINK-SHADED FERN MOTH,**   p. 131
    Callopistria mollissima, ♂, Conn., June
22. **AMERICAN ANGLE SHADES,**   p. 129
    Euplexia benesimilis, ♂, N.C., June

PLATE 27　　　　　　　　　　　　　　　　　　life-size

Groundlings, Midgets, Foresters, and Other Noctuids

1. **RED GROUNDLING,** *Perigea xanthioides,* ♂, Conn., June　　p. 136

2. **DUSKY GROUNDLING,** *Platysenta vecors,* ♀, Ky., May　　p. 137

3. **MOBILE GROUNDLING,** *Platysenta mobilis,* ♂, Fla., March　　p. 136

4. **THE COBBLER,** *Platysenta sutor,* ♂, Ky., Oct.　　p. 137

5. **THE SLOWPOKE,** *Anorthodes tarda,* ♀, Conn., June　　p. 132

6. **CHALCEDONY MIDGET,** *Elaphria chalcedonia,* ♂, Fla., March　　p. 135

7. **FESTIVE MIDGET,** *Elaphria festivoides,* ♂, Conn., June　　p. 135

8. **GOLDENROD STOWAWAY,** *Cirrhophanus triangulifer,* ♂, Md., Sept.　　p. 138

9. **VARIEGATED MIDGET,** *Elaphria versicolor,* ♂, N.C., June　　p. 135

10. **FIGURE-EIGHT SALLOW,** *Psaphida resumens,* ♀, Va., April　　p. 119

11. **ELDER SHOOT BORER MOTH,** *Achatodes zeae,* ♂, N.C., June　　p. 128

12. **BORDERED SALLOW,** *Pyrrhia umbra,* ♀, Ky., Sept.　　p. 140

13. **THE WEDGELING,** *Galgula partita,* ♂, N.Y., Sept.　　p. 136

14. **THE WEDGELING,** *Galgula partita,* ♀, N.S., Aug.　　p. 136

15. **PINK STAR MOTH,** *Derrima stellata,* ♂, Fla., April　　p. 140

16. **FEEBLE GRASS MOTH,** *Amolita fessa,* ♀, Ky., Aug.　　p. 138

17. **OBTUSE YELLOW,** *Stiriodes obtusa,* ♀, Fla., March　　p. 137

18. **GOLD MOTH,** *Basilodes pepita,* ♀, Va., Sept.　　p. 138

19. **MIRANDA MOTH,** *Proxenus miranda,* ♂, N.S., June　　p. 132

20. **COMMON PINKBAND,** *Ogdoconta cinereola,* ♀, Ky., June　　p. 137

21. **AMERICAN DUN-BAR,** *Cosmia calami,* ♀, N.S., Aug.　　p. 139

22. **ORANGE SALLOW,** *Rhodoecia aurantiago,* ♀, S.C., Sept.　　p. 141

23. **BEAUTIFUL WOOD-NYMPH,** *Eudryas grata,* ♂, Ky., June　　p. 139

24. **GRATEFUL MIDGET,** *Elaphria grata,* ♂, Md., Sept.　　p. 136

25. **PEARLY WOOD-NYMPH,** *Eudryas unio,* ♂, Fla., March　　p. 139

Armyworm Moths (2)
and Other Noctuids

PLATE 29   life-size

Flower Moths and Other Noctuids

PLATE 30   life-size

Bird-dropping Moths
and Other Noctuids

PLATE 31   life-size

Looper Moths and Other Noctuids

PLATE 32   life-size

Looper Moths, Underwings (1), and Other Noctuids

PLATE 33   life-size

Underwings (2)

PLATE 34 x ⅔

Underwings (3)

PLATE 35   x ⅔

Underwings (4)

PLATE 36 x ⅔

Underwings (5)

PLATE 37   x $\frac{2}{3}$

Underwings (6) and Zales (1)

PLATE 38   life-size

Zales (2) and Other Catocaline Noctuids

PLATE 39　　　　　　　　　　　　　　　　　life-size

Catocaline and Deltoid Noctuids

PLATE 40 life-size

Deltoid Noctuids (2)

PLATE 41   life-size

Deltoid Noctuids (3)

PLATE 42　　　　　　　　　　　　　　　　　life-size

Deltoid Noctuids (4) and Prominents (1)

PLATE 43   life-size

Prominents (2)

PLATE 44   life-size

Prominents (3) and Tussock Moths (1)

PLATE 45   life-size

Tussock Moths (2) and Thyatirid Moths

PLATE 46   life-size
Hooktip and Inchworm Moths (1)

PLATE 47   life-size

Inchworm Moths (2)

   Note: Because of space limitations, information on
   collection dates or localities had to be omitted for some of
   the moths on this page.

PLATE 48   life-size

Inchworm Moths (3) and Others

PLATE 49　　　　　　　　　　　　　　　　life-size

Inchworm Moths (4)

PLATE 50   life-size

Inchworm Moths (5)

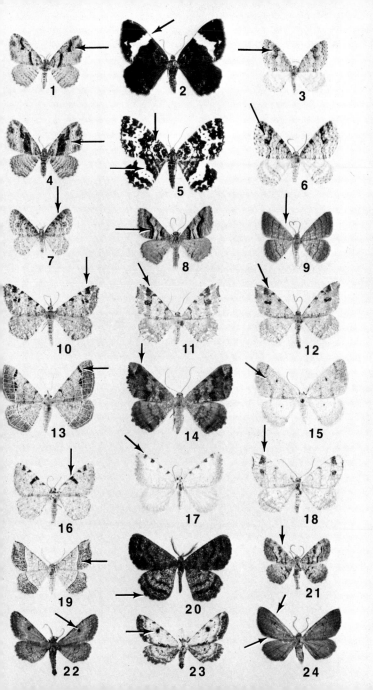

PLATE 51 life-size

Inchworm Moths (6)

PLATE 52   life-size

Inchworm Moths (7)

PLATE 53   life-size

Inchworm Moths (8)

PLATE 54   life-size

Inchworm Moths (9)

PLATE 55   life-size

Inchworm Moths (10)
and Others

PLATE 56   life-size

Inchworm Moths (11)
and Various Micros

1. **FALSE HEMLOCK LOOPER MOTH,**   p. 371
   Nepytia canosaria, ♂, N.S., Sept.
2. **LARGE MAPLE SPANWORM MOTH,**   p. 373
   Prochoerodes transversata, ♂, Ky., July
3. **JEWELED SATYR MOTH,**   p. 360
   Phrygionia argentata, ♂, Fla., May
4. **WHITE-TIPPED BLACK,** *Melanchroia chephise,*   p. 355
   ♀, Fla., Sept.
5. **SKIFF MOTH,** *Prolimacodes badia,* ♂, Fla., Nov.   p. 410
6. **CONFUSED EUSARCA,** *Eusarca confusaria,* ♂,   p. 371
   Ky., Sept.
7. **HAG MOTH,** *Phobetron pithecium,* ♂, N.C., June   p. 410
8. **SADDLEBACK CATERPILLAR MOTH,**   p. 412
   Sibine stimulea, ♂, Fla., May
9. **BLACK-WAVED FLANNEL MOTH,**   p. 412
   Lagoa crispata, ♂, S.C., May
10. **HAG MOTH,** *Phobetron pithecium,* ♀, N.Y., July   p. 410
11. **GRAPE LEAFFOLDER MOTH,**   p. 400
    Desmia funeralis, ♂, Ark., June
12. **SOUTHERN FLANNEL MOTH,**   p. 412
    Megalopyge opercularis, ♂, S.C., Aug.
13. **MOURNFUL THYRIS,** *Thyris sepulchralis,* ♀,   p. 393
    Ky., June
14. *Desmia maculalis,* ♀, S.C., Aug.   p. 400
15. **HAWAIIAN BEET WEBWORM MOTH,**   p. 401
    Spoladea recurvalis, ♂, Va., Sept.
16. **SPOTTED BEET WEBWORM MOTH,**   p. 400
    Hymenia perspectalis, ♀, N.C., July
17. *Pilocrocis ramentalis,* ♀, S.C., Oct.   p. 402
18. **MELONWORM MOTH,** *Diaphania hyalinata,* ♂,   p. 401
    S.C., Sept.
19. *Conchylodes ovulalis,* ♂, S.C., May   p. 402
20. *Nomophila nearctica,* ♀, Ky., Sept.   p. 400
21. *Perispasta caeculalis,* ♂, S.C., April   p. 398
22. *Perispasta caeculalis,* ♀, Ark., July   p. 398
23. **GARDEN WEBWORM MOTH,** *Achyra rantalis,*   p. 398
    ♀, Ark., June
24. *Phlyctaenia coronata tertialis,* ♂, N.C., July   p. 398
25. **CELERY LEAFTIER MOTH,** *Udea rubigalis,* ♂,   p. 399
    Ark., June
26. *Herpetogramma thestialis,* ♂, Ky., June   p. 402

PLATE 57   life-size

Window-winged Moths
and Pyralid Moths

PLATE 58　　　　　　　　　　　　　　　　　life-size

Pyralid Moths, Plume Moths, and Many-plume Moths

PLATE 59 life-size

Pyralid Moths and Tortricid Moths (1)

PLATE 60   life-size

Tortricid Moths (2)
and Clear-winged Moths (1)

PLATE 61   life-size

Tortricid Moths (3), Clear-winged Moths (2), and Other Micros

PLATE 62   life-size

Gelechiid Moths (1) and Other Micros

1. *Urodus parvula,* ♀, Fla., April   p. 431

2. **AMERICAN ERMINE MOTH,**   p. 431
   Yponomeuta multipunctella, ♂, Md., June

3. *Acrolophus popeanella,* ♂, Md., July   p. 452

4. **CURRANT FRUITWORM MOTH,**   p. 434
   Carposina fernaldana, ♀, Ont., Aug.

5. **AILANTHUS WEBWORM MOTH,**   p. 431
   Atteva punctella, ♂, Fla., May

6. *Metzneria lappella,* ♀, N.Y., Aug.   p. 436

7. **REDBUD LEAFFOLDER MOTH,**   p. 437
   Fascista cercerisella, ♂, Md., July

8. *Adela purpurea,* ♂, N.S., May   p. 454

9. **ANGOUMOIS GRAIN MOTH,**   p. 437
   Sitotroga cerealella, ♂, Va., July

10. *Chionodes mediofuscella,* ♀, La., April   p. 437

11. **GOLDENROD GALL MOTH,**   p. 436
    Gnorimoschema gallaesolidaginis, ♂, Ill., Sept.,
    reared

12. **POTATO TUBERWORM MOTH,**   p. 436
    Phthorimaea operculella, ♂, N.S., July

13. **PEACH TWIG BORER MOTH,**   p. 437
    Anarsia lineatella, ♀, Utah, May

14. **SWEETCLOVER ROOT BORER MOTH,**   p. 440
    Walshia miscecolorella, ♂, Ariz., July

15. **SHY COSMET,** *Limnaecia phragmitella,* ♀, Mich.,   p. 439
    July

16. **ACORN MOTH,** *Valentinia glandulella,* ♀, N.C.,   p. 443
    Aug.

17. *Coleophora atromarginata,* ♂, N.C., July   p. 442

18. *Antaeotricha leucillana,* ♂, N.Y., May   p. 446

19. *Ethmia trifurcella,* ♂, Ky., June   p. 445

20. *Antaeotricha schlaegeri,* ♀, N.Y., Sept.   p. 446

21. *Ethmia zelleriella,* ♀, N.Y., May   p. 445

22. *Epermenia imperialella,* ♀, Pa., May   p. 433

23. **EVERGREEN BAGWORM MOTH,**   p. 450
    Thyridopteryx ephemeraeformis, ♂, Ill., Sept.

24. *Cryptothelea gloverii,* ♂, Fla., Nov.   p. 450

PLATE 63 x 2

Clothes Moths, Gelechiids (2), and Other Micros

PLATE 64   x 2

Various Micros

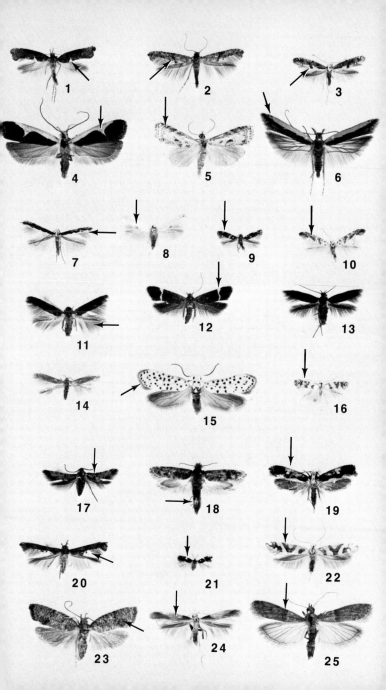

MOURNING UNDERWING
Pl. 35 (4)

Catocala flebilis Grt.

Identification: FW gray, with *diffuse black band* extending from base to outer margin, interrupted by pale gray subreniform spot. Brown shading beyond pm. line and inside reniform spot. Look for white HW fringe. Wingspan 5.4–6.5 cm.

Food: Hickories.

Range: Mass. to N.C., west to Ill., Mo., and Ark. July–Sept. Rare to locally common.

ANGUS'S UNDERWING
Pl. 35 (5, 6)

Catocala angusi Grt.

Identification: Two forms: see Pl. 35. Both forms have *anal dash* beyond zigzag pm. line; ♀ (not shown) of typical form also has a basal dash. FW pale gray in typical form (both sexes) with some brown filling in reniform spot. Form "lucetta" French has *broad black band* from base to outer margin (just below apex), with *distinct break* in median area. HW black in both forms; fringe dark gray, white only at apex. Wingspan 6–7.4 cm.

Food: Hickories and pecan.

Range: Mass. to Ga., west to Ill., Kans., Ark., and Miss. July–Oct. Rare in North, uncommon southward; typical form more common than form "lucetta."

OBSCURE UNDERWING
Pl. 35 (7)

Catocala obscura Stkr.

Identification: FW dull gray; am. and pm. lines black but inconspicuous. Look for *broad whitish st. band* with dark teeth on outer side. Upper ⅔ of HW fringe white, the rest blackish. Wingspan 6–7.2 cm.

Food: Hickories and walnuts.

Range: Mass. and s. Ont. to N.C., west to Ill., Mo., Ark., and Miss. July–Sept. Common southward; uncommon in North.

RESIDUA UNDERWING
Pl. 35 (8)

Catocala residua Grt.

Identification: Similar to Obscure Underwing (above), but *HW fringe mostly black — white only at apex*. St. line of FW usually paler. Look for diffuse black subapical dash in some specimens (shown). Wingspan 6–7.3 cm.

Food: Hickories.

Range: Me. and Ont. to N.C., west to Mich., Ill., Mo., and Miss. July–Sept. More common than Obscure Underwing.

SAPPHO UNDERWING
Pl. 35 (10)

Catocala sappho Stkr.

Identification: *FW white with reddish brown reniform spot* continuing to costa. Lines blackish, heavy only at costa. HW black with white fringe. Wingspan 6.2–7.5 cm.

Food: Pecan trees.
Range: Va. to Fla., west to s. Ill., Mo., and Miss. May–Aug. Locally common southward.

AGRIPPINA UNDERWING   Pl. 34 (11)
Catocala agrippina Stkr.
Identification: FW grayish brown with *warm brown shading* from am. line to st. area; some specimens have a greenish sheen. Subreniform spot usually lighter grayish brown than rest of FW. HW fringe white, with black checkering at ends of veins. Wingspan 6.5–8.5 cm.
Food: Pecan trees.
Range: N.J. to Fla., west to Mo. and Tex. June–Sept. Locally common in South; rare northward.

YELLOW-GRAY UNDERWING   Pl. 34 (10)
Catocala retecta Grt.
Identification: FW pale gray with yellowish brown shading in some specimens (form "luctuosa" Hulst, not shown, which may be a distinct species or subspecies). Pattern distinct, with *2 black dashes near base,* and others below apex and on lower pm. line. HW black with checkered white fringe. Wingspan 6–7.5 cm.
Food: Hickories and walnuts.
Range: Me. and s. Que. to Ga., west to Wisc., Kans., and Ark. July–Oct. Common to abundant; form "luctuosa" is rare.

ULALUME UNDERWING   Pl. 34 (5)
Catocala ulalume Stkr.
Identification: FW mottled light and dark gray (no strong contrasts). Note short basal dash and thickened blackish shade lines below apex and at anal angle (none very conspicuous). Look for a *whitish crescent* accenting am. line at inner margin—often the lightest marking, but not as pronounced as in Tearful Underwing (p. 306, Pl. 35). HW fringe white, checkered. Wingspan 6–7.5 cm.
Food: Hickories.
Range: Va. to n. Fla., west to Ill., Mo., Ark., and Miss. June–Sept. Local and uncommon to rare.

DEJECTED UNDERWING   Pl. 34 (2)
Catocala dejecta Stkr.
Identification: FW mottled gray (more bluish than in Ulalume Underwing, above); usually *more contrast* between black lines and dashes and pale gray areas in this moth. Note *sharp border* between whitish upper median area and black lower median area. Subreniform spot often conspicuous (faint in specimen shown). HW black with white fringe; note teeth at ends of veins. Wingspan 5.6–7.3 cm.
Food: Hickories.
Range: Mass. to n. Fla., west to Mo. and Tex. June–Oct. Uncommon to rare.

INCONSOLABLE UNDERWING
Pl. 34 (1)

Catocala insolabilis Gn.

Identification: FW pale gray with *broken black shade line* just above inner margin. Some brown shading in ♀ (not shown). *HW fringe black* except for thin white edge at apex. Wingspan 6.5–7.5 cm.

Food: Hickories.

Range: Me. and s. Ont. to Fla., west to S.D., Ark., and Miss. June–Aug. Uncommon to rare.

WIDOW UNDERWING
Pl. 34 (4)

Catocala vidua (J.E. Sm.)

Identification: FW pale gray; pattern much like that of Yellow-gray Underwing (p. 305, Pl. 34), but black arc on upper FW heavier, passing *just above* reniform spot (not through it). Note black shading over upper am. and pm. lines and black streak parallel to inner margin. HW fringe white. Wingspan 6.9–8.5 cm.

Food: Hickory, pecan, and walnut trees.

Range: Me. and s. Ont. to n. Fla., west to Wisc., Mo. and n. Ark. July–Oct. Common to abundant throughout most of range.

Similar species: (1) In Marbled Underwing (p. 308, Pl. 37) black arc passes *through* reniform spot on FW. (2) In Yellow-gray Underwing, black FW markings more diffuse, not as heavy.

SAD UNDERWING *Catocala maestosa* (Hulst)
Pl. 34 (9)

Identification: Similar to Widow Underwing (above, Pl. 34) but usually larger. *Black arc above reniform spot of FW is heaviest marking;* no black shade over am. line or above inner margin. Note brown shading along am. and pm. lines, and brown filling in reniform spot. HW fringe white, checkered, narrow. Wingspan 7.8–9.8 cm.

Food: Hickory, pecan, and walnut trees.

Range: L.I., N.Y. to Fla., west to Kans. and Tex. July–Oct.; April–Nov. in Miss. Locally common southward.

TEARFUL UNDERWING
Pl. 35 (3)

Catocala lacrymosa Gn.

Identification: FW mottled dark gray, brown, and black; pattern variable, but look for *whitish crescents* accenting am. and pm. lines *at inner margin*. Distinct forms (not shown) include "evelina" French (wide black band along inner margin of FW); "paulina" Hy. Edw. (FW entirely blackish out to white st. band); and "zelica" French (black basal patch and st. band). HW black with checkered fringe that is mostly white—*black* near anal angle. Wingspan 6–8.2 cm.

Food: Hickories.

Range: Mass. to Fla., west to Wisc., Kans., and Tex. July–Oct. Common except in Northeast.

Similar species: In Ulalume Underwing (p. 305, Pl. 34), FW is

more evenly gray; white am. crescent at inner margin *less distinct.*
HW fringe is *white all the way to anal angle.*

OLDWIFE UNDERWING **Pls. 1 (9); 36 (7, 10)**
Catocala palaeogama Gn.
Identification: FW variable, usually mottled *whitish gray*
(blackish in melanic form "denussa" Ehrman, not shown). Note
orange HW with *irregular black bands* in all forms; *fringe orange
to apex.* Black basal patch and st. band on FW identify form
"phalanga" Grt., Pl. 36 (10). In form "annida" Fager (not shown),
FW is whitish with black reniform spot, subapical spot, and border
along inner margin. Wingspan 6–7 cm.
Food: Larva (Pl. 1) feeds on hickory and walnut trees.
Range: Me. and s. Ont. to S.C., west to S.D., Kans., and Ark.
June–Oct. Common southward.

CLOUDED UNDERWING **Pl. 36 (16)**
Catocala nebulosa Edw.
Identification: FW variable — reddish to yellowish brown, some-
times with a greenish tinge. Prominent *basal patch* darker brown;
ends sharply at am. line. Apical area darker than median area of
FW, but not as dark as basal patch. HW yellowish orange with
broad black bands; fringe yellowish. Wingspan 7.5–8.6 cm.
Food: Unrecorded.
Range: L.I., N.Y. and s. Ont. to n. Fla., west to Wisc., Kans., n.
Ark., and La. July–Oct. Locally common to rare.

YOUTHFUL UNDERWING **Pl. 36 (18)**
Catocala subnata Grt.
Identification: FW mottled light and dark gray with thin, incon-
spicuous black lines. Note *warm brown filling* in reniform spot and
shading beyond pm. line. HW yellowish orange with black bands.
Wingspan 7.5–9 cm.
Food: Butternut, hickories, and walnuts (?).
Range: N.S. to N.C., west to Man., Kans., and Tex. July–Aug.
Uncommon to rare.

THE BRIDE *Catocala neogama* (J.E. Sm.) **Pl. 36 (12)**
Identification: Very similar to Youthful Underwing (above, Pl.
36) but usually smaller and *darker gray* with *heavier markings.*
Hind tibia *flattened,* sparsely and *unevenly spined;* that of Youth-
ful Underwing cylindrical with dense, uniform covering of spines
on outer surface. Wingspan 7–8.5 cm.
Food: Butternut, hickories and walnuts.
Range: Me. and Que. to n. Fla., west to S.D. and Tex. June–Oct.
Common in much of range.

ILIA UNDERWING *Catocala ilia* (Cram.) **Pl. 37 (4, 7)**
Identification: FW extremely variable, may be mottled dark gray
to almost black. Usually some *whitish* in median area. Reniform
spot usually *outlined with white,* or *solid white* (form "conspicua"

Worthington). Note reddish orange median band with *deep scallops* near anal angle of HW. Fringe pale orangish, narrow except at apex. Wingspan 6.5–8.2 cm.

Food: Oaks, including black, burr, red, and white oaks.

Range: Nfld. and Que. to Fla., west throughout our area. June–Sept. One of our most abundant underwings.

Remarks: Also known as the Beloved Underwing or The Wife.

YELLOW-BANDED UNDERWING   Pl. 36 (9)
Catocala cerogama Gn.

Identification: Easily recognized by the *even, deep yellow band* on HW. FW usually brownish gray; note pale band connecting whitish subreniform spot to costa. FW darker brown in melanic form "ruperti" Franc. (not shown). Wingspan 6.4–8.1 cm.

Food: American basswood.

Range: N.S. to N.C., west to Man., S.D. and Mo. July–Oct. Common wherever basswood is plentiful.

WHITE UNDERWING *Catocala relicta* Wlk.   Pl. 35 (9)
Identification: Our only underwing with *black and white bands on HW.* FW varies from gray to blackish and white, providing camouflage when moth rests on birch bark. Wingspan 7–8 cm.

Food: Poplars, quaking aspen, and willows.

Range: Nfld. to Pa., west across Canada, south to Mo. Strays reported from Ky. and Miss. July–Oct. Common northward.

Remarks: Also known as the Forsaken Underwing and the Relict.

MARBLED UNDERWING   Pl. 37 (14)
Catocala marmorata Edw.

Identification: Large; FW pale gray with *curved blackish band* from costa *through* reniform spot to outer margin. HW black and pinkish red. Wingspan 9–9.5 cm.

Food: Unrecorded.

Range: N.H. to S.C., west to Wisc. and Mo. June–Sept. Uncommon to rare.

Similar species: In Widow Underwing (p. 306, Pl. 34) the black arc on upper FW passes *just above* reniform spot.

ONCE-MARRIED UNDERWING   Pl. 37 (9)
Catocala unijuga Wlk.

Identification: FW mottled pale to dark gray and white. Black pm. and white st. lines zigzag. *Orangish red band* on HW only slightly irregular; fringe mostly white. Wingspan 7–9 cm.

Food: Poplars and willows.

Range: Nfld. to Pa., west to Man. and Mo. July–Oct. Common in most of range; very local in Ky.

MOTHER UNDERWING *Catocala parta* Gn.   Pl. 37 (18)
Identification: FW mottled pale gray and brown; note *black dashes* in *basal,* subapical, and anal areas. HW black and pale yellowish orange; black inner band often does not reach inner mar-

gin. HW fringe yellowish orange to apex. Melanics with blackish FW are form "forbesi" Franc. (not shown). Wingspan 7–8.5 cm.
Food: Poplars and willows.
Range: N.S. to Md. and Ky., west to Man., S.D., and Mo. June–Oct. Common to uncommon northward; rare in South.

BRISEIS UNDERWING *Catocala briseis* Edw.   **Pl. 36 (15)**
Identification: FW mottled, *sooty blackish* (rarely lighter gray) with *diffuse whitish st. band* that widens toward costa. Note whitish patch over subreniform spot. HW orangish red with black bands. Wingspan 6–7 cm.
Food: Poplars and willows.
Range: Nfld. to N.J., west across Canada, south to Mich., Ill., and Wisc. Late July–Sept. Uncommon to rare.

SEMIRELICT UNDERWING   **Pl. 37 (1)**
Catocala semirelicta Grt.
Identification: FW white with black lines and shading; diffuse *black line* usually extends *from base to outer margin* (absent in more *uniformly gray* FW of form "atala" Cass., not shown). HW orangish to pinkish red with black bands. Wingspan 6.5–7.5 cm.
Food: Poplars and willows.
Range: N.S. to Me., west across Canada, south into n. Mich. July–Sept. Apparently rare; our most northern underwing.

MESKE'S UNDERWING *Catocala meskei* Grt.   **Pl. 36 (14)**
Identification: Nearly identical to the Once-married Underwing (p. 308, Pl. 37), but gray FW more uniformly dusted with whitish and blackish. HW orangish red with black bands, usually paler in Once-married Underwing; *apex pale orangish* (apex *white* in Once-married Underwing). Wingspan 6.5–7.5 cm.
Food: Cottonwood, other poplars, and willows.
Range: Me. and Que. to N.Y. and Pa., west to Man. and S.C. July–Sept. Uncommon to rare.

JOINED UNDERWING   **Pl. 37 (16)**
Catocala junctura Wlk.
Identification: FW much like that of Once-married Underwing (p. 308, Pl. 37), but usually *uniformly dark gray* with *obscure lines* (specimen shown is unusually dark). In form "julietta" French, black line extends from base of FW to outer margin. HW light orange; black *median band narrower* than in any other large eastern underwing, usually not reaching inner margin. Wingspan 7–8.5 cm.
Food: Willows.
Range: Western N.Y. and Pa. to Ky., west to e. Kans. and Tex. June–Oct. Common westward. Observed in caves in the daytime.

DARLING UNDERWING or BRONZE   **Pl. 37 (20)**
UNDERWING *Catocala cara* Gn.
Identification: *FW deep brown* with *deep green shading* and

black lines. HW banded black and *bright pink*. Form "carissima" Hulst (not shown) has yellowish apical patches on FW. Wingspan 7–8.5 cm.

Food: Poplars and willows, particularly black willow.

Range: N.H. and s. Ont. to Fla., west to S.D. and Tex. July–Oct. Common (form "carissima" more common than typical form southward). Adults hide by day in protected places such as caves or under eaves and bridges.

SLEEPY UNDERWING or PINK UNDERWING *Catocala concumbens* Wlk. Pl. 37 (3)

Identification: FW pale gray with *whitish and tan shading;* lines sharp, thin, black. HW pink (rarely yellow) with black bands; inner black band even, not reaching inner margin. *HW fringe whitish, wide.* Wingspan 6–7.5 cm.

Food: Poplars and willows.

Range: N.S. to N.C. mts., west to Man. and S.D. June–Sept. Locally common northward.

THE SWEETHEART Pl. 37 (13)
Catocala amatrix (Hbn.)

Identification: FW grayish to purplish brown with wavy black lines; am. line usually connected by short lines to subreniform spot. May have a *broken black shade line* from base to outer margin (as shown). *HW pinkish red with black bands;* fringe wide, yellowish white. Wingspan 7.5–9.5 cm.

Food: Poplars and willows; larva seems to prefer cottonwood and black willow.

Range: N.S. to n. Fla., west to S.D. and Tex. July–Oct. Hides by day in caves and other protected places. Locally common to rare.

DELILAH UNDERWING Pl. 36 (11)
Catocala delilah Stkr.

Identification: FW mottled with various shades of brown. Am. and pm. lines black, sharp; *upper ⅔ of am. line* the heaviest marking. HW yellowish orange with black bands; fringe yellowish orange, broad at apex and anal angle. Wingspan 5.8–6.5 cm.

Food: Oaks.

Range: Ill. to Fla., west to Kans. and Tex. Basically a western species; rare eastward. May–June.

MAGDALEN UNDERWING Pl. 36 (13)
Catocala illecta Wlk.

Identification: FW pale gray with thin black lines. HW *deep yellow with black bands;* inner black band does *not* reach inner margin. Wingspan 6–7 cm.

Food: Honey locust and possibly leadplant.

Range: S. Ont. and Ohio to S.C., west to e. Kans. and Tex. May–July. Common toward western limits of range; rare in East.

Remarks: The common name is derived from a synonym, *C. magdalena* Stkr., by which the species was once known.

ABBREVIATED UNDERWING Pl. 32 (10)
Catocala abbreviatella Grt.

Identification: FW grayish brown; *upper am. and pm. lines* sharp, black. Reniform spot hollow; *lower edge heavy.* HW orangish yellow; black marginal band *abruptly broken* near anal angle. Wingspan 4.5–5 cm.

Food: Leadplant.

Range: Minn. and Man. to Tex.; isolated records as far east as Pa. Aug. Sometimes common during the day on milkweed blossoms in prairie habitats in Mo.

MARRIED UNDERWING Pl. 33 (6)
Catocala nuptialis Wlk.

Identification: Similar to Abbreviated Underwing (above), but black *reniform spot complete,* more conspicuous, either solid (as shown) or hollow. Marginal black band of yellowish orange HW *not broken,* but *indented near anal angle.* Wingspan 4–5 cm.

Food: Leadplant; also reported on honey locust and oak.

Range: Ky., Minn., and Man., south to Tex. July–Aug. Uncommon.

Similar species: Whitney's Underwing, *C. whitneyi* Dodge, not shown, has *solid black triangle* formed by am. line, narrowest at costa. Food: Leadplant. Range: Ohio to Tenn., west to Man. and Kans. July–Aug. Emerges later than Married and Abbreviated Underwings where ranges overlap.

THREE-STAFF UNDERWING Pl. 32 (12)
Catocala amestris Stkr.

Identification: FW pale gray with *double black am. and pm. lines* and reniform spot outline. HW yellow with black bands; marginal band broken or complete (complete in form "westcotti" Grt., shown). Wingspan 4–4.5 cm.

Food: Leadplant and locusts.

Range: N.C. to Fla., west to Wisc., S.D., and Tex. July–Aug. northward. Locally common except northward.

MESSALINA UNDERWING not shown
Catocala messalina Gn.

Identification: FW dull gray, gradually darkening in outer $\frac{1}{3}$ of wing; lines evident *only at costa. HW yellowish orange* with *even, unbroken black border* as in False Underwing (p. 168, Pl. 32). Fringe whitish yellow. Wingspan 4–4.5 cm.

Food: Unrecorded.

Range: A southwestern moth, rarely recorded in our area. Known from Va., S.C., Fla., La., Kans., and Tex. in our area. May–June.

SORDID UNDERWING Pl. 33 (3, 5)
Catocala sordida Grt.

Identification: FW mottled gray; *deeply zigzag whitish st. line* usually conspicuous. Black am. and pm. lines either complete and conspicuous, or evident only toward costa. Inner margin of FW bordered with black in form "metalomus" Mayfield, Pl. 33 (5). HW yellow with black bands; marginal band broken near anal angle. Wingspan 3.7–4.5 cm.

Food: Blueberries.

Range: N.S. to Fla., west to Man. and Tex. May–Sept. Common.

GRACEFUL UNDERWING   **Pls. 32 (13), 33 (2), 36 (17)**
Catocala gracilis Edw.

Identification: Similar to Sordid Underwing (above). FW *more mottled; more heavily shaded* along inner margin. Basal dash usually present (but not a reliable feature). Black border of inner margin sharp in form "lemmeri" Mayfield (Pl. 36). Black inner band on yellow HW *does not form complete loop* as it does in Sordid Underwing. Wingspan 4–4.5 cm.

Food: Blueberries.

Range: N.S. to Fla., west to Man., Mo., and Miss. July–Sept. Common in Northeast; rare westward.

Similar species: (1) In Sordid Underwing (above), inner black band of HW *forms complete loop.* (2) Louise's Underwing, *C. louiseae* Bauer (not shown), has whitish zigzag st. line on FW like Andromeda Underwing (below, Pl. 34), and HW orange with black bands; median black band narrow, *ending abruptly* before inner margin. Food: Blueberries. Range: Fla. and Tex. May.

ANDROMEDA UNDERWING   **Pl. 34 (7)**
Catocala andromedae (Gn.)

Identification: Easily recognized by its *small size, black HW,* and *FW pattern* (gray with *black shade line* along inner margin). Underside of FW entirely black except unbroken white median band. Wingspan 4–5 cm.

Food: Blueberries and bog rosemary (?).

Range: Me. and Que. to Fla., west to Mo. and Tex. June–Sept. Common, especially along coast.

HERODIAS UNDERWING   **Pl. 37 (2)**
Catocala herodias Stkr.

Identification: FW gray with fine wood-grain pattern of brown and black. Northern specimens (*C. herodias gerhardi* B. & Benj.) have a *whitish border along FW costa* (shown) that is absent in typical form (*C. herodias herodias*). HW orange-red with black bands and white fringe. Wingspan 5.6–6.5 cm.

Food: Oaks, particularly scrub oak.

Range: Subspecies *gerhardi* is found from Mass. to N.C.; typical form (*C. herodias herodias*) is known from Okla. and Tex. Apparently restricted to oak-pine barrens. July–Aug. Uncommon to rare.

SCARLET UNDERWING   **Pl. 37 (6)**
Catocala coccinata Grt.

Identification: FW mottled light gray; note broad, diffuse *black*

basal dash. Black lines and other dashes may also be heavy. Shade of *bright red* on HW distinctive; fringe white, with some red toward apex in some specimens. Wingspan 5.7-7 cm.
Food: Scrub oak and other oaks.
Range: Locally common throughout our area. June–Sept.

MIRANDA UNDERWING   Pl. 34 (8)
Catocala miranda Hy. Edw.
Identification: FW evenly pale gray, with fine black lines; *no black shading* along inner margin. HW black. Wingspan 3.7–4.5 cm.
Food: Hawthorn.
Range: Mass. to Fla. along coast; inland as far as w. N.C. May–early June. Local; uncommon to rare.
Similar species: (1) Andromeda Underwing (p. 312, Pl. 34) has *black shade* along inner margin of FW. (2) Judith's Underwing, (p. 174, Pl. 34) is larger, more brownish; *underside of wing bases white* (black in Miranda Underwing). (3) Orba Underwing, *C. orba* Kusnezov (not shown), is usually slightly larger, with heavy *black median dash* above inner margin. Food: Hawthorn. Range: S.C. to Fla. (also N.J. ?), west to Tex. May–early June.

ULTRONIA UNDERWING   Pl. 33 (9)
Catocala ultronia (Hbn.)
Identification: Medium-sized, with brown, wood-grained FW, variably tinted with whitish. Note *dark brown subapical patch* and *shading along inner margin,* covering long, thin black basal and anal dashes. HW orangish red with black bands. Wingspan 4.6–6 cm.
Food: Members of the rose family, such as apple and cherry trees.
Range: Common throughout our area. July–Sept.

HAWTHORN UNDERWING   Pl. 33 (8)
Catocala crataegi Saunders
Identification: FW greenish gray in median area; blackish shade in basal area *continues along inner margin* to anal angle. Variable black and brown shading beyond pm. line, especially beyond 2 "teeth" in that line. HW yellowish orange with black bands; marginal band may be broken near anal angle. Wingspan 4–5 cm.
Food: Apple and hawthorn trees.
Range: N.S. to Ga., west to Man. and Ark. Late June–Aug. Uncommon to rare.
Similar species: (1) Texarkana Underwing, *C. texarkana* Brower (not shown), has distinctly *whitish median area;* black am. line does *not* merge with black shade along inner margin. Food: Hawthorn. Range: Fla. to Ark. and Tex. May–June. Locally common. (2) Lincoln Underwing, *C. lincolnana* Brower (not shown), looks like a paler and less heavily marked Hawthorn Underwing, with *dark shading* in lower median area. Food: Hawthorn. Range: Fla. to Ark. Late May–early June. Rare.

WONDERFUL UNDERWING
Pl. 32 (21)

Catocala mira Grt.

Identification: FW uniform light gray; no greenish tint or strong black basal shade as in Hawthorn Underwing (above). Am. and pm. lines farther apart at inner margin. *Subreniform spot* usually conspicuous. HW *deeper* yellowish orange, with unbroken black border; inner band forms a complete loop. Wingspan 4–5 cm.

Food: Hawthorn.

Range: Que. to Fla., west to Man. and Tex. June–Aug., usually 2 weeks later than Hawthorn and Charming Underwings. Common to rare; more common westward.

Similar species: (1) Hawthorn Underwing (above). (2) In Charming Underwing (below, Pl. 33), *am. and pm. lines meet* near inner margin of FW.

WOODY UNDERWING
Pl. 33 (10)

Catocala grynea (Cram.)

Identification: FW uniform greenish gray; orangish brown along inner margin below *black median dash*. Lines fine, broken, black. HW yellowish orange with black bands; black border may have narrow break near anal angle. Wingspan 3.9–5 cm.

Food: Apple, hawthorn, and plum trees.

Range: Me. and s. Ont. to Fla., west to S.D. and Tex. June–Aug. Common in most of range.

PRAECLARA UNDERWING
Pl. 33 (11)

Catocala praeclara Grt. & Rob.

Identification: Similar to Woody Underwing (above), but FW paler greenish gray, with more contrasting brown shading, especially beyond pm. line. Note *black basal dash*. Am. and pm. lines more distinct and more widely separated at inner margin. Black bands on yellowish orange HW *farther apart*. Wingspan 4–5 cm.

Food: Larvae have been reared on chokeberry and juneberry.

Range: N.S. to Fla., west to Minn. and Kans. July–Sept. Common eastward at edges of bogs and barrens; rare westward.

CHARMING UNDERWING
Pl. 33 (16)

Catocala blandula Hulst

Identification: Similar to Hawthorn Underwing (p. 313, Pl. 33), and Wonderful Underwing (above, Pl. 32) but *am. and pm. lines meet* near inner margin. *Basal shade brown,* not black as in Hawthorn Underwing; no greenish tint in median area. Black border of HW usually unbroken. Wingspan 4–5 cm.

Food: Apple and hawthorn.

Range: N.S. to N.C., west to Man., S.D., and Ky. July–Aug. Locally common in Northeast.

TITAN UNDERWING *Catocala titania* Dodge
Pl. 32 (16)

Identification: Our least patterned small underwing. FW pale greenish gray, with usual *markings nearly absent*. HW yellowish

orange with black bands; marginal band may be broken. Wingspan 2–3.8 cm.
Food: Hawthorn.
Range: Pa. to Tenn., west to Mo. June–Aug. Rare eastward.

ALABAMA UNDERWING   Pl. 32 (18)
Catocala alabamae Grt.
Identification: FW greenish gray as in Titan Underwing (above), but *more conspicuously marked.* Am. and pm. lines heavy, sometimes broken; pm. line forms *strong dash near anal angle.* Brown shade beyond pm. line; st. line white, zigzag. HW as in Titan Underwing. Wingspan 3–4 cm.
Food: Chickasaw plum, hawthorns, and wild crabapple.
Range: S.C. to Fla., west to Mo. and Tex. April–June; Aug. Locally common in Fla., but rare or absent in much of overall range northward and westward.

SWEET UNDERWING *Catocala dulciola* Grt.   Pl. 33 (15)
Identification: FW light gray with *black basal dash* and *double am. line;* outer lines obscure. HW yellowish orange with black bands. Wingspan 4–4.5 cm.
Food: Unrecorded.
Range: Northeast N.Y. to western Va., west to Mo. June–early July. Uncommon to rare.

CLINTON'S UNDERWING   Pl. 33 (12)
Catocala clintoni Grt.
Identification: FW pale gray with *sharp black basal dash and more diffuse subapical and anal dashes.* Lines broken, black. HW pale yellowish orange with black bands; marginal band broken and incomplete at anal angle. Wingspan 4.5–5.5 cm.
Food: Apple, hawthorns, and plums.
Range: N.Y. and s. Ont. to Fla., west to Man. and Tex. April–July; Feb.–May in Fla. Usually the first underwing to appear in a given area. Locally common southward, but rare in North.

SIMILAR UNDERWING   Pl. 33 (13)
Catocala similis Edw.
Identification: FW pale gray to dark brownish gray, shaded with warm brown. Am. and pm. lines black, unbroken. Pale *triangular apical patch* along costa. Tear-shaped reniform spot black and gray; open at top but closed at bottom, where it meets subreniform spot. HW light yellowish orange with black bands; marginal band broken near anal angle. Wingspan 3.5–4.5 cm.
Food: Post oak and other oaks.
Range: Me. and Que. to Fla., west to Minn. and Tex. June–July. Sometimes locally common.

LITTLE UNDERWING *Catocala minuta* Edw.   Pl. 33 (14)
Identification: FW mottled light and dark brown; note *white st. line* that *widens toward costa.* Lines black, indistinct except zig-

zag pm. line; black shading along am. line. HW yellowish orange with black bands that bleed into background toward inner margin. Median loop *rounded* (pointed in Little Nymph, below); marginal band *complete*. Wingspan 3.5–4.5 cm.

Food: Honey locust and water locust.

Range: L.I., N.Y., to Fla., west to S.D. and Tex. June–Aug. Sometimes locally common.

GRISATRA UNDERWING   not shown
Catocala grisatra Brower

Identification: FW bluish gray; markings as in Ulalume Underwing (p. 305, Pl. 34), but this moth is *smaller*. Darkest FW markings are *anal dash* and *wide arc* from reniform spot to outer margin below apex. HW bright yellow with black bands; median band does *not* form a complete loop. Wingspan 4.8–5.5 cm.

Food: Hawthorns.

Range: Ga. and Fla. May–June. Very local and uncommon.

LITTLE NYMPH   Pls. 32 (19), 33 (7)
Catocala micronympha Gn.

Identification: Extremely variable; at least 4 forms exist. FW gray, shaded with greenish, brown, white, and black. *No basal dash.* Lines black, obscure to distinct; st. line whitish, usually *prominent at costa.* Broken blackish shade often curves from costa through reniform spot and out to outer margin. HW typically yellowish orange with black bands; black inner loop usually *pointed.* In form "gisela" Meyer (Pl. 32) most of FW is *black.* In form "hero" Hy. Edw. (not shown) most of median area is *white.* In rare form "sargenti" Covell, HW *is all black.* Wingspan 3.5–4.7 cm.

Food: Oaks.

Range: N.H. and s. Ont. to Fla., west to Minn., Kans., and Tex. Late May–Aug.; mostly June–July. Common to abundant.

Remarks: This species is also known as the Little Bride and as the Tiny Nymph Underwing.

CONNUBIAL UNDERWING   Pl. 33 (17, 18)
Catocala connubialis Gn.

Identification: Variable; FW white with *sharp black zigzag lines,* or uniform greenish *gray without distinct pattern* (form "pulverulenta" Brower). FW more whitish, especially in median area, in form "cordelia" Hy. Edw. (not shown). Note *even-edged break in black marginal band* on yellowish orange HW in all forms. Wingspan 3.7–4.7 cm.

Food: Red oak and other oaks.

Range: N.S. to Fla., west to Mo. and Tex. July–Sept. Rare to locally common.

GIRLFRIEND UNDERWING   Pl. 32 (14, 15)
Catocala amica (Hbn.)

Identification: A small underwing with variable FW; note yel-

lowish orange HW has *broken* black marginal band but *no inner black band.* Pl. 32 shows mottled gray and black FW of typical form, and form "curvifascia" Brower, with diffuse *blackish arc* from costa toward outer margin. Not shown are melanic form "nerissa" Hy. Edw. with all blackish FW, and form "suffusa" Beutenmüller, with blackish shading at costa, outer margin, and along inner margin. Wingspan 3.1–4.4 cm.
Food: Oaks, including black and burr oaks.
Range: Me. and s. Ont. to Fla., west to S.D. and Tex. June–Sept. Common.

JAIR UNDERWING *Catocala jair* Stkr.   **not shown**
Identification: Very similar to the Girlfriend Underwing (above, Pl. 32), but *pm. line straighter* and *less toothed.* Prominent brown shading between pm. and st. lines. FW slightly broader and more blunt. HW yellowish orange with black only at border, as in Girlfriend Underwing. Wingspan 3.5–4 cm.
Food: Unrecorded; presumably oaks.
Range: Northern half of Fla.; N.J. Pine Barrens (?). May–June in Fla., where it is local and usually rare.

Subfamily Hypeninae

FLOWING-LINE BOMOLOCHA   Pl. 40 (15)
Bomolocha manalis (Wlk.)
Identification: FW yellowish or light to dark grayish brown; sharp blackish brown median patch *does not reach base or inner margin.* HW dark grayish brown. Wingspan 2.3–2.8 cm.
Food: Unrecorded.
Range: Me. to Fla., west to Minn. and Tex. March–Oct. Uncommon.

BALTIMORE BOMOLOCHA   Pl. 40 (16)
Bomolocha baltimoralis (Gn.)
Identification: FW grayish brown, with whitish tint in ♀ (shown); tint often absent in ♂. Note blackish brown apical dash, and *large dark patch* from base through median area *which does not touch inner margin.* Dark patch usually has white outer edging. HW dark grayish brown. Wingspan 2.6–3.2 cm.
Food: Maples.
Range: N.S. to Fla., west to Wisc., Mo., and Tex. April–Oct. Common.

DIMORPHIC BOMOLOCHA   Pl. 40 (18, 21)
Bomolocha bijugalis (Wlk.)
Identification: FW of ♂ blackish brown with *white spot* on inner margin. FW of ♀ much like Baltimore Bomolocha (above), but *pm. line straighter, farther from outer margin,* and with 1 tooth. Some dark chocolate under blackish brown median patch. HW

dark grayish brown, darker in ♂ than in ♀. Wingspan 2.4–3.1 cm.
Food: Red-osier dogwood.
Range: Common throughout our area. April–Sept. or frost.

MOTTLED BOMOLOCHA   Pl. 40 (19)
Bomolocha palparia (Wlk.)
Identification: Similar to Baltimore Bomolocha (above, Pl. 40) but dark brown median patch *extends to inner margin* (often lighter brown toward inner margin). Basal and outer parts of FW mottled; apical dash broken. Pale areas slightly darker in ♂ (not shown) than in ♀. Wingspan 2.7–3.3 cm.
Food: Oaks (?).
Range: N.S. to Fla., west to Minn. and Tex. April–Oct. Common.

WHITE-LINED BOMOLOCHA   Pl. 40 (17, 20)
Bomolocha abalienalis (Wlk.)
Identification: FW blackish in ♂, dark orangish brown in ♀; am. line white and conspicuous only in ♀. Both sexes have *double, white, broadly rounded pm. line,* close to other white markings in st. area. HW gray, darker in ♂ than in ♀. Wingspan 2.5–3.3 cm; ♂ usually larger than ♀.
Food: Slippery elm.
Range: S. Que. to n. Fla., west to Man. and Tex. April–Aug. Common.

DECEPTIVE BOMOLOCHA   Pl. 40 (22)
Bomolocha deceptalis (Wlk.)
Identification: FW dull grayish brown to blackish brown; lighter beyond *nearly straight, yellowish pm. line.* Note dotted black st. line. ♂ (not shown) darker overall than ♀. Wingspan 2.8–3.5 cm.
Food: Unrecorded.
Range: Me. and Que. to Fla., west to Man. and Tex. April–Aug. Locally common.

GRAY-EDGED BOMOLOCHA   Pl. 41 (1)
Bomolocha madefactalis (Gn.)
Identification: FW grayish brown to blackish brown in ♂; light grayish brown with pinkish gray in basal and st. areas in ♀ (not shown). Median area defined by darker, *slightly sinuous am. and pm. lines* in both sexes; median area darker just inside pm. line. Wingspan 2.5–3.2 cm.
Food: Walnut trees.
Range: Me. and Que. to Ga., west to S.D. and Tex. April–Aug. Common.

SORDID BOMOLOCHA   Pl. 41 (3)
Bomolocha sordidula (Grt.)
Identification: Almost identical to Gray-edged Bomolocha (above) but usually slightly smaller. *No distinct pm. line;* darker *median shade more even,* not darker toward median line. Brownish color duller in ♀ (not shown). Wingspan 2.4–3 cm.

Food: Alder and butternut.
Range: Me. to n. Fla., west to Man., Kans., Ark., and Miss. May–Aug. Considered rare, but probably confused with Gray-edged Bomolocha.

LARGE BOMOLOCHA   Pl. 40 (10)
Bomolocha edictalis (Wlk.)
Identification: Both sexes have a sharply defined, dark grayish brown median area, and a *solid black triangle* representing the reniform spot. Rest of FW yellowish brown with some darker shading in ♂; almost solid dark brown in ♀. Wingspan 3.3–4.2 cm.
Food: Unrecorded.
Range: Me. and Que. to Va. and e. Ky., west to Man. and Mich. July–Aug. Locally common.

GREEN CLOVERWORM MOTH   Pl. 41 (2, 5)
Plathypena scabra (F.)
Identification: Wings drab, blackish brown. *FW narrow; HW broad.* FW pattern ranges from sharp to uniformly dull. Pm. line slightly wavy with a small but conspicuous outward bulge near costa. Wingspan 2.5–3.5 cm.; ♂ usually larger than ♀.
Food: Larva (**Green Cloverworm**) feeds on clover, alfalfa, beans, and other legumes; also strawberry and raspberry plants. A pest, but not usually a serious one.
Range: Throughout our area; abundant in most of range. Adults fly during any warm period in year, but are most common in late summer.

VARIABLE TROPIC   Pl. 39 (18)
Hemeroplanis scopulepes (Haw.)
Identification: *FW variable—* yellow with uneven light brown shading beyond pm. line (as shown), or entirely reddish to dark brown. Pm. line bent below costa. *Black orbicular dot;* reniform spot brown with lighter brown filling. Wingspan 2.3–3 cm.
Food: Unrecorded.
Range: Eastern N.Y. to Fla., west to s. Mo. and Tex. June–July northward; all year in Fla. Common southward.

SIX-SPOTTED GRAY   Pl. 40 (2)
Spargaloma sexpunctata Grt.
Identification: Wings violet gray. Note tiny black orbicular dot and *3 small black spots* in narrow costal triangle near apex. Blackish brown median shade sharply edged on basal side but gradually fades to gray on outer side. Wingspan 2.5–2.9 cm.
Food: Dogbane.
Range: N.S. to Va., west to Neb., Ark., and Miss. May–Sept. Uncommon.

ERNESTINE'S MOTH   Pl. 39 (20)
Phytometra ernestinana (Blanchard)
Identification: FW yellow, sometimes shading to pale olive-

buff toward outer margin. Note deep pink band along basal half of costa and outer margin. *Pink pm. line* straight, broader around tiny black *reniform dot.* HW whitish, usually with pale brown and pink shading. Wingspan 1.8–2 cm.
Food: Unrecorded.
Range: Ga. and Fla., west along Gulf Coast to Tex. Strays recorded in N.Y. and e. Kans. All year southward.

PINK-BORDERED YELLOW   **Pl. 39 (19)**
Phytometra rhodarialis (Wlk.)
Identification: FW yellow with *deep pink band* along basal half of costa; also pink beyond *straight pm. line.* Yellow st. line more distinct in ♂ than in ♀ (shown). HW whitish to gray, often with pink shade toward outer margin. Wingspan 1.8–2.1 cm.
Food: Unrecorded.
Range: N.H. and s. Ont. to Fla., west to Mo. and Tex. June–Sept. Rare northward.

DOUBLE-LINED BROWN   **Pl. 40 (14)**
Hormoschista latipalpis (Wlk.)
Identification: FW grayish brown to blackish brown; median area darker with violet tint. Am. and pm. lines close together, double, dark and light reddish brown. *Black reniform spot touches* inner side of *pm. line* as it turns inward. Markings very obscure in some specimens. HW grayish brown. Wingspan 2–2.2 cm.
Food: Unrecorded.
Range: Wash., D.C. to Fla., west to Ky. and Miss. March–Nov. in South; June–Sept. northward. Uncommon.

Subfamily Hypenodinae

BROKEN-LINE HYPENODES   **Pl. 41 (9)**
Hypenodes fractilinea (Sm.)
Identification: One of our smallest noctuids. FW pale brown with variable grayish shading (extensive to absent). *Am. and pm. lines blackish,* sometimes thin and complete, but *usually dotted.* Dark median shade (shown) found more often in northern specimens; *median shade nearly straight,* outer side accented with whitish. St. line faintly whitish. HW pale grayish brown. Wingspan 1.1–1.4 cm.
Food: Unrecorded.
Range: N.S. and N.B. to ne. Va., west through s. Ont. to Wisc., south to Ky. Also reported from Fla. May–Oct. Locally common.
Similar species: At least 4 other *Hypenodes* species occur in our area, but with more restricted ranges. Most widespread is Large Hypenodes, *H. caducus* (Dyar), not shown, which is typically *larger* (wingspan 1.3–1.5 cm); am. and pm. lines *always complete;* median shade more oblique. Food: Unrecorded. Range: N.S. to Conn., west to Chicago, Ill. area. June–Sept. Rare in collections.

BLACK-SPOTTED SCHRANKIA   Pl. 41 (8)
Schrankia macula (Druce)
Identification: FW brownish; yellowish beyond *straight, oblique pm. line.* Am. line black, broken; reniform dot and dotted terminal line black. HW gray. Wingspan 1.3–1.8 cm.
Food: Bracket fungus.
Range: N. Va. to Fla., west to Mo., Ark., and Miss. May–July. Locally common.

THIN-WINGED OWLET   Pl. 30 (22)
Nigetia formosalis Wlk.
Identification: Easily recognized by the *pointed white FW* with gray shading; costal border and median band *black.* HW gray; black triangle near anal angle. Wingspan 1.6–2 cm.
Food: Unrecorded.
Range: S. Conn. and Ont. to Fla., west to Mo. and Tex. April–Aug.; at least 2 broods. Common.

Subfamily Rivulinae

SPOTTED GRASS MOTH   Pl. 39 (21)
Rivula propinqualis Gn.
Identification: FW light yellow with large, *elliptical, brown blotch* covering 2 small, purplish *reniform dots.* Lines narrow, brown, parallel; some brown shading toward outer margin. HW yellow. Wingspan 1.5–1.9 cm.
Food: Grasses.
Range: Throughout our area. April–Sept. Uncommon.

BENT-LINED TAN *Oxycilla malaca* (Grt.)   Pl. 41 (4)
Identification: Wings pale tan with variable brown shading in median and terminal areas. *Am. and pm. lines* sharp (as shown) or obscure; both lines *sharply bent* just below costa. Look for *2 black dots* inside reniform spot. Some brown shading on HW. Wingspan 1.8–2 cm.
Food: Unrecorded.
Range: S. Que. to S.C., west to Mo. and Ark. April–Sept. Uncommon.

YELLOW-LINED OWLET   Pl. 39 (22)
Colobochyla interpuncta (Grt.)
Identification: FW brown with *3 yellow lines;* note darker brown edging beyond median and pm. lines. Am. line often obscure; *median and pm. lines curve outward—pm. line reaches apex.* Orbicular and reniform spots black. HW grayish brown, darker along outer margin. Wingspan 2–2.4 cm.
Food: Reared successfully on willow leaves.
Range: Mass. and s. Ont. to Fla., west to Mo. and Tex. May–Sept. Rare northward.

Subfamily Herminiinae

AMERICAN IDIA *Idia americalis* (Gn.)   **Pl. 39 (16)**
Identification: FW whitish gray with *some yellowish* in outer parts. Sharp, jagged black lines, *thickest at costa.* Reniform spot filled with yellow. HW has 3 black lines. Fla. specimens paler. Wingspan 2–3 cm.
Food: Lichens.
Range: Very common throughout our area. May–Nov.

COMMON IDIA *Idia aemula* (Hbn.)   **Pl. 41 (12)**
Identification: Similar to American Idia (above) but drabber and more uniformly dark grayish brown. Lines grayish brown and black, but thinner, especially at costa. *Yellowish reniform spot* conspicuous; wider and blackish in Appalachian specimens. Wingspan 2–3 cm.
Food: Dead leaves on forest floor.
Range: Very common throughout our area. April–Nov.

ORANGE-SPOTTED IDIA   **Pl. 41 (10)**
Idia diminuendis (B. & McD.)
Identification: FW dark brown; am. and pm. lines zigzag, but indistinct. Note *round, orangish orbicular and reniform spots.* HW pale brown with 1–2 faint median bands. Wingspan 1.6–1.9 cm.
Food: Unrecorded.
Range: N.S. to Va., west to Iowa and Ark. May–Oct. Uncommon to rare.
Similar species: Rotund Idia, *I. rotundalis* (Wlk.), not shown, is dark *smoky gray;* lines and spots *more obscure;* reniform spot smaller, *more yellowish.* Food: Dead leaves and coral fungus. Range: Common throughout our area. June–Sept.; 2 broods.

SMOKY IDIA *Idia scobialis* (Grt.)   **Pl. 41 (13)**
Identification: FW smoky black with conspicuous *yellowish white broken lines.* Jagged pm. line most complete line. HW similar, with 2 toothed white lines. Wingspan 1.8–2.4 cm.
Food: Unrecorded.
Range: Me. to Fla., west to Mich. and Ky. May–Sept. Uncommon to locally common.

GLOSSY BLACK IDIA   **Pl. 41 (15)**
Idia lubricalis (Gey.)
Identification: Similar to Smoky Idia (above), but larger; FW glossier black, with *jagged dirty whitish lines.* Pm. and st. lines usually complete. HW pale grayish brown with 2 vague lines. Wingspan 2.4–3.6 cm.
Food: Grasses and rotten wood.
Range: Common throughout our area. May–Sept. Comes readily to sugar bait.

DARK-BANDED OWLET   Pl. 41 (11)
Phalaenophana pyramusalis (Wlk.)
Identification: FW dirty white with *gray to grayish brown bands,* especially beyond am. and pm. lines. Am. line straight; pm. and st. lines slightly wavy with darkest shade between them. Look for a black dot at lower end of reniform spot. Wingspan 2.1–2.5 cm.
Food: Dried or wilted leaves.
Range: Throughout our area; uncommon in Southeast. April–Aug.

LETTERED ZANCLOGNATHA   Pl. 41 (16)
Zanclognatha lituralis (Hbn.)
Identification: FW light brown with *3 costal spots,* including *1 at apex.* Reniform spot (if present) is shaped like a *blackish comma.* Wingspan 2.1–2.8 cm.
Food: Dead leaves of trees.
Range: N.S. and Que. to Fla., west to Wisc., Mo., and Tex. May–Aug.; 2 broods. Locally common.

VARIABLE ZANCLOGNATHA   Pl. 41 (17)
Zanclognatha laevigata (Grt.)
Identification: FW extremely variable, ranging from light brown or dark grayish brown to blackish; median area may be same color as ground color, darker, or lighter (as in specimen shown). Pm. line has *squared-off bulge* just below costa; st. line *faint,* slightly *wavy.* Lines and reniform spot may be distinct or obscure. Wingspan 2.5–3.5 cm.
Food: Unrecorded; probably dead leaves.
Range: N.S. and Que. to N.C. mts., west to Man. and Mo. July–Aug. Common.

DARK ZANCLOGNATHA   Pl. 41 (14)
Zanclognatha obscuripennis (Grt.)
Identification: Wings evenly dark smoky gray to reddish brown; reniform spot darker. Am., pm., and st. *lines sharp, even; yellow edging beyond st. line* on FW. Wingspan 2.2–3.2 cm.
Food: Dead leaves.
Range: N.Y. to Fla., west to Mo. and La. April–June; 2 broods. Common.
Similar species: Yellowish Zanclognatha, *Z. jacchusalis* (Wlk.), not shown, is *paler* and *yellowish,* powdered with grayish brown. St. line straight, yellowish, conspicuous on both upper- and undersides of wings. Food: Probably dead leaves. Range: N.S. to Fla., west to Mo. and Ark. April–July. Common.

GRAYISH ZANCLOGNATHA   Pl. 41 (19)
Zanclognatha pedipilalis (Gn.)
Identification: FW and HW light gray to grayish tan (2nd brood dark brownish gray); lines brown. Am. line bends at right angle below costa. Note *narrow bulge in pm. line* (almost a rounded

point). St. line straight, incomplete (*not reaching apex*); no yellow edging. Wingspan 2.4–3 cm.

Food: Dead leaves, including those of soybean.

Range: N.S. and Que. to Fla., west to Kans. and Miss. May–Aug. Locally common.

EARLY ZANCLOGNATHA   Pl. 41 (22)
Zanclognatha cruralis (Gn.)

Identification: Wings pale brown (spring brood) to dark brown (summer brood); lines sharp, darker brown, with yellow tint on st. line. Note *small indentation in bulge* of pm. line. HW brown with 2 darker lines. Wingspan 2.8–3 cm.

Food: Larva reported on balsam fir; probably also feeds on dead leaves.

Range: N.S. to Fla., west to Wisc. and Tex. April–July, usually appearing earlier than related species. Common.

WAVY-LINED ZANCLOGNATHA   Pl. 41 (20)
Zanclognatha ochreipennis (Grt.)

Identification: FW and HW grayish brown, or dull yellowish shaded with light orangish brown. Am. and pm. *lines wavy;* terminal line broken. Checkered fringe on all wings. Wingspan 2.8–3.1 cm.

Food: Probably dead leaves.

Range: Me. to S.C., west to Mo. and La. April–Sept.; 2 broods. Common.

MORBID OWLET *Chytolita morbidalis* (Gn.)   Pl. 41 (24)
Identification: FW pale grayish white; lines diffuse, orangish. Look for small *black dots* over midsection of st. line. HW paler. Wingspan 2.9–3.5 cm.

Food: Dead leaves; larva can be reared on dandelion, grasses, hazelnut, and lettuce.

Range: Me. and Que. to N.C., west to Man. and Ark. in open country. May–Aug. Common.

BLACK-BANDED OWLET   Pl. 41 (7)
Phalaenostola larentioides Grt.

Identification: FW and HW dark violet gray, sometimes reddish brown. Blackish am. and pm. lines fine, wavy; blackish *median and st. bands broad.* Look for fine white edging beyond st. band. Wingspan 1.7–2.4 cm.

Food: Bluegrass and clover; dead grass and leaves.

Range: Me. and Que. to Fla., west to Kans. and Ark. May–Sept.; common in most of range.

PALE EPIDELTA *Epidelta metonalis* (Wlk.)   Pl. 41 (18)
Identification: Antennae broadly bipectinate in ♂; each lateral branch 1 mm long (♀ antennae simple). FW and HW dull yellowish, dusted with light brown. FW often darker in median area and toward apex (not shown). Lines fine, even brown, reniform spot a

sharp, thin crescent. Some specimens have a diffuse, double st. line (not shown). Wingspan 2.2–2.4 cm.
Food: Dead leaves; larva will eat dandelion and lettuce.
Range: Nfld. and Que. to N.C., west to Man. and Mo. June–Aug. Uncommon.
Similar species: Dark Epidelta, *E. eumelusalis* (Wlk.), not shown, has similar markings but is *larger* and *darker;* antennal pectinations shorter (½ mm long) in ♂.

SLANT-LINED OWLET   Pl. 41 (21)
Macrochilo absorptalis (Wlk.)
Identification: FW pale gray, with brown shading inside nearly straight pm. and st. lines. Pm. line oblique. Look for *2 tiny black reniform dots.* Black terminal line fine, complete. Lines continue onto HW. Wingspan 2.2–2.6 cm.
Food: Probably grasses (both dead and alive).
Range: N.S. and Que. to N.C., west to Man. and Mo. June–Aug. Generally uncommon.

SMOKY TETANOLITA   Pl. 41 (6)
Tetanolita mynesalis (Wlk.)
Identification: Fresh specimens can be recognized easily by the solid, *pale yellow reniform spot* contrasting with the shiny blackish FW. Lines inconspicuous—black with some fine whitish accents. HW light grayish brown, with dark lines and shading toward outer margin. Wingspan 2–2.5 cm.
Food: Probably dead leaves.
Range: N.H. and Que. to Fla., west to Mo. and Tex. May–Nov. Common southward.

FLORIDA TETANOLITA   Pl. 41 (23)
Tetanolita floridana (Sm.)
Identification: Similar to Smoky Tetanolita (above), but *FW light gray;* reniform spot narrower and light orange—*not as conspicuous* as in Smoky Tetanolita. Wingspan 2–2.4 cm.
Food: Probably dead leaves.
Range: N.S. to Fla., west to Mo. and Tex. April–Oct.; common all year in deep South.

BENT-WINGED OWLET   Pl. 41 (25)
Bleptina caradrinalis Gn.
Identification: Note *slight bend inward* along costa of FW (FW curves slightly outward in most noctuids). Wings gray, shaded with brown. *Am. and pm. lines jagged;* median line diffuse; *st. line sharp, yellowish.* Spots black; orbicular spot small, reniform spot prominent. Wingspan 2.2–3.2 cm.
Food: Barberry, clover, hickories; also dead leaves of various plants.
Range: Common throughout our area. April–Sept.

LONG-HORNED OWLET
Pl. 42 (3)

Hypenula cacuminalis (Wlk.)

Identification: Similar to *Renia* species (below), but ♂ lacks antennal tuft. Labial palps ("horns") *long, upturned* in both sexes, with a *triangular tuft* at tip. Wings dull—dark grayish brown with fine, scalloped black lines. Note *white dots* in dull orangish reniform spot. Wingspan 2.8–3.9 cm.

Food: Unrecorded.

Range: Se. N.J. to Fla., west to Tex. Common all year in Fla.

CHOCOLATE RENIA
Pl. 42 (1)

Renia nemoralis B. & McD.

Identification: Wings grayish brown in ♂, deep buff to reddish brown or chocolate in ♀; wings may be smooth or mottled. *Am. line dark, even; curves outward* in both sexes. Spots may be more conspicuous than in specimen shown. Note tufts on antennae in ♂ (present in all *Renia* species). Wingspan 2.5–3 cm.

Food: Unrecorded.

Range: Martha's Vineyard, Mass. to Fla., west to Ind. and Tex. July–Aug.

DISCOLORED RENIA *Renia discoloralis* Gn.
Pl. 42 (6)

Identification: FW pale yellowish to dark brown (usually light grayish brown), with darker brown median area and st. band. *Lines dark, deeply scalloped* at intersections with veins. Orbicular and reniform spots pale yellowish; reniform spot represented by 2 black dots, sometimes fused into a *vertical bar* (as shown). Wingspan 3.5–4.5 cm.

Food: Dead leaves of trees.

Range: N.Y. to Fla., west to Mo. and Tex. July–Aug. Common.

FRATERNAL RENIA *Renia fraternalis* Sm.
Pl. 42 (2)

Identification: Wings orange-yellow, sometimes yellowish to grayish brown. Lines toothed, distinct to inconspicuous. Orbicular spot yellowish if present. Look for *black dots* in top and bottom of yellowish reniform spot. Wingspan 2.3–2.5 cm.

Food: Dead leaves.

Range: N.C. to Fla., west to Ark. and Ala. All year in Fla.

SOBER RENIA *Renia sobrialis* (Wlk.)
Pl. 42 (4)

Identification: Wings dark mouse gray, *darker toward outer margins.* FW squared off at apex. Lines blackish, inconspicuous. Orbicular and reniform spots warm brownish or orangish but inconspicuous; black dots in reniform spot sometimes connected. HW lightly frosted with whitish. Tuft on ♂ antenna not as far beyond midpoint as in other *Renia* species. Wingspan 2.4–2.7 cm.

Food: Dead leaves.

Range: N.S. to Fla., west to Mich. and Miss. April–Sept. Uncommon.

AMBIGUOUS MOTH   Pl. 42 (7, 10)
Lascoria ambigualis Wlk.
Identification: Wings brown, variable; *darker beyond straight am. line.* Note *notch* in outer margin of FW in ♂ (absent in ♀). Small black apical dash in both sexes. Wingspan 2.1–2.5 cm.
Food: Ragweed stalks, chrysanthemum, and horseradish.
Range: Me. and Que. to Fla., west to Mo. and Tex. March–Nov. or frost. Common.

DARK-SPOTTED PALTHIS   Pl. 39 (25)
Palthis angulalis (Hbn.)
Identification: FW gray with blackish brown median line that does not reach costa. Blackish brown *reniform spot* usually prominent. Vague orangish patch below apex. Note *very large, tufted labial palps,* characteristic of *Palthis* species. Wingspan 2–2.6 cm.
Food: Alder, birches, blackberry, firs, honeysuckle, red-osier dogwood, serviceberry, and spruces.
Range: Common throughout our area. March–Nov.

FAINT-SPOTTED PALTHIS   Pl. 39 (26)
Palthis asopialis (Gn.)
Identification: Similar to Dark-spotted Palthis (above), but slightly smaller; markings (except *small reniform spot*) usually more distinct. Note dark *subapical triangle,* beyond *yellow st. line.* Wingspan 1.9–2.3 cm.
Food: Beans, coralberry, corn, oaks, and Spanish needles.
Range: Central N.Y. to Fla., west to Mo. and Tex. May–Nov. or frost. Common southward.

PROMINENTS: Family Notodontidae

Medium-sized, stout-bodied moths; mostly drab, brownish to grayish. Wingspan 2.3–6.2 cm, ♀ often notably larger than ♂. Ocelli reduced or absent. Proboscis strongly developed to reduced. Antennae bipectinate in ♂, and in ♀ of some species; simple in others. Tympana ventrally located on 3rd thoracic segment, *pointing downward.* FW rather elongate. Thumblike scale tufts project from inner margin of FW in some species. At rest, wings are held rooflike or rolled, making these moths look like sticks. M_2 *does not arise closer to* M_3 *than to* M_1 on FW or HW (Fig. 26). $Sc+R_1$ of HW usually does *not* touch Rs, but lies *close and parallel to Rs,* above top of discal cell. Rs and M_1 usually *stalked* beyond end of HW discal cell.

Larvae often come in strange shapes (see Pl. 1). Some are green and look like leaves or other parts of food plants; others are gaudily striped. In some species, the larvae feed in groups on leaves. Larvae in *Datana* species lift front and rear parts of body

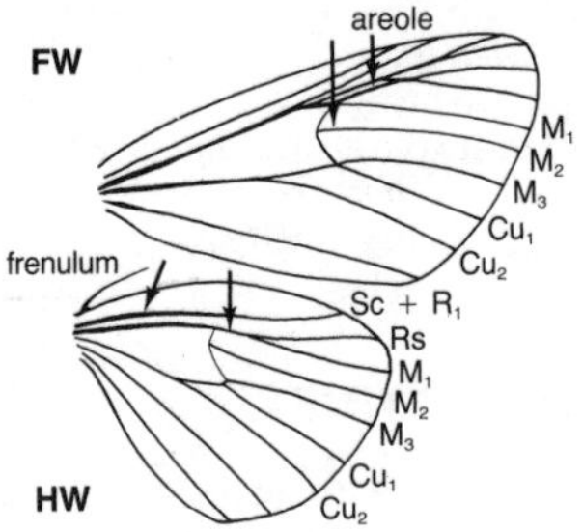

Fig. 26.
Wing venation,
Notodontidae.

and stay motionless when disturbed. Larva spends the winter in hibernation, then pupates, usually in a cell in the soil, or in a loose cocoon on the ground. Some species are serious pests that defoliate forest trees.

SIGMOID PROMINENT   Pl. 42 (11)
Clostera albosigma Fitch
Identification: FW light grayish to smoky brown, deeper brown at apex. Pm. line forms *a prominent white* S just below costa. Wingspan 2.8–3.7 cm.
Food: Poplars and willows.
Range: Throughout our area. Late March–Sept.; 2 broods. Common in most of range, but apparently rare in Southeast.

ANGLE-LINED PROMINENT   Pl. 42 (12)
Clostera inclusa (Hbn.)
Identification: FW pale grayish brown; look for orange tinting near apex, surrounded by some bluish gray shading. *Oblique whitish line* from inner ⅓ of costa *meets bottom of pm. line* at inner margin. HW variably brown with uneven median line. Wingspan 2.3–3.6 cm.
Food: Aspen, poplars, and willows.
Range: Throughout our area to e. Tex. March–Sept. Common, especially northward.

YELLOW-NECKED CATERPILLAR MOTH   Pl. 43 (1)
Datana ministra (Drury)
Identification: A large prominent, with *scalloped FW margin.* FW tawny to reddish brown, with no distinct dark shades (unlike other *Datana* species, below). Orbicular spot inconspicuous, blackish. Am., median, and st. lines darkest markings. HW paler, yellowish. Wingspan 4–5.3 cm.
Food: Larva (**Yellow-necked Caterpillar**) feeds on various trees; sometimes a pest on apple trees.
Range: Common throughout our area. April–Sept.

ANGUS'S DATANA *Datana angusii* Grt. & Rob. **Pl. 43 (5)**
Identification: Distinguished from other *Datana* species by *cool*
light to dark *brown* body and wings (no reddish tint); wings en-
tirely dark brown in some specimens. Wingspan 3.8–4.8 cm.
Food: Birches, butternut, hickories, linden, and walnuts.
Range: N.S. to Fla., west to Mo. and Tex. May–Aug. Common.

DREXEL'S DATANA *Datana drexelii* Hy. Edw. **Pl. 43 (3)**
Identification: Nearly identical to Yellow-necked Caterpillar
Moth (above) but FW slightly *darker* (especially toward costa),
with *less scalloped* outer margin. Orbicular spot sometimes con-
spicuous; HW also darker than in Yellow-necked Caterpillar Moth.
Wingspan 4–5.6 cm.
Food: Birches, blueberry, linden, sassafras, and witch-hazel.
Range: N.S. to S.C., west to Ky. June–Sept. Common.
Similar species: (1) Yellow-necked Caterpillar Moth (p. 328, Pl.
43). (2) Major Datana, *D. major* Grt. & Rob. (not shown), is also
nearly identical, but FW outer margin *even less wavy; darker
brown toward costa* (not tawny to reddish brown, as in Drexel's
Datana). HW more solid orangish brown, like FW. Food: Azalea
and bog rosemary. Range: N.S. to Fla., west to Kans. and Ark.
June–Aug. Locally common in bogs and swamps.

CONTRACTED DATANA **Pl. 43 (7)**
Datana contracta Wlk.
Identification: FW reddish brown; *outer margin not wavy.* Note
wide, conspicuous yellowish shading along lines. HW yellowish
with pale brown shading. Wingspan 3.8–5.5 cm.
Food: Blueberries, chestnut, hickories, oaks, and witch-hazel.
Range: Me. to Fla., west to Wisc. and Ark. June–July. Locally
common.

WALNUT CATERPILLAR MOTH **Pl. 43 (10)**
Datana integerrima Grt. & Rob.
Identification: Similar to Contracted Datana (above), but *yel-
lowish shading* along lines *not as wide* or conspicuous. HW pale
yellowish. Wingspan 3.5–5.5 cm.
Food: Larva (**Walnut Caterpillar**) feeds on hickories, pecan,
walnut, and water oak.
Range: Me. and s. Que. to Fla., west to Minn., Mo., and Tex.
May–Aug. Common.

SPOTTED DATANA **Pl. 43 (8)**
Datana perspicua Grt. & Rob.
Identification: *FW straw yellow* with variable brownish shading
(more extensive in midwestern specimens); note *sharp brown lines*
and conspicuous brown *orbicular and reniform spots.* HW entirely
yellow. Wingspan 4.5–5.6 cm.
Food: Sumacs.
Range: S. Ont. to Fla., west to Mo. and Tex. May–Sept. Common.

WHITE-DOTTED PROMINENT
Pl. 43 (14)

Nadata gibbosa (J.E. Sm.)

Identification: FW yellow with rusty orange to warm brown shading; am. and pm. lines distinct, yellowish. Note *pair of white dots* in reniform spot. Many specimens have less shading than one shown. Wingspan 3.8–5.9 cm.

Food: Birches, cherries, maples, oaks, plums, and other trees.

Range: Common throughout our area. April–Oct.; 2 broods southward.

GEORGIAN PROMINENT
Pl. 42 (8)

Hyperaeschra georgica (H.-S.)

Identification: Note the *thumblike black tuft* midway along inner margin of FW. FW yellowish with gray overlay and black streaks; *am. and pm. lines broken, white.* HW white in ♂, gray in ♀. Wingspan 3.4–4.7 cm.

Food: Oaks.

Range: Me. and Que. to Fla., west to Minn. and Tex. April–Aug. Common.

OVAL-BASED PROMINENT
Pl. 43 (11)

Peridea basitriens (Wlk.)

Identification: Easily identified by the unusual *elliptical pattern* in lower basal area of FW. Black tuft projects from inner margin. Rest of FW gray with fine black veins and inconspicuous scalloped lines. HW whitish with gray terminal line and shading. Wingspan 3.5–5 cm.

Food: Unrecorded.

Range: N.S. to se. Ky., west to Mo. and Miss. April–Oct. Common.

ANGULOSE PROMINENT
Pl. 43 (16)

Peridea angulosa (J.E. Sm.)

Identification: FW mottled gray, with vague white patch in median area toward costa. *Basal, am., and pm. lines double, black;* filled or accented with orangish brown. St. line white. Dark gray tuft projects from inner margin. FW pattern continues onto top of whitish to grayish HW. Wingspan 3.5–5.5 cm.

Food: Oaks.

Range: N.S. to Fla., west to Man. and Tex. May–Oct. Uncommon to common.

CHOCOLATE PROMINENT
Pl. 43 (13)

Peridea ferruginea (Pack.)

Identification: Very similar to Angulose Prominent (above) but FW base and median area *mostly chocolate.* HW whiter. Specimen shown has more white on FW than usual. Wingspan 3.8–5 cm.

Food: Birches.

Range: Throughout our area, at least to cen. Tex. May–Aug. Rare southward.

BLACK-RIMMED PROMINENT   Pl. 42 (15)
Pheosia rimosa Pack.
Identification: FW mostly white with *curved black marking* along costa *near apex;* mixed black, brown, and white area along inner margin. HW white with black marking at anal angle. Wingspan 4.5–6.2 cm.
Food: Poplars and willows.
Range: Nfld. to N.C., west to Man. and Neb. April–Oct. Locally common in some years.

ELEGANT PROMINENT   Pl. 44 (3)
Odontosia elegans (Stkr.)
Identification: FW smooth ash gray with a few fine black streaks; brown shading *darkens toward costa. Fine white streak* extends from FW base; usual lines indistinct or absent. Brown tuft projecting from inner margin usually conspicuous against mostly white HW. Wingspan 4.5–6 cm.
Food: Poplars.
Range: N.S. and Que. to N.J., west to Man. and n. Tex. May–Aug. Rare eastward.

DOUBLE-TOOTHED PROMINENT   Pl. 43 (4)
Nerice bidentata Wlk.
Identification: Easily recognized by the *doubly toothed blackish band* that separates grayish brown lower half of FW from light to dark brown upper half. Note variable white edging along toothed band. HW brown, darker toward margin. Wingspan 3–4 cm.
Food: Elms.
Range: Common throughout our area. April–Sept.

LINDEN PROMINENT   Pl. 42 (13)
Ellida caniplaga (Wlk.)
Identification: FW pale gray mottled with white and warm brown in lower basal, median, and upper st. areas. Lines black, sharp; *am. line triple* toward costa. Reniform spot a *black crescent* surrounded by white. Wingspan 3.4–4.4 cm.
Food: Linden.
Range: Me. and Que. to Fla., west to Man. and e. Tex. April–Oct. Common.

COMMON GLUPHISIA   Pl. 43 (18)
Gluphisia septentrionis Wlk.
Identification: Antennae *broadly bipectinate* in ♂; narrower in ♀. FW dark gray; pattern often obscure. Basal line *deeply indented,* forming 2 *brown-filled loops.* Am. line nearly straight; pm. line usually broadly zigzag. Whitish am. and st. areas. Look for raised glossy black scales in median area (magnification needed). Wingspan 2.5–3.3 cm.
Food: Poplars.
Range: Common throughout our area. April–Sept.

WHITE FURCULA *Furcula borealis* (Guér.)   **Pl. 44 (15)**
Identification: Wings white with striking pattern of *dotted black basal, st. and terminal lines*. Median and upper st. areas filled with dark gray. Wingspan 3.3–4.3 cm.
Food: Poplars, wild cherry, and willows.
Range: Me. to Fla., west to Ill., se. Mo., and Miss. April–Aug. Locally common.

GRAY FURCULA   **Pl. 44 (14)**
Furcula cinerea (Wlk.)
Identification: Similar to White Furcula (above), but FW *light gray* with *darker gray median and st. areas,* or almost entirely dark gray; lines a series of black dots in all forms. HW grayish white. Wingspan 3.1–4.2 cm.
Food: Aspens, birches, poplars and willows.
Range: Common throughout our area. April–Sept.

BLACK-ETCHED PROMINENT   **Pls. 1 (5); 44 (12)**
Cerura scitiscripta Wlk.
Identification: FW white with *sharp, double black lines* and small black reniform spot. Black streaks also extend along veins. HW gray. Fla. specimens (not shown) have reduced black markings and white HW. Wingspan 2.5–4 cm.
Food: Larva (Pl. 1) feeds on poplars, wild cherry, and willows.
Range: Que. to Fla., west to Man. and Tex. April–Sept. Locally common, especially near rivers and lakes.

WHITE-HEADED PROMINENT   **Pl. 43 (2)**
Symmerista albifrons (J.E. Sm.)
Identification: Head yellowish white. FW mottled ash gray with inconspicuous scalloped black lines. Note *irregular white bar* along costa (from am. line to apex), with *tooth* projecting downward just beyond reniform spot. HW gray. Wingspan 3.3–4.5 cm; ♀ larger than ♂.
Food: Oaks.
Range: Common throughout our area. March–Oct.

BLACK-SPOTTED PROMINENT   **Pl. 43 (9, 12)**
Dasylophia anguina (J.E. Sm.)
Identification: Sexually dimorphic. Lower pm. line sharp, rounded in both sexes; *black oval spots* present in lower terminal area. FW gray with black streaking in ♂; shaded with yellowish brown in most of basal and upper median areas in ♀. HW white in ♂, gray in ♀. Wingspan 3–4.1 cm.
Food: Legumes, such as clover, lespedeza, locusts, and wild indigo.
Range: S. Me. and Que. to Fla., west to Man. and Tex. April–Sept. Common.

GRAY-PATCHED PROMINENT   **Pl. 44 (7)**
Dasylophia thyatiroides (Wlk.)
Identification: FW streaked brown and gray, with *gray median area*. Pm. line black, *lower end widened;* look for a vague black

spot near anal angle. HW dark grayish brown. Wingspan 3.6–4.7 cm; ♀ usually larger than ♂.
Food: Hickories and legumes.
Range: N.S. and Que. to n. Fla., west to Mich., Mo., Ark. and Miss. April–Sept. Common.

DRAB PROMINENT *Misogada unicolor* (Pack.)   **Pl. 44 (11)**
Identification: *Dull green* in life, fading to yellowish or grayish brown. *FW almost unmarked;* look for a faint broken pm. line. HW lighter, with faint pm. line. Wingspan 4–5 cm.
Food: Cottonwood and sycamore.
Range: Mass. to n. Fla., west to Mo. and Tex. April–Sept. Locally common.

MOTTLED PROMINENT   **Pl. 42 (20)**
Macrurocampa marthesia (Cram.)
Identification: FW blackish to grayish brown from base to am. line; white, gray and grayish brown mottling beyond it. *Double am. line bends sharply* at midpoint; toothed st. line parallel to outer margin. Melanic specimens dark gray with slight whitish mottling. HW whitish with gray veins and outer margin. Wingspan 3.8–5.5 cm.
Food: Beech, chestnut, maples, oaks, and poplars.
Range: Common throughout our area. April–Sept.
Similar species: White-blotched Heterocampa (below, Pl. 44).

OBLIQUE HETEROCAMPA   **Pl. 43 (17, 19)**
Heterocampa obliqua Pack.
Identification: Sexually dimorphic: FW generally gray in ♂, more brownish in ♀. In both sexes look for a *black edge on inner margin* at base of FW, a *double* blackish am. line, and a *black curved line* formed by black terminal dash meeting inner edge of reniform spot. *Apical patch whitish* in ♂, *pinkish brown* in ♀. HW whitish in ♂, grayish brown in ♀. Wingspan 3.7–5.3 cm.
Food: Oaks.
Range: Common from N.S. to Fla., west to Mo. and Tex. May–Sept.

SMALL HETEROCAMPA   **Pl. 43 (15)**
Heterocampa subrotata Harv.
Identification: Our smallest *Heterocampa* species. FW variable, mixed gray, whitish, greenish, and yellowish brown. Look for *thin black reniform crescent* and *double, brownish,* zigzag lower am. and pm. lines. HW dirty white to gray. Wingspan 2.8–3.6 cm.
Food: Various trees, such as birches, hickories, and maples.
Range: N.Y. to Fla., west to Mo. and Tex. April–Sept. Common.

WHITE-BLOTCHED HETEROCAMPA   **Pl. 44 (1)**
Heterocampa umbrata Wlk.
Identification: FW mottled gray, whitish, brown, and dark green with black lines. Similar to Mottled Prominent (above, Pl. 42) but

usually larger, with *am. line farther from base* and not bent in middle. Look for *white blotch* toward apex, with black reniform crescent at inner edge and *series of black st. wedges* beyond. Melanic specimens have FW almost uniform black. HW white with blackish veins and shading. Wingspan 4.2–6.2 cm.
Food: Oaks.
Range: N.S. to Fla., west to Man. and Ark. April–Sept. Common.

SADDLED PROMINENT or MAPLE   Pl. 44 (6)
PROMINENT *Heterocampa guttivitta* (Wlk.)
Identification: This species and the Wavy-lined Heterocampa (below) are very difficult to distinguish—patterns and colors are similar and variable in both. FW of this moth *deep green with variable gray shading.* Lines and veins black, inconspicuous; st. line a series of small black spots. Reniform spot a *black crescent* within a light gray oval. Melanic specimens much darker gray. HW gray. Wingspan 3.2–4.5 cm; ♀ larger than ♂.
Food: Apple, beech, birches, maples, sumacs, and other trees.
Range: Common throughout our area. April–Sept.

WAVY-LINED HETEROCAMPA   Pl. 44 (4)
Heterocampa biundata Wlk.
Identification: Very similar to Saddled Prominent (above), but usually *larger; more green* on FW (fading to yellowish brown); pattern sharper. Am. and pm. lines double, black, *scalloped,* filled with orange. St. line a series of black wedges. HW gray. Wingspan 3.8–5.6 cm; ♀ larger than ♂.
Food: Beech, birches, cherry, hickories, maple, willows, and other trees.
Range: Common throughout our area, but usually less so than the Saddled Prominent. April–Oct.

VARIABLE OAKLEAF CATERPILLAR   Pl. 42 (16)
MOTH *Lochmaeus manteo* Doubleday
Identification: FW powdery gray, variably shaded with grayish brown; some have a contrasting dark grayish brown patch bounded by reniform spot, pm. line, and costa. Am. and pm. lines black, *double, scalloped,* filled with lighter gray. Reniform spot white, often with black filling. HW gray. Wingspan 3.7–5 cm.
Food: Larva (**Variable Oakleaf Caterpillar**) feeds on beech, birches, elms, hawthorn, linden, oaks, walnut, and other trees.
Range: N.S. to Fla., west to Minn. and Tex. April–Oct. Common.

DOUBLE-LINED PROMINENT   Pl. 42 (14)
Lochmaeus bilineata (Pack.)
Identification: Very similar to Variable Oakleaf Caterpillar Moth (above), but FW more brownish gray. Median area slightly darker than rest of FW; *lines much sharper and less scalloped;* pm. line has 2 concave sections. HW gray. Gulf Coast specimens paler and smaller. Wingspan 3.2–4 cm.

Food: Basswood, beech, birches, elms, linden, and oaks.
Range: Common throughout our area. April–Oct.

MORNING-GLORY PROMINENT   Pl. 42 (19, 21)
Schizura ipomoeae Doubleday

Identification: FW highly variable—usually grayish brown with inconspicuous pattern of fine black streaks and spots (not shown); lines broken, obscure. *Reniform spot blackish,* ringed with ground color. Black-shaded form "cinereofrons" (Pack.), Pl. 42 (19), comprises over $\frac{1}{2}$ of Ky. population. Form "telifer" (Grt.), Pl. 42 (22), is like typical form (not shown), but has *long black streaks* in basal and st. areas. HW dirty white in ♂, dark gray in ♀. Wingspan 3.6–4.7 cm.

Food: Beech, birches, elms, maple, morning-glory, oak, roses and other plants.
Range: Common throughout our area. April–Sept.

CHESTNUT SCHIZURA   Pl. 44 (2)
Schizura badia (Pack.)

Identification: Thorax blackish. FW gray, variably shaded with red. Lines fine, blackish if present. Whitish patch at apex. Black reniform spot a *vertical dash* with *triangular* blackish shade beyond it, *widening* toward outer margin. HW dark brownish. Wingspan 3–3.5 cm.

Food: Northern wild-raisin and other *Viburnum* species.
Range: Throughout our area. May–Sept. Local and uncommon.

UNICORN CATERPILLAR MOTH   Pl. 44 (10)
Schizura unicornis (J.E. Sm.)

Identification: FW dark gray, variably shaded and marked with yellowish, rose and brown, especially along costa and beyond pm. line. *Basal area green* (fading to whitish), bounded by *double black am. line.* Usually a black costal patch near apex and sharp black spots in st. area. HW dirty white in ♂, dark gray in ♀. Wingspan 2.5–3.5 cm.

Food: Larva (**Unicorn Caterpillar**) feeds on birches, cherries, hickory, maples, oaks, roses, willows, and many other trees and shrubs.
Range: Common throughout our area. April–Sept.

PLAIN SCHIZURA   Pl. 42 (17)
Schizura apicalis (Grt. & Rob.)

Identification: FW gray, with brown shading at base and anal angle. Lines blackish, wavy, indistinct. *Black reniform crescent* the heaviest marking. HW dirty white in ♂ with black patch at anal angle; blackish in ♀. Wingspan 2.6–3.2 cm.

Food: Bayberry, blueberries, common waxmyrtle, poplars, and willows.
Range: Me. and Que. to Fla., west to Mo. and Tex. April–Sept. Uncommon.

RED-HUMPED CATERPILLAR MOTH   Pl. 44 (5, 8)
Schizura concinna (J.E. Sm.)
Identification: FW in ♂ yellowish with gray along costa; red overlay toward inner margin. In ♀, red tinting more extensive, replacing yellowish. Usual FW lines absent in both sexes. *Fine black basal dash* and *2 lengthwise dashes* at apex; vague blackish mark at inner margin near anal angle. Discal dot fine, black if present. HW white in ♂, dark gray in ♀. Wingspan 3–3.7 cm.
Food: Apple, blueberries, elms, hickories, maples, persimmon, poplars, walnut, willows, and many other trees and shrubs. Larva (**Red-humped Caterpillar**) more common than adult. May injure apple trees.
Range: Throughout our area. March–Sept. Uncommon as adult.

BLACK-BLOTCHED SCHIZURA   Pl. 44 (16)
Schizura leptinoides (Grt.)
Identification: FW dark gray, usually with *whitish apical patch*. Lines black, double, blurred. *Black reniform spot* usually surrounded by diffuse black shade. HW dirty white in ♂, dark gray in ♀. Wingspan 3.4–4.5 cm.
Food: Apple, beech, oaks, poplars, walnut, and other trees.
Range: Common throughout our area. April–Sept.

RED-WASHED PROMINENT   Pl. 44 (9)
Oligocentria semirufescens (Wlk.)
Identification: FW gray with variable dark grayish brown shading along inner margin and costa (sometimes over almost entire FW). FW variably streaked with yellowish, red and black; usual lines absent. Black basal dash and *reniform dot* usually present. HW yellowish white with gray shading. Wingspan 3–4.5 cm.
Food: Apple, beech, birches, maples, poplars, roses, willows, and other trees and shrubs.
Range: Common throughout our area. May–Sept.

WHITE-STREAKED PROMINENT   Pl. 42 (18)
Oligocentria lignicolor (Wlk.)
Identification: FW light gray, evenly streaked with black and white; note *white streak* at anal angle. Some light brown along inner margin toward base. Lines obscure. *Small black tufts* as reniform dot and midway on inner margin. HW white in ♂, gray in ♀. Wingspan 4.1–5.4 cm.
Food: Beech, birches and oak trees.
Range: Common throughout our area. April–Oct.

PINK PROMINENT   Pl. 43 (6)
Hyparpax aurora (J.E. Sm.)
Identification: *FW bright pink; median area yellow* except along costa. The pink is mixed with yellow, softening the pattern in some individuals. HW white to yellowish, variably shaded with pink toward margin. Wingspan 3–3.6 cm.
Food: Scrub oak and viburnums.

Range: N.S. to Ga., west to Minn., Kans., Ark., and La. April–Sept. Uncommon to rare.

TUSSOCK MOTHS:
Family Lymantriidae

Medium-sized moths; females usually larger than males. Wings mostly brownish to grayish or white. Wings reduced to nubs, or well developed but nonfunctional in females of some species; wingspan 1.5–6.7 cm. Ocelli absent; labial palps well developed; *proboscis reduced or absent. Antennae bipectinate* in both sexes; pectinations (branches) longer in ♂, and usually *tipped with 1–3 long, divergent spines.* Base of M_2 *closer to* M_3 than to M_1 on FW and HW (Fig. 27); 1A and 2A of FW *fused* from base outward. $Sc + R_1$ of HW joins Rs for short distance, forming *larger basal areole* than in related families such as Noctuidae (p. 78).

Larvae generally very hairy, usually with 2 anterior and 2–3 posterior long hair tufts. Stinging hairs present in some species such as the Browntail Moth (p. 340). Larvae feed on foliage of many trees and shrubs but usually not on herbaceous plants. They pupate in a loose cocoon that often incorporates larval hairs. A family of serious forest pests; the Gypsy Moth (p. 340) is the most important one in our area.

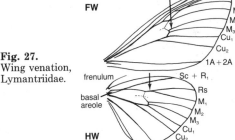

Fig. 27.
Wing venation, Lymantriidae.

TEPHRA TUSSOCK MOTH   Pl. 45 (1)
Dasychira tephra Hbn.
Identification: FW olive to grayish brown, with dark brown *scalloped* lines that are often obscure. Broad, dark lengthwise streaks sometimes present in both sexes. HW dark grayish brown with faint trace of median band. Wingspan 3.1–3.9 cm in ♂; 4.7–5 cm in ♀.
Food: Laurel, water, and white oaks.
Range: S. Md. to s. Fla., west to Mo. and Tex. May–Oct.; 2 broods. Locally common.

SHARP-LINED TUSSOCK MOTH Pl. 45 (6, 9)
Dasychira dorsipennata (B. & McD.)

Identification: Very similar to Tephra Tussock Moth (above), but lines usually *sharper;* median area often contrastingly *whitish,* at least around reniform spot. No lengthwise dark streaks. HW grayish brown with faint median line. Wingspan 3.3–3.8 cm in ♂; 4.8–5.2 cm in ♀.

Food: Larva seems to prefer willows; also feeds on beech, elms, hazelnut, juneberry, and oaks.

Range: N.S. through Appalachians to N.C. mts., west to Man. and Minn. Late June–early Aug.; 1 brood. Locally common.

VARIABLE TUSSOCK MOTH Pl. 45 (3)
Dasychira vagans (B. & McD.)

Identification: Extremely variable; very similar to Sharp-lined Tussock Moth (above), but usually *darker.* Am. line *less distinct;* whitish median patch more noticeable toward costa. No dark-streaked forms. HW brown without median band. Wingspan 3.1–3.9 cm in ♂; 4.7–5.6 cm in ♀.

Food: Deciduous trees such as apple, aspen, balsam poplar, white birch, and willow.

Range: Nfld. to N.C. and Ky. mts., west to Minn. June–Aug. Common northward.

Remarks: The western subspecies, *D. vagans grisea* (B. & McD.), replaces the typical form from Man. to S.D.

YELLOW-BASED TUSSOCK MOTH Pl. 44 (13, 18)
Dasychira basiflava (Pack.)

Identification: Similar to Variable Tussock Moth (above), but FW usually *darker brown,* with *yellowish brown in basal area* (especially in ♂). Median area grayer, whitish toward costa. Am. and pm. lines black, *more sinuous* than in Variable Tussock Moth; both lines *sharply toothed* toward inner margin. Fairly broad lengthwise streak present in some specimens—more often in ♀ than ♂. HW dark grayish brown with faint discal spot and st. line. Wingspan 3–3.9 cm in ♂; 4.2–5.4 cm in ♀.

Food: Oaks; reported as a pest on white oak in Ark.

Range: Mass. and s. Ont. to S.C. (Fla.?), west to Iowa, Mo., and Tex. June–Aug., Oct.; as early as April in n. Fla. Common.

Similar species: Southern Tussock Moth, *D. meridionalis* (B. & McD.), not shown, has *white upper median area* and *nearly straight pm. line* (1 tooth points outward at midpoint; line turns outward above inner margin). Food: Oaks. Range: Fla. west to s. Ark. and se. Tex. April–Oct.

STREAKED TUSSOCK MOTH Pl. 45 (2, 8)
Dasychira obliquata (Grt. & Rob.)

Identification: FW dark brown with extensive dark brown shading; median area usually gray, often whitish toward costa and pm. line in ♀. Long, *thin black basal dash* often present in both sexes (as shown); if present, dash is usually accompanied by other black streaks. Am. line black, *sharply toothed,* especially toward inner margin. Wingspan 3.5-4.3 cm in ♂, 3.9-5.6 cm in ♀.

Food: Beech, birches, black cherry, elms, hickories, and oaks; larva seems to prefer oaks.

Range: S. Que. to Ga. mts., west to Minn., Neb., and Boston Mts. of Ark. June–Sept.; apparently 1 brood. Common.

MANTO TUSSOCK MOTH   Pl. 45 (4, 5)
Dasychira manto (Stkr.)

Identification: FW more *uniformly dark brown* in basal and st. areas than in related species. Median area grayish brown with variable *white patches* in upper median area; white dusting below apex. Am. and pm. lines *thick,* black, complete; am. line *sharply toothed.* Often a thin basal dash, but no lengthwise black streak across FW. HW brown, with vague traces of median and st. lines. Wingspan 3.1-4 cm in ♂; 3.8-4.8 cm in ♀.

Food: Jack and scrub pines.

Range: Md. to s. Fla., west to Ky. and Tex. April–Oct.; 2 broods, perhaps 3 southward. Locally common.

RUSTY TUSSOCK MOTH   Pl. 44 (20)
Orgyia antiqua (L.)

Identification: Male easily recognized by the *rusty brown FW* with a *white to yellowish crescent* just beyond pm. line, near inner margin. Lines brown to blackish, variably distinct. HW orange. Wings absent in ♀ (not shown); body whitish, antennae broadly bipectinate. Our subspecies is *O. antiqua nova* Fitch. Wingspan 2.2-3.1 cm in ♂.

Food: Many trees and shrubs, including alders, apple, cherries, firs, maples, pines, poplars, spruces, and willows.

Range: Holarctic; in our area from Nfld. to Mass. and cen. N.Y., west across Canada, south to Iowa. July–Sept. A day-flier, but males sometimes come to lights.

DEFINITE TUSSOCK MOTH   Pl. 44 (19)
Orgyia definita Pack.

Identification: FW dark grayish brown, with relatively sharp black markings in upper st. area. Note *thin, black costal patch* with black and gray streaks below it, near FW apex. St. line usually sharp, accented by white spot near bottom. HW dark brown, almost black. Wings absent in ♀; ♂ wingspan 2-3.3 cm.

Food: Many deciduous trees, including basswood, birches, oaks, red maple, and willows.

Range: Me. and s. Que. to coastal S.C., west to Ont., Ky., and La. Late Aug.-Oct. northward; April–Oct. (1-2 additional broods) southward. Common.

WHITE-MARKED TUSSOCK MOTH   Pls. 1 (11);
Orgyia leucostigma (J.E. Sm.)   44 (17)
Identification: Similar to Definite Tussock Moth (p. 339); females of these 2 species can be identified only by association with known males. Wings usually grayer in ♂ of this species; median area usually paler. Blackish patch near apex smaller, with no light streaks below it. *White spot* accents lower st. line, as in ♂ Definite Tussock Moth. Wings absent in ♀; ♂ wingspan 2.5–3.5 cm.
Food: Larva (Pl. 1) feeds on over 140 known hosts, including alder, apple, balsam fir, birches, and larch. Sometimes a pest on Christmas tree plantations northward.
Range: Common throughout our area. June–Nov.; 2 broods, usually June–Aug. and Aug.–Nov. One brood in far Northeast (Aug.-Oct.).

GYPSY MOTH   Pls. 1 (13);
Lymantria dispar (L.)   45 (7, 10)
Identification: Sexually dimorphic—♀ much larger and lighter in color. FW brown with yellowish overlay in ♂; HW yellowish to reddish brown. Reniform spot consists of *3 black spots* (usually *merged*) in both sexes; black orbicular dot also present. Wings whitish in ♀, with deeply scalloped gray lines and black spots; terminal line a series of black dots on FW and HW. Wingspan 3–4 cm in ♂; 5.6–6.7 cm in ♀.
Food: Larva (**Gypsy Moth Caterpillar,** Pl. 1) seems to prefer oaks, but will feed on almost any tree or shrub. Known hosts include alder, apple, basswood, birches, box elder, hawthorn, hazelnut, larch, mountain-ash, poplars, rose bushes, sumac, willows, and witch-hazel. Later instars are less particular in their feeding habits than early ones, and can defoliate large tracts of forests in peak years. In woods where larvae are numerous, you can actually hear them feeding.
Range: Now established from N.S. to N.C., west to Mich. and Ill.; in recent years males have been collected in traps as far south and west as Fla. and Mo. July–Aug.; 1 brood.
Remarks: Deliberately introduced from Europe at Medford, Mass. in 1868 or 1869 by Leopold Trouvelot, who hoped to raise this moth for silk production. Unfortunately, some of his moths escaped. By 1889 the Gypsy Moth was doing heavy damage in certain parts of the Boston area; it is now a serious pest throughout much of our area and is expanding its range.

BROWNTAIL MOTH   not shown
Euproctis chrysorrhoea (L.)
Identification: Another white tussock moth, easily distinguished from the ♀ Gypsy Moth (above) by its *orangish to chestnut brown abdomen* ("tail"). Wings and body otherwise entirely white in both sexes. Wingspan 2.8–4 cm.
Food: Larva feeds on many trees and shrubs, but seems to prefer members of the rose family. Apple, bayberry, cherries, oaks, pears,

plums, and willows are major hosts. Once a major defoliating pest in New England states, but now declining (see below).

Range: Introduced from Europe; now apparently confined to seashore habitats on islands in Casco Bay, Me. and Cape Cod, occasionally turning up in other parts of New England. Early July–early Aug.

Remarks: Discovered in Mass. in 1897. At one time its range extended as far north as N.S. and as far south as R.I.

THYATIRID MOTHS:
Family Thyatiridae

Medium-sized moths; wingspan 3–4.6 cm. Superficially similar to noctuid moths (p. 77) and prominents (p. 327), but wing venation differs (Fig. 28): Sc+R_1 of HW *close to but not fused with Rs* (these veins fused near base for short distance in noctuid moths, Figs. 24, 25). Rs and M_1 of HW *arise separately* from top of cell (these veins *stalked* to point beyond cell in prominents, Fig. 26). Vein Cu of HW appears 4-branched in Thyatiridae, 3-branched in Notodontidae, and either 3- or 4-branched in Noctuidae. Ocelli and maxillary palps absent. Labial palps moderately long; proboscis weakly formed, naked (unscaled). *Dorsal tufts* on thorax and abdomen.

Larvae live and feed in loosely rolled leaves of food plant. Only 4 species in the family; all found within our area and treated below.

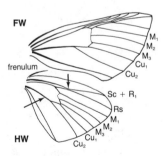

Fig. 28. Wing venation, Thyatiridae.

LETTERED HABROSYNE   Pl. 45 (14)

Habrosyne scripta (Gosse)

Identification: FW yellowish to grayish brown with white costal, am., and pm. areas accented with *pink*. Pm. line of 3–4 fine, black, *looping lines*. HW grayish brown. Wingspan 3–3.9 cm.

Food: Birches, blackberry and other *Rubus* species.

Range: Lab. to w. N.C., west to Man., Ozark Mts. (Ark.), and Miss. May–Aug. Uncommon to rare.

Similar species: Glorious Habrosyne, *H. gloriosa* (Gn.), not shown, is nearly identical; *white am. line* bordering brown basal patch *bent* in *sharp right angle* (not slightly bent as in Lettered Habrosyne); white basal line bordering brown patch *more perpendicular to inner margin*. Food: Unrecorded. Range: Me. to Ky. and westward. April–Sept. Uncommon to rare.

TUFTED THYATIRID   Pl. 45 (11, 15)
Pseudothyatira cymatophoroides (Gn.)
Identification: Note *tuft at anal angle* of FW. FW gray mottled with brownish gray and washed with pinkish at base and in upper median area. Am. and pm. lines black, triple, fused, and more complete in typical dark-marked form; lines expressed only near costa in darker but less heavily marked form. Wingspan 4–4.4 cm.
Food: Alder, birches, maples, oaks, poplars, roses, willows, and other trees and shrubs.
Range: Nfld. to S.C., west to Man., Ark., and Miss. April–Oct.
Remarks: The darker form ("expultrix") is more common.

DOGWOOD THYATIRID   Pl. 45 (12, 13)
Euthyatira pudens (Gn.)
Identification: FW gray with unmistakable pattern of *pinkish white spots* near base, at midpoint of costa, and near apex; smaller spot present at anal angle. The less common form ("pennsylvanica" Sm.) is entirely gray with obscure black lines; sharpest marking is a *black apical dash* beneath pale apical spot (apical dash also present in typical form). Wingspan 4–4.6 cm.
Food: Flowering dogwood.
Range: Nfld. to n. Fla., west to Man. and Tex. Late March–early May. Uncommon to locally common.

HOOKTIP MOTHS:
Family Drepanidae

Medium-sized, broad-winged moths with *FW distinctly hooked* (except in *Eudeilinea* species). *Body shorter* and stouter than in inchworm moths (p. 344). Ocelli absent. Proboscis reduced or absent. Antennae bipectinate in males, except in *Eudeilinea* species. Palps very small. M_2 of FW separated from M_3 by short crossvein (Fig. 29). Humeral angle of HW usually *widened; frenulum reduced or absent*. $Sc + R_1$ of HW *swollen* at base, *not fused* with Rs.
    Larvae lack anal prolegs (rear legs). They feed externally on food plants and pupate in cocoons amid fallen leaves. All known N. American species are treated below.

ARCHED HOOKTIP *Drepana arcuata* Wlk.   Pl. 46 (2)
Identification: Note the unusually *sharp hooked tip* on FW— more pointed than in any of our other hooktip moths. Wings pale yellowish white to orange-yellow. Lines variably distinct; brown

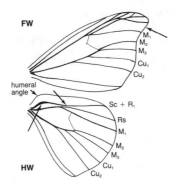

Fig. 29.
Wing venation,
Drepanidae.

st. line widens as it curves toward FW apex. Wingspan 2.4–4 cm.
Food: Alders and birches.
Range: Nfld. to S.C., west to Man. and Mo. April–Sept. Common
except southward.

TWO-LINED HOOKTIP   Pl. 46 (3)
Drepana bilineata (Pack.)
Identification: FW cream to orange-yellow with *scalloped outer
margin* and hooked apex. Am. and pm. lines brown; reniform spot
a black dot. HW pale yellow. Wingspan 2.8–3.3 cm.
Food: Alders, birches, and elms.
Range: Nfld. to N.J., west to Man. and Mich. May–Aug.; 2 broods.
Common.

ROSE HOOKTIP *Oreta rosea* (Wlk.)   Pl. 46 (1)
Identification: Color varies: specimen shown is intermediate between typical all-yellow form and dull pinkish brown form. All
forms have hooked apex and pm. line that *angles back sharply
toward costa* below apex. Wingspan 2.5–3.4 cm.
Food: Birches and viburnums.
Range: Locally common throughout our area. May–Sept., with
stragglers to Nov.

NORTHERN EUDEILINEA   Pl. 48 (21)
Eudeilinea herminiata (Gn.)
Identification: Wings pure white, as in several geometer moths
(next family), but body shorter and stouter, antennae simple in
both sexes. Note black labial palps and shading on forelegs. Am.
and pm. lines very faint, broken or solid, orange-yellow to brown;
pm. line continues onto HW. Specimen shown is more heavily
marked than usual. Wingspan 2.5–2.8 cm.
Food: Dogwoods.
Range: N.S. to N.C., west to Minn. and La. May–Sept.
Similar species: In Florida Eudeilinea, *E. luteifera* Dyar (not
shown), the lines are *more conspicuous.* Food: Unrecorded. Range:
Fla. March–June.

INCHWORM or GEOMETER MOTHS:
Family Geometridae

Small to medium-sized moths, with slender bodies and broad wings. Wingspan 1–6 cm (females wingless in a few species). Ocelli usually absent. Labial palps short, upturned. Proboscis naked (unscaled). Antennae usually bipectinate in ♂, or at least wider than in ♀; ♀ antennae simple. Tympanal cavities located ventrolaterally at base of abdomen, opening anteriorly and usually conspicuous. M_2 of FW *not* usually closer to M_3 than to M_1 (Fig. 30). Veins 1A and 2A fused to FW base. Costa and $Sc+R_1$ of HW *strongly bent* near base; *brace vein* usually connects $Sc+R_1$ to base at frenulum. Rs *fused with* $Sc+R_1$ *briefly* near base, or merely close to it. FW and HW typically similar in color, with lines continuing from FW onto HW (except in many species in subfamily Larentiinae).

Larvae usually twiglike, with first 2–3 pairs of abdominal prolegs absent. Larvae move by extending the front of the body as far forward as possible, then looping the rear of the body up to meet it, hence the name inchworm or measuringworm. They usually feed externally on leaves and pupate in loose cocoons in leaf litter or soil. This is our second largest family of moths, which includes many serious agricultural and forest pests.

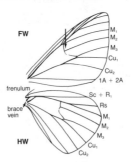

Fig. 30.
Wing venation,
Geometridae.

All 6 N. American subfamilies are represented in our area, and are characterized as follows:

Archiearinae (infants), p. 345 —A small northern group with very hairy bodies. Eyes very small, *oval* (eyes round in other subfamilies). M_2 of HW strongly developed.

Oenochrominae, p. 345—The only species in our area is the Fall Cankerworm Moth (p. 345). Proboscis and wings in ♀ *vestigial.* Body and wings gray.

Ennominae (grays and others), p. 346—Our largest subfamily, with 751 N. American species; it includes the largest inchworm moths as well as many small and medium-sized species. Many are gray, but colors and patterns vary. M_2 of HW *thinner* than M_1 and M_3—sometimes a mere fold in membrane.

Geometrinae (emeralds), p. 373 —The "greens" are small moths, named for their delicate *green color* (a few are yellowish or have brownish spring forms). M_2 arises distinctly *above middle* of discal cells in FW and HW.

Sterrhinae (waves), p. 375 —Similar to the emeralds in size and pattern, but colors vary from white to dark gray and brown— many pastel shades, but not green in our area. $Sc + R_1$ of HW *fused with Rs only at a point or for a short distance,* then sharply diverging, *never fused for more than* $\frac{1}{4}$ *length of discal cell.*

Larentiinae (carpets), p. 379 —Small to medium-sized moths; complex FW pattern often contrasts with simpler HW pattern. $Sc + R_1$ of HW *fused with Rs for more than* $\frac{1}{4}$ *length of discal cell.* Our second largest subfamily of geometers, with 467 N. American species.

Subfamily Archiearinae

THE INFANT *Archiearis infans* (Mösch.)   **Pl. 46 (5)**
Identification: FW brown, dusted with black and white. Diffuse white median, st., and costal patches; st. line white at inner margin. *HW orange* with blackish brown basal bar, discal spot, and *marginal shade*. Wingspan 3–3.3 cm.
Food: Birches.
Range: N.S. to N.J. and Pa., west through Canada south to Minn. March–early May, flying on warm afternoons in birch forests.

Subfamily Oenochrominae

FALL CANKERWORM MOTH   **Pl. 46 (8), 47 (8)**
Alsophila pometaria (Harr.)
Identification: FW light brownish gray in ♂, with complete but inconspicuous toothed, whitish am. and pm. lines, which are edged with darker gray on sides toward each other. *Pm. line sharply inset below costa;* blackish dashes over lines on veins. Faint blackish discal dots on all wings. Wings reduced to nubs in ♀, body not hairy, banded dark and pale gray. ♂ wingspan 2.6–3.2 cm.
Food: Larva (**Fall Cankerworm**) is a pest of apple and other fruit trees and feeds on many other trees and shrubs, such as elms, hackberry, maples, oaks, various members of the rose family, walnut, and willows. Larva has 3 pairs of abdominal prolegs (2 pairs in Spring Cankerworm).
Range: N.S. to n. Fla., west to Man. and Kans. Sept.–May; mostly Oct.–Dec. northward. Common.
Similar species: In ♂ of Spring Cankerworm Moth (p. 358, Pl. 54), FW lines are represented only by *fine black fragments*. Abdomen *spotted* in ♀.

Subfamily Ennominae

COMMON SPRING MOTH   Pl. 49 (23)
Heliomata cycladata Grt. & Rob.

Identification: Wings blackish with terminal line of metallic blue spots. Cream blotches slant from FW costa and inner margin; *1 large cream blotch* fills most of HW. Wingspan 1.7–2.2 cm.

Food: Black locust and honey locust.

Range: Me. and Que. to N.C., west to Ont., Wisc. and Ark. April–June; July northward. A day-flier, but also comes to lights. Common.

RARE SPRING MOTH   Pl. 49 (24)
Heliomata infulata (Grt.)

Identification: Nearly identical to Common Spring Moth (above), but blotches *yellow and narrower*. Wingspan 2–2.5 cm.

Food: Unrecorded.

Range: L.I., N.Y. to N.C., west to w. Pa.; one old record from Fla. May–July. A day-flier. Rare.

VIRGIN MOTH *Protitame virginalis* (Hulst)   Pl. 48 (16)
Identification: Wings white, lightly dusted with grayish brown. Dark grayish brown discal dots. Am. and pm. lines usually double; *pm. line* close to outer margin of FW and *nearly straight* except for a single bend below costa. Some specimens almost unmarked, but look for discal spots on underside of FW and HW. Wingspan 1.9–2.5 cm.

Food: Quaking aspen and bigtooth aspen.

Range: N.S. to Va., west to Man., Miss., and La. Late April–Aug. Locally common.

BROWN-BORDERED GEOMETER   Pl. 50 (19)
Eumacaria latiferrugata (Wlk.)

Identification: Wings light tan to gray, with *darker brown shading* beyond slightly wavy pm. line. Veins light. FW am. line sharply angled; median line straight. Wingspan 2–2.5 cm.

Food: Apple, plum, wild cherry.

Range: Gaspé, Que. to Fla., west to S.D. and e. Tex. April–Sept. Locally common.

LESSER MAPLE SPANWORM MOTH   Pl. 48 (8)
Itame pustularia (Gn.)

Identification: Wings pure white with sharp orange-yellow to brown markings (heaviest as *tops of 4 lines* at FW costa). Pm. line usually most complete line; continues onto HW. Wingspan 1.8–2.7 cm.

Food: Larva (**Lesser Maple Spanworm**) feeds on maples; sometimes a pest.

Range: Nfld. to Fla., west to Man., Neb., and Miss. May–July. May be locally abundant.

CURRANT SPANWORM MOTH   Pl. 51 (8)
Itame ribearia (Fitch)
Identification: Wings *translucent* yellow with *broad, diffuse pm. line* on FW, grayish except over veins. FW basal and pm. areas mostly grayish. Wingspan 3–3.1 cm.
Food: Larva (**Currant Spanworm**) feeds on *Ribes* species, especially black currant.
Range: Me. and Que. to N.J., west to Man. and Mo. May–July. Uncommon.

DRAB ITAME *Itame evagaria* (Hulst)   Pl. 51 (7)
Identification: Wings powdery grayish brown. *4 brown marks* at costa represent tops of lines; lines usually absent in ♂ (shown) except for slight trace of pm. line toward inner margin. Lines complete in ♀; st. area blotched. Wingspan 2.5–3 cm.
Food: Unrecorded; possibly *Ribes* species.
Range: Me. and Que. to Pa., west to N.D. and Mo. June–early Aug. Common.
Similar species: Mousy Itame, *L. argillacearia* (Pack.), not shown, is uniform mouse gray, *not* powdery. ♂ unmarked; ♀ has some yellowish scaling and sometimes traces of spots at costa. Food: Blueberries and *Ribes* species. Range: Same as Drab Itame. Common.

FOUR-SPOTTED ITAME   Pl. 50 (17)
Itame coortaria (Hulst)
Identification: FW powdery light grayish tan, darker brown toward outer margin. Note the *4 sharp, triangular brown spots* along costa—outermost spot sometimes paler or absent. HW paler whitish tan. Wingspan 2.2–2.6 cm.
Food: Apple and hawthorn.
Range: Me. and Ont. to Fla., west to Man. and Tex. May–Aug. Uncommon.

BARRED ITAME *Itame subcessaria* (Wlk.)   Pl. 50 (16)
Identification: Wings powdery light grayish brown with 4 dark brown markings along costa—second one an *even bar, much longer* than other 3 spots. Lower parts of lines thin, variable; may be complete, broken, or absent. Wingspan 2.2–2.8 cm.
Food: Currants and gooseberry.
Range: Nfld. to e. Ky., west to Man., Iowa and S.D. July. Uncommon.

SOUTHERN ITAME *Itame varadaria* (Wlk.)   Pl. 52 (11)
Identification: FW pale brown with faint, diffuse, straight am. and median lines. *Pm. line sharp, concave;* darker brown beyond. Wingspan 1.8–2.2 cm.
Food: Unrecorded.
Range: Coastal S.C. to s. Fla. west along Gulf Coast to Tex. All months southward; spring and summer broods in S.C. Locally common (Fla.).

ORANGE WING *Mellilla xanthometata* (Wlk.)   **Pl. 49 (25)**
Identification: The only geometer moth with a *bright orange HW.* FW varies from gray to brown, with variable but nearly straight lines and black st. spot. Wingspan 1.6–2.1 cm.
Food: Locust trees.
Range: N.J. to S.C., west to Neb. and Tex. April–Oct. Abundant; active both day and night.

PROMISCUOUS ANGLE   **Pl. 49 (19)**
Semiothisa promiscuata Fgn.
Identification: Wings whitish, with tan shading beyond pm. lines. *FW deeply notched* below apex, notch lined with brown. Note the large blackish blotch at midpoint of pm. line, crossed by tan veins and pm. line. Wingspan 2.4–2.8 cm.
Food: Unrecorded.
Range: Md. to Fla., west to Mo. and Tex. April–Sept. Common.
Similar species: Common Angle, *S. aemulataria* (Wlk.), not shown, is slightly smaller and darker, with smaller and paler brown blotch on FW. Hind tibia in ♂ *narrow,* with *no* long hair pencil (see p. 3); Promiscuous Angle has *thickened tibia* with *long hair pencil.* Food: Locust and maples. Range: N.S. to Fla., west to S.D. and Tex. April–Sept. Common.

WOODY ANGLE   **Pl. 49 (22)**
Semiothisa aequiferaria (Wlk.)
Identification: Very similar to Promiscuous and Common Angles (above), but smaller and heavily suffused with *brown.* Black blotch on pm. line of FW *smaller* and less conspicuous than in other two species. Wingspan 1.9–2.4 cm.
Food: Unrecorded.
Range: N.H. to Fla., west to Wisc. and Tex. April–Oct. Common southward; rare in North.

SOUTHERN CHOCOLATE ANGLE   **Pl. 50 (14)**
Semiothisa distribuaria (Hbn.)
Identification: A large *Semiothisa* species, with *chocolate bands* crossing mottled, tan to purplish gray wings. Am. and pm. lines blackish, wavy, complete. Wingspan 2.8–3.5 cm.
Food: Pines.
Range: Coastal N.C. through Fla. to Ark. and e. Tex. All year. Common.

BLURRY CHOCOLATE ANGLE   **Pl. 51 (1)**
Semiothisa transitaria (Wlk.)
Identification: Very similar to Southern Chocolate Angle (above), but smaller and darker; FW lines and *brown bands* usually *blend in more with* purplish *ground color.* Wingspan 2.3–2.6 cm.
Food: Pines.
Range: N.S. to S.C., west to Wisc., Mo., and La. May–Sept. Locally common.

MINOR ANGLE *Semiothisa minorata* (Pack.)   **Pl. 51 (3)**
Identification: FW powdery reddish brown to gray, usually with *warm brown st. band,* often visible only toward costa. Lines usually obscure, except at tops as dark brown costal spots. Pm. line continues as median line across paler HW. Wingspan 1.8–2.4 cm.
Food: Red and white pine.
Range: N.S. to w. N.C., west to Minn. and S.D. May–Aug.; 2 broods. Common.

RED-HEADED INCHWORM MOTH   **Pl. 50 (18)**
Semiothisa bisignata (Wlk.)
Identification: Wings whitish, powdered with light brown. FW st. area sometimes shaded slightly darker. Small blackish costal marks at tops of am., median, and pm. lines. Large *light brown costal spot* near apex, another smaller one usually just outside pm. line. Wingspan 2.1–2.7 cm.
Food: Larva (**Red-headed Inchworm**) feeds on pines.
Range: Nfld. to N.C., west to Minn. and e. Mo. May–Aug.; 2 broods. Locally common.
Similar species: Bicolored Angle, *S. bicolorata* (F.), not shown, is larger; wings powdery *yellowish tan* to pm. line, evenly *darker brown* beyond pm. line on all wings; spots as in Red-headed Inchworm Moth. Food: Pines. Range: N.Y. to Fla. and west. May–Aug. Common.

PALE-MARKED ANGLE   **Pl. 50 (12)**
Semiothisa signaria (Hbn.)
Identification: More lightly marked than preceding species; wings evenly grayish brown. Lines variable, often obscure. Costal spot near apex *light brown, inconspicuous;* lower st. spot may be small, widely divided by pm. line. Our subspecies is *S. signaria dispuncta* (Wlk.). Wingspan 2.4–3 cm.
Food: Firs, hemlocks, larch, pines, spruces, and other conifers.
Range: Lab. to N.C. mts., west across Canada, south to S.D. May–Sept. Common.

WHITE PINE ANGLE   **Pl. 50 (10)**
Semiothisa pinistrobata Fgn.
Identification: This moth and the next 3 species are very similar. Wings mottled with powdery whitish and brown, costal spot near FW apex *blackish brown.* Pm. line wavy. Wingspan 2.2–2.8 cm.
Food: White pine.
Range: N.S. to w. N.C., west to Ont. and Mich. Late May–Aug. Common wherever white pine is abundant.

HEMLOCK ANGLE   **Pl. 50 (11)**
Semiothisa fissinotata (Wlk.)
Identification: Wings powdery brownish gray, less mottled than in White Pine Angle (above) or Granite Moth (below). Spots along

costa and in lower st. area of FW heavy blackish brown—st. spot *larger and darker* than in White Pine Angle (above). Wingspan 2.2–2.5 cm.
Food: Eastern and Carolina hemlocks.
Range: N.S. to Ga. mts., west to Ont. and e. Ky. May–Sept.; 2 broods. Locally common.

GRANITE MOTH *Semiothisa granitata* (Gn.)   **Pl. 49 (21)**
Identification: Almost identical to White Pine Angle (above), but costal spot near FW apex *light to reddish brown* if present. Terminal area often nearly solid grayish brown except below apex. Wingspan 2.2–2.8 cm.
Food: Pitch and scrub pines.
Range: S. Me. to S.C., west to Ohio and Ky. May–Sept.; 2 broods. Common.

MANY-LINED ANGLE   **Pl. 51 (2)**
Semiothisa multilineata (Pack.)
Identification: Wings grayish brown, warm orangish brown beyond pm. line. Lines and shading dark, *straight, vertical.* Wingspan 2.3–2.6 cm.
Food: Unrecorded.
Range: Mass. to Fla., west to Mo. and Ark. April–Sept. Locally common.

THREE-LINED ANGLE   **Pl. 50 (9)**
Semiothisa eremiata (Gn.)
Identification: Wings dark grayish brown, darker toward margins. FW has *3 narrow, solid* grayish brown lines; HW has *2.* Wingspan 2–2.2 cm.
Food: Goat's-rue.
Range: N.H. to Fla., west to Wisc., S.D. and Miss. May–Sept. Uncommon to rare.

FOUR-SPOTTED ANGLE   **Pl. 48 (9)**
Semiothisa quadrinotaria (H.-S.)
Identification: Wings whitish, variably powdered with brown. Note clean-cut brown lines and *round blackish spots* in st. areas of FW and HW. Wingspan 2.3–2.6 cm.
Food: Unrecorded.
Range: Ohio and Va. to n. Fla., west to Kans. and Ark. April–July; Sept. Locally common in deep woods.

CURVE-LINED ANGLE   **Pl. 50 (8)**
Semiothisa continuata (Wlk.)
Identification: Wings varying shades of gray. FW has *heavy black* am. and pm. lines; *pm. line curved* (as shown). Wingspan 2–2.7 cm.
Food: Red cedar; hackberry (?).
Range: Me. to Fla., west to Man. and Tex. March–Oct. Locally common.

FAINT-SPOTTED ANGLE   Pl. 51 (4)
Semiothisa ocellinata (Gn.)
Identification: Wings brownish gray, faintly mottled, with *brown shades beyond pm. line* on FW and its extension onto HW. Black dotting over pm. line, but pattern generally diffuse and soft. Wingspan 2.1–2.7 cm.
Food: Locust trees.
Range: Me. and Que. to Fla., west to Neb., Kans. and La. April–Oct. Common to abundant.

HOLLOW-SPOTTED ANGLE   Pl. 50 (21)
Semiothisa gnophosaria (Gn.)
Identification: Wings dull brown, powdery, with irregular and often obscure blackish lines. (Specimen shown has unusually sharp markings.) Reniform spot on FW a *hollow, vertical ellipse.* Wingspan 1.8–2.3 cm.
Food: Larch and willows.
Range: Ont. to Fla., west to Wisc. and Tex. April–Sept. Common to abundant southward.

PALE-VEINED ECONISTA   Pl. 50 (13)
Econista dislocaria (Pack.)
Identification: Wings grayish brown to ash gray, brown beyond pm. line. *Blackish costal spots* mark tops of FW lines; upper and middle pm. line largely blackish. Note veins outlined with *yellowish white.* Wingspan 2.7–3 cm.
Food: Unrecorded.
Range: Ont. and w. Pa. to e. S.C. and Miss., west to S.D. and Tex. April–June. Uncommon.

SULPHUR MOTH   Pl. 51 (5)
Hesperumia sulphuraria Pack.
Identification: FW pale to deep yellow with reddish brown costal spot near base, *hollow discal spot* and fringe; *darker costal spot* near apex. HW entirely yellow. Some specimens have complete am. and pm. lines, or reddish brown median area. Wingspan 2.9–3.5 cm.
Food: *Ceanothus* species and snowberry.
Range: N.S. to w. Va., westward across s. Canada, south to S.D. and Mo. Late June–Aug. Locally common.

CRANBERRY SPANWORM MOTH   Pl. 50 (20)
Ematurga amitaria (Gn.)
Identification: Wings powdery orange; FW rusty brown in ♂, more whitish and brown in ♀ (not shown). 4 diffuse *dark brown lines* cross FW in both sexes, 3 on HW. Fringe *checkered brown and whitish.* Wingspan of ♂ 2.5–3 cm, ♀ smaller.
Food: Larva (**Cranberry Spanworm**) feeds on arborvitae and other woody plants; sometimes a pest on cranberry.
Range: N.S. to Pa., west to Man. and Minn. Late May–Aug. A day-flier in bogs and wet meadows. Locally common.

UMBER MOTH *Hypomecis umbrosaria* (Hbn.)   **Pl. 52 (6)**
Identification: Wings pale to dark gray with scalloped, jagged black am., pm. and st. lines. Discal spots *elliptical and hollow* on all wings. Wingspan 2.6–4 cm.
Food: Birches and oaks.
Range: Me. to Fla., west to Wisc., Mo., and e. Tex. April–Aug. Common.
Remarks: This moth and the next 24 species are commonly called "grays."

TEXAS GRAY *Glenoides texanaria* (Hulst)   **Pl. 52 (13)**
Identification: Wings gray, slightly mottled. Lines fine, black; *pm. line* sharpest. *Warm brown shading* in st. area on all wings. Wingspan 1.5–2.2 cm.
Food: Unrecorded.
Range: Va. to Fla., west to Mo. and Tex. June–Oct. Common.

DOTTED GRAY *Glena cribrataria* (Gn.)   **Pl. 52 (5)**
Identification: Wings light powdery gray with heavy, *dotted* am., pm., st., and terminal lines; *pm. line strongest.* Double row of black spots on abdomen. Wingspan 2.3–3.1 cm.
Food: Poplars, spruces and willows.
Range: S. Ont. to s. Va., west to Wisc. and Tex. April–May, July–Aug. Uncommon.

BLUEBERRY GRAY *Glena cognataria* (Hbn.)   **Pl. 54 (3)**
Identification: Wings pinkish to violet-gray. Even, wavy pm. line on FW accented with small, *dark spots or dashes* (♂) or vague dark shade (♀, not shown). Am. line represented by 1–2 spots. Wingspan 2–3 cm.
Food: Blueberries.
Range: Coastal N.S. to Fla., west to La.; apparently in bogs and blueberry barrens. May–Aug.; probably 2 broods. Uncommon northward.

FINE-LINED GRAY *Exelis pyrolaria* Gn.   **Pl. 50 (24)**
Identification: Wings dark grayish brown. Am., median, and pm. lines fine, blackish brown, often partly obscured. FW has discal dot, and pm. line that *angles sharply twice* near costa and inner margin. Wingspan 2.2–2.5 cm.
Food: Persimmon and common pipsissewa.
Range: N.Y. to cen. Fla., west to Ill. and La. March–Aug. Locally common southward.

DIMORPHIC GRAY   **Pl. 50 (22, 23)**
Tornos scolopacinarius (Gn.)
Identification: ♂ similar to Fine-lined Gray (above), but wings more brownish and mottled. Discal dot *larger and rounder,* and lines more dotted; fringe checkered. ♀ yellowish tan with brown st. band and gray terminal shade; black discal spot on FW *larger* in ♀ than in ♂. Wingspan 2.1–2.9 cm.

Food: Asters and coreopsis.
Range: S. Conn. to s. Fla., west to s. Wisc. and Tex. Feb.–Nov. Common.

FOUR-BARRED GRAY Pl. 52 (19)
Aethalura intertexta (Wlk.)
Identification: Wings powdery brownish gray. Lines black, broken; *4 bars taper inward* from FW costa. St. line whitish, zigzag on FW and HW. Fringe checkered. Wingspan 2.1–2.5 cm.
Food: Alders and birches.
Range: Nfld. to Fla., west to Man. and Mo. April–July; 2 broods southward. Uncommon.

LARGE PURPLISH GRAY Pl. 52 (17)
Anacamptodes vellivolata (Hulst)
Identification: Wings *bluish to purplish gray,* with warm brown shading in am. and st. areas. Lines black; *median and pm. lines merge* toward inner margin. Wingspan 3–3.5 cm.
Food: Firs, larch, pines, and spruces.
Range: Throughout our area. April–Aug. northward. Locally common in conifer forests, especially in South.

PALE-WINGED GRAY Pl. 52 (16)
Anacamptodes ephyraria (Wlk.)
Identification: Wings whitish gray, with variable overlay of yellowish brown and darker gray. Lines black, pm. line with a *rounded bulge near FW costa.* Note 4 black spots along costa. Discal spots large, hollow on all wings. Wingspan 2.3–2.8 cm.
Food: Ash, birches, choke cherry, elms, balsam fir, gooseberry, hemlock, maples and willows.
Range: Common throughout our area. June–Sept.

SMALL PURPLISH GRAY Pl. 52 (18)
Anacamptodes humaria (Gn.)
Identification: Wings bluish to purplish gray as in Large Purplish Gray (above), but size and lines similar to Pale-winged Gray (see Pl. 52). Pm. line on FW *more toothed inward at top of bulge* than in Pale-winged Gray. Note white dorsal band across basal abdominal segment, followed by a black band. Wingspan 2.4–2.8 cm.
Food: Alfalfa, asparagus, white birch, clover, dewberry, hickory, pecan, persimmon, and soybeans.
Range: Common throughout our area. April–Sept.

BROWN-SHADED GRAY Pl. 52 (14)
Anacamptodes defectaria (Gn.)
Identification: Wings whitish with variable gray mottling; *orangish brown shading* in am. and st. areas. Lines black, sharp— am. and pm. lines usually conspicuous, pm. line scalloped between bulge and costa. Wings dark gray (not whitish) in melanics (not shown), but markings normal. Wingspan 2.4–3.6 cm.
Food: Oaks, poplars, sweet cherry, and willows.

Range: N.J. to Fla., west to Kans. and Tex. Feb.–Nov. Common; may be abundant southward.

BENT-LINE GRAY *Iridopsis larvaria* (Gn.)   **Pl. 52 (9)**
Identification: Wings pale gray to grayish white, less mottled than in Brown-shaded Gray (above), but both moths have brown shading and sharp black lines. Pm. line *more sharply angled* on HW than in any *Anacamptodes* species. Discal spots hollow, more prominent. Melanics evenly dark gray with normal markings. Wingspan 2.6–3.6 cm.
Food: Alders, birches, black cherry, maples, poplars, willows, and other trees.
Range: Nfld. to Ga., west to Man. and Miss. April–Sept. Common.

COMMON GRAY   **Pl. 52 (8)**
Anavitrinella pampinaria (Gn.)
Identification: Wings powdery gray, *heavily mottled* with darker gray and black but no brown. FW pm. line wavy, but not as pronounced a bulge near costa of FW as in *Anacamptodes* species (p. 353) and *not sharply bent* on HW. Discal spots black. White and black abdominal bands as in Small Purplish Gray (p. 353, Pl. 52). Fla. specimens have heavier lines; melanics are dark gray with obscure lines. Wingspan 2.3–3.4 cm.
Food: Apple, ashes, citrus, clover, cotton, elms, pear, poplars, and willows.
Range: Common to abundant throughout our area. April–Oct.

DOUBLE-LINED GRAY *Cleora sublunaria* (Gn.)   **Pl. 52 (4)**
Identification: Wings gray; ♂ sometimes has a greenish tint. Similar to Common Gray (above), but less mottled, especially in median area. *Am. line double, wide; discal spots hollow.* Wingspan 2.5–3 cm.
Food: Sweetfern.
Range: N.Y. and Ont. to Fla., west to Ill. and Tex. Late March–April; May northward.
Similar species: Projecta Gray, *C. projecta* (Wlk.), not shown, is slightly larger, *purplish,* with *whiter median area.* Food: Sweetgale. Range: Que. to Fla., west to Man. and Tex. April–early June. Uncommon to rare.

THE SMALL ENGRAILED   **Pl. 52 (15)**
Ectropis crepuscularia (D. & S.)
Identification: Wings powdery whitish gray, becoming soft brownish gray. Lines darker gray to blackish, toothed, often obscure—pm. line on FW most prominent. Note the 2 distinctive sharp *blackish wedges* in FW st. area. Discal spots obscure or absent. Wingspan 2.6–3.7 cm.
Food: Alders, apple, birches, elms, hemlock, maples, oaks, poplars, willows and other trees.
Range: Common to abundant throughout our area except s. Fla. March–Sept.

PORCELAIN GRAY   Pl. 52 (7)
Protoboarmia porcelaria (Gn.)
Identification: Wings whitish, heavily speckled with brown. Lines blackish brown, curved toward costa. Pm. line usually heaviest on veins, where it forms *triangular spots* pointing outward. St. line zigzag, whitish. Discal spots solid, but usually faint on all wings. Wingspan 2.5–3.5 cm.
Food: Birches, firs, hemlock, larches, oaks, pines, poplars, spruces, white cedar.
Range: Locally common throughout our area. May–Sept.

TULIP-TREE BEAUTY   Pl. 52 (12)
Epimecis hortaria (F.)
Identification: A large moth with very broad wings; outer margin of HW *scalloped.* Pattern variable; typical specimens powdery whitish with *black zigzag lines* across wings. Two other common forms (not shown) exist: (1) In form "dendraria" Gn., *median and st. lines much broader* than other lines; (2) in melanic form "carbonaria" Haim., *wings mostly blackish,* with variable white edging on parts of lines. Wingspan 4.3–5.5 cm.
Food: Pawpaw, poplars, sassafras, and tulip-tree.
Range: Mass. and s. Ont. to Fla., west to Ill., Mo., and Tex. Late March–early Oct. Common.

WHITE-TIPPED BLACK   Pl. 56 (4)
Melanchroia chephise (Cram.)
Identification: *Black, with orange thorax.* FW tips usually *white.* Veins outlined thinly in dark gray. Wingspan 3–4 cm.
Food: Breynia and phyllanthus.
Range: Fla. to s. and cen. Tex. All year. A tropical day-flier; sometimes common.

CANADIAN MELANOLOPHIA   Pl. 52 (3)
Melanolophia canadaria (Gn.)
Identification: Wings whitish, speckled and mottled with brown; grayer northward. Lines distinct, sometimes reduced or absent; *pm. line wavy* when present. Wingspan 2.8–3.6 cm.
Food: Birches, elms, maples, oaks, pines, and *Prunus* species.
Range: Common to abundant throughout our area. March–Sept.; 2 broods.
Remarks: Subspecies *M. canadaria crama* Rindge, occurring roughly from N.J. to n. Ill. and Tenn., is *more mottled* than typical specimens northward. Larger, darker subspecies, *M. canadaria choctawae* Rindge, occurs along coast from Md. to Tex.

SIGNATE MELANOLOPHIA   Pl. 52 (2)
Melanolophia signataria (Wlk.)
Identification: Wings pale gray to brown, usually less mottled than in Canadian Melanolophia (above), which is often almost identical. Pm. line tends to be *straighter* than in Canadian Melanolophia. Wingspan 3–3.5 cm.

Food: Alders, American elm, birches, fir, larch, maples, oaks, poplars, and spruce.
Range: N.S. to Fla., west to Man. and e. Tex. March–Aug. Much less common than Canadian Melanolophia.
Remarks: Larger, darker specimens from w. Fla. are *M. signataria timucuae* Rindge.

POWDER MOTH *Eufidonia notataria* (Wlk.)   **Pl. 51 (6)**
Identification: Wings powdery white in ♂ with heavy reddish brown shading on FW; lines obscure. Wings much paler in ♀, less shaded with brown. *Large discal spots on all wings* in both sexes. Wingspan 2.2–2.6 cm.
Food: Firs, hemlock, larch, spruces, and white pine.
Range: N.S. to W. Va., west to Wisc. and Mo. Late May–July.
Similar species: Sharp-lined Powder Moth, *E. discospilata* (Wlk.), not shown, has *blackish shading* with sharper delineation of dark and white areas. Food: Alders, birches, blueberries, hawthorns, laurels, *Prunus* species, willows, and other trees and shrubs. Range: Nfld. to Mass. and N.Y., west to Wisc. June.

PEPPER-AND-SALT GEOMETER   **Pl. 54 (11)**
Biston betularia (L.)
Identification: The N. American subspecies is *B. betularia cognataria* (Gn.). FW *angled;* wings *white* with dark gray *"peppering."* Lines black. Wings entirely blackish in melanic form "swettaria" (B. & McD.). Wingspan 4–4.5 cm.
Food: Alders, birches, blueberries, elms, hackberries, larch, pecan, *Prunus* species, walnut, willows, and other trees and shrubs.
Range: Holarctic; known in our area from N.S. to w. N.C., west to S.D. and Mo. May–Sept. Common.
Remarks: Known in England as the Peppered Moth, this moth was studied by the late H.B.D. Kettlewell as an example of "industrial melanism." (The melanic form of this species became dominant in areas where smoke from industrial stacks darkened the trees where the moths spend the day.) The typical form is most abundant where lichens cover trees in a "pepper and salt" pattern, enabling the moths to escape detection by birds.

WOOLLY GRAY *Lycia ypsilon* (S.A. Forbes)   **Pl. 54 (5)**
Identification: Body hairy, black. Wings grayish brown in ♂ with *lighter median area;* lines black. ♂ wingspan 3–3.5 cm. ♀ almost wingless.
Food: Apple trees.
Range: N.Y. to Fla., west to Minn. and Tex. April; earlier southward. Locally common.
Similar species: Stout Spanworm Moth, *L. ursaria* (Wlk.), not shown, is extremely hairy. FW *evenly gray* (median area *not* lighter) with 3 blackish lines, often broken into bars; st. line white. ♀ has wings but does not fly. Food: Alders, American elm, basswood, poplars, white ash, white birch, and other broadleaved

trees. Range: Canada, south to N.J. and Iowa. April–June. Locally common.

TWILIGHT MOTH *Lycia rachelae* (Hulst) **Pl. 54 (13)**
Identification: Body *densely hairy* in both sexes, but wings reduced, nearly absent in ♀. *Wings translucent,* grayish white in ♂; veins, base and marginal spots blackish. ♂ wingspan 3.3–3.7 cm.
Food: Apple, birches, choke cherry, elm, poplars, willow, and other trees.
Range: N.H. to Pa.; westward in Canada to Man. Early spring, usually April, sometimes in snowstorms. Thought to be rare, but probably not often sought in season.

ONE-SPOTTED VARIANT Pl. 51 (9, 12)
Hypagyrtis unipunctata (Haw.)
Identification: Note *scalloped HW.* Extremely variable sexually, geographically, and seasonally. Both sexes yellowish tan to orangish, mottled with white, brown and blackish; lines and discal spots on all wings black. FW has *pale st. spot* near costa. Colors in spring specimens, Pl. 51 (9), contrast more than in summer brood, Pl. 51 (12). Females *usually larger, with more deeply scalloped* HW. Melanics commonly occur, but paler spot still visible near FW apex. Wingspan 2–4.7 cm.
Food: Alders, birches, firs, hickories, oaks, pines, willows, and other trees.
Range: Common to abundant throughout our area. April–Sept.; 2–3 broods.

ESTHER MOTH *Hypagyrtis esther* (Barnes) **Pl. 51 (10)**
Identification: Similar to darker forms of One-spotted Variant (above), but *wings evenly violet-gray,* not mottled; reddish brown beyond pm. line. St. spot usually a cleancut *oval* if present. Melanics chocolate. Wingspan 2.5–4.5 cm; ♀ larger than ♂.
Food: Pines.
Range: Mass. to Fla., west to Mo. and Tex. May–Oct. Locally common.

PINE MEASURINGWORM MOTH Pl. 52 (1)
Hypagyrtis piniata (Pack.)
Identification: HW scalloped as in other *Hypagyrtis* species. Wings grayish brown, evenly peppered with black; *no orangish brown* shading. St. spot on FW *white, irregular,* inconspicuous. Lines blackish; pm. line sinuous, toothed. Black discal spots on all wings. Wingspan 2.2–3.5 cm.
Food: Firs, hemlocks, larch, pines, and other conifers.
Range: Nfld. to N.Y. and Pa., across Canada, south to S.D. June–Aug. Common in coniferous forests.

BRENDA'S HYPAGYRTIS Pl. 54 (7)
Hypagyrtis brendae R.L. Heitzman
Identification: Wings smooth, dark violet gray with sharp black

am. and pm. lines, white st. dot, and *orangish brown st. area.*
Wingspan 2.5–4 cm; ♀ larger than ♂.
Food: Unrecorded.
Range: Ky. to w. Mo. and Ark. Late April–Aug.; 2 broods. Locally
common.

THE HALF-WING *Phigalia titea* (Cram.)   **Pl. 52 (21)**
Identification: Wings pale powdery gray. FW lines black, heavy;
pm. line *wavy,* not usually touching *straight, broad median line,*
and *not toothed* toward costa. Melanics darker gray to black. ♀
(not shown) lacks wings; body gray with *no abdominal spines.*
Wingspan of ♂ 3–4 cm.
Food: American basswood, American elm, blueberry, hickories,
maple, oaks and poplars.
Range: Throughout our area; March–April. Usually common.

TOOTHED PHIGALIA   **Pl. 52 (22)**
Phigalia denticulata Hulst
Identification: Similar to the Half-wing (above), but FW more
mottled in ♂ (shown), especially between thin black lines. *Pm. line
sharply toothed near costa,* bulging inward above inner margin,
where it usually approaches median line. Wings reduced to tiny
(2-mm long) nubs in ♀. Wingspan 3–3.7 cm. in ♂.
Food: Unrecorded; probably various trees.
Range: Va. to Fla., west to Mo. and Tex. Dec.–April. Common.

SMALL PHIGALIA   **Pl. 52 (20)**
Phigalia strigataria (Minot)
Identification: Very similar to the Toothed Phigalia (above), but
usually smaller, less mottled, with *straighter pm. line* that *curves
gently* toward inner margin. Wings of ♀ reduced, each less than
1 mm long. ♂ wingspan 3–3.8 cm.
Food: American elm; probably many other trees.
Range: Common throughout our area. March–May or early June
northward; as early as Jan. southward. Emerges earlier than the
Half-wing.

SPRING CANKERWORM MOTH   **Pl. 54 (8)**
Paleacrita vernata (Peck)
Identification: FW in ♂ shiny gray; veins variably accented with
black. Am. line black, *sharply angled;* pm. line fine, black, *bent
inward* toward costa. Black dash inward from outer margin below
apex. Vague whitish st. tint. ♀ gray, wingless. ♂ wingspan 2.2–
3.5 cm.
Food: Larva (**Spring Cankerworm**) feeds on birches, elms, ma-
ples, *Prunus* species and many other deciduous trees and shrubs.
May be a serious defoliating pest.
Range: N.S. to N.C., west to Man. and Tex. Jan.–April southward; March–May in North. Very common.
Similar species: White-spotted Cankerworm Moth, *P. merriccata*
Dyar (not shown), also has gray, wingless ♀. ♂ almost identical,

but has *1 bulge* on each antennal segment, while Spring Cankerworm Moth has 2. Conspicuous *white discal spot* on FW, absent in Spring Cankerworm Moth. Food: Unrecorded. Range: Ont. to Fla., west to Mo. and Tex. March–May. Uncommon.

LINDEN LOOPER MOTH   **Pls. 1 (14),**
or WINTER MOTH *Erannis tiliaria* (Harr.)   **47 (6), 51 (13)**
Identification: Wings in ♂ broad; FW pale straw yellow to fawn brown, either uniform or darker beyond pm. line. *Pm. line bends outward, then back inward* to meet costa. May have discal spots. HW cream. ♀ wingless; body and legs mottled *black and white.* Wingspan in ♂ 3.2–4.2 cm.
Food: Larva (**Linden Looper**) may be a serious forest pest, attacking American basswood, apple, ashes, beech, birches, elms, maples, oaks, poplars, *Prunus* species and *Ribes* species.
Range: Nfld. to Va., west to Man. and Kans. Oct.–early Dec. Uncommon to locally abundant, usually varying from year to year in a given area.

BLUISH SPRING MOTH   **Pl. 49 (18)**
Lomographa semiclarata (Wlk.)
Identification: FW white, but appears *slightly bluish* due to black shading and lines. HW shiny white with *black discal dot,* faint median line, and sharp terminal line of dots. Wingspan 1.8–2.2 cm.
Food: Alders, juneberries, chokeberries, hawthorns, poplars, and *Prunus* species.
Range: Nfld. to w. S.C., west across Canada, south to Mo. and S.D. Late March–April; to June northward. A day-flier, sometimes mistaken for a butterfly.

WHITE SPRING MOTH   **Pl. 48 (10)**
Lomographa vestaliata (Gn.)
Identification: Wings shiny *translucent white,* without markings. (The tiny black dots on specimen shown are pinholes.) Wingspan 1.5–2.6 cm.
Food: Apple, hawthorn, hornbeam, maples, *Prunus* species, and snowberries.
Range: Common throughout our area except in peninsular Fla. March–Sept. Often encountered during the day.

GRAY SPRING MOTH   **Pl. 50 (15)**
Lomographa glomeraria (Grt.)
Identification: Wings pale powdery gray. FW has sharp *black discal dot* and diffuse brownish am. and pm. lines. *Pm. line curves* and continues on paler HW. Terminal line thin, sharp, brown. Wingspan 2.2–2.6 cm.
Food: *Prunus* species and possibly hawthorn.
Range: Nfld. to Fla., west to Man. and Tex. April–May. May be very common.

JEWELED SATYR MOTH   Pl. 56 (3)
Phrygionia argentata (Dru.)
Identification: Wings grayish brown, crossed by yellow bands that are lined with *silvery blue.* HW has red spot and shading in terminal area. Wingspan 2.4–2.7 cm.
Food: Marlberry.
Range: Cen. to s. Fla. and tropics. All year; flight resembles that of satyrid butterflies in shaded swamps. Comes to lights.

YELLOW-DUSTED CREAM MOTH   Pl. 48 (7)
Cabera erythemaria Gn.
Identification: Wings cream to white with rough yellowish dusting. Faint, slightly irregular, yellowish am., median, and pm. lines on all wings, roughly *parallel* to each other. Wingspan 2.1–2.8 cm.
Food: Birch, blueberry, poplars, and willows.
Range: Nfld. to w. N.C., west across Canada, south to Ill. and Minn. May–Aug. Common northward.

PINK-STRIPED WILLOW SPANWORM   Pl. 48 (13)
MOTH *Cabera variolaria* Gn.
Identification: Wings pure white, but not shiny and translucent as in White Spring Moth, Pl. 48 (13). Front of head and forelegs yellowish brown to orange. Very *faint traces* of yellowish to grayish brown *lines* in some specimens. Wingspan 2.2–2.7 cm.
Food: Poplars and willows.
Range: Nfld. to w. N.C., west across Canada, south to Neb. June–Sept. Common northward.

FOUR-LINED CABERA   Pl. 48 (12)
Cabera quadrifasciaria (Pack.)
Identification: Smooth, creamy white with *4 parallel, grayish brown lines* on FW, 3 on HW. Wingspan 2.5–2.7 cm.
Food: Unrecorded.
Range: Ohio to n. Ky., west to Neb., Kans., and Ark. May–early June. Uncommon to rare.

BROAD-LINED ERASTRIA   Pl. 49 (20)
Erastria coloraria (F.)
Identification: Wings dull gray to brown in spring brood, straw yellow to olive in summer brood (shown). Am. and median lines variably complete. *Pm. line complete,* diffuse, *curved slightly outward,* often with diffuse spot just beyond it at midpoint. Underside yellow, variably tinted with bright pink in summer form. Wingspan 2.7–3.7 cm.
Food: Jersey tea; also possibly clover and *Rubus* species.
Range: Conn. to Fla., west to Minn., Neb., and Tex. April–July; 2 broods. Locally common; often seen during the day.
Similar species: Thin-lined Erastria, *E. cruentaria* (Hbn.), not shown, has sharper FW apex and *thinner,* more sharply defined pm. line that meets costa *farther out* than in Broad-lined Erastria. Colors same, but underside marked with orange to reddish purple.

Food: Blackberry. Range: Wash., D.C. to Fla., west to Mo. and Tex. April–Sept.; 2 broods.

BLACK-DOTTED RUDDY   Pl. 54 (1)
Thysanopyga intractata (Wlk.)

Identification: Wings deep orange to dull reddish brown with 3 darker, indistinct lines. Pm. line on FW irregular, accented outwardly with *whitish dots*. Discal dots on all wings sharp, black. Wingspan 2.1–3.1 cm.

Food: Unrecorded.

Range: Mass. to Fla., west to Wisc. and Tex. July northward. Common in South only.

COMMON LYTROSIS   Pl. 52 (10)
Lytrosis unitaria (H.-S.)

Identification: Large; wings pale gray to yellow and yellowish brown. Male (shown) is heavily shaded and streaked with brown and blackish beyond pm. line of FW and over entire HW; *pm. line black, nearly straight.* ♀ larger, *more uniform pale ash gray* with some brown toward outer margin. Wingspan 4.6–5.7 cm.

Food: Hawthorn, pin oak, and sugar maple.

Range: S. Que. to Fla., west to N.D. and Tex. Mid–May to mid–Aug. Sometimes locally common.

Similar species: Sinuous Lytrosis, *L. sinuosa* Rindge (not shown), is nearly identical, but more yellowish. Am. line more complete, with more contrastingly brownish basal area. Lower part of pm. line has a *distinct bulge* just above inner margin. Food: Unrecorded. Range: Southern N.J. to Fla., west to Mo., Ark., and Miss. April–July.

THE SAW-WING *Euchlaena serrata* (Dru.)   Pl. 51 (15)

Identification: Wings yellow with *reddish brown shading* (almost solid) beyond pm. line. Reddish brown shading in basal area and forming median line, and as general powdering of yellow areas. *Sawtoothed* outer wing margins give this species its name. Wingspan 3.6–5 cm.

Food: Apple, blueberries, and maples.

Range: Que. and Me. to Fla., west to Minn., Neb., and Mo. Late April–Aug. Rare southward.

OBTUSE EUCHLAENA   Pl. 51 (16)
Euchlaena obtusaria (Hbn.)

Identification: Wings smooth purplish to brownish gray; slightly darker beyond pm. line. Median area has variable yellowish tint. Look for a small *bluish black apical dash* and *1–2 spots* at outer margin near FW apex. Tiny black discal dots on all wings. Wingspan 2.7–4.8 cm.

Food: Rose and impatiens.

Range: N.J. to Fla., west to Man. and Tex. April–Sept. Common.

Similar species: Muzaria Euchlaena, *E. muzaria* (Wlk.), not shown, has *gray or whitish basal area,* with no yellowish tint or dusting. Food: Reared on wild cherry. Range: N.S. to Fla., west to S.D. June–July.

JOHNSON'S EUCHLAENA   Pl. 51 (11)
Euchlaena johnsonaria (Fitch)

Identification: FW outer margin *scalloped* in ♂, more *deeply so* in ♀ (not shown). ♂ orange-yellow; reddish brown with blackish blotches beyond pm. line. ♀ uniformly orange-brown with blotches; lines very fine in both sexes. Wingspan 2.6–3.7 cm.

Food: Hawthorn, oaks, *Prunus* species, white ash, white birch, white elm, and willows.

Range: N.S. to w. N.C. and Miss., west to Man. and Tex. May–Sept.; 2 broods. Moderately common.

DEEP YELLOW EUCHLAENA   Pl. 51 (17)
Euchlaena amoenaria (Gn.)

Identification: Wings straw to orangish yellow with reddish brown or blackish st. band. Area beyond pm. line grayish brown (spring brood) to rusty brown (summer). Note pale *yellow apical patch.* Wingspan 3–4.9 cm.

Food: Unrecorded.

Range: Mass. to Fla., west to Wisc. and e. Tex. May–Sept.; 2 broods. Common.

FORKED EUCHLAENA   Pl. 51 (14)
Euchlaena pectinaria (D. & S.)

Identification: Wings pale straw yellow, with variably heavy dusting of black and variable brownish shading beyond pm. line. Discal dots black, prominent. *Pm. line forked* into 2 lines at inner margin, continuing onto HW, where it *again diverges* into straight inner and rounded outer lines before rejoining toward anal margin. Wingspan 3–4.6 cm.

Food: Wild cherry.

Range: N.J. to Fla., west to Man. and e. Tex. April–Aug. Common.

MOTTLED EUCHLAENA   Pl. 51 (20)
Euchlaena tigrinaria (Gn.)

Identification: Wings bright orange-yellow (fawn brown in some specimens), darker beyond fine, *single pm. line.* Overall black speckling heaviest of our *Euchlaena* species. Wingspan 3.3–4.1 cm.

Food: Oak, quaking aspen, and white birch.

Range: Me. to Va., west to Man. and Tex. April–Aug. Common.

LEAST-MARKED EUCHLAENA   Pl. 51 (19)
Euchlaena irraria (B. & McD.)

Identification: Wings powdery yellowish or brownish gray. FW has faint brown am. line and sinuous, usually complete pm. line. Note *dark brown shade* beyond lower half of pm. line, fading back to ground color toward outer margin. Discal spots blackish, usually prominent on all wings. Wingspan 3.7–4.8 cm.

Food: Oaks, quaking aspen, and sugar maple.

Range: N.S. to N.C., west to Man. and Mo. Ozarks. Late May–June. Sometimes locally common.

FALSE CROCUS GEOMETER   **Pl. 51 (18)**
Xanthotype urticaria Swett
Identification: Wings usually bright, deep yellow, with *many purplish brown blotches* and spots, more so in ♂ than ♀. Wingspan 3–4 cm; ♀ larger than ♂.
Food: Catnip, goldenrods, ground-ivy, red-osier dogwood, rhodora azalea, and possibly alders.
Range: Nfld. to Ga., west to Man., Kans., and Ark. May–Nov. Locally common.
Similar species: (1) Crocus Geometer (below), has *paler* yellow wings with *less mottling*. (2) Rufous Geometer, *X. rufaria* Swett (not shown), is smaller and deeper yellow, with *reddish coppery fringe*. Food: Unrecorded. Range: N.C. to Fla., west to Miss. April–Oct.

CROCUS GEOMETER   **Pl. 51 (21)**
Xanthotype sospeta (Dru.)
Identification: Largest and palest yellow of our *Xanthotype* species. Purplish brown *spotting sparse* in ♂, sparser still or absent in ♀. Wingspan 3.5–4.8 cm; ♀ larger than ♂.
Food: Recorded on basswood, dogwoods, elms, hickories, *Polygonum* species, red maple, *Ribes* species, and strawberry.
Range: N.S. to Fla., west across Canada, south to Tenn., Mo., and Neb. April–Oct.; June–July northward. Common.

HONEST PERO *Pero honestaria* (Wlk.)   **Pl. 54 (17)**
Identification: Outer margins *scalloped.* Sinuous, sharp pm. border between dark median and lighter st. areas marks our *Pero* species. ♂ usually *blackish gray,* ♀ brown with *no mottling* and little striation; markings black. Ventral plate on 8th segment has lateral lobe not visible when viewed from below under magnification (visible in Hübner's Pero, below). Wingspan 3.4–3.6 cm.
Food: Black locust, American larch, and wild cherry.
Range: Common throughout our area; April–Sept.

HÜBNER'S PERO *Pero hubneraria* (Gn.)   **Pl. 54 (16)**
Identification: Very similar to Honest Pero (above), but ♂ *brown* (not dark gray), with a variable purplish tint. Lateral lobe of 8th sternite ventrally visible in ♂ (not visible in ♂ Honest Pero). ♀ best identified by association with ♂. Wingspan 3.1–3.7 cm.
Food: Alder, buffalo berry, and willows.
Range: Me. and Que. to Fla., west to Man. and Mo. March–Sept. Common.

MORRISON'S PERO   **Pl. 54 (14)**
Pero morrisonaria (Hy. Edw.)
Identification: Similar to preceding 2 *Pero* species, but usually slightly larger. FW *heavily mottled* with black and brown. Wingspan 3.4–4 cm.

Food: Balsam fir, birches, larch, white pine, white spruce, and other trees.
Range: Nfld. to N.C. mts., west across Canada, south at least to Wisc. and Minn. May–July. Locally common.

OAK BEAUTY   Pl. 54 (2)
Nacophora quernaria (J.E. Sm.)
Identification: Wings powdery light to dark olive brown, with variable *white patch* at FW apex and *white edging along black am. and pm. lines,* at least to costa. ♀ larger, with *much broader white areas.* Blackish melanics common. Wingspan 3.7–5.6 cm.
Food: Balsam, basswood, hawthorn, quaking aspen, wild cherry, willow, white birch, and white elm.
Range: Common throughout our area. March–Oct.

PALE BEAUTY *Campaea perlata* (Gn.)   Pl. 48 (14)
Identification: Wings and body pale greenish to grayish white, often yellowish when faded. FW am. and pm. lines *nearly straight, faint,* darker grayish accented with white. Pm. line continues onto HW. Wingspan 2.8–5.1 cm; ♀ much larger than ♂.
Food: A variety of trees; some hosts include alders, birches, firs, elms, maples, oaks, poplars, and willows.
Range: Lab. to w. N.C. and Tenn., west across Canada, south to Mo. and S.D.; also reported from Fla. May–Sept.; 2 broods. Common.

MAPLE SPANWORM MOTH   Pl. 55 (9)
Ennomos magnaria Gn.
Identification: Wings deeply, unevenly scalloped. Bright orange-yellow, variably spotted with brown and *shaded with reddish brown* toward outer margin. Wingspan 4.3–6 cm; ♀ larger than ♂.
Food: Deciduous trees such as alders, ashes, aspen, basswood, elms, hickories, maples, oaks, and poplars. Larva (**Maple Spanworm**) is a forest pest.
Range: Nfld. to n. Fla., west across Canada, south to S.D., Mo., and Miss. Aug.–Oct. Common to abundant.

ELM SPANWORM MOTH   Pl. 48 (5)
Ennomos subsignaria (Hbn.)
Identification: Pure white except for yellow branches on bipectinate antennae. Easily separated from other all-white species by *angled outer margin* of FW. Wingspan 3–4.2 cm.
Food: Apple, birches, elms, maples, oaks, and many other trees and shrubs. Larva (**Elm Spanworm**) sometimes a serious pest.
Range: N.S. to s. Fla., west to Man., S.D., Mo., and La. Common to rare.

COMMON PETROPHORA   Pl. 55 (6)
Petrophora divisata Hbn.
Identification: Wings yellowish tan with reddish brown dusting. Am. and pm. lines in FW thin, brown. *Pm. line* on FW and HW

curves slightly; note darker brown shading beyond it. Wingspan 2.5–3.2 cm.
Food: Probably ferns.
Range: N.Y. to Fla., west to Miss. in coastal marshes. April–June (March southward). Locally common.
Similar species: Northern Petrophora, *P. subaequaria* (Wlk.), not shown, is *brown;* lines similar but *pm. line double.* Food: Ferns. Range: N.S. to W.Va., west to Wisc. May–Aug. Uncommon.

PALE HOMOCHLODES   Pl. 53 (7)
Homochlodes fritillaria (Gn.)
Identification: Wings light brown, speckled with blackish brown. Lines obscure; faint pm. line on FW *edged with white,* evident *at costa* and as *white spot at midpoint* of pm. line. Wingspan 2.6–3.1 cm.
Food: Brake and other ferns.
Range: Nfld. to Fla., west to Wisc. April–July. Uncommon.
Similar species: Dark Homochlodes, *H. disconventa* (Wlk.), not shown, is *darker brown,* with blackish shading. Whitish spot very *small;* lines brown, diffuse. Food: Probably ferns. Range: Me. to Va. and Ky. May–July.

KENT'S GEOMETER   Pl. 55 (3)
Selenia kentaria (Grt. & Rob.)
Identification: Wings orange-yellow with *whitish dusting,* heaviest *toward FW costa.* FW am., median, and pm. lines orangish brown. Double median line on underside of HW has white edging beyond it. Wingspan 3.3–5.2 cm.
Food: Basswood, beeches, birches, maples, oaks, and other forest trees.
Range: N.S. to Va., west to Alta. and Mo. March–early Aug.
Similar species: Northern Selenia, *S. alciphearia* Wlk., not shown, has *white edging inside* double pm. line on underside of HW. Food: Maples. Range: Canada south to Mass., N.Y., and Wisc. May–Oct.

PALE METANEMA   Pl. 54 (9)
Metanema inatomaria Gn.
Identification: Wings gray. FW has indented outer margin, thin yellowish am. and pm. lines, and reddish brown *discal spot.* Wingspan 2.5–3.6 cm.
Food: Forest trees such as aspens, birch, hazel, poplars, willow firs, and pines.
Range: Nfld. to N.J., Ky., and Miss., west across Canada, south to Mo. May–Sept. Locally common to rare.

DARK METANEMA   Pl. 54 (6)
Metanema determinata Wlk.
Identification: Similar to Pale Metanema (above), but *darker gray.* Lines broader; double pm. line reaches costa closer to apex. *Smaller,* black discal spot or none. Wingspan 2.4–3 cm.

Food: Ash, aspen, and willows.
Range: Nfld. to N.J. and Ky., west across Canada, south to Mo. May–Aug. Uncommon to rare.

RUDDY METARRANTHIS Pl. 53 (15)
Metarranthis duaria (Gn.)
Identification: The *broad, pointed* FW of *Metarranthis* species makes them easy to recognize, but further study is still needed to characterize some of the 12 eastern species. Wings of Ruddy Metarranthis are reddish to yellowish gray with black dusting. FW has diffuse, blackish am. and pm. lines that are *broken where they cross veins;* pm. line bent, sometimes at right angle. Wingspan 3.5–4 cm.
Food: Alder, aspen, basswood, blueberries, choke cherry, linden, oak, wild cherry, and willows.
Range: Nfld. to e. S.C., west across Canada, south to Mo. and Miss. April–June. Locally common to rare.

ANGLED METARRANTHIS Pl. 53 (10)
Metarranthis angularia B. & McD.
Identification: Similar to Ruddy Metarranthis (above), but *pm. line more angled.* Wings have coarse blackish dusting over solid reddish purple shading in all but median area and apex of FW, especially in ♂. Wingspan 3.1–4.4 cm.
Food: Choke cherry and wild cherry.
Range: Me. and Que. to Ga., west to Wisc. and Mo. April–July. Locally common.

COMMON METARRANTHIS Pl. 54 (20)
Metarranthis hypochraria (H.-S.)
Identification: Wings powdery yellowish white with brown lines and shading. Shading especially heavy *inside sharply bent pm. line* and its continuation onto HW. Wingspan 3.2–4.3 cm.
Food: Apple, blueberry, choke cherry, sassafras, and wild cherry.
Range: N.S. to S.C., west to Minn., Mo., and Miss. May–June. Common.
Similar species: Pale Metarranthis, *M. indeclinata* (Wlk.), not shown, is nearly identical, but *brown shading and dusting much paler.* Food: Apple, persimmons, sassafras, and wild cherry. Range: Me. and Que. to Ky., west to Minn. May–July.

PURPLISH METARRANTHIS Pl. 54 (19)
Metarranthis homuraria (Grt. & Rob.)
Identification: A small Metarranthis with deeply *scalloped outer margin on* HW. Wings dark red, purplish red, or brown with darker blotches. *Pm. line* on FW forms *sharp right angle.* Wingspan 2.6–3.2 cm.
Food: Probably many plants in the rose family; records confused.
Range: Me. to Fla., west to Mo. and La. April–Oct. Common.

YELLOW-WASHED METARRANTHIS   Pl. 53 (11)
Metarranthis obfirmaria (Hbn.)
Identification: Wings light brown, dark reddish brown in FW basal area and beyond pm. line on all wings. HW tinted with *deep yellow* on costal half; black discal spot. Wingspan 2.6–3.6 cm.
Food: Blueberries, choke cherry, and oaks.
Range: N.S. to Fla., west to Wisc. and Tex. April–July. Sometimes common in much of range.

SCALLOP MOTH *Cepphis armataria* (H.-S.)   Pl. 54 (4)
Identification: All wings *deeply scalloped;* brown with dark purplish brown lines. Pm. line of FW *double.* HW lines overlaid with purple. Wingspan 2.6–3.3 cm.
Food: Apple, birches, currants, gooseberry, and maples.
Range: N.S. and Que. to N.C., west to Man. and Mo.; late June–July; 2nd brood sometimes in Aug. Uncommon.

AMERICAN BARRED UMBER   Pl. 53 (8)
Anagoga occiduaria (Wlk.)
Identification: Powdery reddish brown with solid darker brown median area bounded by *sharp, nearly straight am. line.* Violet shading beyond pm. line in some specimens, occasionally blending with median area to form larger darkened part of FW. Wingspan 2.6–3.2 cm.
Food: Alders, aspen, birches, fir, hemlock, spruce, wild-raisin, and others.
Range: Nfld. to N.C., west across Canada, south to S.D. April–July. Moderately common.

DOGWOOD PROBOLE *Probole nyssaria* (Gn.)   Pl. 53 (12)
Identification: Spring brood (shown) is whitish with brown dusting, often forming network pattern in median area of FW; heavier brown shading beyond pm. line. *Pm. line strongly toothed;* upper part of line from tooth to costa *indented.* Summer brood (not shown) has purplish red band inside am. line, and solid purplish red shading beyond pm. line. Wingspan 2.6–3.5 cm.
Food: Dogwoods.
Range: Me. and Que. to Fla., westward throughout our area. March–Aug.; 2 broods. Common.

FRIENDLY PROBOLE *Probole amicaria* (H.-S.)   Pl. 53 (9)
Identification: Similar to Dogwood Probole (above), but pm. line not as strongly toothed, and upper part of line between tooth and FW costa nearly *straight,* not indented. Median area pale, with brown streaks along veins; solid reddish to purplish shading beyond pm. line. Spring and summer broods very similar. Wingspan 2.3–3.4 cm.
Food: Sourwood and probably other trees.
Range: S. New England to Va., west to Wisc. and Ill. April–Aug.; 2 broods. Locally common.
Similar species: (1) Alien Probole, *P. alienaria* H.-S. (not

shown), is paler, usually without solid purplish red border on wings, except in Me. and e. Canada, where it may closely resemble Friendly Probole. Food: Many woody plants. Range: Common throughout our area. May–Aug. (2) Heath Probole, *P. nepiasaria* (Wlk.), not shown, is mostly reddish, with solid purplish red shading inside am. line and beyond pm. line; usually *orange* in median area. Food: Sheep laurel and dwarf cornel. Range: N.S. to Ga. and Ky. in acid soil habitats; southward in mountains only. May–Aug. Uncommon.

LEMON PLAGODIS *Plagodis serinaria* H.-S. **Pl. 53 (2)**
Identification: Largest of our *Plagodis* species, easily recognized by the *pale lemon yellow FW* with brown to rose lines and *pink shading.* HW white. Some specimens have reduced dark markings. Wingspan 2.7–3.8 cm.
Food: Aspen, basswood, birches, black cherry, linden, maples, and oaks.
Range: N.S. to w. N.C., west to Man. and n. Mo. April–June; to July northward. Moderately common.

PURPLE PLAGODIS *Plagodis kuetzingi* (Grt.) **Pl. 53 (5)**
Identification: Wings orange-yellow with *dark purple shading* beyond pm. lines. FW has brown speckling and shading in basal area. Pm. line curved, *diffuse* in upper half, and *closer to base* of FW than in other *Plagodis* species. Wingspan 2.6–3 cm.
Food: Ashes.
Range: N.S. to Va. and Tenn., west to Wisc., Ill., and Ky. May–July. Uncommon to rare.

STRAIGHT-LINED PLAGODIS **Pl. 53 (1)**
Plagodis phlogosaria (Gn.)
Identification: Pm. line of FW even, complete; usually *straight,* sometimes bulging slightly outward. Summer brood (shown) brown with tan basal area on HW; some purple beyond pm. line. Discal spots absent. Spring brood (not shown) orange-yellow with purple shading beyond pm. line, except at costa. Wingspan 2.2–3.3 cm.
Food: Many trees, including alders, basswood, birches, black cherry, and choke cherry.
Range: Nfld. to w. N.C., west across Canada, south to Mo. and S.D. April–Aug. Common.

FERVID PLAGODIS **Pl. 53 (3)**
Plagodis fervidaria (H.-S.)
Identification: Wings yellow. Spring specimens (shown) have faint vertical brown streaks on FW. Pm. line *broad,* complete; straight or bulging slightly outward. HW with gray shading at anal angle. Summer brood (form "arrogaria" Hulst, not shown) has much *gray shading* on FW; pm. line visible only at costa and toward inner margin. Discal spots small to absent. Wingspan 2.3–3.1 cm.

Food: Ashes, birches, maples, oaks, sour cherry, and spruce.
Range: Me. to n. Fla., west to Minn., S.D., and Tex. April–Sept.; 2 broods. Common.

HOLLOW-SPOTTED PLAGODIS   Pl. 53 (4, 6)
Plagodis alcoolaria (Gn.)
Identification: Wings yellowish white, shaded with orangish brown; lines orangish to blackish brown. *Pm. line curves outward* and meets costa *closer to apex* than in other *Plagodis* species; discal spot large. Summer brood (form "kempii" Hulst) is paler yellow with fewer markings than spring brood. Wingspan 2.6–3.5 cm.
Food: Basswood, beeches, birches, chestnut, maples, and oaks.
Range: N.S. to Ga., west to Man., S.D., Mo., and Miss. Late March–Sept.; 2 broods. Common.

GRAY SPRUCE LOOPER MOTH   Pl. 53 (18)
Caripeta divisata Wlk.
Identification: FW dull grayish brown, with brown shading along costa. Lines black, toothed, accented with white; large *white discal spot* outlined in black. Wingspan 2.7–3.8 cm.
Food: Larva (**Gray Spruce Looper**) feeds on conifers such as balsam fir, hemlock, spruces, and white pine.
Range: Nfld. to Fla. (old record), west across Canada, south to Minn. June–July. Locally common.

NORTHERN PINE LOOPER MOTH   Pl. 53 (13)
Caripeta piniata (Pack.)
Identification: FW orangish brown; basal and st. areas *streaked with white*. Sharply angled am. and wavy pm. lines bordered with white. Discal spots white, irregular. HW cream with orange lines between veins. Wingspan 3–3.8 cm.
Food: White, jack, and red pines; also white spruce.
Range: Nfld. to N.C., west across Canada, south to Minn. July–Aug. Uncommon southward.

BROWN PINE LOOPER MOTH   Pl. 53 (17)
Caripeta angustiorata Wlk.
Identification: FW reddish to orangish brown; median area smooth. Am. and pm. lines black, edged with white. Am. line has *sharp point;* pm. line *straighter* than in other *Caripeta* species. St. shade line grayish. HW pale tan. Wingspan 2.8–3.1 cm.
Food: Larva (**Brown Pine Looper**) feeds on firs, white and other pines, spruces, and larch.
Range: Nfld. to N.C., west across Canada, south to Minn. July–Aug. Uncommon southward.

SOUTHERN PINE LOOPER MOTH   Pl. 53 (16)
Caripeta aretaria (Wlk.)
Identification: *FW orangish brown along costa* to pm. line; median area reddish to orangish brown. Am. and pm. lines accented

with white; st. line black-shaded. HW pale gray, darkest of our *Caripeta* species. Wingspan 3.5–4 cm.

Food: Pupa found on red pine.

Range: Va. and W. Va. to Fla., west to Ark. April, late Aug.; Jan.–March in Fla. Uncommon to rare.

STRAW BESMA   Pl. 53 (21)
Besma endropiaria (Grt. & Rob.)

Identification: Wings shiny, pale straw yellow, slightly translucent, faintly striated and veined with *pale brown*. FW has 3 brown lines; am. line often connected to pm. line by a *short crossbar* near inner margin (as shown). St. line thin, rounded, *fading away* below midpoint. Wingspan 3–3.6 cm.

Food: Sugar maple.

Range: N.S. and Que. to N.C., west to Man. and Mo. May–June. Locally common.

OAK BESMA   Pl. 53 (19, 20)
Besma quercivoraria (Gn.)

Identification: Variable and sexually dimorphic. Wings pale straw yellow with pale brown powdering and vein outlines. FW has sharp *black discal dot*. In ♂ pm. line is faint and slightly indented, with heavy purplish to orangish brown shading beyond it (on both wings). Am. line on FW often connected to pm. line by a *short bar* across median area in ♂. Wings in ♀ more sharply angled, sparsely speckled with orangish brown. Am. and pm. lines on FW orangish brown, sharp; pm. line continues onto HW. Diffuse grayish spot near anal angle in some specimens (not shown). Wingspan 2.7–4.1 cm.

Food: Elms, oaks, poplar, willows, and white spruce.

Range: Common throughout our area. April–Sept.; 2 broods.

HEMLOCK LOOPER MOTH   Pl. 54 (21)
Lambdina fiscellaria (Gn.)

Identification: Wings slightly translucent, cream to mouse gray. HW has *small tooth* at outer margin. Lines brown, sharp, sometimes shaded with darker brown on sides of median area; *pm. line strongly bent* on all wings. Wingspan 3.2–4.5 cm.

Food: Firs, hemlocks, oaks, and spruces.

Range: Lab. to S.C. and Miss., west across Canada, south to Tex. Aug.–Oct. Common.

YELLOW-HEADED LOOPER MOTH   Pl. 54 (18)
Lambdina pellucidaria (Grt. & Rob.)

Identification: Wings translucent mouse gray, with some yellow on head and thorax. Lines darker gray, diffuse, *not edged with cream* as in Curve-lined Looper Moth (p. 371). Wingspan 2.9–4 cm.

Food: Oaks and pines.

Range: Me. to Fla., west to Mo. and Tex. Late April–May. Usually common.

CURVE-LINED LOOPER MOTH   Pl. 54 (15)
Lambdina fervidaria (Hbn.)
Identification: Our subspecies is *L. fervidaria athasaria* (Wlk.).
Wings translucent cream, variably dusted with grayish brown.
Lines sharp, *edged with cream* on sides away from median area.
Pm. line on all wings *gently curved, not sharply bent* as in Hemlock Looper Moth (above). Wingspan 2.5–3.7 cm., spring specimens
usually small.
Food: White oak.
Range: N.S. to N.C., west to S.D. and Mo. April–Aug.; 2 broods.
Common.

CHAIN-DOTTED GEOMETER   Pl. 48 (19)
Cingilia catenaria (Dru.)
Identification: Wings white to pale grayish with am., pm., and
terminal lines of *black dots.* Wingspan 3–4 cm.
Food: Sometimes a pest on alders, arborvitae, blueberries, goldenrod, grasses, maples, oaks, pines, roses, sweetfern, and willows.
Range: N.S. and Que. to N.J., west to Man. and Minn. Sept.–Oct.
Locally common.

FALSE HEMLOCK LOOPER MOTH   Pl. 56 (1)
Nepytia canosaria (Wlk.)
Identification: Wings white dusted with gray. FW am. and pm.
lines black, *toothed.* HW paler. Fringe checkered. Wingspan 2.5–
3.2 cm.
Food: Larva (**False Hemlock Looper**) feeds on fir, hemlock,
pines, spruces, and other conifers.
Range: Nfld. to mts. of Va. and e. Ky., west across Canada, south
to Minn. Late July–Oct. Locally common.
Similar species: Southern Nepytia, *N. semiclusaria* (Wlk.), not
shown, is larger, *smoother dark gray* with less contrasting lines.
Food: Pines. Range: N.C. to Fla. and westward along Gulf Coast.
All year.

SHARP-LINED YELLOW   Pl. 53 (14)
Sicya macularia (Harr.)
Identification: FW angled; *bright yellow* with a fine, nearly
straight pm. line. Reddish shading beyond pm. line variable (heavy
to absent). Wingspan 2.4–3.5 cm.
Food: Alder, ashes, birch, *Ceanothus* species, poplar, spiraea, and
willow.
Range: Nfld. to Va., west across Canada, south to ne. Mo. and
S.D. June–July. Locally common.

CONFUSED EUSARCA   Pl. 56 (6)
Eusarca confusaria Hbn.
Identification: Wings yellowish tan, with variable grayish brown
dusting; some specimens dark brown except along lines and veins.
Straight brown *pm. line fades out or hooks inward* just below
apex. Tiny black discal spots on all wings. Wingspan 2.9–4.1 cm.

Food: Asters, clover, dandelion, goldenrod, and other composites.
Range: Very common throughout our area. April–Oct.

YELLOW SLANT-LINE *Tetracis crocallata* Gn.   **Pl. 55 (7)**
Identification: Wings pale orange-yellow to yellow, often lightly powdered with brown. Am. line absent. *Brown pm. line* usually *broad, complete* from apex to inner margin of FW; pm. line continues onto HW in summer brood only (shown). Discal dots black. Wingspan 2.5–4.5 cm.
Food: Alder, chestnut, sumac, and willows.
Range: N.S. to S.C. (a single Fla. record), west to Man. and Tex. April–Aug.; 2 broods. Common northward.

WHITE SLANT-LINE   **Pl. 55 (4)**
Tetracis cachexiata Gn.
Identification: Similar to Yellow Slant-line (above), but FW paler, yellowish to cream. Pm. line orangish, reaching costa just before FW apex, *not* continued onto HW. *HW white.* Wingspan 3.8–5 cm.
Food: Ash, birches, cherry, elms, maples, oaks, pines, sheep laurel, sweetfern, willows, and other trees and shrubs.
Range: N.S. to Fla., west to Man. and Ark. April–June. Common.

SNOWY GEOMETER   **Pl. 48 (6)**
Eugonobapta nivosaria (Gn.)
Identification: Pure gleaming white. HW *pointed.* Black discal dots sometimes present on underside of all wings. Wingspan 2.1–3.3 cm.
Food: Unrecorded.
Range: Me. and Que. to w. N.C., west to Man. and Mo. May–Aug.; 2 broods. Locally common.

CURVE-TOOTHED GEOMETER   **Pl. 55 (1)**
Eutrapela clemataria (J.E. Sm.)
Identification: Wings brownish gray, mottled brown on yellowish tan. Pm. line fine, mostly straight, turning sharply back toward costa; short *upper section curves inward.* Wing margins *gently scalloped.* Wingspan 3.8–5.6 cm; ♀ larger than ♂.
Food: Ash, aspen, basswood, birches, elms, fir, maples, poplars, willows, and other trees.
Range: Common throughout our area. April–Aug.
Similar species: In the Large Maple Spanworm Moth (p. 373, Pl. 56), short upper section of pm. line on FW *curves outward;* wing margins *not scalloped.*

JUNIPER GEOMETER   **Pl. 54 (10)**
Patalene olyzonaria (Wlk.)
Identification: Our subspecies is *P. olyzonaria puber* (Grt. & Rob.). FW *hooked* at tip, more sharply in ♀ than in ♂. Wings orangish to reddish brown. Pm. line sharp, hooking back toward FW costa as in Curve-toothed Geometer (above). Wingspan 2.1–1.3 cm.

Food: Junipers; pines (?).
Range: N.H. to Fla., west to Wisc., Mo. and Tex. April–Nov. Common southward.

LARGE MAPLE SPANWORM MOTH   Pl. 56 (2)
Prochoerodes transversata (Dru.)
Identification: Similar to Curve-toothed Geometer (above), but wing margins *not scalloped.* Short upper section of pm. line *curves outward,* not inward. Wingspan 3.5–5 cm.
Food: Larva (**Large Maple Spanworm**) feeds on apple, blueberries, cherries, currant, geranium, grasses, maples, oaks, soybean, sweetfern, walnut, and other plants.
Range: Common throughout our area. April–Oct.

VARIABLE ANTEPIONE   Pl. 55 (2, 5)
Antepione thisoaria (Gn.)
Identification: Seasonally and sexually dimorphic; most reliable marking is *dark triangular patch* near apex of FW (absent in summer ♀, not shown). Most forms also have some dark accents (sometimes a distinct double spot) at lower end of pm. line. Wings mottled fawn brown in spring brood (both sexes); usually more yellowish in summer brood (compare forms on Pl. 55). Summer ♂ bright yellow with reddish brown shading beyond pm. line; summer ♀ (not shown) *all yellow.* All forms were found in 1 brood reared in Nova Scotia. Wingspan 2.7–4 cm.
Food: Apple, maple, persimmon, sumac, and other plants.
Range: N.S. to w. N.C. and Miss., west to Wisc., Neb., and Tex. April–Oct. Locally common.

HORNED SPANWORM MOTH   Pl. 54 (12)
Nematocampa limbata (Haw.)
Identification: Wings light straw yellow to cream; veins and lines brown. Am. line single. Pm. line double—*lines far apart* at costa but *touching* below it, then separating again. Purplish to brown shading beyond pm. line variably heavy on all wings. Wingspan 1.9–2.5 cm.
Food: Larva (**Horned Spanworm**) feeds on apple, birches, lindens, hickories, maples, oaks, pear, *Ribes* species, strawberry, and many other low plants and trees.
Range: Local and uncommon throughout our area. May–Aug.

Subfamily Geometrinae

RED-BORDERED EMERALD   Pl. 46 (4)
Nemoria lixaria (Gn.)
Identification: Wings pale green with jagged white am. and pm. lines and *red terminal lines.* Tiny black discal dots on all wings; fringe checkered red and white. Abdominal *spots white ringed with red.* Melanic specimens brownish green with dark brown lines and fringe. Wingspan 2–3 cm.

Food: Red oak.
Range: Coastal N.J. to Fla., west to Ark. and e. Tex. April–June; July–Oct. northward; all year in deep South. Common.

RED-FRONTED EMERALD   Pl. 46 (6)
Nemoria rubrifrontaria (Pack.)
Identification: Similar to Red-bordered Emerald (above), but *without* discal dots and red terminal line. White am. and pm. lines straighter. Red shading on head (frons), legs and FW base at costa; outer scales of fringe may be pinkish. Look for 3–4 white spots ringed with red on abdomen. Wingspan 2.1–2.5 cm.
Food: Northern bayberry, *Ceanothus* species, sheep laurel, winged sumac, sweetfern, and sweetgale.
Range: N.S. to N.C., west to S.D. and Kans. April–Aug.; 2 or more broods southward. Common.

SHOWY EMERALD *Dichorda iridaria* (Gn.)   Pl. 46 (7)
Identification: Body and wings pale to deep green with *wide, straight, white am. and pm. lines* on FW; no am. line on HW. Black discal dots on all wings. Fla. specimens with sharper lines are *D. iridaria latipennis* (Hulst). Wingspan 2–3 cm.
Food: Staghorn sumac and winged sumac.
Range: N.S. and Que. to Fla., west to Wisc. and Tex. April–Aug.; 2 broods. Moderately common.

WAVY-LINED EMERALD   Pl. 46 (9)
Synchlora aerata (F.)
Identification: Body and wings pale yellowish green; frons may be green, red, or brownish. Abdominal spots merge to form a *white stripe.* Toothed white lines on FW curve outward, and continue onto HW. Northern specimens are *S. aerata albolineata* (Pack.), and are larger, with deeper green, more opaque wings that have more jagged lines. Wingspan 1.3–2.4 cm.
Food: Many plants, including asters, coneflowers, coreopsis, *Erigeron* species, huckleberry, ragweeds, and raspberry fruits.
Range: Nfld. to N.C. and Ala., west to Man., south to Tex. Subspecies *albolineata* occurs north of Conn. and Ill. May–Oct.; 2–3 broods. Common.
Similar species: Southern Emerald, *S. frondaria* Gn., subspecies *denticularia* (Wlk.), not shown, is usually smaller; pm. line of FW more jagged. Food: Blackberry, chrysanthemum, Spanish needles and other plants. Range: Va. to Fla., west to Tex. March–Oct. in Miss.; all year farther south. Common.

BLACKBERRY LOOPER MOTH   Pl. 46 (12)
Chlorochlamys chloroleucaria (Gn.)
Identification: Antennae broadly bipectinate in ♂ (shown). Wings grayish green, fading to yellowish. Costa, am. and pm. lines *cream; pm. line straight* or nearly so. Wingspan 1.4–2.3 cm.
Food: Larva (**Blackberry Looper**) feeds on blackberry fruits; also on petals of various composite flowers, such as asters, *Comp-*

tonia species, coneflowers, and sunflowers; and on ox-eye daisy.
Range: Common throughout our area except in extreme s. Fla.
April–Nov.
Similar species: Thin-lined Chlorochlamys, *C. phyllinaria*
(Zell.), not shown, has thinner, whiter lines; *pm. line curves outward.* Food: Unrecorded. Range: Ga. west to Neb. and Tex. June–
Sept.

ANGLE-WINGED EMERALD   Pl. 46 (11)
Chloropteryx tepperaria (Hulst)
Identification: Wings grayish to olive green in fresh specimens,
fading to yellowish. Am. and pm. lines white, dotted, inconspicuous; fine brown terminal line and checkered fringe. *HW sharply
pointed,* unlike HW of any other green geometer in our area. Wingspan 1.5–2.2 cm.
Food: Baldcypress and eastern hemlock.
Range: Va. to Fla., west to Mo. and Tex. May–early Sept.;
2 broods, but usually not common.

PISTACHIO EMERALD   Pl. 46 (10)
Hethemia pistasciaria (Gn.)
Identification: Deep yellowish to grayish green when fresh, drying to various greens, yellows, orange, or brown. Am. and pm. lines
dotted, white, inconspicuous. *HW squared off* but *not* sharply
pointed. Antennae simple. Wingspan 1.6–3.1 cm.
Food: Blueberries and oaks.
Range: N.S. to Fla., west to N.D., nw. Ark., and La. April–July;
1 brood. Moderately common.

Subfamily Sterrhinae

DRAB BROWN WAVE   Pl. 47 (5)
Lobocleta ossularia (Gey.)
Identification: Wings tan to dark brown with darker brown lines
and discal spots. *Median line* on FW *broadest line, bent inward*
below midpoint and continuing onto HW. Wingspan 1–1.6 cm.
Food: Bedstraws (*Galium* species), chickweed, clover, and strawberry.
Range: Mass. to Fla., west to Mo. and Tex. March–Oct. Common.

STRAIGHT-LINED WAVE   Pl. 47 (2)
Lobocleta plemyraria (Gn.)
Identification: Light to dark brown, variably tinted with orange
or yellowish; *lines straighter* than in Drab Brown Wave (above);
median line less prominent. Wingspan 1.3–2 cm.
Food: Unrecorded.
Range: N.J. to Fla., west to S.D. and Tex. June–Sept. Uncommon.

NOTCH-WINGED WAVE   Pl. 46 (17, 18)
Idaea furciferata (Pack.)
Identification: HW in ♂ has *deep notch,* absent in ♀. FW tan in

both sexes, with dull reddish brown lines and shading. ♀ slightly darker, with *sharper st. band*. Wingspan 1.4–1.8 cm.
Food: Reared on clover and dandelion.
Range: Md. to n. Fla., west to Mo. and Tex. June–July northward. Locally common in some areas.

### RED-BORDERED WAVE	Pl. 46 (16)
Idaea demissaria (Hbn.)
Identification: Wings tan with reddish to brown lines and shading at margins, if present. Am. and median lines diffuse, sometimes absent; *pm. line curves outward* except near anal angle; sometimes the only line. Fringe red. Wingspan 1.4–1.9 cm.
Food: Unrecorded; probably a variety of low plants.
Range: N.H. and s. Que. to Fla., west to Neb. and Tex. April–Oct. Common.

DOT-LINED WAVE *Idaea tacturata* (Wlk.)	**Pl. 48 (22)**
Identification: Wings pearly white, almost translucent; FW has 4 variably conspicuous, brownish, *dotted* or zigzag *lines* that continue onto HW. *Pm. line* usually thickest; st. line usually overlaid with *fine blackish dots*. Tiny black discal dot on all wings, and variable scattering of blackish scales. Wingspan 1.3–2.1 cm.
Food: Reared on clover.
Range: Coastal S.C. through Fla. to coastal se. Tex. All year. Locally common.

RIPPLED WAVE *Idaea obfusaria* (Wlk.)	**Pl. 48 (4)**
Identification: Wings white with prominent black discal dots on all wings. Pm. line black, *very irregular;* other lines pale yellowish brown. Wingspan 1.5–2.5 cm.
Food: Clover and dandelion; probably other low plants.
Range: Se. N.J. to Fla., west to Mo. and Tex. June–Sept.; mostly July. Locally common southward.

### COMMON TAN WAVE	Pl. 46 (19)
Pleuroprucha insulsaria (Gn.)
Identification: Wings powdery tan to brown. Lines inconspicuous, finely toothed, *parallel* to outer margin. Am. and pm. lines paler than ground color, usually overlaid with brown dots. *St. line more heavily dotted.* Melanics dark gray; lines may be absent. Wingspan 1.4–2.1 cm.
Food: American bittersweet, bedstraws (*Galium* species), chestnut, corn, goldenrod flowers, oaks, willows, and other plants.
Range: Common throughout our area. May–Oct.

### SWEETFERN GEOMETER	Pl. 46 (23)
Cyclophora pendulinaria (Gn.)
Identification: Wings white or various shades of gray to blackish brown (melanics). Note the *hollow discal spots—round* on FW, *oval* on HW. Am. and pm. lines sharpest, but usually broken to

dotted; median line more diffuse; shading also variable. Wingspan 1.7–2.5 cm.
Food: Alder, beech, blueberries, Sampson's snakeroot, and sweetfern.
Range: Lab. to N.C. and Miss., west through s. Canada, south to nw. Ark. April–Sept. Common northward.

PACKARD'S WAVE   Pl. 46 (20)
Cyclophora packardi (Prout)
Identification: *Discal spots hollow* as in Sweetfern Geometer (above), but wings *yellowish to orangish brown,* not mottled. Am. and pm. lines made of gray dots; solid gray median line sometimes present. Discal spots often *white-filled.* Wingspan 1.7–2.3 cm.
Food: Unrecorded; possibly oak or sweetfern.
Range: Mass. to Fla., west to Mo. and Tex. April–Sept. Locally common.

CHICKWEED GEOMETER   Pl. 46 (21)
Haematopis grataria (F.)
Identification: Easily identified by the *yellow wings* with variably defined *pink lines* and discal spots. HW brighter yellow; median line crosses discal spot. In form "annettearia" Haim. (not shown), wings are *entirely pink.* Wingspan 1.8–2.6 cm.
Food: Chickweeds, clovers, knotweed, smartweeds, and other low plants.
Range: Me. and s. Ont. to n. Fla., west to Man. and Tex. April–Nov. Abundant in most of range; often flies in fields during daytime. Form "annettearia" seems to be limited to the Ohio Valley and upper Miss. Valley.

CROSS-LINED WAVE   Pl. 46 (14)
Calothysanis amaturaria (Wlk.)
Identification: FW *hooked;* HW *pointed.* Oblique brown *pm. line seems to cross thin st. line* below FW apex, continues onto HW. Wingspan 2–2.8 cm.
Food: Buckwheat, *Polygonum cristatum*, and dock.
Range: Mass. to Fla., west to Kans. and Tex. May–Sept. May be common in open fields during the day.

SMALL FROSTED WAVE   Pl. 48 (23)
Scopula lautaria (Hbn.)
Identification: Wings white with uneven brownish shading beyond sharp pm. line. FW has *2 blackish blotches* on outer edge of pm. line; *blotch at inner margin* usually larger. Tiny black discal dots on all wings. Wingspan 1.1–1.6 cm.
Food: Low plants; can be reared on clover.
Range: Coastal S.C. through Fla. to La. All year. Common.

FROSTED TAN WAVE   Pl. 47 (3)
Scopula cacuminaria (Morr.)
Identification: Wings cream to tannish. Black dorsal spots on

abdomen. Lines pale brown with black dots over pm. and terminal lines. *Blackish shading* beyond pm. line, *heaviest near anal angles* of FW and HW. Outer margin of HW pointed. Wingspan 1.8–2.3 cm.
Food: Reared on dandelion and lettuce.
Range: N.S. to N.C., west to Man. and Tex. May–Sept.; apparently 2 broods. Local and uncommon.

CHALKY WAVE *Scopula purata* (Gn.)   **Pl. 48 (15)**
Identification: Wings pure, chalky white with *blackish shading beyond wavy black pm. line,* which continues onto HW. Pm. shading broadest toward inner margin. Note black discal dots and dotted terminal line. Wingspan 1.7–2.2 cm.
Food: Reared on dandelion.
Range: N.H. to cen. Fla. along Atlantic Coast, and along Gulf Coast to Miss. June–Aug. northward; April–July in South. Very local and uncommon.

LARGE LACE-BORDER   **Pl. 48 (2, 3)**
Scopula limboundata (Haw.)
Identification: Wings cream to yellowish. Lines yellowish to tan; *pm. line* usually most conspicuous, with *2 bulges* below costa. *Much black shading beyond pm. line* on all wings in typical form, Pl. 48 (2); shading reduced to large spot at inner margin of FW in form "relevata" (Swett), not shown, and totally absent in form "enucleata" (Gn.), Pl. 48 (3). Discal spots sharp, blackish on all wings. Wingspan 2–3 cm.
Food: Apple, bedstraws (*Galium* species), blueberries, clovers, dandelion, meadow-beauty, wild cherry, and others.
Range: Common throughout our area. May–Sept.
Remarks: This moth and other white waves resemble washed-out bird droppings when they rest with their wings outstretched on broad leaves of low forest plants.

SIMPLE WAVE *Scopula junctaria* (Wlk.)   **Pl. 48 (1)**
Identification: Similar to unshaded form ("enucleata") of Large Lace-border (above), but wings purer white. Median and pm. lines similar in sharpness, but *pm. line lacks double bulge* in upper half, and never has blackish shading beyond it. Discal spots faint, often absent. Wingspan 2–2.6 cm.
Food: Chickweed, clover, elm, and other plants.
Range: Nfld. to N.J., west to Man. and S.D. June–Aug. Locally common in hardwood forests.
Similar species: Four-lined Wave, *S. quadrilineata* (Pack.), not shown, is almost identical, but *pm. line almost perfectly straight.* Food: Clover and *Pyrus* species. Range: N.S. to Pa., west to w. Ont. and Ill. June–July. Less common than Simple Wave.

FRIGID WAVE *Scopula frigidaria* (Mösch.)   **Pl. 46 (22)**
Identification: Wings powdery whitish gray to light brown. Lines darker brown; only *pm. line* is prominent, *bulging slightly out-*

ward at about midpoint and continuing onto HW. Discal spots usually absent. Wingspan 1.8–2.6 cm.
Food: Unrecorded.
Range: Lab. to Me., west through Canada, south to Wisc. June–Aug. Common in boreal and arctic habitats.

SOFT-LINED WAVE   Pl. 46 (15)
Scopula inductata (Gn.)
Identification: Wings warm grayish brown, usually with 5 soft, wavy lines; *median and pm. lines* most conspicuous. Discal dots small, black. Wingspan 1.7–2.4 cm.
Food: Aster, clover, dandelion, ragweeds, sweet clover, and various *Prunus* species.
Range: Common throughout our area. May–Sept.

DARK-RIBBONED WAVE   Pl. 46 (13)
Leptostales rubromarginaria (Pack.)
Identification: Wings dull orange to orangish brown; median area may be solid purplish brown (as shown). Am., pm., and st. lines *purplish brown, wavy.* Wingspan 1.4–2 cm.
Food: Unrecorded.
Range: S. Que. to Fla., west across Canada, south to Tex. April–Aug. More common inland than along coast.

Subfamily Larentiinae

MARBLED CARPET   Pl. 49 (3)
Dysstroma truncata (Hufn.)
Identification: Extremely variable; basal area light grayish brown with some brown or orange, median area *white to gray.* Pm. area gray with brown or orange shading, strongest toward costa. Our N. American subspecies is *D. truncata traversata* (Kellicott). Wingspan 2.6–3.2 cm.
Food: Alders, plantain, strawberry, Virginia creeper, willows, and other plants.
Range: Holarctic; Lab. to N.C. mts. in our area, west through Canada, south to Mo. June–Aug. Common northward.

ORANGE-BARRED CARPET   Pl. 49 (6)
Dysstroma hersiliata (Gn.)
Identification: Basal and median areas of FW usually gray, with an *even orange bar* in am. area. Median area rusty in some specimens. Note orange and white patch in upper st. area, *beyond deep cleft* (sharp tooth) in pm. line. HW whitish. Wingspan 2.5–2.9 cm.
Food: Currant.
Range: Lab. to Pa. mts., west across Canada, south to Minn. June–Aug. Common.
Similar species: Similar forms of Marbled Carpet Moth (above) have only a *slight tooth* in upper pm. line.

LESSER GRAPEVINE LOOPER MOTH   Pl. 49 (5)
Eulithis diversilineata (Hbn.)
Identification: FW *hooked* at apex; orange-yellow with brown lines. Pm. line heaviest; note *sharp tooth* at midpoint. *Median area* shaded with pale brown, especially in lower half, which is *solid* (not crossed by 2 fine lines, as in Greater Grapevine Moth, not shown). Discal spot small or absent. Wingspan 2.8–3.3 cm.
Food: Larva (**Lesser Grapevine Looper**) feeds on grapes and Virginia creeper; not a serious pest.
Range: Throughout our area. Late May–Oct. Common.
Similar species: (1) Greater Grapevine Looper Moth, *E. gracilineata* (Gn.), not shown, is *paler;* median area completely *crossed by 2 fine lines* with no brown shading between them. Food and range same as for Lesser Grapevine Looper Moth. (2) In Dimorphic Eulithis, *E. molliculata* (Wlk.), not shown, wings are reddish brown in ♂, bright orange-yellow in ♀. Both sexes have a *brown patch* near FW apex, accented with white scallops. Food: Ninebark. Range: Que. to Pa., west to Ont. and Minn. June–Aug. (3) Chevron Moth, *E. testata* (L.), not shown, is colored like ♀ Dimorphic Eulithis, but *lacks patch* near FW apex; median line *sharply angled.* Food: Poplars and willows. Range: Nfld. to N.J., west across Canada, south to Minn. June–Sept.

WHITE EULITHIS *Eulithis explanata* (Wlk.)   Pl. 47 (24)
Identification: FW white with gray basal, median, and terminal shading, heaviest just below apex. Gray shading in median area may be broken into upper and lower patches by variably wide, *white band* crossing median area. Am. and pm. lines obscure, scalloped; *st. line white, zigzag.* Discal spot black. HW white with gray shading and traces of lines, heaviest toward anal angle. Wingspan 2.8–3.5 cm.
Food: Blueberries.
Range: Lab. to N.C. mts., west across Canada, south to Minn. June–Sept. Locally common.

BLACK-BANDED CARPET   Pl. 47 (21)
Eustroma semiatrata (Hulst)
Identification: Very similar to White Eulithis (above), but basal and larger median area blackish gray. More yellowish white in am. band and st. area. *Pm. line more angled* than in White Eulithis, with a large bulge that almost reaches outer margin. Wingspan 2.8–3.5 cm.
Food: Willow-herb.
Range: Lab. to Catskill Mts., N.Y., west across Canada, south to S.D. July–Aug.

DARK-BANDED GEOMETER   Pl. 47 (15)
Ecliptopera atricolorata (Grt. & Rob.)
Identification: FW black, marbled with narrow white lines; sharply angled am. line often *touches pm. line,* bisecting median

area and sometimes separating it into *large upper* and *small lower* parts. HW dark gray with white median line. Wingspan 2.8–3.2 cm.
Food: Unrecorded.
Range: S. Que. to n. Fla., west to Mo., Ark., and Miss. May–July. Locally common.
Similar species: The Small Phoenix, *E. silaceata* (D. & S.), not shown, is slightly smaller, *duller*, with more rounded pm. line. Am. and pm. lines always *widely separated*. Food: Impatiens and willow-herb. Range: Lab. to Me., west to Man. and Wisc. May–Sept. Uncommon.

BLACK-DASHED HYDRIOMENA   Pl. 47 (12)
Hydriomena divisaria (Wlk.)
Identification: FW grayish to brown (mostly brown in some specimens) with *no greenish tint;* some pink scales usually present in am. and st. areas. Pattern variable, very similar to that of other *Hydriomena* species (below); markings usually less conspicuous in northern specimens. Median area often black at inner margin; *black apical dash* usually merges with another dash beyond pm. line. HW variably grayish; pm. and st. lines faint. Wingspan 2.4–3 cm.
Food: Balsam fir, pine, and white spruce.
Range: Nfld. to N.C., west to Man. and Wisc. Late April–early July. Uncommon.

RENOUNCED HYDRIOMENA   Pl. 49 (9)
Hydriomena renunciata (Wlk.)
Identification: Difficult to distinguish from the next 2 *Hydriomena* species—pattern very similar in all 3 moths. FW variable but mostly brown and gray with a slight greenish tint. Pm. line broad, scalloped. Width of upper median area and pm. line somewhat distinctive, but specialists study genitalia of ♂ under a microscope to confirm identifications: uncus (Fig. 5, p. 6) deeply forked in this species, less deeply forked (only halfway to base or less) in other 2 species. HW whitish, shaded with gray. Wingspan 2.7–3 cm.
Food: Alder.
Range: Lab. and Que. to Ky., west through Canada, south to Ill. and Mo. (?). May–Aug. Common northward.
Remarks: This moth and the next 2 species are among the most widespread and common in our area of the 56 N. American *Hydriomena* species.

TRANSFIGURED HYDRIOMENA   Pl. 49 (8)
Hydriomena transfigurata Swett
Identification: Very similar to the other *Hydriomena* species, but median area of FW *relatively narrow*. FW extremely variable—grayish brown in dark areas, greenish white in light areas (including median area). Pm. line scalloped. Specimens from the Northeast are paler than those westward (Manitoba) and southward (Del. to n. Fla.); darker specimens are *H. transfigurata manitoba*

B. & McD. HW light to dark grayish brown. Wingspan 2.6–3.3 cm.
Food: Pines.
Range: N.S. to n. Fla., west to Man. and Tex. Late March–early May. Common.

SHARP GREEN HYDRIOMENA   Pl. 49 (4)
Hydriomena pluviata (Gn.)
Identification: Very similar to the previous 2 moths, but upper median area of FW usually *wider*; pm. line and other *markings sharper*. Pm. line usually bends deeply outward, but *not scalloped*. Specimens south of N.J. (*H. pluviata meridianata* McD.) darker than northern form. HW grayish brown. Wingspan 2.6–3 cm.
Food: Unrecorded.
Range: Me. to n. Fla., west to e. Kans. and Tex. Feb.–April southward; into June northward. Common.

TISSUE MOTH *Triphosa haesitata* (Gn.)   **Pl. 47 (16)**
Identification: FW wood brown, sometimes tinted with pinkish; note complex pattern of *light and dark scalloped lines*, mostly parallel. Basal and st. lines white; darkest area is blackish shading beyond upper pm. line. Upper median area warm brown; blotches along outer margin also warm brown (note *large blotch* halfway between apex and anal angle). HW pale grayish brown with fainter scalloped lines. Our subspecies is *T. haesitata affirmaria* (Wlk.). Wingspan 3.5–4 cm.
Food: Buckthorns, cascara (*Rhamnus* species), European barberry, hawthorn, oak, *Pisonia aculeata*, and wild plum.
Range: Lab. to N.C., west to Man. and Mo. May–Sept. Uncommon.

BARBERRY GEOMETER   Pls. 47 (18), 49 (14)
Coryphista meadii (Pack.)
Identification: Two forms: typical form (Pl. 47) is all dark brown like Tissue Moth (above); form "badiaria" (Hy. Edw.) has orangish brown am. and st. bands (Pl. 49). In both forms FW *apex sharper* than in Tissue Moth, and *tooth* toward top of pm. line more pronounced. FW not blotched with dark brown. HW pale grayish brown with variably distinct lines. Wingspan 3–3.6 cm.
Food: Barberry.
Range: Me. to Fla., west to Wisc. and Tex. May–Oct.; several broods. These moths can be flushed near their food plants during the day.

FERGUSON'S SCALLOP SHELL   Pl. 47 (13)
Hydria prunivorata (Fgn.)
Identification: Wings brown, with many fine *scalloped lines* of black, brown, and yellowish. St. line most conspicuous. Pattern continues onto HW. Wingspan 2.7–3.5 cm.
Food: Wild cherry. Larvae live together in nests formed by tying leaves together.

Range: N.S. to S.C., west to Wisc., Mo., and Miss. May–Sept. Locally common.

Similar species: In the Scallop Shell, *H. undulata* (L.), not shown, *pattern less sharp* and bright, but so similar that the 2 species can best be distinguished by genitalia and larval characteristics. Food: Azalea, spiraea, rhodora azalea, and willows; larvae *solitary* (not colonial). Range: Holarctic; Lab. to Me. in our area, west through Canada, south to Minn. May–Aug.

SPEAR-MARKED BLACK   Pl. 50 (2)
Rheumaptera hastata (L.)

Identification: FW black with *broad white pm. band*, often *dotted with black*. White st. wedges at costa and opposite tooth of pm. band. HW may have thin white median band, but no white at apex. Wingspan 2.5–3.3 cm.

Food: Alders, birches, blueberries, hazelnut, poplars, sweetfern, sweetgale, willows, and other trees and shrubs.

Range: Lab. to N.C. and Tenn., west across Canada, south to S.D. June–July. A day-flier.

WHITE-BANDED BLACK   Pl. 50 (5)
Rheumaptera subhastata (Nolcken)

Identification: Wings black, but with more extensive bold white markings than in Spear-marked Black (above). Note wide *white median band* on HW. Wingspan 3–3.4 cm.

Food: Alders, northern bayberry, and sweetgale.

Range: Lab. to Me., west across Canada in bogs. June–July; a day-flier.

WHITE-RIBBONED CARPET   Pl. 47 (20)
Mesoleuca ruficillata (Gn.)

Identification: Wide, pure *white median band* contrasts with solid black areas near base and along costa of FW. Note black discal dots on all wings. Basal area solid blackish; black patch on costa from pm. to st. lines. HW white with gray median line and terminal border. Wingspan 2.5–2.8 cm.

Food: Birches and blackberry.

Range: Lab. to mts. of N.C. and Ky., west through Canada, south to Wisc. May–Aug. Common northward.

DOUBLE-BANDED CARPET   Pl. 47 (4)
Spargania magnoliata Gn.

Identification: FW gray with *white am. and pm. bands* and *up to 10 scalloped, dark gray lines* variably shaded with black. Discal spot large, black. HW dirty white shaded with gray, usually with a slight salmon-pink tint. Terminal line black; fringe white. Wingspan 1.9–2.7 cm.

Food: Willow-herbs (*Epilobium* species) and evening-primrose.

Range: Nfld. to N.C., west across Canada, south to Wisc. May–Aug.; 2 broods.

SQUARE-PATCHED CARPET　　　　　　Pl. 49 (16)
Perizoma basaliata (Wlk.)
Identification: Basal, median, and apical areas on FW dark gray. Am. and st. areas brown. Note *black square* opposite tooth on pm. line; black discal dots on all wings. Pattern often obscure. HW pale gray. Wingspan 1.9–2.1 cm.
Food: Unrecorded.
Range: Lab. to N.C. mts., west to Man. and Wisc. July–Sept. Sometimes locally common.

MANY-LINED CARPET　　　　　　Pl. 49 (13)
Anticlea multiferata (Wlk.)
Identification: FW brownish maroon with many fine, vertical, *parallel yellowish lines.* Wingspan 1.9–2.5 cm.
Food: Willow-herb.
Range: Lab. to N.C. and Miss., west through Canada, south to ne. Okla. and La. April–Aug.; most southern records are for April and May. Moderately common.

SHINY GRAY CARPET　　　　　　Pl. 49 (1)
Stamnodes gibbicostata (Wlk.)
Identification: Wings smooth, shiny brownish gray. FW markings most distinct *at costa*—note tops of white lines and black peppering. All fringes checkered black and whitish. Wingspan 2.5–3.1 cm.
Food: Unrecorded.
Range: Que. to W. Va. and Ky., west to Wisc., Neb., and Mo. Sept.–Oct. Uncommon.

LABRADOR CARPET　　　　　　Pl. 49 (10)
Xanthorhoe labradorensis (Pack.)
Identification: This and the next 2 species represent about 13 similar, mostly northern *Xanthorhoe* species in our area. Wings pale gray in Labrador Carpet, with *heavy, straight, black am. line* and pale brown median area on FW. Wingspan 2–2.5 cm.
Food: Cabbage, hemlock, peppergrass, radish, sweet alyssum, and other plants.
Range: Lab. to N.C., Miss., and La., west through Canada, south to Wisc. May–Aug. Common; 2 broods northward.

RED TWIN-SPOT　　　　　　Pl. 49 (7)
Xanthorhoe ferrugata (Clerck)
Identification: Wings grayish to light tan, with reddish brown shading in basal area of FW. Note *double black spot* near outer margin of FW. Median area reddish brown, sometimes blackish (as shown); edged by irregular white pm. line with broad tooth. *Dark brown blotch* accents top of pm. line, which is double at costa. Wingspan 1.8–2.5 cm.
Food: Low plants, such as common chickweed, ground ivy, and *Polygonum* species.

Range: Lab. to Va., west to Man. and Minn. April–Sept.; 2 broods. Common.

TOOTHED BROWN CARPET   Pl. 47 (1)
Xanthorhoe lacustrata (Gn.)

Identification: Similar to Red Twin-spot (above, Pl. 49), but slightly larger; median area narrower and dark brown (not reddish brown). Dark spot at outer margin brown (not black), *more diffuse*. This moth also resembles Sharp-angled Carpet (below, Pl. 47), but pm. line bordering dark median area is *indented* above tooth, and dark apical patch is *irregular* (not square). HW gray, crossed by vague wavy lines. Wingspan 2–2.6 cm.

Food: Birches, blackberries and other *Rubus* species, hawthorns, impatiens, and willows.

Range: Common throughout our area, though not recorded between N.C. and Fla. March–Sept.; 2 broods.

WHITE-BANDED TOOTHED CARPET   Pl. 47 (23)
Epirrhoe alternata (Müller)

Identification: Wings have wide *white st. bands*. Basal, median and terminal areas of FW gray, median and upper st. areas sometimes darker gray. FW discal spot a vertical black oval. HW paler. Wingspan 1.9–2.5 cm.

Food: Bedstraws (*Galium* species).

Range: Lab. to W. Va., west through Canada, south to Minn. May–Sept. Locally common northward.

SHARP-ANGLED CARPET   Pl. 47 (22)
Euphyia unangulata (Haw.)

Identification: FW brownish; pattern similar to that of Toothed Brown Carpet (above), but basal area usually *darker, pm. line nearly straight above tooth*, and dark blotches at outer margin less conspicuous. Dark *apical patch almost square*. HW grayish with whitish scalloped lines. Our subspecies of this European moth is *E. unangulata intermediata* (Gn.). Wingspan 2.3–2.7 cm.

Food: Chickweed, elm, impatiens, and mustard.

Range: Lab. to N.C., west to Man. and Wisc. May–Sept.; 2 broods. Common northward.

THE GEM *Orthonama obstipata* (F.)   Pl. 49 (12, 15)

Identification: Wings yellowish brown in ♂, darker from base to median line, with tiny *black discal dot* on FW. Lines generally obscure; note oblique *blackish dash* from st. line to FW apex. FW in ♀ maroon; lines accented with white dots. Tiny black discal dot *encircled with white*. HW duller brownish. Wingspan 1.5–2.2 cm.

Food: Wide variety of plants, such as chrysanthemums, dock, elms, mayweed, *Polygonum* species, and ragworts (*Senecio* species).

Range: Worldwide; dies out in colder areas each year, but repopulates rapidly the following spring. April–Oct.; several broods. Very common.

BENT-LINE CARPET   Pl. 50 (1, 4)
Orthonama centrostrigaria (Woll.)

Identification: Wings pale gray with many fine, broken, dotted or scalloped lines. Median area in ♂ defined by wide blackish am. line and *curved upper half* of pm. line (lower half *absent*). Median area same color as rest of FW in ♂; *darker brown* in ♀. Tiny black discal dots on all wings. Wingspan 1.7–2.3 cm.

Food: Low plants, such as knotweed and smartweed.

Range: Common throughout our area from Me. and Que. south and west. March–Oct.

SOMBER CARPET   Pl. 47 (25)
Disclisioprocta stellata (Gn.)

Identification: Wings deep brown; am. and pm. areas sometimes paler yellowish, especially southward. Lines *black, wavy;* pm. line heaviest. Look for white filling in am. and pm. lines and white spotting in st. area. Wingspan 2.5–3.3 cm.

Food: Amaranth and devil's claws.

Range: Tropical, straying north as far as N.S. and Mich. July–Nov. northward; common during any warm period southward.

UNADORNED CARPET   Pl. 50 (7)
Hydrelia inornata (Hulst)

Identification: Wings pale powdery gray, usually *darker along costa*. Lines very diffuse, blotchy, grayish brown, especially at middle of pm. line on FW. Discal dots black. Wingspan 1.7–2.2 cm.

Food: White and yellow birch.

Range: N.S. and Que. to N.C., west to Minn. and se. Mo. May–Aug. Locally common.

FRAGILE WHITE CARPET   Pl. 48 (18)
Hydrelia albifera (Wlk.)

Identification: Body and wings white. Look for a yellow bar on upper half of frons. FW has wide, wavy, *yellow pm. line* and narrower, broken am. and st. lines. Tiny *black discal dot* on each wing. Wingspan 1.6–1.7 cm.

Food: Alternate-leaf and red-osier dogwoods; white birch.

Range: Nfld. to se. Ky., west to Man., Mo. and Miss. Late May–Aug.; 2 broods. Common northward.

THE WELSH WAVE *Venusia cambrica* Curtis   Pl. 50 (6)
Identification: FW pale powdery gray with irregular black lines. Am. line double, heavy at costa; pm. line heaviest, with *2 black dashes* just beyond midpoint. HW white with gray lines. Wingspan 2.3–2.5 cm.

Food: Alders, apple, birch, black cottonwood, mountain-ash, serviceberry, and willow.

Range: Lab. to N.C. mts., west across Canada, south to Mich. May–Aug.; 2 broods. Common in northern forest habitats.

BROWN-SHADED CARPET   Pl. 50 (3)
Venusia comptaria (Wlk.)
Identification: Very similar to the Welsh Wave (above), but smaller and duller gray, lines less sharp. Upper half of pm. line on FW thickened, with 1–2 small black dashes beyond middle of line. Brown shading in upper median and pm. areas. HW paler grayish. Wingspan 1.6–2.2 cm.
Food: Alders, beeches, and birches.
Range: N.S. and Gaspé, Que., to Va. and Miss., west to Wisc. and Mo. April–early May. Common.

WHITE-STRIPED BLACK   Pl. 47 (9)
Trichodezia albovittata (Gn.)
Identification: Wings black with *white bar* across FW, narrowing and meeting terminal white wedge near inner margin. HW fringe black, white toward outer angle. Wingspan 2–2.5 cm.
Food: Impatiens.
Range: Lab. to N.C., west to Man. and Mo. April–Sept.; 2 broods. A common day-flier in woodlands.

THE BEGGAR *Eubaphe mendica* (Wlk.)   Pl. 49 (17)
Identification: Wings translucent pale yellow; FW crossed by 2 irregular lines of *fused bluish gray spots*. Note single spot midway along outer margin of FW. Wingspan 2.1–3 cm.
Food: Maples and violets.
Range: Common throughout our area. May–Sept.; 3 broods.

THE LITTLE BEGGAR   Pl. 49 (11)
Eubaphe meridiana (Slosson)
Identification: Very similar to The Beggar (above), but *smaller* and *more orangish.* FW spots representing am. and pm. lines small, *not fused.* Wingspan 1.8–2.5 cm.
Food: Unrecorded.
Range: Eastern N.Y. to Fla., west to Ky. and Miss. June–Aug. northward. Uncommon northward.

BROWN BARK CARPET   Pl. 47 (14)
Horisme intestinata (Gn.)
Identification: Wings dirty yellowish brown with many wavy dark gray to black lines, making moth look brownish overall. FW pm. line *deeply scalloped;* discal spots small, blackish. Black basal bar on HW aligns with black bar across base of abdomen. Wingspan 2.1–3.2 cm.
Food: Unrecorded; European relatives feed on clematis.
Range: Common throughout our area. April–Oct.; 2 broods.

COMMON EUPITHECIA   Pl. 47 (17)
Eupithecia miserulata Grt.
Identification: This and the next species are among the most common and widespread of about 40 *Eupithecia* species in our area. Mostly northern; many are so similar that they are impossi-

ble to identify without studying genitalia. Common Eupithecia has broad wings and heavy, round, *black discal spots* on dirty gray wings. Wingspan 1.2–2 cm.
Food: Aster, clover, coneflower, hoptree, junipers, *Myrica* species, oaks, wild cherry and willows.
Range: Common throughout our area; April–Oct.

## HEREFORD'S EUPITHECIA					Pl. 47 (19)
Eupithecia herefordaria C. & S.
Identification: Wings grayish brown. FW extremely long, *narrow*, and *pointed*. Pm. line darker, with slightly paler band beyond it; other lines very faint. Discal spots on all wings faint. Wingspan 1.4–2.1 cm.
Food: Unrecorded.
Range: Pa. to S.C. and Ala., west to Mo. April–early May. Locally common.

## OLIVE-AND-BLACK CARPET					Pl. 46 (25)
Acasis viridata (Pack.)
Identification: FW mottled olive green, fading to yellowish in collections. Note blackish median and st. shades and fine black vein outlines; lower part of pm. line *double, white*. HW grayish brown with darker median line. Wingspan 1.8–2 cm.
Food: Northern wild-raisin.
Range: Lab. to Va. and e. Ky., west across Canada, south to Wisc. Also reported from Fla. May–July. Usually common.

## MOTTLED GRAY CARPET					Pl. 47 (7)
Cladara limitaria (Wlk.)
Identification: Frons and vertex (top of head) white, with a black line between them. FW white mottled with pale green and gray. Pm. line fine, sharp, usually complete; angled sharply at discal spot and *curving evenly inward* below that bend. HW grayish. Wingspan 2.1–2.8 cm.
Food: Sheep laurel and conifers.
Range: Lab. to N.C., west across Canada, south to Mo. April–June. Common.
Similar species: Angle-lined Carpet, *C. anguilineata* (Grt. & Rob.), not shown, is generally *duller*, grayish brown with less contrasting pattern; grayish brown scaling on frons. Food: Unrecorded. Range: Same as for Mottled Gray Carpet, but more common southward.

## THE SCRIBBLER					Pl. 46 (24)
Cladara atroliturata (Wlk.)
Identification: FW white with *pale green bands* and *irregular black lines* and spots. HW grayish with faint lines in outer half. Wingspan 2.5–3 cm.
Food: Alders, birches, maples, and willows.
Range: Nfld. to Va., west to w. Ont., Wisc., and Ky.; also old

records from Tex. April–May; into June northward. Locally common.

POWDERED BIGWING   Pl. 48 (11)
Lobophora nivigerata Wlk.
Identification: FW powdery gray marked with 4 darker gray bands, heaviest at costa. *Discal spot diffuse*, blackish. HW white with tiny black discal dot and faint median line. FW in melanic specimens almost unmarked, dark gray. Wingspan 2.1–2.5 cm.
Food: Balsam poplar, speckled alder, white birch, willow, but mostly trembling aspen.
Range: Nfld. to N.C. mts., west across Canada, south to Wisc. and Minn. May–July. Common northward.

THREE-PATCHED BIGWING   Pl. 47 (11)
Heterophleps refusaria (Wlk.)
Identification: FW much bigger than HW. FW powdery gray, with *3 blackish costal patches;* 2 patches represent tops of dotted am. and pm. lines. HW paler gray. Wingspan 2.3–3 cm.
Food: Unrecorded.
Range: Que. and Me. to N.C. mts., west to Man. and n. Mo. May–July. Uncommon.

THREE-SPOTTED FILLIP   Pl. 47 (10)
Heterophleps triguttaria H.-S.
Identification: FW broad, shiny, pale brown, with *3 dark brown costal patches* as in Three-patched Bigwing (above); outer patch smallest. Am. and pm. lines even, faint, paler than ground color. HW slightly paler and much smaller than FW. Wingspan 1.8–2.4 cm.
Food: Maples.
Range: N.S. and Que. to Fla., west to Wisc., Kans. and Miss. April–Sept. Locally common.

THE BAD-WING *Dyspteris abortivaria* (H.-S.)   Pl. 49 (2)
Identification: Easily recognized by *pale bluish green wings* with *white lines* and discal spots. FW *much larger* than HW, the latter often difficult to pull into position for spreading—hence the common name. Wingspan 2–2.8 cm.
Food: Grapes.
Range: Common throughout our area. Mid-April to Aug.

EPIPLEMID MOTHS:
Family Epiplemidae

Medium to small moths with broad wings, superficially similar to inchworm moths (previous family). Wingspan 1.5–2.2 cm. *Wing margins irregular,* especially on HW (Fig. 31). R_5 and M_1 of FW *stalked;* M_3 and Cu_1 *not* stalked; M_2 *arises closer to M_1* than to

M_3. Sc + R_1 of HW *fused*, diverging from Rs at base; frenulum present.

Early larval stages feed communally in webs; later instars are more exposed. A large family in the neotropics, but represented by only 8 N. American species, only 2 of which are widespread in our area.

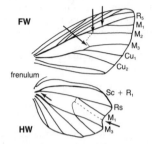

Fig. 31.
Wing venation,
Epiplemidae.

GRAY SCOOPWING *Callizzia amorata* Pack.   **Pl. 55 (13)**
Identification: Outer margin of FW *even*, slightly rounded. Wings brownish gray. Lines, terminal spot on FW and median shade of HW blackish. HW margin deeply scooped. Wingspan 1.5–2.2 cm.
Food: Honeysuckle.
Range: N.S. to Fla., west to Man. and Tex. April–Sept. Uncommon to locally common.

BROWN SCOOPWING   **Pl. 55 (12)**
Calledapteryx dryopterata Grt.
Identification: Wings reddish to orangish brown. FW has *large scoop* in outer margin, lined with dark brown. Wingspan 1.8–2.2 cm.
Food: Smooth blackhaw (*Viburnum prunifolium*) and southern wild-raisin (*V. nudum*).
Range: Que. to Fla., west to Man. and Ark. May–Aug. Uncommon.

Microlepidoptera

PLUME MOTHS:
Family Pterophoridae

Medium to small moths, either unmarked or patterned. Wingspan 1.3–4.1 cm. Easily recognized by long, slender legs and ⊤-shaped appearance when at rest, with rolled wings held at right angles to the body (see rear endpapers). Outer margin of FW *deeply notched*. HW divided into *3 fringed lobes* that look like plumes (Fig. 32); compare with many-plume moths (Fig. 54, p. 435).

Larvae usually leafrollers or borers. The Grape Plume Moth, *Geina periscelidactyla* (Fitch), not shown, is a widely distributed pest on grapes.

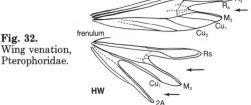

Fig. 32.
Wing venation,
Pterophoridae.

Platyptilia carduidactyla (Riley)　　　　　　　　**Pl. 58 (21)**
Identification: FW brown with *darker costal border* that widens to form a *triangle* at top of pm. line; st. line edged on both sides with white. HW gray with tiny black triangle on anal margin. Wingspan 1.8–2.7 cm.
Food: Thistles.
Range: Lab. to Va., west across Canada, south to Tex. April–Sept. Common.

Emmelina monodactyla (L.)　　　　　　　　**Pl. 58 (19)**
Identification: Wings pale grayish to pinkish brown, flecked with dark brown. *Heaviest dark brown spot* at *point* of FW split; other vague brown spots on outer costa and each branch formed by split. All 3 branches of HW linear; broad fringe on anal branch. Wingspan 1.8–2.8 cm.
Food: Common morning-glory, *Convolvulus* species, lamb's-quarters, orache, and sweet joe-pye-weed.
Range: Common throughout our area. March–Sept.

HYBLAEID MOTHS:
Family Hyblaeidae

Medium-sized moths with unique HW pattern; wingspan of our only species is 2.8–3.2 cm. Maxillary palps well developed; labial palps long,

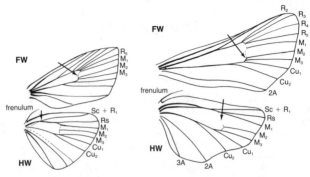

Fig. 33. Wing venation, Hyblaeidae.

Fig. 34. Wing venation, Thyrididae.

projecting forward, beaklike. Antennae simple. Proboscis long, naked. Discal cell of FW *open*. All veins *unstalked* (Fig. 33); M_2 arises closer to M_3 than to M_1. Sc of HW *joins Rs briefly* near base.

Larva feeds in silken network between leaves of various plants; pupates in cocoon in foliage, leaf litter, or soil.

ORANGE-PATCHED HYBLAEA   Pl. 42 (9)
Hyblaea puera (Cram.)
Identification: FW brown, variably mottled with darker brown and speckled with tiny black dots. HW blackish with long median and smaller marginal *orange patches;* median patch sometimes *divided* into 2. Wingspan 2.8–3.2 cm.
Food: *Kigelia pinnata, Tabebuia avellandae,* tulip-tree, and *Tecomaria capensis.*
Range: A tropical moth; common in peninsular Fla. in all months. Flies to lights; also found during day on blossoms of plants such as day jessamine (*Cestrum diurnum*).

WINDOW-WINGED MOTHS:
Family Thyrididae

Small to medium, stout-bodied moths with moderately broad wings; wingspan 1.2–4.2 cm. Species shown have *translucent, windowlike spots* in wings. Labial palps upturned; 2nd segment broad, bladelike. Proboscis well developed, naked. Outer margins of wings wavy (Fig. 34). Discal cell of FW *open*, with R and M endings *unstalked* (R_3 and R_4 stalked in tropical species in Gulf Coast area, not shown). M_2 arises close to M_3. Sc and Rs of HW either fused at midpoint, or separate but close together; discal cell of HW *open*. 1A absent on FW and HW.

Larvae are leaf rollers or borers in stems and twigs of host plants. Adults of species included here are day-fliers and may be more common than collections indicate.

SPOTTED THYRIS *Thyris maculata* Harr.   Pl. 57 (2)
Identification: Wings blackish with inconspicuous orange spots. Note

round, *translucent whitish spot* in median area of FW; 2 other spots close together on HW. Wingspan 1.2–1.5 cm.
Food: Clematis and *Houstonia* species.
Range: Que. to N.C., west to Kans. and Miss. May–Sept. Local and uncommon.

MOURNFUL THYRIS *Thyris sepulchralis* Guér.   **Pl. 56 (13)**
Identification: Wings black with large median and other smaller *white spots;* those at margins give wings a ragged look. HW has white median patch. Wingspan 1.5–2.3 cm.
Food: Clematis and grapes.
Range: Me. to Fla., west to Mo. and Tex. April–Aug. Uncommon, but conspicuous when seen flying in daytime because of bold pattern.

EYED DYSODIA *Dysodia oculatana* Clem.   **Pl. 57 (1)**
Identification: Wings dull, mottled metallic orange and brown, with broad and narrow brown lines. FW has small translucent reniform spot; larger, *crescent-shaped* spot on HW. Wingspan 1.8–2.1 cm.
Food: Beans and *Eupatorium ageratoides;* larva bores into stems and is also a leaf roller.
Range: Pa. to Fla., west to Mo. and Miss. May–Aug. Uncommon in much of range.

PYRALID MOTHS:
Family Pyralidae

Small to medium-sized (rarely medium to large) moths comprising the third largest moth family in N. America. Wingspan 0.9–3.7 cm (a few subtropical species measure up to 6.2 cm). Antennae usually simple. Labial palps usually *long, projecting* forward or upward; maxillary palps usually visible, though small. Proboscis usually present, scaled at base. Tympanal cavities on underside of abdomen near base open forward, toward hind coxae. FW triangular to elongate. These moths hold their wings out to the side, fold them flat, or roll them up, making their bodies look like sticks. M_2 of FW arises close to M_3 (Fig. 35); $Sc + R_1$ of HW *fused or very close together* well beyond end of discal cell, then separating, so first vein from costa appears forked. Usually 3 anal veins.

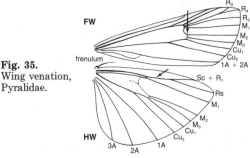

Fig. 35. Wing venation, Pyralidae.

Larval habits vary, but larva usually concealed when feeding—some species bore into plant tissues; others roll leaves or form webs on them. Some caterpillars in this family are scavengers on dried or decaying organic matter, some feed on scale insects, and some live in nests of bees and other Hymenoptera. Members of subfamily Nymphulinae are the Lepidoptera that are best adapted to aquatic life—the larvae have tracheal gills that enable them to extract oxygen from the water. Many pyralids are important pests of crops, stored food products, and beehives.

The species included here represent 14 of the 18 subfamilies into which the family is divided. A brief synopsis of those subfamilies follows, with references to pages where coverage of species in those subfamilies begins.

Scopariinae, p. 395—Mostly small, gray to brown moths; FW triangular with *tufts of black scales*. Labial palps beaklike. Larvae feed on mosses or bore in roots of flowering plants.

Nymphulinae, p. 395—Small, delicate moths; FW narrow, usually with a complex pattern of lines. HW has a row of *shiny metallic spots* along outer margin in many species. Larvae usually aquatic, eating water plants; many have tracheal gills.

Odontiinae, p. 396—Similar to Pyraustinae (below) but with a single flap over tympanum. FW usually has *scaled tuft* at inner margin near base. Larvae of known species vary in habits: some are leaf miners, others form webs, and still others feed on seeds.

Glaphyriinae, p. 396—Small, broad-winged moths; am. and pm. lines of FW usually sharply defined. *Tufts* of modified scales usually present on upperside of HW and underside of FW. Larval feeding habits diverse.

Evergestinae, p. 397—Similar to Pyraustinae (below), differing mainly in genitalic features. Broad-winged; HW *broadly rounded*. Larvae feed mostly on plants in the mustard and caper families.

Pyraustinae, p. 397—Our largest pyralid subfamily. Body slender, wings broad, as in geometer moths (Geometridae, p. 344), but abdomen *as long* as end of HW *or longer* (shorter in most Geometridae). Many species are brightly patterned. Larvae fold leaves, or bore in stems and fruits of food plants.

Schoenobiinae, p. 403—Small to large moths; FW long and narrow. Most species tan or white, not as sharply patterned as *Scirpophaga perstrialis* (p. 403, Pl. 58). Larvae feed mostly on aquatic and semiaquatic grasses and other monocots, boring in the stems.

Crambinae, p. 403—Mostly brown, gray, or white moths, either with little FW pattern, or *streaked* with silver lines. FW *long, narrow*, rolled up, giving moth a *sticklike* appearance at rest. Labial palps beaklike. Larvae are webworms or stem borers; some are major pests of turf grasses, rice, or sugar cane.

Pyralinae, p. 404—FW triangular, without scale tufts; lines usually sharp. Many species rest with *wings outspread*, and *abdomen curled upward* between them. Larvae feed mostly on decaying plant matter and stored food products.

Chrysauginae, p. 405—Maxillary palps *absent;* legs conspicuously *tufted* with scales. FW somewhat squared; in ♂ FW costa usually distorted, tufted, or rolled to form *cone* near base. Wings of many species fold flat over body at rest; moths often stand high on legs. Larval habits vary.

Epipaschiinae, p. 406—Mostly grayish moths; median area of FW usually well defined. *Tufts* of scales usually present. Wings are folded flat at rest. Some larvae are leaf rollers.

Galleriinae, p. 406—A small group of small to medium-sized, grayish or brownish moths; FW has *no sharp pattern*. *No hood* over tympanum; R_3 and R_4 of FW *stalked* (Fig. 35). Outer margin of FW indented in Wax Moth (p. 406, Pl. 58). Larvae live in bee and wasp nests, where they feed on wax and other materials.

Phycitinae, p. 406—A large group of mostly grayish, obscurely marked moths. FW *narrow, triangular*, with *only 4* radial veins (R_3 combined with R_4). Moths usually rest with front of body upcurved. Larvae roll or fold leaves, bore into stems or fruits, or feed on decaying matter or stored food products. Several species are serious pests.

Peoriinae, p. 407—A small group similar to Phycitinae (above), but distinguished by ♂ genitalic differences and more compressed lobes on ♀ ovipositor. *Pale costal border* on darker FW identifies many species. Life cycles unknown.

Subfamily Scopariinae

Eudonia heterosalis (McD.)   **not shown**
Identification: Wings gray, mottled with grayish brown. Am. and pm. *lines black with white edging*. Black orbicular, claviform, and reniform spots inconspicuous, obscured by mottling. Fringe checkered gray and grayish brown. Wingspan 0.9–1.1 cm.
Food: Unrecorded.
Range: N.S. to Fla., west to Ont. and La. May–Oct. Common.

Subfamily Nymphulinae

Munroessa icciusalis (Wlk.)   **Pl. 57 (25)**
Identification: Wings bright lemon yellow, brown beyond pm. line in some specimens. Lines black, *broken, edged with white;* median area white on all wings. Wingspan 1.6–2.6 cm.
Food: Aquatic plants, such as buckbean, duckweed, eelgrass, pondweeds, and sedges. Larva and pupa protected by a case made of plant parts.
Range: Locally common throughout our area. June–Sept.

Munroessa gyralis (Hulst)   **Pl. 57 (26)**
Identification: FW orangish brown to deep grayish brown; lines of ♂ black with white edging. Am. and pm. *lines connected* at upper and lower ⅓ to form *loops* from costa and inner margin. Terminal line white. ♀ usually unmarked. HW whitish to gray. Wingspan 1.6–3 cm; ♀ larger than ♂.
Food: Waterlilies. Larva eats leaves first, later bores into petioles.
Range: N.S. to Fla., west to Man. and e. Tex. July–Oct.; every month in Fla.

Synclita obliteralis (Wlk.)   **Pl. 57 (27)**
Identification: Sexually dimorphic: ♂ smaller and more broad-winged than ♀. Wings grayish brown, with dark brown shading and whitish lines. Reniform spot a *whitish crescent*. In ♀ (shown) the light areas are paler than in ♂; ♀ also less sharply marked. Wingspan 1–2.2 cm.
Food: Duckweed, pondweeds, waterlilies, and other aquatic plants; larva makes a case out of plant parts. A minor pest of aquatic ornamentals; sometimes a problem in greenhouses.
Range: Common throughout our area. May–Aug.

Parapoynx obscuralis (Grt.)   **Pl. 57 (29)**
Identification: HW white, with even *brown st. band* and *orange border*. FW of ♂ white with variable brown shading; FW of ♀ nearly all dark brown. Wingspan 1.7–2.6 cm.
Food: Eelgrass, pondweed, yellow waterlily, and other aquatic plants; larva a casemaker.
Range: N.S. to Fla., west to Wisc. and cen. Tex. June–Aug. Locally common.

Petrophila bifascialis (Rob.)   **Pl. 57 (28)**
Identification: Wings whitish with grayish brown shading and orangish brown transverse bands. Note the blackish reniform spot and *metallic silver patches* on FW, toward anal angle and in median band. Silver patches also present within *row of black spots* along outer margin of HW. Wingspan 1.1–2.4 cm.
Food: Larva scrapes diatoms and other algae from rocks in fast-moving streams, where it lives in a silken web.
Range: N.S. to Va., west to Ont. and Tex. Aug.–Sept. northward. Locally common. May be found as far south as Fla.

Subfamily Odontiinae

Eustixia pupula Hbn.   **Pl. 48 (17)**
Identification: The pattern of *black spots on silvery white wings* is unmistakable. Wingspan 1.2–1.6 cm.
Food: Peppergrass and cabbage.
Range: Mass. and s. Ont. to Fla., west to Mo. and Tex. May–Aug.; 2 broods. Common.

Subfamily Glaphyriinae

Dicymolomia julianalis (Wlk.)   **Pl. 57 (6)**
Identification: Wings variably dark reddish brown; upper median area of FW *white*. Upper half of pm. line black. Note the *black median blotch* and *terminal dots* on HW. Wingspan 1.2–2 cm.
Food: Cattail heads and stems, dead cotton bolls, milk-vetch, prickly pear, and thistle; larva also eats eggs of bagworm moths.
Range: N.S. to Fla., west to Ill., Ark. and Tex. May–Oct. Common.

Subfamily Evergestinae

PURPLE-BACKED CABBAGEWORM MOTH   Pl. 57 (13)
Evergestis pallidata (Hufn.)
Identification: Wings straw yellow with grayish brown shading and sharp median and pm. lines. Note *ringlike marking* as part of upper median area. HW white toward base. Wingspan 2–2.9 cm.
Food: Bitter-cress, cabbage, radish, turnip, and other plants in the mustard family.
Range: Common from Nfld. to Va., west across Canada, south to Ky. and Miss. (?). May–Sept.

Evergestis unimacula (Grt. & Rob.)   **Pl. 58 (3)**
Identification: Wings dull gray to grayish brown, with large *yellow oblong spot* near apex on costa of FW; smaller spot near inner margin. Larger paler yellow blotch toward costa of HW. Wingspan 1.8–2.2 cm.
Food: Unrecorded.
Range: S. Ont. to N.C., west to Ill. and Ark. May–Aug. Uncommon.

Subfamily Pyraustinae

Crocidophora pustuliferalis Led.   **Pl. 58 (5)**
Identification: FW shiny pale orangish to brownish yellow. Note *sharp, evenly scalloped, dark pm. and st. lines* and dotted terminal line on all wings. Wingspan 2.3–2.5 cm.
Food: Canes (*Arundinaria* species).
Range: Va. to Fla., west to Ky., Ark., and Miss. May–July. Common southward.

Crocidophora tuberculalis Led.   **Pl. 57 (10)**
Identification: Wings translucent straw yellow with *broad, pale grayish brown terminal bands* on all wings. Pm. line narrower but complete, continuing onto HW. Wingspan 1.5–1.7 cm.
Food: Unrecorded.
Range: Common from Que. to n. Fla., west to Mo. and Miss. May–Aug.

EUROPEAN CORN BORER MOTH   Pl. 57 (20, 21)
Ostrinia nubilalis (Hbn.)
Identification: Sexually dimorphic: wings mostly grayish brown in ♂, deep yellow *around discal spot* and beyond pm. line of FW; yellow blotch on HW. Wings yellow in ♀, with grayish brown lines. Note *large notch* in toothed pm. line near inner margin. Wingspan 2.4–3.2 cm; ♀ larger than ♂.
Food: Corn; larva (**European Corn Borer**) tunnels in stalks and cuts leaves off at bases. Probably our most serious corn pest. Also feeds on asters, beans, dahlias, potato, and other plants.
Range: Throughout our area except s. Fla. and coastal plain areas of South. April–Oct.; 1 brood in North, 3 southward. Common. Introduced about 1908 or 1909 from Europe.

Perispasta caeculalis Zell.   **Pl. 56 (21, 22)**
Identification: Wings dark grayish brown in both sexes, with FW *outer margins indented* and lined with white. White FW dash in discal area in ♂ but not in ♀. Wingspan 1.3–1.9 cm.
Food: Unrecorded.
Range: Common throughout our area. April–Aug.

Phlyctaenia coronata (Hufn.)   **Pl. 56 (24)**
Identification: The N. American subspecies is *P. coronata tertialis* (Gn.). Wings dull grayish brown with pale yellow spots and accents along darker lines. Note *large yellow spots* outside pm. line on FW and HW. Wingspan 1.8–2.2 cm.
Food: Alders, elderberry, hickories, viburnums, and other plants.
Range: Nfld. to Fla., west across Canada, south to La. May–Aug. Common.

Anania funebris (Ström)   **Pl. 58 (2)**
Identification: Wings black, with *2 pale yellowish white spots* on each wing. The N. American species is *A. funebris glomeralis* (Wlk.). Wingspan 1.8–2.2 cm.
Food: Goldenrod.
Range: Holarctic; Nfld. to s. N.C. in our area, west across Canada, south to Mich. and Minn. May–early July. Common; found in fields during the day.

GARDEN WEBWORM MOTH   **Pl. 56 (23)**
Achyra rantalis (Gn.)
Identification: FW orange, brown or grayish brown in varying shades. Am. and pm. lines diffuse, slightly darker than ground color; pm. line *edged with paler color*. Orbicular and reniform spots usually present. HW usually colored as FW but lighter; median line present in costal half. Wingspan 1.8–2.2 cm.
Food: Larva (**Garden Webworm**) feeds on alfalfa, beans, clover, corn, peas, strawberries, and many other low plants.
Range: Me. and s. Que. to Fla., west to Kans. and Tex. April–Nov.; 4 or more broods. Common.

Helvibotys helvialis (Wlk.)   **Pl. 57 (12)**
Identification: Wings shiny, pale yellow. Am. and pm. lines pale reddish brown; pm. line curved as shown. Note *2 dots* toward FW costa in median area—outer one larger. HW has brown median line and terminal shade. Wingspan 1–2.2 cm.
Food: Amaranth and beets.
Range: Me. and s. Ont. to Fla. Keys, west to Ky. and Tex. March–Oct. Locally common.

Pyrausta signatalis (Wlk.)   **Pl. 57 (23)**
Identification: FW rose pink, crossed by sharp, narrow, *toothed, pale yellow am. and pm. lines* (lines sometimes less complete than shown). HW yellowish, shaded with brown. Wingspan 1.5–2.2 cm.
Food: Horsemint and probably other mints.
Range: N.J. and s. Ont. to S.C., west to Minn., S.D., and Tex. May–Sept.

Pyrausta bicoloralis (Gn.)   **Pl. 57 (17)**
Identification: Wings deep orangish yellow with *wide outer borders* of dark reddish brown, becoming blackish at margins. Lines reddish brown but inconspicuous. Wingspan 1.4–1.9 cm.
Food: Unrecorded.
Range: N.S. to Fla., west to Mich. and Tex. June–Sept.

Pyrausta subsequalis (Gn.)   **Pl. 57 (19)**
Identification: FW in ♀ (shown) sharply patterned orange or yellow and blackish; HW black with *3 bright orange bands.* FW in ♂ dull grayish brown; HW black with 1–2 dull orange bands. Wingspan 1.6–2.1 cm.
Food: Thistles.
Range: Throughout our area. May–Aug.
Similar species: *P. orphisalis* Wlk., not shown, is slightly smaller. FW dark brown with a *large orange pm. spot* near costa; wide orange pm. band on HW. Food: Savory and *Monarda* species. Range: Throughout our area. May–Aug.

Pyrausta tyralis (Gn.)   **Pl. 57 (24)**
Identification: Similar to *P. signatalis* (above, Pl. 57), but FW *deep crimson* with wider, *deeper yellow lines.* HW crimson, orangish toward base. Wingspan 1.2–1.6 cm.
Food: Wild coffee.
Range: N.Y. to Fla., west to Ill. and Tex. June–Oct. Common southward.

Pyrausta acrionalis (Wlk.)   **Pl. 57 (22)**
Identification: FW deep rose to violet; *yellow along costa* near apex, and along terminal areas and fringes of all wings. Am. and pm. lines edged unevenly with yellow; median blotches also yellow. HW rose to gray with thin yellow median bar. Wingspan 1.4–1.8 cm.
Food: Mints.
Range: N.S. to Fla., west to Man., Mo., and Tex. April–Oct. Common.

Pyrausta niveicilialis (Grt.)   **Pl. 58 (4)**
Identification: Wings dark grayish brown with *white fringes;* yellowish brown outer edging of pm. line usually present toward FW costa. Wingspan 1.8–2.7 cm.
Food: Unrecorded.
Range: S. Ont. to Fla. and westward. April–Oct. Local; usually uncommon.

CELERY LEAFTIER MOTH   **Pl. 56 (25)**
Udea rubigalis (Gn.)
Identification: Very similar to *A. rantalis* (p. 398, Pl. 56), but *pm. line sharper and darker.* HW has faint, even pm. line and black discal *spot.* Wingspan 1.6–2 cm.
Food: Many low plants. Larva (**Celery Leaftier**) attacks beans, beets, celery, and spinach; may also be a pest in greenhouses.
Range: Common throughout our area. Feb.–Nov.

Diacme elealis (Wlk.)   **Pl. 57 (9)**
Identification: Wings straw yellow with grayish brown lines, costal edging, and wide borders. FW has *2 large spots along costa,* representing tops of am. and median lines. Wingspan 1.7–2.3 cm.
Food: Unrecorded.
Range: Va. to Fla., west to Ky. and Tex. April–Sept. Common southward.

Epipagis huronalis (Gn.)   **Pl. 57 (11)**
Identification: *FW very narrow;* acutely pointed in ♂, less so in ♀ (shown). Wings translucent white, tinted with pale yellow; lines, veins, and apical areas yellowish brown to dark brown. HW crossed by *2 sharp brown lines.* Wingspan 2–2.5 cm.
Food: Unrecorded.
Range: N.C. and Ky. to Fla., west to Ark. and Tex. May–Sept. Common southward.

Nomophila nearctica Mun.   **Pl. 56 (20)**
Identification: FW narrow, rounded at tip, brown with fine grayish brown veins and streaks. Heaviest markings are large grayish brown orbicular, claviform, and reniform *spots* and *curved midsection* of pm. line. HW lighter, unmarked. Wingspan 2.4–3.5 cm.
Food: Wide variety of low plants such as celery, grasses, *Polygonum* species, and sweet clover.
Range: Common to abundant throughout our area, sometimes migrating to the far north. April–Oct.

GRAPE LEAFFOLDER MOTH   **Pl. 56 (11)**
Desmia funeralis (Hbn.)
Identification: Head black with a *few white scales.* FW long, narrow, and pointed; black, with 2 white spots. Note *large white blotch* on each HW. Fringes partly white. Wingspan 2.1–2.8 cm.
Food: Larva (**Grape Leaffolder**) feeds on evening-primrose and redbud as well as on wild and domestic grapes, but apparently not a major vineyard pest.
Range: Common throughout our area. April–Sept.; 2–3 broods. Frequently seen in the daytime, but also comes to lights at night.

Desmia maculalis Westwood   **Pl. 56 (14)**
Identification: Almost identical to Grape Leaffolder Moth (above) but usually *slightly smaller;* look for prominent *white patch* on top of head (slight white scaling in Grape Leaffolder Moth). White wing spots not reliable features, since they vary between sexes in both species. Wingspan 1.8–2.4 cm.
Food: Probably same as for Grape Leaffolder; records unreliable due to confusion between the 2 species.
Range: Va. to Fla., west to Ky. Probably occurs more widely, but records confused. May–Sept. Less common than Grape Leaffolder Moth.

SPOTTED BEET WEBWORM MOTH   **Pl. 56 (16)**
Hymenia perspectalis (Hbn.)
Identification: Wings dark brown with white lines. FW median line broken, *very narrow toward inner margin.* HW median line complete,

somewhat tapering, with an *outward bulge* at midpoint. Wingspan 1.6–2.2 cm.
Food: Larva (**Spotted Beet Webworm**) feeds on amaranth, beets, chard, potatoes, and various green house plants.
Range: Me. to Fla., west to Mich., Ill., and Tex. May–Nov. Common.

HAWAIIAN BEET WEBWORM MOTH Pl. 56 (15)
Spoladea recurvalis (F.)
Identification: Similar to Spotted Beet Webworm Moth (above), but white lines *sharper* and *broader. No* outward bulge in HW median line. Wingspan 1.9–2.1 cm.
Food: Larva (**Hawaiian Beet Webworm**) feeds on amaranth, beets, chard, and various weeds; sometimes a pest.
Range: N.Y. to Fla., west to Ill. and Tex. May; Aug.–Oct.; 2 broods. Common southward and in the tropics.

Blepharomastix ranalis (Gn.) Pl. 57 (7)
Identification: Wings shiny; pale yellowish tan, with sharp brown spots and lines. Orbicular and reniform spots hollow. Pm. line *turns sharply inward, then downward* before meeting inner margin. Wingspan 1.6–2 cm.
Food: Leaves of a *Chenopodium* species.
Range: Ont. to Fla., west to Mo. and Tex. April–Oct. Common.

PICKLEWORM MOTH Pl. 57 (5)
Diaphania nitidalis (Stoll)
Identification: Wings iridescent purplish brown. FW has translucent yellow *patch that continues* onto HW, filling all but broad marginal brown HW border. Note conspicuous anal tuft, present in both sexes of *Diaphania* species. Wingspan 2.5–3.2 cm.
Food: Larva (**Pickleworm**) feeds on stems, blossoms, and fruits of cucumbers, gourds, melons and squashes; a pest southward.
Range: Me. to Fla., west to Neb. and Tex. Aug.–Oct.; all months in Fla., where it is common.

MELONWORM MOTH Pl. 56 (18)
Diaphania hyalinata (L.)
Identification: Wings pearly translucent white. FW has *broad black costal border* that continues on *outer margins* of all wings; black band also extends across thorax. Note anal tufts. Wingspan 2.7–3 cm.
Food: Cucumber, melons, pumpkins and squash; larva prefers foliage. A pest in Gulf states.
Range: Que. to Fla. west to Kans. and Tex. Oct.–Nov. northward; all months except Feb. and Dec. in Fla., where it is common.

Palpita magniferalis (Wlk.) Pl. 58 (1)
Identification: Wings pearly translucent gray with *black speckling* and diffuse *black median band.* HW brownish. Wingspan 2.3–2.7 cm.
Food: Ashes.
Range: Me. and Que. to Fla., west to Man. and Tex. April–Oct. Common to abundant.

Polygrammodes flavidalis (Gn.)   **Pl. 57 (16)**
Identification: Wings pearly white overlaid with yellow, especially toward margins. FW has *5 irregular brown lines*. Note *brown orbicular dot*. Wingspan 2.4–3.5 cm.
Food: Ironweed; larva bores into roots.
Range: N.Y. to Fla., west to Ill. and e. Tex. June–Sept. Common.

Polygrammodes langdonalis (Grt.)   **Pl. 57 (18)**
Identification: Wings pale translucent cream to yellow with *iridescent purplish brown* basal shading, fragments of lines, discal spots, and broad st. bands. Wingspan 2.6–3.3 cm.
Food: Ironweed.
Range: N.J. to Tenn., west to Ill. Late June–Aug. Rare.

Compacta capitalis (Grt.)   **Pl. 57 (15)**
Identification: Wings translucent pearly white with narrow blackish brown lines and small, *hollow orbicular spot*. Wingspan 3–3.7 cm.
Food: Unrecorded.
Range: Va. to Fla., west to Ill. and Tex. June. Rare.

BASSWOOD LEAFROLLER MOTH   **Pl. 57 (14)**
Pantographa limata (Grt. & Rob.)
Identification: Wings white with yellow and brown shading. Sharpest markings are brown lines, especially terminal lines, *hollow* orbicular, claviform, and reniform *spots*. Wingspan 3–3.7 cm.
Food: Larva (**Basswood Leafroller**) feeds on basswood, oaks, and rock elms.
Range: Me. and Que. to n. Fla., west to w. Ont. and Tex. April–Aug. Common.

Herpetogramma thestealis (Wlk.)   **Pl. 56 (26)**
Identification: Body long, slender. Wings yellowish white with *purple sheen;* lines, veins and spots dark brown. FW has heavy brown shading along costa and outer margin. St. line *deeply zigzag* on all wings. Wingspan 2.8–3.3 cm.
Food: Euonymus, hazelnut, and linden.
Range: Me. to Fla., west to Man. and Tex. May–Sept. Common.

Pilocrocis ramentalis Led.   **Pl. 56 (17)**
Identification: Wings evenly dark grayish brown, with *3 irregular white lines* on FW, 1 on HW. Wingspan 2.4–2.9 cm.
Food: Button hemp, cardinal's guard, and false nettle (Fla.).
Range: N.Y. to Fla., west to Ont. and Tex. Sept.–early Nov. northward. Common.

Conchylodes ovulalis (Gn.)   **Pl. 56 (19)**
Identification: Wings white with violet sheen. FW marked with *6 blackish brown lines* and prominent *hollow reniform spot*. Wingspan 2.3–2.8 cm.
Food: Unrecorded.
Range: W. Pa. to Fla., west to Mo. and Tex. May–Sept. Common.

Subfamily Schoenobiinae

Scirpophaga perstrialis (Hbn.)   **Pl. 58 (18)**
Identification: FW dark brown with even, *silvery white stripe* from base to apex. HW white with slight grayish brown shading. Body very long. Wingspan 2.6–3.5 cm.
Food: Larva bores in aquatic and marsh plants, possibly only in sedges and other reedy plants.
Range: Mass. to Fla., west to Mich. and Tex. All months in Fla. Rare northward; very local.

Subfamily Crambinae

Crambus agitatellus Clem.   **Pl. 58 (12)**
Identification: FW squared as in other *Crambus* species; tiny black dots among silvery scales along terminal line. Lower half of FW deep yellow, upper half white, crossed by *sharply angled brown pm. line* and *thin, rounded st. line.* Blackish streaks extend from pm. line to outer margin; HW white with gray shading. Wingspan 1.7–2.2 cm.
Food: Grasses and other low plants.
Range: Me. to W. Va., west to Ind., Ky., and Tex. June–Aug. Common.

Crambus laqueatellus Clem.   **Pl. 58 (10)**
Identification: Similar to *C. agitatellus* (above) but larger, with narrower FW. Note *silvery white border* along costa, bisected by *brown lengthwise streak. Faint dark streaks* extend inward from outer margin (not just row of terminal dots, as in *C. agitatellus*). Pm. and st. lines barely visible; streaks do not contrast much with FW ground color. Wingspan 2.3–3 cm.
Food: Mosses.
Range: Me. to S.C. and Miss., west to Ky., Ark., and Tex. April–July. Common.

VAGABOND CRAMBUS   **Pl. 58 (14)**
Agriphila vulgivagella (Clem.)
Identification: FW yellowish tan with sharp grayish brown *streaks between veins*; 7 black terminal *dots.* FW *fringe golden bronze.* Wingspan 2–3.9 cm.
Food: Various grasses, including grains.
Range: Throughout our area. Late Aug.–Oct. Locally common.

SOD WEBWORM MOTH   **Pl. 58 (11)**
Pediasia trisecta (Wlk.)
Identification: FW yellowish gray streaked and dusted with brown. 2–3 variably conspicuous *oblique, blackish marks* represent middle of pm. and st. lines. Note *3 white streaks* in outer margin or fringe of FW. HW whitish with brown shading. Wingspan 2.3–3 cm.
Food: Grasses. Larva (**Sod Webworm**) spins webbing and can kill large patches of lawn turf, on which it is a major pest.
Range: Me. to N.C. and Miss., west to Man. and Tex. May–Aug.; Aug.–Oct. 2 broods. Common to abundant; moths fly low above lawns during the day but also come to lights.

Microcrambus elegans (Clem.)   **Pl. 64 (5)**
Identification: Wings silvery white. FW variably *shaded with brown*, heaviest in upper pm. area. St. line sharp, even, parallel to outer margin. Look for 7 blackish terminal dots. Wingspan 1.2–1.5 cm.
Food: Grasses.
Range: Me. and Ont. to Fla., west to Kans. and the Gulf Coast. April–Sept. Common.

Urola nivalis (Dru.)   **Pl. 48 (20)**
Identification: *Silvery white.* FW has dark brown terminal line and *tiny spot* midway on inner margin; fringe paler brown. HW translucent white (looks gray on black background). Wingspan 1.5–2.3 cm.
Food: Grasses.
Range: Me. and s. Canada to Fla., west to Ill. and Tex. May–Sept.; 2 broods. Common southward.

Vaxi auratella (Clem.)   **Pl. 59 (7)**
Identification: Wings silvery white. Yellow median line on FW *widens* toward inner margin where it connects with narrow yellow terminal line. Wingspan 1.5–1.8 cm.
Food: Unrecorded.
Range: Me. and Que. to Fla., west to Man. and Tex. June–Aug.
Similar species: In *V. critica* (Fbs.), not shown, median line yellow but *does not widen* toward inner margin. Food: Unrecorded. Range: Me. and S. Ont. to Fla., west at least to e. Ky. June–Aug.; March–July in Fla.

Subfamily Pyralinae

MEAL MOTH *Pyralis farinalis* L.   **Pl. 59 (1)**
Identification: Wings dull brownish scarlet. FW *olive brown* in median area, defined by *white am. and pm. lines* that continue onto HW. Wingspan 1.5–3 cm.
Food: Larva a serious pest of stored grain and grain products.
Range: Common throughout our area. All year.

GREASE MOTH *Aglossa cuprina* Zell.   **Pl. 58 (6)**
Identification: FW yellowish tan, *heavily mottled with dull red and gray;* median area sometimes mostly gray. Usually greasy looking. Lines zigzag, gray. Orbicular spot usually filled with ground color and some *red*. HW dirty whitish. Wingspan 1.8–2.7 cm.
Food: Unrecorded; a related species is a scavenger.
Range: N.H. to Fla., west to Ky. and Tex. June–Sept. Locally common.

CLOVER HAYWORM MOTH   **Pl. 59 (3)**
Hypsopygia costalis (F.)
Identification: Wings rose, grayish in some specimens. Note the *very wide yellow fringes* on all wings. Am. and pm. lines yellow, broadened at costa to form spots. Wingspan 1.3–1.9 cm.
Food: Larva (**Clover Hayworm**) feeds on stored hay; sometimes a pest.
Range: Me. to N.C., west to Ky. and Miss. May–Sept. Common.

Herculia infimbrialis Dyar   **Pl. 59 (8)**
Identification: Larger and *much paler rose* than Clover Hayworm Moth (above), but tops of am. and pm. lines usually less widened at costa; lower pm. line curves slightly inward. *Fringes pale rose.* Wingspan 2–2.5 cm.
Food: Unrecorded.
Range: Me. to S.C., west to Ky. May–Sept. Uncommon.

Herculia olinalis (Gn.)   **Pl. 59 (4)**
Identification: Similar to Clover Hayworm Moth (above), but slightly larger; ground color varies from rose to deep purplish. Widened *tops of* am. and pm. *lines more triangular.* Yellow fringes narrower. Wingspan 1.6–2.4 cm.
Food: Oaks.
Range: Common throughout our area. May–Sept.

Subfamily Chrysauginae

Galasa nigrinodis (Zell.)   **Pl. 59 (6)**
Identification: FW dull red with gray accenting *slight dip* at middle of costa. Lines whitish, usually distinct only at costa. HW whitish to gray. Wingspan 1.3–2 cm.
Food: Larva ties together and eats dead leaves of boxwood.
Range: S. Me. and Ont. to Fla., west to Man. and Tex. June–Sept. Common.

Tosale oviplagalis (Wlk.)   **Pl. 58 (7, 9)**
Identification: Sexually dimorphic: FW dull reddish brown and gray in ♂; gray in ♀, sometimes with reddish brown shading. *Large dark blotch in am. area* in both sexes. ♂ also has large round blotch along HW costa; HW unmarked in ♀. Wingspan 1.3–1.7 cm.
Food: Unrecorded.
Range: N.Y. to Fla., west to Ill. and Tex. May–Sept. Common.

Clydonopteron tecomae Riley   **Pl. 59 (5)**
Identification: *FW costa very wavy.* FW brownish crimson, washed with orange to pm. line; some gray shading in st. area. White dash inward from costa at top of pm. line. Wingspan 1.5–2.5 cm.
Food: Trumpet creeper; larva feeds and pupates in seedpods.
Range: Wash., D.C. to Fla., west to Mo. and e. Tex. May–Aug. Locally common.

Condylolomia participialis Grt.   **Pl. 59 (2)**
Identification: FW pale gray to yellowish, with an *olive tint* when fresh; reddish shading toward outer margin. Faint, even, am. and pm. lines. FW in ♂ has *fold with dark scale tuft* on costa. HW dark gray. Wingspan 1.2–1.5 cm.
Food: *Myrica* species (?).
Range: Mass. to w. N.C., west to Ill. and Miss. June–Aug. Common.

Subfamily *Epipaschiinae*

Epipaschia superatalis Clem.	**Pl. 58 (17)**
Identification: Wings grayish tan, dusted variably with gray and black; reddish brown beyond *toothed* black *pm. line.* Am. line black, widest at costa. Discal dot black. Wingspan 1.7–2.5 cm.
Food: Unrecorded.
Range: N.H. and Ont. to Fla., west to Ky. and La. Late May–Aug. Common.

Tetralopha asperatella (Clem.)	**Pl. 58 (15)**
Identification: FW gray with some brown shading, darkest toward base; *median area white.* Am. line double, nearly straight. Pm. line more diffuse; upper half bulges outward. HW dark grayish brown. Wingspan 2–2.5 cm.
Food: Reported on beech, elm, hickory, honey locust, hornbeam, maples, and staghorn sumac.
Range: N.S. to Fla., west to Wisc. and Tex. Late May–Aug. Common.

Subfamily *Galleriinae*

GREATER WAX MOTH	**Pl. 58 (13, 16)**
Galleria mellonella (L.)
Identification: FW outer margin *concave,* more deeply so in ♂ than in ♀. FW gray, with broad brown shade along inner margin, narrowing to anal angle; variable black streaking. Vague curved pm. line of black dots. HW dirty translucent whitish with variable light grayish brown shading. Wingspan 2.5–3.5 cm.; ♀ larger than ♂.
Food: Beeswax; larva forms webs over combs in neglected hives.
Range: Worldwide; common wherever honeybees occur in our area. July–Oct. northward. Adult sometimes flies to lights.
Similar species: Lesser Wax Moth, *Achroia grisella* (F.), not shown, is *smaller* (wingspan 1.7–2.2 cm.). Wings shaped much like those of *Urodus parvula* (p. 431, Pl. 62), but FW uniform gray, HW paler gray; *frons yellow.* Food: Beeswax, dried apples and other fruits, crude sugar, pollen, and dead insects. A minor pest. Range: Worldwide. Adults fly during any warm period of the year.

Omphalocera munroei Martin	**Pl. 58 (8)**
Identification: FW dark red, *basal area yellowish*; median area darker than beyond toothed pm. line. Discal spot a yellowish vertical dash. Wingspan 2.9–3.7 cm.
Food: Larva bores into pawpaw fruit.
Range: Wash., D.C. to Fla., west to s. Ill. and Tex. Late July–early Aug. Uncommon.

Subfamily *Phycitinae*

Euzophera ostricolorella Hulst	**Pl. 59 (10)**
Identification: FW long and narrow; maroon, with gray median area

defined by *paler gray am. and pm. lines*. HW shiny grayish. Wingspan 3.4–4.1 cm.

Food: Tulip-tree.

Range: N.Y. to Fla., west to Ky. and Miss. May–early Nov. Common.

Similar species: *E. magnolialis* Capps (not shown) is an almost identical species recently described from the deep South; larva feeds on evergreen magnolia.

INDIAN-MEAL MOTH   Pl. 58 (20)
Plodia interpunctella (Hbn.)

Identification: FW base tan to gray with greenish tint when fresh, fading after death. Outer part *dull reddish brown*, crossed by irregular, inconspicuous, shiny lead-colored lines. HW translucent dirty whitish with grayish brown terminal line. Wingspan 1.1–1.6 cm.

Food: A major pest of stored grains, grain products, and dried vegetable products.

Range: Worldwide. All stages of life cycle may be found indoors all year; moth flies to lights outside in warm months.

Similar species: Mediterranean Flour Moth, *Anagasta kuehniella* (Zell.), not shown, infests the same materials and has same distribution and habits as Indian-meal Moth. FW evenly pale bluish gray to gray. *Zigzag* am. line and *toothed* pm. line *paler*, edged with darker gray. Discal spot darker gray. HW translucent white. Another major pest of cereals.

ALMOND MOTH   Pl. 64 (25)
Cadra cautella (Wlk.)

Identification: FW variable, brownish to blackish gray; *straight, almost vertical am. line* separates *paler basal area* from rest of FW. Pm. and st. lines darker gray, sometimes obscure. HW translucent, dark along veins and outer margin (including fringe). Wingspan 1.1–2 cm.

Food: Figs and other dried fruits, nuts, and grains; sometimes a minor pest in honeycombs.

Range: Worldwide, but not common in any part of our area. Adults fly in all months in warm habitats.

Remarks: Also known as the Dried Currant Moth or Fig Moth.

Similar species: (1) The Raisin Moth, *C. figulilella* (Gregson), not shown, is almost identical; am. line sometimes more oblique, but not a reliable feature. Same food, range, and habits as for Almond Moth. (2) Indian-meal Moth (above) also has pale basal area and straight, vertical am. line, but outer FW *reddish brown*.

Subfamily Peoriinae

Peoria approximella (Wlk.)   Pl. 59 (9)

Identification: FW deep pink; costa and inner margins bordered with yellowish white. Some *blackish* along basal half of costa. HW translucent whitish. Wingspan 1.4–2 cm.

Food: Unrecorded.

Range: N.S. to s. Ga., west to Man. and Tex. May–Sept. Common.

PLANTHOPPER PARASITE MOTHS:
Family Epipyropidae

Small; wingspan 0.9–1 cm. Wings blackish, broad. Antennae *bipectinate* to tip in *both sexes*. All FW *veins unstalked* (Fig. 36). *Sc of HW fused with R_1* from base to outer margin. Rs well separated from Sc + R_1. Frenulum a single spine in both sexes.

Eggs laid on plants frequented by planthoppers (Homoptera, super-family Fulgoroidea). First-instar larva attaches itself to the planthopper, on which it becomes an ectoparasite, sucking body fluids from the abdomen beneath the wings. Some life-cycle details are still not known for our single N. American species.

PLANTHOPPER PARASITE MOTH   **Pl. 57 (3)**
Fulgoraecia exigua (Hy. Edw.)
Identification: Smoky black; *wings broad, unmarked.* Antennae bipectinate with very long branches for length of shaft. Wingspan 0.9–1 cm.
Food: Larva (**Planthopper Parasite**) sucks body fluids from various planthoppers.
Range: N.J. and Pa. to cen. Fla., west to Mo. and Tex. June–Oct. Uncommon to common.
Similar species: Small bagworm moths such as *Cryptothelea gloverii* (p. 450, Pl. 62) have similar black, unmarked, broad wings, but are *larger* (wingspan at least 1.4 cm) and have shorter branches on their bipectinate antennae.

SLUG CATERPILLAR MOTHS:
Family Limacodidae

Medium to medium-small moths with stout, often hairy bodies and broad, rounded wings. Wingspan 1.5–4.3 cm. Most are brown or yellow-ish with contrasting FW markings. Head small, retracted; labial palps short; maxillary palps and proboscis short or absent. Antennae bipectinate in δ, at least in basal half. Radial veins of FW branched (Fig. 37); M_2 *arises near* M_3; *2 complete* anal veins; *3A fused with 2A* not far from FW base. Sc + R_1 and Rs of HW *fused* for short distance *at or before middle of discal cell;* 3 anal veins.

Larvae naked to densely hairy (Pl. 1), usually with *stinging hairs.* Thoracic legs short. Like slugs, these caterpillars move with a gliding motion, with abdominal prolegs replaced by suckers. Slug caterpillars feed on many woody and herbaceous plants. Larva overwinters in loose, oval cocoon. About 50 N. American species.

Tortricidia testacea Pack.   **Pl. 55 (24)**
Identification: FW yellow-brown, with *dark brown veins.* Broad, dif-fuse *orange brown shade* from apex to middle of median area. HW cream. Wingspan 1.5–2.6 cm.
Food: Beeches, birches, black cherry, chestnut, oaks, and witch-hazel.
Range: N.S. to sw. Va., west to Man., Mo., and Miss. April–Aug. Com-mon.

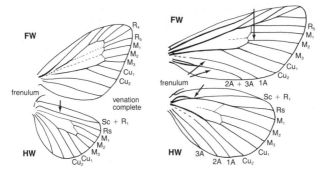

Fig. 36. Wing venation, Epipyropidae.

Fig. 37. Wing venation, Limacodidae.

Tortricidia flexuosa (Grt.)   Pl. 55 (19)
Identification: FW pale yellow to orange-yellow. Faint, diffuse brown pm. and st. *lines join below costa* to form an *inverted* ∪. Area between lines sometimes solid brown. HW cream. Wingspan 1.5–2.5 cm.
Food: Apple, black cherry, chestnut, hazelnut, hickory, oak, and plum trees.
Range: N.S. to Va., west to Mo. and Miss. April–Aug. Common.

Packardia geminata (Pack.)   Pl. 55 (22)
Identification: Wings cream to light straw yellow, with brown veins and shading between pm. and st. lines of FW. *1-3 sharp white terminal spots* near anal angle. Wingspan 1.7–2.5 cm.
Food: Birches, hickories, oaks, spruce, and other trees and shrubs.
Range: N.S. to w. N.C., west to Wisc. and n. Ark. May–July. Uncommon.

Lithacodes fasciola (H.-S.)   Pl. 55 (23)
Identification: FW orangish brown, crossed by *toothed white pm. line.* Gray and brown shading beyond line. St. line rounded, dark brown; curves from top of pm. line to outer margin. Wingspan 1.8–2.5 cm.
Food: Apple, beeches, birches, elms, hickories, linden, oaks, willows, and other trees and shrubs.
Range: Common throughout our area. April–early Sept.

Apoda y-inversum (Pack.)   Pl. 55 (21)
Identification: FW light orange-yellow. Am. and pm. lines dark brown, sometimes with dark brown shading between. *2 thinner lines form an* X near anal angle. HW paler. Wingspan 2.1–3 cm.
Food: Beeches, hickories, ironwood, and oaks.
Range: Gaspé, Que. to Fla., west to s. Ont., Ark. and Miss. May–Aug. Common.

Apoda biguttata (Pack.)   Pl. 55 (25)
Identification: FW brown in basal half, gray in outer half, 2 halves

separated by oblique yellow median line. Dark brown patch at apex; *dark brown spot* on inner margin near anal angle—both edged with yellow. HW even grayish brown. Wingspan 1.9–3 cm.

Food: Blue beech, hickories, and oaks.

Range: N.S. and Que. to Fla., west to Mo. and Tex. April–Aug. Locally common.

SKIFF MOTH *Prolimacodes badia* (Hbn.)   **Pl. 56 (5)**
Identification: FW pale brown tinted with white at base. Dark brown along costa near base widens to form a *semicircular patch* covering most of FW, narrowing to costa at apex. Patch has blackish reniform dot and lower edge *bordered with white*. HW brown. Wingspan 2.4–3.5 cm.

Food: Birches, blueberries, chestnut, hornbeams, *Myrica* species, oaks, poplars, *Prunus* species, willows, and other woody plants.

Range: N.H. to Fla., west to s. Ont., Mo., Ark., and Miss. May–Sept. Common; sometimes abundant in Fla.

Isochaetes beutenmuelleri (Hy. Edw.)   **Pl. 55 (20)**
Identification: FW yellowish with vague orangish brown lines and shading; sharpest marking a circular *brown spot* at midpoint between pm. and st. shades. ♀ darker than ♂ (shown); the spot thicker and blackish. Wingspan 1.9–2.4 cm.

Food: Swamp oak.

Range: Se. N.Y. to Fla., west to Mo. and Miss. June–Aug. Uncommon.

HAG MOTH   **Pls. 1 (2); 56 (7, 10)**
Phobetron pithecium (J.E. Sm.)
Identification: Body black. Wings in ♂ *translucent*; veins, margins, vague lines and discal spot black. HW black along inner margin. FW in ♀ mixed *yellow and brown*; irregular am. and pm. lines and discal spot *black*. HW smoky blackish. Wingspan 2–2.8 cm; ♀ larger than ♂.

Food: Apple, ashes, birches, chestnut, dogwoods, hickories, oaks, persimmon, willows, and other woody plants. Larva (**Monkey Slug,** Pl. 1) has stinging hairs.

Range: Me. and Que. to Fla., west to Neb., Ark., and Miss. May–Sept. Uncommon as adult.

NASON'S SLUG MOTH   **Pl. 55 (16)**
Natada nasoni (Grt.)
Identification: FW yellowish tan with heavy brown shading except toward apex and outer margin. 2 even *dark brown lines converge* toward apex, but do not meet. ♀ paler brown. Wingspan 1.6–2.9 cm.

Food: Beeches, chestnuts, hickories, hornbeams, oaks, and other trees and shrubs.

Range: Me. to Fla., west to Mo. and Miss. June–Aug. Uncommon.

Isa textula (H.-S.)   **Pl. 55 (17)**
Identification: FW brown; inconspicuous *gray shading* in pm. area and apical half of terminal area. *No prominent markings*. HW brown. Wingspan 1.7–2.5 cm.

Food: Elms, hickories, lindens, maples, oaks, *Prunus* species, and other trees and shrubs.
Range: Mass. and s. Ont. to Fla., west to Mo. and Miss. May–Aug. Locally common.

Adoneta spinuloides (H.-S.)   **Pl. 55 (15)**
Identification: FW light to dark brown with black veins and median streak. Pm. line *white, wavy*, expressed *only* toward costa and inner margin. HW pale grayish brown. Wingspan 1.6–2.4 cm.
Food: Beeches, birches, chestnut, linden, *Prunus* species, willows, and other trees and shrubs.
Range: N.H. and Que. to N.C. (Fla.?); west to Mo. and Miss. May–Sept. Common northward.

Monoleuca semifascia (Wlk.)   **Pl. 55 (18)**
Identification: FW brown, sometimes reddish brown; only marking a narrow, *wavy, silvery white to yellowish line* above inner margin. Wingspan 1.9–2.7 cm.
Food: Unrecorded.
Range: N.C. to Fla., west to Mo. and Tex. June–Aug. Uncommon northward.

SPINY OAK-SLUG MOTH   **Pl. 55 (10, 14)**
Euclea delphinii (Bdv.)
Identification: FW brown with some orange and purplish shading. *Green patches* in median area bordered with *white*, varying from large to nearly absent. Discal streak brown to black. HW brown. Wingspan 1.9–3.1 cm.
Food: Larva (**Spiny Oak-slug**) feeds on apple, beeches, chestnut, linden, maples, oaks, *Prunus* species, sycamore, willows, and other woody plants.
Range: Me. and s. Que. to Fla., west to Mo. and La. May–Aug. Common.

SMALLER PARASA   **Pl. 55 (11)**
Parasa chloris (H.-S.)
Identification: Thorax green. FW brown with large *green patch* that has a *nearly straight outer edge*. No darker brown patch in brown terminal border as in Stinging Rose Caterpillar Moth (below). HW yellowish with broad brownish border. Wingspan 1.8–2.7 cm.
Food: Woody plants, such as apple, dogwood, elms, and oaks.
Range: N.Y. to Fla., west to Mo. and Miss. May–Aug. More common than Stinging Rose Caterpillar Moth.

STINGING ROSE CATERPILLAR MOTH   **Pl. 55 (8)**
Parasa indetermina (Bdv.)
Identification: Similar to Smaller Parasa (above), but larger. Outer edge of green patch on FW *more rounded*. Look for *dark brown patch* in lighter brown outer margin. HW yellowish with narrow brown border. Wingspan 2.3–3 cm.
Food: Larva (**Stinging Rose Caterpillar**) feeds on apple, dogwood, hickory, maples, oaks, poplars, and rose bushes.
Range: N.Y. to Fla., west to Mo. and Tex. June–July. Uncommon.

SADDLEBACK CATERPILLAR MOTH   Pls. 1 (8); 56 (8)
Sibine stimulea (Clem.)
Identification: Wings glossy dark chocolate brown with black shading; *1 white dot* near FW base, *1-3 more* near apex. HW paler brown. Wingspan 2.6–4.3 cm; ♀ larger than ♂.
Food: Many plants, including apple, asters, blueberries, citrus, corn, dogwoods, elms, grapes, linden, maples, oaks, *Prunus* species, sunflowers, and viburnums. Larva (**Saddleback Caterpillar,** Pl. 1) can inflict a painful *sting* with sharp bristles on its body.
Range: Mass. to Fla., west to e. Mo. and Tex. June–July. Uncommon to common; larva often more commonly found than adult.

FLANNEL MOTHS:
Family Megalopygidae

Medium-sized moths, with *stout, hairy* bodies. Wings broad, usually with some *wrinkled hair-scales* on FW near costa; wingspan 2.4–4 cm. Mouth parts reduced, hidden in dense hair; antennae in ♂ broadly bipectinate to apex. Wings usually white, yellow, or brownish, with almost no markings. Veins R_2 to R_5 of FW *branch* beyond end of discal cell (Fig. 38); M_2 arises close to M_3; 2 anal veins. Sc + R_1 and Rs *fused* along top of discal cell *except at base*; 3 anal veins. Frenulum reduced in *Megalopyge* species (below).
    Larvae have stinging hairs hidden among tufts of dense, soft hairs. They feed externally on various trees and shrubs. Only 11 species in N. America, 3 in our area.

BLACK-WAVED FLANNEL MOTH   Pl. 56 (9)
Lagoa crispata (Pack.)
Identification: Body and wings pale yellowish cream. FW costa has several *sharp, wavy black lines* with variable brownish shading beneath them. HW unmarked. Wingspan 2.5–4 cm.
Food: Alder, apple, birches, blackberry, *Myrica* species, oaks, poplars, *Prunus* species, sassafras, willows, and other trees and shrubs.
Range: N.H. to Fla., west to Mo. and La. May–Oct. Common in most of range.
Remarks: This species is called the White Flannel Moth in Holland's *Moth Book*, but that name is better suited to *Norape ovina* (p. 413, Pl. 13).

SOUTHERN FLANNEL MOTH   Pl. 56 (12)
Megalopyge opercularis (J.E. Sm.)
Identification: Wings and body cream; thorax and FW base *orangish*. Some *blackish* and white along basal ⅔ of FW costa, but no sharp wing pattern. Wingspan 2.4–3.6 cm.
Food: Almond, apple, hackberry, oaks, orange, pecan, persimmon, roses, and other trees and shrubs.
Range: Md. to Fla., west to Mo. and Tex. Strays to N.Y. and Pa. All months and common southward.
Similar species: Yellow Flannel Moth, *Lagoa pyxidifera* (J.E. Sm.),

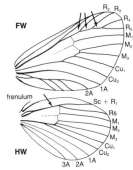

Fig. 38. Wing venation, Megalopygidae.

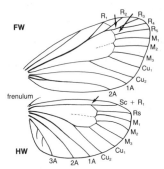

Fig. 39. Wing venation, Zygaenidae.

not shown, is *entirely orange-yellow, without* markings. Food: Blueberries, oaks, and plum. Range: Pa. to Fla., west to Miss. All year. Common southward.

WHITE FLANNEL MOTH   Pl. 13 (15)
Norape ovina (Sepp)
Identification: Wings and body pure, *gleaming white;* separated from other all-white moths by wing shape and *stout, hairy body.* HW rounded. Branches of ♂ antennae orangish. Wingspan 2.7–3.3 cm.
Food: Hackberry and redbud.
Range: Wash., D.C. to Fla., west to se. Mo. and La. April–May; July–Sept. Rare northward; common in Fla.

SMOKY MOTHS:
Family Zygaenidae

Medium to medium-small moths, with translucent smoky gray to blackish wings. Wingspan 1.6–2.8 cm. Adults have ocelli and prominent chaetosemata (bristle patches above eyes—see Fig. 1, p. 2). *Antennae slightly widened, bipectinate in* ♂. Labial palps short, upturned; proboscis naked. Wings narrow to broad; FW rounded at tip. All branches of R arise *separately* from outer end of FW discal cell, or R_3 and R_4 *short-stalked* (Fig. 39) in some species. 1A and 2A present in FW. Sc + R_1 and Rs of HW *fused* from base to near end of discal cell. 1A, 2A, and usually 3A well developed.

These moths are day-fliers, and may be collected as they visit flowers. Larvae feed externally, skeletonizing leaves of members of the grape family.

GRAPELEAF SKELETONIZER MOTH   Pl. 57 (8)
Harrisina americana (Guér.)
Identification: Body black with *red to orange collar.* Wings very narrow, translucent black. Wingspan 1.8–2.8 cm.

Food: Ampelopsis, grapes, redbud, and Virginia creeper. Larvae (**Grapeleaf Skeletonizer**) feeds in groups lined up side by side.

Range: N.H. to Fla., west to Mo. and Tex. April–Oct.

Similar species: Yellow-collared Scape Moth (p. 75, Pl. 11), is *larger,* with a *yellow collar* and more contrastingly translucent HW.

ORANGE-PATCHED SMOKY MOTH   Pl. 57 (4)
Pyromorpha dimidiata H.-S.

Identification: Wings black and *translucent* except for *orange basal half of FW* from costa to vein 1A. Wingspan 1.8–2.8 cm.

Food: Reported feeding on underside of fallen oak leaves.

Range: N.Y. to Fla., west to Man., Mo., and Miss. May–July. Locally common.

Similar species: Black-and-yellow Lichen Moth (p. 61, Pl. 11), has *opaque black and brighter orange* wings; base of HW also orange.

COCHYLID MOTHS:
Family Cochylidae

Small to medium-small moths, wingspan 0.8–2.7 cm. Head scales rough. Ocelli small. Proboscis small or absent, naked if present. Labial palps medium to long, rough-scaled, projecting forward and looking beaklike. Wings moderately long, narrow, and rounded (Fig. 40); *FW usually bent slightly downward at tip,* especially noticeable in live specimens. FW has an areole; Cu$_2$ arises from *outer* $\frac{1}{4}$ of discal cell; *1A absent* (see Tortricidae, next family). HW trapezoidal, broad as FW; Rs and M$_1$ *close together* (as shown) or stalked.

Larval habits vary: some are leaf tiers or miners; others bore in seeds, stems, and other plant parts. Formerly known as Phaloniidae, this family includes about 110 N. American species named so far; many others have yet to be described.

Carolella sartana (Hbn.)   Pl. 63 (24)
Identification: FW orange-yellow, light brown, or gray; median band dark brown, twice as wide at inner margin as at costa. St. line *curved, becoming narrower toward apex* but *not* touching it. HW gray. Wingspan 1–1.4 cm.

Food: Unrecorded.

Range: Pa. to Fla., west to La. All year in Fla.; Aug. northward.

Hysterosia birdana Bsk.   Pl. 60 (13)
Identification: FW gray, shaded with brown, *darkest beyond curved pm. line,* palest in basal area. HW paler grayish brown. Wingspan 1.9–2.7 cm.

Food: Larva bores in roots of sunflowers.

Range: N.Y. to Fla., west to Ky. Late July–Sept. Common.

Conchylis oenotherana Riley   Pl. 61 (3)
Identification: A tiny moth, easily recognized by the *dull yellow base* and *deep pink outer half* of FW. HW dark grayish brown. Wingspan 0.9–1.2 cm.

Food: Evening-primrose.

Range: Me. to Fla., west to Kans. and Ark. Late May–Oct.

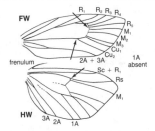

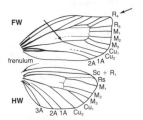

Fig. 40. Wing venation, Cochylidae.

Fig. 41. Wing venation, Tortricidae.

TORTRICID MOTHS:
Family Tortricidae

Small to medium-small moths; wingspan 1–3.3 cm. Head usually rough-scaled; ocelli usually present. Proboscis naked; antennae usually threadlike (filiform). Maxillary palps very small; labial palps usually *project forward,* apical segment *turned down.* Wings moderately broad (Fig. 41); FW usually *squared off* at apex. Costal margin strongly arched or wavy in some species; accessory cell present or absent. Vein Cu_2 arises *before outer $\frac{3}{4}$* of discal cell; 1A evident at outer margin and for a small distance inward. HW broad; 2–3 anal veins. At rest, wings held like a flattened roof, making moth resemble an arrowhead.

Moths in subfamily Olethreutinae (below), sometimes considered a separate family, tend to be brownish to grayish with complex, poorly contrasting FW lines and mottling. *Fringe* of *long hair-scales* usually *along base of* Cu on upper side of HW (except in *Cydia* species, in which M_1 is close to M_2 at tip). R_4 and R_5 *separate* (Fig. 41), or M_2, M_3, and Cu_1 of FW *divergent or parallel.* Moths in subfamily Tortricinae (p. 417) lack fringe along base of Cu and usually have paler FW— reddish, yellowish, or pale brown, with sharper pattern. R_4 and R_5 of FW often *stalked or fused;* M_2, M_3, and Cu_1 *divergent or parallel.*

Larvae are leaf rollers, leaf tiers, or borers in roots, stems, or fruits. Many are serious forest and orchard pests. Also of interest is the Mexican Jumping Bean Moth, *Cydia deshaisiana* (Lucas), not shown, which is sold as a novelty in the hollow seed of its foodplant, *Sebastiana.* The "bean" jumps when the larva throws itself against the seed's wall; the adult emerges by pushing through the bean's shell.

Subfamily Olethreutinae

Olethreutes ferriferana (Wlk.)   **Pl. 58 (22)**
Identification: FW powdery light gray; dark brown basal blotch has straight outer edge. Note the large, *dark brown trapezoidal patch* near FW apex, narrowing toward outer margin. Wingspan 1.5–1.8 cm.

Food: Hydrangea.
Range: Me. to N.C., west to Ky. and Tex. June–July. Common.

Eucosma robinsonana (Grt.)   **Pl. 60 (2)**
Identification: FW crossed by pale and dark brown *stripes*. 2 basal stripes silvery white; outer 2 stripes silvery white only toward costa. HW pale grayish brown. Wingspan 1–1.8 cm.
Food: Unrecorded; probably roots of some asters.
Range: N.J. to Fla., west to Kans. and Tex. Late April–June; Aug.-Oct.; 2 broods.

Eucosma dorsisignatana (Clem.)   **Pl. 58 (24)**
Identification: FW ash gray to brown with faint whitish lines. *Dark brown patch* on inner margin near base; larger, paler brown median patch bounded by costa and pm. line. Markings reduced or absent in some specimens. Wingspan 1.2–2.2 cm.
Food: Roots of goldenrods.
Range: Me. and Que. to N.C., west to Man. and Tex. July–early Oct. Common.

BIDENS BORER MOTH   **Pl. 60 (3)**
Epiblema otiosana (Clem.)
Identification: FW mixed gray, brown, and black; *large silvery white blotch* extends inward from inner margin. Large, rounded whitish spot at anal angle usually inconspicuous because of dark speckling. Wingspan 1.2–2 cm.
Food: Ragweed, Spanish needles, and *Polygonum* species; larva (**Bidens Borer**) bores in wood and pith of stems.
Range: Me. and Ont. to Fla., west to Kans. and Tex. Late May–Sept. Common.

CODLING MOTH   **Pl. 60 (1)**
Cydia pomonella (L.)
Identification: Gray-tipped brown scales make FW look striated. Heavy *dark brown st. line* curves upward and outward from inner margin near anal angle and *loops over* lower terminal area to form an *oval spot*. Wingspan 1.5–2.2 cm.
Food: Fruits of apple, cherry, peach, pear, quince, and walnut trees. A major pest of apple trees.
Range: Originally from Eurasia; now locally common wherever apple trees grow in our area. April–Nov.; 2 broods.

FILBERTWORM MOTH   **Pl. 60 (4)**
Melissopus latiferreanus (Wlsm.)
Identification: FW varies widely from tan to rust or various shades of dark brown. 3 *metallic bands* across FW also vary from brassy to coppery or lead-colored; middle band widest and most complete. HW brownish gray. Wingspan 1.4–1.9 cm.
Food: Larva (**Filbertworm**) feeds on young beechnuts, chestnut burs, or "oak apples" (galls of cynipid wasps on oak trees); filberts (?).
Range: Me. and s. Que. to Fla., west to Kans. and Tex. June–Oct.; 2 broods. Common.

Ecdytolopha punctidiscana (Dyar)   **Pl. 60 (5)**
Identification: FW mixed dark gray, grayish brown, and black. Note *tiny white reniform dot* in black median shade band. HW dark gray. Wingspan 1.7–2.5 cm.
Food: Unrecorded.
Range: Mass. to Fla., west to e. Kans. and Tex. April–Sept. Common.

LOCUST TWIG BORER MOTH   **Pl. 60 (6)**
Ecdytolopha insiticiana Zell.
Identification: FW mottled gray, dark brown, and black, with black speckling beyond oblique pm. line. Note *blackish spots* near FW apex and on inner margin near anal angle. HW grayish brown. Wingspan 2–2.7 cm.
Food: Larva bores into twigs of locust trees and wisteria.
Range: Me. and Ont. to Fla., west to Man. and Tex. Late April–Sept. Common.

Subfamily *Tortricinae*

OAK LEAFTIER MOTH   **Pl. 59 (26)**
Croesia semipurpurana (Kft.)
Identification: FW *bright yellow* at base and along costa and outer margin; *large brown blotch* (dusted with metallic gray scales) covers most of FW. FW blotch sometimes smaller, faint brown instead of dark brown and gray. HW gray; fringe white. Wingspan 1.5–1.6 cm.
Food: Larva (**Oak Leaftier**) feeds on oaks.
Range: N.S. to n. Fla., west to Mo. and Tex. June–July. Locally common.

Croesia curvalana (Kft.)   **Pl. 59 (27)**
Identification: Very similar to Oak Leaftier Moth (above), but with *yellow reniform spot* on FW; brown patch more *reddish*. Wingspan 1.4–1.6 cm.
Food: Reported on huckleberry.
Range: Me. to Fla., west to Mo. and Ark. May–Aug. Locally common.

Acleris subnivana (Wlk.)   **Pl. 60 (23)**
Identification: FW white; similar to Gray-banded Leafroller Moth (p. 418, Pl. 60), but smaller. Costal margin curves inward slightly above *black triangular patch*. HW gray. Wingspan 1.2–1.5 cm.
Food: Red oak; ironweed (?).
Range: N.S. to Ky., west across Canada, south to Tex. April–Aug.; Nov. Common.

Acleris chalybeana (Fern.)   **Pl. 60 (11)**
Identification: FW dark gray; *black basal patch* usually conspicuous. Broad *triangular patch* points inward from costa and may blend with ground color. HW dark grayish brown. Wingspan 1.9–2.2 cm.
Food: Apple, beeches, birches, maples, and oaks.
Range: Me. and Que. to Va., west to Man. and Ky. April–May; July–Nov. Locally common.

Acleris logiana (Cl.)   Pl. 60 (14)

Identification: FW pearly gray, variably streaked with brown; traces of brown lines. Brown costal triangle present in some specimens; sharpest marking is straight *black discal dash*. HW pale gray. Our N. American subspecies is *A. logiana placidana* (Rob.). Wingspan 1.6–2.1 cm.

Food: Birches and viburnums.

Range: Holarctic; Me. and Que. to n. Fla. in our area, west across Canada, south to Mo. March–Nov. Common.

THREE-LINED LEAFROLLER MOTH   Pl. 59 (17)
Pandemis limitata (Rob.)

Identification: FW pale reddish brown, crossed by darker basal and median *bands edged* with slightly *paler brown*. Similar coloring in rounded costal patch near apex. HW whitish with variable gray shading in lower half. White band across abdomen at base. Wingspan 1.6–2.6 cm.

Food: Larva (**Three-lined Leafroller**) feeds on alders, apple, ashes, aspen, birches, elms, maples, oaks, and many other trees. A pest on apple trees.

Range: Me. and Que. to Ga., west to Kans. and Tex. March to mid-Sept.; 2 broods. Common.

RED-BANDED LEAFROLLER MOTH   Pl. 61 (1, 2)
Argyrotaenia velutinana (Wlk.)

Identification: FW orangish and grayish brown. FW in ♂ has oblique median band that is *blackish* in upper half, *brown* in lower half. Small black triangle at costa near apex. ♀ generally larger; median band broader, *entirely brown*. Black costal triangle larger than in ♂. HW whitish with heavy gray shading. Wingspan 1.1–1.8 cm.

Food: Larva (**Red-banded Leafroller**) is the most serious pest of apple trees, eating fruits and foliage; it also attacks cherries, grapes, peaches, plums, spruces, vegetables, and many other plants.

Range: Me. and Que. to Ga., west to Kans. and Tex. March to mid-Sept.; 2 broods. Common.

Argyrotaenia quercifoliana (Fitch)   Pl. 61 (4)

Identification: FW yellowish cream with golden brown speckling. Median and pm. lines brown, oblique, usually complete. Median line joins partial terminal line to form a *hollow circle* in st. area. HW pure white with slight yellow shading in lower half. Wingspan 1.6–2.4 cm.

Food: Oaks, witch-hazel, and buckthorn (?).

Range: Common throughout our area. May–July.

Argyrotaenia alisellana (Rob.)   Pl. 60 (12)

Identification: FW brown with *cream blotches and spots* in basal area and along costa and outer margin. HW white. Wingspan 1.8–2.5 cm.

Food: Oaks.

Range: Me. and Que. to Fla., west to Wisc. and Ark. May–Sept. Locally common.

GRAY-BANDED LEAFROLLER MOTH   Pl. 60 (10)
Argyrotaenia mariana (Fern.)

Identification: FW white with wide, triangular black *costal patch*

divided by *gray line.* Some orange-yellow, brown, and blackish shades and flecks. HW gray. Wingspan 1.6–2.4 cm.
Food: Larva (**Gray-banded Leafroller**) feeds on apple, beeches, birches, blueberries, oaks, and willows. An orchard pest in N.S.
Range: N.S. to Fla., west to Man. and Ky. April–July. Common.

Choristoneura fractivittana (Clem.) **Pl. 59 (20, 21)**
Identification: FW orange-yellow with brown shading; ♂ usually smaller and darker than ♀. Uneven, oblique median band brown, with *ground color across* upper part in ♂, *less* so in ♀. Narrow brown subapical patch at costa linked to median band in ♂, separate in ♀. HW dark gray in ♂, tan with gray shade in lower half in ♀. Wingspan 1.6–2.8 cm.
Food: Apple, beeches, birches, elms, oaks, and *Rubus* species.
Range: Me. and Que. to N.C. and Miss., west across Canada, south to Tex. May–Aug.; 2 broods. Common.

SPOTTED FIREWORM MOTH **Pl. 59 (22)**
Choristoneura parallela (Rob.)
Identification: FW light reddish to orange-brown. Similar to Three-lined Leafroller Moth (above, Pl. 59), but basal area usually not dark; bands not edged with paler border, and am. line less distinct. Look for 2 *dark brown costal patches;* patch near FW apex continues along outer margin as paler terminal band. HW orange-yellow to tan; may have gray shading in lower half. Wingspan 1.9–2.5 cm.
Food: Larva (**Spotted Fireworm**) feeds on blueberries, citrus, cranberry, flowering almond, gardenia, goldenrods, roses, and sheep laurel. A pest on cranberry in Northeast.
Range: Me. and Ont. to Fla., west to Mo. and Miss. May–Sept. Common.

OBLIQUE-BANDED LEAFROLLER **Pl. 59 (23, 24)**
MOTH *Choristoneura rosaceana* (Harr.)
Identification: Similar to Spotted Fireworm Moth (above), but usually larger and darker reddish brown. FW in ♂ has *costal fold* from base to top of am. line, where dark scale tuft lies flat, forming a *dark spot* absent in similar species (magnification needed). HW *pale orange-yellow* in ♂; *deep yellow* in ♀; may have gray shading in lower third. Wingspan 1.7–3.3 cm; ♀ much larger than ♂.
Food: Larva (**Oblique-banded Leafroller**) a pest of apple. Also feeds on holly, oaks, pines, roses, and other woody plants.
Range: Common throughout our area. Late April–Oct.; 2 broods in much of range.

SPRUCE BUDWORM MOTH **Pl. 59 (28)**
Choristoneura fumiferana (Clem.)
Identification: Extremely variable. FW strongly mottled orangish brown and yellowish, usually with gray to black spot or bar in middle. *2 cream patches* at costa and 1 at inner margin. HW dark gray. Wingspan 2.1–3 cm.
Food: Larva (**Spruce Budworm**) is a major forest pest, attacking firs and spruces and, less commonly, larches and pines.
Range: Lab. to Va., west across Canada, south to Tex. June–Aug.

Sometimes abundant in northern coniferous forests; southern records may be strays.

FRUIT-TREE LEAFROLLER MOTH   Pl. 59 (19)
Archips argyrospila (Wlk.)
Identification: FW cream and yellow, heavily mottled with reddish to blackish brown. 2 *whitish costal spots* are sharpest markings. HW dark gray. Wingspan 1.4–2.4 cm.
Food: Larva (**Fruit-tree Leafroller**) a pest of apple and pear; to a lesser extent, apricot, cherries, peaches and plums. Feeds on many plants, including alfalfa, beans, blueberries, cedar, grapes, elms, oaks, onions and *Prunus* species.
Range: Common throughout our area. June to mid-Aug.

OAK WEBWORM MOTH   Pl. 59 (16)
Archips fervidana (Clem.)
Identification: FW orangish brown with gray in outer ¼. Look for a *dark triangle* formed by 2 costal and 1 median dark brown to blackish spots. HW dark gray. Wingspan 1.8–2.5 cm.
Food: Larva (**Oak Webworm**) feeds on hickories and oaks.
Range: Me. and Que. to N.C., west to Wisc. and Ark. Mid-June to early Sept. Common.

Archips purpurana (Clem.)   Pl. 60 (9)
Identification: Note the *deep inward curve* of costal and outer margins near apex. FW uniformly purplish brown, or pale brown with darker brown streaks and median band. HW white, shaded with gray in lower half. Wingspan 1.8–2.7 cm.
Food: Apple, blueberries, geranium, goldenrod, sassafras, strawberry, violets, willows, and other plants.
Range: Throughout our area. Late June–Aug. Locally common.

Syndemis afflictana (Wlk.)   Pl. 60 (8)
Identification: FW mottled gray. Broad, oblique, whitish *median bar* edged with black on outer side; other black lines usually inconspicuous. Wingspan 1.8–2.3 cm.
Food: Firs, mountain alder, white birch, and willows.
Range: Nfld. to Va., west to Ont. and Tex. April–July. Locally common.

WHITE TRIANGLE TORTRIX   Pl. 59 (18)
Clepsis persicana (Fitch)
Identification: FW orange and brown with *silvery white costal triangle* that *curves* outward; terminal line white. HW gray with white fringe. Wingspan 1.5–2.2 cm.
Food: Over 40 trees, including alders, apple, birches, firs, maples, tamarack, and spruces.
Range: Lab. to Va., west across Canada, south to Minn. June–Aug. Common northward.

Clepsis melaleucana (Wlk.)   Pl. 59 (25)
Identification: FW yellowish cream; purplish brown blotch toward anal angle is crossed by oblique median band of slightly darker ground color. *Paler brownish patch* at costa near apex. HW gray. Wingspan 1.8–2.5 cm.

Food: Apple, blue cohosh, mandrake, Solomon's-seal, and trilliums.
Range: Nfld. to N.C., west to Man., Minn., and Ky. May–July. Common.

GARDEN TORTRIX   Pl. 63 (23)
Ptycholoma peritana (Clem.)
Identification: FW orange-yellow, with blackish subapical *spot at costa* and oblique median band that *narrows* below costa. HW grayish brown with shiny white fringe. Wingspan 1–1.5 cm.
Food: Strawberries and other low herbaceous plants; larva seems to prefer dying leaves on the ground.
Range: Common throughout our area. May–Sept.

SPARGANOTHIS FRUITWORM MOTH   Pl. 59 (12)
Sparganothis sulfureana (Clem.)
Identification: FW bright lemon yellow, longer in ♀ than in ♂. Variable overlay of orange *netlike pattern*. Orange brown am. and pm. lines variably wide and complete, usually *meeting* above inner margin to form a *vague* V. HW pale grayish to orangish, but never pure white. Wingspan 1–2 cm.
Food: Larva (**Sparganothis Fruitworm**) feeds on alfalfa, apple, carrot, choke cherry, clover, corn, elms, pines, willows, and other plants. A pest of cranberry.
Range: Common throughout our area. May–Oct.; 2 broods.

Sparganothis reticulatana (Clem.)   Pl. 59 (13)
Identification: Similar to Sparganothis Fruitworm Moth (above), but orange netlike pattern heavier. Thick brown am. line oblique. Pm. line a *large brown blotch* at costa, dividing to form an *inverted* Y toward inner margin. HW yellowish white. Wingspan 1.5–1.7 cm.
Food: Alders, apple, ashes, asters, beeches, birches, blueberries, cherries, maples, oaks, pear, persimmon, and other trees and shrubs.
Range: Common throughout our area. June–Aug.

Sparganothis pettitana (Rob.)   Pl. 59 (11)
Identification: FW *lemon yellow*, either unmarked or with variable orange to brownish mottling along costa, vaguely representing tops of am. and pm. lines (shown). *HW pure white*. Wingspan 1.9–2.7 cm.
Food: Basswood, birches, hickories, maples, oaks, and other trees.
Range: N.S. to Fla., west across Canada, south to Kans. and Ark. May–July. Common, at least eastward.

Platynota flavedana Clem.   Pl. 59 (14, 15)
Identification: FW in ♂ orangish brown, shaded with blackish brown *except* near outer margin. FW in ♀ marked with lighter blackish brown than in ♂, heaviest toward costa as diffuse median and st. bands. HW *orangish brown* in both sexes. Wingspan 1.2–1.6 cm.
Food: Apple, clover, maples, roses, sassafras, strawberries, and other plants.
Range: Me. to Fla., west to Kans. and Tex. April–Oct.; 2–3 broods. Common.

TUFTED APPLE-BUD MOTH   Pl. 60 (16)
Platynota idaeusalis (Wlk.)
Identification: FW ash gray with obscure blackish and brown shad-

ing. Thin st. and terminal lines and small *squarish patch* at middle of outer margin. HW grayish brown. Wingspan 1.2–2.5 cm.
Food: Apple, ashes, black walnut, boxelder, clover, goldenrod, pines, willows, and other plants.
Range: Common throughout our area. May–Sept.

Amorbia humerosana Clem.   **Pl. 60 (7)**
Identification: FW mottled pale and medium gray, dotted with black. *Brown shading* along inner margin. No sharp pattern. HW gray. Wingspan 2.1–3 cm.
Food: Alders, apple, huckleberries, pines, poison ivy, sumac, and other trees and shrubs.
Range: Common throughout our area. April–early July.

CARPENTERWORM and LEOPARD MOTHS:
Family Cossidae

These are our largest microlepidoptera; wingspan 2.5–8.5 cm. Head scales erect; no ocelli. *Antennae bipectinate* in ♂, *filiform* (threadlike) in ♀. Labial palps short to long and upturned; other mouth parts vestigial. Body heavy; abdomen extends beyond HW as in sphinx moths (p. 30), but these moths can be distinguished from sphinx moths by differences in the antennae and the appearance of the wings (these moths look duller and greasier). Wing venation considered primitive, but similar to butterflies in some respects. FW has an *areole,* some R endings stalked, and veins 1A and 2A *complete.* HW broad with *3 anal veins* (Fig. 42). Pattern usually consists of dark mottling on pale wings.
    Larvae bore in various trees, sometimes causing considerable damage. Some species take 2–4 years to complete their life cycles.

BLACK-LINED CARPENTERWORM MOTH   **Pl. 60 (18)**
Inguromorpha basalis (Wlk.)
Identification: Wings generally dark gray, FW with some white tinting and network of fine, dark lines on and between veins. Heaviest markings are straight *black basal line* and *crescent* at apex. Wingspan 2.6–3.8 cm.
Food: Unrecorded; probably a borer in trees.
Range: Se. N.J. to Fla., west to Mo. and Ark. May–Aug. Common southward.

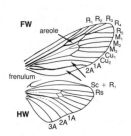

Fig. 42.
Wing venation,
Cossidae.

ANNA CARPENTERWORM MOTH   Pl. 60 (15)
Givera anna (Dyar)
Identification: Similar to Black-lined Carpenterworm Moth (above), but smaller and more *brownish* gray, with dark-edged, *white discal spot* and no heavy lines on FW. Wingspan 2.5–3.6 cm.
Food: Larva bores in pine trunks.
Range: Se. N.J. to Fla., west to Mo. and Ark. May–Aug. Common locally in deep South.

PECAN CARPENTERWORM MOTH   Pl. 7 (4)
Cossula magnifica (Stkr.)
Identification: FW gray and white with tiny black vertical dashes. Elliptical brown *terminal patch* set off by *dark brown st. line.* HW dark grayish brown. Wingspan 3.2–4.5 cm.
Food: Larva (**Pecan Carpenterworm**) bores in wood of hickories, oaks, pecan, and persimmon.
Range: Coastal N.C. to s. Fla., west to Miss. March–June. Locally common.

CARPENTERWORM MOTH   Pl. 7 (6, 9)
Prionoxystus robiniae (Peck)
Identification: FW in ♀ mottled gray and blackish, slightly translucent. FW in ♂ less sharply mottled. HW *yellow* with black outer border in ♂, *no yellow* in ♀. Wingspan 4.3–8.5 cm; ♀ larger than ♂.
Food: Larva (**Carpenterworm**) bores in wood of ash, chestnut, locusts, oaks, poplars, willows, and other trees. Life cycle takes 3–4 years. Larval tunnels decrease the value of hardwood lumber.
Range: Throughout our area. April–Oct., mostly June–July.
Similar species: (1) Little Carpenterworm Moth (below). (2) Leopard Moth, *Zeuzera pyrina* (L.), not shown. Wings white with bluish black spots over FW; HW all white or with a few spots. Abdomen bluish black. *Antennae* in ♂ *bipectinate* in basal half only (whole length in Carpenterworm Moth). Food: Elms, maples, and other trees. Range: Introduced from Europe before 1879. Me. to Philadelphia, Pa. area. May–Sept.; a 2-year life cycle.

LITTLE CARPENTERWORM MOTH   Pl. 7 (7)
Prionoxystus macmurtrei (Guér.)
Identification: Both sexes similar to ♀ Carpenterworm Moth (above), but smaller. Wings *more translucent;* black markings are *thin, vertical lines* rather than large blotches. HW translucent gray. Wingspan 5.2–7.5 cm.
Food: Larva (**Little Carpenterworm**) bores in ash, maples, and oaks.
Range: Que. to Fla., west to Minn. and Tex. April–July.

CHOREUTID MOTHS:
Family Choreutidae

Small; wingspan 0.9–1.4 cm. Head scales smooth; proboscis scaled at base. Antennae of some species have triangular scale tuft extending from lower side of base. Labial palps long, upcurved, pointed, with *long stiff hair-scales* on underside of 2nd segment. Wings broad (Fig. 43).

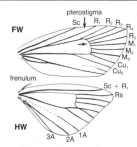

Fig. 43. Wing venation, Choreutidae.

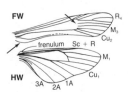

Fig. 44. Wing venation, Sesiidae.

FW *membrane thickened along costa* between Sc and R_1; 8 of 10 veins extending from discal cell arise from its outer margin. HW has 3 anal veins.

Choreutid moths are mostly dark in color. Most are day-fliers that do not come to lights, so a net or Malaise trap (p. 17) should be used to collect them. Larvae are mostly surface feeders on living plants; a few species live in hollow stems of food plants such as thistle.

Prochoreutis inflatella (Clem.)   **Pl. 63 (1)**
Identification: FW dark brown with metallic blackish shading and white median dusting. Curved pm. and partial st. lines metallic purple or green with orange-yellow between them. Note *sharp white triangle* at costa near apex. HW smoky grayish brown, pointed at outer angle. Wingspan 0.9–1.1 cm.
Food: Larva skeletonizes the leaves of mad-dog skullcap.
Range: Que. to Fla., west to Man. and e. Tex. June–Sept. Common.
Similar species: Apple-and-thorn Skeletonizer, *Choreutis pariana* (Cl.), not shown, is slightly larger; FW *chocolate brown* with some faint *paler lines*. Food: Apple and hawthorn. Range: Introduced from Europe into New England about 1917; now found almost everywhere apples grow in our area. Aug. Apparently not an important pest.

CLEAR-WINGED MOTHS:
Family Sesiidae

Medium to small moths; wingspan 1.4–4.6 cm. Easily recognized by *transparent areas* on all wings, or HW only. Most of these moths look very *wasplike*. Head smooth; ocelli conspicuous. Antennae simple to bipectinate, *widening* gradually then *narrowing* again to tip. Proboscis unscaled. FW long and narrow, flaring beyond open end (*unveined outer margin*) of discal cell, from which most vein endings arise (Fig. 44). FW folds downward along inner margin, with a row of *tiny curved spines* that interlock with the fold; similar *spines along HW costa* help hold the wings together. HW broader than FW, but narrow at base. Sc and R parallel and close together in *costal fold; all 3 anal veins present*.

Larvae bore in roots, stems, and trunks of many herbaceous and woody plants. Some are serious pests of garden crops, fruit trees, and forest trees, Sesiid moths are day-fliers; only the Maple Callus Borer (p. 426) comes to lights. Look for these moths on food plants, flowers, or resting on leaves—or trap them with captive females, pheromone bait, or a Malaise trap (p. 17). It is a challenge to collect these moths, since they not only look like wasps, but move like them as well—some species even mimic the threatening posture (of the abdomen) of many wasps.

RASPBERRY CROWN BORER MOTH   Pl. 61 (8)
Pennisetia marginata (Harr.)

Identification: Our only sesiid *without a tuft* of hair-scales on tip of antenna. Body black, with yellow markings on thorax and abdomen. Wings transparent, with brownish borders. Wingspan 2.5–3 cm.

Food: Larva (**Raspberry Crown Borer**) feeds on leaves of blackberries and raspberries.

Range: Nfld. to N.C., west to Ont., Mo. and Miss. July–Oct.

Remarks: These moths mimic yellowjackets in behavior and appearance, and may be common around brambles of host plants.

OAK STUMP BORER MOTH   Pl. 61 (12)
Paranthrene asilipennis (Bdv.)

Identification: FW transparent in ♂ (shown), edged with a mixture of reddish and brownish black. Reniform spot *red* edged with *brown*. FW in ♀ (not shown) dark brown, transparent only in *small triangle* near anal angle. Abdomen blackish with thin yellow bands in both sexes. Wingspan 2.8–4.6 cm.

Food: Oaks. Larva bores in low part of trunk, roots, and stumps.

Range: Mass. to Fla., west to Wisc., Kans., and Tex. April–July. Life cycle takes 2 years. Moths may be common in woods with fresh-cut stumps.

HORNET CLEARWING   Pl. 61 (6)
Paranthrene simulans (Grt.)

Identification: Body black with yellow markings. Abdomen yellow except for *black basal patch* crossed by *yellow band*. FW brown in costal half, transparent in lower half. Orange replaces yellow in some specimens. A mimic of hornets. Wingspan 2.7–4 cm.

Food: Chestnut and oaks.

Range: N.S. to Fla., west to Minn., Mo., and Miss. May–June. Life cycle takes 2 years. Not commonly collected because of its close resemblance to hornets.

GRAPE ROOT BORER MOTH   Pl. 60 (24)
Vitacea polistiformis (Harr.)

Identification: *Body and FW black* shaded with brown; HW transparent. Abdominal segments 2 and 4 have even, pale yellow bands. Head and *legs mostly orange*. Resembles paper wasp. Wingspan 2.6–6.4 cm.

Food: Larva (**Grape Root Borer**) bores in roots of wild and cultivated grapes.

Range: N.Y. to Fla., west to Mo. and Tex. April–Sept. Life cycle takes

2 years. May be locally common when a population is found, but rare in general collections because of its effective mimicry of paper wasps.

SQUASH VINE BORER MOTH Pl. 61 (9)
Melittia cucurbitae (Harr.)

Identification: Conspicuous *orange abdomen* with black spots and *long, bushy,* orange and black hind legs. Body and FW black with greenish iridescence; HW transparent. Wingspan 2.5–3.2 cm.

Food: A pest of squashes, gourds, and pumpkins. Larva bores into plant stems.

Range: Throughout our area. April–Nov.; 2 broods southward. May be very common where host plants grow. I have found these moths on milkweed blossoms in my garden.

DOGWOOD BORER MOTH Pl. 60 (21)
Synanthedon scitula (Harr.)

Identification: Body black with yellow abdominal *stripes* (stripe on segment 4 much *heavier* than others). Wings transparent with brown outer margin on FW. Hind tibia yellow with black band between spurs. Wingspan 1.4–2 cm.

Food: Many trees, such as apple, beech, birches, black cherry, chestnut, dogwood, oaks, and pecan, on which it may be a pest.

Range: Common throughout our area. May–Sept.

LESSER PEACHTREE BORER MOTH Pl. 60 (17)
Synanthedon pictipes (Grt. & Rob.)

Identification: Similar to ♂ Peachtree Borer Moth (p. 427, Pl. 60), but *smaller;* area between antennae *black* (not yellow-tufted, as in Peachtree Borer Moth). FW has some yellow dusting on blackish brown areas, especially on underside. Wingspan 1.5–2.5 cm.

Food: Larva (**Lesser Peachtree Borer**) feeds on peach trees, but is not as serious a pest as the Peachtree Borer; this species also feeds on wild cherry and wild plum.

Range: N.S. to Fla., west to Minn. and Tex. April–Sept.; 2 broods. Locally common.

RILEY'S CLEARWING Pl. 61 (5)
Synanthedon rileyana (Hy. Edw.)

Identification: Wings transparent with brownish black borders variably powdered with orangish red. *Orangish red reniform bar* on FW. Thorax and abdomen black with yellow lines and bands. Wingspan 1.8–3 cm.

Food: Horsenettle.

Range: N.Y. to Fla., west to Wisc., Kans., and Tex. June–Sept. Common.

MAPLE CALLUS BORER MOTH Pl. 61 (7)
Synanthedon acerni (Clem.)

Identification: *Red tuft* at tip of abdomen and *yellow* in st. area of FW identify this species. Wingspan 1.8–2.5 cm.

Food: Larva (**Maple Callus Borer**) bores in maples.

Range: Common throughout our area. April–Aug. Our only clear-wing moth regularly attracted to lights.

PEACHTREE BORER MOTH   Pl. 60 (19, 20)
Synanthedon exitiosa (Say)

Identification: Body in ♂ black with *yellow collar,* and yellow bands or streaks on thorax, abdomen, and legs. Wings transparent with black borders. Body bluish black in ♀, with *red to orange abdominal crossband;* FW entirely *black.* Wingspan 1.4–3.3 cm.

Food: Apricot, peach, plums, and other *Prunus* species. Larva (**Peachtree Borer**) bores into trunks of trees from 8 cm below soil to about 30 cm above surface. A major pest of peach trees.

Range: Common throughout our area. May–Sept.; 1 brood per year.

LILAC BORER MOTH or ASH BORER MOTH   Pl. 60 (22)
Podosesia syringae (Harr.)

Identification: Body reddish brown and blackish. FW *transparent only in basal half;* outer half *brown.* Whitish to yellow streak on upper side of abdomen near base. A striking mimic of paper wasps (*Polistes* species). Wingspan 2.5–3.8 cm.

Food: Larva (**Lilac** or **Ash Borer**) bores in ashes, fringetree, lilacs, and privet.

Range: Common throughout our area, but easily overlooked because of its resemblance to wasps. May–July.

Similar species: Banded Ash Clearwing, *P. aureocincta* Purrington & Nielsen (not shown) is almost identical, but has *orangish yellow band* on 4th abdominal segment, which Lilac Borer Moth lacks. Food and range as in Lilac Borer Moth, but adults fly in *late Aug.-Sept.* Locally common.

EUPATORIUM BORER MOTH   Pl. 61 (10)
Carmenta bassiformis (Wlk.)

Identification: Wings transparent, but with a *broad, dark border* on FW. Thorax purplish black; abdomen also purplish black with *yellow bands* in both sexes. Note width of bands, especially on abdominal segments 3 and 5: those bands narrower in ♀ (shown); all bands nearly same width in ♂ (not shown). Antennae all black in ♂; black with a white section in ♀. Wingspan 1.8–2.6 cm.

Food: Roots of ironweed and joe-pye-weed.

Range: Mass. to Fla., west to Wisc., Kans., and Tex. Late May–Sept. Sometimes locally common.

HELIODINID MOTHS:
Family Heliodinidae

Very small moths; wingspan 0.7–1.5 cm. Head smooth-scaled; labial palps short to moderate in length, sometimes drooping; proboscis unscaled. Note *whorls of bristles* on hind tibia and tarsal segments. Wings very narrow—*lancelike to linear* (Fig. 45). Wing venation varies: most heliodinid moths have 8–10 veins from discal cell to margins. R_1 extends from about *middle of cell* to costal margin; *at least 3 veins extend from cell apex.* (No discal cell on FW and only 3–4 veins in *Cycloplasis* species, not shown.) HW veins reduced; Sc + R_1 well separated from Rs.

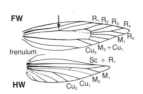

Fig. 45. Wing venation, Heliodinidae.

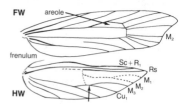

Fig. 46. Wing venation, Acrolepiidae.

Adults are often brilliantly colored with metallic markings; they hold their hindlegs upward when resting. Larval feeding habits vary: larvae are either leaf miners or external feeders (on leaf surface).

Heliodines bella (Cham.) **Pl. 63 (2)**
Identification: FW deep orange; look for 2 *metallic gray spots* at costa, 2 more at inner margin. Base, terminal area, and *fringe* of FW, HW, and body dark gray. Wingspan 0.7–0.8 cm.
Food: Chinquapin blossoms and velvetbean (*Stizolobium*).
Range: Ky. to Fla., west to Kans. and Tex. June; Aug.–Sept.; 2 broods. Common.

Heliodines nyctaginella Gibson **Pl. 64 (17)**
Identification: FW metallic orange, like *H. bella* (above), but *larger*. Note 5 metallic gray *spots* along costa—2 spots nearest FW base *connected;* 3 more spots along inner margin. Wingspan 1–1.1 cm.
Food: Four-o'clocks.
Range: Ohio to Man., Iowa, and Ark. Mid-May–mid-Sept.

ACROLEPIID MOTHS:
Family Acrolepiidae

Very small moths; wingspan 0.9–1 cm. Head mostly smooth-scaled, with a few erect hairs toward back of vertex (Fig. 2, p. 2). Maxillary palps long, *folded;* labial palps long, upturned, tapering. Wings lance-like; FW slightly hooked and HW somewhat *trapezoidal* (Fig. 46). Venation nearly complete; note FW areole. Similar to argyresthiid moths (Fig. 48, below) and ermine moths (Fig. 49, p. 430) but *no pterostigma* on FW. M_3 and Cu_1 of HW *stalked.* Argyresthiid moths also differ in having large hair tuft on vertex and no maxillary palps.
Larvae may tie and skeletonize leaves, or bore in bulbs of food plants. Only 3 N. American species known.

Acrolepiopsis incertella (Cham.) **Pl. 64 (1)**
Identification: FW brown with some blackish shading. Narrow *white*

triangle points inward from midpoint of inner margin. HW gray. Wingspan 0.9–1 cm.
Food: Larvae have been reported skeletonizing greenbriar leaves and boring in bulbs of lilies.
Range: N.H. to Ky., west to Ark. April–Sept.

DOUGLASIID MOTHS:
Family Douglasiidae

Very small moths; the only species in our area has a wingspan of 0.7–1 cm. Head smooth-scaled; ocelli large, prominent; proboscis unscaled. Wings narrow, lancelike (Fig. 47); R_5 and M_1 of FW *stalked.* HW lacks discal cell; Rs follows *long axis* of wing to apex, with *1 branch* to costa (about $\frac{2}{3}$ distance from base).

Larvae are leaf miners. Only 5 N. American species; 1 in eastern N. America.

Tinagma obscurofasciella (Cham.)   **Pl. 63 (21)**
Identification: Body and FW grayish brown. Note *darker* median and st. bands; median band *edged with white.* HW grayish brown. Wingspan 0.7–1 cm.
Food: A leaf miner in various plants in the rose family.
Range: Ont. to N.Y., s. Ohio, and cen. Ky. April–May.

ARGYRESTHIID MOTHS:
Family Argyresthiidae

Small to very small moths; wingspan 0.7–1.4 cm. Vertex of head rough-scaled; frons smooth. Ocelli present (except in *Argyresthia* species, below). Wings very narrow, lancelike (Fig. 48); venation similar to that of ermine moths (Yponomeutidae, Fig. 49), the family in which argyresthiid moths were included until recently. These moths are usually much smaller than ermine moths and have a *more lancelike HW;* M_1 and M_2 *stalked.* FW *membrane thickened* (pterostigma present) along costa, between veins Sc and R_1 in both families.

These moths are often white, yellowish, or brown; some look metal-

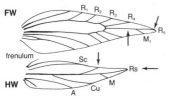

Fig. 47. Wing venation, Douglasiidae.

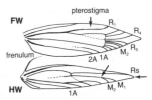

Fig. 48. Wing venation, Argyresthiidae.

lic. At rest, head is held downward and body projects upward at an angle. Larvae are leaf miners, or borers in twigs, buds, or fruits. Pupation occurs in white cocoon, usually in larval tunnel.

Argyresthia annettella Bsk.   Pl. 64 (16)
Identification: FW silvery white, crossed by *3 irregular*, broken *gold bands;* median band Y-*shaped*, enclosing white spot at costa. Wingspan 0.7–0.9 cm.
Food: Juniper.
Range: Conn. to s. Ohio. June–July.

Argyresthia calliphanes Meyr.   Pl. 64 (22)
Identification: Head, thorax, and wings gleaming white. FW has broad, even coppery basal line, V-*shaped median band*, and white-dotted terminal line. HW gray. Wingspan 1.3–1.4 cm.
Food: Alders.
Range: Me. and Ont. to N.Y., west across Canada, south to Mich. and S.D. June–Aug.

APPLE FRUIT MOTH   Pl. 64 (3)
Argyresthia conjugella Zell.
Identification: Thorax white with brown tegulae. Costal half of FW brown, lower half white; note *blackish square* at middle of inner margin. HW gray. Wingspan 1.1–3 cm.
Food: Larva bores in berries of mountain ash and developing fruit of apple trees.
Range: A European moth, accidentally introduced into N. America; discovered in B.C. in 1897. N.Y. to Fla. and westward across s. Canada. Late June–July.

Argyresthia oreasella Clem.   Pl. 63 (3)
Identification: FW silvery white with white streaks. *Median band* and combined st. and terminal bands oblique and irregular, *gold and brown*. Note 2 white dots enclosed by terminal band near apex. HW gray. Wingspan 1–1.2 cm.
Food: Choke cherry, oaks, and pin cherry.
Range: Que. to W. Va., west to Man. and Mo. Late June–July.

ERMINE MOTHS:
Family Yponomeutidae

Medium-small moths; wingspan 1.2–3 cm. Head and labial palps smooth-scaled; maxillary palps have *1–2 segments; no ocelli.* Glyphipterigid moths (p. 432) are similar but usually smaller, with 1, 3, or 4 segments in each maxillary palp and *conspicuous ocelli.* In ermine moths the wings are usually blunt, not lancelike; venation nearly complete (Fig. 49). FW usually has pterostigma at costa between Sc and R_1. Wing pattern often colorful, or white with black dots.

Ermine moth larvae live together in webbing spun over leaves of food plant and pupate in loose webbing. Adult moths at rest roll their wings and look like sticks, much like the pyralid moths in subfamily Crambinae (p. 403).

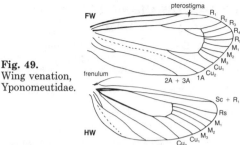

Fig. 49.
Wing venation,
Yponomeutidae.

AILANTHUS WEBWORM MOTH Pls. 61 (13); 62 (5)
Atteva punctella (Cram.)
Identification: FW orange, with *4 bands of yellow spots* outlined in black. Spots smaller in Florida population (Pl. 62), which until recently was considered a separate species, *A. floridana* (Neum.). HW smoky gray. Wingspan 1.8–3 cm.
Food: Ailanthus and paradise tree. Larva (**Ailanthus Webworm**) lives in communal webs.
Range: N.Y. to Fla., west to Neb. and Tex. March–Nov. Common.

Lactura pupula (Hbn.) Pl. 61 (11)
Identification: FW white with sharp, thin black lines and usually 5 dashes. *HW salmon-pink.* Wingspan 1.7–2.5 cm.
Food: Reported on saffron plum (*Bumelia celastrina*) in Fla.
Range: Ky. to Fla., west to Kans. and Tex. April–Aug. Common southward.

Urodus parvula (Hy. Edw.) Pl. 62 (1)
Identification: Dull, smoky black body and wings. *No markings* on wings; HW *translucent*. Wingspan 2–2.9 cm.
Food: Bumelia, hibiscus, oaks, orange, and redbay. Cocoon a fine netlike chamber attached to food plant by a filament.
Range: Wash., D.C. and Va. to Fla., west to Miss. All year southward, where it is common.

BROWN-BORDERED ERMINE MOTH Pl. 64 (15)
Yponomeuta atomocella Dyar
Identification: FW white with black dots and *pinkish brown fringe;* HW and abdomen also pinkish brown. Wingspan 1.7–2 cm.
Food: Hoptree.
Range: S. Ohio to Ill., Mo., and Tex. April–June. Uncommon to rare.

AMERICAN ERMINE MOTH Pl. 62 (2)
Yponomeuta multipunctella Clem.
Identification: FW white with black dots, as in Brown-bordered Ermine Moth (above), but *no* pinkish brown fringe. HW gray in ♂ (shown), white in ♀. Wingspan 1.7–2 cm.
Food: Euonymous. Caterpillars feed in groups.
Range: N.Y. to Fla., west to Mich., Mo., and Miss. Late May–early July. Locally common southward.

DIAMONDBACK MOTHS:
Family Plutellidae

Small moths; wingspan 1.2–1.5 cm. Head scales slightly rough; labial palps upturned, with long triangular tuft on 2nd segment. Ocelli present. Wings elongate, *narrowly rounded at apex* (Fig. 50); R_4 and R_5 of FW *not* stalked; M_1 and M_2 of HW *stalked or very close together* in basal $\frac{1}{3}$ or more of their length beyond discal cell. Antennae held outward when moth is at rest.

Larvae feed individually in tied leaves or in groups amid masses of silk webbing. They pupate in loose, meshwork cocoons.

DIAMONDBACK MOTH *Plutella xylostella* (L.)   **Pl. 60 (25)**
Identification: FW in ♂ dark gray or brown, with *irregular white band* along inner margin; coloring darkest just above white band. FW paler in ♀, so contrast with inner margin border less pronounced. HW gray. White FW markings form a "diamond" when moth folds its wings together. Wingspan 1.2–1.5 cm.
Food: A minor pest of cabbage and other plants in the mustard family; also feeds on candytuft and sweet alyssum. Larvae eat holes in underside of leaves and pupate in meshlike cocoons attached to leaves.
Range: Throughout our area. April–Oct.; many broods. Introduced from Europe before 1850.
Similar species: In Mimosa Webworm Moth, *Homadaula anisocentra* Meyr. (not shown), FW is broader than in Diamondback Moth. FW *gleaming dark gray* with sparse covering of *black spots;* st. and terminal lines are rows of black dots. HW solid dark gray. Wingspan 1.2–1.6 cm. Food: Ornamental mimosa and honey locust trees. Larvae feed in silken webbing and may defoliate much of host tree. Range: Md. to Fla., west to Great Plains and Tex. An Asian moth discovered in Wash., D.C. in 1943. May–Sept.; many broods.

GLYPHIPTERIGID MOTHS:
Family Glyphipterigidae

Very small moths, usually blackish with iridescent silver markings; some species are more colorful. Wingspan 0.7–1.4 cm. Head smooth-scaled. Labial palps upturned beyond vertex; palps smooth-scaled, or 2nd segment slightly tufted. Proboscis *unscaled; ocelli large and conspicuous.* FW broad, usually with rounded apex and distinct anal angle (Fig. 51). Four of 10 veins from discal cell reach FW costa; R_4 and R_5 sometimes stalked; Cu_2 arises from outer $\frac{1}{4}$ of cell. HW usually narrower, shorter than FW. *Rs and M_1 arise separately.*

In species for which life history is known, larvae bore in stems and leaves.

Diploschizia impigritella (Clem.)   **Pl. 63 (5)**
Identification: FW dark brown, with some paler scales in outer area. 5 small white bars taper inward from costa. Note the *long, curving white line* tapering from inner margin toward apex, and the large, black apical spot. FW fringes broad, brown with gray outer halves. HW dark gray. Wingspan 0.7–0.8 cm.

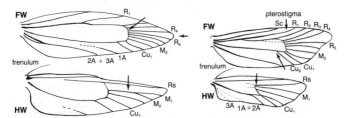

Fig. 50. Wing venation, Plutellidae.

Fig. 51. Wing venation, Glyphipterigidae.

Food: *Cyperus* species; larva bores in stems and leaf bases.
Range: N. S. to Fla., west to Iowa and Tex. May–Aug. Locally common.

EPERMENIID MOTHS:
Family Eperminiidae

Small, yellowish to grayish moths; wingspan 0.9–1.8 cm in our few species. Head smooth-scaled; labial palps long, upcurved; proboscis reduced, unscaled. *Stiff bristles* on upper and lower side of hind tibia. Wings lancelike (Fig. 52). FW has 10 veins arising from discal cell, 4 of them extending to costa; R_5 *originates before middle* of cell. Fringe broad, particularly at anal angle, emphasizing hooked appearance of FW; *small scale tufts* on inner margin. HW narrow; Rs and M_1 stalked or *very close together* at base.

Larvae usually mine in leaves, preferring plants in the parsley family (Umbelliferae). At least 1 species feeds in flowers and seeds.

Epermenia imperialella Bsk.   **Pl. 62 (22)**
Identification: Straw yellow with orange-yellow shading. *FW apex hooked;* outer margin edged with brown. HW pale gray with yellow fringe. Wingspan 1.5–1.8 cm.
Food: Unrecorded.
Range: Pa. and Man.   June.

Epermenia cicutaella Kft.   **Pl. 64 (2)**
Identification: FW white to yellowish, mottled with blackish and grayish brown, *heaviest at median band.* 2 bar-shaped spots sometimes present; blackish tufts in fringe of inner margin. HW gray. Wingspan 1.2–1.4 cm.
Food: Flowers and seeds of water-hemlock (*Cicuta maculata*); also reported on caraway and *Perideridia* species.
Range: Que., N.H., N.Y., N.J., and Ky. July.

Epermenia pimpinella Murt.   **Pl. 64 (20)**
Identification: FW reddish to brownish gray, variably powdered with white. 3 blackish reniform dots sometimes present. Inner margin fringe

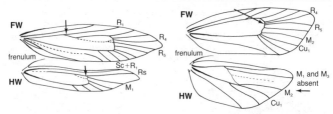

Fig. 52. Wing venation, Epermeniidae.

Fig. 53. Wing venation, Carposinidae.

of gray hairy scales with *5-6 tufts* of broad, blackish brown scales. (Outer margin fringe of broad blackish brown scales.) HW gray. Wingspan 0.9–1.2 cm.

Food: Yellow pimpernel (*Taenidia integerimma*).
Range: Ohio to N.C. and S.C., west to Mo. and Ark. May–July.

CARPOSINID MOTHS:
Family Carposinidae

A small group of small moths; wingspan about 1–2 cm. Wings rather broad; FW pattern characterized by *tufts* of dark, *raised* scales. FW has 10 unstalked veins arising from discal cell; R_4 arises *well apart* from R_5. M_1 and M_3 *absent* on HW; M_2 arises from *bottom* of discal cell (Fig. 53).

Larvae bore in fruits, plant shoots, and gum oozing from fruit trees. Pupation usually occurs in a cocoon in the soil.

CURRANT FRUITWORM MOTH   Pl. 62 (4)
Carposina fernaldana Bsk.
Identification: FW gray with fine darker checkering along costa. Vague pattern of raised *white and blackish tufts* on FW, heaviest as *black basal dot* and *bar or patch* in upper median area. HW translucent gray. Wingspan 1.8–1.9 cm.
Food: Larva (**Currant Fruitworm**) feeds on fruits of currant, hawthorn, and other plants in the rose family and the saxifrage family.
Range: Ont. and N.Y. to Miss., west to Ill. and Mo. April–June and Aug.-Oct. broods.

MANY-PLUME MOTHS:
Family Alucitidae

Moderately small moths; the only species in our area has a wingspan of 1.2–1.4 cm. *All wings are divided* almost to bases into. *6 plumelike branches* (Fig. 54). Head smooth-scaled. Labial palps long, rough-scaled. Proboscis naked (unscaled). These moths traditionally have been considered close relatives of the plume moths (p. 391), which also have divided wings (FW with 2 branches, HW 3), but the many-plume moths are now grouped with the next 3 families on the basis of their naked proboscis and characteristics of the immature stages.

Larvae tunnel in shoots, buds, and flowers of food plants, sometimes producing galls. They pupate in a cocoon on the ground or on food plant. Adult moths do not roll up their wings at rest as plume moths do.

SIX-PLUME MOTH *Alucita hexadactyla* L.   **Pl. 58 (23)**
Identification: *All wings divided* into 6 feathery branches. Spread specimens show faint pattern of dark and light gray vertical bands (see Pl. 58). Wingspan 1.2–1.4 cm.
Food: Honeysuckles (?). In Europe, larva feeds on flowers of *Centaurea* and *Knautia* species.
Range: Holarctic; Ont. to N.Y., west across Canada, south to S.D. in our area. March–July. Locally common.
Remarks: This is the only many-plume moth that has been described in our area; it may have been introduced from Europe.

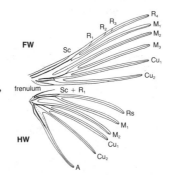

Fig. 54. Wing venation, Alucitidae.

GELECHIID MOTHS:
Family Gelechiidae

A large, diverse family of small to very small moths; wingspan 0.7–2.5 cm (mostly 1–2 cm). Head smooth-scaled; maxillary palps 4-segmented, folded over base of proboscis. Labial palps long, upcurved; 3rd segment *long and tapering* (Fig. 55A). Long hair-scales on hind tibia. FW narrowly rounded or pointed at tip (Fig. 55B); R_4 and R_5 usually *stalked,* R_5 ending at costa. HW of most species *trapezoidal,* drawn out to point at apex; outer margin *concave below apex* (Fig. 55B). Rs and M_1 of HW usually *close together* toward base, or *stalked.*

Larval habits vary widely: our species include leaf miners, folders and tiers; stem gall makers; and fruit and seed feeders. The Pink Bollworm, *Pectinophora gossypiella* (Saund.), not shown, is a serious pest that bores in cotton bolls. A number of pests that eat stored grain products belong to this family.

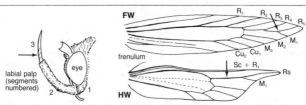

Fig. 55. A (*left*) Head (detail), Gelechiidae. **B** (*right*) Wing venation, Gelechiidae.

Metzneria lappella (L.)   **Pl. 62 (6)**
Identification: FW yellow with *dull brown streaks;* no definite pattern—brown heaviest along costa near middle. HW gray. Wingspan 1.2–1.9 cm.
Food: Burs of burdock.
Range: Me. and Que. to Fla., west to Ont. and Mo. April–Aug. Introduced from Europe or Asia.

Aristotelia roseosuffusella (Clem.)   **Pl. 63 (6)**
Identification: FW white; *4 black bars* extend inward from costa—basal bars do not reach inner margin. 3rd bar complete, with pink shading on each side, at inner margin, and at yellowish brown reniform spot. 4th bar curves from apex to meet 3rd bar. Apex and fringe of FW white. HW gray. Wingspan 1–1.1 cm.
Food: Clover.
Range: Common throughout our area. June–Oct.

Aristotelia rubidella (Clem.)   **Pl. 63 (19)**
Identification: FW gray with pink and brownish mottling that *increases* toward outer margin. Subapical area generally blackish. HW gray. Wingspan 0.9–1.1 cm.
Food: Unrecorded.
Range: Me. to Fla., west to cen. Mo. and Tex. May–Aug.

GOLDENROD GALL MOTH   **Pl. 62 (11)**
Gnorimoschema gallaesolidaginis (Riley)
Identification: FW powdery gray, grayish brown, and white. Large curved blackish patch with *whitish edging* along its bottom extends downward from costa. HW dark gray. Wingspan 2.2–2.5 cm.
Food: Goldenrods. Larva forms a stem gall that is more tapered and less spherical than that of the Gall Fly (Tephritidae), which is commonly seen in late summer.
Range: Common throughout our area. Aug.–Oct.

POTATO TUBERWORM MOTH   **Pl. 62 (12)**
Phthorimaea operculella (Zell.)
Identification: Antennae ringed with black and gray. FW gray with orange-yellow to brown streaks, heaviest in upper FW except in terminal area. HW gray with long fringe. Wingspan 1.2–1.9 cm.
Food: Larva (**Potato Tuberworm**) feeds on leaves, stems and fruits of nightshade family. A pest of stored potatoes and tobacco.
Range: Throughout our area. A continuous breeder in all months when protected from cold. Introduced from South America.

Chionodes mediofuscella (Clem.)   **Pl. 62 (10)**
Identification: *Tan basal patch* of FW *wider at inner margin* than at costa. Note grayish brown to blackish shade, set off sharply by black am. line. St. and apical areas variable, mixed tan and blackish. HW gray. Wingspan 1–1.6 cm.
Food: Seeds of great ragweed.
Range: Me. to Fla., west to Mo., Ark., and La. March–Sept. Common.

REDBUD LEAFFOLDER MOTH   Pl. 62 (7)
Fascista cercerisella (Cham.)
Identification: Head white; thorax and FW shiny black. FW has *3 white costal spots* (largest near base), and another white spot at anal angle. HW pale gray. Wingspan 1.3–1.6 cm.
Food: Redbud. Larva (**Redbud Leaffolder**) ties leaves together with silk.
Range: Md. and Pa. to Fla., west to Kans. and Tex. April–Sept.

Anacampsis agrimoniella (Clem.)   **Pl. 64 (12)**
Identification: Outer half of FW black; basal half and all of HW dark gray. White pm. line crosses FW, *widest at costa.* Wingspan 1.2–1.4 cm.
Food: Larva a leaf roller on *Agrimonia eupatoria.*
Range: N.Y. to Ga., west to Ill. and Ky. May–Sept.

PEACH TWIG BORER MOTH   Pl. 62 (13)
Anarsia lineatella Zell.
Identification: FW mottled gray and whitish. Sharpest marking is *black spot* at middle of costa; smaller black spot closer to FW base. HW gray. Wingspan 1–1.5 cm.
Food: Peach and plums. Spring larva bores tunnels in twigs and buds; later generations attack twigs and fruits.
Range: Throughout our area; a minor pest in eastern states. May–Aug.; 3–4 broods.

ANGOUMOIS GRAIN MOTH   Pl. 62 (9)
Sitotroga cerealella (Olivier)
Identification: Wings silky yellow to pale tan. Some have *no markings;* others are *streaked and dotted* with blackish and brown, especially *toward apex* of FW. Wingspan 1.1–1.6 cm.
Food: Larva feeds in kernels of corn, wheat, and other stored grain, leaving 1 or 2 holes in each damaged kernel.
Range: Throughout our area. Introduced from Europe, where it was first noted in Angoumois Province, France, in 1736. Adults fly all year.
Similar species: Casemaking Clothes Moth (p. 452, Pl. 63) is similar in color and FW markings, but its HW outline is *rounded,* not trapezoidal. Larva prefers woolens and other animal products and does not make holes in grain kernels.

PALMERWORM MOTH   Pl. 64 (6)
Dichomeris ligulella Hbn.
Identification: FW long and narrow, dark grayish brown. Look for darker reniform spot and other small dots. *Costal half* of FW *cream* in some specimens (shown). HW bluish gray, translucent. Triangular scale tuft on 2nd segment of labial palp (magnification needed). Wingspan 1.5–1.8 cm.
Food: Larva (**Palmerworm**) feeds on hackberries, hazelnuts, oaks,

and apple trees, on which it is sometimes a pest.
Range: Common throughout our area. April–Oct.

Trichotaphe flavocostella (Clem.) **Pl. 64 (4)**
Identification: FW purplish black. *Cream costal border* does not reach apex; note *spur* pointing inward in pm. area. HW gray. Wingspan 1.5–1.8 cm.
Food: Goldenrods and sunflowers.
Range: Me. to Fla., west to Man., Mo., and Miss. May–Aug. Common.

SCYTHRIDID MOTHS:
Family Scythrididae

Very small moths; wingspan 0.9–1.4 cm. Most are dull or dark. Head smooth-scaled; short maxillary palps fold over base of proboscis. Labial palps long, upcurved, but barely reach top of head at most. Antennal base not swollen. *Long hairs* on hind tibia. Wings narrow, lancelike (Fig. 56). FW has 9 veins arising from discal cell; R_2 arises *near apex* of cell, *far* from R_1; R_4 and R_5 stalked; R_5 ends below apex on outer margin. HW lancelike but has discal cell and complete venation; Rs *parallel* to M_1 as they arise from end of cell.

Larvae of most species known are leaf miners or skeletonizers. This small family needs much further study.

Scythris eboracensis (Zell.) **Pl. 64 (13)**
Identification: Body and wings iridescent brownish black; *no markings*. Wingspan 0.9–1.2 cm.
Food: Larva forms web and feeds on thistle heads.
Range: Me. to Fla., west to Mo. and Tex. May–July and late Aug.–Sept.; 2 broods. Locally common.

COSMOPTERIGID MOTHS:
Family Cosmopterigidae

A moderately large family of small to minute moths; wingspan 0.4–2.6 cm. Head smooth-scaled. Labial palps long, curving upward; often *sickle-shaped*. FW and HW lancelike. FW shape varies from narrow (Fig. 57) to extremely narrow; HW usually extremely narrow. Wings often brightly marked. Combination of *narrow wings* (especially if FW extremely narrow) and *poorly developed vein 1A* in FW (either *absent, or incomplete* to outer margin) usually identifies cosmopterigids, but examination of genitalic features of ♂ is the only sure way to distinguish all species in this family from those in closely related families. If FW broader and rounded at apex (as shown in Fig. 57), *lack of vein 1A* in HW separates cosmopterigids from blastobasid and oecophorid moths (pp. 443 and 444), in which vein 1A is present at least at outer margin. Also, in blastobasids, FW usually *thickened at costa* (Fig. 61). In agonoxenids, tips of labial palps are *flattened;* genitalic features are also distinctive. Gelechiid moths have pointed, *trapezoidal* HW (Fig. 55B, p. 436). Identification of ♀ cosmopterigids can be confirmed only by association with a known ♂ .

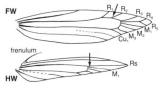

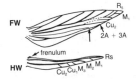

Fig. 56. Wing venation, Scythrididae.

Fig. 57. Wing venation, Cosmopterigidae.

Larval feeding habits vary among cosmopterigids: some species are leaf miners; others form stem or root galls, or feed on seeds, flower buds, or dead plant material.

Euclemensia bassettella (Clem.) **Pl. 61 (18)**
Identification: Body and wings gleaming black. FW overlaid with *bright orange,* except for black basal bar, *costal spot,* and large area from apex along margins. Wingspan 0.9–1.4 cm.
Food: Larva parasitizes scale insects of the genus *Kermes* (gall-like coccids).
Range: N.H. and s. Ont. to Fla., west to Kans. and Tex. May–Sept. Common.

Cosmopterix gemmiferella Clem. **Pl. 63 (8)**
Identification: Body and wings blackish brown; antennae and FW *white-tipped.* Wide orange median band of FW accented with *silver am. and pm. lines;* other silver markings include lines on head, line and spot on thorax, and 4 short basal streaks on FW. HW blackish, very thin, with wide fringe. Wingspan 0.9–1.2 cm.
Food: Larva mines leaves of panic-grass (*Panicum dichotomum*).
Range: Me. and Que. to Fla., west to Mo., Ark., and La. June–July; April–May southward. Common.

SHY COSMET *Limnaecia phragmitella* Staint. **Pl. 62 (15)**
Identification: Shiny yellowish tan FW has 2 white-ringed, *dark brown dots* in am. and pm. areas. Some dark brown shading near apex. HW tan, shaded with gray. Wingspan 1.5–2 cm.
Food: Flowers and developing seeds of cattails.
Range: N.S. to Va., west to Ont. and Okla. June–Aug. Common.

Triclonella pergandeella Bsk. **Pl. 61 (14)**
Identification: Basal and median area of FW dull yellow; *black* beyond curved pm. line. Look for a tiny black median dot. HW pale gray. Wingspan 1–1.3 cm.
Food: Butterfly pea and lespedeza; larva a leaf miner.
Range: Wash., D.C. to Fla., west to Kans. and Tex. March–Sept.; 2–3 broods. Common.

Periploca ceanothiella (Cosens) **Pl. 64 (11)**
Identification: Head, thorax, and FW *gleaming black;* abdomen and wide *fringe* of FW gray. Second segment of labial palp *twice as long* as third. HW gray, nearly all fringe. Wingspan 0.9–1.2 cm.

Food: New Jersey tea.
Range: Que. to N.Y., west to S.D. May–July.
Similar species: *P. gleditschiaeella* (Cham.), not shown, is superficially identical, but 2nd and 3rd segments of labial palp *same length.*
Food: Honey locust. Range: Md. to s. Ohio and Ky. May–June.

SWEETCLOVER ROOT BORER MOTH   Pl. 62 (14)
Walshia miscecolorella (Cham.)
Identification: Head, thorax and FW blackish. FW basal patch has 2 tufts; note *pale yellow median band,* also with tufts. St. area mottled reddish brown and blackish; more tufts along outer half of inner margin. HW gray; broad fringes on all wings. Wingspan 1–1.8 cm.
Food: Larva (**Sweetclover Root Borer**) bores in stems and roots of bull thistle, lupines, sweetclovers and other legumes.
Range: Me. to Fla., west across Canada, south to Tex. May–Nov.; 2 broods.

AGONOXENID MOTHS:
Family Agonoxenidae

Very small moths; wingspan 0.8–1 cm. Similar to both casebearer moths (p. 441) and elachistid moths (p. 443); some researchers believe agonoxenid moths and casebearers belong to the same family. Head smooth-scaled. Frons very oblique. Labial palps very long; *outermost segment flattened.* Wings narrow, lancelike (Fig. 58); 9 veins extend from FW discal cell, R_5 and M_1 *stalked.* Rs of HW *straight, well separated* from Sc + R_1 at base (close together in casebearers); Rs and M *not forked* as in elachistids (Fig. 62).

Larvae feed in loose silken webs on undersides of leaves and in bark; they pupate in a double-layered cocoon. Some species feed on palms in the tropics—one species is a pest on coconut palms. Only 6 species in N. America.

LINDEN BARK BORER MOTH   Pl. 63 (4)
Glyphipteryx linneella (Cl.)
Identification: Wings shiny black. Large elliptical *orange patch* on FW does not touch any wing margin, and contains 3 silvery black spots. Broad HW fringe. Wingspan 1 cm.

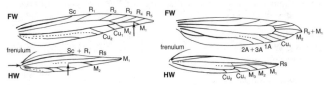

Fig. 58. Wing venation, Agonoxenidae.

Fig. 59. Wing venation, Momphidae.

Food: Larva (**Linden Bark Borer**) bores in bark of basswood in U.S. (feeds on linden trees in Europe).
Range: A European moth; discovered near N.Y.C. in 1928. Mass. to N.J. and s. N.Y., west to Mich. Late May–July.

MOMPHID MOTHS:
Family Momphidae

Small to very small moths; wingspan 0.8–1.6 cm. This family now includes only 1 genus (*Mompha*) with about 36 N. American species. Wings (Fig. 59) very similar to those of narrow-winged species of blastobasid moths (Fig. 61, p. 443), but FW *lacks pterostigma; anal veins usually absent* from HW. Momphid moths are also nearly identical to elachistid moths (p. 443); specialists use genitalic features to separate them.

In species for which life histories are known, momphid caterpillars feed in buds and seed capsules of evening-primroses and related plants. Blastobasid larvae feed on dead leaves or fallen nuts; elachistid larvae mine leaves of grasses and sedges.

Mompha circumscriptella (Zell.)   **Pl. 61 (27)**
Identification: FW shining white; outer half usually mottled with pale yellowish to grayish brown and black. *Gray triangular patch* on costa near base. Broad fringes on all wings, especially on gray HW. Wingspan 0.9–1.2 cm.
Food: Seed capsules of evening-primroses.
Range: N.J. to Fla., west to Mo. and Tex. May–Oct. Locally common.

Mompha eloisella (Clem.)   **Pl. 61 (28)**
Identification: Similar to *M. circumscriptella* (above), but larger. Look for 1 basal and 2 am. *black dots* on FW. Yellowish brown V-shaped lines fill st. and terminal areas, paralleling pointed apex and blackish point formed by fringe. HW gray with broad fringe. Wingspan 0.8–1.5 cm.
Food: Stems of evening-primroses.
Range: Common throughout our area. May–Aug.

CASEBEARER MOTHS:
Family Coleophoridae

Small to very small moths; wingspan 0.5–2.6 cm. Head smooth-scaled. Each antenna thickly scaled, tufted at base; shaft often ringed with alternating light and dark scales. Labial palps have 3 segments; 3rd segment usually upturned. Abdominal segments have *2 conspicuous dorsal patches of spines*. Wings lancelike (Fig. 60), usually all 1 color; sometimes streaked or dusted with other colors, but usual FW lines or markings absent. Apex of FW discal cell closer to inner margin than to costa. R_2 arises from top of cell *far from apex,* about halfway between R_1 and R_3. M_1 *absent.* If present, veins Cu_1 and Cu_2 are *very short* and directed toward outer margin.

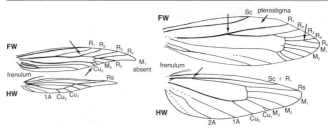

Fig. 60. Wing venation, Coleophoridae.

Fig. 61. Wing venation, Blastobasidae.

Larvae mine in leaves, seeds, and (rarely) stems; they are known as casebearers because they live in portable cases made from plant material and frass (excrement), held together with silk spun by the larvae. Larval cases are sometimes distinctive enough to be useful in identifying species. So far 169 species have been recognized in N. America but many more are present; much research needs to be done on this family.

Coleophora atromarginata Braun   **Pl. 62 (17)**
Identification: FW white; *costa and veins* of outer half *yellowish brown,* becoming *dark brown* toward apex. HW dark, gray with broad fringe. Wingspan 1–1.5 cm.
Food: Red oak and swamp white oak; also recorded on birch, cherry, hazelnut, hickory, and ironwood.
Range: N.S. to S.C., west to Man. and Ark. May–Aug.

LARCH CASEBEARER MOTH   **Pl. 64 (14)**
Coleophora laricella (Hbn.)
Identification: Wings shiny dark gray with no markings; wings turn brownish in old specimens. Each antenna *ringed with dark and pale gray* (use magnification). Wingspan 0.9–1 cm.
Food: Larches. Larva mines in needles, causing considerable damage (most noticeable in spring as empty needles shrivel and die). Larva (**Larch Casebearer**) overwinters in cigar-shaped case attached to base of leaf bud.
Range: A European moth, first found in Mass. in 1886. Nfld. to N.Y., west to Wisc. and Ohio. June–July.

Coleophora spissicornis (Haw.)   **Pl. 63 (7)**
Identification: Wings metallic dark brown with no markings. Each antenna *ringed* with brown and white beyond *thickened* basal half. Wingspan 1.1–1.2 cm.
Food: Clover seeds.
Range: Common throughout our area. May–Aug.

Homaledra heptathalama Bsk.   **Pl. 61 (15)**
Identification: FW tan, entirely *bordered with brown.* Note *2 silvery white spots* in center of FW—inner spot tear-shaped. HW shiny yellowish tan with broad fringe. Wingspan 1.8–2.6 cm.

Food: Cabbage palm. Larva makes mud "house" in 7 distinct parts on mid-vein of frond near the tip.
Range: Fla. March–Oct. Common.

BLASTOBASID MOTHS:
Family Blastobasidae

A large family (over 300 species) of small to very small moths; wingspan 0.8–1.6 cm. Most species are gray, brownish, whitish, or yellowish, without striking patterns. Head scales *smooth and long, curling down* over face. Labial palps long, upturned; usually reaching beyond top of head (but very short and directed forward in some species). FW broad, rounded to lancelike. Most species have a distinct *pterostigma* (thickened membrane) along FW costa between veins Sc and R_1 (Fig. 61). R_1 arises in *basal half or middle* of large discal cell; R_2 arises near apex of cell. R_4 and R_5 *stalked* for much of length, usually from end of discal cell. HW usually narrower than FW; Sc + R_1 usually *fused with Rs for short distance* near base.

Larvae are scavengers on decaying plants, or borers in nuts already attacked by other insects. Taxonomy and life history of species in this family not well known; still in need of much study.

Glyphidocera lactiflosella (Cham.) **Pl. 63 (22)**
Identification: FW whitish with blackish dusting and terminal line. Usually 5 blackish dots—*all but 3rd dot* lined up in a row along FW. HW whitish with gray shading. Wingspan 1.2–1.3 cm.
Food: Unrecorded.
Range: Md. to Fla., west to Tex. May–Sept.

ACORN MOTH *Valentinia glandulella* (Riley) **Pl. 62 (16)**
Identification: FW mottled powdery pale and darker gray, darkest in median area. Am. line bent, whitish; 1 black median dot and 2 reniform *dots form triangle.* Terminal line a series of dark gray dots. HW shiny gray. Wingspan 1.5–2.5 cm.
Food: Larva feeds inside acorns and chestnuts.
Range: Throughout our area. April–Sept.

ELACHISTID MOTHS:
Family Elachistidae

A small family of very small moths (wingspan 0.6–1.1 cm). Usually gray to brown or black, with white to silvery markings. Head smooth-scaled; vertex slightly rough in some species. Wings broadly lancelike; FW slightly broader than HW (Fig. 62). Discal cell complete only in FW; incompletely closed if present in HW. In FW, vein R_1 arises from *top* of discal cell, near middle; 8–9 veins extend from cell (5 or fewer to costa from top of cell; only 1–2 from cell apex). Rs and M_1 of HW *forked* well toward HW apex.

In this family, larvae mine leaves of grasses and sedges, then pupate

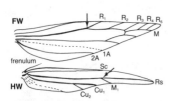

Fig. 62. Wing venation, Elachistidae.

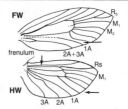

Fig. 63. Wing venation, Oecophoridae.

in loose, meshlike cocoons or as naked pupae attached to plants or other objects by a silken girdle around the middle.

Cosmiotes illectella Clem.   **Pl. 64 (9)**
Identification: FW grayish brown, mottled with grayish white, especially toward outer margin. Complete white am. band; white *pm. band broken* at middle. HW gray. Wingspan 0.6–0.8 cm.
Food: Larva mines in leaves of grasses such as Kentucky bluegrass, bottle-brush grass, and timothy.
Range: Mass. and Ont. to Tenn., west to Mich. and Mo. April–Sept.

OECOPHORID MOTHS:
Family Oecophoridae

Very small to medium-sized moths; wingspan 0.3–3 cm (usually closer to 3 cm). Head smooth-scaled; labial palps usually upturned. FW rather broad, often squarish as in some tortricid moths (Pl. 61); apex and outer margin *rounded* (Fig. 63). Vein *1A present,* at least at *outer margin* of FW. HW variable—usually broad; rounded to lancelike, but *outer margin rounded* (as shown). Rs and M_1 of HW usually separate and parallel, except in subfamilies Stenomatinae (*Antaeotricha* species, Pl. 62) and Peleopodinae (not shown).

Larvae usually feed concealed in webs or in rolled or tied leaves of food plant. Some feed on dead leaves or animal carcasses, or on decaying fungi. These moths pupate in their larval shelters or in other parts of food plant, or on the ground or below its surface.

A large family with 7 N. American subfamilies, 4 of which are treated in this guide: Drepressariinae (*Agonopterix, Machimia,* and *Psilocorsis* species), Ethmiinae (*Ethmia* species), Stenomatinae (*Antaeotricha* species), and Oecophorinae (*Callima* and *Mathildana* species). Some researchers treat subfamilies Ethmiinae and Stenomatinae as separate families (Ethmiidae and Stenomidae).

Agonopterix robiniella (Pack.)   **Pl. 61 (20)**
Identification: FW reddish to yellowish orange, variably mottled with brown and sparsely peppered with black. Vague *gray line curves outward* from midpoint of costa, then back to meet inner margin; sometimes a branch toward anal angle. Black discal dot often present. HW gray. Wingspan 1.7–2.3 cm.

Food: Black locust and oaks.
Range: N.S. to mts. of Ga., west to Mo. and Ark. June–Oct. Common.

GOLD-STRIPED LEAFTIER MOTH   Pl. 61 (19)
Machimia tentoriferella Clem.
Identification: FW yellowish gray to grayish brown. Note *2 sharp blackish dots* in am. and reniform positions that form a *triangle* with *more diffuse spot* on inner margin. Diffuse pm. line usually present. HW pale grayish brown. Wingspan 2–2.6 cm.
Food: Ash, elms, maples, oaks, and many other trees. Larva (**Gold-striped Leaftier**) rolls or ties leaves of food plant together.
Range: N.S. to Va., west to Iowa and Miss. June–July; Sept.-Oct. Common.

Psilocorsis quercicella Clem.   **Pl. 64 (23)**
Identification: FW usually pale yellow or yellowish orange with contrasting gray fringe. FW crossed by several brownish orange blotches and a vague, dark brownish gray *oblique median band.* Adterminal line complete from costa to anal angle but not solid—a series of black dots. HW variably dark grayish brown. Wingspan 1.2–1.5 cm.
Food: Larva has been reared on beech, chestnut and various oaks.
Range: N.S. to Fla., west to Kans. and Tex. May–Sept.; 2 broods. Common.
Similar species: (1) In *P. relexella* Clem. (below) FW is darker. (2) In *P. cryptolechiella* (Cham.), not shown, FW is usually paler orange or yellow, with several thin, *dark gray to brown transverse lines* (not blotches); adterminal line runs *only halfway* from costa to anal angle. Fringe darker gray or brownish. Food: Chestnut, locust, northern bayberry; reared on oaks. Range: Me. to n. Fla., west to Ark. and Tex. April–Sept.; 2 broods.

Psilocorsis reflexella Clem.   **Pl. 61 (21)**
Identification: Similar to *P. quercicella* (above), but slightly *larger;* FW *darker* with fine grayish brown mottling over yellowish brown ground color. Blackish am. and discal dots, and oblique, dark brown *pm. line* usually faintly visible. HW grayish brown. Wingspan 1.6–2.5 cm.
Food: Aspen, basswood, beech, birches, hickories, maples, and oaks. Larva is a leaf tier.
Range: Me. and Que. to Fla., west to Wisc. and Tex. March–Sept. Common.

Ethmia zelleriella (Cham.)   **Pl. 62 (21)**
Identification: Easily recognized by the *yellow abdomen* and grayish white FW marked with sharp, elongate black spots. HW shiny translucent white, with gray shading. Wingspan 2.2–2.7 cm.
Food: Phacelias.
Range: S. Que. to N.C., west to Mo. and Tex. April–July. May be locally common.

Ethmia trifurcella (Cham.)   **Pl. 62 (19)**
Identification: FW white with *broad, broken, black shade* in costal half. Terminal line a series of tiny black dots. HW gray. Wingspan 1.6–1.9 cm.

Food: Wild comfrey (*Cynoglossum virginianum*).
Range: Pa. to Fla., west to Mo. June–Sept. Probably 2 broods.

Antaeotricha schlaegeri (Zell.)   **Pl. 62 (20)**
Identification: At rest, this moth resembles bird droppings on leaves.
Note brownish black tuft toward rear edge of thorax. Wings white; FW
has *large gray basal patch* near inner margin, st. patch, and 3 terminal
lines (middle one *dotted*). Look for a brown scale tuft on inner margin,
near base of FW. Wingspan 2.1–3 cm.
Food: White oak and possibly white birch.
Range: Que. and Mass. to N.C., west to Kans. and Tex. April–Aug.
Common.

Antaeotricha leucillana (Zell.)   **Pl. 62 (18)**
Identification: Very similar to *A. schlaegeri* (above), but smaller,
with *less gray near base* of FW on inner margin. Thoracic tuft usually
paler. To confirm identification, specialists examine genitalia of ♂
(uncus forked at tip in *A. leucillana;* simple, curved in *A. schlaegeri*).
Wingspan 1.5–2.3 cm.
Food: Ashes, basswood, birches, elms, maples, oaks, poplars, willows,
and other trees.
Range: Common throughout our area. April–Aug.

Callima argenticinctella Clem.   **Pl. 61 (16)**
Identification: Each antenna ringed with black and white scales. FW
orange, including fringe; lines white, edged with black. Note *white
reniform spot* at costa. Brown basal patch, rounded patch along inner
margin near anal angle, and mixed brown and white shade in st. area.
HW gray. Wingspan 1.1–1.2 cm.
Food: Larva has been reared on corn plants; found under bark of elm
trees in the wild.
Range: N.S. to S.C., west to Kans. and Tex. May–early Sept.; as early
as March in Tex. Common.

Mathildana newmanella (Clem.)   **Pl. 61 (17)**
Identification: FW metallic blackish brown, with *2 yellow to orange
streaks*—one extending from base, the other above and just beyond the
first streak (looks like 1 marking without magnification). HW paler
brown with broad fringe. Wingspan 1.5–1.8 cm.
Food: Larva feeds in web under bark of standing dead trees such as
apple trees.
Range: Me. and s. Que. to w. N.C., west to Ohio and Ark. April–June.

LEAF BLOTCH MINER MOTHS:
Family Gracillariidae

Small to minute moths; wingspan 0.4–2 cm. Usually colorful, with *long
fringes* on FW and HW (Pl. 61). Top of head rough- to smooth-scaled.
Antennae long; eye-cap (Fig. 4, p. 3) sometimes present at base. If
present, maxillary palps short, projecting forward. Labial palps well
developed, sometimes long and upturned; 3rd segment usually at slight
angle to 2nd segment. Wings lancelike (Fig. 64). FW discal cell long,
with 8 or fewer veins extending from it to margins—usually no more

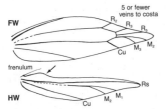

Fig. 64.
Wing venation,
Gracillariidae.

than 4 veins to costa (5 in genus *Callisto,* not shown). HW *very narrow; costal margin* usually *dips inward* not far from base, making basal part look humped.

Larvae usually form blotch mines in leaves (serpentine mines with dark line of frass down center in genus *Phyllocnistis,* not shown). These moths usually pupate in their mines. Adults often *elevate front of body* while at rest, pushing tips of folded wings against surface on which they are resting.

Caloptilia murtfeldtella (Bsk.) **Pl. 61 (23)**
Identification: Thorax yellow with orangish brown markings. FW pale yellow with orangish brown shading at base and apex; thin orangish streaks run lengthwise along wing. Fringe scales just below apex tipped with grayish brown, forming *4 sharp, parallel lines* (magnification needed). HW grayish brown. Wingspan 1.8–2 cm.
Food: Unrecorded.
Range: S. Ohio and Ky., west to Mo. and Ark. June, Sept.

Caloptilia superbifrontella (Clem.) **Pl. 64 (24)**
Identification: Head, thorax, and FW gleaming lemon yellow. FW has broad, semicircular *yellow median patch* flanked by large *brownish and iridescent purple patches* in basal and terminal areas; orange along inner margin. HW dark gray. Wingspan 1.1–1.3 cm.
Food: Witch-hazel; larva rolls leaf of food plant into a cone.
Range: N.H. to S.C., west to Ky. and Ark. June–Aug.

Micrurapteryx salicifoliella (Cham.) **Pl. 64 (7)**
Identification: Head and thorax white. FW long, narrow; dark brown with blackish shading (especially along irregular *broad white border* of inner margin). Incomplete white lines curve inward from outer half of costa and blend into brown st. area. Note black spot at apex. HW gray; extremely thin with broad fringe. Wingspan 0.9–1 cm.
Food: Willows; larva forms a blotch mine in leaf.
Range: Ohio to Ky., west to Mo. Oct.–Nov. Common.

Cameraria conglomeratella (Zell.) **Pl. 63 (9)**
Identification: Each antenna white with brown rings. FW golden brown; 2 short, straight *white costal dashes* slant toward anal angle. White st. line forked, with branch to costa near apex. Dark brown shading beyond dashes and lines, heaviest along outer margin. HW gray, with wide fringe. Wingspan 0.6–0.9 cm.
Food: Oaks; larva forms a blotch mine in leaf.
Range: N.Y. and N.J. to Fla., west to Mo. and Tex. March–June; Sept.–Oct.; at least 2 broods.

SOLITARY OAK LEAFMINER MOTH   Pl. 64 (10)
Cameraria hamadryadella (Clem.)

Identification: Head and thorax white; abdomen gray. FW covered with gray-tipped white scales; FW pure white in basal area and beyond *lead-gray median and pm. bands.* Gray-tipped white scales form 2–3 basal spots and interrupt pm. band above middle. HW gray, very narrow; fringes of both wings shiny grayish white. Wingspan 0.6–0.9 cm.
Food: Hornbeam, magnolias, and oaks; larva (**Solitary Oak Leafminer**) a pest that forms blotch mines in leaves.
Range: S. Que. to N.C., west to w. Ont. and Ky. April–Aug. Common.

Cameraria obstrictella (Clem.)   Pl. 63 (11)

Identification: FW reddish brown, crossed by *3 silver bands.* Blackish edging beyond silver bands and black shading in apical area. HW dark gray, with *broad fringe.* Wingspan 0.7–0.8 cm.
Food: Oaks, usually chestnut oak. Larval mine usually Y-shaped.
Range: Me. to Pa., west to Ohio and Ky. April–early Aug.

LYONETIID MOTHS:
Family Lyonetiidae

Tiny moths; wingspan 0.4–1.1 cm. Vertex covered with *rough, bristly scales,* but scales of frons smooth. Base of each antenna usually surrounded by an *eye-cap* (Fig. 65A). No ocelli or maxillary palps. Labial palps short, drooping. Wings lancelike, ending in *narrow points* (Fig. 65B); 3–4 veins extend from top of FW discal cell to costa. R_1 arises from discal cell well toward base of FW. HW linear, with extensive fringe. Rs often extends *through middle* of wing to apex.

Larval habits vary; in *Bucculatrix* (our largest genus), larvae make whitish serpentine mines in leaves and leave a fine black line of frass down center of mine. In most species, later instars skeletonize leaves. These moths usually pupate in a ribbed, whitish cocoon formed along twig of food plant. Cocoon of each species is distinctive, sometimes distinctive enough to identify the species.

BIRCH SKELETONIZER MOTH   Pl. 63 (16)
Bucculatrix canadensisella Cham.

Identification: FW brown to grayish brown, variably mottled with white; *white spots* on inner margin with *darker brown* between them. Blackish brown shading at apex continues into apical fringe. HW pale gray. Wingspan 0.7–0.9 cm.
Food: Birches; larva (**Birch Skeletonizer**) makes a twisted, linear mine in leaf.
Range: Nfld. to w. N.C. and e. Tenn., west across Canada, south to Minn. May–July. Common.

OAK SKELETONIZER MOTH   Pl. 63 (12)
Bucculatrix ainsliella Murt.

Identification: Head and body white with brown shading. FW shiny brown with white base. Whitish *am. and pm. bands broken* in middle. White median streak extends inward from costa, and some white in

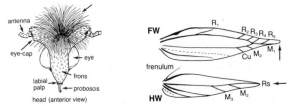

Fig. 65. A (*left*) Head (anterior view), Lyonetiidae. **B** (*right*) Wing venation, Lyonetiidae.

terminal area below *dark brown spot* at apex. Note brown spot beyond am. line at inner margin. HW pale silvery gray. Wingspan 0.7–0.8 cm.
Food: Chestnut and oaks; larva (**Oak Skeletonizer**) makes thread-like mine along leaf midrib.
Range: N.S. to S.C., west to Minn. and Mo. April–early Aug. Common.

CEREAL STEM MOTH:
Family Ochsenheimeriidae

Head rough-scaled, including antennae, which look like *shaggy horns*. Frons broad. Compound eyes small; ocelli prominent. R_5 of FW ends at costa, *very close to apex*. Base of vein M present on HW (Fig. 66).
   This family includes 23 species worldwide, all in the same genus (*Ochsenheimeria*). Our only N. American species was recently introduced, and its known range is limited. If it spreads, it may become a serious pest on grains in the future.

CEREAL STEM MOTH   **Pl. 64 (18)**
Ochsenheimeria vacculella F. v. Rösslerstamm
Identification: Body grayish brown, with *yellowish band on abdomen*. FW grayish brown, dotted and blotched with yellowish to light brown, lighter toward outer margin. HW whitish in basal half, light grayish brown beyond median line. Wingspan 1.1–1.4 cm.
Food: Various grasses, including winter wheat. A pest of cereals.
Range: A Eurasian moth, accidentally introduced into the U.S. sometime before 1964. Reported in N.Y., Pa., and Ohio. June–Sept.

Fig. 66.
Wing venation,
Ochsenheimeriidae.

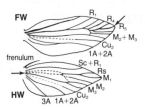

BAGWORM MOTHS:
Family Psychidae

A small family of small to medium-sized moths. Wings usually absent or vestigial (reduced to small nubs) in ♀; wingspan in ♂ 1.2–3.6 cm. Males black in most of our species; wings usually unmarked. Abdomen usually long and tapering. Veins *1A and 2A of FW fused* to form apex of *basal areole* (Fig. 67), then continuing as a single vein to outer margin. HW may be broad (as shown) or narrower; 2–3 anal veins present. Mouth parts vestigial in adults of both sexes; antennae, eyes, and legs absent in females of some species.

Larvae (bagworms) form characteristic *spindle-shaped silken cases* covered with bits of leaves, twigs, or other debris; each larva enlarges its case as it grows. These moths pupate in the larval case after it is attached to a twig with silk. In most species, ♀ does not leave the case, but attracts males by emitting pheromones (chemical sex attractants) from her abdomen. To mate, ♂ thrusts his abdomen through the open lower end of the case. The ♀ lays her eggs in the case; when they hatch, larvae crawl away to feed and form their own silken cases.

Cryptothelea gloverii (Pack.)   **Pl. 62 (24)**
Identification: Wings in ♂ evenly dark, *smoky grayish brown.* Antennae bipectinate in ♂; segments 22–24 of each antenna have thick branches. Wing scales hairlike; no FW pattern. HW broadly rounded. ♀ wingless, usually does not leave case. Wingspan of ♂ 1.4–1.8 cm.
Food: Acacia, avocado, citrus, guava, hawthorn, oaks, yuccas, and other plants. Larva has also been reported eating scale insects.
Range: Coastal S.C. to Fla., west to Tex. All year.

EVERGREEN BAGWORM MOTH   **Pls. 2 (3), 62 (23)**
Thyridopteryx ephemeraeformis (Haw.)
Identification: Body in ♂ entirely black. Wings also entirely black but usually *translucent* from loss of scales after emergence from larval case. Abdomen long, *tapering.* ♀ entirely wingless and does not leave larval case. Wingspan of ♂ 1.7–3.6 cm.
Food: Larva (**Evergreen Bagworm**) feeds on many trees, shrubs, and herbaceous plants. A pest of ornamentals, particularly red cedar. Larva attaches its case (Pl. 2) with silk to twig of food plant.
Range: Mass. to s. Fla., west to Neb. and Tex. Sept–Oct. April–June records may represent release of individuals reared indoors. Common.

CLOTHES MOTHS and OTHERS:
Family Tineidae

A fairly large family of small to medium-small moths; wingspan 0.7–3.6 cm. Most species are dark, but some species that are important as pests are pale, with or without markings. Head scales very rough in most species; maxillary palps variable—5-segmented to absent. Labial palps almost always have *stout hairs* projecting from 2nd segment. Wings

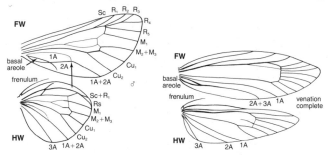

Fig. 67. Wing venation, Psychidae (♂ only).

Fig. 68. Wing venation, Tineidae.

broadly lancelike to somewhat rounded at tips; venation *complete* (*all anal veins present*) in most genera (Fig. 68).

Larvae eat a variety of food including dead plant and animal matter, fungi, wool, and similar materials; *Acrolophus* species feed on roots of grasses. Most larvae form cases similar to those of casebearers (p. 441); *Acrolophus* species form silken tunnels among roots of grasses.

Limits of subfamilies within this family not yet clearly defined. *Acrolophus* species are grouped in subfamily Acrolophinae, which some researchers have treated as a separate family (Acrolophidae).

EUROPEAN GRAIN MOTH or WOLF MOTH   Pl. 63 (10)
Nemapogon granella (L.)
Identification: FW cream-colored, heavily spotted with metallic brown; look for *6 brown spots* along costa. HW gray. Wingspan 1.1–1.2 cm.
Food: Grains of all kinds (both in fields and in storage). Webbing holding kernels together is sign of larval infestation. Larva also reared from dried mushrooms and shelf fungus. Not an important pest.
Range: Throughout our area; introduced from Europe. July. Uncommon.

Acrolophus morus (Grt.)   Pl. 61 (24)
Identification: Body more slender than in other *Acrolophus* species. FW blackish in ♂, dull yellowish brown in ♀; both variably speckled with darker brown or black. Note vague *blackish bar* in lower median area and reniform spot. FW outer margin slightly brownish in ♀. HW dark grayish brown in both sexes. Wingspan 2.5–3.3 cm.
Food: Birches.
Range: N.H. to Fla., west to Minn. and Ky. Sept–early Nov. Locally common.

Acrolophus plumifrontella (Clem.)   Pl. 61 (22)
Identification: FW brown tinted with red, generally speckled with darker brown. Diffuse darker brown reniform spot and *2 squarish spots* side by side near inner margin. Palps very hairy. HW grayish brown. Wingspan 2.6–3.6 cm.

Food: Unrecorded.
Range: N.H. to Fla., west to Neb. and Tex. April–Oct. Common.

Acrolophus popeanella (Clem.)   **Pl. 62 (3)**
Identification: FW yellowish to reddish brown, sometimes purplish, heavily streaked and mottled with dark grayish brown. Note *median spot near inner margin* of FW; variable black basal streak and reniform blotch also present. Area between basal streak and median spot whitish; whitish border along basal $\frac{2}{3}$ of inner margin. HW grayish brown. Wingspan 2.4–3.3 cm.
Food: Roots of red clover.
Range: N.J. to Fla., west to Neb. and Tex. May–Sept. Common.

CASEMAKING CLOTHES MOTH   Pl. 63 (14)
Tinea pellionella L.
Identification: FW shiny grayish tan to gray; slightly darker brown *reniform spot* and, in fresh specimens, a similar spot in median area. HW grayish. Wingspan 1–1.5 cm.
Food: Woolens, furs, feathers, and similar animal products. Also reported eating dried plant materials such as almonds, ginger, and tobacco. Larva lives in a small, tubular white case.
Range: Throughout our area. All year indoors. Less common in homes than Webbing Clothes Moth (below, Pl. 63), so not as serious a pest.
Similar species: Two other moths in our area look almost identical (specialists dissect genitalia of males to confirm identification), but are even less common: (1) *T. dubiella* Staint. and (2) *T. translucens* Meyr. (not shown). Larval habits also similar. Another household pest, (3) the Angoumois Grain Moth (p. 437, Pl. 62) is similar in color and FW markings, but has *trapezoidal HW* and different larval feeding habits—larva bores holes into kernels of corn and other grains.

CARPET MOTH *Trichophaga tapetzella* (L.)   **Pl. 63 (20)**
Identification: FW white with blackish basal area; the *border* between black and white *oblique, straight* and *sharp*. Gray and black spotting in white area, especially at apex. HW pale shiny gray with broad fringe. Wingspan 1.2–2.4 cm.
Food: A pest on furs, skins, felt, carpets, and other animal materials. Also reported feeding on wallpaper and fecal pellets of owls.
Range: Worldwide, throughout our area but not yet reported from Fla. and some other states. All year. The rarest of our clothes moths.

Monopis dorsistrigella (Clem.)   **Pl. 64 (19)**
Identification: Head and thorax white; tegulae and FW blackish brown. Large *white spot* on costa, near midpoint; uneven white border along inner margin. HW dark gray. Wingspan 1.2–1.4 cm.
Food: Unrecorded.
Range: Me. to N.C., west to s. Ont. and Mo. June–July.

WEBBING CLOTHES MOTH   Pl. 63 (15)
Tineola bisselliella (Hummel)
Identification: FW uniformly *shiny golden tan*; usually unmarked, but dark reniform dot sometimes present. Head has some reddish brown hair-scales. HW paler than FW, slightly translucent. Wingspan 1.2–1.5 cm.

Food: Woolens, furs, feathers, brushes made from animal bristles, dead insects, dried animal carcasses, pollen, and other dried plant and animal products. Larvae form silken tunnels or mats over material on which they are feeding. The most important clothes moth pest in our area.
Range: Worldwide; occurring throughout our area. All months indoors.

SHIELD BEARER MOTHS:
Family Heliozelidae

Tiny moths; wingspan 0.4–1 cm. FW usually has metallic markings. Head entirely smooth-scaled. Maxillary palps minute; labial palps short, drooping. Proboscis short, scaled at base. Wings lancelike, with variable venation: if discal cell is present (as shown in Fig. 69), 4 veins extend from cell to costa and inner margin of FW, as in *Antispila* and *Heliozela* species; if discal cell is absent, 4 veins extend to FW costa and 3–4 to inner margin (3 veins in *Coptodisca* species, not shown). Veins R_5 and M_1 *stalked*. HW veins reduced; Rs widely separated from $Sc + R_1$.

Larvae form small blotch mines in leaves of various broad-leaved plants, packing much frass in oldest parts of each leaf mine. A characteristic oval "shield" is cut from the food plant to form the cocoon, hence the name shield bearer. Cocoon drops to ground or is bound by silk to leaf litter on the ground.

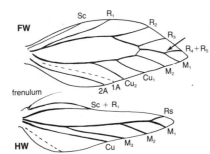

Fig. 69.
Wing venation,
Heliozelidae.

TUPELO LEAFMINER MOTH   Pl. 63 (18)
Antispila nysaefoliella Clem.
Identification: FW dark gleaming greenish brown. Broad silver to *golden am. band,* which is *narrower at costa* than at inner margin. Triangular median patch at inner margin; another represents top of pm. line at costa. HW dark gray with broad fringe. Wingspan 0.7–0.8 cm.
Food: Larva mines leaves of tupelo and black gum trees.
Range: N.Y. to Wash., D.C., west to Ohio. May.

YUCCA and FAIRY MOTHS:
Family Incurvariidae

Small to medium-small moths; wingspan 0.9–3.3 cm. Antennae short to very long; simple. Wings rounded at tips; aculeae (tiny spines) present on FW. FW venation usually complete; R_5 *extends to costa near apex* (Fig. 70A). HW nearly as wide as FW. Females have strong ovipositors, used to pierce plants when eggs are laid. Larvae either form cases or bore in stems, seeds, or fruits of host plants.

Some researchers treat the 3 subfamilies described below as separate families. The 3 species of incurvariid moths described below represent each subfamily respectively:

Incurvariinae—Small, usually dark moths. Maxillary palp conspicuous, folded down: length of folded part $= \frac{1}{2}$ width of head. Older larvae make cases from plant material.

Prodoxinae (yucca moths)—Mostly white. Length of folded part of maxillary palp $= \frac{2}{3}$ width of head. Females of genus *Tegeticula* have curved "tentacles" (Fig. 70B), which are used to collect pollen from yuccas.

Adelinae (fairy moths)—Easily recognized by their *extremely long antennae* (1–$1\frac{1}{4}$ times length of FW or longer), unique in our area. Larvae make silken cases.

MAPLE LEAFCUTTER MOTH   Pl. 63 (17)
Paraclemensia acerifoliella (Fitch)
Identification: *Head orange;* antennae black. FW dark metallic blue to greenish blue with no markings. HW gray. Wingspan 0.9–1.2 cm.
Food: Beeches, birches, huckleberries, maples, and oaks. Larva (**Maple Leafcutter**) starts out as a leaf miner, and later cuts 2 circular pieces from a leaf to form a turtlelike "shell" or case that it carries about. Occasionally a pest.
Range: Nfld. to N.C., west to Ont., Mich., and Ky. April–June.

YUCCA MOTH *Tegeticula yuccasella* (Riley)   Pl. 48 (24)
Identification: *FW pure white,* without markings. HW gray with

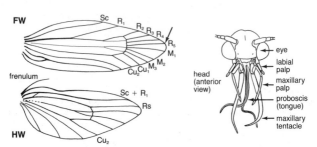

Fig. 70. A (*left*) Wing venation, Incurvariidae (*Tegeticula yuccasella*). **B** (*right*) Head (anterior view), Incurvariidae (*Tegeticula* sp.)

white fringe. Maxillary palp in ♀ bears a long, curved "tentacle" (Fig. 70B) for collecting pollen from yuccas. Wingspan 1.5–3.3 cm.
Food: Yuccas; usually *Yucca filamentosa* in our area. ♀ punctures pistil of flower, inserts 1 egg per puncture, and then packs pollen into opening. This ensures pollinization of the flower and a seed supply for the larvae to feed on.
Range: Mass. and s. Ont. to s. Fla., west to N.D. and Tex. May–early July. Adults emerge when yucca plants bloom.

Adela purpurea Wlk. **Pl. 62 (8)**
Identification: *Antennae long*—each antenna 3 times length of FW in ♂; antennae short in ♀. FW dark greenish, bluish, or purplish with *white pm. band* and small white streak on costa near apex. HW translucent gray. Wingspan 1.4–1.5 cm.
Food: Larval food unrecorded; adults reported on willow blossoms.
Range: N.S. to N.J., west to Man. April–June.

TISCHERIID MOTHS:
Family Tischeriidae

Very small moths; wingspan 0.6–1.1 cm. *Tuft* of rough scales on top of head (vertex) contrasts with smooth scales on frons. Maxillary palps small; labial palps short. Proboscis scaled toward base. Wings narrow, drawn out to *sharp points* (Fig. 71). FW costa *bulges* slightly outward. Areole (accessory cell) may be up to half as long as discal cell; 5 veins from top of cells *end at costa, between vein Sc and FW apex.* HW veins reduced, *unbranched.* Frenulum in ♂ normal; 2 small bristles form frenulum in ♀.

Larvae mine leaves of plants in the composite, beech, mallow, and rose families. Leaf mines are characteristically shaped like trumpets or blotches, often at leaf margins. Pupation occurs in leaf mine.

About 30 of the 47 N. American species of *Tischeria,* the only genus in the family, occur in our area. Although taxonomy of this family was recently revised by the late Annette F. Braun, more species probably await discovery.

Tischeria zelleriella Clem. **Pl. 63 (13)**
Identification: FW bright, shiny orange-yellow, with *reddish or*

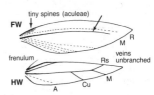

Fig. 71. Wing venation, Tischeriidae (*Tischeria* sp.)

Fig. 72. Wing venation, Opostegidae.

brownish shading toward apex. No markings. HW gray. Wingspan 0.75–0.95 cm.

Food: Larva mines leaves of chestnut and oak trees.

Range: Que. to n. Fla., west to Ont., Mo. and Tex. March–Aug.

OPOSTEGID MOTHS:
Family Opostegidae

Tiny moths; wingspan 0.4–0.9 cm. First segment of each antenna a large *eye-cap* that covers eye and base of FW. Wings narrow, lancelike; tiny spines (aculeae) present, but only near base of FW. FW veins *unbranched,* and *only 1 vein* (M) *is distinctly thick and tubular* (Fig. 72).

Larvae mine stems or leaves, but life cycles are incompletely known for most of the 7 species of *Opostega,* the only N. American genus in the family.

Opostega quadristrigella Cham.   **Pl. 64 (8)**
Identification: FW shiny white with *brownish gray dash* midway along inner margin. Tiny black dot at wingtip. HW gray. Wingspan 0.8–0.9 cm.

Food: Currants and gooseberry; larva mines in fibrous inner lining of bark.

Range: Mass. to Fla., west to Ark. and Tex. May–late June.

NEPTICULID MOTHS:
Family Nepticulidae

Among our tiniest moths; wingspan 0.3–0.7 cm. Basal segment of each antenna enlarged, concave beneath, forming an *eye-cap.* Labial palps short; maxillary palps long and folded. Wings narrow, pointed; *venation reduced, branched* (Fig. 73). Tiny spines (aculeae) scattered over wing (magnification needed). Frenulum a strong spine in ♂, reduced to a few minute bristles in ♀, but FW and HW held together by a row of *curved costal bristles* near HW base (Fig. 73, bottom).

Larvae mine in leaves or bark of trees, sometimes producing tiny galls. Leaf mines linear, at least in early instars; changing to blotches in later instars in some species. Adults can run and fly fast and erratically; it is easiest to collect them in crevices of tree bark, where they rest with their wings folded flat (edges meet down the back). These habits, plus their small size, explain why so few have been collected. Many species are still undiscovered; life histories of many are unknown.

Ectoedemia virgulae (Braun)   **Pl. 64 (21)**
Identification: Look for brownish yellow scale tuft on frons and whitish eye-caps; antennae brown. FW black with *silver fringe* and *curved median band,* widest at costa. HW gray. Wingspan 0.4–0.5 cm.

Food: Larva mines leaves of hazelnut trees.

Range: Ohio, Fla., and Tex. May, July.

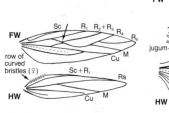

Fig. 73. Wing venation,
Nepticulidae.

Fig. 74. Wing venation,
Hepialidae.

GHOST MOTHS or SWIFTS:
Family Hepialidae

Our only large to medium-sized moths (wingspan 2.5–10 cm) with a
fingerlike *jugum* on inner margin of FW, near base (Fig. 74). Our few
species are usually yellowish, brownish, or grayish, with silver markings
on FW. Antennae usually short with beadlike segments. Wings covered
with tiny spines (aculeae) that are visible only under magnification.
Venation similar, *complete* on FW and HW (Fig. 74); *humeral vein*
strong in both wings.

Larvae bore in roots of trees and perhaps some other plants. Life
cycle takes 1–2 years. Adults are short-lived and do not feed. The dart-
ing, zigzag flight of these moths at dusk prompted the name "swifts."
Since they seldom come to lights or bait they are rare in collections, but
may be numerous when found in mating swarms.

Sthenopis species (below) are large with pointed FW apex (Pl. 7);
Hepialus species are smaller (wingspan 2.5–5 cm), with more rounded
FW apex, as shown in Fig. 74.

SILVER-SPOTTED GHOST MOTH   Pl. 7 (10)
Sthenopis argenteomaculatus (Harr.)
Identification: One of our largest "micros," with gray to tan FW
crossed by irregular dark bands. Note silver dot near base and *silver
triangle* beyond it. HW gray in ♂, yellowish in ♀ (shown). Wingspan
6.5–10 cm.
Food: Larva bores in roots of alders that are partially submerged in
water. Life cycle takes 2 years.
Range: N.S. to Va., west to Minn. June–Aug. Swarms of males fly near
alder groves in dancing patterns; females enter swarms to mate. Moths
fly at dusk, and are not attracted to lights or bait.

ERIOCRANIID MOTHS:
Family Eriocraniidae

Tiny day-fliers with nonfunctional mandibles; proboscis short but
functional (adults feed on various liquids). Middle tibia bears *1 spur*.

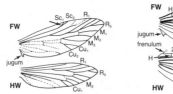

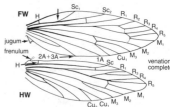

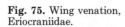

Fig. 75. Wing venation, Eriocraniidae.

Fig. 76. Wing venation, Micropterygidae.

Wings have tiny spines (aculeae) in basal patches; venation complete, similar in FW and HW (Fig. 75). Sc of FW *forked far from base; jugum* present toward base on inner margin; small frenulum may also be present.

Larva (early instars) makes linear mine in leaves of broad-leaved trees; later instars form blotch mines. Pupa has loose appendages, including movable mandibles for cutting through tough cocoon in which it pupates underground. Adults emerge in spring; they are short-lived. Rare in collections.

Dyseriocrania griseocapitella (Wlsm.)   **Pl. 61 (25)**
Identification: Head and thorax have mixed white and grayish brown hair scales. FW *metallic brown* mixed with iridescent blue and purple scales (visible under magnification). HW gray. Wingspan 0.9–1.3 cm.
Food: Larva mines leaves of chestnut, chinquapin, and oaks.
Range: N.S. to Fla., west to Ill. and Miss. April–May; 1 brood, which emerges as early as Feb. southward.

MANDIBULATE MOTHS:
Family Micropterigidae

Very small, dark moths with short fringes on wings; wingspan 0.9–1.2 cm. Our only adult moths with *functional mandibles,* used for eating pollen. FW and HW very similar in size, shape, and venation (Fig. 76); tiny spines (aculeae) present. Sc of FW *forked* before its midpoint; small *jugum* at base on inner margin.

Larva sluglike; feeds on mosses and liverworts. Pupa has sharp mandibles for cutting its way out of parchmentlike cocoon. The 2 N. American species are rarely collected, and are best sought in daytime in beds of mosses and liverworts.

Epimartyria auricrinella Wlsm.   **Pl. 61 (26)**
Identification: FW dark gray with coppery scales that look iridescent (mostly metallic purple with some gold) under magnification; no markings. Top of head (vertex) covered with *long orange-yellow hair-scales.* Wingspan 0.9–1.2 cm.
Food: Liverworts.
Range: Ont. to N.C., west to Ky. May. Best collected by sweeping a net over liverwort beds during the day.

Glossary

The definitions which follow are specific to the way the terms are used in this book, although some of the terms have additional meanings in other areas of biology. Many of these terms are used widely throughout this Guide. Others that appear infrequently are followed by references to the pages or illustrations where they are introduced. More extensive glossaries include Torre-Bueno's *A Glossary of Entomology;* and those in Borror, DeLong, and Triplehorn; and Borror and White (see Bibliography, p. 464).

Abdomen: One of the 3 body regions of an insect; composed of 10 segments in Lepidoptera. The last 3 segments are usually highly modified to form the genitalia.

Accessory cell: See **areole.**

Aculea (*pl.,* aculeae): Minute, fixed spines in the wing membranes of some microlepidoptera (Fig. 72, p. 456).

Adterminal line: A line parallel to the outer margin of FW and just inside the terminal line (see front endpapers).

Am. line: The antemedial line, which separates the basal and median areas (see front endpapers).

Anal angle: Angle of wing formed by the outer margin and inner margin; called the *tornus* in some books (see front endpapers).

Anal veins (A): Unbranched, longitudinal wing veins, usually 1–3 in number, between vein Cu and the inner margin. These veins are numbered from Cu downward (1A, 2A, 3A). They may be fused from the wing base or at some point beyond the base (see front endpapers).

Androconia: Specialized scales on the abdomen, legs, or wings of males for dispersal of sex pheromones (p. 3).

Antenna: A multi-segmented sensory appendage on the head at the inside edge of each compound eye. **Simple** antenna: Threadlike, without lateral branches. **Bipectinate** antenna: Featherlike, with 2 branches on most segments. A **quadripectinate** (doubly bipectinate) antenna has 4 branches (2 pairs). **Serrate** antenna: Sawtoothed. See also **capitate.**

Areole: A small area of wing membrane surrounded completely by veins which have come together; an **accessory cell.** Usually formed by branches of vein R, or at the wing base (see **basal areole**).

Basal areole: An areole at the base of a wing, as in Lymantriidae (p. 337).

Basal line: Transverse line of FW, nearest the wing base in the typical noctuid pattern (see front endpapers).

Bipectinate: See **antenna.**

Capitate: Antenna type found in butterflies but not in N. American moths. Threadlike filament widens at tip to form a knob.

Case: A silken, cocoonlike structure formed by larvae of some species for shelter (see Coleophoridae, p. 442; Psychidae, and Tineidae, p. 450).

Caterpillar: Larval form in Lepidoptera.

Cell: A space in the wing entirely surrounded by veins (see **discal cell, areole**).

Chaetosema (*pl.*, chaetosemata): A small sensory tubercle located above each compound eye in some families of microlepidoptera (see Fig. 1, p. 2).

Chorion: The shell of the insect egg.

Chrysalis (*pl.*, chrysalids): Pupa of butterfly.

Claviform spot: Spot on the FW beneath the orbicular spot in the typical noctuid pattern (see front endpapers).

Cocoon: Protective covering made of silk and/or other materials by the caterpillar prior to pupation (see Pl. 2). Compare with **case,** which the caterpillar makes earlier to protect itself during the larval stage; a case may also serve as a cocoon during pupation.

Cocoon cutter: A ridgelike process on the head of some microlepidoptera adults which enables them to penetrate their pupal "skin" and cocoon when they are ready to emerge.

Collar: In dorsal view, the anterior (front) part of the prothorax, consisting of 2 flattened, mushroom-shaped lobes, the **patagia** (see rear endpapers).

Compound eye: Insect eye composed of many individual receptive units, represented on the surface by hexagonal divisions called facets (see Fig. 1, p. 2).

Costa (C): An unbranched vein forming the anterior (costal) margin of each wing; the costal margin itself is also often referred to as the **costa** (see front endpapers).

Coxa: The basal segment of the insect leg (see rear endpapers).

Cremaster: Extension of the posterior tip (abdomen) of the pupa in Lepidoptera, usually bearing a group of hooked setae (**crochets**) for attachment to the inside of the cocoon or place of pupation. (See Fig. 10, p. 10).

Crepuscular: Active or flying during twilight.

Crochets: Curved spines or hooks on the bottom surface of an abdominal proleg of a caterpillar or the cremaster of a pupa.

Cubitus (Cu): A longitudinal wing vein between veins Media (M) and 1A; normally ends in 2 branches (see front endpapers).

Cutworm: A type of caterpillar in many noctuid species that damages tender young plants by eating into the stems at ground level. Some species are serious agricultural pests.

Dash: A sharp, short, usually black line on the FW of many moths, such as *Acronicta* (p. 81) and *Catocala* (p. 172) species.

Diapause: A state of arrested growth and development during the insect life cycle.

Dimorphic: Having 2 distinctively different forms within a species. *Sexually dimorphic*—a condition in which the form or pattern of the male differs from that of the female.

Discal cell: A large cell from the wing base that widens as it extends outward through the middle of the wing, bordered by veins R and Cu; basal part of vein M usually not visible (see front endpapers).

Discal spot (discal dot): A spot toward the end of the discal cell, most often expressed on the HW; called a *discal dot* if small and sharply defined.

Diurnal: Active or flying during the day.

Dorsal: Pertaining to the upper surface.

Exoskeleton: The outer body wall, or integument, in arthropods. Normally hardened to serve as a skeleton as well as a protective covering.

Eye-cap: Broadened segment (scape), at the base of the antenna, that partially covers the compound eye in some microlepidoptera (Fig. 4, p. 3).

Epiphysis: Spinelike or leaflike appendage on the tibia of the foreleg, possibly used for cleaning antennae and mouth parts (see rear endpapers).

Femur: Segment of the insect leg between the trochanter and the tibia: usually large (see rear endpapers).

Forewing (FW): The anterior wing, arising from the mesothorax (see rear endpapers).

Frass: Excrement of caterpillars; usually in pellet form.

Frenulum: A single spine (in males) or multiple spines (in most females) that project anteriorly (toward the front) from the base of the HW. Held by the *retinaculum* (a membranous hook or series of bristles) on the underside of the FW to join the FW to the HW so the wings can work in unison during flight. Absent in some moth families, including some of those with a jugum. See also **jugum.**

Fringe: Border of hair-scales along the outer margins of the wings, projecting beyond the end of the wing membrane.

Frons: Front of the insect head, between the compound eyes and above the mouth parts (Fig. 2, p. 2). Sometimes called the *front.*

Hind wing (HW): The posterior wing, arising from the metathorax.

Holarctic: Occurring in the northern hemisphere around the world.

Hood: Small flap at the base of the abdomen, covering the tympanal cavity at the posterior end (rear) of the metathorax.

Humeral angle: Sharp angle of the costa near the base of the HW, conspicuous in some moths (see front endpapers).

Instar: The period between molts in the larval stage of the insect life cycle. The newly-hatched caterpillar would be referred to as the *first instar larva.*

Jugum: A fingerlike extension of the FW from the inner margin near the base in some primitive microlepidoptera (Figs. 74–76). The jugum holds the FW and HW together in flight by overlapping the HW near the base (p. 4).

Larva: The caterpillar, or growing stage of the life cycle in Lepidoptera; the stage between the egg and the pupa.

Labial palp(s): A pair of segmented (usually 3-segmented) appendages that project forward and usually curve upward from the lower part of the head (Fig. 1, p. 2). Sensory in function. Usually covered with scales. Labial palps are usually larger and more conspicuous than maxillary palps.

Lashes: Bristles grouped at the upper margin of the compound eye in some species of microlepidoptera (Fig. 3, p. 3).

Macrolepidoptera: Lepidoptera that are mostly large; butterflies, plus moths of superfamilies Sphingoidea, Bombycoidea, Mimallonoidea, Noctuoidea, Geometroidea, and Drepanoidea (see p. 30).

Mandible: The main chewing mouth part in caterpillars and adults of a few primitive moth families (p. 3).

Maxillary palp(s): Segmented appendages extending from the lower part of the head, one on each side of the proboscis (Fig. 1, p. 2). May be 5-segmented and folded (as in some microlepidoptera), or consist of 1-4 segments; absent in some species.

Media (M): A longitudinal wing vein between veins R and Cu, usually with 3 branches toward the outer margin (see front endpapers). The basal half of this vein is absent in most Lepidoptera, leaving a **discal cell.**

Median area: An area at the middle of the wing, usually bounded by the am. and pm. lines (see front endpapers).

Median line: A transverse line extending through the middle of the median area of the FW or HW in some moths (see front endpapers).

Melanic: An individual of a species that has unusually dark (sometimes solid black) coloration. May recur often enough to be referred to as a form (see Pl. 17, for example).

Mesothorax: The middle segment of the thorax, which bears the forewings and middle legs (see rear endpapers).

Metamorphosis: Distinct change in form during postembryonic development. Insects, such as Lepidoptera, with 4-stage metamorphosis (egg, larva, pupa, and adult) are said to undergo **complete metamorphosis** (also called the *holometabolous* type).

Metathorax: The most posterior of the 3 thoracic segments, which bears the hind legs and hind wings (see rear endpapers).

Microlepidoptera: All the moths except superfamilies designated above as macrolepidoptera. These moths are usually small to tiny, but some, such as Cossidae (p. 422), are medium to large.

Mine: Excavation in plant tissue made by tunneling larva.

Nearctic: Geographic region including North America from Greenland down through the Mexican highlands.

Neotropical: Geographic region including South America, Central America, and the West Indies, extending north to the southern limits of the Nearctic Region.

Nocturnal: Active or flying normally at night, as most moths do.

Orbicular spot: A round or elliptical spot in the median area of FW (toward costa) in the typical noctuid pattern (see front endpapers).

Ovum (*pl.,* ova): Scientific name for the insect egg—the first of 4 stages in the life cycle of Lepidoptera.

Patagium (*pl.,* patagia): See **collar** and rear endpapers.

Pedicel: The second antennal segment, between the scape and the base of the shaft (Fig. 2, p. 2).

Pheromone: A chemical substance secreted by an animal. One type is the sex attractant, released by both male and female moths.

Pm. line: The postmedial line, which separates the median area from the subterminal area in the typical noctuid pattern (see front endpapers).

Proboscis: The double coiled tongue of adult Lepidoptera, which can be extended to take in liquid food and water (Fig. 1, p. 2).

Prothorax: The most anterior of the 3 thoracic segments; capped dorsally by the pronotum. The prothorax bears forelegs but no wings (see rear endpapers).

Pterostigma: Thickened area along costa in FW membrane in some microlepidoptera; usually between veins Sc and R_1. (See Fig. 43, p. 424).

Pupa: Quiescent stage in life cycle of insects that undergo complete metamorphosis, during which larval features are replaced by adult characteristics. *Pupation* is the formation of the pupal stage.

Radial sector (Rs): The stalk of veins R_2–R_5, beyond the point where it branches from R_1 (see front endpapers).

Radius (R): Longitudinal wing vein between veins Sc and M; R usually ends in 5 branches, which often fuse to create **areoles** at the upper end of the discal cell in the FW (see front endpapers).

Reniform spot: A spot, usually kidney-shaped, in the outer part of the FW, toward the costa, in the typical noctuid pattern (see front endpapers).

Scale: A modified seta, or bristle, which may be flattened or hairlike. Scales cover the body, wings, and other appendages in most Lepidoptera. Those on the wings usually overlap each other like shingles on a roof.

Scape: The basal segment of an insect antenna, which is broadened to form an **eye-cap** in some families of microlepidoptera (Fig. 2, p. 2).

Serrate: See **antenna.**

Seta (*pl.*, setae): A bristle which emerges from the exoskeleton. Modified to form scales in adult Lepidoptera.

Shaft: The outer part of the antenna, beyond the pedicel; called the *flagellum* in some books (Fig. 4, p. 3).

Spine: A sharp, *immovable* outgrowth of the exoskeleton. Compare with **spur.**

Spinneret: Silk-spinning organ near the mouth of a caterpillar.

Spur: An elongate, sharp outgrowth from the exoskeleton; similar to a spine, but *movable.*

Subcosta (Sc): A longitudinal wing vein between costa and R (see front endpapers); usually unbranched in Lepidoptera, and may be fused with R_1 in HW.

Subreniform spot: A spot just below the reniform spot in some moths that have the typical noctuid pattern (see front endpapers).

Tegula (*pl.*, tegulae): A small appendage (usually clothed with scales) attached to the prothorax just above and in front of the FW base, curling over the costa and covering the base (see rear endpapers).

Terminal line: The line closest to and parallel to the outer margin of the wing (see front endpapers).

Tarsus (*pl.*, tarsi): Group of small segments (*tarsal segments*) beyond the tibia on an insect leg (see rear endpapers). Lepidoptera usually have 5 tarsal segments, with spines on each segment in most cases.

Thorax: The middle of the 3 body regions in insects, which consists of 3 segments: the **prothorax, mesothorax,** and **metathorax** (see rear endpapers).

Tibia (*pl.*, **tibiae**): The long, narrow segment of the leg between the femur and tarsus, which is often spined (see rear endpapers). Males of some species have tibiae that are modified for pheromone dispersal.

Trochanter: Very small segment of an insect leg, between the coxa and the femur (see rear endpapers). Absent in some species, at least in 1 or more of the 3 pairs of legs.

Tympanum (*pl.*, **tympana**): The membrane-covered cavity that serves as the hearing organ for many moth species; usually located on the lower side of the metathorax, toward the rear.

Veins: Tubular branching rods that extend from the bases to the margins of the wings and provide support for the wing membrane.

Venation: Pattern of formation and branching of veins in wings, usually characteristic of moth families, subfamilies, and genera. Very useful in identification.

Ventral: Pertaining to the lower surface.

Vertex: The top of the insect head (Fig. 1, p. 2).

Bibliography

Much of the information in this *Field Guide* came from publications such as those listed below. Space limitations prohibit inclusion of all but a few major sources, but many additional references can be found in the bibliographies of the works cited here. As your interest in moths grows, you may wish to obtain some of these works for more complete coverage of the moths in our area. Look for the titles below in major libraries. Some are also available from supply houses (see p. 466).

Selected References

Borror, D.J., D.M. DeLong, and C.A. Triplehorn. 1981. *Introduction to the Study of Insects.* 5th ed. Philadelphia: Saunders.

Borror, D.J. and R.E. White. 1970. *A Field Guide to the Insects.* Boston: Houghton Mifflin.

Brimley, C.S. 1938. *The Insects of North Carolina.* Raleigh: North Carolina Dept. of Agriculture, Div. of Entomology. Supplement, 1942. Supplements 2 (1950) and 3 (1967) by D.L. Wray.

Brower, A.E. 1974–83. *A List of the Lepidoptera of Maine.* Orono: University of Maine Technical Bulletin 66 (Part 1, 1974, Macrolepidoptera); 109 (Part 2, 1983, Microlepidoptera, partial).

Crumb, S.E. 1956. *The Larvae of the Phalaenidae.* U.S. Dept. of Agriculture Technical Bulletin 1135.

Ferguson, D.C. 1955. *The Lepidoptera of Nova Scotia.* Bulletin 2, Nova Scotia Museum.

———. 1971–72. *The Moths of America North of Mexico.* Fascicles 20.2A (1971) and 20.2B (1972): Bombycoidea, Saturniidae. London: Curwen Press.

———. 1978. *The Moths of America North of Mexico.* Fascicle 22.2: Noctuoidea, Lymantriidae. London: Curwen Press.

Forbes, W.T.M. 1923–60. *Lepidoptera of New York and Neighboring States.* Ithaca, New York: Cornell University Agriculture Experiment Station Memoirs 68 (Part I, 1923), 274 (Part II, 1948), 329 (Part III, 1954), and 371 (Part IV, 1960).

Franclemont, J.G. 1973. *The Moths of America North of Mexico.* Fascicle 20.1: Mimallonoidea and Bombycoidea (in part). London: Curwen Press.

Hodges, R.W. 1971. *The Moths of America North of Mexico.* Fascicle 21: Sphingoidea. London: Curwen Press.

———. 1974. *The Moths of America North of Mexico.* Fascicle 6.2: Gelechioidea, Oecophoridae. London: Curwen Press.

———. 1978. *The Moths of America North of Mexico.* Fascicle 6.1: Gelechioidea, Cosmopterigidae. London: Curwen Press.

Hodges, R.W., *et al.* 1983. *Check List of the Lepidoptera of America North of Mexico.* London: Curwen Press.

Holland, W.J. 1903. *The Moth Book.* New York: Doubleday, Page & Co.; reprinted 1968 with updating by A.E. Brower. New York: Dover.

Kimball, C.P. 1965. *Arthropods of Florida and Neighboring Land Areas,* Vol. 1: *Lepidoptera of Florida.* Gainesville: Div. of Plant Industry, Florida Dept. of Agriculture.

Klots, A.B. 1951. *A Field Guide to the Butterflies of North America East of the Great Plains.* Boston: Houghton Mifflin.

McDunnough, J.H. 1938–39. *Check List of the Lepidoptera of Canada and the United States of America.* Part 1, Macrolepidoptera (1938); Part 2, Microlepidoptera (1939). Southern California Academy of Science Memoirs 1 and 2.

McGuffin, W.C. 1967–81. *Guide to the Geometridae of Canada (Lepidoptera).* Memoirs of the Entomological Society of Canada 50 (Part 1, 1967), 86 (Part 2, 1972), 101 (Part 3, 1977), and 117 (Part 4, 1981).

Moore, S. 1955. *An Annotated List of the Moths of Michigan, Exclusive of the Tineoidea (Lepidoptera).* University of Michigan Museum of Zoology Miscellaneous Publication 88.

Morris, R.F. 1980. *Butterflies and Moths of Newfoundland and Labrador.* Hull, Quebec: Canadian Government Publications Centre.

Munroe, E.G. 1972–76. *The Moths of America North of Mexico.* Fascicles 13.1 (A–C) and 13.2 (A–B): Pyraloidea, Pyralidae. London: Curwen Press.

McGugan, B.M., and R.M. Prentice (eds.). 1958–65. *Forest Lepidoptera of Canada Recorded by the Forest Insect Survey,* Vols. 1–4. Canada Department of Forestry, Bulletin 128 and Publications 1013, 1034, and 1142. (Vol. 1 ed. by McGugan; Vols. 2–4 by Prentice).

Rindge, F.H. 1961. *Revision of the Nacophorini (Lepidoptera, Geometridae).* American Museum of Natural History Bulletin 123.

Rockburne, E.W. and J.D. Lafontaine. 1976. *The Cutworm Moths of Ontario and Quebec.* Canadian Dept. of Agriculture Publication 1593.

Sargent, T.D. 1976. *Legion of Night: The Underwing Moths.* Amherst: University of Massachusetts Press.

Sutherland, D.W.S. 1978. *Common Names of Insects and Related Organisms.* College Park, Maryland: Entomological Society of America.

Tietz, H.M. 1972. *An Index to the Described Life Histories, Early Stages and Hosts of the Macrolepidoptera of the Continental United States and Canada.* 2 volumes. Sarasota, Florida: The Allyn Museum of Entomology.

de la Torre-Bueno, J.R. 1937. *A Glossary of Entomology.* Lancaster, Pennsylvania: Science Press. Supplement A, 1960, ed. by G.S. Tulloch. New York: Brooklyn Entomological Society.

Tuxen, S.L. 1970. *Taxonomist's Glossary of Genitalia in Insects.* Rev. ed. Copenhagen: Enjar Munksgaard.

Villiard, P. 1969. *Moths and How to Rear Them.* New York: Funk & Wagnall's.

Societies for Lepidopterists in North America

The Lepidopterists' Society, Department of Biology, University of Louisville, Louisville, KY 40292. Publishes *Journal, News,* and *Memoirs* of the Lepidopterists' Society.

Lepidoptera Research Foundation, Santa Barbara Museum of Natural History, 2559 Puesta del Sol Rd., Santa Barbara, CA 93105. Publishes *Journal of Research on the Lepidoptera.*

Supply Houses

BioQuip Products, P.O. Box 61, Santa Monica, CA 90406. (equipment, chemicals, books)

Carolina Biological Supply Co., Burlington, NC 27215. (equipment, chemicals)

E.W. Classey, Ltd., Park Rd., Faringdon, Oxon, SN7 7DR, England. (current and out-of-print books)

Entomological Reprint Specialists, P.O. Box 77224, Dockweiler Station, Los Angeles, CA 90007 (current and reprinted books)

Ianni Butterfly Enterprises, P.O. Box 81171, Cleveland, OH 44181. (insect pins; tropical specimens)

Insect Museum Supply (Jack R. Powers), 1021 8th Ave. South, Moorhead, MN 56560 (printed labels; insect pins)

Ward's Natural Science Establishment, Inc., P.O. Box 92912, Rochester, NY 14603. (equipment, chemicals)

Species Author Names

In this guide, as in many other works, the names of many authors who are credited with first describing species are abbreviated to conserve space.

Abbreviation	Author's Names
B.	Barnes, William
B. & Benj.	Barnes, Wm. and Benjamin, F.H.
B. & McD.	Barnes, Wm. and McDunnough, J.H.
Bdv.	Boisduval, Jean A.
Benj.	Benjamin, Foster H.
Bsk.	Busck, August
Btlr.	Butler
Cass.	Cassino, Samuel E.
C. & S.	Cassino, S.E., and Swett, L.W.
Cham.	Chambers, Victor T.
Clem.	Clemens, J. Brackenridge
Cl.	Clerck, C.A.
Cram.	Cramer, Pieter
Curt.	Curtis, John
D. & S.	Denis and Schiffermüller
Dru.	Drury
Hy. Edw.	Edwards, Henry
Edw.	Edwards, William H.
Esp.	Esper, Eugen J.C.
F.	Fabricius, Johann C.
Fgn.	Ferguson, Douglas C.
Fern.	Fernald, Charles H.
Fbs.	Forbes, William T.M.
Franc.	Franclemont, John G.
Free.	Freeman, T.N.
Gey.	Geyer, Carl
Grossb.	Grossbeck, John A.
Grt.	Grote, August R.
Grt. & Rob.	Grote, A.R., and Robinson, C.T.
Gn.	Guenée, Achille
Guér.	Guérin-Méneville, Félix E.
Haim.	Haimbach, Frank
Hamp.	Hampson, Sir George F.
Harr.	Harris, Thaddeus W.
Harv.	Harvey, Francis L.
Haw.	Haworth, Adrian H.

Abbreviation	Author's Names
H.-S.	Herrich-Schäffer, G.A.W.
Hbn.	Hübner, Jacob
Hufn.	Hufnagel
Kft.	Kearfott, William D.
Kby.	Kirby, William F.
Led.	Lederer, Julius
L.	Linnaeus, Carolus (Carl von Linné)
Lint.	Lintner, James A.
McD.	McDunnough, James H.
Meyr.	Meyrick, Edward
Morr.	Morrison, Herbert K.
Mösch.	Möschler, Heinrich B.
Murt.	Murtfeldt, Mary E.
Neum.	Neumoegen, Berthold
Ochs.	Ochsenheimer, Ferdinand
Pack.	Packard, Alpheus S.
Reak.	Reakirt, Tryon
Rob.	Robinson, Coleman T.
R. & J.	Rothschild, W. and Jordan, K.
Saund.	Saunders, William
Sm.	Smith, John B.
Sm., J.E.	Smith, James E.
Sm., S.I.	Smith, S.I.
Snell.	Snellen, Pieter C.T.
Staint.	Stainton, Henry T.
Steph.	Stephens, James F.
Stkr.	Strecker, Herman
Sulz.	Sulzer, Johann H.
Tr.	Treitschke, F.
Wlk.	Walker, Francis
Wlsm.	Walsingham, Lord Thomas
Woll.	Wollaston, Thomas V.
Zell.	Zeller, Philipp C.

Index

Because of space limitations, the following index includes only scientific and common names of families, subfamilies, genera, and species treated in this book. Other names, such as those of superfamilies, subspecies, and forms, are omitted. As in other Field Guides, to avoid duplication, references to plate numbers are given *after common names only* (not after scientific names), except for species of microlepidoptera that have not been assigned common names. Plate numbers are shown in **boldface;** other numbers (not in boldface) refer to pages in the text.

469

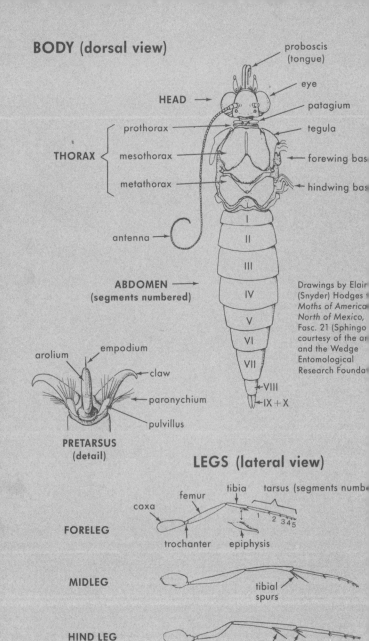

BODY (dorsal view)

proboscis (tongue)

eye

HEAD →

patagium

prothorax

tegula

THORAX { mesothorax

forewing bas

metathorax

hindwing bas

antenna →

I

II

III

ABDOMEN →
(segments numbered)

IV

V

VI

VII

VIII

IX + X

Drawings by Elair
(Snyder) Hodges
Moths of America
North of Mexico,
Fasc. 21 (Sphingo
courtesy of the ar
and the Wedge
Entomological
Research Founda

arolium   empodium

claw

paronychium

pulvillus

PRETARSUS
(detail)

LEGS (lateral view)

femur   tibia   tarsus (segments numbe

coxa

1 2 3 4 5

FORELEG

trochanter   epiphysis

MIDLEG

tibial spurs

HIND LEG

tibial spurs